*Now available

ISAIAH 1–39

with
AN INTRODUCTION TO
PROPHETIC LITERATURE

MARVIN A. SWEENEY

The Forms of the Old Testament Literature
VOLUME XVI
Rolf P. Knierim and Gene M. Tucker, editors

WILLIAM B. EERDMANS PUBLISHING COMPANY
GRAND RAPIDS, MICHIGAN / CAMBRIDGE, U.K.

© 1996 Wm. B. Eerdmans Publishing Co.
255 Jefferson Ave. S.E., Grand Rapids, Michigan 49503 /
P. O. Box 163, Cambridge CB3 9BA U.K.

Printed in the United States of America

02 01 00 99 98 97 96   7 6 5 4 3 2 1

Library of Congress Cataloging-in-Publication Data

Sweeney, Marvin A. (Marvin Alan), 1953-
Isaiah 1-39: with an introduction to prophetic literature /
Marvin A. Sweeney.
p.   cm.   — (The forms of the Old Testament literature; v. 16)
Includes bibliographical references and index.
ISBN 0-8028-4100-7 (pbk.: alk. paper)
1. Bible. O.T. Isaiah I-XXXIX — Commentaries. 2. Prophets.
I. Title.   II. Series.
BS1515.3.S94   1996
224'.10663 — dc20   95-50492
                                       CIP

For
Doll and Gramps

CONTENTS

ABBREVIATIONS AND SYMBOLS

I. MISCELLANEOUS ABBREVIATIONS AND SYMBOLS

Akk.	Akkadian
cf.	compare
col(s).	column(s)
Diss.	Dissertation
DtrH	Deuteronomistic History
ed.	editor(s), edited by; edition
e.g.	for example
esp.	especially
ET	English translation
et al.	*et alii* (and others)
f(f).	following verse(s), page(s), line(s)
Fest.	*Festschrift*
Hebr.	Hebrew
idem	the same
i.e.	*id est* (that is)
l(l).	line(s)
LXX	Septuagint
MS(S)	manuscript(s)
MT	Masoretic Text
n(n).	note(s)
n.s.	new series
NT	New Testament
OT	Old Testament
p(p).	page(s)
pl(s).	plate(s)
PN	personal name
repr.	reprint
rev.	revised
sic	so, thus (indicating an error transcribed from the original)

s.v.	*sub voce* (under the word)
TJ	Targum Jonathan
tr.	translator(s), translated by
v(v).	verse(s)
vol(s).	volume(s)
VS(S).	version(s)
*	When placed after a text citation, the asterisk indicates a hypothetical form presumed to underlie the present form of the text
→	the arrow indicates a cross reference to another section of the commentary
=	equals, is equivalent to

II. PUBLICATIONS

AASOR	Annual of the American Schools of Oriental Research
AB	Anchor Bible
ABD	*Anchor Bible Dictionary*
ABS	Archaeology and Biblical Studies
ACEBT	*Amsterdamse Cahiers voor Exegese en Bijbelse Theologie*
AcOr	*Acta Orientalia*
AION	*Annali del'istituto universiterio orientale di Napoli,* Pubblicazioni
AJSL	*American Journal of Semitic Languages and Literatures*
AJT	*American Journal of Theology*
Alt, *KS*	A. Alt, *Kleine Schriften zur Geschichte des Volkes Israel* (3 vols.; Munich: Beck, 1953)
ALUOS	*Annual of the Leeds University Oriental Society*
AnBib	Analecta Biblica
ANET	J. B. Pritchard, ed., *Ancient Near Eastern Texts Relating to the Old Testament* (3rd ed.; Princeton: Princeton University, 1969)
AnOr	Analecta Orientalia
AOAT	Alter Orient und Altes Testament
ARAB	D. D. Luckenbill, ed., *Ancient Records of Assyria and Babylonia* (2 vols.; Chicago: University of Chicago Press, 1926-27)
ArOr	*Archiv orientální*
ARW	*Archiv für Religionswissenschaft*
ASTI	*Annual of the Swedish Theological Institute in Jerusalem*
ATANT	Abhandlungen zur Theologie des Alten und Neuen Testaments
ATD	Das Alt Testament Deutsch
ATR	*Anglican Theological Review*
ATSAT	Arbeiten zur Text und Sprache des Alten Testament

AUM	Andrews University Monographs
AusBR	*Australian Biblical Review*
AUSS	*Andrews University Seminary Studies*
AzT	Arbeiten zur Theologie
BA	*Biblical Archaeologist*
BASOR	*Bulletin of the American Schools of Oriental Research*
BAT	Botschaft des Alten Testament
BBB	Bonner biblische Beiträge
BBET	Beiträge zur biblischen Exegese und Theologie
BDB	F. Brown, S. R. Driver, and C. A. Briggs, *Hebrew and English Lexicon of the Old Testament* (rev. ed.; Oxford: Oxford University Press, 1957)
BEATAJ	Beiträge zur Exegese des Alten Testaments und Antike Judentums
BETL	Biblioteca Ephemeridum Theologicarum Lovaniensium
BEvT	Beiträge zur evangelischen Theologie
BHS	K. Elliger and K. Rudolph, eds., *Biblia Hebraica Stuttgartensia* (Stuttgart: Deutsche Bibelstiftung, 1977)
Bib	*Biblica*
BibB	Biblische Beiträge
BibIll	*Bible Illustrator*
BibLeb	*Bibel und Leben*
BibOr	Biblical et orientalia
BibS(N)	Biblische Studien (Neukirchen, 1951-)
BIOSCS	*Bulletin of the International Organization of Septuagint and Cognate Studies*
BJRL	*Bulletin of the John Rylands University Library of Manchester*
BJS	Brown Judaic Studies
BKAT	Biblischer Kommentar: Altes Testament
BLS	Bible and Literature Series
BMS	BIBAL Monograph Series
BN	*Biblische Notizen*
BO	*Bibliotheca orientalis*
BOuT	De Boeken van het Oude Testament
BR	*Biblical Research*
BSac	*Bibliotheca Sacra*
BT	*The Bible Translator*
BTFT	*Bijdragen: Tijdschrift voor Filosofie en Theologie*
BTS	Biblisch-Theologische Studien
BWANT	Beiträge zur Wissenschaft vom Alten und Neuen Testament
BZ	*Biblische Zeitschrift*
BZAW	Beihefte zur Zeitschrift für die alttestamentliche Wissenschaft
CAT	Commentaire de l'Ancien Testament
CBC	Cambridge Bible Commentary
CBQ	*Catholic Biblical Quarterly*
CBQMS	Catholic Biblical Quarterly Monograph Series

CBSC	Cambridge Bible for Schools and Colleges
CC	Continental Commentary
CentB	Century Bible
ConBOT	Coniectanea biblica, Old Testament
ConJud	*Conservative Judaism*
CR:BS	*Currents in Research: Biblical Studies*
CTM	Calwer theologische Monographien
DBSup	*Dictionnaire de la Bible, Supplément*
DD	*Dor le-Dor*
EBib	Études bibliques
EF	Erträge der Forschung
EHAT	Exegetisches Handbuch zum Alten Testament
EncJud	*Encyclopedia Judaica* (1971)
ErIs	*Eretz Israel*
EstBib	*Estudios biblicos*
ETL	*Ephemerides theologicae lovanienses*
ETR	*Études Théologiques et Religieuses*
EvT	*Evangelische Theologie*
ExAud	*Ex Auditu*
ExpB	Expositor's Bible
ExpTim	*Expository Times*
FAT	Forschungen zur Altes Testament
FB	Forschung zur Bibel
FOTL	Forms of the Old Testament Literature
FRLANT	Forschungen zur Religion und Literatur des Alten und Neuen Testaments
HAR	*Hebrew Annual Review*
HAT	Handbuch zum Alten Testament
HDR	Harvard Dissertations in Religion
HKAT	Handkommentar zum Alten Testament
HSAT	*Die heilige Schrift des Alten Testaments* (Kautzsch) (4th ed.; Tübingen, 1922-23), ed. Bertholet
HSM	Harvard Semitic Monographs
HSS	Harvard Semitic Series
HTR	*Harvard Theological Review*
HTS	Harvard Theological Studies
HUCA	*Hebrew Union College Annual*
HUCM	Hebrew Union College Monographs
IB	*Interpreter's Bible*
ICC	International Critical Commentary
IDB	*Interpreter's Dictionary of the Bible*
IDBSup	Supplementary volume to *IDB*
IEJ	*Israel Exploration Journal*
Int	*Interpretation*
IOS	*Israel Oriental Studies*
IRT	Issues in Religion and Theology
JAOS	*Journal of the American Oriental Society*

JARCE	*Journal of the American Research Center in Egypt*
JBL	*Journal of Biblical Literature*
JBQ	*Jewish Bible Quarterly*
JBR	*Journal of Bible and Religion*
JCS	*Journal of Cuneiform Studies*
JEA	*Journal of Egyptian Archaeology*
JETS	*Journal of the Evangelical Theological Society*
JNES	*Journal of Near Eastern Studies*
JNSL	*Journal of Northwest Semitic Languages*
JQR	*Jewish Quarterly Review*
JR	*Journal of Religion*
JSOT	*Journal for the Study of the Old Testament*
JSOTSup	Journal for the Study of the Old Testament Supplement Series
JSS	*Journal of Semitic Studies*
JTS	*Journal of Theological Studies*
KAT	Kommentar zum Alten Testament
KB	L. Koehler and W. Baumgartner, *Lexicon in Veteris Testamenti libros*
KEH	Kurzgefasstes exegetisches Handbuch zum Alten Testament
KHC	Kurzer Hand-Commentar zum Alten Testament
LBC	Layman's Bible Commentary
LD	Lectio divina
LQ	*Lutheran Quarterly*
LUÅ	Lunds universitets årsskrift
MGWJ	*Monatsschrift für Geschichte und Wissenschaft des Judentums*
MIOF	*Mitteilungen des Instituts für Orientforschung*
NCB	New Century Bible
NEB	Neue Echter Bibel
NGTT	*Nederduits Gereformeerde Teologiese Tydskrif*
NICOT	New International Commentary on the Old Testament
NRSV	*New Revised Standard Version*
NRT	*Nouvelle revue théologique*
NTT	*Nederlands Theologisch Tijdschrift*
OBO	Orbis biblicus et orientalis
OBT	Overtures to Biblical Theology
OLZ	*Orientalische Literaturzeitung*
OrAnt	*Oriens antiquus*
OTE	*Old Testament Essays*
OTL	Old Testament Library
OTS	*Oudtestamentische Studiën*
OTWSA	Ou-Testamentiese Werkgemeenskap in Suid-Afrika
PEFQS	*Palestine Exploration Fund Quarterly Statement*
PEGLMBS	*Proceedings, Eastern Great Lakes and Midwest Biblical Societies*
PEQ	*Palestine Exploration Quarterly*
PJ	*Palästinajahrbuch*
POS	Pretoria Oriental Series

PSB	*Princeton Seminary Bulletin*
PTMS	Pittsburgh Theological Monograph Series
RB	*Revue biblique*
REJ	*Revue des Études Juives*
RGG	*Die Religion in Geschichte und Gegenwart*
RHPR	*Revue d'histoire et de philosophie religieuses*
RHR	*Revue de l'histoire des religions*
RivB	*Revista biblica*
RSPT	*Revue de Sciences Philosophiques et Théologieuses*
RSR	*Recherches de science religieuse*
RSV	*Revised Standard Version*
SacPag	*Sacra Pagina*
SAT	Die Schriften des Alten Testaments
SB	Sources bibliques
SBL	Society of Biblical Literature
SBLDS	Society of Biblical Literature Dissertation Series
SBLMS	Society of Biblical Literature Monograph Series
SBLSCS	Society of Biblical Literature Septuagint and Cognate Studies
SBM	Stuttgarter biblische Monographien
SBS	Stuttgarter Bibelstudien
SBT	Studies in Biblical Theology
SEÅ	*Svensk exegetisk årsbok*
Sem	*Semitica*
SJOT	*Scandinavian Journal of the Old Testament*
SJT	*Scottish Journal of Theology*
SSN	Studia semitica neerlandica
ST	*Studia Theologica*
TA	*Tel Aviv*
TBC	Torch Bible Commentary
TBT	*The Bible Today*
TBü	Theologische Bücherei
TDOT	G. J. Botterweck and H. Ringgren, eds., *Theological Dictionary of the Old Testament* (Eng. tr.; 12 vols.; Grand Rapids: Eerdmans, 1974-)
ThStK	*Theologische Studien und Kritiken*
TLZ	*Theologische Literaturzeitung*
TRu	*Theologische Rundschau*
TS	Theologische Studien
TThSt	Trierer Theologische Studien
TTZ	*Trierer theologische Zeitschrift*
TynB	*Tyndale Bulletin*
TZ	*Theologische Zeitschrift*
UF	*Ugarit Forschungen*
USQR	*Union Seminary Quarterly Review*
UUÅ	Uppsala universitets årsskrift
VF	*Verkündigung und Forschung*
VT	*Vetus Testamentum*

VTSup	Vetus Testamentum, Supplements
WBC	Word Biblical Commentary
WF	Wege der Forschung
WMANT	Wissenschaftliche Monographien zum Alten und Neuen Testament
WO	*Die Welt des Orients*
WZHalle	*Wissenschaftliche Zeitschrift der Martin-Luther-Universität*
ZAH	*Zeitschrift für Althebräistik*
ZAW	*Zeitschrift für die alttestamentliche Wissenschaft*
ZBK	Zürcher Bibel Kommentar
ZDMG	*Zeitschrift der deutschen morgenländischen Gesellschaft*
ZDPV	*Zeitschrift des deutschen Palästinavereins*
ZKTh	*Zeitschrift für Katholische Theologie*
ZRGG	*Zeitschrift für Religions- und Geistesgeschichte*
ZTK	*Zeitschrift für Theologie und Kirche*

Editors' Foreword

THIS BOOK is the ninth in a series of twenty-four volumes planned for publication throughout the nineteen-eighties and nineteen-nineties. The series eventually will present a form-critical analysis of every book and each unit of the Old Testament (Hebrew Bible) according to a standard outline and methodology. The aims of the work are fundamentally exegetical, attempting to understand the biblical literature from the viewpoint of a particular set of questions. Each volume in the series will also give an account of the history of the form-critical discussion of the material in question, attempt to bring consistency to the terminology for the genres and formulas of the biblical literature, and expose the exegetical procedure in such a way as to enable students and pastors to engage in their own analysis and interpretation. It is hoped, therefore, that the audience will be a broad one, including not only biblical scholars but also students, pastors, priests, and rabbis who are engaged in biblical interpretation.

There is a difference between the planned order of appearance of the individual volumes and their position in the series. While the series follows basically the sequence of the books of the Hebrew Bible, the individual volumes will appear in accordance with the projected working schedules of the individual contributors. The number of twenty-four volumes has been chosen for merely practical reasons that make it necessary to combine several biblical books in one volume at times, and at times to have two authors contribute to the same volume. Volume XIII is an exception to the arrangement according to the sequence of the Hebrew canon in that it omits Lamentations. The commentary on Lamentations will be published with that on the book of Psalms.

The initiation of this series is the result of deliberations and plans that began some twenty years ago. At that time the current editors perceived the need for a comprehensive reference work that would enable scholars and students of the Hebrew scriptures to gain from the insights that form-critical work had accumulated throughout seven decades, and at the same time to participate more effectively in such work themselves. An international and interconfessional team of scholars was assembled and has been expanded in recent years.

Several possible approaches and formats for publication presented themselves. The work could not be a handbook of the form-critical method with some examples of its application. Nor would it be satisfactory to present an encyclopedia of the genres identified in the Old Testament literature. The reference work would have to demonstrate the method on all of the texts, and identify genres only through the actual interpretation of the texts themselves. Hence, the work had to be a commentary following the sequence of the books in the Hebrew Bible (the Kittel edition of the *Biblia hebraica* then and the *Biblia hebraica stuttgartensia* now).

The main purpose of this project is to lead the student to the Old Testament texts themselves, and not just to form-critical studies of the texts. It should be stressed that the commentary is confined to the form-critical interpretation of the texts. Consequently, the reader should not expect here a full-fledged exegetical commentary that deals with the broad range of issues concerning the meaning of the text. In order to keep the focus as clearly as possible on a particular set of questions, matters of text, translation, philology, verse-by-verse explanation, etc. are raised only when they appear directly relevant to the form-critical analysis and interpretation.

The adoption of a commentary format with specific categories for the analysis of the texts rests upon a conclusion that has become crucial for all form-critical work. If the results of form criticism are to be verifiable and generally intelligible, then the determination of typical forms and genres, their settings and functions, has to take place through the analysis of the forms in and of the texts themselves. This leads to two consequences for the volumes in this series. First, each interpretation of a text begins with the presentation of the *structure* of that text in outline form. The ensuing discussion of this structure attempts to distinguish the typical from the individual or unique elements, and to proceed on this basis to the determination of the *genre,* its *setting,* and its *intention.* Traditio-historical factors are discussed throughout this process where relevant; e.g., is there evidence of a written or oral stage of the material earlier than the actual text before the reader?

Second, the interpretation of the texts accepts the fundamental premise that we possess all texts basically at their latest written stages—technically speaking, at the levels of the final redactions. Any access to the texts, therefore, must confront and analyze that latest edition first, i.e., a specific version of that edition as represented in a particular text tradition. Consequently, the commentary proceeds from the analysis of the larger literary corpora created by the redactions back to any prior discernible stages in their literary history. Larger units are examined first, and then their subsections. Therefore, in most instances the first unit examined in terms of structure, genre, setting, and intention is the entire biblical book in question; next the commentary treats the individual larger and then smaller units.

The original plan of the project was to record critically all the relevant results of previous form-critical studies concerning the texts in question. While this remains one of the goals of the series, it had to be expanded to allow for more of the research of the individual contributors. This approach has proved to be important not only with regard to the ongoing insights of the contributors but also in view of the significant developments that have taken place in the field in recent years. The team of scholars responsible for the series is committed to following a basic design throughout the commentary, but differences of emphasis and even to some extent of approach will be recognized as more volumes appear. Each author will ultimately be responsible for his own contribution.

The use of the commentary is by and large self-explanatory, but a few comments may prove helpful to the reader. This work is designed to be used alongside the Hebrew text or a translation of the Bible. The format of the interpretation of the texts, large or small, is the same throughout, except in cases where the biblical material itself suggests a different form of presentation. Individual books and major literary corpora are introduced by a general bibliography referring to wider information on the subjects discussed and to works relevant for the subunits of that literary body. Whenever available, a special form-critical bibliography for a specific unit under discussion will conclude the discussion of that unit. In the outline of the structure of units, the system of sigla attempts to indicate the relationship and interdependence of the parts within that structure. The traditional chapter and verse divisions of the Hebrew text, as well as the versification of the *New Revised Standard Version,* are supplied in the right-hand margin of the outlines.

In addition to the commentary on the biblical book, this volume includes a glossary of the genres discussed in the commentary. Many of the definitions in the glossary were prepared by Professor Sweeney, but some have arisen from the work of other members of the project on other parts of the Old Testament. Each subsequent volume will include such a glossary. Eventually, upon the completion of the commentary series, all of the glossaries will be revised in the light of the analysis of each book of the Old Testament and published as Volume XXIII of the series. The individual volumes will not contain special indices, but the indices for the entire series will be published as Volume XXIV.

The editors acknowledge with appreciation the contribution of numerous persons and institutions to the work of the project. All of the contributors have received significant financial, secretarial, and student assistance from their respective institutions. In particular, the editors have received extensive support from their universities. Without such concrete expressions of encouragement the work scarcely could have gone on. At Claremont, the Institute for Antiquity and Christianity has from its own inception provided office facilities, a supportive staff, and the atmosphere that stimulates not only individual but also team research. Emory University and the Candler School of Theology have likewise provided tangible support and encouragement. The editors are particularly indebted to Professor Timothy Beal of Eckerd College for his extraordinary editorial assistance in the preparation of this volume while he was a graduate student at Emory University, and to Dr. and Mrs. J. E. Williams for their generous financial support of our work.

ROLF P. KNIERIM
GENE M. TUCKER

PREFACE

For the last five years, it has been an honor and a privilege to write this commentary on Isaiah 1–39. I have benefited greatly and learned much, not only from Isaiah but also from the many people and institutions with whom I have had the pleasure to be associated during this time. It is now my pleasure to thank those who have done so much for me.

First, I would like to thank the editors of the Forms of the Old Testament Literature Commentary Series, Rolf P. Knierim and Gene M. Tucker, for inviting me to contribute the present volume. As my teacher, Rolf initially directed my dissertation on Isaiah, and has continued to show his confidence in me in many ways. As editor, Gene has provided constant support and encouragement as well as a free hand to test and express ideas. I am especially indebted to him and to his assistant, Timothy Beal, for their hard work on this project and for saving me from many errors. Any that remain are, of course, my own.

I would also like to express my thanks to the members of the Society of Biblical Literature Seminar on the Formation of the Book of Isaiah for their collegiality and intellectual stimulation. The Isaiah seminar has brought me into contact with some of the finest minds and issues in contemporary Isaiah scholarship. I would especially like to thank Roy F. Melugin, who cochairs the seminar with me, for the many hours of conversation we have shared at conferences and over the phone on Isaiah and methodological issues in the study of biblical literature. In addition, I would like to thank the Steering Committee members, David Carr, Ronald Clements, Edgar Conrad, Katheryn Pfisterer Darr, Rolf Rendtorff, Christopher Seitz, and Gary Stansell, for their continuous support and hard work. I am also grateful to the many individuals, both members of the seminar and others, who have contributed greatly to the study of Isaiah and have shared their insights with me. I look forward to a continuing association with these fine people as the seminar progresses.

I have benefited greatly from a great deal of institutional support as well. A postdoctoral fellowship from the Yad Hanadiv/Barecha Foundation provided the funding for my appointment as a Visiting Post-doctoral Fellow in Jewish Studies at the Hebrew University of Jerusalem during the 1989-90 academic year. During that period I was priviledged to study David Kimchi's commentary on Isaiah with Moshe Greenberg, from whom I learned much about philological exegesis. A grant from the Dorot Research Foundation provided the funds for my appointment as Dorot Research Professor at the W. F. Albright Institute in Jerusalem during the 1993-94 academic year, where I completed the editorial work on this volume. In both cases, I am indebted to the University of Miami for enabling me to accept these appointments by granting a sabbatical, a leave of absence, and support funds. In addition, the university provided Max Orovitz Summer Stipends in the Humanities to support my work in 1990, 1992, and 1993. Daniel Pals, chairperson of the Department of Religious Studies, and deans David Wilson and Ross Murfin of the College of Arts and Sciences have played particularly instrumental roles in facilitating the writing of this commentary. My colleagues and students at Miami have provided much scholarly stimulation and personal support during the course of this project. Although I am leaving the university for a new position, I look forward to a close association with them in the coming years.

Finally, I would like to thank my family, Maimunah and Leah, for their understanding and love. Likewise, my father, my grandparents, my brothers, my sister-in-law, and my nieces and nephews have always reminded me of the best of this world.

I would like to dedicate this volume to my grandfather, Sam Dorman, and to the memory of my grandmother, Minnie Lee Stein Dorman. Both have been a constant source of love and inspiration to me throughout the years.

JERUSALEM, MAY 1994

Introduction to the Prophetic Literature

BIBLIOGRAPHY

G. W. Ahlström, *Joel and the Temple Cult of Jerusalem* (VTSup 21; Leiden: Brill, 1971); F. Ahuis, *Der klagende Gerichtsprophet: Studien zur Klage in der Überlieferung von den alttestamentlichen Gerichtspropheten* (Stuttgart: Calwer, 1982); R. Bach, *Die Aufforderung zur Flucht und zum Kampf im alttestamentliche Prophetenspruch* (WMANT 9; Neukirchen: Neukirchener, 1962); S. E. Balentine, "The Prophet as Intercessor: A Reassessment," *JBL* 103 (1984) 161-73; E. Balla, *Die Droh- und Scheltworte des Amos* (Leipzig: A. Edelmann, 1926); K. Baltzer, *Die Biographie der Propheten* (Neukirchen: Neukirchener, 1975); idem, "Considerations Regarding the Office and Calling of the Prophet," *HTR* 61 (1968) 567-81; J. Barton, *Reading the Old Testament: Method in Biblical Study* (Philadelphia: Westminster, 1984); F. Baumgärtel, "Die Formel *nĕ'um JHWH*," *ZAW* 73 (1961) 277-90; idem, "Zu den Gottesnamen in den Büchern Jeremia und Ezechiel," in *Verbannung und Heimkehr* (*Fest.* W. Rudolph; ed. A. Kuschke; Tübingen: Mohr, 1961) 1-29; W. Baumgartner, "Joel 1 und 2," in *Beiträge zur alttestamentliche Wissenschaft* (BZAW 34; ed. K. Marti; Giessen: Töpelmann, 1920) 10-19; idem, *Die Klagegedichte des Jeremia* (BZAW 32; Giessen: Töpelmann, 1917); J. Begrich, "Die priesterliche Heilsorakel," in *Gesammelte Studien zum Alten Testament* (TBü 21; Munich: Kaiser, 1964) 217-31 (repr. from *ZAW* 52 [1934] 81-92); idem, "Die priesterliche Tora," in *Werden und Wesen des Alten Testaments* (ed. P. Volz et al.; BZAW 66; Berlin: Töpelmann, 1936) 63-88; idem, *Studien zu Deuterojesaja* (BWANT 77; Stuttgart: Kohlhammer, 1938; repr. TBü 20; 2nd ed.; Munich: Kaiser, 1969); W. H. Bellinger Jr., *Psalmody and Prophecy* (JSOTSup 27; Sheffield: JSOT Press, 1984); A. Bentzen, *Introduction to the Old Testament* (2nd ed.; 2 vols.; Copenhagen: Gad, 1952); idem, "The Ritual Background of Amos i 2–ii 16," *OTS* 8 (1950) 85-99; P. L. Berger, "Charisma and Religious Innovation: The Social Location of Israelite Prophecy," *American Sociological Review* 28 (1963) 940-50; R. V. Bergren, *The Prophets and the Law* (HUCM 4; Cincinnati: Hebrew Union College — Jewish Institute of Religion, 1974); K. Bernhardt, *Die gattungsgeschichtliche Forschung am Alten Testament als exegetische Methode* (Berlin: Evangelische Verlagsanstalt, 1959); J. M. Berridge, *Prophet, People, and the Word of YHWH: An Examination of the Form and Content in the Proclamation of the Prophet Jeremiah* (Zurich: EVZ, 1970); W. Beyerlin, *Die Kulttraditionen Israels in der Verkündigung des Propheten Micha* (FRLANT 72; Göttingen: Vandenhoeck & Ruprecht, 1959); J. Blenkinsopp, *A History of Prophecy in Israel: From the Settlement in the Land to the Hellenistic Period* (Philadelphia: Westminster, 1983); idem, *Prophecy and Canon: A Contribution to the Study of Jewish Origins* (Notre Dame: University of Notre Dame Press, 1977); H.-J. Boecker, "Anklagereden und Verteidigungsreden im Alten Testament," *EvT* 20 (1960) 398-412; idem, "Bemerkungen zur formgeschichtlichen Terminologie des Buches Maleachi," *ZAW* 78 (1966) 78-80; idem, *Redeformen des Rechtslebens im Alten Testament* (2nd ed.; WMANT 14; Neukirchen-Vluyn: Neukirchener, 1970); B. A. Bozak, *Life "Anew": A Literary-Theological Study of Jer. 30–31* (AnBib 122; Rome: Biblical Institute Press, 1991); J. Bright, "The Prophetic Reminiscence: Its Place and Function in the Book of Jeremiah," *Biblical Essays, 1966* (OTWSA 9; Pretoria: OTWSA, 1966) 11-30; C. Budde, "Das hebräische Klagelied," *ZAW* 2 (1882) 1-52; K. Budde, "Ein althebräisches Klagelied," *ZAW* 3 (1883) 299-306; M. J. Buss, *The Prophetic Word of Hosea: A Morphological Study* (BZAW 111; Berlin: Töpelmann, 1969); M. J. Buss, ed., *Encounter with the Text: Form and History in the Hebrew Bible* (Missoula: Scholars Press; Philadelphia: Fortress, 1979); R. P. Carroll, *Jeremiah* (OTL; Philadelphia: Westminster, 1986); idem, "Prophecy and Society," in *The World of Ancient Israel: Sociological, Anthropological and Political Persepctives* (ed. R. E. Clements; Cambridge: University Press, 1989) 203-25; idem, *When Prophecy Failed: Cognitive Dissonance in the Prophetic Traditions of the Old Testament* (New York: Seabury, 1979); B. S. Childs, "The Canonical Shape of the Prophetic Literature," *Int* 32 (1978) 46-55; idem, *Introduction to the Old Testament as Scripture* (Philadelphia: Fortress, 1979); D. L. Christensen, *Transformation of the War Oracle in Old Testament Prophecy: Studies in the Oracles against the Nations* (HDR 3; Missoula: Scholars Press, 1975); R. E. Clements, *One Hundred Years of Old Testament Interpretation* (Philadelphia: Westminster, 1976); idem, "Patterns in the Prophetic Canon," in *Canon and Authority: Essays in Old Testament Religion and Theology* (ed. B. O. Long and G. W. Coats; Philadelphia: Fortress, 1977) 42-55; idem, "Patterns in the Prophetic Canon: Healing the Blind," in *Canon, Theology, and Old Testament Interpretation* (*Fest.* B. S. Childs; ed. G. M. Tucker et al.; Philadelphia: Fortress, 1988) 189-200; idem, *Prophecy and Covenant* (SBT 1/43; London: SCM, 1965); idem, *Prophecy and Tradition* (Atlanta: John Knox, 1975); idem, "The Prophet and His Editors," in *The Bible in Three Dimensions* (JSOTSup 87; Sheffield: JSOT Press, 1990) 203-20; R. J. Clifford, "The Use of HÔY in the Prophets," *CBQ* 28 (1966) 458-64; R. J. Coggins et al., eds., *Israel's Prophetic Tradition* (*Fest.* P. R. Ackroyd; Cambridge: University Press, 1982); E. W. Conrad, *Fear Not Warrior: A Study of 'al tira' Pericopes in the Hebrew Scriptures* (BJS 75; Chico: Scholars Press, 1985); idem, "Second Isaiah and the Priestly Oracle of Salvation," *ZAW* 93 (1981) 234-46; J. L. Crenshaw, *Hymnic Affirmation of Divine Justice: The Doxologies of Amos and Related Texts in the Old Testament* (SBLDS 24; Missoula: Scholars Press, 1975); idem, *Prophetic Conflict: Its Effect upon Israelite Religion* (BZAW 124; Berlin: de Gruyter, 1971); idem, "YHWH Ṣĕbaʾôt Šĕmô: A Form-Critical Analysis," *ZAW* 81 (1969) 156-75; R. C. Culley and T. W. Overholt, eds., *Anthropological Perspectives on Old Testament Prophecy* (Semeia 21; Chico: Scholars Press, 1982); D. R. Daniels, "Is There a 'Prophetic Lawsuit' Genre?" *ZAW* 99 (1987) 339-60; M. De Roche,

2

"YHWH's *rîb* against Israel: A Reassessment of the So-Called 'Prophetic Lawsuit' in the Preexilic Prophets," *JBL* 102 (1983) 563-74; S. J. De Vries, *1 and 2 Chronicles* (FOTL XI; Grand Rapids: Eerdmans, 1989); M. Dietrich, *Prophetie und Geschichte* (Göttingen: Vandenhoeck & Ruprecht, 1972); H. M. Dion, "The Patriarchal Traditions and the Literary Form of the 'Oracle of Salvation,' " *CBQ* 29 (1967) 198-206; P.-E. Dion, "The 'Fear Not' Formula and Holy War," *CBQ* 32 (1970) 565-70; O. Eissfeldt, *The Old Testament: An Introduction* (tr. P. Ackroyd; New York: Harper & Row, 1965); idem, "The Prophetic Literature" (tr. D. R. Ap-Thomas), in *The Old Testament and Modern Study* (ed. H. H. Rowley; Oxford: Clarendon, 1951) 114-61; idem, "Zur Überlieferungs-geschichte der Prophetenbücher des Alten Testaments," *Kleine Schriften* (1966) 3:55-60 (repr. from *TLZ* 73 [1948] 529-34); F. Ellermeier, *Prophetie in Mari und Israel* (Herzberg: E. Jungfer, 1968); J. Fichtner, "Jesaja unter den Weisen," *TLZ* 74 (1949) 75-80; M. H. Floyd, "Prophetic Complaints about the Fulfillment of Oracles in Habakkuk 1:2-17 and Jeremiah 15:10-18," *JBL* 110 (1991) 397-418; G. Fohrer, "Die Gattung der Berichte über symbolische Handlungen der Propheten," in *Studien zur alttestamentlichen Prophetie (1949-1965)* (BZAW 99; Berlin: Töpelmann, 1967) 92-112 (repr. from *ZAW* 64 [1952] 101-20); idem, "Micha 1," in *Das ferne und nahe Wort* (*Fest.* L. Rost; ed. F. Maas; BZAW 105; Berlin: Töpelmann, 1967) 65-80; idem, "Neuere Literatur zur alttestament-lichen Prophetie," *TRu* 19 (1951) 277-346; 20 (1952) 193-271, 295-361; idem, "Neue Literatur zur alttestamentlichen Prophetie (1961-1970)," *TRu* 40 (1975) 193-209, 337-77; 41 (1976) 1-12; idem, "Prophetie und Magie," in *Studien zur alttestamentlichen Pro-phetie (1949-1965)* (BZAW 99; Berlin: Töpelmann, 1967) 242-64; idem, "Remarks on Modern Interpretation of the Prophets," *JBL* 80 (1961) 309-19; idem, "Zehn Jahre Literatur zur alttestamentlichen Prophetie (1950-1960)," *TRu* 28 (1962) 1-75, 235-97, 301-74; idem, *Die symbolischen Handlungen der Propheten* (2nd ed.; ATANT 54; Zurich: Zwingli, 1968); B. Gemser, "The *rîb*- or Controversy-Pattern in Hebrew Mentality," in *Wisdom in Israel and in the Ancient Near East* (*Fest.* H. H. Rowley; ed. M. Noth and D. W. Thomas; VTSup 3; Leiden: Brill, 1955) 120-37; B. Gerhardsson, "Mündliche und schriftliche Tradition der Prophetenbücher," *TZ* 17 (1961) 216-20; E. Gerstenberger, "Jeremiah's Complaints: Observations on Jer 15:10-21," *JBL* 82 (1963) 393-408; idem, "The Woe-Oracles of the Prophets," *JBL* 81 (1962) 249-63; Y. Gitay, "Deutero-Isaiah: Oral or Written?" *JBL* 99 (1980) 185-97; idem, *Isaiah and His Audience: The Structure and Meaning of Isaiah 1–12* (SSN 30; Assen/Maastricht: Van Gorcum, 1991); idem, *Prophecy and Persuasion: A Study of Isaiah 40–48* (Bonn: Linguistica Biblica, 1981); F. J. Goldbaum, "Two Hebrew Quasi-Adverbs *lkn* and *’kn*," *JNES* 23 (1964) 132-35; D. E. Gowan, "Habak-kuk and Wisdom," *Perspective* 9 (1968) 157-66; A. Graffy, *A Prophet Confronts His People: The Disputation Speech in the Prophets* (AnBib 104; Rome: Biblical Institute, 1984); P. Grech, "Interprophetic Re-interpretation and Old Testament Eschatology," *Augustinianum* 9 (1969) 235-65; F. Greenspahn, "Why Prophecy Ceased," *JBL* 108 (1989) 37-49; H. Gressmann, *Die älteste Geschichtsschreibung und Prophetie Israels* (SAT 2/1; Göttingen: Vandenhoeck & Ruprecht, 1910); idem, "Die literarische Analyse Deuterojesajas," *ZAW* 34 (1914) 254-97; idem, *Der Messias* (FRLANT 34; Göttingen: Vandenhoeck & Ruprecht, 1929); H. Gross, "Gab es in Israel ein 'prophetisches Amt'?" *TTZ* 73 (1964) 336-49; H. Gunkel, "Einleitungen," in H. Schmidt, *Die grossen Propheten* (2nd ed.; SAT 2/2; Göttingen: Vandenhoeck & Ruprecht, 1923) IX-LXX; idem, *Die israelitische Literatur* (Darmstadt: Wissenschaftliche Buchgesellschaft, 1963; repr. from *Die orientalischen Litera-turen* [ed. P. Hinneberg; 2nd ed.; Leipzig: Teubner, 1925] 53-112); idem, "Jesaia 33, eine

3

prophetische Liturgie," *ZAW* 42 (1924) 177-208; idem, "Propheten II: Seit Amos," *RGG*[2] (= "The Israelite Prophecy from the Time of Amos," in *Twentieth Century Theology in the Making* [ed. J. Pelikan; tr. R. A. Wilson; New York: Harper & Row, 1969] 48-75); A. H. J. Gunneweg, *Mündliche und schriftliche Tradition der vorexilischen Prophetenbücher als Problem der neueren Prophetenforschung* (FRLANT 73; Göttingen: Vandenhoeck & Ruprecht, 1959); idem, "Ordinationsformular oder Berufungsbericht in Jeremia 1," in *Glaube, Geist, Geschichte (Fest.* E. Benz; ed. G. Müller and W. Zeller; Leiden: Brill, 1967) 91-98; N. Habel, "The Form and Significance of the Call Narratives," *ZAW* 77 (1965) 297-323; D. G. Hagstrom, *The Coherence of the Book of Micah: A Literary Analysis* (SBLDS 89; Atlanta: Scholars Press, 1988); A. Haldar, *Associations of Cult Prophets among the Ancient Semites* (Uppsala: Almqvist & Wiksell, 1945); B. Halpern, "The Ritual Background of Zechariah's Temple Song," *CBQ* 40 (1978) 167-90; R. M. Hals, *Ezekiel* (FOTL XIX; Grand Rapids: Eerdmans, 1989); M. Haran, "From Early to Classical Prophecy: Continuity and Change," *VT* 27 (1977) 385-97; C. Hardmeier, *Prophetie im Streit vor dem Untergang Judas* (BZAW 187; Berlin: de Gruyter, 1990); idem, *Texttheorie und biblische Exegese: Zur rhetorischen Funktion der Trauermetaphorik in der Prophetie* (BEvT 79; Munich: Kaiser, 1978); P. B. Harner, "The Salvation Oracle in Second Isaiah," *JBL* 88 (1969) 418-34; J. Harvey, *Le plaidoyer prophétique contre Israël après la rupture de l'alliance* (Montreal: Bellarmin, 1967); idem, "Le 'rîb-Pattern,' réquisitoire prophétique sur la rupture de l'alliance," *Bib* 43 (1962) 172-96; J. H. Hayes, "The History of the Form-Critical Study of Prophecy," in *SBL 1973 Seminar Papers* (ed. G. McRae; vol. 1; Cambridge: Society of Biblical Literature, 1973) 60-99; idem, *An Introduction to Old Testament Study* (Nashville: Abingdon, 1979); idem, "Prophetism at Mari and Old Testament Parallels," *ATR* 49 (1967) 397-409; idem, "The Usage of Oracles against Foreign Nations in Ancient Israel," *JBL* 87 (1968) 81-92; J. Hempel, *Die althebräische Literatur und ihr hellenistisch-jüdisches Nachleben* (Wildpark-Potsdam: Akademische Verlagsgesellschaft, 1934); idem, *Worte der Propheten* (Berlin: Töpelmann, 1949); M.-L. Henry, *Prophet und Tradition: Versuch einer Problemstellung* (BZAW 116; Berlin: de Gruyter, 1969); R. Hentschke, *Die Stellung der vorexilischen Schriftpropheten zum Kultus* (BZAW 75; Berlin: Töpelmann, 1957); S. Herrmann, "Prophetie in Israel und Ägypten: Recht und Grenze eines Vergleichs," *Congress Volume, Bonn 1962* (VTSup 9; Leiden: Brill, 1963) 47-65; idem, *Ursprung und Funktion der Prophetie im alten Israel* (Opladen: Westdeutscher, 1976); F. Hesse, "Wurzelt die prophetische Gerichtsrede im israelitische Kult?" *ZAW* 65 (1953) 45-53; D. R. Hillers, *Treaty-Curses and the Old Testament Prophets* (BibOr 16; Rome: Pontifical Biblical Institute, 1964); Y. Hoffman, *The Prophecies against Foreign Nations in the Bible* (Tel Aviv: Tel Aviv University, 1977) (in Hebrew); J. S. Holladay Jr., "Assyrian Statecraft and the Prophets of Israel," *HTR* 63 (1970) 29-51; W. L. Holladay, *The Architecture of Jeremiah 1–20* (Lewisburg; Associated University Presses, 1976); idem, "Isa. iii 10-11: An Archaic Wisdom Passage," *VT* 18 (1968) 481-87; idem, *Jeremiah* (2 vols.; Hermeneia; Philadelphia: Fortress, 1986–89); idem, "The Recovery of Poetic Passages of Jeremiah," *JBL* 85 (1966) 401-35; G. Hölscher, *Die Profeten* (Leipzig: Hinrichs, 1914); F. Horst, "Die Visionsschilderungen der alttestamentlichen Propheten," *EvT* 20 (1960) 193-205; P. R. House, *The Unity of the Twelve* (JSOTSup 97; BLS 27; Sheffield: Almond, 1990); H. Huffmon, "The Covenant Lawsuit in the Prophets," *JBL* 78 (1959) 285-95; idem, "The Origins of Prophecy," in *Magnalia Dei: The Mighty Acts of God (Fest.* G. E. Wright; ed. F. M. Cross et al.; Garden City: Doubleday, 1976) 171-86; idem, "Prophecy in the Mari Letters," in *Biblical Archeologist Reader* 3 (ed. E. F. Campbell Jr. and D. N. Freedman; Garden City: Doubleday, 1970)

199-224 (repr. from *BA* 31 [1968] 101-24); P. Humbert, "Die Herausforderungsformel *'hinnenî êlēkâ,'*" *ZAW* 51 (1933) 101-8; A. Vanlier Hunter, *Seek the Lord! A Study of the Meaning and Function of the Exhortations in Amos, Hosea, Isaiah, Micah, and Zephaniah* (Baltimore: St. Mary's Seminary and University, 1982); H. Jahnow, *Das hebräische Leichenlied im Rahmen der Völkerdichtung* (BZAW 36; Giessen: Töpelmann, 1923); W. Janzen, *Mourning Cry and Woe Oracle* (BZAW 125; Berlin: de Gruyter, 1972); E. S. Jenni, *Die politischen Voraussagen der Propheten* (Zurich: Zwingli, 1956); C. Jeremias, *Die Nachtgesichte des Sacharja: Untersuchungen zu ihrer Stellung im Zusammenhang der Visionsberichte im Alten Testament und zu ihrem Bildmaterial* (FRLANT 117; Göttingen: Vandenhoeck & Ruprecht, 1977); J. Jeremias, Kultprophetie und Geschichtsverkündigung in der späten Königszeit Israels (WMANT 35; Neukirchen-Vluyn: Neukirchener, 1970); A. S. Johnson, *The Cultic Prophet in Ancient Israel* (2nd ed.; Cardiff: University of Wales, 1962); O. Kaiser, *Introduction to the Old Testament: A Presentation of Its Results and Problems* (tr. J. Sturdy; Minneapolis: Augsburg, 1975); idem, *Isaiah 1–12* (tr. J. Bowden; 2nd ed.; OTL; Philadelphia: Westminster, 1983); idem, *Isaiah 13–39* (tr. R. A. Wilson; OTL; Philadelphia: Westminster, 1974); A. S. Kapelrud, "Cult and Prophetic Words," *ST* 4 (1951) 5-12; M. Kessler, "Form-Critical Suggestions on Jer 36," *CBQ* 28 (1966) 389-401; idem, "Jeremiah Chapters 26–45 Reconsidered," *JNES* 27 (1968) 81-88; R. Kilian, "Die prophetischen Berufungsberichte," in *Theologie im Wandel* (Freiburg: E. Wewel, 1967) 356-76; W. Klatt, *Hermann Gunkel* (FRLANT 100; Göttingen: Vandenhoeck & Ruprecht, 1969); R. P. Knierim, "Criticism of Literary Features, Form, Tradition, and Redaction," in *The Hebrew Bible and Its Modern Interpreters* (ed. D. A. Knight and G. M. Tucker; Chico: Scholars Press, 1985) 123-65; idem, "Old Testament Form Criticism Reconsidered," *Int* 27 (1973) 435-68; K. Koch, "Die Entstehung der sozialen Kritik bei den Propheten," in *Probleme biblischer Theologie (Fest. G. von Rad; ed. H. W. Wolff; Munich: Kaiser, 1971) 236-57; idem, *The Growth of the Biblical Tradition: The Form-Critical Method* (tr. S. Cupitt; New York: Scribner's, 1969); K. Koch et al., *Amos: Untersucht mit den Methoden einer strukturalen Formgeschichte* (3 vols.; AOAT 30; Kevelaer: Butzon & Bercker; Neukirchen-Vluyn: Neukirchener, 1976); L. Köhler, "Der Botenspruch," in *Kleine Lichter* (Zurich: Zwingli, 1945) 11-17; idem, *Deuterojesaja (Jesaja 40–55) stilkritisch untersucht* (BZAW 37; Giessen: Töpelmann, 1923); H. Kosmala, "Form and Structure of Isaiah 58," *ASTI* 5 (1967) 69-81; H.-J. Kraus, *Die prophetische Verkündigung des Rechts in Israel* (TS 51; Zurich: Evangelischer, 1957); J. Levenson, *Theology of the Program of Restoration of Ezekiel 40–48* (HSM 10; Missoula: Scholars Press and Harvard Semitic Museum, 1976); J. Limburg, "The Root *ryb* and the Prophetic Lawsuit Speeches," *JBL* 88 (1969) 291-304; J. Lindblom, *Die literarische Gattung des prophetischen Literatur* (UUÅ Theologi 1; Uppsala: Lundquistska, 1924); idem, *Prophecy in Ancient Israel* (Philadelphia: Fortress, 1967); idem, "Wisdom in the Old Testament Prophets," in *Wisdom in Israel and in the Ancient Near East (Fest. H. H. Rowley; ed. M. Noth and D. W. Thomas; VTSup 3; Leiden: Brill, 1955) 192-204; W. Lofthouse, "Thus hath JHVH Said," *AJSL* 40 (1923-24) 231-51; B. O. Long, "Divination as Model for Literary Form," in *Language in Religious Practice* (ed. W. J. Samarin; Rowley, MA: Newbury House, 1976) 84-100; idem, "The Effect of Divination upon Israelite Literature," *JBL* 92 (1973) 489-97; idem, *1 Kings; with an Introduction to Historical Literature* (FOTL IX; Grand Rapids: Eerdmans, 1984); idem, "Prophetic Authority as Social Reality," in *Canon and Authority: Essays in Old Testament Religion and Theology* (ed. B. O. Long and G. W. Coats; Philadelphia: Fortress, 1977)

3-20; idem, "Prophetic Call Traditions and Reports of Visions," *ZAW* 84 (1972) 494-500; idem, "Recent Field Studies in Oral Literature and the Question of *Sitz im Leben*," *Semeia* 5 (1976) 35-49; idem, "Recent Field Studies in Oral Literature and Their Bearing on OT Criticism," *VT* 26 (1976) 187-98; idem, "Reports of Visions Among the Prophets," *JBL* 95 (1976) 353-65; idem, *2 Kings* (FOTL X; Grand Rapids: Eerdmans, 1991); "The Social Setting for Prophetic Miracle Stories," *Semeia* 3 (1975) 46-63; idem, "Two Question and Answer Schemata in the Prophets," *JBL* 90 (1971) 129-39; J. R. Lundbom, *Jeremiah: A Study in Ancient Hebrew Rhetoric* (SBLDS 18; Missoula: Scholars Press, 1975); idem, "Poetic Structure and Prophetic Rhetoric in Hosea," *VT* 29 (1979) 300-308; W. McKane, "Prophecy and Prophetic Literature," in *Tradition and Interpretation: Essays by Members of the Society for Old Testament Study* (ed. G. W. Anderson; Oxford: Clarendon, 1979) 163-88; idem, "Prophet and Institution," *ZAW* 94 (1982) 251-66; A. Malamat, "Prophetic Revelations in New Documents from Mari and the Bible," *Volume du Congrès, Genève 1965* (VTSup 15; Leiden: Brill, 1966) 207-27; W. E. March, "Prophecy," in *Old Testament Form Criticism* (ed. J. H. Hayes; San Antonio: Trinity University, 1974) 141-77; idem, "Redaction Criticism and the Formation of Prophetic Books," in *SBL 1977 Seminar Papers* (ed. P. J. Achtemeier; Missoula: Scholars Press, 1977) 87-101; L. Markert, *Struktur und Bezeichnung des Scheltworts: Eine gattungskritische Studie anhand des Amosbuches* (BZAW 140; Berlin: de Gruyter, 1977); R. A. Mason, "The Purpose of the 'Editorial Framework' of the Book of Haggai," *VT* 27 (1977) 413-21; M. P. Matheney, "Interpretation of Hebrew Prophetic Symbol Act," *Encounter* 29 (1968) 256-67; F. Matheus, *Singt dem Herrn ein neues Lied: Die Hymnen Deuterojesajas* (SBS 141; Stuttgart: Katholisches Bibelwerk, 1990); J. L. Mays and P. J. Achtemeier, eds., *Interpreting the Prophets* (Philadelphia: Fortress, 1987); S. A. Meier, *The Messenger in the Ancient Semitic World* (HSM 45; Atlanta: Scholars Press, 1988); idem, *Speaking of Speaking: Marking Direct Discourse in the Hebrew Bible* (VTSup 46; Leiden: Brill, 1992); R. F. Melugin, "The Conventional and the Creative in Isaiah's Judgment Oracles," *CBQ* 36 (1974) 301-11; idem, "Deutero-Isaiah and Form Criticism," *VT* 21 (1971) 326-37; idem, *The Formation of Isaiah 40–55* (BZAW 141; Berlin: de Gruyter, 1976); idem, "Muilenburg, Form Criticism, and Theological Exegesis," in *Encounter with the Text: Form and History in the Hebrew Bible* (ed. M. J. Buss; Philadelphia: Fortress; Missoula: Scholars Press, 1979) 91-99; W. L. Moran, "New Evidence from Mari on the History of Prophecy," *Bib* 50 (1969) 15-56; S. Mowinckel, *Prophecy and Tradition* (Oslo: J. Dybwad, 1946); idem, *Psalmenstudien,* vol. 3: *Kultprophetie und prophetische Psalmen* (repr. Amsterdam: P. Schippers, 1966); idem, *Zur Komposition des Buches Jeremia* (Kristiana: J. Dybwad, 1914); J. Muilenburg, "Baruch the Scribe," in *Proclamation and Presence (Fest.* G. H. Davies; ed. J. I. Durham and J. R. Porter; London: SCM, 1970) 215-38; idem, "The Book of Isaiah, Chapters 40–66," *IB* 5 (1956) 381-773; idem, "Form Criticism and Beyond," *JBL* 88 (1969) 1-18; idem, "The Linguistic and Rhetorical Usages of the Particle *kî* in the Old Testament," *HUCA* 32 (1961) 135-60; idem, "The 'Office' of the Prophet in Ancient Israel," in *The Bible in Modern Scholarship* (ed. J. P. Hyatt; Nashville: Abingdon, 1965) 74-97; D. F. Murray, "The Rhetoric of Disputation: Re-examination of a Prophetic Genre," *JSOT* 38 (1987) 95-121; R. Murray, "Prophecy and the Cult," in *Israel's Prophetic Tradition (Fest.* P. R. Ackroyd; ed. R. J. Coggins et al.; Cambridge: University Press, 1982) 200-216; P. H. A. Neumann, "Prophetenforschung seit Heinrich Ewald," in *Das Prophetenverständnis in der deutschsprachigen Forschung seit Heinrich Ewald* (ed. P. H. A. Neumann; WF 307; Darmstadt: Wissenschaftliche Buchgesellschaft,

1979) 1-51; E. W. Nicholson, *Preaching to the Exiles: A Study of the Prose Tradition in the Book of Jeremiah* (Oxford: Blackwell, 1970); S. Niditch, *The Symbolic Vision in Biblical Tradition* (HSM 30; Chico: Scholars Press, 1983); E. Nielsen, "Deuterojesaja: Erwägungen zur Formkritik, Traditions- und Redaktionsgeschichte," *VT* 20 (1970) 190-205; K. Nielsen, "Das Bild des Gerichts (*Rib*-Pattern) in Jes. I–XII," *VT* 29 (1979) 309-24; idem, *YHWH as Prosecutor and Judge: An Investigation of the Prophetic Lawsuit (Rîb-Pattern)* (tr. F. Cryer; JSOTSup 9; Sheffield: JSOT Press, 1978); E. Noort, *Untersuchungen zum Gottesbescheid in Mari: Die 'Mari-prophetie' in der alttestamentlichen Forschung* (AOAT 202; Kevelaer: Butzon & Bercker; Neukirchen-Vluyn: Neukirchener, 1977); R. North, "Angel-Prophet or Satan-Prophet?" *ZAW* 82 (1970) 31-67; H. M. Orlinsky, "The Seer in Ancient Israel," *OrAnt* 4 (1965) 153-74; G. S. Ogden, "Prophetic Oracles Against Foreign Nations and Psalms of Communal Lament: The Relationship of Psalm 137 to Jeremiah 49:7-22 and Obadiah," *JSOT* 24 (1982) 89-97; T. W. Overholt, *Channels of Prophecy: The Social Dynamics of Prophetic Activity* (Minneapolis: Fortress, 1989); idem, "Commanding the Prophets: Amos and the Problem of Prophetic Authority," *CBQ* 41 (1979) 517-32; idem, "The Ghost Dance of 1890 and the Nature of the Prophetic Process," *Ethnohistory* 21 (1974) 37-63; idem, "Jeremiah and the Nature of the Prophetic Process," in *Scripture in History and Theology* (Fest. J. C. Rylaarsdam; ed. A. L. Merrill and T. W. Overholt; PTMS 17; Pittsburgh: Pickwick, 1977) 129-50; idem, "Jeremiah 2 and the Problem of 'Audience Reaction,' " *CBQ* 41 (1979) 262-73; idem, *The Threat of Falsehood: A Study in the Theology of the Book of Jeremiah* (SBT 2/15; Naperville: Allenson, 1970); S. B. Parker, "Possession Trance and Prophecy in Pre-exilic Israel," *VT* 28 (1978) 271-85; D. Patrick and A. Scult, *Rhetoric and Biblical Interpretation* (JSOTSup 86; BLS 26; Sheffield: Almond, 1990); D. L. Petersen, "Israelite Prophecy: Change versus Continuity," *Congress Volume, Leuven 1989* (ed. J. A. Emerton; VTSup 43; Leiden: Brill, 1991) 190-203; idem, *Late Israelite Prophecy: Studies in Deutero-Prophetic Literature and in Chronicles* (SBLMS 23; Missoula: Scholars Press, 1977); idem, "The Oracles against the Nations: A Form-Critical Analysis," in *SBL 1975 Seminar Papers* (ed. G. McRae; Missoula: Scholars Press, 1975) 1:39-61; idem, *The Roles of Israel's Prophets* (JSOTSup 17; Sheffield: JSOT Press, 1981); D. L. Petersen, ed., *Prophecy in Israel* (IRT 10; Philadelphia: Fortress, 1986); E. Pfeiffer, "Die Disputationsworte im Buche Maleachi," *EvT* 19 (1959) 546-68; G. Quell, "Der Kultprophet," *TLZ* 81 (1956) 402-3; idem, *Wahre und falsche Propheten* (Gütersloh: Bertelsmann, 1952); K. von Rabenau, "Die Form des Rätsels im Buche Hesekiel," *WZHalle* 7 (1957-58) 1055-57; G. von Rad, *Old Testament Theology* 2 (tr. D. Stalker; New York: Harper & Row, 1965); T. Raitt, "The Prophetic Summons to Repentance," *ZAW* 83 (1971) 30-49; G. W. Ramsey, "Speech-Forms in Hebrew Law and Prophetic Oracles," *JBL* 96 (1977) 45-58; B. Reicke, "Liturgical Traditions in Mic. 7," *HTR* 60 (1967) 349-67; R. Rendtorff, "Botenformel und Botenspruch," *ZAW* 74 (1962) 165-77; idem, "Erwägungen zur Frühgeschichte des Prophetentums in Israel," *ZTK* 59 (1962) 145-67; idem, *The Old Testament: An Introduction* (tr. J. Bowden; Philadelphia: Fortress, 1986); idem, "Priesterliche Kulttheologie und prophetische Kultpolemik," *TLZ* 81 (1956) 339-52; idem, "Zum Gebrauch der Formel *ne'um JHWH* im Jeremiabuch," *ZAW* 66 (1954) 27-37; H. G. Reventlow, *Das Amt des Propheten bei Amos* (FRLANT 80; Göttingen: Vandenhoeck & Ruprecht, 1962); idem, "Gattung und Überlieferung in der 'Tempelrede Jeremias,' Jer 7 und 26," *ZAW* 81 (1969) 315-52; idem, *Liturgie und prophetisches Ich bei Jeremia* (Gütersloh: G. Mohn, 1963); idem, "Prophetenamt und Mittleramt," *ZTK* 58 (1961)

269-84; idem, *Wächter über Israel: Ezechiel und seine Tradition* (BZAW 82; Berlin: Töpelmann, 1962); W. Richter, *Exegese als Literaturwissenschaft: Entwurf einer alttestamentlichen Literaturtheorie und Methodologie* (Göttingen: Vandenhoeck & Ruprecht, 1971); idem, *Die sogennanten vorprophetischen Berufungsberichte* (FRLANT 101; Göttingen: Vandenhoeck & Ruprecht, 1970); C. Rietzschel, *Das Problem der Urrolle: Ein Beitrag zur Redaktionsgeschichte des Jeremiabuches* (Gütersloh: G. Mohn, 1966); A. Rofé, "The Arrangement of the Book of Jeremiah," *ZAW* 101 (1989) 390-98; idem, "Classes in the Prophetical Stories: Didactic Legenda and Parable," *Studies on Prophecy* (VTSup 26; Leiden: Brill, 1974) 143-64; idem, "The Classification of the Prophetical Stories," *JBL* 89 (1970) 427-40; idem, *The Prophetical Stories* (Jerusalem: Magnes, 1988); J. F. Ross, "Prophecy in Hamath, Israel, and Mari," *HTR* 63 (1970) 1-28; idem, "The Prophet as YHWH's Messenger," in *Israel's Prophetic Heritage* (*Fest.* J. Muilenburg; ed. B. W. Anderson and W. Harrelson; New York: Harper & Row, 1962) 98-107; H. H. Rowley, "The Nature of Old Testament Prophecy in the Light of Recent Study," *HTR* 38 (1945) 1-38; J. A. Sanders, "Hermeneutics in True and False Prophecy," in *Canon and Authority: Essays in Old Testament Religion and Theology* (ed. B. O. Long and G. W. Coats; Philadelphia: Fortress, 1977) 21-41; H. Schmidt, *Die grossen Propheten* (2nd ed.; SAT 2/2; Göttingen: Vandenhoeck & Ruprecht, 1923); W. H. Schmidt, *Zukunftsgewissheit und Gegenwartskritik: Grundzüge prophetischer Verkündigung* (BibS[N] 64; Neukirchen-Vluyn: Neukirchener, 1973); R. B. Y. Scott, "The Literary Structure of Isaiah's Oracles," in *Studies in Old Testament Prophecy* (*Fest.* T. H. Robinson; ed. H. H. Rowley; Edinburgh: T. & T. Clark, 1950) 175-86; I. P. Seierstad, *Die Offenbarungserlebnisse der Propheten Amos, Jesaja und Jeremia: Eine Untersuchung der Erlebnisvorgänge unter besonderer Berücksichtigung ihrer religiös-sittlichen Art und Auswirkung* (2nd ed.; Oslo: Universitetsforlaget, 1965); C. R. Seitz, "The Prophet Moses and the Canonical Shape of Jeremiah," *ZAW* 101 (1989) 3-27; idem, *Theology in Conflict: Reactions to the Exile in the Book of Jeremiah* (BZAW 176; Berlin: de Gruyter, 1989); E. Sellin and G. Fohrer, *Introduction to the Old Testament* (tr. D. Green; Nashville: Abingdon, 1968); K. Seybold, *Das davidische Königtum im Zeugnis der Propheten* (FRLANT 107; Göttingen: Vandenhoeck & Ruprecht, 1972); M. Sister, "Die Typen der prophetischen Visionen in der Bibel," *MGWJ* 78 (1934) 399-430; W. A. Smalley, "Recursion Patterns and the Sectioning of Amos," *BT* 30 (1979) 118-27; W. D. Stacey, *Prophetic Drama in the Old Testament* (London: Epworth, 1990); O. H. Steck, *Der Abschluss der Prophetie im Alten Testament: Ein Versuch zur Frage der Vorgeschichte des Kanons* (BTS 17; Neukirchen-Vluyn: Neukirchener, 1991); idem, "Theological Streams of Tradition," in *Tradition and Theology in the Old Testament* (ed. D. A. Knight; Philadelphia: Fortress, 1977) 183-214; M. A. Sweeney, "Concerning the Structure and Generic Character of the Book of Nahum," *ZAW* 104 (1992) 364-77; idem, "A Form-Critical Reassessment of the Book of Zephaniah," *CBQ* 53 (1991) 388-408; idem, *Isaiah 1-4 and the Post-Exilic Understanding of the Isaianic Tradition* (BZAW 171; Berlin: de Gruyter, 1988); idem, "Structure, Genre, and Intent in the Book of Habakkuk," *VT* 41 (1991) 63-83; K. A. Tångberg, *Die prophetische Mahnrede: Form- und traditionsgeschichtliche Studien zum prophetischen Umkehrruf* (FRLANT 143; Göttingen: Vandenhoeck & Ruprecht, 1987); S. Terrien, "Amos and Wisdom," in *Israel's Prophetic Heritage* (*Fest.* J. Muilenburg; ed. B. W. Anderson and W. Harrelson; New York: Harper & Row, 1962) 108-15; R. J. Tournay, *Seeing and Hearing God with the Psalms: The Prophetic Liturgy of the Second Temple in Jerusalem* (tr. J. E. Crowley; JSOTSup 118; Sheffield: JSOT Press, 1991); M. Tsevat,

"The Neo-Assyrian and Neo-Babylonian Vassal Oaths and the Prophet Ezekiel," *JBL* 78 (1959) 199-204; G. M. Tucker, *Form Criticism of the Old Testament* (Philadelphia: Fortress, 1971); idem, "Prophecy and the Prophetic Literature," in *The Hebrew Bible and Its Modern Interpreters* (ed. D. A. Knight and G. M. Tucker; Chico: Scholars Press, 1985) 325-68; idem, "Prophetic Authenticity: A Form-Critical Study of Amos 7:10-17," *Int* 27 (1973) 423-34; idem, "Prophetic Speech," *Int* 32 (1978) 31-45; idem, "Prophetic Superscriptions and the Growth of a Canon," in *Canon and Authority: Essays in Old Testament Religion and Theology* (ed. B. O. Long and G. W. Coats; Philadelphia: Fortress, 1977) 56-70; H. Utzschneider, *Hosea, Prophet vor dem Ende: Zum Verhältnis von Geschichte und Institution in der alttestamentlichen Prophetie* (OBO 31; Göttingen: Vandenhoeck & Ruprecht; Freiburg: Universitätsverlag, 1980); W. Vogels, "Les récits de vocation des prophètes," *NRT* 95 (1973) 3-24; J. Vollmer, *Geschichtliche Rückblicke und Motive in der Prophetie des Amos, Hosea, und Jesaja* (BZAW 119; Berlin: de Gruyter, 1971); H. E. von Waldow, *Der traditionsgeschichtliche Hintergrund der prophetischen Gerichtsreden* (BZAW 85; Berlin: Töpelmann, 1963); S. D. Walters, "Prophecy in Mari and Israel," *JBL* 89 (1970) 78-81; G. Wanke, "*'ôy* und *hôy*," *ZAW* 78 (1966) 215-18; idem, *Untersuchungen zur sogenannten Baruchschrift* (BZAW 122; Berlin: de Gruyter, 1971); G. Warmuth, *Das Mahnwort: Seine Bedeutung für die Verkündigung der vorexilischen Propheten Amos, Hosea, Micha, Jesaja und Jeremia* (BBET 1; Frankfurt: Lang, 1976); R. D. Weis, "A Definition of the Genre *Maśśa'* in the Hebrew Bible" (Diss., Claremont Graduate School, 1986); A. Weiser, *The Old Testament: Its Formation and Development* (tr. D. M. Barton; New York: Association, 1961); C. Westermann, *Basic Forms of Prophetic Speech* (tr. H. C. White; Cambridge: Lutterworth; Louisville: Westminster/John Knox, 1991; repr. from Philadelphia: Westminster, 1967); idem, "Das Heilswort bei Deuterojesaja," *EvT* 24 (1964) 355-73; idem, *Isaiah 40–66* (tr. D. Stalker; OTL; Philadelphia: Westminster, 1969); idem, "Die Mari-Briefe und die Prophetie in Israel," in *Forschung am Alten Testament* (TBü 24; Munich: Kaiser, 1964) 171-88; idem, *Prophetic Oracles of Salvation in the Old Testament* (tr. K. Crim; Louisville: Westminster/John Knox, 1991); idem, *Sprache und Struktur der Prophetie Deuterojesajas* (CTM 11; Stuttgart: Calwer, 1981); idem, "The Way of the Promise Through the Old Testament" (tr. L. Gaston and B. W. Anderson), in *The Old Testament and Christian Faith* (ed. B. W. Anderson; New York: Harper & Row, 1963) 200-224; idem, "Zur Erforschung und zum Verständnis der prophetischen Heilsworte," *ZAW* 98 (1986) 1-13; J. W. Whedbee, *Isaiah and Wisdom* (Nashville: Abingdon, 1971); H. Wildberger, *Jesaja* (BKAT X/1-3; Neukirchen-Vluyn: Neukirchener, 1972-82); idem, *JHWHwort und prophetische Rede bei Jeremia* (Zurich: Zwingli, 1942); idem, *JHWHs Eigentumsvolk: Eine Studie zur Traditionsgeschchte und Theologie des Erwählungsgedankens* (ATANT 37; Zurich: Zwingli, 1960); J. G. Williams, "The Alas-Oracles of the Eighth Century Prophets," *HUCA* 38 (1967) 75-91; idem, "The Social Location of Israelite Prophecy," *JAAR* 37 (1969) 153-65; J. T. Willis, "Redaction Criticism and Historical Reconstruction," in *Encounter with the Text: Form and History in the Hebrew Bible* (ed. M. J. Buss; SBL Semeia Supp.; Philadelphia: Fortress; Missoula: Scholars Press, 1979) 83-89; R. R. Wilson, "Early Israelite Prophecy," *Int* 32 (1978) 3-16; idem, "Form-Critical Investigation of the Prophetic Literature: The Present Situation," in *SBL 1973 Seminar Papers* (ed. G. W. MacRae; vol. 1; Cambridge, MA: Society of Biblical Literature, 1973) 100-121; idem, "Prophecy and Ecstasy: A Reexamination," *JBL* 98 (1979) 321-37; idem, *Prophecy and Society in Ancient Israel* (Philadelphia: Fortress, 1980); idem, "Prophecy and Society in

Ancient Israel: The Present State of the Inquiry," in *SBL 1977 Seminar Papers* (ed. P. J. Achtemeier; Missoula: Scholars Press, 1977) 341-58; H. W. Wolff, *Amos the Prophet* (tr. F. R. McCurley; Philadelphia: Fortress, 1973); idem, "Der Aufruf zur Volksklage," *ZAW* 76 (1964) 48-56; idem, "Die Begründungen der prophetischen Heils- und Unheils- sprüche," *ZAW* 52 (1934) 1-22; idem, "Der Gerichtsverständnis der alttestamentlichen Prophetie," *EvT* 20 (1960) 218-35; idem, *Haggai* (tr. M. Kohl; CC; Minneapolis: Augs- burg, 1988); idem, "Hauptprobleme alttestamentlicher Prophetie," *EvT* 16 (1955) 446-68; idem, *Hosea* (tr. G. Stansell; Hermeneia; Philadelphia: Fortress, 1977); idem, "Hoseas geistige Heimat," *TLZ* 81 (1956) 83-94; idem, *Joel and Amos* (tr. W. Janzen, S. D. McBride Jr., and C. A. Muenchow; Hermeneia; Philadelphia: Fortress, 1977); idem, *Micah* (tr. G. Stansell; CC; Minneapolis: Fortress, 1990); idem, *Obadiah and Jonah* (tr. M. Kohl; CC; Minneapolis: Augsburg, 1986); idem, "Prophecy from the Eighth through the Fifth Century" (tr. W. S. Towner with J. E. Heebink), *Int* 32 (1978) 17-30; idem, "Das Thema 'Umkehr' in der alttestamentlichen Prophetie," *ZTK* 48 (1951) 129-48; idem, "Wie verstand Micha von Moreschet sein prophetisches Amt?" *Congress Volume, Göttingen 1977* (VTSup 29; Leiden: Brill, 1978) 403-17; idem, *Das Zitat im Prophe- tenspruch* (BEvT; Munich: Kaiser, 1937); G. E. Wright, "The Lawsuit of God: A Form- Critical Study of Deuteronomy 32," in *Israel's Prophetic Heritage* (*Fest.* J. Muilenburg; ed. B. W. Anderson and W. Harrelson; New York: Harper, 1962) 26-67; E. Würthwein, "Amos-Studien," *ZAW* 62 (1949-50) 10-52; idem, "Kultpolemik oder Kultbescheid? Beobachtungen zum Thema 'Prophetie und Kult,' " in *Tradition und Situation: Studien zur alttestamentlichen Prophetie* (ed. E. Würthwein and O. Kaiser: Göttingen: Vanden- hoeck & Ruprecht, 1963) 115-31; idem, "Der Ursprung der prophetischen Gerichtsrede," *ZTK* 49 (1952) 1-16; G. A. Yee, *Composition and Tradition in the Book of Hosea: A Redaction Critical Investigation* (SBLDS 102; Atlanta: Scholars Press, 1987); W. Zim- merli, *Ezekiel* (tr. R. E. Clements and J. D. Martin; 2 vols.; Hermeneia; Philadelphia: Fortress, 1979- 83); idem, "Prophetic Proclamation and Reinterpretation," in *Tradition and Theology in the Old Testament* (ed. D. A. Knight; Philadelphia: Fortress, 1977) 69-100; idem, "Vom Prophetenwort zum Prophetenbuch," *TLZ* 104 (1979) 481-96; idem, "The Word of Divine Self-Manifestation (Proof Saying), a Prophetic Genre," in *I Am YHWH* (tr. D. W. Stott; Atlanta: Knox, 1982) 99-110.

I. FORM CRITICISM AND PROPHETIC LITERATURE

Throughout most of the 20th century, form-critical research on the prophetic literature of the Hebrew Bible has been based largely on the premises laid down by Hermann Gunkel. In considering the nature of prophetic literature and the social functions of the prophets, Gunkel observed that "the prophets were not originally writers but speakers" ("The Prophets as Writers and Poets," in Pe- tersen, ed., *Prophecy in Israel,* 24). Prophets functioned in relation to their setting in the life of the people, and they delivered their messages to their Israelite and Judean audiences in oral speeches spoken in the temple, the royal court, the streets of the city, or in other locations that might provide a suitable setting for prophetic speech. Gunkel was heavily influenced by the Romanticist conceptions of the time, which posited the spontaneous but alogical genius of the primitive mind in contrast to the calm and well-reasoned reflection of the modern thinker and writer. Because the prophets were speakers, they employed short, self-contained speech units, often blurted out in a state of uncontrolled ecstasy, as their basic form of discourse. Such short speech units were easily memorized, and they were later placed into collections of the prophet's words that lacked any sense of logical organization or indication of the settings in which they were spoken. Such collections of prophetic oracles eventually formed the basis of the prophetic books that were written centuries after the deaths of the prophets as a means to preserve their sacred words for future generations.

As a result, most form-critical research on prophetic literature focuses on the forms or genres of prophetic *speech,* but there has been relatively little interest in the forms of prophetic *writing* except as a means to identify the speech forms. Gunkel argued that although the prophets were some of the most original thinkers in ancient Israel and Judah, they were dependent on traditional, stereotyped speech patterns or genres that determined the forms of their oral expression and thereby made it possible to identify and reconstruct the "original" forms of prophetic speech. Such a concern presupposes that the primary object of research is the word of the prophet him- or herself, and that the later editorial additions and literary supplements to the "original" prophetic collections stand as obstacles to the recovery of the prophetic word. The written work of later editors and tradents of the prophetic traditions was regarded as the work of "lesser intellects" (Gunkel, "Prophets as Writers and Poets," 23), who generally did not understand the significance of the prophetic message that they transmitted and frequently corrupted it by adding their own "irrelevant and very dull" comments and interpretations (see Koch, *Growth,* 57). Consequently, a great deal of early form-critical research concentrated on stripping away the "inferior" work of later redactors and tradents by using genre as a criterion to identify and reconstruct the theologically significant "original" prophetic speeches.

The nature of the prophetic literature, and indeed of the Hebrew Bible in general, poses a fundamental problem for such a conception of the form-critical enterprise. There is clear evidence of the presence of later writings in the prophetic literature that do not stem from the original prophet. One needs only to read the narratives about the prophets in Amos 7:10-17, Isaiah 36–39, Jeremiah 52, or the anonymous writings in Isaiah 40–66 or Zechariah 9–14 to recognize this point. But the prophetic literature of the Hebrew Bible does not distinguish between the "original" words of the prophets and the writings of the later redactors and tradents. Rather, an entire prophetic book is presented to the form critic in its totality, and it is in the form of the prophetic book that the prophetic message lays a claim to religious authority and interpretation. In interpreting the prophetic literature, the exegete cannot simply claim that some part of that literature is a worthy representation of the prophetic message and that some other part is less so.

The final form of the prophetic book in its entirety must therefore stand as the basis for form-critical exegesis. It is the only form in which the prophetic message is presented. This does not, however, negate the need to determine the history of the book's composition. It is necessary to distinguish between earlier and later material within the prophetic literature in order to understand the interaction between the prophetic message and the communities that accepted it and understood it as such, and thereby defined it as religiously significant. Such interaction demonstrates the continued vitality of the prophetic message. It points to the fact that the prophetic message was not read exclusively as an archival chronicle of past prophetic speeches delivered to an earlier Israelite or Judean community. Rather, the prophetic literature was preserved, transmitted, supplemented, and reformulated because later writers and communities believed that it addressed them and their situations respectively (see Clements, "Prophet").

This is especially evident in books such as Isaiah and Zechariah, which add deutero-prophetic literature to material that stems from or reflects the original prophet. Critical scholars are aware that Isaiah 40–66 and Zechariah 9–14 were written by anonymous prophets long after the lifetimes of Isaiah ben Amoz or Zechariah ben Berechiah ben Iddo, but these deutero-prophetic writings are presented as part of the message of the original prophet. Although Isaiah spoke about the Assyrian invasions and Zechariah spoke about the early Persian period restoration, later editors believed that Isaiah also addressed the Babylonian and Persian periods and that Zechariah also addressed the Hellenistic period, and these editers presented the messages of these prophets accordingly in the present forms of their respective books. The same principle applies to other prophetic books as well. The frequent references to Judah in the book of Hosea, a prophet who spoke exclusively to the northern kingdom of Israel, indicate that his message was read in relation to the Judean community following the collapse of the northern kingdom of Israel in the late 8th century (see Yee). The notice of the restoration of the "fallen booth of David" in Amos 9:11-15 speaks to the aspirations of the Jewish community in Jerusalem during the early Persian period that sought to restore Zerubbabel to the Davidic throne (see Wolff, *Joel and Amos,* 352-53). Likewise, the vision of the restored temple in Ezekiel 40–48 addresses the concerns of the same community that sought to restore the temple (see Levenson), and this vision has continued to function within Judaism as a description of the "Third Temple," which will be established at the end of days.

Although the words and actions of the original prophets initiated the composition of the prophetic literature, the writings of the later editors and tradents completed it. Obviously, they saw something of value in the words of the original prophets that prompted them to understand these words as an address to them and to their own situations. Only by investigating the process by which such later tradents understood, reformulated, and reapplied the earlier words of the prophets can the form critic identify the impetus for the preservation, growth, and continued vitality of the prophetic tradition. In order to understand fully the meaning and significance of the prophetic literature in relation to the communities that produced it, the form critic must account for the prophetic book in its entirety. This means that the form critic must consider *both* the "original" prophetic speech forms *and* the later material that defines the present form, insofar as they can be identified. The setting of a text form therefore includes both its *Sitz im Leben* ("setting in life") and its *Sitz im Literatur* ("setting in literature"; cf. Richter, *Exegese,* 148).

As a result of this challenge, form critics have paid increasing attention to the role of redaction criticism in their research. Redaction criticism is the study of the editorial formation of biblical literature. It is essentially a literary discipline, but like form criticism it is concerned with the social reality that stands behind a literary text in that it attempts to identify the work, setting, and intentions of the anonymous tradents who edited and shaped biblical literature into its present form. The extent to which the two methods can be separated is debatable. Each is necessarily dependent on the other, and the two methods together investigate different aspects of the same essential question. Whereas form criticism tends to focus on the oral or preliterary forms and settings of a text, redaction criticism focuses on its literary forms and settings. Because prophetic books are literary in nature, form criticism requires redaction criticism to identify the prophetic forms that constitute the object of its research. But redaction criticism also requires form criticism to identify earlier material, and thereby to provide the basis for understanding the later literary formulation. Together, form criticism and redaction criticism address the overall formation of prophetic books.

At this point form critics and redaction critics are faced with a fundamental problem in the study of prophetic literature. The final forms of the prophetic books constitute the necessary starting point for form- and redaction-critical research. They are the products of the books' final redactors, who selected, interpreted, arranged, supplemented, and perhaps reformulated the prophetic traditions. In short, redactors are not simply mechanistic editors; they are authors in their own right who employ the works of earlier authors when composing their own redactional works. Consequently, the present form of the prophetic literature reflects the redactors' understanding of the prophetic message, which may or may not be the same as that of the earlier authors or prophets whose works appear within the book.

Because the form critic cannot assume that a prophetic book contains preredactional forms, redaction-critical questions must be addressed from the outset (see Knierim, "Criticism," esp. 153-58; cf. March, "Redaction Criticism"). Only after the form, genre, setting, and intention of the final form of the text have been defined can the exegete look to the earlier forms that may or may not be present within that final form. In general, the identification of prior material is based on the detection of inconsistencies in the literary form, thematic concerns, or conceptual outlook of the prophetic book. Such inconsistencies may indicate the presence of work by different authors in the same text. But this does not account for the redactor who does his or her work so well that such inconsistencies are no longer evident, nor does it account for the redactor whose viewpoint or literary techniques are in fundamental agreement with those of the earlier form of the text. Barton (pp. 56-58) refers to "the disappearing redactor" whose work may not be detectable within a text, thereby raising questions about the ability of form and redaction criticism to reconstruct the compositional history of a text. Such questions do not negate the validity of attempts to reconstruct the compositional history of a text, however, for ample evidence exists for the presence of earlier text forms throughout the prophetic literature (see Willis). But it does point to the limits of form and redaction criticism in that the reconstruction of a compositional history may not always be possible. Even when reconstruction is possible, it can never be considered as absolutely definitive; it can only be considered as the best possible hypothesis for the compositional history of the text. But then, human thought in general, and scientific or scholarly thought in particular, is inherently hypothetical.

This increased attention to the *literary* character of prophetic literature has changed the way in which form critics view the nature of prophetic *speech* as well. Scholars have come to recognize the literary coherence of prophetic literature, whether they recognize it as a product of an original author or as a redactional composition. Whereas Gunkel argued that distinctive genres constituted short, self-contained speech units as the basic form of prophetic discourse, an increasing number of scholars have followed Muilenberg ("Form Criticism") in maintaining that generic distinctions within a prophetic text may well represent a rhetorical device within a larger text that an author employs to create an impression or to make a particular point to his or her audience. The result has been an increasing interest in rhetorical criticism, including consideration of the persuasive character of prophetic speech and longer, distinctively formulated textual units as the basic forms of prophetic speech (e.g., Patrick and Scult; Gitay, *Isaiah and His Audience*). A number of scholars have likewise turned to studies of prophetic literature as textual phenomonena and have attempted to define the literary coherence of prophetic texts without consideration of their compositional history (e.g., Bozak; Hagstrom).

Such studies demonstrate that each text is uniquely formulated as a distinct literary composition with its own structure, characteristics, and aims. This has important implications for form critics in that the focus on larger textual units demonstrates the basic interrelationship between typical elements of genre and the unique formulation of individual texts (see Melugin, "Muilenberg"). Each text is a unique composition that employs its own vocabulary and concepts, and displays its own structure, forms, and intentions. Genres can determine the overall form of a distinct prophetic text, but they do not necessarily do so. Typical generic elements frequently function *within* a text and play a role in its composition or formulation, but they do not necessarily dictate its composition or formulation. Instead, the author's intentions dictate the composition and formulation of a text, including the choice of generic elements and language. The recognition of this interrelationship is essential to a full understanding of textual formation and meaning in prophetic literature: Each text is unique even though it employs typical elements of genre. Genres do not always define texts; they function within them as compositional tools.

Finally, the social setting of prophecy and prophetic literature continues to attract the attention of scholars (Carroll, "Prophecy and Society"; Petersen, *Roles;* Wilson, *Prophecy and Society*). Prophetic literature provides varying perspectives on the prophets of ancient Israel and Judah, and it points to different social settings for prophetic activity. Some are priests. Ezekiel and Zechariah represent the Zadokite line of priests who officiated at the Jerusalem temple, whereas Samuel and Jeremiah represent the Elide line who officiated initially at the Shiloh sanctuary and later resided in Anathoth after Solomon expelled Abiathar from the Jerusalem temple. Others are closely associated with the royal houses of Israel and Judah in varying capacities. In the northern kingdom of Israel, for example, Elijah and Elisha are presented as opponents to the royal house of Omri who supported Jehu in his successful coup d'état; Hosea, who is identified simply as a cuckolded husband, presents a scathing indictment of the northern monarchy; and Amos, identified as a Judean herdsman and dresser of sycamore trees, presents a severe critique of Jeroboam II's administration. In Judah the prophets tend to be more supportive of the monarchy. Nathan is credited with providing the foundational oracle for the establishment of the Davidic dynasty; Isaiah appears to have functioned as an advisor to Ahaz and Hezekiah; Zephaniah may well have been descended from Hezekiah (Zeph 1:1); and Haggai supports the restoration of Zerubbabel to the Davidic throne. Some, such as Joel, Obadiah, Nahum, and Habakkuk, may well have been cultic prophets who functioned in relation to the temple liturgy. Others, such as Micah and Amos, appear to have their roots in outlying villages.

Consequently, scholars have had some difficulties in specifying the definition of a prophet or in locating the social role of prophecy (see Petersen, *Prophecy in Israel*, 1-21; Carroll, "Prophecy and Society"). Nevertheless, two major social settings for prophecy and prophetic literature are evident: the temple and the royal court. This is no accident: the temple and the king constitute the two most fundamental institutions of ancient Israel and Judah as well as of ancient Near Eastern societies in general. Furthermore, the two are interrelated in that kings generally found and support temples in the ancient world, and temples legitimize the kings (e.g., David and Solomon founded the Jerusalem temple, which then served as a symbol for YHWH's eternal promise to the house of David). The activities and sayings of the prophets generally gravitate around these two institutions, either in opposition or in support. In this regard, it is noteworthy that prophecy ends in Judah shortly after the demise of the Davidic dynasty. Furthermore, the temple may well have been the location for the preservation, composition, and performance of prophetic books. Prophets appear to have played a significant role in the temple liturgy by the Second Temple period, and the affinities between the Psalms and various poetic compositions in the prophetic books indicate that prophetic books may well have constituted part of the temple liturgy (see R. Murray; Bellinger; Tournay). Such a setting would naturally provide the context for the appropriation of prophetic literature by the postexilic Jewish community.

II. THE GENRES OF PROPHETIC LITERATURE

Prophetic literature employs a variety of genres that derive from both the literary setting of prophetic writing and the social setting of prophetic speech. In addition, a number of characteristic genres appear to have been adapted from non-prophetic forms.

A. Prophetic Book

The PROPHETIC BOOK is the literary presentation of the sayings of a particular prophet. Every prophetic book begins with a SUPERSCRIPTION or some sort of narrative introduction that identifies the prophet to whom the book is attributed or whom the book describes. Narrative material by or about the prophet may also be included to provide a historical, social, ideological, or literary context by which the prophet's sayings are to be understood. In some cases, not all of the prophetic material derives from the prophet to whom the book is attributed (e.g., Isaiah 40–66; Zechariah 9–14). Nevertheless, such material is presented as if it is the product of the prophet in question.

There are at least four prophetic books in the Hebrew Bible (Isaiah, Jeremiah, Ezekiel, Twelve Prophets) or as many as fifteen (Isaiah, Jeremiah, Ezekiel, Hosea, Joel, Amos, Obadiah, Jonah, Micah, Nahum, Habakkuk, Zephaniah, Haggai, Zechariah, Malachi). The reason for the discrepancy is that scholars are just beginning to consider the book of the Twelve Prophets as a discrete book in and of itself rather than as a collection of twelve individual prophetic books (see Steck, *Der Abschluss,* 30-73; and House). Furthermore, there is some uncertainty as to whether Malachi constitutes a distinct prophetic book or an appendix to the book of Zechariah (see Weis, 253, 379-404, and the literature cited there).

In the prophetic books, the SUPERSCRIPTION normally appears at the beginning of the book in various forms (see Tucker, "Prophetic Superscriptions"). It generally includes a brief indication of author, date, and subject (e.g., Isa 1:1; Hos 1:1; Joel 1:1; Amos 1:1; Mic 1:1; Nah 1:1; Zeph 1:1; Hag 1:1; Zech 1:1). Three books begin with a more elaborate narrative introduction that includes elements of the SUPERSCRIPTION (Jer 1:1-3; Ezek 1:1-3; Jon 1:1). It may also identify the book generically as the "words" (Jer 1:1; Amos 1:1), "vision" (Isa 1:1; Obad 1:1; Nah 1:1), "pronouncement" (Hab 1:1; Mal 1:1), or "book" (Nah 1:1) of the prophet. Most frequently it identifies the book as the "word of YHWH" that came to the prophet (e.g., Ezek 1:1-3; Hos 1:1; Joel 1:1; Jon 1:1; Mic 1:1; Zeph 1:1; Hag 1:1; Zech 1:1; Mal 1:1). PROPHETIC BOOKS also may include SUPERSCRIPTIONS for textual blocks within the book (e.g., Isa 2:1 [chs. 2–4]; 13:1 [chs. 13–23]; Jer 46:1 [chs. 46–51]) or for individual compositions within the book (e.g., Isa 14:28; 15:1; 17:1; 19:1; 21:1, 11, 13; 22:1; 23:1; 30:6; 38:9; Jer 7:1; 11:1; 14:1; 18:1; 21:1; 23:9; 25:1-2; 26:1; 27:1; 29:1-3; 30:1; 32:1; 34:1; 35:1; 36:1; 40:1; 44:1; 45:1; 46:2, 13; 47:1; 48:1; 49:1, 7, 23, 28, 34; 50:1; 51:59; Hab 3:1; Hag 2:1, 10, 20; Zech 1:7; 7:1; 9:1; 12:1). Several prophets, including Jeremiah, Zechariah, and especially Ezekiel, employ first-person reporting language that can function as a SUPERSCRIPTION. For example, "The word of YHWH came to me (saying)" (Jer 2:1; Ezek 6:1; 7:1; Zech 6:9).

Some scholars consider PROPHETIC BOOKS as completed collections of the message of the prophet (Hals, 352-53), but this view must be reconsidered for several reasons. First, there are no criteria by which to determine if a prophetic book is a complete collection of the sayings of a prophet. Scholars simply do not know whether material stemming from the prophet in question failed to be included, either intentionally or accidentally, in the book that bears the prophet's

16

name. The existence of two distinct forms of the book of Jeremiah in the Greek and Masoretic traditions, each with a different structure, arrangement, and, to some extent, contents, certainly testifies to the fact that the full inclusion of the prophet's materials, or material attributed to the prophet, is not a criterion for the definition of a prophetic book. Second, not all the material in a prophetic book necessarily stems from or relates to the prophet. The oracles of Second and Third Isaiah in Isaiah 40–55 and 56–66 and those of Second and Third Zechariah in Zechariah 9–11 and 12–14 attest to the fact that the writings of later anonymous authors can be included within a prophetic book as a means to represent an extension or fulfillment of the prophet's message. Third, prophetic books can be labeled as a collection only in the most general sense. While research into the structure and intention of prophetic books is a relatively recent phenomenon, it has nonetheless already made clear that each book has a distinctive structure that indicates a specific intention in composing the book in the first place. Prophetic books are simply not haphazard or incoherent collections of prophetic oracles as Gunkel conceived them; rather, they are well-planned compositions with specific aims.

Part of the task of form- and redaction-critical research is to determine the principles of composition that appear within the individual prophetic books. Scholars frequently presuppose that prophetic books are arranged according to a tripartite schema that includes (1) judgment against Israel/Judah; (2) judgment against the nations; and (3) promise for Israel/Judah and the nations (e.g., Sellin-Fohrer, *Introduction,* 361-62), but investigation of the structure and themes of individual texts demonstrates that this pattern is not consistently observable (e.g., Sweeney, "Form-Critical Reassessment"). In general, prophetic books tend to focus on the punishment and restoration of Israel/Judah, with emphasis on the latter (Clements, "Patterns," in *Canon and Authority,* 1977). But the specific structural principle varies book by book. It may be chronological, as in the cases of Ezekiel, Haggai, and Zechariah, which supply narrative indications of date throughout. It may be generic, as in the cases of Isaiah and Zephaniah, which are presented as prophetic EXHORTATIONS (see this commentary on Isaiah; and Sweeney, "Form-Critical Reassessment"); Nahum, which is presented as a prophetic DISPUTATION (Sweeney, "Nahum"); or Habakkuk, which is presented as a PROPHETIC PRONOUNCEMENT followed by a PRAYER (Sweeney, "Habakkuk"). It also may be governed by a narrative presentation, as in the case of Jonah.

Finally, the setting for the composition and reading of prophetic books appears to be within the temple in Jerusalem. A number of prophetic books contain liturgical texts, such as Isaiah 12, 33, and Habakkuk 3 (R. Murray, 210-16); the HYMNS of Second Isaiah (Matheus); the DOXOLOGIES of Amos (Crenshaw, *Hymnic Affirmations*); the book of Joel (Ahlström); and the partial ACROSTIC of Nahum (J. Jeremias, *Kultprophetie,* 11-55). The liturgical character of these texts indicates that the prophetic books of which they are a part were read as part of the temple liturgy. The affinities of these texts with the various Psalms (Mowinckel, *Psalmenstudien*) and references to the prophetical functions of the Second Temple Levitical singers (Tournay, 34-45) demonstrate the potential use of prophetic texts in a liturgical setting. Furthermore, the continued reinterpretation and expansion of prophetic materials and the interest in supplying SUPERSCRIPTIONS that identified the prophet, the nature of the prophetic literature, and its historical setting indicate that these texts were studied in a context that accepted the past word of the prophets as a contemporary address to the postexilic Jewish community centered around the Second Temple (see Tucker, "Prophetic Superscriptions").

B. Prophetic Narrative

Prophetic literature contains a wide variety of narratives written by or about prophets. Such narratives point to the literary setting of prophecy, in which later tradents preserve traditions about the prophets or attempt to reflect on the significance of the prophet's words or activities. In some cases, prophetic narratives are autobiographical in form, which suggests that the actual writing of prophetic literature began with the prophets themselves. This indicates that prophets must be considered as writers as well as speakers, and that prophecy is both a literary and an oral phenomenon. It further indicates that prophets can be considered not only as non- or irrational ecstatic shaman figures, but also as clear rational thinkers who reflect upon and interpret their ecstatic experiences. It is in such reflection and writing that prophetic literature is produced, both by the prophets themselves and by the tradents of the prophetic traditions. This suggests a thread of continuity between the original prophets and their later redactors.

Perhaps one of the most characteristic of the prophetic genres is the prophetic VISION REPORT. It is usually an autobiographical form that recounts what a prophet sees or hears as an inner perception or private experience. It typically contains (1) an announcement of the vision that employs forms of the verb r'h, "to see," in order to state that the prophet "saw" or "was made to see" the vision; (2) a transition to the vision indicated by wĕhinnēh, "and behold"; and (3) the vision sequence itself, which usually begins with one or more visual images followed by scenes, sounds, voices, dialogues, and movements that help to explain the significance of the vision (Sister; Long, "Reports of Visions"). Horst initially identified three types of prophetic vision reports, including the "presence vision," which recounts the prophet's experience in the presence of YHWH, the "word assonance vision," in which the vision is based on a wordplay involving similar-sounding words (e.g., Amos 8:1-2), and the "event vision," which focuses on an event such as the fall of Babylon (Isa 21:1-10).

Long ("Reports of Visions") has since refined this analysis by identifying the following three types: (1) the "oracle vision," which employs a question-and-answer dialogue to convey the significance of a simple visionary image (Amos 7:7-8; Jer 1:11-14; 24:1-10; Zech 5:1-4); (2) the "dramatic word vision," which depicts a supramundane heavenly scene or dramatic action to convey a word of God that presages a future event in the mundane realm (Amos 7:1-6; Ezek 9:1-10; Jer 38:21-22; Zech 1:8-17; cf. Isaiah 6); and (3) the "revelatory-mysteries-vision," which employs symbolic imagery and a dialogue between the prophet and a divine guide to convey veiled secrets of divine activity and future events (Zech 2:3-4; 4:1-6a, 10b-11, 13-14; 5:5-8; cf. Daniel 8; 10–12). Prophetic VISION REPORTS may well have been set in the context of divination where they functioned as a means to answer individuals who approached a prophet to determine divine intentions (see 2 Kgs 8:7-15; Ezekiel 14; 20; Jer 38:21-23; cf. Long, "Effect of Divination"). In their present literary contexts, they serve as a means to authenticate and convey the prophetic message.

The REPORT OF A PROPHETIC WORD is a narrating genre that functions in a similar manner to authenticate and convey a prophetic message. It typically begins with the PROPHETIC WORD FORMULA, which combines the phrase *dĕbar-yhwh* ("the word of YHWH") with the verb *hāyâ* ("to be, happen"), the preposition *'el* ("unto"), and the name of the prophet or the pronoun "me" (e.g., *haddābār 'ăšer-hāyâ 'el-yirmĕyāhû mē'ēt yhwh*, "the word that was to Jeremiah from YHWH," Jer 35:1; *wayĕhî dĕbar-yhwh 'ēlay lē'mōr*, "and the word of YHWH was to me saying," Ezek 14:2). This is combined with other narrative elements that specify the setting of the prophetic word, and it is followed by a quotation of the word of YHWH to the prophet. Examples appear in Jer 21:1-10; 32:1-44; 34:8-22; 35:1-19; Ezek 14:1-11; 20:1-44. The genre is closely related to the REPORT OF A PROPHETIC REVELATION, which employs a similar form and structure to convey a private message from YHWH to a prophet in a narrative context (e.g., 1 Sam 15:10-11; 2 Sam 7:4-16; 1 Kgs 16:1-4; 17:2-4, 8-9; 21:28-29). The intention of the REPORT OF A PROPHETIC WORD reflects its literary setting in that it grows out of a concern to preserve and convey the public statements of a prophet and to relate those statements to specific historical circumstances. It is generally considered to be a later redactional form that developed from the writing of historical narratives. But the formal and functional similarities to autobiographical statements in which the prophet reports the reception of a divine word (e.g., Jer 2:1; Ezek 6:1; 12:1, 17, 21; 13:1; 26:1; 29:1; cf. Isa 8:1, 5; Jer 3:6) suggest that the REPORT OF A PROPHETIC WORD may well have developed out of autobiographical reports by the prophets of a word from YHWH.

The REPORT OF A SYMBOLIC ACTION is a 1st- or 3rd-person narrative that describes the prophet's performance of an act intended to symbolize YHWH's intentions or actions toward the people. The symbolic action frequently accompanies a prophetic word or vision, and it functions as a sign to confirm the efficacy of that word or vision. Examples appear in Hosea 1; 3; Isa 7:3; 8:1-4; 20:1-6; Jer 13:1-11; 16:1-4, 5-7, 8-9; 32:1-15; Ezek 4:1–5:17; 12:1-20; 37:15-28; cf. 1 Kgs 11:29-39; 22:11). Fohrer's analysis ("Die Gattung"; *Die symbolischen Handlungen*) demonstrates that the form typically contains three elements: (1) an instruction to perform a symbolic act; (2) the report that the act was performed; and (3) a statement that interprets the significance of the act. Fohrer relates the REPORT OF THE SYMBOLIC ACT to sympathetic magic by which YHWH is compelled to act in the prescribed manner ("Prophetie und Magie"). In contrast, Stacey's analysis of the dramatic elements and cultic functions of these reports demonstrates that they function as a means to introduce and express divine action, but they do not cause it. When employed by the prophet, such acts illustrate and thereby reinforce the efficacy of the prophet's message to his or her audience. The genre serves a similar function in its literary contexts where it aids in reinforcing and illustrating the prophet's entire message as expressed in writing. Because the genre appears in both first- and third-person forms, it testifies to the origins of prophetic writing among the prophets themselves and its subsequent development among their tradents. The REPORT OF AN EXPRESSIVE ACTION is similar, but it generally employs simpler actions or gestures (e.g., Ezekiel 6; see Zimmerli, *Ezekiel*, 1:182-83).

The prophetic VOCATION ACCOUNT is presented as an autobiographical narrative of the prophet's experience in which he or she was initially called by YHWH, ordained, or commissioned to convey YHWH's message. Zimmerli (*Ezekiel*, 1:97-100) demonstrates that there are two basic types. One appears to be modeled on the prophetic VISION REPORT in that it presents a report of a vision in the heavenly court of YHWH in which the deity commissions the prophet to speak (e.g., Isaiah 6; Ezekiel 1–3; cf. 2 Kgs 22:19-23). The other emphasizes a very personal experience of YHWH in which the coming word of God replaces the visionary experience (e.g., Jer 1:4-10; cf. Exodus 3–4; Judg 6:11-14). Habel's analysis of the "call narratives" demonstrates that a number of consistent elements appear within these reports, including a divine confrontation, an introductory word, a commission, an objection, a reassurance, and a sign. He concludes that the form derives from settings in which ambassadors or messengers present their credentials (e.g., Gen 24:35-48), and its purpose is to authenticate the prophet as YHWH's representative.

The autobiographical character of the prophetic VOCATION REPORTS has been challenged in various studies that point to the traditional elements that shape them (e.g., Reventlow, *Liturgie*). The most important is that by Long ("Prophetic Authority"), who notes that actions, not accounts of call, are generally used by charismatics to authenticate themselves and thereby to deflect criticism. Long points to the literary function of the prophetic VOCATION ACCOUNTS, showing how they highlight the theological themes of their respective prophetic books and thereby vindicate the prophet as a spokesperson for the truth. Long identifies the prophetic book's tradents as the most likely source for such accounts, insofar as they are interested in defending their own legitimacy by appealing to the authority of the original master. Nevertheless, this view overlooks the role that traditional elements play in shaping a prophet's self-understanding and the capacity of the prophet to reflect upon that self-understanding and the message that is delivered. Both Jeremiah and Ezekiel are priests and regularly employ images and tradition elements from their respective backgrounds in the Elide and Zadokite priestly lines. Isaiah appears to have close ties with the royal house of David. For example, his vision of YHWH enthroned in the temple (Isaiah 6) reflects images of the Davidic monarch and the perspective of one who stands at the king's position by the pillar at the entrance to the temple (2 Kgs 11:14; 23:2). The prophetic VOCATION ACCOUNTS may not present a fully accurate account of the prophet's initial experience, but they may well convey the prophet's reflection upon the significance of that experience and thereby serve as a means to authenticate the prophet's message. Such accounts do not require a public oral setting; rather, they may indicate the earliest stages of the writing of the prophet's tradition.

The PROPHETIC STORY is basically a narrative in which the prophet plays a central role in conveying the narrator's aims in writing the story. Rofé's study of the PROPHETIC STORIES identifies a variety of subgenres, based primarily on content and aim (Rofé, *Prophetical Stories;* cf. idem, "Classification"; "Classes").

In the most general sense, the PROPHETIC LEGEND focuses on the prophet as an exemplar of virtue, goodness, piety, and divine favor in order to edify its audience or to inculcate religious devotion. The "simple legenda" (2 Kgs 2:19-22, 23-24; 4:1-7, 38-41, 42-44; 6:1-7; 13:20-21) recount the performance of a miracle that demonstrates the prophet's or the holy person's power over nature employed for the benefit and veneration of the people. The "elaborations of the legenda" (2 Kgs 1:2-17a; 4:8-37) display a fully developed plot that explains the circumstances of the miracle. The "vita" (see the Elisha cycle in 1 Kgs 19:19–2 Kgs 13:19; esp. 2 Kgs 2:1-18 on the ascension of Elijah) attempts to describe the origins and end of the prophet or holy person. The genre presupposes a large existing body of legenda and results in the presentation of a "biography of legenda" (Rofé, *Prophetical Stories,* 42).

The "political legenda" (2 Kgs 6:8-23; 6:24–7:20) place the prophet in the arena of politics in order to overcome an opponent who attempts to belittle the holy person's abilities. The details of political events found in these legenda occur commonly in historiography. Like historiography, "prophetic historiography" (2 Kgs 9:1–10:28; 18:13–19:37 [cf. Isaiah 36–37]; 2 Kgs 20:12-19 [cf. Isaiah 39]) treats a series of continuous political events, avoids supernatural explanations, attempts to be historically accurate, and suggests causal relationships. It differs, however, in that a prophetic word is often sufficient cause for an event, and the adherence to or rejection of that word is frequently the cause of the success or failure of major characters. The "prophetic biography" does not attempt to glorify the prophet as "holy person." Instead, it contains details of political events in the lifetime of the prophet, and it aspires to authenticity and historical accuracy. Although the biographical material in Jeremiah 26–36 and 37–43 represents the closest example in the Hebrew Bible, it is not a true biography. It does not present a continuous account of the prophet's life, but is subsumed into the overall structure of the book of Jeremiah. Furthermore, the presentation of Jeremiah may be more fictional than historical in order to serve the apologetic interests of the prophet's later disciples (see esp. Carroll, *Jeremiah;* Seitz, *Theology in Conflict*). This is particularly evident in the prophetic CONFRONTATION STORIES (Amos 7:10-17; Jeremiah 6; 19:1-2; 26; 27–28; 36; cf. Isaiah 36–37), which recount the vindication of the prophet following a confrontation by opponents and their punishment.

The "ethical legenda" (e.g., Num 20:1-13; 2 Kgs 4:1-7, 18-37; 5; 20:1-11 [cf. Isaiah 38]) emphasize the power of prayer and the word of YHWH in order to concentrate on the *significance* rather than the *fact* of the miracle. The "exemplum" (e.g., 1 Kgs 22:1-28) employs the example of a historically recognized prophet or the opponents of a prophet to teach a moral, whereas the closely related "parable" (e.g., Jonah; 1 Kings 13) instructs by means of an imaginary incident. The "epic" (e.g., 1 Kgs 16:29–19:18) surpasses the miracle-working primitivism of the legenda to focus on an idea that dominates the prophet's life struggle, for example, the choice of YHWH over Baal in the Elijah cycle. Finally, the "martyrology" (Jer 38:28b; 39:3, 11-14; 40:1-6) presents a believer who, at the risk of his life, testifies to the existence of God before nonbelievers.

PROPHETIC STORIES are never written by the prophet; they are always written about the prophet. Their function is to venerate the prophet, to edify the audience, and to impart moral or religious instruction. They must therefore be considered as the products of the tradents of the prophetic traditions. Insofar as they appear in both historiographical literature and in the books of the prophets themselves, they point to the interrelationship between the composition of historical works, such as the DtrH (Joshua, Judges, Samuel, and Kings), and the prophetic books (e.g., Isaiah, Jeremiah, Amos, and Jonah).

C. Prophetic Speech

Although the forms of prophetic literature testify to the extensive writing activities of the prophets from the later monarchy through the early postexilic era, prophets appear to have functioned first and foremost as speakers. Prophetic literature contains a wide variety of genres that are characteristic of prophetic speech. Many of these forms appear to derive from social settings outside prophecy itself, which demonstrates that the prophets were not isolated figures; rather, they were well rooted in the life of the people and aware of the world around them.

One of the most basic speech forms employed by the prophets is the ORACLE. An ORACLE is a divine communication presented through an intermediary such as a priest, prophet, or seer. ORACLES may be delivered in response to an inquiry (cf. Num 22:7-12, 19-20; Josh 7:6-15; Judg 1:1-2; 1 Sam 23:2, 10-11; 2 Sam 5:23-24), or they may be unsolicited. The ORACLE itself has no specific form, but it is generally indicated by presence of the ORACULAR FORMULA, nĕ'um yhwh, "utterance of YHWH," at its beginning, middle, or end (on the rhetorical use of this form, see Meier, *Speaking of Speaking*, 298-314). Examples appear throughout prophetic literature, frequently in conjunction with other prophetic speech forms (Isa 14:4-23; 17:1-6; 30:1-5; 41:10-16; Jer 1:4-10; 30:1-3; Ezek 11:7-13; 24:9-14; Hos 11:1-11; Amos 2:6-16; Nah 2:14; Zeph 1:2-3; etc.; cf. Num 24:3-9, 15-24). The setting of the ORACLE appears to be a formal oracular inquiry through dreams, Urim, or the prophets (1 Sam 28:6), perhaps in a cultic context (cf. Numbers 22–24).

The PROPHETIC PRONOUNCEMENT or *maśśā'* is a standard prophetic form of discourse in which the prophet attempts to explain how YHWH's actions will be manifest in the realm of human affairs (for full discussion of this form, see Weis). The genre has no specific formal structure, other than an identification of the text as a *maśśā'*, "pronouncement, burden" (*RSV* "oracle"), in a superscription (e.g., Isa 13:1; 14:28; 30:6; Nah 1:1; Hab 1:1; Zech 9:1; 12:1; Mal 1:1). The term itself derives from the verb *nś'*, "to lift up," and it may well have been employed in a setting of oracular inquiry (Jer 23:16-40; cf. Num 24:3, 21, 23). The PRONOUNCEMENT appears to be based on a revelatory experience or vision; it is analytical in character, and it is spoken in response to a particular situation in human events.

The MESSENGER SPEECH appears frequently in prophetic literature, although one can hardly characterize it as a distinctive prophetic form. It is essentially a report of an oral message delivered by a messenger, in which the words dictated by the sender are repeated literally to the recipient (cf. Gen 32:1-5). The form is identified by the appearance of the MESSENGER FORMULA, *kōh 'āmar* PN, "thus says PN." In prophetic literature the form appears as *kōh 'āmar yhwh*, "thus says YHWH," or as *'āmar yhwh*, "says YHWH," since YHWH is the one who sends the prophet as a messenger; otherwise, it has no distinguishing characteristics. It frequently appears with or presupposes a COMMISSION in which a prophet is charged to speak on behalf of YHWH (see 2 Sam 7:4; 1 Kgs 12:22; 19; 21:17; 2 Kgs 20:4; Hosea 1; Amos 7:10-17; Isaiah 6; 7:3-9; Jeremiah 1; 2:1-2; 7:1; 17:19; 26:1-2; 35:1-2). The form then includes several key elements: (1) the PROPHETIC WORD FORMULA, which identifies YHWH as the one who commissions the message; (2) the COMMISSIONING FORMULA, "go and say," directed to the addressee; and (3) the MESSENGER FORMULA, followed by the message.

Westermann (*Basic Forms,* 90-128; cf. Ross) attempts to define the MESSENGER SPEECH as a characteristic prophetic speech form, based on the appearance of the MESSENGER FORMULA in prophetic texts from the Mari letters. But Ellermeier demonstrates that the MESSENGER SPEECH form appears too infrequently in the Mari letters to be identified as a characteristic prophetic form. Likewise, Rendtorff ("Botenformel") and North ("Angel-Prophet") raise questions as to whether the MESSENGER SPEECH form can be isolated from other generic elements in prophetic speech as a primary prophetic form. More recently, Meier's study of the MESSENGER FORMULA and its frequent use in Jeremiah and Ezekiel points to a potential association of the form with 6th-century Persian royal inscriptions issued by the Persian monarch as a form of royal proclamation (*Speaking of Speaking,* 272-98; cf. *Messenger*). Not all the prophets employ the MESSENGER SPEECH form (it is lacking in Hosea, Joel, Habakkuk, and Zechariah), but its association with royal proclamations indicates the self-conception of many prophets as representatives of YHWH, the ultimate monarch. In this regard, it is probably no accident that the form was increasingly used at a time when Assyrian and later conquerors issued royal proclamations to their vassals in Israel and Judah (cf. J. S. Holladay).

Perhaps the most basic form of prophetic speech is the PROPHETIC ANNOUNCEMENT or PROPHECY. It can be considered as a genre only in the broadest sense in that it has no specific form other than an unsolicited announcement by a prophet of future events or future actions by YHWH. In this regard, it complements the solicited prophetic ORACLE discussed above. Depending on its specific form and content, the PROPHETIC ANNOUNCEMENT can appear in a number of variations that announce both judgment and salvation.

One of the most widely recognized subgenres of the PROPHETIC ANNOUNCEMENT is the PROPHETIC JUDGMENT SPEECH in which the prophet speaks on behalf of YHWH to announce disaster to individuals, groups, or nations. It includes a statement of the reasons for judgment, a logical connective, such as *lākēn,* "therefore," and the ANNOUNCEMENT OF JUDGMENT, often in combination with the MESSENGER FORMULA. Examples include Mic 3:9-12; Isa 8:6-8;

and Jer 11:9-12. In cases where a punishment is decreed without reason, the ANNOUNCEMENT OF JUDGMENT functions separately as an independent genre (e.g., 2 Kgs 20:1 [Isa 38:1]; Jer 22:10, 11-12; 22:24-27, 28-29, 30; 37:17). According to Westermann (*Basic Forms,* 161-63), these announcements are delivered in response to an inquiry by the king. This could indicate an origin for the form in situations of oracular inquiry, although the genre and its variations, the PROPHETIC ANNOUNCEMENT OF PUNISHMENT AGAINST AN INDIVIDUAL and the PROPHETIC ANNOUNCEMENT OF PUNISHMENT AGAINST THE PEOPLE, appear to be heavily influenced by juridical language.

The PROPHETIC ANNOUNCEMENT OF PUNISHMENT AGAINST AN IN-DIVIDUAL is a prophetic word that announces coming disaster to an individual (e.g., 1 Sam 2:27-36; Amos 7:14-17; Jer 20:1-6) or to a group of individuals (e.g., 1 Kgs 14:7-11; Jer 23:2, 9-12, 13-15). It is distinguished as a variation of the PROPHETIC JUDGMENT SPEECH in that it employs a more direct accusation against the individual. The form was initially identified by Westermann (*Basic Forms,* 129-68), who noted the necessary interrelationship between Gunkel's separate categories of "threat" (*Drohrede*) and "reproach" (*Scheltrede*), and combined them into a single form that he called the "prophecy of judgment." The result is a two-part structure that appears to reflect the sequence of ancient Israelite juridical proceedings. The "indictment" (Westermann: "reason" or "accusation") presents the cause of punishment in which the defendant is accused of a crime in the law court. The "verdict" (Westermann: "announcement of judgment"), introduced frequently by *lākēn,* "therefore," and the MES-SENGER FORMULA, presents the punishment of the defendant by YHWH as the necessary consequence of the crime. Examples include Amos 7:14-17; Jer 20:1-6; 23:2, 9-12, and 13-15. Koch's analysis of the form (*Growth,* 210-13) avoids the juridical setting in favor of a private revelation to the prophet. He therefore labels the form as the "prophecy of disaster," and argues that it includes three basic elements: (1) the "indication of the situation" or "diatribe," which presents the situation in need of remedy; (2) the "prediction of disaster" or "threat," which constitutes the real substance of the prophecy and emphasizes its future character; and (3) the "concluding characterization" or "motive clause," which usually describes the sender or the recipients of the prophecy. Westermann's two-part form has a clear advantage in that it emphasizes the causative principle underlying the genre and its dependence on the legal sphere, which Koch acknowledges. Koch's terminology and overall conception of the form have the advantage of recognizing that the PROPHETIC ANNOUNCEMENT OF PUNISHMENT AGAINST AN INDIVIDUAL is not inherently a legal form, but indicates the experience and motivations of the prophet in relation to the social circumstances that he or she addresses.

According to Westermann, the PROPHETIC ANNOUNCEMENT OF PUNISH-MENT AGAINST THE PEOPLE is a development of a previous genre that addresses the entire nation (*Basic Forms,* 169-89). It, too, employs a direct accusation (e.g., Amos 2:1-3, 4-5; 4:1-3; Hos 2:7-9; Isa 30:12-14; Mic 3:1-4). The basic two-part structure is somewhat more complicated, but it is essentially similar to the PROPHETIC ANNOUNCEMENT OF PUNISHMENT AGAINST AN INDIVIDUAL, in that both the "reason" and the "announcement of intervention of God" are expanded and the occurrence of the phrase "therefore, thus says YHWH," is inconsistent. At times, the structural sequence can be inverted to present an analysis of the cause of disaster. In that case, it functions as a PROPHETIC EXPLANATION OF PUNISHMENT (e.g., Isa 5:1-11; Jer 2:26-28; Ezek 22:23-31; 23:5-10; Amos 9:8-10). Westermann attributes these changes to the eventual decline and dissolution of the form, but they seem instead to reflect the prophets' rhetorical adaptation of the form in relation to national collapse during the Assyrian and Babylonian periods.

A variation of the PROPHETIC JUDGMENT SPEECH appears as the PROPHET-IC PROOF SAYING, also known as the SELF-DISCLOSURE ORACLE, in which a prophet announces punishment against an individual, group, or nation, and argues that the punishment will convince the recipient to recognize YHWH's sovereign identity (see Zimmerli, "Word"). Examples appear in 1 Kgs 20:13, 28; Isa 41:17-20; 49:22-26; Ezek 12:19-20; 25:6-7; and 25:8b-11. The primary form contains two elements: (1) the announcement of punishment, and (2) the RECOGNITION FORMULA, "and you shall know that I am YHWH" (e.g., Ezek 12:19-20). An expanded three-part form prefixes the reason for punishment and a logical transition to the announcement of punishment (e.g., Ezek 26:6-7, 8b-11).

The counterpart to the PROPHETIC JUDGMENT SPEECH is the PROPHECY OF SALVATION, in which a prophet speaks on behalf of YHWH to announce salvation to individuals, groups, or the nation. Examples include Isa 7:7-9; Jer 28:2-4; 31:2-6; 34:4; Amos 9:11-12, 13-15; and Mic 5:10-20. According to Koch (*Growth,* 213-15), the structure of the PROPHECY OF SALVATION is basically similar to the "prophecy of disaster" in that it corresponds to his three-part schema discussed above: (1) an "indication of the situation," often introduced by an "appeal for attention" or *ya'an kî,* "forasmuch as," which may indicate YHWH's actions to alter the present situation; (2) a "prediction of salvation" or "promise," frequently introduced by *lākēn,* "therefore," and followed by a negative statement formulated with an imperfect verb or a positive statement formulated with *hinnēnî,* "behold, I," and a participle; and (3) a "concluding characterization," which refers to the one who authorizes the promise, pre-sumably YHWH. At times, the "indication of the situation" is missing (cf. Isa 29:18-21, 22-24; Jer 33:10-11, 12-13; Mic 4:1-4; 5:7-9).

According to Westermann (*Prophetic Oracles,* 14), the PROPHECY OF SALVATION is more properly termed the "proclamation of salvation" in keeping with the prophetic character of the form. The basic pattern of the PROPHECY OF SALVATION includes a proclamation of deliverance followed by blessing, which may refer to prosperity in preexilic times and restoration of a state of well-being after the collapse in 587 B.C.E. It has a long history of use, but the most important developments in the form take place in the exilic and postexilic periods, espe-cially in relation to the ORACLE OF SALVATION found in Deutero-Isaiah (Isa 41:8-13, 14-16; 43:1-7; 44:1-5). Begrich ("Das priesterliche Heilsorakel") ar-gued that Deutero-Isaiah derived the ORACLE OF SALVATION from a priestly form that offered assurance to the petition of an individual in a lament ceremony. Westermann (*Prophetic Oracles,* 42-43) follows by arguing that the "proclama-tion of salvation" originates in a cultic situation of lament calling for YHWH's intervention. This is illustrated in Deutero-Isaiah where the "promise of salvation" includes a "call of reassurance" that employs the characteristic REASSURANCE FORMULA, "fear not," the "basis of reassurance in the perfect tense or a nominal form," and the "future-oriented basis," which is identical with the "proclamation of salvation." According to Westermann, this sets the pattern for the independent examples of the PROPHECY OF SALVATION that appear in Deutero-Isaiah and in other prophetic writings as independent texts and supplements to prior texts throughout the exilic and postexilic periods. Prior to the exile, the PROPHETIC ORACLES OF SALVATION proclaim deliverance from a coming threat and the destruction of enemies; after 587, they proclaim deliverance from exile without regaining political or military power. Ultimately, Westermann's analysis points to both a cultic setting for prophecy and an interest in reinterpreting older prophetic tradition within the prophetic corpus. Given the dependence of the form on the priestly ORACLE OF SALVATION and its similarities to the ANNOUNCEMENT OF JUDGMENT, the origins of the PROPHETIC ANNOUNCEMENT OF SALVATION might also be traced to oracular inquiry.

A special form of the PROPHECY OF SALVATION appears as the ANNOUNCEMENT OF A ROYAL SAVIOR, in which the prophet announces and describes the rule of a just and righteous king. Examples appear in Isa 11:1-10; 32:1-8; Jer 23:5-6; 33:15-16; and Mic 5:1-4. There is no set structure, but characteristic elements include the announcement of the new king's reign, his names, a description of the righteousness and peace that will characterize his rule, and descriptions of social, cosmic, or political chaos that preceded and necessitated the new king's rule. The form was employed extensively in Egypt and Mesopotamia (see Wildberger, *Jesaja*, 438-42), where it functioned retrospectively as a means to justify the rule of a new king or usurper.

A special form of the PROPHETIC ANNOUNCEMENT is the PROPHECY CONCERNING A FOREIGN NATION. The form is identified primarily by content in that it focuses on the punishment or destruction of a foreign nation by an enemy. It generally presents the destruction as an event that is currently taking place or that will take place in the near future. PROPHECIES CONCERNING FOREIGN NATIONS appear frequently in series (Isaiah 13–23; Jeremiah 46–51; Ezekiel 25–32; Amos 1–2; Zeph 2:4-15), but they may appear individually as well (e.g., Isaiah 34; Obadiah; Nahum). The primary intent appears to be to identify the destruction of a foreign nation as an act by YHWH. In this respect, the form resembles the PROPHETIC PRONOUNCEMENT with which it is frequently identified (see Isaiah 13–23). The form ultimately addresses Israel even though it is ostensibly addressed to another nation. It can employ a variety of genres. According to D. L. Christensen, the setting of the form is in the holy war traditions, where it functioned as a means to curse Israel's enemies (Deut 20:1-4; 1 Kings 22; Christensen, *Prophecy and War in Ancient Israel: Studies in the Oracles against the Nations in Old Testament Prophecy* [BMS 3; Berkeley: BIBAL, 1989]). He argues that the basic structure includes the "summons to battle" (i.e., SUMMONS TO WAR; cf. Bach), the "summons to flight" (cf. Bach), announcements of victory or defeat, and victory and TAUNT songs. He further maintains that the form underwent two major transformations: (1) Amos employed the form to announce judgment against Israel as well as against the nations; and (2) Jeremiah employed the form as a means to project restoration for Israel and Zion. A cultic setting is likely, initially as an execration ritual designed to curse enemies, and later in conjunction with the liturgical announcement of YHWH's sovereignty (cf. Psalms 2; 46; 48; 76).

The ANNOUNCEMENT OF REPRIEVE is a type of oracle that announces YHWH's intent to mitigate a promised punishment to an individual. Its typical elements include (1) an allusion to some act of penitence by the person addressed; (2) the reason for the reprieve; and (3) the reprieve itself. Examples appear in 1 Kgs 21:29; 2 Kgs 22:18-20; and 2 Chr 12:7-8. It is uncertain whether the ANNOUNCEMENT OF REPRIEVE ever constituted an independent genre of prophetic speech. All examples occur as a part of the SCHEMA OF REPRIEVE, a narrative form that appears to be the product of late redactional composition of the narrative books.

The PROPHETIC ANNOUNCEMENT OF A SIGN is a characteristically prophetic form in which the prophet announces that an event will take place in the future that will confirm the prophetic word. It is identified by three characteristic elements: (1) a declaration of an event as a sign from YHWH, e.g., "This shall be the sign to you from YHWH"; (2) a subordinate clause stating the significance of the sign; and (3) a description of the event that will constitute the sign. Examples appear in 1 Kgs 13:3; Isa 37:30-32 (2 Kgs 19:29-31); Isa 38:7-8 (2 Kgs 20:9-10); and Jer 44:29-30. The settings of such announcements vary according to the circumstances in which they were delivered, but they seem to be rooted in the practice of oracular inquiry from prophets (cf. Isa 7:10).

Other characteristic prophetic genres employ language derived from a variety of settings, including the legal, cultic, educational, and royal spheres of life.

The TRIAL GENRES relate to juridical procedure and a courtroom setting, which may be located in "secular law" as decided in the gates of a city (Ruth 4) and the royal court (1 Kgs 3:16-28; cf. 2 Sam 12:1-15) or in "sacred law" as decided in a cultic setting (Joshua 7; Jeremiah 26). The primary form is known as the "trial speech," the "*rîb* [i.e., 'controversy'] pattern" or the "covenant lawsuit." Begrich (*Studien,* 26-48) described the form in detail, and it has been extensively discussed since (see K. Nielsen, *YHWH as Prosecutor,* 5-26). Examples appear in Isaiah 1; 41:1-5, 21-29; 42:18-25; 43:8-15, 22-28; 44:6-8; 50:1-3; Jeremiah 2; Hosea 4; and Micah 6. Westermann (*Sprache und Struktur,* 51-61) identifies three basic elements in the examples from Deutero-Isaiah: (1) the summons to trial; (2) the trial proper, which includes speeches by the plaintiff and defendant; and (3) the sentencing. Harvey's more general study *(Le plaidoyer)* identifies five: (1) an introductory call to a hearing; (2) the questioning of witnesses and statement of accusation; (3) an address by the prosecutor delineating YHWH's gracious acts; (4) reference to the uselessness of cultic acts of compensation; and (5) a declaration of guilt and sentencing. The form may express YHWH's accusations against the gods of the nations or against Israel. Various settings have been proposed, including standard court procedure (Begrich, *Studien;* Westermann, *Sprache und Struktur;* idem, *Basic Forms,* 199-200; Boecker, *Redeformen*), the cult (Würthwein, "Der Ursprung"), and international treaty formulations (Harvey, *Le plaidoyer;* Limburg). Others see the roots of the form in secular or international law, but locate the TRIAL GENRES in traditions of the covenant between YHWH and Israel (Huffmon; K. Nielsen, *YHWH as Prosecutor;* von Waldow; Wright). A number of recent studies challenge the existence of a specific "lawsuit" form since such texts lack a common word field and consistent literary structure (De Roche; Daniels), but these studies tend to apply overly rigid criteria and thereby overlook the role played by the rhetorical use of typical forms in the composition of a unique text.

The prophetic DISPUTATION speech is frequently related to the TRIAL GENRES in that they are designed to argue against a particular viewpoint and thereby support the interrogations that take place in a courtroom setting. Although most of the examples appear in prophetic literature (Isa 8:16–9:6 [*RSV* 7]; 40:27-31; 49:14-25; Jer 31:29-30; 33:23-26; Ezek 11:2-12; 11:14-17; 12:21-28; 18:1-20; 20:32-44; 33:10-20, 23-29; 37:11b-13; Mic 2:6-11; Hag 1:2-11; Mal 1:2-5; 1:6–2:9, 10-16; 2:17–3:5, 6-12, and 13-21; cf. Nahum), the original setting of the form does not appear to be law or even prophecy, but wisdom, in which contrasting viewpoints are analyzed and evaluated (cf. Job). Graffy argues that the structure of the form comprises two basic elements: (1) the quotation of the opinion to be disputed; and (2) the refutation of that opinion. D. F. Murray refines this position by demonstrating that the surface structure can vary according to the rhetorical purpose of the author. Three basic elements appear in the deep structure of the text: (1) the thesis to be disputed; (2) the counterthesis for which the speaker argues; and (3) the dispute or argumentation itself.

The WOE ORACLE appears commonly in prophetic literature as a means to criticize specific actions and attitudes of people, and to announce punishment against them. They may occur individually (Amos 5:18-20; 6:1-7; Isa 1:4; 3:11; 10:5) or in series (Isa 5:8-24; Hab 2:6-20). The form is identified by (1) the introductory exclamation *hôy*, "woe!" followed by a participle or a noun that describes the action or people in question; and (2) additional material employing various forms to elaborate upon the situation. Westermann (*Basic Forms,* 194-98) identifies it as a variation of the PROPHETIC JUDGMENT SPEECH that ultimately derived from cursing ceremonies directed against Israel's enemies. Gerstenberger ("Woe Oracles") and Whedbee (pp. 80-110) argue that it stems from wisdom circles that contrast ideal and foolish actions in order to warn against undesirable behavior. Other scholars associate the exclamation with funerary rituals of lamentation (cf. 1 Kgs 13:30; Clifford; Wanke; Williams, "Alas-Oracles"; Janzen, *Mourning Cry;* Hardmeier, *Texttheorie*). Although Hardmeier posits the origins of the form in the funerary lament, his study of the rhetorical usage of the "woe" forms demonstrates that the prophets employed it as rhetorical speech device to attract the hearer's attention (cf. Zech 2:10).

The PROPHETIC INSTRUCTION, also known as PROPHETIC TORAH, is a didactic form employed by prophets to offer guidance to an individual or group. It is frequently linked to the PRIESTLY TORAH, in which priests give authoritative instruction in response to a question concerning cultic purity or other sacred matters (e.g., Hag 2:11-13; Isa 1:10-17; Jer 7:21; Amos 5:21-24; Mic 6:6-8). Not all instances of PROPHETIC INSTRUCTION presuppose cultic issues (cf. Isa 8:11-15; Amos 3:3-8), nor do they exclusively combine reproof with INSTRUCTION (Westermann, *Basic Forms,* 203-4; cf. Isaiah 5–12; 28–33, which combine

INSTRUCTION with reproof, but lead ultimately to the ANNOUNCEMENT OF A ROYAL SAVIOR). It seems much more likely that both the PRIESTLY TORAH and the PROPHETIC INSTRUCTION derive ultimately from the more generalized IN-STRUCTION genre characteristic of the wisdom tradition (e.g., Proverbs 1–9; 22:17–24:22). Various prophets, including Amos, Micah, and Isaiah, have been associated with the wisdom tradition (cf. Wolff, *Amos the Prophet;* idem, "Wie verstand Micha?"; Fichtner; Whedbee), but this may reflect nothing more than the means by which literate persons were educated in ancient Israelite and Judean society (cf. J. L. Crenshaw, "Education in Ancient Israel," *JBL* 104 [1985] 601-15). The specific form of PROPHETIC INSTRUCTION may vary, but characteristic wisdom forms, such as COMMANDS, PROHIBITIONS, RHETORICAL QUESTIONS, CALLS TO ATTENTION, EXHORTATIONS, ADMONITIONS, PARABLES, etc., appear frequently.

The prophetic EXHORTATION is an address form employed to persuade an audience to follow a particular course of action. It complements the ADMONI-TION, which attempts to persuade against a particular course of action. Together, the two forms constitute PARENESIS, which is an address to an individual or group that attempts to persuade with reference to a goal. The form varies in that it employs an assortment of generic components, including CALLS TO ATTEN-TION, COMMANDS, PROHIBITIONS, INSTRUCTIONS, MOTIVE CLAUSES, etc. The setting appears to be any situation of public or private address (see Deuteronomy 6–11; Josh 1:2-9; 1 Kgs 2:2-9; 1 Chr 28:8, 20-21; 2 Chr 15:7), although the form appears to be rooted in wisdom instruction (cf. Prov 1:8-19) or cultic instruction (Psalms 1; 50; 95). In the discussion of prophetic literature, the form is generally associated with the motif of repentance, and its existence as an independent genre of prophetic speech is contested. Wolff ("Das Thema"; cf. Warmuth; Hunter) argues that the motif of repentance is subsumed under PRO-PHETIC ANNOUNCEMENTS OF PUNISHMENT or SALVATION. Raitt argues that the "summons to repentance" is an independent prophetic genre that can appear in association with prophecies of disaster. It consists of two basic elements: (1) an "appeal," with messenger formula, vocative, and admonition; and (2) the "mo-tivation," with promise, accusation, and threat (cf. Tångberg). The objections to seeing the PROPHETIC EXHORTATION as a discrete form with a distinctive struc-ture and word field are well founded, but opponents of the genre overlook the means by which exhortational elements shape the prophecies of disaster and define their intent. Given the social role of prophets as interpreters of divine intent and spokespersons for YHWH, and given their future orientation, it makes little sense to maintain that the prophets simply announced judgment without attempting to influence their addressees. Otherwise, they had little reason to speak.

Finally, a number of prophetic texts may be classified as PROPHETIC LITURGIES (Isaiah 12; 33; Jeremiah 14; Joel 1–2; Habakkuk; Nahum). There is no set form to a PROPHETIC LITURGY; rather, the prophetic texts employ standard liturgical genres such as HYMNS (Isaiah 12), PRAYERS (Habakkuk 3), COM-PLAINTS (Jeremiah 14; Joel 1–2), ENTRANCE LITURGIES (Isaiah 33), THANKS-GIVING SONGS (Isaiah 12), THEOPHANIES (Habakkuk 3), ZION SONGS (Isa 2:2-4; Mic 4:1-4), and DOXOLOGIES (Amos 4:13; 5:8-9; 9:5-6). PROPHETIC LITURGIES apparently reflect the cultic setting in which prophetic literature was performed and perhaps produced. Furthermore, the frequent use of standard liturgical forms by the prophets in their own speech, such as the COMPLAINT (e.g., Jer 15:10-18; 18:18-23; 20:7-9; Hab 1:2-17; see Baumgartner, *Die Klagegedichte;* Ahuis; Floyd) and other liturgically based forms discussed above, further testifies to an association between the prophets and the cult.

Chapter 1

INTRODUCTION TO THE
BOOK OF ISAIAH

Bibliography

P. R. Ackroyd, "Isaiah," in *The Interpreter's One-Volume Commentary on the Bible* (ed. C. M. Layman; Nashville: Abingdon, 1971) 329-71; idem, "Isaiah I–XII: Presentation of a Prophet," *Congress Volume, Göttingen 1977* (VTSup 29; Leiden: Brill, 1978) 16-48 (repr. in *Studies in the Religious Tradition of the Old Testament* [London: SCM, 1987] 79-104, 266-74); idem, "Isaiah 36–39: Structure and Function," in *Von Kanaan bis Kerala* (*Fest.* J. P. M. van der Ploeg; ed. J. R. Nelis et al.; AOAT 211; Neukirchen-Vluyn: Neukirchener, 1982) 3-21 (repr. in *Studies,* 105-20, 274-78); R. Albertz, "Das Deuterojesaja-Buch als Fortschreibung der Jesaja-Prophetie," in *Die hebräische Bibel und ihre zweifache Nachgeschichte* (*Fest.* R. Rendtorff; ed. E. Blum et al.; Neukirchen-Vluyn: Neukirchener, 1990), 241-56; O. T. Allis, *The Unity of Isaiah: A Study in Prophecy* (Philadelphia: Presbyterian and Reformed, 1950); R. Althann, "Yom, 'Time' and Some Texts in Isaiah," *JNWSL* 11 (1983) 3-8; B. W. Anderson, "The Apocalyptic Rendering of the Isaiah Tradition," in *The Social World of Formative Christianity and Judaism* (*Fest.* H. C. Kee; ed. J. Neusner et al.; Philadelphia: Fortress, 1988) 17-38; R. T. Anderson, "Was Isaiah a Scribe?" *JBL* 79 (1960) 57-58; A. G. Auld, "Poetry, Prophecy, Hermeneutic: Recent Studies in Isaiah," *SJT* 33 (1980) 567-81; P. Auvray, *Isaïe 1–39* (SB; Paris: Gabalda, 1972); H. Barth, *Die Jesaja-Worte in der Josiazeit: Israel und Assur als Thema einer produktiven Neuinterpretation der Jesajaüberlieferung* (WMANT 48; Neukirchen-Vluyn: Neukirchener, 1977); J. Barton, "Begründungsversuche der prophetischen Unheilsankündigung im Alten Testament," *EvT* 47 (1987) 427-35; idem, "Ethics in Isaiah of Jerusalem," *JTS* 32 (1981) 1-18; E. Beaucamp, "D'Isaïe à son livre: A propos d'un ouvrage récent," *Liber Annuus* 33 (1983) 75-98; J. Becker, *Isaias — Der Prophet und sein Buch* (SBS 30; Stuttgart: Katholisches Bibelwerk, 1968); P. C. Beentjes, "De 'Redaktionsgeschichte' van Jesaja I–XXXV," *BTFT* 40 (1979) 168-72; G. Beer, "Zur Zukunftserwartung Jesajas," in *Studien zur semitischen Philologie und Religionsgeschichte* (*Fest.* J. Wellhausen; ed. K. Marti; BZAW 27; Giessen: Töpelmann, 1914) 13-35; A. Bentzen, *Jesaja,* vol. 1: *Jes. 1–39* (Copenhagen: Gad, 1944); W. A. M. Beuken, "Isa. 56:9–57:13 — An Example of the

Isaianic Legacy of Trito-Isaiah," in *Tradition and Reinterpretation in Jewish and Early Christian Literature (Fest.* J. C. H. Lebram; ed. J. W. Van Henten et al.; Leiden: Brill, 1986) 48-64; idem, "Isaiah Chapters LXV–LXVI: Trito-Isaiah and the Closure of the Book of Isaiah," *Congress Volume, Leuven 1989* (ed. J. A. Emerton; VTSup 43; Leiden: Brill, 1991) 204-21; idem, "Isaiah 34: Lament in Isaianic Context," in *OTE* 5 (1992) 78-102; idem, "Jesaja 33 als Spiegeltext im Jesajabuch," *ETL* 67 (1991) 5-35; J. A. Bewer, *The Book of Isaiah* (2 vols.; New York: Harper, 1950); H. Birkeland, *Zum hebräischen Traditionswesen: Die Komposition der prophetischen Bücher des Alten Testament* (Oslo: Dybwad, 1938); S. Blank, *Prophetic Faith in Isaiah* (New York: Harper, 1958); idem, "Traces of Prophetic Agony in Isaiah," *HUCA* 27 (1956) 81-92; J. Boehmer, " 'JHWHs Lehrlinge' im Buch Jesaja," *ARW* 33 (1936) 171-75; T. A. Boorgaart, "Reflections on Restoration: A Study of Prophecies in Micah and Isaiah about the Restoration of Northern Israel" (Diss., Groningen University, 1981); D. Bourguet, "Pourquoi à-t-on rassemblé des oracles si divers sous le titre d'Esaïe?" *ETR* 58 (1983) 171-79; C. Boutflower, *The Book of Isaiah, Chaps. 1–39, in the Light of Assyrian Monuments* (London: SPCK, 1930); P. Bovati, "Le langage juridique du prophète Isaïe," in *The Book of Isaiah/Le livre d'Isaïe: Les oracles et leurs relectures unité et complexité de l'ouvrage* (ed. J. Vermeylen; BETL 81; Leuven: Leuven University Press and Peeters, 1989) 177-96; G. H. Box, *The Book of Isaiah* (London: Pitman, 1908); C. J. Bredenkamp, *Der Prophet Jesaia* (Erlangen: Deichert, 1887); C. Brekelmans, "Deuteronomistic Influence in Isaiah 1–12," in *The Book of Isaiah/Le livre d'Isaïe* (ed. J. Vermeylen; BETL 81; Leuven: Leuven University Press and Peeters, 1989) 167-76; J. Bright, "Isaiah I," in *Peake's Commentary on the Bible* (ed. M. Black and H. H. Rowley; London and New York: Nelson, 1962) 489-515; W. H. Brownlee, *The Meaning of the Qumran Scrolls for the Bible* (New York: Oxford University Press, 1964); W. Brueggemann, "Unity and Dynamic in the Isaiah Tradition," *JSOT* 29 (1984) 89-107; K. Budde, "Über die Schranken die Jesajas prophetischer Botschaft zu setzen sind," *ZAW* 41 (1923) 154-203; D. M. Carr, "Reaching for Unity in Isaiah," *JSOT* 57 (1993) 61- 80; idem, "What Can We Say about the Tradition History of Isaiah?" in *Society of Biblical Literature 1992 Seminar Papers* (ed. E. H. Lovering Jr.; Atlanta: Scholars Press, 1992) 583-97; R. P. Carroll, "Inner Tradition Shifts in Meaning in Isaiah 1–11," *ExpTim* 89 (1977-78) 301-4; idem, *When Prophecy Failed: Cognitive Dissonance in the Prophetic Traditions of the Old Testament* (New York: Seabury, 1979); L. Černy, *The Day of YHWH and Some Relevant Problems* (Prague: University Karlovy, 1948); T. K. Cheyne, *Introduction to the Book of Isaiah* (London: Adam and Charles Black, 1895); idem, *The Prophecies of Isaiah* (2 vols.; London: Paul, Trench, Trübner, 1889); B. S. Childs, *Introduction to the Old Testament as Scripture* (Philadelphia: Fortress, 1979) 311-38; idem, *Isaiah and the Assyrian Crisis* (SBT 2/3; London: SCM, 1967); R. E. Clements, "Beyond Tradition-History: Deutero-Isaianic Development of First Isaiah's Themes," *JSOT* 31 (1985) 95-113; idem, "Isaiah," in *The Books of the Bible,* vol. 1: *The Old Testament/The Hebrew Bible* (ed. B. W. Anderson; New York: Scribner's, 1989) 247-79; idem, *Isaiah 1–39* (NCB; London: Marshall, Morgan and Scott; Grand Rapids: Eerdmans, 1980); idem, "The Prophecies of Isaiah and the Fall of Jerusalem in 587 B.C.," *VT* 30 (1980) 421-36; idem, *Prophecy and Tradition* (Atlanta: John Knox, 1975); idem, "The Unity of the Book of Isaiah," *Int* 36 (1982) 117-29; A. Condamin, *Le Livre d'Isaïe: Introduction* (EBib; Paris: Gabalda, 1940); idem, *Le Livre d'Isaïe: Traduction critique avec notes et commentaires* (EBib; Paris: Lecoffre, 1905); E. W. Conrad, "Isaiah and the

Abraham Connection," *AJT* 2 (1988) 382-93; idem, *Reading Isaiah* (OBT; Minneapolis: Fortress, 1991); idem, "The Royal Narratives and the Structure of the Book of Isaiah," *JSOT* 41 (1988) 67- 81; J. Coppens, "Les espérances messianiques du Proto- Isaïe et leurs prétendues relectures," *ETL* 44 (1968) 491-97; D. H. Coorley, "Messianic Prophecy in First Isaiah," *AJSL* 39 (1922-23) 220-24; C. H. Cornill, "Die Composition des Buches Jesajas," *ZAW* 4 (1884) 83-105; G. I. Davies, "The Destiny of the Nations in the Book of Isaiah," in *The Book of Isaiah/Le livre d'Isaïe* (ed. J. Vermeylen; BETL 81; Leuven: Leuven University Press and Peeters, 1989) 93-120; S. Deck, *Die Gerichtsbotschaft Jesajas: Charakter und Begründung* (FB 67; Würzburg: Echter, 1991); F. Delitzsch, *Biblical Commentary on the Prophecies of Isaiah* (tr. J. Martin; 2 vols.; repr. Grand Rapids: Eerdmans, 1954); B. Dicou, "Literary Function and Literary History of Isaiah 34," *BN* 58 (1991) 30-45; W. Dietrich, *Jesaja und die Politik* (BEvT 74; Munich: Kaiser, 1976); A. Dillmann, *Der Prophet Jesaja* (Leipzig: Hirzel, 1890); W. J. Doorly, *Isaiah of Jerusalem: An Introduction* (New York and Mahwah: Paulist, 1992); P. Dreyfus, "La doctrine du reste d'Israël chez la prophète Isaïe," *RSPT* 39 (1955) 361-86; G. R. Driver, "Isaiah I–XXXIX: Textual and Linguistic Problems," *JSS* 13 (1968) 36-57; S. R. Driver, *Isaiah: His Life and Times* (London: Nesbet, 2nd ed. 1897); idem, "Linguistic and Textual Problems: Isaiah I–XXXIX," *JTS* 38 (1937) 36-50; B. Duhm, *Das Buch Jesaia* (5th ed.; HKAT; Göttingen: Vandenhoeck & Ruprecht, 1968); W. J. Dumbrell, "The Purpose of the Book of Isaiah," *TynB* 36 (1985) 111-28; J. H. Eaton, "The Isaiah Tradition," in *Israel's Prophetic Tradition* (*Fest.* P. R. Ackroyd; ed. R. Coggins et al.; Cambridge: University Press, 1982) 58-76; idem, "The Origin of the Book of Isaiah," *VT* 9 (1959) 138-57; A. B. Ehrlich, *Randglossen zur hebräischen Bibel textkritisches, sprachliches und sachliches,* vol. 4: *Jesaia, Jeremia* (Leipzig: Hinrichs, 1912); W. Eichrodt, *Der Heilige in Israel: Jesaja 1–12* (BAT 17/1; Stuttgart: Calwer, 1960); idem, *Der Herr der Geschichte: Jesaja 13–23 und 28–39* (BAT 17/2; Stuttgart: Calwer, 1967); idem, "Prophet and Covenant: Observations on the Exegesis of Isaiah," in *Proclamation and Presence* (*Fest.* G. H. Davies; ed. J. I. Durham and J. R. Porter; London: SCM, 1970) 167-88; I. Eitan, "A Contribution to Isaiah Exegesis," *HUCA* 12-13 (1937-38) 55-88; K. Elliger, *Deuterojesaja in seinem Verhältnis zu Tritojesaja* (BWANT 63; Stuttgart: Kohlhammer, 1933); C. A. Evans, "On Isaiah's Use of Israel's Sacred Tradition," *BZ* 30 (1986) 92-99; idem, "On the Unity and Parallel Structure of Isaiah," *VT* 38 (1988) 129-47; H. Ewald, *Die Propheten des Alten Bundes* (2nd ed.; 3 vols.; Göttingen: Vandenhoeck & Ruprecht, 1867); F. Feldman, *Das Buch Isaias* (EHAT 14/1; Münster: Aschendorff, 1925); A. Feuillet, "Bibliographie choisie sur le livre d'Isaïe," in *Études d'exégèse et de la théologie biblique A.T.* (Paris: Gabalda, 1975) 501-8; idem, "La communauté messianique dans la prédication d'Isaïe," *Bible et Vie Chretienne* 20 (1957-58) 38-52; idem, "Introduction au livre d'Isaïe," in *Études d'exégèse et de la théologie biblique A.T.* (Paris: Gabalda, 1975) 19-201; idem, "Isaïe (Le livre d')," *DBSup* 4 (1947) 647-729; idem, "Le messianisme du livre d'Isaïe: Ses rapports avec l'histoire et les traditions d'Israël," in *Études d'exégèse et de la théologie biblique A.T.* (Paris: Gabalda, 1975) 223-59 (repr. from *RSR* 36 [1949] 182-228); R. Fey, *Amos und Jesaja: Abhängigkeit und Eigenständigkeit des Jesaja* (WMANT 12; Neukirchen: Neukirchener, 1963); J. Fichtner, "Jesaja unter den Weisen," *TLZ* 74 (1949) 75-80; idem, "JHWHs Plan in der Botschaft des Jesaja," *ZAW* 63 (1951) 16-33; idem, "Die 'Umkehrung' in der prophetischen Botschaft: Eine Studie zu dem Verhältnis von Schuld und Gericht in der Verkündigung Jesajas," *TLZ* 78 (1953) 459-66; J. Fischer, *Das Buch Isaias,* vol. 1: *Kap. 1–39* (HSAT 7/1/1; Bonn: Hanstein, 1937); G. Fohrer, *Das Buch Jesaja* (2nd ed.;

3 vols.; ZBK; Zurich and Stuttgart: Zwingli, 1964-67); idem, "Entstehung, Komposition, und Überlieferung von Jesaja 1–39," in *Studien zur alttestamentlichen Prophetie (1949-1965)* (BZAW 99; Berlin: Töpelmann, 1967) 113-47 (tr. of *ALUOS* 3 [1961] 3-38); idem, "Jesaja 1 als Zusammenfassung der Verkündigung Jesajas," *ZAW* 74 (1962) 251-68 (repr. in *Studien zur alttestamentlichen Prophetie (1949-1965)* [BZAW 99; Berlin: Töpelmann, 1967] 148-66); idem, "The Origin, Composition, and Tradition of Isaiah I–XXIX," *ALUOS* 3 (1961) 3-38; idem, "Wandlungen Jesajas," in *Studien alttestamentlichen Texten und Themen (1966-1972)* (BZAW 155; Berlin and New York: de Gruyter, 1981) 11-23 (repr. from *Festschrift für Wilhelm Eilers* [ed. G. Wiessner; Wiesbaden: Harrassowitz, 1967] 58-71); C. Franke, "The Function of the Oracles Against Babylon in Isaiah 14 and 47," in *Society of Biblical Literature 1993 Seminar Papers* (ed. E. H. Lovering Jr.; Atlanta: Scholars Press, 1993), 250-59; K. Fullerton, "The Book of Isaiah: Critical Problems and a New Commentary," *HTR* 6 (1913) 478-520; idem, "Viewpoints in the Discussion of Isaiah's Hopes for the Future," *JBL* 41 (1922) 1-101; T. J. Gaehr, "Shear-jashub; or the Remnant Sections in Isaiah," *BSac* 79 (1922) 363-71; W. Gesenius, *Philologisch-kritischer und historiker Commentar über den Jesaia* (3 vols.; Leipzig: F. C. W. Vogel, 1821); H. Gevaryahu, "Isaiah: How the Book Entered Holy Writ," *JBQ* 18 (1989-90) 206-12; idem, "The School of Isaiah, Biography and Transmission of the Book of Isaiah," *DD* 18 (1989-90) 62-68; H. L. Ginsberg, "Isaiah, First Isaiah," *EncJud* 9, 44-60; idem, "Isaiah in the Light of History," *ConJud* 22/1 (1967) 1-18; idem, *The Supernatural in the Prophets, with Special Reference to Isaiah* (Cinncinati: Hebrew Union College Press, 1979); Y. Gitay, "The Effectiveness of Isaiah's Speech," *JQR* 75 (1984) 162-72; idem, "Isaiah and His Audience," *Prooftexts* 3 (1983) 223-30; idem, *Isaiah and His Audience: The Structure and Meaning of Isaiah 1–12* (Assen and Maastricht: Van Gorcum, 1991); idem, "Isaiah and the Syro-Ephraimite War," in *The Book of Isaiah/Le livre d'Isaïe* (ed. J. Vermeylen; BETL 81; Leuven: Leuven University Press and Peeters, 1989) 217-30; idem, "Oratorical Rhetoric: The Question of Prophetic Language with Special Attention to Isaiah," *ACEBT* 10 (1989) 72-83; B. Gosse, "Isaïe 1 dans la rédaction du livre d'Isaïe," *ZAW* 104 (1992) 52-66; idem, "Isaïe vi et la tradition isaïenne," *VT* 42 (1992) 340-49; idem, *Isaïe 13,1–14,23 dans la tradition littéraire du livre d'Isaïe et dans la tradition des oracles contre les nations* (OBO 78; Freiburg: Universitätsverlag; Göttingen: Vandenhoeck & Ruprecht, 1988); idem, "Isaïe 34–35: Le chatiment d'Edom et des nations, salut pour Sion: Contribution à l'étude de la rédaction du livre d'Isaïe," *ZAW* 102 (1990) 396-404; idem, "Isaïe 52,13–53,12 et Isaïe 6," *RB* 98 (1991) 537-43; idem, "Michée 4,1-5, Isaïe 2,1-5 et les rédacteurs finaux du livre d'Isaïe," *ZAW* 105 (1993) 98-102; H. Graetz, "Isaiah XXXIV and XXXV," *JQR* 4 (1891) 1-8; G. B. Gray, *A Critical and Exegetical Commentary on the Book of Isaiah I–XXVII* (ICC; Edinburgh: T. & T. Clark, 1912); H. Gressmann, *Der Messias* (FRLANT 34; Göttingen: Vandenhoeck & Ruprecht, 1929); H. Gross, *Die Idee des ewigen und allgemeinen Weltfriedens im Alten Orient und im Alten Testament* (TThSt 7; Trier: Paulinus, 1956); E. Haag, "Der Weg zum Baum es Lebens: Ein Paradiesmotiv im Buch Jesaja," in *Künder des Wortes* (*Fest.* J. Schreiner; ed. L. Ruppert et al.; Würzburg: Echter, 1982) 35-52; R. Halas, "The Universalism of Isaias," *CBQ* 12 (1950) 162-70; C. Hardmeier, "Jesajaforschung im Umbruch," *VF* 31 (1986) 3-31; idem, *Texttheorie und biblische Exegese: Zur rhetorischen Funktion der Trauermetaphorik in der Prophetie* (BEvT 79; Munich: Kaiser, 1978); G. F. Hasel, *The Remnant: The History and Theology of the Remnant Idea from Genesis to*

Isaiah (3rd ed.; AUM 5; Berrien Springs: Andrews University Press, 1980); J. Hayes and S. Irvine, *Isaiah, the Eighth-century Prophet: His Times and His Preaching* (Nashville: Abingdon, 1987); A. S. Herbert, *The Book of the Prophet Isaiah, Chapters 1–39* (CBC; Cambridge: University Press, 1973); H.-J. Hermisson, "Zukunftserwartung und Gegenwartskritik in der Verkündigung Jesajas," *EvT* 33 (1973) 54-77; V. Herntrich, *Der Prophet Jesaja, Kapitel 1–12* (ATD 17; Göttingen: Vandenhoeck & Ruprecht, 1957); H. W. Hertzberg, *Der Erste Jesaja* (Kassel: Oncken, 1952); W. Hill, "Book of Isaiah," *New Catholic Encyclopedia* 7 (1967) 666-71; F. Hitzig, *Der Prophet Jesaja* (Heidelberg: Winter, 1833); H. W. Hoffmann, *Die Intention der Verkündigung Jesajas* (BZAW 136; Berlin and New York: de Gruyter, 1974); J. Høgenhaven, *Gott und Volk bei Jesaja: Eine Untersuchung zur biblischen Theologie* (Leiden: Brill, 1988); W. L. Holladay, *Isaiah: Scroll of a Prophetic Heritage* (Grand Rapids: Eerdmans, 1978); G. Hölscher, "Jesaja," *TLZ* 77 (1952) 683-94; F. Huber, *JHWH, Juda und die anderen Völker beim Propheten Jesaja* (BZAW 137; Berlin and New York: de Gruyter, 1976); S. A. Irvine, *Isaiah, Ahaz, and the Syro-Ephraimitic Crisis* (SBLDS 123; Atlanta: Scholars, 1990); E. Jacob, *Esaïe 1–12* (CAT VIII/A; Geneva: Labor et Fides, 1987); J. Jensen, *The Use of tôrâ by Isaiah: His Debate with the Wisdom Tradition* (CBQMS 3; Washington: Catholic Biblical Association, 1973); idem, "Weal and Woe in Isaiah: Consistency and Continuity," *CBQ* 43 (1981) 167-87; idem, "YHWH's Plan in Isaiah and in the Rest of the Old Testament," *CBQ* 48 (1986) 443-55; J. Jensen and W. H. Irwin, "Isaiah 1–39," in *The New Jerome Biblical Commentary* (ed. R. E. Brown et al.; Englewood Cliffs: Prentice-Hall, 1990) 229-48; K. Jeppesen, *Jesajas Bog fortolket* (Copenhagen: Det Danske Bibelselskab, 1988); D. Jones, "The Traditio of the Oracles of Isaiah of Jerusalem," *ZAW* 67 (1955) 226-46; H. Junker, "Ursprung und Grundzüge des Messiasbildes bei Isajas," *Volume du Congrès, Strasbourg 1956* (VTSup 4; Leiden: Brill, 1957) 181-96; O. Kaiser, "Geschichtliche Erfahrung und eschatologische Erwartung: Ein Beitrag zur Geschichte der alttestamentlichen Eschatologie im Jesajabuch," in *Von der Gegenwartsbedeutung des Alten Testaments* (Göttingen: Vandenhoeck & Ruprecht, 1984) 167-80; idem, *Isaiah 1–12* (tr. R. A. Wilson; OTL; Philadelphia: Westminster, 1972; 2nd ed.; tr. J. Bowden; 1983); idem, *Isaiah 13–39* (tr. R. A. Wilson; OTL; Philadelphia: Westminster, 1974); idem, "Literarkritik und Tendenzkritik. Überlegungen zur Methode des Jesajaexegese," in *The Book of Isaiah/Le livre d'Isaïe* (ed. J. Vermeylen; BETL 81; Leuven: Leuven University Press and Peeters, 1989) 55-71; idem, "Die Verkündigung des Propheten Jesaja im Jahre 701," *ZAW* 81 (1969) 304-14; O. Keel, "Rechttun oder Annahme des drohenden Gerichts?" *BZ* 21 (1977) 200-218; C. A. Keller, "Das quietistische Element in der Botschaft des Jesaja," *TZ* 11 (1955) 81-97; R. H. Kenneth, *The Composition of the Book of Isaiah in the Light of History and Archaeology* (London: British Academy, 1910); K. Kiesow, *Exodustexte im Jesajabuch* (OBO 24; Fribourg: Éditions Universitaires; Göttingen: Vandenhoeck & Ruprecht, 1979); R. Kilian, *Jesaja 1–12* (NEB 17; Würzburg: Echter, 1986); idem, *Jesaja 1–39* (EF 200; Darmstadt: Wissenschaftliche Buchgesellschaft, 1983); idem, "Der Verstockungsauftrag Jesajas," in *Bausteine biblischer Theologie (Fest.* G. J. Botterweck; ed. H.-J. Fabry; BBB 50; Cologne and Bonn: P. Hanstein, 1977) 209-25; E. J. Kissane, *The Book of Isaiah*, vol. 1 (Dublin: Browne and Nolan, 1941; 2nd ed. 1960); J. Klausner, *The Messianic Idea in Israel* (tr. W. F. Stinespring; London: George Allen and Unwin, 1956); K. Koch, "Damnation and Salvation — Prophetic Metahistory and the Rise of Eschatology in the Book of Isaiah," *ExAud* 6 (1990) 5-13; idem, "Ezra and the Origins of Judaism," *JSS* 19 (1974) 173-97;

35

idem, "Zur Geschichte der Erwählungsvorstellung in Israel," *ZAW* 67 (1955) 205-26; E. König, *Das Buch Jesaja* (Gütersloh: Bertelsmann, 1926); R. G. Kratz, *Kyros im Deuterojesaja-Buch: Redaktionsgeschichtliche Untersuchungen zu Entstehung und Theologie von Jes 40–55* (FAT 1; Tübingen: Mohr [Siebeck], 1991); A. Laato, *Who is Immanuel? The Rise and Foundering of Isaiah's Messianic Expectations* (Abo: Abo Academy Press, 1988); R. Lack, *La symbolique du livre d'Isaïe* (AnBib 59; Rome: Biblical Institute, 1973); A. LeFèvre, "L'expression 'en ce jour-là' dans le livre d'Isaïe," in *Mélanges Bibliques* (Fest. A. Robert; Paris: Bloud et Gay, 1957) 174-79; T. Lescow, "Das Geburtsmotiv in den messianischen Weissagungen bei Jesaja und Micha," *ZAW* 79 (1967) 172-207; E. A. Leslie, *Isaiah, Chronologically Arranged, Translated, and Interpreted* (New York: Abingdon, 1963); L. J. Liebreich, "The Compilation of the Book of Isaiah," *JQR* 46 (1955-56) 259-77; 47 (1956-57) 114-38; idem, "The Position of Chapter Six in the Book of Isaiah," *HUCA* 25 (1954) 37-40; O. Loretz, "Der Glaube des Propheten Isaias an das Gottesreich," *ZKTh* 82 (1960) 40-73, 159-81; P. Machinist, "Assyria and Its Image in the First Isaiah," *JAOS* 103 (1983) 719-37; R. Margalioth, *The Indivisible Isaiah: Evidence for the Single Authorship of the Prophetic Book* (New York: Yeshiva University, 1964); R. J. Marshall, "The Structure of Isaiah 1–12," *BR* 7 (1962) 19-32; idem, "The Unity of Isaiah 1–12," *LQ* 14 (1962) 21-38; K. Marti, *Das Buch Jesaja* (KHAT 10; Tübingen: Mohr [Siebeck], 1900); R. Martin-Achard, "Esaïe et Jérémie aux prises avec les problèmes politiques: Contribution à l'étude du thème: Prophétie et politique," *RHPR* 47 (1967) 208-24; idem, "Sagesse de Dieu et sagesse humaine chez Ésaïe," in *La Branche d'Amandier* (Fest. W. Vischer; Montpellier: Causse, Graille, Castelnau, 1960) 137-44; J. Mauchline, *Isaiah 1–39* (TBC; New York: Macmillan, 1962); R. Melugin, "The Conventional and the Creative in Isaiah's Judgment Oracles," *CBQ* 36 (1974) 301-11; idem, *The Formation of Isaiah 40–55* (BZAW 141; Berlin and New York: de Gruyter, 1976); W. R. Millar, "Isaiah, Book of (Isaiah 24–27 [Little Apocalypse])," *ABD;* P. D. Miscall, "Isaiah: The Labyrinth of Images," *Semeia* 54 (1991) 103-21; J. Milgrom, "Did Isaiah Prophesy During the Reign of Uzziah?" *VT* 14 (1964) 164-82; H. G. Mitchell, "Isaiah on the Fate of His People and Their Capital," *JBL* 37 (1918) 149-62; J. Morgenstern, "Further Light from the Book of Isaiah upon the Catastrophe of 485 B.C.," *HUCA* 37 (1966) 1-28; F. L. Moriarty, "Isaiah 1–39," in *Jerome Bible Commentary* (ed. R. Brown et al.; Englewood Cliffs: Prentice-Hall, 1968), 265-82; S. Mowinckel, *He That Cometh* (tr. G. W. Anderson; Nashville and New York: Abingdon, 1954); idem, *Jesaja-Disiplene: Profetien fra Jesaja til Jeremia* (Oslo: Dybwad, 1926); idem, "Die Komposition des Jesajabuches Kap. 1–39," *AcOr* 11 (1933) 267-92; idem, *Prophecy and Tradition* (Oslo: Dybwad, 1946); H.-P. Müller, "Zur Funktion des Mythischen in der Prophetie des Jesaja," *Kairos* 13 (1971) 266-81; B. D. Napier, "Isaiah and the Isaian," *Volume du Congrès, Genève 1965* (VTSup 15; Leiden: Brill, 1966) 240-51; H. Niehr, "Bedeutung und Funktion kanaanäischer Traditions-elements in der Sozialkritik Jesajas," *BZ* 28 (1984) 69-81; K. Nielsen, "Das Bild des Gerichts (Rib Pattern) in Jes. I–XII," *VT* 29 (1979) 309-24; idem, *There Is Hope for a Tree: The Tree as Metaphor in Isaiah* (tr. C. and F. Crowley; JSOTSup 65; Sheffield: JSOT Press, 1989); J. N. Oswalt, *The Book of Isaiah, Chapters 1–39* (NICOT; Grand Rapids: Eerdmans, 1986); C. R. North, "Isaiah," *IDB;* H. Odeberg, *Trito-Isaiah (55–66): A Literary and Linguistic Analysis* (UUÅ, Theologi 1; Uppsala: Almqvist and Wiksell, 1931); A.-M. Pelletier, "Le livre d'Isaïe et le temps de l'histoire," *NRT* 112 (1990) 30-43; D. L. Petersen, *Haggai and Zechariah 1–8* (OTL; Philadelphia:

Westminster, 1984); A. Petitjean, "Représentations littéraires de Dieu chez Isaïe: Introduction à la théologie isaïenne," *Revue Diocésaine de Namur* 21 (1967) 143-62; M. Pope, "Isaiah 34 in Relation to Isaiah 35, 40–66," *JBL* 71 (1952) 235-43; W. Popper, "A Suggestion as to the Sequence of Some Prophecies in the First Isaiah," *HUCA* 1 (1924) 79-96; O. Procksch, *Jesaja I–XXXIX* (KAT 9; Leipzig: Deichert, 1930); Y. Radday, "Two Computerized Statistical-linguistic Tests Concerning the Unity of Isaiah," *JBL* 89 (1970) 319-24; idem, *The Unity of Isaiah in the Light of Statistical Linguistics* (Hildesheim: H. A. Gerstenberg, 1973); idem, "Vocabulary Eccentricity and the Unity of Isaiah," *Tarbiz* 39 (1969-70) 323-41 (Hebrew); H. Renard, "Le messianisme dans la première partie du livre d'Isaïe," *SacPag* 1 (1959) 398-407; R. Rendtorff, "The Book of Isaiah: A Complex Unity: Synchronic and Diachronic Reading," in *Society of Biblical Literature 1991 Seminar Papers* (ed. E. H. Lovering Jr.; Atlanta: Scholars Press, 1991) 8-20; idem, "Jesaja 6 im Rahmen der Komposition des Jesajabuches," in *The Book of Isaiah/Le livre d'Isaïe* (ed. J. Vermeylen; BETL 81; Leuven: Leuven University Press and Peeters, 1989) 73-82; idem, "Isaiah 56:1 as a Key to the Formation of the Book of Isaiah," in *Canon and Theology* (tr. and ed. M. Kohl; OBT; Minneapolis: Augsburg Fortress, 1993) 181-89; idem, "Zur Komposition des Buches Jesajas," *VT* 34 (1984) 295-320; J. J. M. Roberts, "Isaiah in Old Testament Theology," *Int* 36 (1982) 130-43; A. Rofé, "How is the Word Fulfilled? Isaiah 55:6-11 within the Theological Debate of Its Time," in *Canon, Theology, and Old Testament Interpretation* (*Fest.* B. S. Childs; ed. G. M. Tucker et al.; Philadelphia: Fortress, 1988) 246-61; J. Ruck, "Isaiah and the Prophetic Disciple," *TBT* 21 (1983) 399-405; G. Sauer, "Die Umkehrforderung in der Verkündigung Jesajas," in *Wort — Gebot — Glaube* (*Fest.* W. Eichrodt; ed. H.-J. Stoebe; ATANT 59; Zurich: Zwingli, 1970) 277-95; J. F. A. Sawyer, "Daughter of Zion and Servant of the Lord in Isaiah: A Comparison," *JSOT* 44 (1989) 89-107; idem, *Isaiah* (2 vols.; Daily Study Bible; Philadelphia: Westminster, 1984-86); C. Schedl, *Rufer des Heils in heilloser Zeit: Der Prophet Jesajah Kapitel i–xii logotechnisch und bibeltheologisch erklärt* (Paderborn: Schöningh, 1973); H. Schmidt, *Die Grossen Propheten* (SAT 2/2; Göttingen: Vandenhoeck & Ruprecht, 1915); W. H. Schmidt, "Die Einheit der Verkündigung Jesajas: Versuch einer Zusammenschau," *EvT* 37 (1977) 260-72; idem, "Jerusalemer El-Traditionen bei Jesaja: Ein religionsgeschichtlicher Vergleich zum Vorstellungskreis des göttlichen Königtums," *ZRGG* 16 (1964) 302-13; J. J. Schmitt, *Isaiah and His Interpreters* (New York: Paulist, 1986); R. Schoenstene, "An Image of the Promised Land: Jerusalem in Isaiah," *TBT* 29 (1991) 9-13; A. Schoors, "Isaiah, the Minister of Royal Anointment?" *OTS* 20 (1977) 85-107; idem, *Jesaja I* (BOuT 9A; Roermond: J. J. Romen en Zonen, 1972); J. Schreiner, *Sion-Jerusalem, JHWHs Königssitz* (Munich: Kösel, 1963); idem, "Das Buch jesajanischer Schule," in *Wort und Botschaft: Eine theologische und kritische Einführung in die Probleme des Alten Testaments* (Würzburg: Echter, 1967) 143-62; K.-D. Schunck, "Strukturlinien in der Entwicklung der Vorstellung vom 'Tag JHWHs,'" *VT* 14 (1964) 319-30; R. B. Y. Scott, "The Book of Isaiah, Chapters 1–39," *IB;* idem, "The Literary Structure of Isaiah's Oracles," in *Studies in Old Testament Prophecy* (*Fest.* T. H. Robinson; ed. H. H. Rowley; Edinburgh: T. & T. Clark, 1950) 175-86; I. P. Seierstad, *Die Offenbarungserlebnisse der Propheten Amos, Jesaja und Jeremia* (2nd ed.; Oslo: Universitetsforlaget, 1965); C. R. Seitz, "The Divine Council: Temporal Transition and New Prophecy in the Book of Isaiah," *JBL* 109 (1990) 229-47; idem, "Isaiah, Book of (First Isaiah)," *ABD;* idem, "Isaiah 1–66: Making Sense of the Whole," in *Reading and Preaching the Book of Isaiah* (ed. C. R. Seitz; Philadelphia: Fortress, 1988) 105-26; idem,

Zion's Final Destiny: The Development of the Book of Isaiah (Minneapolis: Fortress, 1991); G. T. Sheppard, "The Anti-Assyrian Redaction and the Canonical Context of Isaiah 1–39," *JBL* 104 (1985) 193-216; idem, "The Book of Isaiah: Competing Structures According to a Late Modern Description of Its Shape and Scope," in *Society of Biblical Literature 1992 Seminar Papers* (ed. E. H. Lovering Jr.; Atlanta: Scholars Press, 1992) 549-82; idem, "Isaiah 1–39," in *Harper's Bible Commentary* (ed. J. L. Mays et al.; San Francisco: Harper & Row, 1988) 542-70; P. Skehan, "Isaias and the Teaching of the Book of Wisdom," *CBQ* 2 (1940) 289-99; J. Skinner, *The Book of the Prophet Isaiah, Chapters 1–39* (CBC; Cambridge: University Press, 1905); I. W. Slotki, *Isaiah* (Soncino; London: Soncino, 1949); J. Smart, *History and Theology in Second Isaiah: A Commentary on Isaiah 35, 40–66* (Philadelphia: Westminster, 1965); G. A. Smith, *The Book of Isaiah* (2 vols.; ExpB; New York: A. C. Armstrong, 1905); J. M. P. Smith, "Isaiah and the Future," *AJSL* 40 (1923-24) 252-58; L. P. Smith, "The Messianic Ideal of Isaiah," *JBL* 36 (1917) 158-212; O. H. Steck, *Bereitete Heimkehr: Jesaja 35 als redaktionelle Brücke zwischen dem Ersten und dem Zweiten Jesaja* (SBS 121; Stuttgart: Katholisches Bibelwerk, 1985); idem, " '. . . ein kleiner Knabe kann sie leiten': Beobachtungen zum Tierfrieden in Jesaja 11,6-8 und 65,25," in *Alttestamentlicher Glaube und Biblische Theologie* (*Fest.* H. D. Preuss; ed. J. Hausmann and H.-J. Zobel; Stuttgart: Kohlhammer, 1992) 104-13; idem, *Friedensvorstellungen im alten Jerusalem: Psalmen — Jesaja — Deuterojesaja* (TS 111; Zurich: Theologisches Verlag, 1972); idem, *Studien zu Tritojesaja* (BZAW 203; Berlin and New York: de Gruyter, 1991); idem, "Tritojesaja im Jesajabuch," in *The Book of Isaiah/Le livre d'Isaïe* (ed. J. Vermeylen; BETL 81; Leuven: Leuven University Press and Peeters, 1989) 361-406; U. Stegemann, "Der Restgedanke bei Isaias," *BZ* 13 (1969) 161-86; J. Steinmann, *Le prophete Isaïe, sa vie, son oeuvre et son temps* (LD 5; Paris: Cerf, 1950); M. A. Sweeney, "The Book of Isaiah in Recent Research," *CRBS* 1 (1993) 141-62; idem, *Isaiah 1–4 and the Post-Exilic Understanding of the Isaianic Tradition* (BZAW 171; Berlin and New York: de Gruyter, 1988); idem, "On Multiple Settings in the Book of Isaiah," in *Society of Biblical Literature 1993 Seminar Papers* (ed. E. H. Lovering Jr.; Atlanta: Scholars Press, 1993) 267-73; idem, "Textual Citations in Isaiah 24–27: Toward an Understanding of the Redactional Function of Chapters 24–27 in the Book of Isaiah," *JBL* 107 (1988) 39-52; A. J. Tomasino, "Isaiah 1.1–2.4 and 63–66, and the Composition of the Isaianic Corpus," *JSOT* 57 (1993) 81-98; C. C. Torrey, *The Second Isaiah: A New Interpretation* (Edinburgh: T. & T. Clark, 1928); N. H. Tur-Sinai, "A Contribution to the Understanding of Isaiah i–xii," *Scripta Hierosolymitana* 8 (1961) 154-88; J. Vermeylen, *Du prophète Isaïe à l'apocalyptique* (2 vols.; EBib; Paris: Gabalda, 1977-78); idem, "Le Proto-Isaïe et la sagesse d'Israël," in *La Sagesse de l'Ancien Testament* (ed. M. Gilbert; BETL 51; Leuven: Peeters, 1979) 39-58; idem, "L'unité du livre d'Isaïe," in *The Book of Isaiah/Le livre d'Isaïe* (ed. J. Vermeylen; BETL 81; Leuven: Leuven University Press and Peeters, 1989) 11-53; J. Vermeylen, ed., *The Book of Isaiah/Le livre d'Isaïe* (BETL 81; Leuven: Leuven University Press and Peeters, 1989); E. Vogt, "Jesaja und die drohende Eroberung Palälestinas durch Tiglatpileser," in *Wort, Lied und Gottespruch,* vol. 2: *Beiträge zu Psalmen und Propheten* (*Fest.* J. Ziegler; ed. J. Schreiner; FB 2; Würzburg: Echter; Stuttgart: Katholisches Bibelwerk, 1972) 249-55; idem, "Sennacherib und die letzte Tätigkeit Jesajas," *Bib* 47 (1966) 427-37; J. Vollmer, *Geschichtliche Rückblicke und Motive in der Prophetie des Amos, Hosea, und Jesaja* (BZAW 119; Berlin: de Gruyter, 1971); T. C. Vriezen, "Essentials of the Theology of Isaiah," in *Israel's Prophetic Heritage* (*Fest.* J. Muilenburg; ed. B. W.

Anderson and W. Harrelson; London: SCM, 1962) 128-46; G. W. Wade, *The Book of the Prophet Isaiah* (Westminster Commentary; London: Methuen, 1911); J. M. Ward, *Amos and Isaiah: Prophets of the Word of God* (Nashville and New York: Abingdon, 1969); idem, "Isaiah," *IDBSup;* J. D. W. Watts, *Isaiah 1–33* (WBC 24; Waco: Word, 1985); idem, *Isaiah 34–66* (WBC 25; Waco: Word, 1987); B. G. Webb, "Zion in Transformation: A Literary Approach to Isaiah," in *The Bible in Three Dimensions* (ed. D. J. A. Clines et al.; JSOTSup 87; Sheffield: JSOT Press, 1990) 65-84; P. Wegner, *An Examination of Kingship and Messianic Expectation in Isaiah 1–35* (Lewiston: Mellen, 1992); W. Werner, *Studien zur alttestamentlichen Vorstellung vom Plan JHWHs* (BZAW 173; Berlin and New York: de Gruyter, 1988); idem, *Eschatologische Texte in Jesaja 1–39: Messias, Heiliger Rest, Völker* (FB 46; Würzburg: Echter, 1982); J. W. Whedbee, *Isaiah and Wisdom* (Nashville: Abingdon, 1971); H. Wildberger, "Gottesnamen und Gottesepitheta bei Jesaja," *JHWH und sein Volk* (TBü 66; Munich: Kaiser, 1973) 219- 48; idem, *Jesaja* (BKAT 10/1-3; Neukirchen-Vluyn: Neukirchener, 1972-82); idem, "Jesajas Verständnis der Geschichte," *Congress Volume, Bonn 1962* (VTSup 9; Leiden: Brill, 1963) 83-117; idem, *Königsherrschaft Gottes: Jesaja 1–39* (2 vols.; Neukirchen-Vluyn: Neukirchener, 1984); F. Wilke, *Jesaja und Assur: Eine exegetisch-historische Untersuchung zur Politik des Propheten Jesaja* (Leipzig: Weicher, 1905); G. E. Wright, *Isaiah* (LBC; Richmond: John Knox, 1964); E. J. Young, *The Book of Isaiah* (3 vols.; NICOT; Grand Rapids: Eerdmans, 1965-72); J. Ziegler, *Das Buch Isaias* (Echter Bibel; Würzburg: Echter, 1958); idem, "Zum literarischen Aufbau verschiedener Stücke im Buche des Propheten Isaias," *BZ* 21 (1933) 131-49, 237-54; W. Zimmerli, "Gottesrecht bei den Propheten Amos, Hosea und Jesaja," in *Werden und Wirken des Alten Testaments* (*Fest.* C. Westermann; ed. R. Albertz et al.; Göttingen: Vandenhoeck & Ruprecht; Neukirchen-Vluyn: Neukirchener, 1980) 216-35; idem, "Verkündigung und Sprache der Botschaft Jesajas," in *Gesammelte Aufsätze,* vol. 2: *Studien zur alttestamentlichen Theologie und Prophetie* (TBü 51; Munich: Kaiser, 1974) 73-87.

THE VISION OF ISAIAH BEN AMOZ: PROPHETIC EXHORTATION TO JERUSALEM/JUDAH TO ADHERE TO YHWH, ISAIAH 1:1–66:24

Structure

I. Concerning YHWH's plans for worldwide
   sovereignty at Zion   1:1–33:24
   A. Prologue to the book of Isaiah:
      introductory parenesis concerning YHWH's
      intention to purify Jerusalem   1:1-31
   B. Prophetic instruction concerning YHWH's
      projected plans to establish worldwide
      sovereignty at Zion: announcement of
      Day of YHWH   2:1–33:24
      1. Prophetic announcement concerning
         preparation of Zion for its role as center
         for YHWH's world rule   2:1–4:6

    c. Prophetic instruction concerning process
        of selection for reconstituted
        covenant community   63:1–66:24

During most of the 20th century, it has been customary to treat Isaiah 1–39 as a distinct prophetic book. This is based on the historical presuppositions that stand behind Duhm's identification of First, Second, and Third Isaiah within the book as a whole. Duhm's paradigm holds that chs. 1–39 must be associated with the 8th-century prophet, Isaiah ben Amoz; that chs. 40–55 are the work of an anonymous prophet of the Babylonian exile identified only as Deutero-Isaiah; and that chs. 56–66 reflect the work of a postexilic prophet identified as Trito-Isaiah. But more recent research on the literary character of the book of Isaiah has called this decision into question (for a survey of current scholarly opinion, see Sweeney, "Recent Research"). Although chs. 1–39 clearly portray an 8th-century historical setting much earlier than that of chs. 40–55 or 56–66, there is no evidence that chs. 1–39 ever constituted a distinct prophetic book separate from their present literary context in the book of Isaiah. Literary, exegetical, and thematic links between the various parts of the book demonstrate that, although Isaiah was composed over the course of some four centuries, it now constitutes a single literary entity (for detailed summaries of the following, see Sweeney, "Recent Research"; idem, *Isaiah 1–4*, 1-25).

Overall, the first part of the book projects judgment and subsequent restoration whereas the second part announces that the judgment has ended and restoration is beginning; consequently the "former things" or prophecies of judgment in First Isaiah give way to the "new things" or prophecies of restoration in Second Isaiah (see esp. Becker; Childs, *Introduction,* 311-38). Other links include: (1) the lexical associations between chs. 1 and 65–66 that demonstrate that these chapters form a literary inclusion for the entire book (see esp. Lack; Sweeney, *Isaiah 1–4*, 21-24; Beuken, "Isaiah LXV–LXVI"; Tomasino); (2) the portrayal of Babylon as the symbol of world power arrayed against YHWH in both halves of the book (see esp. Gosse, *Isaïe 13,1–14,23;* Franke); (3) the transitional function of chs. 36–39, which anticipate the Babylonian exile (39:6-7) and contrast the faithful Hezekiah with the faithless Ahaz of ch. 7 (see esp. Ackroyd, "Isaiah 36–39"; Sweeney, *Isaiah 1–4*, 12-17); (4) the theme of a new exodus (see esp. Steck, *Bereitete Heimkehr,* esp. 45-79; Sweeney, *Isaiah 1–4*, 17-20); (5) the theme of Israel's blindness and deafness that will come to an end in the age of redemption (see esp. Clements, "Beyond Tradition History"); and (6) the themes of *mišpāṭ,* "justice," and *ṣĕdāqâ,* "righteousness," that permeate the entire book (see esp. Rendtorff, "Zur Komposition"). Furthermore, various studies demonstrate that texts in the second part of Isaiah make explicit reference to or develop themes from the first part of the book, including the references to 8:6 in 66:10-14 (Sweeney, "On *ûmĕśôś*"); the citation of 11:6, 9 in 65:25 (Childs, *Introduction,* 330; Steck, " '. . . ein kleiner Knabe' "; J. van Ruiten, "The Intertextual Relationship Between Isaiah 65, 25 and Isaiah 11, 6-9," *The Scriptures and the Scrolls* (VTSup 49; *Fest.* A. S. van der Woude; eds. F. García Martínez et al.; Leiden: E. J. Brill, 1992) 31-42; and the above-mentioned references to ch. 1 in chs. 65–66. Finally, a number of studies have demonstrated that the material in the first part of the book is organized to address issues that pertain to the exilic or postexilic periods (e.g., Jones; Ackroyd, "Isaiah I–XII"; Clements, "Prophecies"). Consequently, treatment of the structure, genre, setting, and intention of chs. 1–39 must account for these chapters in relation to the entire book of Isaiah.

Even when the book of Isaiah is considered as a literary whole, there is no evidence that Duhm's divisions of First, Second, and Third Isaiah constitute the literary structure of the book. Because of the focus on Isaiah ben Amoz and Hezekiah during Sennacherib's siege of Jerusalem in chs. 36–39, most scholars have been inclined to treat chs. 1–39 as a literary unit in which these narratives close the traditions concerning the 8th-century prophet. But more recent studies by Melugin, Ackroyd, and Seitz demonstrate that chs. 36–39 do not close the traditions of First Isaiah; rather, they introduce the writings that now appear in chs. 40ff. Taking his cue from Isaiah's prophecy of Babylonian exile in 39:6-7, Melugin (*Formation,* 177) states that "the closest thing to a setting for chs. 40ff. is the prophecy of Isaiah to Hezekiah concerning the exile to Babylon." Ackroyd ("Isaiah 36–39") builds on this observation to argue that chs. 36–39 deliberately contrast Hezekiah's faithfulness with the portrayal of Ahaz's faithlessness in 6:1–9:6 (*RSV* 7) in order to idealize Hezekiah as an example of hope for the disaster of the Babylonian exile. Seitz ("Divine Council") follows up by demonstrating that 40:1-11 cannot be considered as a traditional call narrative for Deutero-Isaiah, since the prophetic call has already been issued in ch. 6; rather, 40:1-11 represents a renewal of the prophetic commission addressed to the servant Israel and Zion. It is noteworthy that the book of Isaiah does not identify a new prophet in ch. 40. Consequently, chs. 40–66 must be considered as part of "The Vision of Isaiah ben Amoz" (1:1). In essence, chs. 40–66 are presented as part of the prophecy of the 8th-century prophet addressed to the situations of the Babylonian exile and the early postexilic period.

The transitional function of chs. 34–35 also plays a major role in defining the structure of the book of Isaiah. Critical scholars argue frequently that chs. 34–35 were composed much later than chs. 1–33, and some argue that these chapters, especially ch. 35, may well stem from Deutero-Isaiah or the prophet's immediate circle of tradents (Graetz; Torrey; Pope; Smart; Kiesow). Others point to the transitional function of these chapters in that both reflect on themes of judgment from chs. 1–33 but point forward to new opportunities for salvation and restoration in the second half of the book. Dicou notes the thematic correspondences between ch. 34 on the one hand and, on the other hand, the prologue in ch. 1, the oracle against Babylon in ch. 13, and the oracle against Edom in 63:1-6. He argues that ch. 34 may once have concluded an early form of the book of Isaiah, and that together with chs. 1 and 13, ch. 34 formed the "frame." But the parallel with ch. 1 and the association with ch. 35 and 63:1-6 indicate that ch. 34 points forward as well as backward, so that the chapter introduces the second half of the book as well. Beuken's study of ch. 34 ("Isaiah 34") demonstrates its transitional character in that it anticipates the nations' opportunity to recognize YHWH in Deutero-Isaiah, following their judgment in chs. 1–33. Ch. 34 likewise anticipates the final judgment of YHWH against the wicked in chs. 65–66 that will result in the nations' recognition of YHWH's worldwide sovereignty. Steck's study of ch. 35 (*Bereitete Heimkehr*, 45-79) likewise points to the "bridging function" of this chapter that presupposes the end of punishment and anticipates the return to Zion announced in 11:11-16; 27:12-13; 40:1-11; and 62:10-12. It is noteworthy that chs. 32 and 33 play a similar transitional role in that they sum up major concerns of chs. 1–33 and thereby conclude these chapters. Ch. 32 anticipates the peaceful reign of the righteous Davidic monarch announced in 9:1-6 (*RSV* 2-7) and 11:1-16, and Isaiah 33 anticipates the downfall of the "treacherous" enemy (Assyria; Babylon) that opposed YHWH and oppressed Israel throughout the first part of the book (cf. Beuken, "Jesaja 33"; for a full discussion of the transitional roles of these chapters, see the commentary below). In this regard, the concluding command in 34:16-17 to "read from the book of YHWH" in order to confirm the realization of YHWH's commands indicates that the realized prophecies of chs. 1–33 serve as the basis for accepting the unrealized prophecies that dominate the second half of the book.

The transitional functions of chs. 32–33; 34–35 and 36–39 indicate that the structure of the book of Isaiah falls into two basic parts: chs. 1–33 and chs. 34–66 (cf. Brownlee; Evans; Gosse, "Isaïe 34–35"). Several additional considerations support this contention. First, both sections begin with a call to attention that is directed to the world or cosmos at large to witness YHWH's punishment against Israel in ch. 1 and against the nations in ch. 34 (cf. Brownlee; Evans). Isa 1:2 is addressed to "the heavens" and "the earth," and 34:1 is addressed to the "nations," "peoples," "the earth and all that fills it," and "the world and all that comes from it." In each case, the call to witness punishment corresponds to a major concern in the respective portion of the book. The call to witness Israel's punishment in ch. 1 corresponds to the overall concern with the punishment or purification of Jerusalem, Judah, and Israel in chs. 1–33. Such punishment or purification demonstrates YHWH's sovereignty over the people in these chapters. Likewise, the call to witness the nations' punishment in ch. 34 corresponds to the overall concern to establish YHWH's worldwide sovereignty in chs. 34–66. In this case, the redemption of Israel and Jerusalem serves as a signal to the nations that YHWH's worldwide rule is manifest in Zion and that the nations will be included in YHWH's plans.

Second, chs. 1–33 anticipate the punishment and subsequent restoration of Jerusalem, Judah, and Israel. In chs. 34–66, this punishment is completed and the restoration is now taking place. Likewise, chs. 1–33 anticipate the downfall of the enemy oppressor (ch. 33), identified primarily as Assyria (10:5-34; 14:24-27) but also as Babylon (13:1–14:23). Chs. 34–66 presuppose the downfall of YHWH's and Zion's major enemies, including Edom (ch. 34; 63:1-6) and Babylon (chs. 46–47) in the age of Zion's restoration. Throughout chs. 1–33, this scenario of punishment is identified with the concept of the "Day of YHWH," directed against both Israel (2:12) and Babylon (13:6, 9; cf. 22:5). This "Day of YHWH" apparently provides the referent for the formula *bayyôm hahû'*, "in that day," and its variations that appear frequently in chs. 1–33 beginning in 2:11 and ending in 31:7 (the occurrence of the formula in 52:6 is an exceptional reference to Assyrian oppression in Second Isaiah). But the references to the "Day of YHWH's vengeance" *(yôm nāqām lĕyhwh)* throughout chs. 34–66 express YHWH's punishment of Edom (34:8; 63:14) and the anticipated final punishment of the wicked (61:2; cf. 35:4; 59:17; cf. Gosse, "Isaïe 34–35").

Third, chs. 1–33 anticipate the reign of a righteous Davidic monarch that will inaugurate a period of peace for the people (9:1-6 [*RSV* 2-7]; 11:1-16; 32:1-20). In chs. 34–66, the Davidic covenant is still in force for the people (55:3), but these chapters portray the rule of Cyrus as the initial manifestation of YHWH's righteous rule in Zion (44:24-28; 45:1-7; 60–62; 65–66). Furthermore, YHWH's righteous rule is portrayed as the ultimate fulfillment of the promises of chs. 2–4. Although both chs. 1–33 and chs. 34–66 anticipate YHWH's worldwide sovereignty, a major shift takes place beginning in ch. 34. The material in chs. 1–33 presents YHWH's plans for such sovereignty entirely as a future event, but the material in chs. 34–66 presupposes that the process has already begun. The downfall of both Edom and Babylon as well as the rise of Cyrus in these chapters are presented as established facts. Unlike chs. 1–33, which point to no instance in which Isaiah's prophecies are realized, chs. 34–66 point to these events as proof that the prophetic statements are coming to pass. The downfall of Edom (ch. 34; 63:1-6), the Assyrian monarch (chs. 36–37), and Babylon (chs. 46–47) all represent a partial fulfillment of the prophet's statements that the oppressor will fall, and the rise of Cyrus (44:24-28; 45:1-7; cf. Kratz) represents a partial fulfillment of the prophet's predictions of the reign of a righteous monarch. In both instances, these events legitimize the anticipation of a final destruction of the wicked and a full manifestation of the reign of YHWH in chs. 65–66.

Thus the structure of the book of Isaiah comprises two major subunits. Chs. 1–33 focus on the projection of YHWH's plans to establish worldwide sovereignty at Zion, and chs. 34–66 focus on the realization of YHWH's plans for the establishment of worldwide sovereignty at Zion. Whereas chs. 1–33 are wholly anticipatory, chs. 34–66 present the process as a current event. The downfall of Edom, the Assyrian monarch, and Babylon, on the one hand, and the rise of Cyrus, on the other, partially fulfill the promises found in chs. 1–33 and support the contention of chs. 34–66 that YHWH's worldwide sovereignty is about to be manifested. In this context, chs. 1–33 thereby legitimize expectations for the final realization of YHWH's full sovereignty at Zion. The reader simply has to read the first part of the book to know that the prophecies in the second part will indeed be realized (34:16-17).

The demarcation and identification of the various textual blocks within chs. 1–33, including chs. 1; 2–4; 5–12; 13–23; 24–27; and 28–33, are discussed in the commentary below. Within these chapters, it is clear that the parenesis concerning the purification of Jerusalem in ch. 1 is distinguished from the balance of the material in chs. 2–33. As noted above, ch. 1 forms an inclusion with chs. 65–66 for the book of Isaiah as a whole. Scholars generally consider ch. 1 as the prologue to the entire book in that it focuses on the punishment, purification, and redemption of Jerusalem, which appears to be the major concern of the book of Isaiah as a whole (Fohrer, "Jesaja 1"; Sweeney, *Isaiah 1–4*, 27-32). Isa 1:1 serves as the superscription for the entire book as well as for ch. 1 in that it identifies the object of Isaiah's vision as Judah and Jerusalem, and the historical context as the days of the Judean kings mentioned throughout the book of Isaiah, including Uzziah (6:1; 7:1), Jotham (7:1), Ahaz (ch. 7; 14:28), and Hezekiah (chs. 36–39). Finally, its parenetic character is distinguished from the prophetic announcements, pronouncements, and instructions that follow in chs. 2–33.

Isaiah 2:1 likewise begins with a superscription that identifies the following material as "the word that Isaiah ben Amoz saw concerning Judah and Jerusalem." Many scholars follow Ackroyd ("A Note on Isaiah 2, 1," *ZAW* 75 [1963] 320-21), who maintains that 2:1 applies only to 2:2-5 in order to identify it as an authentic word of Isaiah. But the parallel formulation of 13:1, "the pronouncement [*RSV* 'oracle'] of Babylon that Isaiah ben Amoz saw," the exclusive concern of chs. 2–4 with Judah and Jerusalem, and the absence of reference to the kings of Judah indicate that 2:1 applies to a much broader context that follows upon ch. 1. Isa 2:1 appears to have been composed in relation to chs. 2–4, which focus explicitly on the future of Judah and Jerusalem; but in its present literary context, 2:1 appears to serve as the superscription for an entire block of material in chs. 2–33. With their focus on Zion/Jerusalem, Jacob/Israel, and the nations, chs. 2–4 seem to take up major concerns that appear throughout chs. 5–33 as well. Chs. 5–12 focus especially on the northern kingdom of Israel, frequently identified as "Jacob" (2:5, 6; cf. 4:2-6), its fall to the Assyrian empire, and its anticipated return to the Davidic monarchy. Chs. 13–23 focus especially on the fate of the nations who ascend to Mt. Zion to hear YHWH's Torah in 2:2-4. Chs. 24–27 likewise focus on the role of Zion as the center for YHWH's gathering of the nations following worldwide punishment. Finally, chs. 28–33 return to a concern with the punishment and projected restoration of Jerusalem in analogy to that of northern Israel, a concern that appears in chs. 2–4 as well.

The association between chs. 2–4 and the balance of the material in chs. 5–33 is also evident in that chs. 5–33 refer frequently to chs. 2–4. The first major reference to the concept of the "Day of YHWH" appears in 2:12 (cf. 13:6, 9; 22:5), and the many occurrences of the formula *bayyôm hahû'* throughout chs. 2–33 (viz., from 2:11 to 31:7) refer back to it. The vineyard imagery in 5:1-7 reflects that of 3:14. Isa 5:15-16 cites the formula "man is bowed down, and men are brought low, and the eyes of the haughty are humbled. But YHWH Sabaoth is exalted in justice," which takes up the language of 2:9, 11, and 17. The reference to the "Day of YHWH" in the oracle against Babylon in 13:6, 9 reiterates the occurrence of the motif in 2:12, and the statement in 13:11, "I will put an end to the pride of the arrogant, and lay low the haughtiness of the ruthless," likewise reflects the language of 2:9, 11, and 17. Chs. 24–27 contain numerous citations of earlier texts. In addition to references to the vineyard song in 5:1-7, and the pronouncements concerning Babylon and Damascus in chs. 13 and 17, these chapters cite the language of 2:9-17 in the condemnation of Moab (25:11b-12) and the anonymous city (26:5) as well as language for the protection of Zion in 4:5-6 and 32:1-2 (25:4-5; for a full discussion of textual citations in chs. 24–27, see the commentary below and Sweeney, "Textual Citations"; idem, "New Gleanings from an Old Vineyard: Isaiah 27 Reconsidered," *Early Jewish and Christian Exegesis* (*Fest.* W. H. Brownlee; eds. C. A. Evans and W. F. Stinespring; Atlanta: Scholars Press, 1987) 51-66. Likewise, 28:5-6 cites language from 4:2-6 to describe YHWH's sovereignty (cf. 32:1-2), and 31:6-7 refers to the casting away of "his idols of silver and his idols of gold, which your hands have sinfully made for you," which takes up the language of 2:7-8, 18, and 20.

The various textual blocks that constitute chs. 2–33 alternate between prophetic announcements that focus on the proclamation of the Day of YHWH for Zion (chs. 2–4) and the nations (chs. 13–27), and prophetic instruction that describes the significance of YHWH's actions for Jacob/Israel (chs. 5–12) and Jerusalem (chs. 28–33). It is noteworthy that such prophetic instruction culminates in material that predicts the coming of a royal savior (9:1-6 [*RSV* 2-7]; 11:1-16; and 32:1-20), and thereby reiterates the themes of YHWH's kingship that appear in chs. 2–4 and 24–27. Thus chs. 2–4 constitute a prophetic announcement concerning the preparation of Zion on the Day of YHWH for its role as the center for YHWH's worldwide rule. Chs. 5–12 constitute a prophetic instruction concerning the significance of the Assyrian judgment against Jacob/Israel, and thereby anticipate the reunification of Judah and Israel with the restoration of Davidic rule over the northern kingdom. Chs. 5–12 therefore take up the concern with Jacob and the remnant of Israel expressed in 2:5 and 4:2. Chs. 13–27 constitute a prophetic announcement concerning the preparation of the nations on the Day of YHWH for YHWH's worldwide rule. Scholars have frequently noted an association between chs. 13–23 and chs. 24–27 in that the prophetic announcement of YHWH's new world order, with its portrayal of the gathering of the nations at Zion, provides a climactic conclusion for the pronouncements against the nations in chs. 13–23 (e.g., Clements, *Isaiah 1–39*, 196-97; Vermeylen, *Du prophète*, 35; Skinner, lxviii-lxix; Sweeney, *Isaiah 1–4*, 62-63; Wildberger, *Jesaja*, 892-93). The theme of the gathering of the nations at Zion likewise reiterates the ascent of the nations to Zion in 2:2-4, and the focus on Israel's redemption in these chapters reiterates the concern with Jacob/Israel in chs. 2–4 and chs. 5–12. Finally, chs. 28–33 constitute prophetic instruction concerning YHWH's plans for Jerusalem. The portrayal of Jerusalem's judgment in these chapters culminates in the announcement of a royal savior in ch. 32 and the downfall of the oppressor in ch. 33. Chs. 28–33 thereby recapitulate the concerns expressed throughout chs. 2–27, and return to the theme of the purification or preparation of Zion that introduces this segment of Isaiah in chs. 2–4.

Clearly, the constituent textual blocks of chs. 2–33 work together to instruct the reader on the significance of the announcements that are made concerning the Day of YHWH and the preparations for YHWH's worldwide sovereignty. Consequently, chs. 2–33 constitute prophetic instruction concerning YHWH's projected plans to establish worldwide sovereignty. Essentially, this instruction is presented in the form of an announcement of the Day of YHWH.

The second half of Isaiah, chs. 34–66, focuses on the realization of YHWH's plans for worldwide sovereignty at Zion. As noted in the discussion above, the downfall of Edom, the Assyrian monarch, and Babylon provides the basis for the projection of the full realization of YHWH's worldwide sovereignty in these chapters. Yet within chs. 34–66, it is clear that a major structural division exists between chs. 34–54 and 55–66. Whereas chs. 34–54 present the realization of YHWH's worldwide sovereignty at Zion as an unimpeded, contemporaneous event that is unfolding before the eyes of the reader, chs. 55–66 present the full realization of YHWH's sovereignty as an event that will take place following the purging of the wicked in Zion and throughout the world. The concern with the continued presence of evil permeates chs. 56–66. These chapters begin with criteria for those to be included in YHWH's covenant and condemnations of irresponsible leadership in the community in 56:9-12, and they conclude with lurid condemnations of the wicked together with further definitions of those to be included in YHWH's new heavens and new earth in chs. 65–66.

Isaiah 55 plays a particularly important role within the structure of chs. 34–66. This chapter was apparently composed as the conclusion to the writings of Deutero-Isaiah in chs. 40–55 in that it is formulated as an exhortation that directs the reader to hold fast to the covenant of YHWH in light of the redemption of Zion announced throughout the writings of Deutero-Isaiah. But when one considers it in relation to its present literary context within the book of Isaiah as a whole, ch. 55 no longer functions as the conclusion to chs. 40–55. The introductory *hôy*, "woe" (*RSV* "Ho"), in 55:1 distinguishes the following material from the preceding summary-appraisal in 54:17b, and indicates the beginning of a new unit. The feminine singular address forms directed to Zion in ch. 54 give way to masculine plural address forms, like those of ch. 56, directed to the people. The concern with adherence to YHWH's covenant in 55:1-5 is reiterated in 56:4-5; 59:21; and 61:8. The invitation in 55:1-5 by personified Wisdom to be a guest at her table is specified by the exhortation to follow YHWH in 55:6-13, which defines the benefits for continued adherence to YHWH and alludes to the consequences for the wicked who forsake YHWH's way. Ch. 55 serves as an introduction to chs. 56–66 that exhorts the reader to choose to be part of the covenant community that will emerge following YHWH's final judgment against the wicked articulated throughout chs. 56–66. In this regard, it is noteworthy that various scholars persistently maintain that ch. 55 is part of the writings of Trito-Isaiah (see Elliger, 135-67; Rofé, "How is the Word Fulfilled?" and the literature cited there). Ch. 55 defines the entire text block in chs. 55–66 as a prophetic exhortation to adhere to YHWH's covenant in that it calls upon the reader to maintain the covenant in ch. 55 and then defines the constitution of the community that will maintain that covenant once the wicked are punished in chs. 56–66.

The overall instructional character of the material in chs. 34–54 and its focus on the imminent manifestation of YHWH's universal sovereignty at Zion indicate that these chapters constitute a long prophetic instruction concerning the realization of YHWH's worldwide sovereignty at Zion. This unit is introduced by the prophetic instruction concerning YHWH's power to return the redeemed exiles to Zion in chs. 34–35, which serves as a sort of prologue for the second half of the book by emphasizing the themes of the downfall of the wicked and the redemption of the righteous in a restored Zion (for the demarcation and identification of this unit, see the commentary below). It is followed by the royal narratives concerning YHWH's deliverance of Jerusalem and Hezekiah in chs. 36–39, which reinforce the themes of YHWH's protection of Zion and the righteous for whom the idealized Hezekiah serves as a model (see the commentary below). Both of these textual blocks serve as an introduction to the prophetic instruction that YHWH is maintaining the covenant and restoring Zion in chs. 40–54.

Unfortunately, a full discussion of the structure of chs. 40–54 is not possible in the context of a commentary devoted only to chs. 1–39, but it is necessary to outline the structure of chs. 40–54 in order to account for the literary context of chs. 1–39. A detailed discussion of these chapters appears in Sweeney (*Isaiah 1–4*, 65-95). Essentially, the argumentative or disputational character of these chapters indicates that they constitute a prophetic instruction that YHWH is maintaining the covenant and restoring Zion. They begin with a renewed prophetic commission in 40:1-11 to announce YHWH's restoration of Zion (cf. Seitz, "Divine Council"). The instruction proper in 40:12–54:17 includes five basic contentions: (1) that YHWH is the master of creation (40:12-31); (2) that YHWH is the master of human events (41:1–42:13); (3) that YHWH is the redeemer of Israel (42:14–44:23); (4) that YHWH will use the pagan king Cyrus for the restoration of Zion (44:24–48:22); and (5) that YHWH is restoring Zion (chs. 49–54). The structure of this unit is clearly designed to lead the reader to the conclusion that YHWH's restoration of Zion is now taking place.

Finally, the prophetic exhortation in chs. 55–66 to adhere to YHWH's covenant concludes the book by returning to the concerns initially expressed in the prologue in ch. 1 (for a full discussion of these chapters, see Sweeney, *Isaiah 1–4*, 87-92). Following the initial exhortation proper in ch. 55, prophetic instruction concerning the reconstituted covenant community in Zion provides substantiation that YHWH's sovereignty will in fact be realized. Chs. 56–59 constitute prophetic instruction concerning the proper observance of the covenant; chs. 60–62 constitute a prophetic announcement of salvation for the reconstituted covenant community; and chs. 63–66 constitute a prophetic instruction concerning the process of selection for the reconstituted covenant community. By providing instruction into the nature, requirements, and ultimate fate of the reconstituted covenant community, these chapters aid in convincing the reader to become a part of that community and to adhere to the covenant with YHWH.

Genre

Broadly speaking, the book of Isaiah may be identified as an example of the PROPHETIC BOOK genre in that it presents an assemblage of prophetic oracles identified with the prophet, Isaiah ben Amoz. But this classification presents problems since research on the genre PROPHETIC BOOK remains in its infancy. The genre is generally described in archival terms as a collection, or collection of collections, of the oracles of a particular prophet. The genre has no set structure or form, although many scholars maintain that a PROPHETIC BOOK typically contains a tripartite arrangement of oracles of judgment against Israel/Judah, oracles of judgment against the nations, and oracles of salvation for Israel/Judah and the world at large. The setting is generally identified as that of liturgical worship in the temple or other worship settings, and the intention is described in terms of an interest in preserving the words of the prophet.

Certainly, the book of Isaiah contains oracles of judgment and promise against Israel, Judah, and the nations, all under the heading of a SUPERSCRIPTION that identifies the entire book as "The vision of Isaiah ben Amoz that he saw concerning Judah and Jerusalem in the days of Uzziah, Jotham, Ahaz, Hezekiah, the kings of Judah." Furthermore, the narrative traditions concerning Isaiah's actions in chs. 6–7; 20; and 36–39 point to an archival interest. Moreover, various compositions in the book, such as chs. 12; 33; and 60–62 point to a potential liturgical setting.

But questions must be raised about the archival conception of a PROPHETIC BOOK. The abundant evidence of redaction, supplementation, and reinterpretation throughout the prophetic literature of the Hebrew Bible calls into question the view that PROPHETIC BOOKS are designed primarily to *preserve* the words of the prophets. The current debate concerning the interrelationship between the historical figures of the prophets and the images of the prophets presented in prophetic literature attests to the view that the interests of those who assembled PROPHETIC BOOKS were not confined to archival preservation (e.g., the debate on Jeremiah posits radically different views on the historical prophet and his presentation in the book of Jeremiah; see R. P. Carroll, "Radical Clashes of Will and Style: Recent Commentary Writing on the Book of Jeremiah," *JSOT* 45 [1989] 99-114). Furthermore, PROPHETIC BOOKS appear to be designed to address issues of importance for the present or future of the Jewish community. The book of Ezekiel is concerned with promoting the restoration of the temple in Jerusalem and offers an interpretation of the destruction of Jerusalem that maintains that the city was offered as a sacrifice in order to purify it from contamination. The addition of materials concerning Judah in the book of Hosea indicates that the call to return to YHWH in Hosea 14 has been reinterpreted as a call for the repentance of Judah by the book's redactors so that Judah might avoid the judgment visited upon the northern kingdom of Israel (see T. Naumann, *Hoseas Erben: Strukturen der Nachinterpretation im Buch Hosea* [BWANT 131; Stuttgart: Kohlhammer, 1991]). The addition of Zechariah 9–14 to the traditions of the historical prophet appears to be designed to extend the implications of Zechariah's visions of restoration into the later Hellenistic period.

The evidence of extensive redaction and reinterpretation in the book of Isaiah certainly demonstrates that the function of the book is not merely to preserve the words of the prophet Isaiah. In its present form, the book of Isaiah addresses the Judean community and calls for action or response. The Deutero-Isaiah traditions clearly call for the Judean community to begin the return to Zion from Babylonian captivity, and the Trito-Isaiah traditions call upon its readers to hold firm to the covenant to await the manifestation of YHWH's worldwide sovereignty. When viewed in relation to these traditions, those of Isaiah ben Amoz are clearly designed to support these calls for action. They are presented as the foundation on which the traditions of Deutero- and Trito-Isaiah build. That the traditions of Isaiah ben Amoz are redacted and reinterpreted to assume this role so that the entire book is presented as "the vision of Isaiah ben Amoz" demonstrates that concern with the past intermingles with concern for the present and the future in the book of Isaiah. A PROPHETIC BOOK offers not only an archival vision of the past for the Jewish community but also a programmatic vision for the future.

The generic identification of the book of Isaiah as a prophetic EXHORTA-TION therefore assumes central importance in considering the genre and form of this particular PROPHETIC BOOK. An EXHORTATION is designed to motivate its audience to pursue a particular course of action or to adopt a particular set of ideas or teachings. In the case of the book of Isaiah, the prophetic EXHOR-TATION functions as a means to convince the Judean community to maintain the covenant with YHWH in that the manifestation of YHWH's world rule is about to take place. It asks that the audience wait for the final purge of the wicked from the city, and it supports its contentions by pointing to the partial realization of Isaiah's prophecies concerning the downfall of Jerusalem's oppressors and the restoration of Zion.

Within the superstructure of the book of Isaiah, the specific form of the EXHORTATION appears only in chs. 1 and 55, but the strategic placement of these chapters in relation to the rest of the book insures that they determine its overall generic character. The PARENESIS in ch. 1 combines elements of EXHORTATION with its counterpart, ADMONITION, which attempts to convince an audience against a particular course of action, in order to provide a prologue for the book of Isaiah. The placement of PARENETIC material at the head of the book determines the context by which the rest of the material is read. The balance of the book then supports the initial call for action in ch. 1 in that the presentation of Isaiah's prophecies and traditions about the prophet provides the basis on which the audience will make its decision. Insofar as the book points to the realization of the prophecies of Isaiah, and demonstrates that past punishment is a means to prepare Jerusalem for its future at the center of YHWH's worldwide rule, the audience will be prepared to accept the call for action inherent in the PARENESIS of ch. 1.

This call for action, or a decision on the part of the audience, is reiterated at the end of the book in chs. 55–66. The identification of this entire block as an EXHORTATION is determined by the initial EXHORTATION proper in ch. 55. Like ch. 1, the initial placement of ch. 55 at the head of this textual block determines its generic identification, since the material presented in chs. 56–66 supports the call for action or decision in ch. 55. Essentially, ch. 55 calls upon the audience to maintain its covenant with YHWH, and the material in chs. 56–66 supports that call by defining the qualities necessary for inclusion in YHWH's covenant and by portraying the final judgment that will be visited on those who choose not to become part of YHWH's scheme. Altogether, these chapters portray a bright future of peace, based on the prophecies of Isaiah ben Amoz, for those who choose to adhere to YHWH's covenant.

EXHORTATION is frequently combined with INSTRUCTION in order to provide a basis for the acceptance of the call to act. INSTRUCTION essentially offers its audience guidance on various topics or issues. In the case of the book of Isaiah, prophetic INSTRUCTION appears to be the dominant genre for chs. 2–33; 34–54; and 56–66. Again, the identification of these textual blocks as prophetic INSTRUCTION is based on the strategic placement of instructional materials in relation to other generic entities, such as PROPHETIC ANNOUNCEMENT (chs. 2–4; 13–27; 60–62) and ROYAL NARRATIVE (chs. 36–39). When prophetic INSTRUC-TION in chs. 5–12 and 28–33 is combined with the PROPHETIC ANNOUNCEMENTS of chs. 2–4 and 13–27, the result is a composition that explains the significance of the announcements concerning the meaning of the Day of YHWH and YHWH's plans to establish worldwide sovereignty in Zion. In essence, the instructional material in chs. 5–12 and 28–33 explains how these grandiose plans are to be realized: Israel, the nations, and Jerusalem must be punished and cleansed before YHWH's sovereignty can be manifested. The instructional material in chs. 2–33 thereby provides the basis for accepting the call for action inherent in ch. 1.

The instructional material in chs. 34–66 plays a similar role. The prophetic INSTRUCTION in chs. 34–35 (see the commentary for a detailed discussion of these chapters) sets the tone for the material that follows by presenting some basic theses of the book of Isaiah: YHWH will punish Israel's oppressors and restore the people to Zion. The instructional material in chs. 40–54 demonstrates how this will be realized by employing forms of argumentation characteristic of the DISPUTATION. Thus chs. 40–54 argue a number of subpoints that support the larger thesis, i.e., YHWH is master of creation, controls human events, redeems Israel, employs Cyrus as a redeemer, and restores Zion. Altogether, these subpoints support the contention that YHWH is acting to overthrow the oppressors, restore the people to Zion, and thereby to establish worldwide sovereignty at Zion. The instructional material in chs. 56–66 likewise supports the larger claims of the book in that it instructs the audience in the criteria for covenant participation and points out the benefits of adherence to YHWH's covenant. Again, such INSTRUCTION is designed to support the prophetic EXHORTATION that dominates the generic character of the book of Isaiah.

Setting

The book of Isaiah presents itself as a single literary work, but a detailed analysis of its contents demonstrates that it is a composite work written over the course of some four centuries. The present commentary identifies four major stages in the composition of the book of Isaiah: (1) the final form of the book in Isaiah 1–66, which was produced in relation to the reforms of Ezra and Nehemiah in the mid- to late 5th century B.C.E.; (2) a late-6th-century edition of the book in chs. 2–32*; 35–55; and 60–62, which was produced in conjunction with the return of the Babylonian exiles to Jerusalem and the building of the Second Temple; (3) a late-7th-century edition comprising chs. 5–23*; 27–32; and 36–37, which was written to support King Josiah's program of national and religious reform; and (4) various texts found throughout chs. 1–32* that stem from the 8th-century prophet, Isaiah ben Amoz.

The final redaction of the book was designed to support the reforms of Ezra and Nehemiah. Although it comprises all 66 chapters of the book, the redaction appears to be an expansion of the 6th-century edition of the book (discussed below). This redaction produced the present form of several major textual blocks in Isaiah, including chs. 1; 2–4; 28–33; 34–35; and 55–66. In each case, it employed earlier textual material but added its own material to produce the present form of the text. Thus the 5th-century redaction is responsible for the composition of 1:1, 19-20, 27-28; 2:1; 4:3-6; 33; 34; 56–59;

and 63–66. In the case of chs. 56–59 and 63–66, it is likely that the redaction employed earlier material composed during the course of the 5th century, but the limits of the present context preclude full discussion of these texts (see esp. Seizo Sekine, *Die Tritojesajanische Sammlung (Jes 56–66) Redaktions-geschichtlich Untersucht* [BZAW 175; Berlin and New York: de Gruyter, 1989]; and Steck, *Studien zu Tritojesaja;* for a summary of discussion on Trito-Isaiah, see Grace I. Emmerson, *Isaiah 56–66* [OT Guides; Sheffield: JSOT Press, 1992]).

There are a number of reasons for dating the final form of the book of Isaiah to the period of Ezra and Nehemiah during the latter part of the 5th century. First, the universal or worldwide perspective of the book of Isaiah appears to include nations that made up the Persian empire. The pronouncements concerning the nations play a particularly important role at this point in that the nations listed therein, including Babylon (13:1–14:23; cf. chs. 46–47), Assyria (14:24-27; cf. 10:5-34), Philistia (14:28-32), Moab (chs. 15–16), Aram and Israel (ch. 17; cf. ch. 5; 9:7 [*RSV* 8]–10:4), Ethiopia and Egypt (chs. 18–20), Midbar-Yam (i.e., the Tigris-Euphrates delta region; 21:1-10), Dumah (21:11-12), Arabia (the north Arabia desert region; 21:13-17), Jerusalem (ch. 22; cf. chs. 1–4; 28–31), and Tyre (ch. 23), were all incorporated into the Persian empire during the late 6th through 5th century. Likewise, the former territory of Edom (ch. 34; 63:1-6) was also included in the Persian empire. Greece is notably absent, which precludes a date in the Hellenistic period. Persia is not listed as one of the nations subjected to YHWH's judgment, but 21:1-10 identifies Elam and Media as the powers responsible for the fall of Babylon (identified with Midbar-Yam). Moreover, 44:24-28 and 45:1-7 identify the Persian monarch Cyrus as YHWH's anointed king and temple builder.

Babylon (13:1–14:23; chs. 46–47) appears to represent the head of the nations and the major enemy of YHWH in the book of Isaiah. In 539 Babylon submitted to the Achaemenid-Persian monarch Cyrus, whose empire represented a federation of Persia and Media. The book of Isaiah appears to equate Cyrus's rule over Babylon, and indeed Achaemenid-Persian rule over the nations, with YHWH's worldwide sovereignty (see Kratz). In the context of the 5th-century edition of Isaiah, Cyrus and the later Achaemenid rulers serve as the agents for the manifestation of YHWH's rule over the nations from Zion. Judea was a Persian province during the period of Ezra and Nehemiah, and both of these men received their appointments — Ezra as priest and Nehemiah as governor of Judah — from the Persian monarch. Furthermore, although the early Isaiah traditions look forward to the rule of an ideal Davidic monarch (9:1-6 [*RSV* 2-7]; 11; 32), the later materials presuppose the rule of Cyrus (45:1-7) and YHWH (chs. 65–66), but not that of a Davidic monarch. Rather, the Davidic promise is applied to the people at large (55:3).

Second, it is clear that although the final form of Isaiah presupposes that the temple in Jerusalem has been rebuilt (see chs. 56; 60–62; but contra 63:7–64:12; 66), the full manifestation of YHWH's rule from Zion has not yet occurred (see chs. 65–66). Such a situation corresponds to the circumstances of the latter part of the 5th century when Nehemiah and Ezra returned to Jerusalem. Although the temple had been rebuilt in 520-515, Nehemiah returned to Jerusalem in 445 to find the city virtually deserted and the temple ignored due to the inability of its inhabitants to protect themselves. Nehemiah took measures to protect and repopulate Jerusalem and to insure the support of the temple during the course of his administration (see Nehemiah 1–7; 11–13). Ezra, who appears to have arrived in the latter part of the 5th century, enacted a religious reform program based on the Torah or Five Books of Moses that was designed to protect the identity of the people and to reinforce the centrality of the temple in postexilic Jewish life (see Ezra; Nehemiah 8–10).

The efforts of both of these men were directed toward achieving an ideal Jewish community, based on Torah and built around the temple in Jerusalem. The final form of the book of Isaiah looks forward to a similar ideal. Furthermore, it envisions YHWH's rule of Israel and the nations from Zion as one based on Torah (Isa 2:2-5, esp. v. 3). Although it is unlikely that the author of this passage intended "Torah" to refer to the Five Books of Moses, it would be understood as such in a late-5th-century context (cf. Sheppard, "Book of Isaiah," esp. 578-82). In this respect, the final form of the book of Isaiah presents itself as an expression of YHWH's Torah to Israel at a time when the postexilic Jewish community was reconstituting itself on the basis of Mosaic Torah.

Third, the present form of the book of Isaiah presupposes a clear distinction between the righteous and the wicked within the community and calls upon its audience to identify with the righteous. Many scholars follow Paul Hanson (*The Dawn of Apocalyptic* [Philadelphia: Fortress, 1975]), who argues that such a distinction in Trito-Isaiah and other texts from this period indicates a conflict between a prophetic-visionary party and a priestly group within the postexilic Jewish community. In relation to the book of Isaiah, such a conflict would pit the authors of Trito-Isaiah, who advocate a covenant that will include eunuchs, foreigners, and the nations at large (cf. 56:1-8; 66:18-24), against the supporters of Ezra and Nehemiah, who advocate a covenant based on Mosaic Torah that excludes foreign participation. This position presupposes that the inclusion of eunuchs and gentiles in Trito-Isaiah stands in conflict with the prohibition against intermarriage enacted under Ezra and Nehemiah (Ezra 9–10; Neh 13:23-31).

But this argument overlooks several important considerations. First, on the one hand, the Trito-Isaiah traditions do not address the issue of intermarriage; they address the issue of proper observance of the covenant. They argue that a eunuch or a foreigner who keeps the covenant by observing the Sabbath and refraining from evil shall be accepted in YHWH's temple. On the other hand, the Ezra-Nehemiah traditions do not exclude the eunuch or the foreigner who adopts the covenant of Judaism. They speak only about the prohibition against intermarriage as a means to avoid pollutions and abominations of the gentiles and thereby to protect the covenant (Ezra 9). This prohibition is based on Exod 34:11-16 and Deut 7:1-5, which prohibit intermarriage with various nations as a means to avoid apostasy, and on Deut 23:3-8, which excludes Ammonites and Moabites from the community as well as Edomites and Egyptians to the third generation.

Interestingly, the Ezra traditions indicate that only the foreign wives and children are banished; nothing is said about foreign husbands. Most scholars assume that the Jewish wives of foreign men would have abandoned Judaism to follow their pagan husbands, and consequently there would have been no need to banish the foreign husbands since they were not part of the community in the first place. But no consideration is given to the possibility that such husbands might have adopted the observances of Judaism. In the case of such a conversion, there would have been no need to banish a foreign husband since he would have become part of the community by adopting the covenant. The foreigners mentioned in Trito-Isaiah are not those who are banished by Ezra; they are foreign men who observe the covenant and therefore convert to Judaism. J. Blenkinsopp (*Ezra-Nehemiah: A Commentary* [OTL; Philadelphia: Westminster, 1988] 178) notes that both Trito-Isaiah (Isa 66:2, 5) and Ezra (Ezra 9:4; 10:3) employ the participle *ḥārēd*, "he who trembles," to refer to those who observe the covenant as "those who tremble" *(ḥărēdîm)* at the word of YHWH. Apart from 1 Sam 4:13, these are the only occurrences of this term in the Hebrew Bible. Both Isaiah and Ezra-Nehemiah employ the same terminology to describe those who observe the covenant in the early Persian period; both polemicize against those who fail to observe the covenant; both emphasize observance of the sabbath as the cornerstone of the covenant (Isa 56:1-8; 58:13-14; Neh 9:14; 10:31; 13:15-22); both emphasize YHWH's Torah; both support the centrality of the temple; and neither precludes the participation of eunuchs or those foreigners who convert to Judaism. It would appear, therefore, that both traditions are in fundamental agreement on the nature of covenant observance in postexilic Judaism.

This proposal has implications for understanding the polemic against the wicked in the book of Isaiah. Both Isaiah and Ezra-Nehemiah polemicize against those who do not observe the covenant; it would appear that both polemicize against those who fail to observe Ezra's understanding of the covenant. Insofar as the book of Isaiah constitutes an exhortation to adhere to YHWH's covenant, it becomes an exhortation to support the reform program of Ezra and Nehemiah. This conclusion is borne out by the relationship between the book of Isaiah and Ezra's return to Jerusalem. Koch ("Ezra") and J. G. McConville ("Ezra-Nehemiah and the Fulfillment of Prophecy," *VT* 36 [1986] 205-24) demonstrate that Ezra's program is presented as a fulfillment of prophecy in the book of Isaiah, insofar as Ezra refers to the people as the "holy seed" (Ezra 9:2; cf. Isa 6:13) and a "remnant" (Ezra 9:8; cf. Isa 4:2; 10:20; 37:31-32), and insofar as Ezra's return to Jerusalem is presented as a second exodus in keeping with the renewed exodus proclaimed in the book of Isaiah.

As noted in the commentary to Isaiah 12 and 35 below, these texts indicate that the book of Isaiah may well have been employed liturgically in the Jerusalem temple. It is entirely possible that Ezra's reading of the Torah in Nehemiah 8–10 included a reading of the book of Isaiah as well. Ezra's reading took place during the festival of Sukkot, or Booths, which stresses the themes of the ingathering of the grape and olive harvest, the beginning of the rainy season, and the ingathering of the people of Israel from the exodus at the end of the forty years of wandering in the wilderness. Such themes would correspond well to those of the book of Isaiah, which stresses the ingathering of the harvest and renewed creation together with the ingathering of the exiles (e.g., 11:11–12:6; 27:12-13; 35:8-10; 40:1-11; 62:10-12; see further below). This would facilitate the community's understanding of the Torah by pointing out that the experiences of disaster at the hands of Assyria and Babylonia, as well as restoration under Persian rule, were designed to lead to the purification of Jerusalem and renewal of the covenant that was currently underway in the time of Ezra.

A reading of the book of Isaiah, with its exhortation to adhere to YHWH's covenant and its emphasis on YHWH's Torah, would provide an ideal means to garner support for Ezra's program of reform and restoration. It would also point to a Levitical context for the preservation and reinterpretation of the Isaiah tradition. That context might in turn be identified with the so-called Isaianic school posited by Mowinckel *(Jesaja-Disiplene; Prophecy and Tradition),* Schreiner ("Das Buch jesajanischer Schule"), and Eaton ("Isaiah Tradition"; "Origin"). The Levites are identified as the interpreters of Torah in Neh 8:7-8, and Levitical singers are identified as prophets in the Second Temple period (1 Chronicles 15; 25; 2 Chronicles 20; 29; for a full discussion, see R. J. Tournay, *Seeing and Hearing God with the Psalms: The Prophetic Liturgy of the Second Temple in Jerusalem* [tr. J. E. Crowley; JSOTSup 118; Sheffield: JSOT Press, 1991]; Petersen, *Late Israelite Prophecy*). Such a Levitical context would account for the Deuteronomic character of Isaiah 1, which seems to reflect the Levitical sermon form.

The late-6th-century edition of the book of Isaiah, which comprises chs. 2–32*; 35–55; and 60–62, appears to have been composed in conjunction with the building of the Second Temple in Jerusalem. This redaction is responsible for the basic form of several major textual blocks, including 2:2–4:2; 24–27; 35; and 60–62. In addition, it provided the oracle concerning Babylon at the head of the oracles concerning the nations in chs. 13–23, and it added and reformulated material from 2 Kings 18–20 in Isaiah 36–39. Although it employed and organized a great deal of earlier material, it also composed various texts, including 2:2-4, 5; 4:2; 13:2-22; 14:1-2, 3-4a, 22-23; 24–26; 35; and 60–62 (on the composition of chs. 60–62 in relation to an edition of the book of Isaiah prior to its final form, see the studies by Steck in *Studien zu Tritojesaja* and *Bereitete Heimkehr,* esp. 45-79).

Various features of this edition indicate its historical setting in relation to the building of the Second Temple in 520-515. First, the premise for the entire edition appears at the outset in 2:2-4, which announces YHWH's worldwide sovereignty and recognition by the nations at Zion. This announcement serves as the basis for the invitation issued to Jacob/Israel in 2:5 to join the nations in recognizing YHWH and thereby to participate in YHWH's new world order. It also concludes in chs. 60–62 with a portrayal of the nations' recognition of YHWH at Zion and the new role that Israel will have as the priests in the midst of the world (see esp. 61:6). Not only is Zion the site for YHWH's temple, but other biblical texts associated with the building of the Second Temple in Jerusalem emphasize similar themes. Thus Haggai envisions an influx of the nations to recognize YHWH's sovereignty as a consequence of the building of the Second Temple (see esp. Hag 2:1-9) to garner support for its construction. Zechariah 1–8 likewise portrays the building of the Second Temple as an event of worldwide significance that demonstrates YHWH's control of the cosmos. These chapters conclude with a portrayal of the nations coming to Jerusalem to entreat YHWH with language similar to that of Isa 2:2-4 (see Zech 8:20-23; Petersen, *Haggai and Zechariah 1-8,* 312-20). The rebuilding of the temple in Jerusalem and the role that Israel will assume in relation to the nations thereby becomes the basis for the message of Isaiah in the 6th-century edition of the book.

Second, this edition of the book of Isaiah places a special emphasis on the return of the exiles to Zion. The motif appears at key points throughout the book, including 11:11-16; 27:12-13; 35:8-10; 40:1-11; 48:17-22; 52:11-12; 54:1-17; 55:12-13; and 62:10-12 (cf. Steck, *Bereitete Heimkehr,* 59-69). It is well known that Jews began to return to Jerusalem following Cyrus's decree in 539, which permitted them to do so (see 2 Chr 36:22-23; Ezra 1:1-11). The return is portrayed as a new exodus from Assyria and Egypt (Isa 11:11-16; 27:12-13), but it later portrays Babylon as the location from which the exiles return (48:17-22; 52:11-12). The focus on the downfall of Babylon throughout the edition therefore takes on an especially important role. Babylon is clearly the major enemy of YHWH whose defeat initiates the return of the exiles to Jerusalem in the traditions of Deutero-Isaiah (see chs. 46-47; 48). But Babylon also assumes this role in the first part of the book. Although Assyria is the major oppressor of Israel and Judah in the traditions of Proto-Isaiah, the oracle concerning the downfall of Babylon in ch. 13 is placed at the head of the oracles against the nations in chs. 13-23, which signifies Babylon's role as the major enemy of YHWH. Furthermore, 14:24-27 indicates that Babylon will fill this role in place of Assyria and that Babylon's fate will be analogous to that of Assyria. As the commentary to chs. 13-14 demonstrates, this is the work of the 6th-century redaction of Isaiah, which composed 13:2-22 and reformulated traditions concerning Assyria in 14:1-27 in order to portray Babylon in this manner. Likewise, the demise of the anonymous city and the manifestation of YHWH's rule over the nations in chs. 24-26 provide the basis for the restoration of the exiles in ch. 27. Clearly, the fall of the Babylonian empire to Cyrus during the years 545-539, along with the subsequent return of Jewish exiles to Jerusalem during the years that followed, forms a major premise of the 6th-century edition of Isaiah.

Third, the 6th-century edition of the book of Isaiah portrays Cyrus as the royal deliverer who acts on behalf of YHWH to rebuild the temple and to redeem the exiles. Cyrus is explicitly named to this role in 44:24-28 and 45:1-7, and he is presupposed in various other texts from Deutero-Isaiah (41:2-3, 25; 45:13; 46:11; and 48:14-15; see Kratz, 15). This is particularly significant in the light of the promises of a royal savior from the house of David that appear throughout the traditions of Proto-Isaiah (9:1-6 [*RSV* 2-7]; 11:1-16; 32:1-20). Cyrus is obviously not a member of the Davidic house, but the 6th-century edition of Isaiah nevertheless portrays him as the royal figure who acts on YHWH's behalf to bring about the promises made in the first part of the book. The 6th-century edition of Isaiah maintains that the Davidic covenant is still intact, but it applies the promise to the people, not to a monarch from the Davidic line (see 55:3). Yet it also presupposes that YHWH is the true ruler, not the Davidic monarch, and that YHWH's rule in fact fulfills the promises of the first part of the book. Such a view accounts for the political realities of Judah during the early Persian period in which Judah was subject to Persia. Although there was sentiment for the installation of Zerubbabel as monarch and the renewal of the Davidic line during the period of the rebuilding (Hag 2:20-23; cf. Zechariah 4), such plans proved to be impossible in the light of Persian rule. The 6th-century edition of Isaiah wisely equates YHWH's rule with that of the Persian monarchy. It thereby reflects the period in which the Second Temple was completed (ca. 515) and in which Zerubbabel disappeared from the scene and Davidic pretentions came to an end (cf. Zech 6:9-14; Petersen, *Haggai and Zechariah 1–8*, 272-81).

The great deal of hymnic material contained in the 6th-century edition of the book of Isaiah suggests a potential liturgical use for the book (chs. 12; 24–27; 35; 42:10-13; 44:23; 45:8; 48:20-21; 49:13; 51:3; 52:9-10; 54:1-3; 60–62; see Frank Matheus, *Singt dem Herrn ein neues Lied: Die Hymnen Deuterojesajas* [SBS 141; Stuttgart: Katholisches Bibelwerk, 1990], esp. 152-71, who examines the function of these hymns in the larger structure of Deutero-Isaiah and draws out implications for the composition of the entire book). When the potential liturgical function of the book is considered in relation to the historical setting of the building of the Second Temple, it seems likely that this edition of Isaiah may well have functioned as part of the liturgy of the dedication of the Second Temple. In keeping with tradition, the Second Temple was dedicated during the festival of Sukkot (Ezra 3:1-7; cf. 1 Kings 8; 2 Chronicles 5–7), which commemorates the exodus tradition of forty years of wilderness wandering and the ingathering of the people of Israel into the promised land. Sukkot occurs in the seventh month at the time of the ingathering of the grape and olive harvests. In Israel it also begins the rainy season, which causes the land to bloom with new plants and flowers. Insofar as the 6th-century edition of Isaiah stresses the theme of the return of the exiles to Zion in the context of the renewal of creation (e.g., chs. 12; 35; 40:1-11), it would provide an appropriate liturgical text for Sukkot and the dedication of the Second Temple.

The late-7th-century edition of the book of Isaiah, which comprises chs. 5–12; 14–23*; 27; 28–32; and 36–37, appears to have been written in order to support and legitimize the Judean king Josiah's program of national and religious restoration in Jerusalem during the years 639-609. This redaction employed earlier Isaianic traditions, and it is largely responsible for the present form of several major textual blocks, including chs. 5–12; 14–23*; 27; and 36–37. A number of texts were composed for this redaction, including a reworked form of ch. 7 (vv. 1-4, 10, 18-19, 21-25); 15:2b; 16:13-14; 20; 23:1a, 15-18; 27; 30:19-33; 32:1-8, 15-20; and the inclusion of a reworked form of 2 Kings 18–19 in Isaiah 36–37. In addition, it includes Isa 19:18-25, which may have been added to the Isaiah tradition during the first half the 7th century. Although it is difficult to be certain about the final form of this redaction, its organization appears to include four major textual blocks: (1) oracles concerning the Assyrian punishment of northern Israel and the demise of Assyria, which conclude with an announcement of a royal savior and the return of Israel to the house of David in chs. 5–12; (2) oracles concerning the nations headed by Assyria, which culminate in the return of exiles in chs. 14–23*; 27; (3) oracles concerning Jerusalem, which culminate in an announcement of a royal savior in chs. 28–32; and (4) an appended narrative concerning YHWH's deliverance of Jerusalem in chs. 36–37.

A number of considerations support the association of the 7th-century edition of Isaiah with King Josiah's reform (for discussion of the Josianic redaction of Isaiah, see esp. Barth; Vermeylen, *Du prophète;* Clements, *Isaiah 1–39*). First, this edition maintains that Israel's and Judah's subjugation to the Assyrian empire was deliberately brought about by YHWH as part of a divine plan to purge the people of evil and then to restore them to unity under the authority of the Davidic dynasty. Thus the leaders of the northern kingdom of Israel are portrayed as abusive leaders, lacking in justice and religious perspective, who exploit their own people (5:8-24; 9:7 [*RSV* 8]–10:4) for material gain. Likewise, Judah's leaders, particularly King Ahaz, are portrayed as lacking faith in the basic premise of the Davidic tradition, namely, that YHWH would guarantee the security of Jerusalem and the Davidic dynasty. Assyria thereby becomes a tool by which YHWH punishes the leaders of the people for wrongdoing. Once the land is purged of its unfit leaders, the way is cleared for the reunification of the people under righteous Davidic rule centered in Zion (9:1-6 [*RSV* 2-7]; 11:1-16; 32:1-20). This corresponds to the goals of Josiah's reform program in that he attempted to reunite the former northern kingdom of Israel with the southern kingdom of Judah under Davidic rule in Jerusalem. In this regard, it is noteworthy that the ideal Davidic monarch is described in terms that recall Josiah specifically (e.g., 11:1-16, which describes the reign of a small boy, the attempt to reunify Israel and Judah, etc.).

Second, the demise of the Assyrian empire plays a major role in this redaction. Although Assyria is summoned by YHWH to act as a tool of punishment against the people of Israel and Judah (5:26-30), Assyria's abuse of this role, especially the Assyrian king's boast that he will threaten Jerusalem and YHWH, results in YHWH's decision to destroy the Assyrians (10:5-34; cf. 14:24-27). This provides a theological rationale for the demise of the Assyrian empire in the latter part of the 7th century. Josiah's reforms, including his bid for national independence and his attempt to extend his rule over the former northern kingdom of Israel, coincides with the decline of Assyrian power following the death of Assurbanipal in 627. By presenting the subjugation of Judah to Assyria and the subsequent fall of Assyria as acts of YHWH, the 7th-century edition provides theological legitimation to Josiah's reform by maintaining that the restoration of Davidic rule over a united kingdom is the purpose for YHWH's introduction of the Assyrians in the first place.

Third, the oracles against the nations in this edition do not present a worldwide perspective, but focus on those nations that were of concern to Josiah's plans. Assyria (10:5-34; 14:5-27) and Egypt (chs. 18–20) were the major powers that posed obstacles to Josiah's plans. Philistia (14:28-32), Moab (chs. 15–16), and Aram/Israel (ch. 17) were countries over which Josiah apparently intended to extend his rule. Southern Babylonia and the Arabian desert regions (21:1-10, 11-12, 13-17) were allies of Judah and were apparently among the first countries to break free of Assyrian control, and Tyre was envisioned as a trading partner (ch. 23), much as Hiram of Tyre had been for David and Solomon.

Finally, the 7th-century edition of Isaiah gives special attention to motifs associated with the exodus and the ingathering of the exiles from Assyria and Egypt (viz., 11:11-16; 27:12-13). This would suggest the possibility that this edition of Isaiah was read publicly in a liturgical context at the Jerusalem temple. Possible settings include Josiah's Passover celebration (2 Kgs 23:21-23) or the festival of Sukkot, at which time the refurbished temple may well have been dedicated and the Torah/book of the covenant (perhaps a form of Deuteronomy) read to the people (2 Kgs 23:1-3; cf. Deut 31:9-13). Sukkot seems to be the more likely candidate as this was the festival of temple dedication, and this edition of the book begins with an analogy between Israel and a vineyard in Isa 5:1-7. In such a setting, the liturgical reading of the book of Isaiah would reinforce the themes of the festival, and would aid in identifying the king with YHWH's purposes in establishing the temple and festival system. It would thereby legitimize Josiah's rule and reform as actions in keeping with YHWH's purposes.

Material written by the 8th-century prophet, Isaiah ben Amoz, appears throughout chs. 1*; 2–4*; 5–10; 14–23*; and 28–32*. The oracles stem from various periods in the prophet's career, including the Syro-Ephraimite War (735-732; 1:21-26, 27-31; 5:1-24; 6:1-11 [12-13]; 7:2-17*, 20; 8:1-15; 8:16–9:6 [RSV 7]; 15:1b–16:12; and 29:15-24), the fall of Samaria and the early reign of the Assyrian monarch Sargon II (724-720; 5:25-30; 9:7 [RSV 8]–10:4; 10:5-34; 14:24-27; 17–18; 19:1-17; and 29:1-14), Hezekiah's revolt against Assyria, including both the period of his preparations and the revolt itself (715-701; 1:2-9, 10-18; 2:6-19; 3:1-9, 12-15, 16–4:1; 14:4b-21, 28-32; 22:1b-14, 15-25; 23:1b-14; 28; 30:1-18; 31; and 32:9-14), and Sennacherib's attacks against the Chaldean prince Merodach-baladan (691-689; 21:1-10, 11-12, 13-17).

It is difficult to say whether there was an 8th-century book of Isaiah, although there do appear to be collections of material relating to different periods. Such collections include the autobiographical material in 6:1–9:6* (RSV 7*) that pertains to the Syro-Ephraimite War, an expanded version of this collection in 5:1–10:34; 14:24-27 that is directed against Hezekiah's plans to revolt against Assyria, and chs. 28–32*, which are also directed against Hezekiah's revolt. Many of the oracles against the nations in chs. 14–23, beginning with the oracle against Philistia in 14:28-32, appear to derive from the reign of Hezekiah, and it is possible that they constitute a distinct collection of oracles against nations that would fall to Assyria. Such a collection would demonstrate that these nations were judged by YHWH and thereby would be employed to convince Hezekiah that the Assyrian invasion was an act of divine judgment.

Unlike the later editions of the book of Isaiah, there is no evidence that the writings of the prophet were ever employed in an 8th-century liturgical context. Rather, Isaiah appears to have functioned as a royal advisor, and his writings appear to have been employed in the context of discussions concerning Ahaz's and Hezekiah's foreign policy as a means to convince the monarchs to adopt particular courses of action. From the narratives preserved in ch. 7, and later memories of the prophet presented in chs. 36–39, Isaiah seems to have had access to the Davidic kings and presented his analysis of the situation and his recommendations for action (cf. Nathan, who seems to have had similar access to the king in 2 Samuel 7; 12; and 1 Kings 1). Altogether, Isaiah appears to have been an isolationist who advised against foreign alliances with Assyria during the Syro-Ephraimite War, with Egypt and Philistia during the periods of the

Israelite and Philistine revolts, and again with Egypt and Tyre during the period of Hezekiah's revolt. The basis for his opposition is both theological and pragmatic. On the one hand, YHWH alone guaranteed the security of Jerusalem and the Davidic dynasty; alliance with a foreign power constituted betrayal of the theological foundations on which the Davidic state was based. On the other hand, Judah could not hope to stand against the power of the Assyrian empire. Thus the best policy was to accept Assyrian suzerainty as an act of YHWH. According to Isaiah, such a policy would eventually lead to the restoration of the Davidic empire and thereby demonstrate the power of YHWH to act on behalf of Jerusalem, the house of David, and the people at large. This positive outlook concerning Jerusalem and the house of David apparently constitutes the basis for the continued growth of the book of Isaiah over the next four centuries.

Intention

On the basis of the discussions of structure, genre, and setting above, it is clear that the intention of the final form of the book of Isaiah is to convince its Judean audience to adhere to the covenant with YHWH promoted by the reforms of Ezra and Nehemiah. The book presents itself as the work of a single prophet who projects the future manifestation of YHWH's worldwide sovereignty centered on Zion, and exhorts the audience to identify themselves with YHWH and thereby to assume a central role in the midst of the nations.

One of the central principles of the book appears in the statement "the word of our God will stand forever" (Isa 40:8), and the reiterations of this theme in 14:27 ("for the LORD of hosts has purposed, and who will annul it? His hand is stretched out, and who will turn it back?") and 55:11 ("so shall my word be which goes forth from my mouth; it shall not return to me empty, but it shall accomplish that which I purpose, and prosper in the thing for which I sent it"). The placement of this statement in 55:11 is strategic in that this text heads the final exhortation of the book, which attempts to convince the audience that the "vision" articulated by Isaiah ben Amoz in the days of kings Uzziah, Jotham, Ahaz, and Hezekiah (cf. 1:1) will in fact take place despite the obstacles faced by Judah during the late 5th century. To this end, the structure of the book plays a role in that, following the initial parenesis, the first part of the book presents Isaiah's prophecies from the Assyrian period that project YHWH's rule and Zion's glory as a result of the purging process initiated by the Assyrian invasions.

The second half of the book then presents the manifestation of YHWH's rule as an event that is presently taking place and that requires the faithful patience of the audience for full realization. By presupposing the fall of Assyria, Edom, and Babylon, together with YHWH's protection of Zion and the return of the exiles, the second half of the book testifies to the principle that YHWH's word will stand forever and that the promises of divine sovereignty from Zion will in fact be realized. It reinforces this perspective by directing the reader to "read from the book of YHWH," apparently a reference to the first half of Isaiah, in order to confirm the realization of YHWH's commands (34:16-17). The book thereby presents a theological interpretation of Jerusalem's history that argues that the invasions of Assyria and Babylon were acts of YHWH designed to purge the city of evil and to prepare it to assume its role as YHWH's capital. In this regard, the faithful Hezekiah, who turns to YHWH in a time of crisis and thereby achieves deliverance for his city and a cure from his sickness (chs. 36–39), provides a model for the people to continue their adherence to the covenant despite the difficulties that they might face.

The final form of Isaiah essentially identifies YHWH's purposes with the rule of the Persian empire, but the focus on worldwide upheaval and the destruction of the wicked (66:18-24) indicates that even the Persian political order will be overthrown as YHWH's rule is manifested and recognized by the nations. This concern reflects the political and social circumstances of the Persian empire during the 5th century, when it was plagued by internal instability. Furthermore, the theme of the destruction of the wicked also addresses the Jerusalem/Judean community itself in that the wicked are identified as those who reject YHWH by refusing to join in Ezra's reform, whereas the righteous are those who support the program. In this regard, the final manifestation of YHWH's sovereignty will fulfill the oracles promising a royal savior in the first part of the book, and the revelation of YHWH's Torah at Zion (2:2-4) will be identified with the revelation of Torah that stands at the basis of Ezra's reform program.

The intention of the 6th-century edition of the book of Isaiah runs along somewhat similar lines, although its purpose is to garner support for the newly built Second Temple. It, too, employs the principle that YHWH's word will stand forever, but it differs in that the manifestation of YHWH's rule in Zion is presented as an event that is now being realized with the construction of the Second Temple. Again, the past history of Jerusalem's tribulations is presented as a process by which the city is purged of evil and prepared for its role as the center for YHWH's world rule; and again, YHWH's rule is presented as the fulfillment of the oracles promising a royal savior. In this context, the narratives concerning YHWH's deliverance of Jerusalem and Hezekiah present Hezekiah as a faithful role model for the people. Because the manifestation of YHWH's rule is portrayed as a contemporary event, there is less need to present an exhortation — the audience will not have to wait long to see the full manifestation of YHWH's rule and Zion's glory. Rather, the rise of the Persian empire and the overthrow of Babylonia constitute the realization of YHWH's rule. The 6th-century edition of Isaiah presupposes that the nations, including Persia, will recognize YHWH's sovereignty once the temple is established and will stream to Zion to hear YHWH's Torah. In this context, Israel will stand at the center of the nations to act as YHWH's priests.

The intention of the 7th-century edition of the book of Isaiah is to support and to legitimize the reign and reform program of King Josiah of Judah. In many respects, it functions as an announcement of a royal savior in that it presents Josiah's reign as the culmination of a historical cycle of suffering and restoration on the part of the people of Israel and Judah. To this end, it presents the fall of the northern kingdom of Israel to Assyria as part of a divine plan to return the northern kingdom to Davidic rule, and depicts the downfall of Assyria as a punishment by YHWH for excessive cruelty against Israel and for arrogance against Jerusalem and its God. In addition to Assyria, Josiah's other major enemy,

Egypt, is subjected to divine punishment. Other nations that are expected to fall into the Josianic orbit, including Philistia, Moab, Aram, and Tyre, are also included in the scenario of judgment that will ultimately lead to the glory of the renewed Davidic empire. Jerusalem likewise suffers as it is purged of the evil represented by the faithlessness of Ahaz and his like, but the city ultimately triumphs as the capital of the newly restored Davidic empire when the promised just ruler of the royal house of David assumes the throne. It is noteworthy that promises of a royal savior and the return of the exiled people conclude every major section of this edition (11:1–12:6; 27:1-13; and 32:1-20). In this respect, Josiah is portrayed as the monarch promised by the prophet Isaiah during the period of the Assyrian invasions. His program of religious reform and national restoration, designed to purge the people of non-YHWHistic practices and to reestablish the Jerusalem-centered Davidic state, is presented as the ultimate object of Isaiah's prophecies.

Finally, the intention of the writings of Isaiah ben Amoz appear to be politically as well as theologically oriented in that they are intended to persuade the monarchs of Judah to avoid alliances with foreign powers that might lead to military confrontation with a potential invader. In all cases, his advice is motivated by the ideology of the Davidic dynasty, which maintains that YHWH alone will protect Jerusalem and the house of David from outside threat. Although Isaiah is frequently portrayed as a prophet of judgment, his judgment prophecies are motivated by the rejection of YHWH's guarantee of protection by the Davidic monarchs and the people. Thus Isaiah counsels Ahaz against alliance with Assyria to stave off the threat of the Syro-Ephraimite invasion. But when Ahaz rejects this advice, Isaiah condemns him for faithlessness and argues that continued neutrality will see the reunification of Israel and Judah under Davidic rule once the Assyrians have defeated the northern kingdom of Israel (7:1–9:6* [RSV 7*]). Likewise, Isaiah opposes Hezekiah's plans to ally with Egypt, the Philistines, and Tyre in an attempted revolt against the Assyrian empire. Given Egypt's reputation for unreliability and internal instability (chs. 18–19) and past experience with the power of the Assyrians, it would be foolhardy to challenge the Assyrians. According to Isaiah, such alliances invite punishment from YHWH because they constitute a fundamental rejection of the theological basis for the existence of the Davidic state. If Hezekiah will trust in YHWH's promises and avoid a confrontation, Jerusalem will endure oppression from the Assyrians, but eventually YHWH will deliver the city (ch. 31).

Isaiah is ultimately a prophet of salvation (cf. b. B. Bat. 14b), and it is this perspective that motivates the continued growth of the book from the time of the 8th-century prophet to the emergence of the final edition of chs. 1–66 in the late 5th century.

Chapter 2

THE INDIVIDUAL UNITS
OF ISAIAH 1:1–39:8

PROLOGUE: INTRODUCTORY PARENESIS, 1:1-31

Structure

The boundaries of this unit are marked by the superscription in v. 1, which plays a dual role as the title for the entire book of Isaiah as well as the introduction to ch. 1. This chapter contains a number of originally independent units that will be discussed individually in separate sections of the commentary below. But various features of the text demonstrate that these units have been editorially combined, supplemented, and arranged so that the chapter now constitutes a coherent structural and rhetorical whole that requires treatment as a distinct text. These features include the catchword links between the chapter's subunits, the overall trial genre pattern, and the parenetic rhetorical strategy that permeates the entire chapter.

Because of its distinctive generic character and its function as the introduction that identifies the following material, the superscription in v. 1 constitutes the first major structural subunit of this chapter. Consequently, vv. 2-31 constitute the second subunit of the chapter.

It is clear that the prophet is portrayed as the speaker throughout 1:2-31. Although speeches by YHWH appear in vv. 2b-3, 11*-17, 18*-20, 24b-26, their contexts, the various YHWH speech formulas (vv. 2a*, 11a*, 18a*, 20b*), and the oracular formula in v. 24a all indicate that the prophet is portrayed as quoting YHWH in the context of his own discourse. Consequently, the structure of this chapter is not constituted by shifts in the speaker but by other factors. These factors include elements of the trial genre pattern, the objects of the prophet's discussion, and other literary, rhetorical, and thematic features of the text.

Within 1:2-31, the first major textual subunit is vv. 2-20. Although this section contains four distinct generic units addressed either to the "heavens" and the "earth" (vv. 2-3) or to the people (vv. 4-9, 10-17, 18-20), these sections are bound together as a coherent unit by several features.

The first is catchword connections. Vv. 2-3 and vv. 4-9 are tied together by the appearance of *bānîm,* "sons" (v. 2b), and *bānîm mašḥîtîm,* "corrupt sons" (v. 4a). Vv. 4-9 and vv. 10-17 are linked by the mention of "Sodom and Gomorrah" (vv. 9 and 10), by the appearance of *tôsîpû sārâ,* "that you would add apostasy" (v. 5a) and *lōʾ tôsîpû hābîʾ minḥat-šāwʾ,* "do not again bring a false grain offering" (v. 13a), and by the mention of *zeraʿ mĕrēʿîm,* "wicked seed" (v. 4a), and *ḥidlû hārēaʿ,* "cease doing evil" (v. 16b). Vv. 10-17 and vv. 18-20 are linked by imagery rather than by catchwords. V. 15b portrays hands full of blood from the sacrificial animals slaughtered at the temple altar, and v. 18 emphasizes the "redness" of sins. Likewise, v. 16a demands that the people cleanse and purify themselves, and v. 18 offers them the opportunity to do so. Both v. 17 and v. 18 employ legal terminology in their references to the people's repentance: *diršû mišpāṭ,* "seek justice," in v. 17 and *wĕniwwākĕhâ,* "and we shall arbitrate," in v. 18. Finally, vv. 2-20 are demarcated by a catchword *inclusio, kî yhwh dibbēr,* "for YHWH has spoken," in v. 2 and *kî pî yhwh dibbēr,* "for the mouth of YHWH has spoken," in v. 20.

The second unifying feature is the focus on the *people* and their need to change their patterns of behavior. Although vv. 2-3 are cast as a direct address to the heavens and earth, YHWH's statements in vv. 2b-3 clearly concern the people of Israel and the fact that they lack understanding. Vv. 4-9 directly address the people as indicated by the introductory "woe" formula in v. 4 and the 2nd-person masculine plural address form employed throughout these verses. The main point of this section is that the people's suffering was caused by their own wickedness and rejection of YHWH. Vv. 10-17 again address the people as indicated by the call to attention formula directed to the "rulers of Sodom" and the "people of Gomorrah" in v. 10 and the 2nd-person masculine plural address forms used throughout the section. Again, it focuses on the people's wrongdoing but provides instruction on how to correct their deeds. Finally, vv. 18-20 address the people as indicated by continued use of the 2nd-person masculine form of address. These verses convey an offer of repentance to the people.

The third concerns the legal character of the language employed in vv. 2-20 and relates to the focus on the people and their wrongdoing mentioned above. This text is heavily influenced by the trial genre pattern and employs a sequence of elements that appear in this genre prior to court action. Vv. 2-3 contain the opening appeal to heaven and earth to serve as witnesses and state the basic charge against the people. Vv. 4-9 substantiate the charge of rebellion against YHWH by pointing to the present suffering of the people as proof of their wrongdoing. Vv. 10-17 lay out explicit instructions concerning activity that is and is not acceptable to YHWH. Finally, vv. 18-20 contain the appeal to begin the legal proceeding that will determine the people's fate.

The second major structural subunit in vv. 2-31 is vv. 21-31. As with vv. 2-20, this section contains a number of distinct generic entities (vv. 21-26, 27-28, 29-31), but here too they are bound together as a coherent textual subunit by several factors.

Again, the first is catchword connections. Vv. 21-26 and vv. 27-28 are connected by the appearance of *mišpāṭ*, "justice," and *ṣedeq/ṣĕdāqâ*, "righteousness," in vv. 21 and 27 (cf. v. 26). Likewise, the appearance of *yaḥdāw*, "together," in v. 28 and v. 31 provides a link between vv. 27-28 and vv. 29-31.

The second concerns semantics and syntax, and pertains to vv. 27-28 and vv. 29-31. V. 29 begins with the particle *kî*, "because" or "for," which establishes a semantic and syntactical connection between v. 28 and v. 29, indicating that the sinners who perish will do so because of their "oaks" or "terebinths" and their "gardens," which bring them shame. Furthermore, the reading *yēbōšû*, "they shall be ashamed," provides a further link between v. 29 and v. 28. The 3rd-person masculine form of this verb appears out of place in the context of vv. 29-31, which employs 2nd-person masculine plural verbs. Although some medieval Hebrew MSS and TJ change the verb to a 2nd-person form (*tēbōšû*, "you shall be ashamed"), conforming to the other governing verbs of vv. 29-31, the text should stand as is. The change is not made in other MS traditions, indicating the validity of the reading. It facilitates the transition between v. 28 and vv. 29-31 and apparently marks the work of an editor who joined vv. 29-31 to the preceding text. By this means, vv. 29-31 were structurally subsumed under vv. 27-28 where they function as an explication of the fate of the sinners identified in v. 28.

The third unifying factor for vv. 21-31 concerns theme and imagery. Vv. 21-26 emphasize a purge of Jerusalem in which the corrupt elements of the city's leadership will be removed by YHWH as one removes slag when smelting metal. The result, of course, will be a purified city restored to its former righteousness. Vv. 27-28 build on this theme by emphasizing the distinction in character and fate between those who "repent" or return to YHWH and those who continue their rebellious ways. In describing the redemption of Zion, v. 27 emphasizes the "justice" and "righteousness" that formerly characterized the city according to v. 21. The sinners will perish according to v. 28 much like the slag. Vv. 29-31 also build on the themes and imagery of the preceding material, focusing on the destruction of the "oaks" or "terebinths" and the "gardens" in which the sinners delighted. Such terebinths and gardens are symbolic of the Canaanite nature cult and represent the abandonment of YHWH. In this respect, vv. 29-31 draw on the theme of Jerusalem's harlotry mentioned at the beginning of v. 21, insofar as harlotry and the pursuit of Canaanite nature religion are often employed as a metaphors for the abandonment of YHWH. The destruction of the terebinths and gardens in vv. 29-31 corresponds to the destruction of the sinners in v. 28.

The fourth unifying factor is the focus on the *city* and its fate, as opposed to the people in vv. 2-20. Vv. 21-26 employ both 3rd-person feminine singular language and 2nd-person feminine singular direct address forms in reference to the city of Jerusalem to discuss the city's corrupt state and the purge that will take place. Likewise, v. 27, the dominant verse of vv. 27-31, employs 3rd-person feminine singular grammatical forms in reference to Zion. No choice is offered to the city, although it is clear from the reference to "her repenters" in v. 27 that the people residing there must choose repentance or face destruction.

Finally, a number of additional factors indicate that vv. 2-20 and vv. 21-31 function together to form the larger unit of text.

Again, the first is catchword connections. The charge that the judges do not judge the widows and orphans fairly in v. 23 contrasts directly with the commands to "judge the orphan" and "plead for the widow" in v. 17. The appearance of *mĕlē'ătî mišpāṭ*, "full of justice," in v. 21 contrasts with *yĕdêkem dāmîm mālē'û*, "your hands are full of blood," in v. 15. Likewise, *mišpāṭ* in vv. 21 and 27 points back to the command *diršû mišpāṭ*, "seek justice," in v. 17. Finally, the mention of *pōšĕ'îm*, "rebels," *ḥaṭṭā'îm*, "sinners," and *'ōzĕbê yhwh*, "forsakers of YHWH," in v. 28 corresponds to similar terminology for the wicked in v. 2 (*wĕhēm pāšĕû bî*, "and they rebelled against me") and in v. 4 (*gôy ḥōṭē'*, "sinful nation," and *'āzĕbû 'et-yhwh*, "they have forsaken YHWH").

The second is thematic. Vv. 2-20 accuse the people of sinning against YHWH and offer forgiveness to those who repent and conform to YHWH's instructions. Vv. 21-31 announce a general purge of the wicked in Zion and redemption of the city together with those who repent.

The third relates to the trial genre pattern in this chapter. Vv. 2-20 focus on an accusation against the wicked among the people and other facets of the legal proceeding prior to final judgment. Vv. 21-31 announce the judgment against the wicked.

Genre

Isaiah 1 is constituted by a number of generic entities. This is due in part to the editorial composition of this text and to the nature of the dominant generic patterns that constitute its final form: the TRIAL GENRE pattern and PARENESIS. Due to the various settings in which they appear, neither of these genres has an absolutely fixed structure or form, and both employ a variety of other generic forms in their individual examples. In the case of Isaiah 1, the TRIAL GENRE constitutes the basic structure of the text and the PARENESIS constitutes its primary function.

Following the SUPERSCRIPTION in v. 1, vv. 2-31 are organized according to the pattern of a legal proceeding in which YHWH is the plaintiff and Israel is the defendant. Vv. 2-20 constitute the ACCUSATION SPEECH insofar as the prophet acts as spokesperson on YHWH's behalf. All elements of this speech pertain to that aspect of the proceeding prior to final judgment. The introductory CALL TO ATTENTION directed to heaven and earth in v. 2a is a common feature of the TRIAL GENRE that establishes the two witnesses required for the proceedings. YHWH's accusation against Israel, namely, that Israel has rebelled against YHWH, appears in vv. 2b-3 in the form of a LAMENT. Vv. 4-9 employ a WOE STATEMENT, a RHETORICAL QUESTION, and a description of the land's desolate state to admonish the people against continued wrongdoing. The PROPHETIC TORAH in vv. 10-17 provides instruction as to what YHWH requires from the people. Finally, vv. 18-20 contain YHWH's APPEAL to begin the proceeding. Vv. 21-31 then constitute the SPEECH of the judge. It begins with vv. 21-26, which are based in the ANNOUNCEMENT OF JUDGMENT pattern, but constitute an ANNOUNCEMENT of the rehabilitation or purge of Zion. Vv. 27-31 explicate the meaning of this announcement by emphasizing a clear distinction between the respective fates of Zion's "repenters" and those who persist in rebellion against YHWH.

Although the TRIAL GENRE sets the basic structure of this chapter, several features of the text indicate that the TRIAL GENRE does not fully constitute the generic function of this text. Instead, the primary function of this chapter is constituted by its parenetic character. The primary goal does not appear to be the conviction and punishment of the defendant, but an attempt to persuade the people to change their behavior and thus to avoid the punishment. No speech of defense appears in this chapter, apparently because the people's actions are considered indefensible from the perspective of the text. Instead, the people are afforded the opportunity to respond to the charges by changing their behavior. This is evident in the appearance of the rhetorical question of v. 5 ("Why would you be smitten further that you continue apostasy?"), the instructions for righteous behavior in vv. 16-17, and YHWH's offer to cleanse the sins of those who are willing to change in vv. 18-20. It is also apparent in the "Speech of the Judge," insofar as vv. 27-31 offer redemption for the repenters and destruction for the rebellious. In this respect, ch. 1 contains both the positive elements of EXHORTATION and the negative elements of ADMONITION as aspects of its parenetic character.

Setting

The setting of ch. 1 must be considered in relation to the composite nature of this text. Although this chapter includes a great deal of material that derives from the 8th-century prophet, a number of its features indicate that its final form is the product of a mid- to late-5th-century redaction. Consequently, the settings of the individual subunits differ markedly from that of the final form.

A great deal of tension and inconsistency indicates the composite nature of ch. 1. Not all of its constituent subunits were composed in relation to one another. Some were composed independently and later combined and arranged into their present form.

Such tensions clearly exist within vv. 2-20. Vv. 4-9 presuppose a foreign invasion of the land of Judah, presumably that by Sennacherib in 701. Although Willis has claimed that vv. 10-17 must be understood in relation to Sennacherib's invasion, insofar as sacrificial offerings tend to increase in a time of emergency, the routine nature of the festivals mentioned in vv. 13-14 indicates that vv. 10-17 presuppose a time of relative peace. The only hints of violence appear in vv. 4-9 and vv. 18-20. Thus an editor apparently associated vv. 10-17 with Sennacherib's invasion and placed these verses in relation to the other passages in the context of vv. 2-20.

There is also evidence of such tension between vv. 2-20 and vv. 21-31. The purge of the city mentioned in these verses may well reflect or anticipate the Assyrian invasion of Judah insofar as the Assyrians were known for deporting the government officials and other leading figures of conquered enemies. In fact, Sennacherib reports such a deportation of Judeans following his invasion of 701 (*ANET,* 288). Nevertheless, it is striking that vv. 21-31 focus only on the city of Jerusalem, whereas vv. 2-20 appear to refer to the entire people of Israel (cf. v. 2). Likewise, vv. 21-26 focus only on the leaders of the city, whereas vv. 2-20 specify the entire nation (vv. 3, 4) or the leaders together with the people (v. 10). Clearly, the chapter progressively narrows its focus from all Israel to the city of Jerusalem and from the entire people to only the leaders, but the tensions in this text suggest that this is an editorial scheme achieved by placing disparate texts together.

There is also tension within vv. 21-31. Whereas vv. 21-26 speak of a purge of Zion's leaders, vv. 27-28 speak in much more general terms of the "repenters" and "rebels" with no consideration of their leadership status. Furthermore, as noted above, vv. 29-31 were editorially attached to v. 28 as an explication of the fate of the wicked.

Indeed, vv. 27-28 play a particularly key role in organizing and interpreting the various components of this chapter. Much of its vocabulary reflects that of other passages, such as *mišpāṭ,* "justice" (cf. vv. 17, 21); *wĕšābêhā,* "her repenters" (cf. v. 26); *biṣdāqâ,* "in righteousness" (cf. vv. 21, 26); *pōšĕʿîm,* "rebels" (cf. v. 2); *wĕḥaṭṭāʾîm,* "and sinners" (cf. vv. 4, 18); *yaḥdāw,* "together" (cf. v. 31); and *wĕʿōzĕbê yhwh,* "and those who forsake YHWH" (cf. v. 4). Such lexical connections enable vv. 27-28 to draw out the major themes of the preceding material, namely, the punishment of wickedness and rebellion against YHWH and the need for justice and righteousness. It is striking in this respect that vv. 27-28 distinguish between the redemption of the righteous as opposed to destruction of the wicked. Although the punishment of the people is presupposed throughout the chapter, such a clear distinction appears elsewhere only in vv. 19-20. Many scholars view these verses as a secondary expansion of v. 18 because of their introduction of violence in a passage that emphasizes YHWH's offer of forgiveness to the people while drawing on Deuteronomistic vocabulary and concepts (cf. Deut 1:26; 1 Sam 12:14-15). In this respect, it is important to note that the concept of repentance expressed by the verb *šûb* in v. 27 is also an important feature of Deuteronomistic literature. Furthermore, vv. 19-20 take up the vocabulary and themes from the preceding material, including the YHWH speech formula of v. 20b (cf. v. 2a) and the wordplay on the verbal root *ʾkl,* "to eat," in vv. 19 and 20a (cf. v. 7b). As noted above, they are instrumental in associating vv. 10-17 with vv. 4-9.

These considerations indicate that vv. 27-28 and vv. 19-20 play a constitutive role in the redaction of this chapter. They organize and draw major themes and concepts from the earlier material of this text. But in doing so, they change its character and add something new by emphasizing a dualistic concept of reward or redemption for the repenters and punishment or destruction for those who refuse (cf. v. 20a) to repent.

There are a number of indications that this redaction took place in the mid- to late 5th century. The first is the concern with the reward and punishment scheme, which is typical of the Deuteronomistic literature from the exilic and early Persian periods (e.g., DtrH; Jeremiah). This does not require that Isaiah is the literary product of a Deuteronomistic school, as Vermeylen maintains (*Du prophète,* 37-111; cf. Kaiser, *Isaiah 1–12,* passim); rather, it simply indicates a concern with reward and punishment (see Brekelmans). The second is the interest in making clear distinctions between the righteous and the wicked, which is typical of the early apocalyptic literature that begins to emerge in the 5th century. Furthermore, the application of the reward-punishment scheme to these two groups is especially characteristic of Trito-Isaiah (cf. chs. 65–66) and the reforms of Ezra and Nehemiah. Likewise, the interest in Zion's redemption and "her returners," whether understood as "those who repent" or "those who return [from exile]," is characteristic of the early Persian period, particularly the time of Ezra and Nehemiah (mid- to late 5th century).

Although much of this text was composed in the late 8th century, a number of features take on special significance when read in relation to the period of Ezra and Nehemiah, and suggest the reasons for the interest in editing and re-presenting Isaiah's oracles during the mid- to late 5th century. The desolate state of Jerusalem and the land of Judah corresponds to the situation of this period, as does the image of an isolated city (vv. 4-9). Certainly, Nehemiah's workmen understood the rewards of eating the good of the land or the threat of dying by the sword as they worked to rebuild the city and protect themselves at the same time (Neh 4:9-13). Likewise, purging the city of the wicked, including corrupt leadership (vv. 21-26) and religious syncretists (vv. 29-31), and reestablishing a correct understanding of temple sacrifice in relation to the moral concerns of YHWH's Torah (vv. 10-17) were special focuses of Ezra's and Nehemiah's reforms. The parenetic form and Deuteronomic concerns are characteristic of Levitical teaching and preaching, which certainly played a major role in Ezra's program for reestablishing the covenant (cf. Neh 8:9-12). Finally, the sequence "Judah and Jerusalem," which appears in the superscription in v. 1, is a characteristic designation of the land in this period.

Finally, a large number of catchwords connect ch. 1 and chs. 65–66 (see Liebreich, "Compilation"; Lack, 139-41; Sweeney, *Isaiah 1–4,* 21-24; cf. Conrad, *Reading Isaiah,* 83-116). Chs. 65–66 draw out some of the characteristic themes of ch. 1, including cultic abuse, the separation of the righteous and unrighteous, and the punishment of the apostates and triumph of the elect. These connections indicate that chs. 65–66 were composed in relation to ch. 1, and that these two blocks of material form a redactional envelope for the final 5th-century edition of the book of Isaiah.

Intention

On the basis of both its structure and generic characteristics, the intention of this text is clearly to motivate a basic change in the behavior of its audience. It maintains that present patterns of behavior are immoral and contrary to the Torah of YHWH, and that such immorality is the cause of present difficulties suffered by the audience, namely, a desolate land and an isolated and besieged Jerusalem. The text proceeds by offering the audience the opportunity to conform its behavior to YHWH's requirements to do justice and righteousness and thus to accept YHWH's offer of forgiveness and life in a redeemed Zion. Key elements in this offer include the rhetorical question in v. 5 that asks why the people should suffer further punishment by continuing their apostasy, vv. 16-17 that define YHWH's requirements for justice and righteousness, vv. 18-20 that present YHWH's offer, and v. 27 that describes the reward for those who accept. The text also makes clear, however, that those who refuse YHWH's offer will suffer further punishment and ultimate destruction when YHWH purges Jerusalem of its wrongdoers (cf. vv. 19-20, 28-31). Consequently, it employs a combination of positive exhortation and negative admonition to achieve its purpose.

When one considers this text in relation to its mid- to late-5th-century setting, it is also clear that one must view the purpose of the final form of the text in relation to the reform and restoration program of Ezra and Nehemiah. Isa 1:10 calls upon the people to "give ear to the Torah of our God," indicating that Isaiah 1 and the book of Isaiah as a whole appear to have been composed to support Ezra's reform based on Mosaic Torah (Nehemiah 8–10). As indicated in the Introduction to this commentary, there is no indication that "Torah" in Isa 1:10 and elsewhere refers to Mosaic Torah (contra Sheppard, "Book of Isaiah," esp. 578-82), but 56:1-8 and 66:18-21 do not contradict Ezra's exclusion of gentiles and other prohibited persons from the Jewish community. Rather, the book of Isaiah appears to offer an alternative understanding of Torah as prophetic revelation. Isaiah 1 points to the desperate circumstances of Judah and Jerusalem at that time, and the threat of further difficulties, which confronted Ezra and Nehemiah. By presenting the alternatives of reward for the repenters and destruction for the rebels, it attempts to persuade the people that the understanding of Torah presented in Isaiah offers the means to achieving a secure and righteous Jerusalem or *qiryâ ne'ĕmānâ*, "faithful/secure city" (vv. 21, 26).

Finally, one should note that, in its present position, ch. 1 serves as the prologue of the book of Isaiah. The oracles contained in this chapter summarize the main themes and message of the book: the punishment of Israel and Judah and the restoration of the people around Jerusalem by YHWH.

Bibliography

→ bibliography at "Introduction to the Prophetic Literature." K. Budde, "Zu Jesaja 1–5," *ZAW* 49 (1931) 16-40, 182-211; 50 (1932) 38-72; G. Fohrer, "Jesaja 1 als Zusammenfassung der Verkündigung Jesajas," in *Studien zur alttestamentlichen Prophetie (1949-1965)* (BZAW 99; Berlin: Töpelmann, 1967) 148-66 (repr. from *ZAW* 74 [1962] 251-68);

Y. Gitay, "Reflections on the Study of Prophetic Discourse: The Question of Isaiah I 2-20," *VT* 33 (1983) 207-21; B. Gosse, "Isaïe 1 dans la rédaction du livre d'Isaïe," *ZAW* 104 (1992) 52-66; A. Luc, "Isaiah 1 as Structural Introduction," *ZAW* 101 (1989) 115; A. Mattioli, "Due schemi letterari negli oracoli d'introduzione al libro d'Isaia: Is. 1,1-31," *RivB* 14 (1966) 345-64; S. Niditch, "The Composition of Isaiah 1," *Bib* 61 (1980) 509-29; L. G. Rignell, "Isaiah Chapter I," *ST* 11 (1957) 140-58; J. J. M. Roberts, "Form, Syntax, and Redaction in Isaiah 1:2-20," *PSB* 3 (1982) 293-306; E. Robertson, "Isaiah Chapter I," *ZAW* 52 (1934) 231-36; J. D. W. Watts, "The Formation of Isaiah 1: Its Context in Chapters 1-4," in *SBL 1978 Seminar Papers,* vol. 1 (ed. P. Achtemeier; Missoula: Scholars Press, 1978) 109-19; J. T. Willis, "The First Pericope in the Book of Isaiah," *VT* 34 (1984) 63-77.

SUPERSCRIPTION: TITLE OF THE BOOK OF ISAIAH, 1:1

Structure

I. Title proper: the vision of Isaiah ben Amoz	1aα
II. Specification of vision	1aβ-b
A. Concerning subject of vision: Judah and Jerusalem	1aβ
B. Concerning time of vision: reigns of Uzziah, Jotham, Ahaz, and Hezekiah	1b

The structure of v. 1 is determined by the syntactical structure of the sentence. The title, "The Vision of Isaiah ben Amoz," is specified by a relative clause that states the subject of the prophet's vision, i.e., Judah and Jerusalem, and the time when he saw it, i.e., during the reigns of the Judean kings Uzziah, Jotham, Ahaz, and Hezekiah.

Genre

This verse is clearly a SUPERSCRIPTION insofar as it defines the work that follows. Because it stands at the beginning of the book of Isaiah and defines its generic character, its author, its subject, and the time of its purported composition, 1:1 also serves as the title for the entire book (cf. 2 Chr 32:32).

Setting

Although the setting of this verse is notoriously difficult to define, there are indications of a postexilic origin. The primary evidence is the designation "Judah and Jerusalem." Jones's studies have demonstrated that "Judah and Jerusalem" serve as the stereotyped designation for the exilic and postexilic Jewish community, appearing some 20 times in Chronicles-Ezra-Nehemiah as well as in other literature from this period. Isaiah's speeches generally employ the order

"Jerusalem and Judah" (cf. Isa 3:1, 8; 5:3; 22:21), whereas the framework materials of the book, which do not derive from the prophet, employ "Judah and Jerusalem" (cf. 1:1; 2:1; 36:7). Likewise, the term *ḥāzôn,* "vision," as a designation for a prophetic book appears elsewhere only for the late-7th-century Nahum (Nah 1:1) and the 6th-century Obadiah (Obad 1). In view of these considerations, it is best to place the composition of this verse in a relatively late period. Because it functions in relation to the entire book of Isaiah and in relation to ch. 1, both of which achieve their final form in the mid- to late 5th century, 1:1 must be dated to the mid- to late 5th century.

Intention

This verse clearly functions as the title for the book of Isaiah. It is certainly recognized as such in 2 Chr 32:32 and Sir 48:22. Its placement at the head of the book and its characterization of the book's contents testify to this role. Several other factors confirm this function. First, the kings mentioned in this verse are found throughout the book. Second, the two other major superscriptions of the book in Isa 2:1 and 13:1 contain the relative clause *'ăšer ḥāzâ yěša'yāhû ben-'āmôṣ,* "which Isaiah ben Amoz saw." The reappearance of this clause in 2:1 and 13:1 indicates that in the present form of the book the latter are subsumed structurally under 1:1 and that the *dābār,* "word," of 2:1 and the *maśśā',* "pronouncement," of 13:1 are considered as aspects of Isaiah's overall vision. Other prophetic superscriptions likewise associate visionary experience with *dābār* (Mic 1:1; Amos 1:1; cf. Ezek 1:1-3) and *maśśā'* (Nah 1:1; Hab 1:1).

Isaiah 1:1 also functions in relation to ch. 1, specifically insofar as this chapter serves as the prologue to the entire book of Isaiah by presenting a compendium of material that summarizes the message of the book. In this respect, one should recognize that although the book contains a great deal of material concerning Israel and the nations in addition to Judah and Jerusalem, the book focuses on their relation to Judah and Jerusalem and their significance for understanding Judah's and Jerusalem's experience and role in YHWH's plans. This is especially clear in chs. 40–66, where the reestablishment of Judah and Jerusalem will result in the "new heaven and earth."

Finally, the purpose of the superscription is to identify the entire book of Isaiah as "the vision of Isaiah ben Amoz." Although chs. 40–66 and much of chs. 1–39 were clearly composed long after the lifetime of the prophet, the entire book is presented as his vision. In this respect, it is important to note the future orientation of the term *ḥāzôn,* "vision." It is used elsewhere in the titles of prophetic books as a designation for Nahum's prediction of the fall of Nineveh (Nah 1:1) and Obadiah's prediction of the fall of Edom (Obad 1) as these events concern the future of Israel and Judah. In the case of Isaiah, it is used to predict the eventual restoration of Judah and Jerusalem and its significance for the world.

Bibliography

H. M. I. Gevaryahu, "Biblical Colophons: A Source for 'Biography' of Authors, Texts, and Books," *Congress Volume, Edinburgh 1974* (VTSup 28; Leiden: Brill, 1975) 42-59.

ANNOUNCEMENT OF YHWH'S ACCUSATION
AGAINST ISRAEL, 1:2-3

Structure

I. Introduction: summons of witnesses	2a
A. Call to attention to heaven and earth	2aα
B. Motivation: prophetic speech formula	2aβ
II. Accusation speech by YHWH against Israel: lament form	2b-3
A. Father speech: complaint against children for improper behavior	2b
B. Wisdom allegory: Israel's lack of knowledge	3
1. Analogy of ox and ass	3a
2. Israel's lack of knowledge	3b

The boundaries of this passage are determined by the introductory call to attention in v. 2a, the *hôy,* "woe," of v. 4 that introduces a new address to the people, and the passage's characterization as the prophet's transmission of a speech by YHWH.

The speech pattern also determines the structure of the unit. The prophet is the speaker in v. 2a, which contains both his imperative address to heaven and earth and the prophetic speech formula providing the motivation for heaven and earth to listen. YHWH's speech follows in vv. 2b-3, which employ a 1st-person singular address concerning Israel.

The use of allegorical language indicates the two parts of this speech. V. 2b employs the language of a father complaining about his children's misbehavior to state YHWH's basic accusation that the people have rebelled against him. V. 3 employs an allegorical comparison of the people with oxen and asses to demonstrate Israel's lack of understanding.

Genre

The genre of this passage must be defined as a PROPHETIC ANNOUNCEMENT of YHWH's ACCUSATION against Israel on the basis of its characterization as the prophet's transmission of a SPEECH by YHWH and the contents of the speech. In formulating this announcement, the author employs a number of subordinate generic elements. The CALL TO ATTENTION formula is a typical means for a public presentation or address and functions in a variety of contexts. Here it is addressed to heaven and earth and corresponds to the pattern of the TRIAL

GENRE, which frequently call heaven and earth as witnesses to a legal proceeding by YHWH. The PROPHETIC SPEECH formula is a common indicator of divine speech in prophetic literature. YHWH's statement is cast in the form of a LAMENT insofar as the accusation of rebellion also relates YHWH's sorrow at the demonstration of Israel's ignorance. Whedbee's study is particularly useful in pointing to the wisdom background of the allegorical language in v. 3. Observations of the natural world and the application of the principles observed to human life are particularly characteristic of wisdom ALLEGORY. Furthermore, the element of surprise is employed in the ALLEGORY insofar as Israel is not explicitly identified as the object of YHWH's COMPLAINT until the end of the speech. Nevertheless, this wisdom ALLEGORY serves the legal purpose of this passage insofar as it reinforces YHWH's point that the people have rebelled.

Setting

Isaiah's use of wisdom forms and traditions as part of his rhetorical repertoire is well established. Both allegorical language (cf. 5:1-7; 28:23-29) and comparisons of the people to children (cf. 29:23; 30:1, 9) are common in his oracles. Although his use of the root *pš'*, "to rebel," to characterize the actions of the people often refers to a political act of rebellion (cf. R. Knierim, *Die Hauptbegriffe für Sünde im Alten Testament* [Gütersloh: G. Mohn, 1965] 180) and may characterize Isaiah's condemnation of the people for relying on political alliances rather than on YHWH for protection, the lack of specific information in this passage hampers attempts to define its historical setting. The lack of such information indicates that the passage was never an independent unit. Furthermore, the links to vv. 4-9 mentioned in the discussion of ch. 1 as a whole (above) suggest that it was composed in relation to 1:4-9, which has to do with the specific historical circumstances of Sennacherib's invasion of Judah in 701 B.C.E.

Intention

The primary intention of this unit is clearly to convey the accusation that the people of Israel have rebelled against YHWH. As such, it serves as the introduction to the trial genre that constitutes the structure of vv. 2-31. In keeping with the parenetic function of vv. 2-31 discussed above, however, YHWH's statement that the people lack understanding plays an important role in defining the intent of this unit. The ox and ass are deliberately employed because they are well known for their lack of understanding. When Israel is compared to them, the intended effect is to demonstrate that the people should know what even these animals are capable of understanding, i.e., the identity of their master and the source of their livelihood. This indicates that the underlying intention of this passage is not merely to accuse but to open the means for the people's return to YHWH. By pointing to the people's lack of understanding, the passage demonstrates the need for instruction. When read in relation to the following material in vv. 4-9, especially the RHETORICAL QUESTION of v. 5

that suggests that the suffering can stop, vv. 2-3 initiate the offering of repentance that is the basis of the parenetic character of vv. 2-31. Consequently, the intention of this chapter is not only to accuse but also to point to the possibility of resolving the accusation.

Bibliography

A. J. Bjørndalen, *Untersuchungen zur allegorischen Rede der Propheten Amos und Jesaja* (BZAW 165; Berlin and New York: de Gruyter, 1986) 177-85; idem, "Zur Frage der Echtheit von Jesaja 1,2-3; 1,4-7 und 5,1-7," *NTT* 83 (1982) 89-100; E. W. Davies, *Prophecy and Ethics: Isaiah and the Ethical Traditions of Israel* (JSOTSup 16; Sheffield: JSOT, 1981) 40-64; M. Delcor, "Les attaches littéraires, l'origine et la signification de l'expression biblique 'prendre à temoin le ciel et la terre,' " *VT* 16 (1966) 8-25; I. von Loewenclau, "Zur Auslegung von Jesaja 1,2-3," *EvT* 26 (1966) 294-308; C. Westermann, "The Role of the Lament in the Theology of the Old Testament," *Int* 28 (1974) 20-38.

ADMONITION AGAINST CONTINUED WRONGDOING, 1:4-9

Structure

I. Woe oracle: accusation concerning Israel's apostasy	4
A. Woe address: characterization of people as sinful	4a
B. Substantiation of characterization: accusation proper	4b
II. Motivation to cease apostasy: threat concerning continued apostasy	5-9
A. Rhetorical question concerning continued apostasy	5a
B. Basis for question	5b-9
1. Sickness of people: allegory	5b-6
2. Desolation of land	7
3. Isolation of Jerusalem	8
4. Remnant of people	9

The boundaries of this unit are defined by the introductory WOE ORACLE in v. 4, its consistent rhetorical character as an address by the prophet to the people, and the introductory CALL TO ATTENTION in v. 10, which begins a new unit.

Despite the shifts in pronouns from 3rd-person plural in v. 4, to 2nd-person masculine plural in vv. 5-8, to 1st-person plural in v. 9, the entire text constitutes the prophet's address to the people. Roberts and Hillers have demonstrated that the vocative character of the woe oracles and the use of the 1st-person plural address form in v. 9 are simply rhetorical devices by which the speaker identifies with the suffering of the audience. Although the authenticity of v. 9 has been challenged on the basis of its change in form, its use of the remnant motif, and its use of the Sodom and Gomorrah motif (Crüsemann, 163ff.; Barth, *Jesaja-Worte,* 190-91), one should bear in mind that the prophet's fate was bound up with that of the people and that following Sennacherib's devastation of the land, it was quite appropriate to speak of Jerusalem as a "remnant" of the land of Judah.

The structure of this text is determined by its two major generic elements: the WOE ORACLE in v. 4 and the RHETORICAL QUESTION in v. 5a, and their respective address forms.

Verse 4 is distinguished from the rest of the unit by its WOE ORACLE form and its use of 3rd-person plural address language. V. 4a contains the woe address to the people that characterizes them as a "sinning nation," "people heavy with guilt," "wicked seed," and "corrupt children" (*RSV* "sinful nation, people laden with iniquity, offspring of evil doers, sons who deal corruptly"). V. 4b employs 3rd-person plural verbal forms to state the substantiation for this characterization, i.e., the people "have abandoned [*RSV* 'forsaken'] YHWH" and "despised the Holy One of Israel."

The key to this passage is the RHETORICAL QUESTION in v. 5a: "Why will you be smitten again that you continue apostasy [*RSV* 'to rebel']?" Here the language shifts to 2nd-person plural address form and challenges the audience to change its situation. The intent of the question is clearly to convey to the people that they are responsible for their current misfortunes and that they are capable of ending their suffering by ending their apostasy. Vv. 5b-9 provide the motivation to make such a change by employing four images to point out the desperate situation of the people. They include an allegorical portrayal of a sick and wounded people (vv. 5b-6), a description of a desolate land overrun with foreigners (v. 7), a metaphorical portrayal of Jerusalem standing isolated like an agricultural field hut (v. 8), and the prophet's statement that the people would have become like Sodom and Gomorrah had YHWH not allowed a remnant to survive (v. 9).

Genre

The genre of this text must be defined as ADMONITION insofar as its primary purpose is to dissuade the audience from its current course of behavior. It also contains a number of subordinate generic elements that work together to achieve this purpose.

The first subordinate element is the *hôy* or WOE ORACLE form in v. 4. The WOE ORACLE has been derived from funeral lamentations and wisdom circles and seems to function as an exclamation of suffering or warning. Here the latter is the case. V. 4 conveys an accusation concerning the people's apostasy, but the balance of the unit provides the opportunity for the people to correct their behavior.

The second is the RHETORICAL QUESTION in v. 5a. Clearly, no answer is expected for this question since its purpose is to point out that the people bear responsibility for their present suffering and that they have the power to stop it by changing the behavior that caused the suffering in the first place.

The third is the ALLEGORY and metaphorical language of vv. 5b-9, which reinforce the point made by the RHETORICAL QUESTION. The vivid images of oozing sores, devouring aliens, a lonely *sukkâ*, "field hut" or "booth," and the infamous Sodom and Gomorrah combine to emphasize the people's desperate situation.

Finally, an element of threat is implicit in this passage. It offers the possibility of ending the suffering if the people will change their behavior to conform to the divine will. The suffering will continue if they do not.

Setting

Although attempts have been made to connect this passage with the Syro-Ephraimite invasion of Judah in 734 B.C.E. or the Babylonian siege of Jerusalem in 588-587, a number of factors demonstrate that Sennacherib's invasion of Judah and blockade of Jerusalem in 701 is the historical setting of this text (contra Ben Zvi). The portrayal of a devastated countryside overrun with foreigners certainly corresponds to Sennacherib's claim that he captured forty-six fortified Judean cities (*ANET,* 288). The portrayal of an isolated Jerusalem also corresponds to Sennacherib's description of his campaign and his claim to have blockaded the city. The appearance of the phrase *kĕʿîr nĕṣûrâ* presents no problem for this understanding. Literally translated, the phrase means "like a watched/guarded city," and is generally understood either as "like a fortified city" or as "like a besieged city." Jerusalem was clearly fortified at this time, as indicated by Sennacherib's claims to have employed sappers against the city. Although Sennacherib does not claim to have placed the city under full siege as the bulk of his army was concentrated elsewhere, his control of the approaches to the city demonstrates that Jerusalem was "watched" or "guarded."

Claims that the setting of this passage must be the Syro-Ephraimite invasion of 734 cannot be substantiated because there is no evidence that the countryside was overrun or that Jerusalem was isolated as portrayed in vv. 7-8. Likewise, attempts to connect the passage to the Babylonian invasions of the early 6th century are unnecessary because the "remnant" imagery of v. 9 is entirely appropriate to the 701 setting. After Sennacherib had destroyed forty-six Judean cities and carried off over 200,000 inhabitants, Jerusalem was certainly a remnant. As Ben Zvi notes, this passage lacks specific references to its historical background, but this enables 1:4-9 to be read in relation to various historical settings.

Intention

The intention of this passage is clearly linked to the RHETORICAL QUESTION of v. 5a. Here the prophet informs the people that they have the power to end their suffering by ending their apostasy *(sārâ).* The prophet has already established that the people's course of action constitutes a rejection of YHWH in v. 4. The problem is to determine what exactly he means by "apostasy" in this passage. It can hardly refer to the practice of sacrifice that the prophet condemns in the following verses since this would have no influence on the invading Assyrian army. As noted above, this passage must be read in conjunction with vv. 2-3, which accuse the people of "rebellion," employing the term *pāšaʿ,* which often refers to a political act of rebellion (e.g., 2 Kgs 8:20). Because he views the establishment of the Assyrian hegemony over Judah as an act of YHWH (5:25-30; 7:18-25; 8:1-4), Isaiah is consistently opposed to revolt against the Assyrians (30:1-4; 31:1-3; 39:1-8). In this case, the use of the term *sārâ* is particularly important. Its literal meaning is "turning away," generally understood as apostasy from YHWH. It is related to the verbal root *swr*, which is also used to describe the rebellious nature of the people when they attempt to make an alliance with Egypt against Assyria (30:1). With these considerations in mind, one should note that cessation of hostilities against the Assyrians is the one action that the people can take to put an end to the suffering described in this passage. Such a perspective on Isaiah's intention is supported by the narrative in chs. 36–37. According to these chapters, it is only when Hezekiah gives up his reliance on his own means of defense and places his confidence solely in YHWH that YHWH takes action to destroy the Assyrian and army and to relieve the people of their suffering.

Bibliography

E. Ben Zvi, "Isaiah 1,4-9, Isaiah, and the Events of 701 BCE in Judah," *SJOT* 5 (1991) 95-111; Bjørndalen, *Untersuchungen* (→ 1:2-3), 189-208; idem, "Zur Frage der Echtheit" (→ 1:2-3); F. Crüsemann, *Studien zur Formgeschichte von Hymnus und Danklied in Israel* (WMANT 32; Neukirchen: Neukirchener, 1969) 163ff.; H. Donner, *Israel unter den Völkern: Die Stellung der klassischen Propheten des 8. Jahrhunderts v. Chr. zur Aussenpolitik der Könige von Israel und Juda* (VTSup 11; Leiden: Brill, 1964) 119-21; F. J. Gonçalves, *L'expèdition de Sennachérib en Palestine dans la littérature hébraïque ancienne* (Louvain-la-Neuve: Institut Orientaliste, 1986) 245-54; J. Hausmann, *Israels Rest: Studien zum Selbstverständnis der nachexilischen Gemeinde* (BWANT 124; Stuttgart, Berlin, Cologne, Mainz: Kohlhammer, 1987) 139-41; N. A. Van Uchelen, "Isaiah I 9 — Text and Context," *OTS* 21 (1981) 155-63; W. Werner, *Eschatologische Texte in Jesaja 1–39: Messias, Heiliger Rest, Völker* (2nd ed.; FB 46; Würzburg: Echter, 1986) 118-33; idem, "Israel in der Entscheidung: Überlegungen zur Datierung und zur theologischen Aussage von Jes 1,4-9," in *Eschatologie* (*Fest.* E. Neuhäusler; ed. R. Kilian, K. Funk, and P. Fassl; St. Ottilien: EOS, 1981) 59-72; J. T. Willis, "An Important Passage for Determining the Historical Setting of a Prophetic Oracle — Isaiah 1.7-8," *ST* 39 (1985) 151-69.

PROPHETIC TORAH ON PROPER SERVICE TO YHWH, 1:10-17

Structure

I. Call to instruction   10
   A. To the "rulers of Sodom"   10a
   B. To the "people of Gomorrah"   10b
II. Quotation of YHWH's torah speech   11-17

The boundaries of this unit are determined by the introductory imperative call to instruction in v. 10, its characterization as the prophet's presentation of a speech by YHWH, and its concern with instructing the people. V. 18, with its proposal for a legal proceeding and its own speech formula, marks the beginning of a new unit.

The basic structure of this unit is determined by its characterization as the prophet's presentation of a speech by YHWH. The unit begins with the prophet's imperative address to the audience, identified as the "rulers of Sodom" and "people of Gomorrah," to hear the "word of YHWH" and the "torah/instruction of our God." The YHWH speech formula in v. 11aα_2 and the 1st-person address form directed to a 2nd-person plural audience indicate that vv. 11-17 constitute the prophet's quotation of YHWH's speech.

The two RHETORICAL QUESTIONS in vv. 11-12 and the instructions in vv. 13-17 set the structure of YHWH's speech in that the rhetorical questions establish the need for the INSTRUCTIONS that follow. The first question (v. 11) asks why the people are making sacrifices when YHWH neither needs nor wants them. The second question (v. 12) asks who requested such activities in YHWH's courts in the first place. If YHWH is asking these questions, there can be no satisfactory answer. Because the people are making sacrifices that YHWH neither needs nor requests, they obviously need instruction in proper service to YHWH. The instructions in vv. 13-17 is expressed both negatively and positively. The negative instruction consists of one prohibition against the continued bringing of false or worthless offerings *(minḥat šāw')* in v. 13aα and the reasons for the PROHIBITION in vv. 13aβ-15: YHWH is unwilling to endure such activities (vv. 13aβ-14); YHWH will not respond (v. 15a); the people's hands are full of blood (v. 15b). The positive instruction then appears in vv. 16-17 as a progression of nine COMMANDS: wash, be purified, remove evil, stop doing evil, learn to do good, seek justice, correct oppression, judge the orphan, and plead for the widow.

Genre

The genre of this unit is based in the PRIESTLY TORAH, but it has been modified to fit the needs of the situation and the prophet's purpose so that its present generic character is PROPHETIC TORAH. The text begins with a specialized form of the CALL TO ATTENTION formula known as the CALL TO INSTRUCTION, which commonly appears in the wisdom tradition. It directs the audience's attention to the following torah SPEECH and indicates the prophet's role in presenting this INSTRUCTION. Within the SPEECH itself, the usual torah question and torah answer have been modified. YHWH speaks in place of the priest. Furthermore, the two RHETORICAL QUESTIONS do not request information concerning proper cultic procedure as is common in the PRIESTLY TORAH form. Instead, these common wisdom forms question the very legitimacy of the sacrifices performed by the people. The INSTRUCTION proper appears in vv. 13-17, including a PROHIBITION against false offerings and commands to the people to purify themselves and seek justice.

Setting

The setting of this unit is clearly not the same as that of vv. 4-9. There is no indication of Sennacherib's invasion in this text despite the appearance of the voluntary offerings, *zebaḥ,* "sacrifice" (understood as *šělāmîm,* "peace offerings"), and *ʿōlôt,* "whole burnt offerings," which were often utilized in times of emergency (Hayes and Irvine, 75; cf. Willis, 76). Instead, the routine nature of the festival observances mentioned in v. 13 (new moon, sabbath, etc.) presupposes the normal functions of the temple service. Such an emphasis on the condemnation of cultic practice must be seen in relation to Hezekiah's cultic reforms (2 Kgs 18:1-8). Hezekiah's closing of worship sites in the countryside and the removal of syncretistic worship objects would surely have focused attention on the services performed in the temple of Jerusalem. The basis for Isaiah's opposition to such activity does not appear to be opposition to the cult in and of itself. After all, he emphasizes the condemnation of "false offerings" in v. 13, not the practice of offering in general. Instead, the basis of his opposition appears to be the relationship between Hezekiah's religious reforms and his policy of preparing for armed revolt against the Assyrians. Consequently, this passage must be placed prior to Hezekiah's revolt against Sennacherib in 701 B.C.E., sometime during the period 715-701.

Intention

Although this passage is often understood as a blanket condemnation of cultic practice, the prophet's emphasis on condemning "false offerings" (v. 13) and the historical setting of the passage indicate a different agenda. One must keep in mind that the temple served not only as the religious center of the country but also as the symbol of its independence and the power of the Davidic dynasty that established it. Isaiah's condemnation of these cultic practices is based on their relation to Hezekiah's plans for revolt. Consequently, he condemns false offerings here not because they are inherently evil but because they are performed in conjunction with a national policy that Isaiah considers to be fundamentally wrong. He maintains consistently that the security of the country depends on YHWH's guarantee of protection, not on foreign alliances and armed confrontation with Assyria. Isaiah considers Hezekiah's policies to be a rejection of YHWH's guarantee of protection to the country. In the context of such a policy, he condemns the temple service as false and hypocritical.

A secondary issue is whether the passage contains any offer of forgiveness to the people. A number of scholars claim that no offer of forgiveness appears here because Isaiah did not expect any change in the people's behavior. Consequently, the intent of the passage focuses entirely on condemning the people. Such a view violates the plain meaning of the text. The basis for repentance is offered in the positive instructions of vv. 16-17. Whether Isaiah expected the people to meet these requirements is irrelevant. Furthermore, the relationship of this unit to vv. 18-20, which explicitly offer the opportunity for repentance to the people, supports this understanding of vv. 10-17.

Bibliography

→ bibliography at "Introduction to the Prophetic Literature" for Begrich, "Die priester-liche Tora"; Hunter, *Seek the Lord,* 176-90; Tångberg, *Mahnrede,* 61-64; Warmuth, *Mahnwort,* 74-80. Jensen, *Use of tôrâ* (→ "Introduction to the Book of Isaiah"), 65-84; T. Lescow, "Die dreistufige Tora: Beobachtungen zu einer Form," *ZAW* 82 (1970) 362-79; G. Stansell, *Micah and Isaiah: A Form and Tradition Historical Comparison* (SBLDS 85; Atlanta: Scholars Press, 1988) 115-17.

APPEAL TO BEGIN LEGAL PROCEEDING, 1:18-20

Structure

I. Invitation to arbitration	18a
A. Invitation proper	18aα
B. YHWH speech formula	18aβ
II. Elaboration concerning incentives for arbitration	18b-20
A. Statements of incentive	18b-20bα
1. YHWH's offer of vindication	18b
a. First statement	18bα
b. Second statement	18bβ
2. YHWH's conditions	19-20bα
a. Positive	19
1) Case: people obey	19a
2) Positive result	19b

b. Negative	20a-bα
1) Case: people disobey	20a
2) Negative result	20bα
B. YHWH authorization formula	20bβ

Although this text is cast in the form of the prophet's quotation of a speech by YHWH, the new speech formula in v. 18aβ distinguishes it from vv. 10-17 and indicates that it is a new unit. The YHWH SPEECH FORMULA in v. 20bβ marks the end of the unit.

The structure of the unit is determined by the introductory cohortative address in v. 18a and the four conditional statements that follow in vv. 18b-20. Furthermore, each section concludes with a YHWH speech formula (vv. 18aβ, 20bβ). The contents of the cohortative address in v. 18a indicate that it functions as YHWH's invitation to the people to engage in arbitration. The conditional statements provide incentive to accept this invitation by explaining the terms. The form and content of these statements indicate that they function as two sets of pairs. The first pair (vv. 18bα, 18bβ) employs 3rd-person plural imperfect verbs stating YHWH's offer to forgive sins. The second pair (vv. 19, 20a-bα) employs 2nd-person plural imperfect verbs to state the consequences for acceptance or rejection of YHWH's offer. If the people accept, they eat the good of the land. If they refuse, they are consumed by the sword.

Genre

The cohortative form of the initial statement and the use of the legal technical term *niwwākĕhâ*, "let us arbitrate," characterize the entire unit as an APPEAL to begin a legal proceeding. Such an appeal functions as part of the TRIAL GENRE as a request for a legal judgment. The YHWH SPEECH FORMULAS further characterize this unit as the prophet's quotation of YHWH's appeal to begin a legal proceeding.

Setting

The absence of specific information concerning the people's sins or of the circumstances for which this text was composed indicates that it does not constitute an originally independent unit. A number of factors suggest that it was composed in relation to vv. 10-17. These include the red/crimson imagery for the sins of the people that corresponds to the blood imagery of v. 15b; the transformation of red sins to white that corresponds to the concern for cleansing evil in v. 16; the mention of sins becoming like wool that relates to the sheep in v. 11; the use of forensic language that corresponds to the concern for justice and the proper judgment of widows and orphans in v. 17; and the 2nd-person plural address form that continues that of vv. 10-17. It is interesting to note, however, that the first four parallels appear only in v. 18. Vv. 19-20 employ a 2nd-person plural address form, but the use of 2nd-person plural verbs disrupts the 3rd-person plural verb pattern of v. 18. Furthermore, these verses introduce the threat of warfare and the concern for eating from the land, which are entirely foreign to the concerns of vv. 10-17 or v. 18 but appear prominently in vv. 4-9. Because their language corresponds to that of the framework speeches that constitute the structure of the DtrH (cf. Deut 1:26; 1 Sam 12:14-15), vv. 19-20 appear to be an addition made by a writer who was heavily influenced by Deuteronomistic ideology. On the basis of these considerations, v. 18 must be deemed part of vv. 10-17 and dated to 715-701 b.c.e., whereas vv. 19-20 must be a 5th-century addition. As argued above, the purpose of this addition was to combine vv. 2-9 and vv. 10-18 together into a single unit.

Intention

Despite its small size, this passage has been the subject of a great deal of scholarly discussion, which Willis has admirably summarized. Although the plain meaning of the text presents an offer of divine forgiveness, this understanding has been contested on several grounds. Some have argued that the conditional statements in v. 18b are actually Rhetorical Questions: "While your sins are as scarlet, how can they be white as snow? While they are red like crimson, how can they be as wool?" (Tur-Sinai, 156). This interpretation is undermined by the absence of the *he* interrogative, which frequently marks questions in the Hebrew Bible. Others have understood these statements as ironic, sarcastic, or as a judge's quotation of statements by the accused that are to be refuted; such interpretations, however, are highly subjective and relate to the view that Isaiah's judgment perspective left no room for forgiveness. An additional basis for these understandings has been that it is impossible for red to change to white just as it is impossible for the people's sins to be forgiven, but this is precisely the point of the passage. At the same time, it is important to keep in mind that these are conditional statements. No unconditional offer of forgiveness appears here. Instead, it is an offer to repent, change behavior, and then be forgiven.

This understanding of vv. 18-20 as an offer of forgiveness based on repentance is particularly clear when these verses are read in relation to vv. 10-17. In the original form of this passage, v. 18 would have been the concluding statement and thus would have provided the incentive for the positive instructions of vv. 16-17. In the context of the 5th-century redaction of ch. 1, which emphasizes a land devastated by foreign invasion, vv. 18-20 play a similar role in relation to vv. 2-17, except that they add the reward of enjoying a secure land or the threat of death as additional incentives.

Bibliography

→ bibliography at "Introduction to the Prophetic Literature" for Raitt, "Prophetic Summons"; Tångberg, *Mahnrede,* 64-65; Warmuth, *Mahnwort,* 80-82. J. Goldingay, "If Your Sins Are Like Scarlet . . . (Isaiah 1:18)," *ST* 35 (1981) 137-44; E. Kutsch, " 'Wir wollen miteinander rechten': Zu Form und Aussage von Jes 1,18-20," in *Kleine Schriften zum Alten Testament* (ed. L. Schmidt and K. Eberlein; BZAW 168; Berlin and New York: de Gruyter, 1986; repr. from *Künder des Wortes — J. Schreiner* [Würzburg: Echter, 1982] 23-33) 146-56; Lescow, "Die dreistufige Tora" (→ 1:10-17); J. Schoneveld, "Jesaja I 18-20," *VT* 13 (1963) 342-44; Tur-Sinai, "Contribution" (→ "Introduction to the Book of Isaiah"); C. Westermann, *Prophetic Oracles of Salvation,* 239-40; J. T. Willis, "On the Interpretation of Isaiah 1:18," *JSOT* 25 (1983) 35-54.

PROPHETIC ANNOUNCEMENT OF ZION'S REHABILITATION, 1:21-26

Structure

I. Indictment of Jerusalem's leaders	21-23
A. Lamentation concerning corrupt state of city	21
B. Specific accusations	22-23
1. Evidence of corruption	22
2. Reason for corruption: leaders	23
II. Announcement of cleansing judgment	24-26
A. Expanded oracle formula	24a
B. YHWH's announcement of cleansing judgment	24b-26
1. Woe speech concerning YHWH's replacement of corrupt leaders	24b-26a
2. Result: Jerusalem's character restored	26b

The boundaries of this unit are marked by the initial *'êkâ,* "alas!" of v. 21, which commonly introduces a dirge or lamentation, and the appearance of *qiryâ nĕ'ĕmānâ,* "the trustworthy city," in both v. 21 and v. 26, which constitutes a rhetorical inclusion for the passage. As noted above, vv. 27-31 constitute a related but separate unit in the larger structure of ch. 1.

The structure of this unit is determined by its speech patterns, content, and generic character based on the prophetic judgment speech. Vv. 21-23 contain a speech by the prophet concerning the corrupt state of the city. Vv. 24-26 contain the prophet's quotation of YHWH's speech concerning actions to be taken against the leaders of the city. When read together, vv. 21-23 constitute an indictment speech against the leaders of Jerusalem, and vv. 24-26 constitute an announcement of judgment against the leaders.

Within vv. 21-23, v. 21 contains a lament concerning the corrupt state of Jerusalem formulated in 3rd-person descriptive language. Vv. 22-23 shift to 2nd-person feminine forms in a direct address to the city. These verses contain specific accusations concerning the evidence for the corrupt state of the city, impure silver, and diluted wine, and the reason for the city's decline, namely, the corrupt character of its leaders.

Verses 24-26 include an expanded oracular formula (v. 24a) and the speech by YHWH (vv. 24b-26). The first part of YHWH's speech is formulated as a woe speech in vv. 24b-26a. This section includes a chain of six 1st-person verbal statements, linked by *wāws*, concerning YHWH's plans to remove the corrupt leaders and replace them with proper judges and advisors. The second part of the speech states the result in v. 26b: Jerusalem will again be called the "trustworthy city."

Genre

The overall genre of this passage is based in the PROPHETIC JUDGMENT SPEECH. As noted above, vv. 21-23 constitute an indictment speech in that they focus on the corrupt state of the city and assign the blame to its leaders. Vv. 24-26 constitute an ANNOUNCEMENT OF JUDGMENT in that they announce the projected removal and replacement of the corrupt leaders. One should note, however, that the basic concern of this passage is not with the city's leaders and their punishment but with the city itself and its restoration. Consequently, the genre has been modified here to announce the cleansing or rehabilitation of Jerusalem.

The unit employs a number of subordinate generic elements to achieve its ends. The first is the LAMENTATION over Jerusalem in v. 21. The verse employs a form very similar to that of a DIRGE for an individual, including the initial *'êkâ*, "alas!" and the 3/2 *qînâ* meter in v. 21a. V. 24a contains an expanded form of the ORACULAR FORMULA, which has been prefixed with *lākēn*, "therefore," in keeping with the standard form of the PROPHETIC JUDGMENT SPEECH, which governs the unit overall. Finally, the exclamation *hôy*, "woe!" introduces YHWH's ANNOUNCEMENT OF JUDGMENT. The statements do not conform to the standard form of the WOE ORACLE, however, and it is likely that the *hôy* finds its way into this oracle because of its association with mourning for the dead (cf. 1 Kgs 13:30) and the LAMENTATION in v. 21.

Setting

The metaphorical use of foundry imagery in this passage is characteristic of Isaiah and indicates that the prophet is the author. The prophet's emphasis on the removal of public officials may well presuppose the Assyrian practice of deporting such officials from conquered regions. Nevertheless, the focus on impure silver, diluted wine, and the general concerns for societal justice suggest that no immediate crisis for Judah stands behind this passage. Instead, the passage presupposes normal trading conditions and an awareness of Assyrian policies toward its victims. Consequently, the setting for this passage can be any time between 732 B.C.E., following the first Assyrian defeat of the northern kingdom of Israel, and 701, when Hezekiah began his revolt against Assyria. Isaiah commonly employed the experience of Israel as an example of what could happen to Judah (cf. 28:1-29).

Intention

The intention of this passage is clearly to voice Isaiah's opposition to Jerusalem's leaders. When read against the background of the Assyrian policy of deporting government officials, it indicates that Isaiah views the Assyrians as YHWH's tool for punishing those responsible for social corruption in the city.

Bibliography

J. T. Willis, "Lament Reversed — Isaiah 1,21ff," *ZAW* 98 (1986) 236-48.

PROPHETIC ANNOUNCEMENT OF ZION'S REDEMPTION, 1:27-31

Structure

I. Announcement of redemption to Zion for Zion and her repenters	27
II. Announcement of annihilation for sinners	28-31
A. Basic statement	28
B. Metaphorical elaboration	29-31
1. Statement concerning shame of sinners	29
2. Metaphorical statement concerning consequences	30-31

Although vv. 27-31 are related to vv. 21-26 in the larger structure of ch. 1, the abrupt change to a statement of Zion's redemption and the shift from 2nd-person address forms to 3rd-person announcement language define these verses as a new structural unit. The superscription in 2:1 marks the beginning of the next major section of the book of Isaiah.

The structure of this unit is defined by the contrasting statement concerning the redemption of Zion and her "repenters" in v. 27 and the annihilation of sinners in v. 28. As noted above, vv. 29-31 are connected to v. 28 by the particle *kî*, "for," and the editorial modification of *tēbōšû*, "you shall be ashamed," to *yēbōšû*, "they shall be ashamed," in v. 29. These verses elaborate on the fate of the sinners by comparing them to a dry oak or a dry garden destroyed by fire. V. 29 states that they shall be ashamed of their oaks and gardens. Vv. 30-31 apply the metaphor, claiming that they shall perish like a withering oak or a dry garden that catches fire and burns.

Genre

Because the redemption of Zion requires the annihilation of its sinners, v. 27 defines the generic character of this passage as an ANNOUNCEMENT OF REDEMP-

TION. The contents of vv. 29-31 define them as a metaphorical ANNOUNCEMENT OF PUNISHMENT in their original form. In their present context, vv. 29-31 elaborate on the fate of the sinners announced in v. 28.

Setting

As noted in the overview of ch. 1, vv. 27-28 constitute a mid- to late-5th-century redactional addition to the material in ch. 1. This is due to their role in organizing and interpreting the preceding material, their introduction of a distinction between the fates of the righteous and the wicked, their emphasis on violence in relation to the earlier materials, and their relation to Deuteronomistic literature. By contrast, vv. 29-31 appear to be the work of Isaiah, albeit modified by the editorial work evident in v. 29. The metaphorical technique is quite common throughout the prophet's oracles and the image of the tree is one of the leading themes of his work (cf. K. Nielsen, *Tree*). Although the oracles lack specific historical information, its emphasis on oaks and gardens here indicates a concern with syncretistic nature cult practices and suggests a period prior to the reign of Hezekiah as the setting for this oracle.

Intention

As discussed above, the intention of the present form of this passage is to organize and interpret the contents of ch. 1 in order to present the book of Isaiah as an alternative form of the torah presupposed in Nehemiah's and Ezra's reform program. The original intent of vv. 29-31 is somewhat difficult to establish since they appear to be a fragment of a text that was composed for an entirely different context. Isaiah clearly employs the images of nature cult syncretism to condemn the subjects of this passage, but the lack of more specific information prevents secure conclusions.

PROPHETIC ANNOUNCEMENT CONCERNING THE CLEANSING OF ZION FOR ITS ROLE AS THE CENTER FOR YHWH'S WORLD RULE, 2:1–4:6

Structure

The boundaries of this larger unit are determined by a combination of formal and thematic elements. The superscription in 2:1 marks its beginning and designates it as Isaiah's word concerning Judah and Jerusalem. Furthermore, the following material is formulated with 3rd-person announcement language and 2nd-person address forms until ch. 5, which begins with a 1st-person address. Although the emphasis is clearly on Jerusalem or Zion, the concern with Judah and Jerusalem appears consistently throughout this unit. In some cases, this is explicit (2:2-4; 3:1-15; 3:16–4:1), but in others it is expressed somewhat elliptically. For example, 2:5 and 2:6ff. refer to the "house of Jacob," which is sometimes understood as a reference to the northern kingdom of Israel (Cazelles, "Isaïe II 2-5," 412-13; Roberts, "Isaiah 2," 293-94). But, as Wildberger's discussions have shown (*Jesaja*, 83-87; "Völkerwallfahrt," 66-69, 78-79), "house of Jacob" in vv. 5 and 6 must be correlated with "God of Jacob" in v. 3. The term *'ĕlōhê ya'ăqōb*, "God of Jacob," is a typical designation for YHWH in the Zion psalms and refers to YHWH as God of all Israel, based in the Jerusalem temple. Likewise, the emphasis on Zion and Jerusalem as the remnant of Israel in 4:2-6 indicates the central concern with Jerusalem and its environs (cf. 4:5) following the demise of the rest of Israel. The primary aspect of this concern is the focus on the Temple Mount (2:2, 3; 4:5-6) at the beginning and end of this unit. But ch. 5 begins a new section, which continues through ch. 12, that is concerned with both Israel and Judah (cf. 5:7; 9:7-8; 11:13-14; 12:6). Finally, the unit is held together by frequent references to the "Day of YHWH" announced in 2:12 (cf. 2:20; 3:7; 3:18; 4:1; 4:2), although one should note that the other subunits of chs. 1–39 also refer to the "Day of YHWH," which indicates the programmatic character of chs. 2–4 within the book.

Isaiah 2–4 is clearly a composite unit. Its editors employed texts that were written for distinct purposes in various historical settings. The result is a composition that presents an ideal portrayal of Zion's role as the center for YHWH's rule of all nations and then explains how Zion is to be prepared for this role. Its generic characterization as a PROPHETIC ANNOUNCEMENT offers no fixed structural pattern in that it employs a number of generic entities to achieve its ends. Instead, the structure of this text is constituted by a combination of its formal, syntactical, and rhetorical features together with its thematic content, and this determines the interrelationships of the various subunits.

A key element in this structure is the contrast between the ideal Zion presented in 2:2-4 and the current state of its people that must be overcome to achieve this ideal in 2:5–4:6. This is frequently expressed through metaphorical use of the imagery of height and depth. On the one hand, the ideal Zion is portrayed as the highest and most exalted mountain (2:2). On the other hand, the portrayal of the people employs symbols of height to emphasize their self-pride and failure to rely on YHWH (2:12-16). In the view of the text, this indicates that the people are in fact low and debased (2:9, 11, 17). The Day of YHWH will therefore correct this situation by stripping away all symbols of human pride so that YHWH's exalted status will be manifested (2:10-21; 3:1-9; 3:16–4:1).

The superscription in 2:1 constitutes the first major structural unit of chs. 2–4 (Tucker, "Prophetic Superscriptions," 57-58). The body of the text in 2:2–4:6 constitutes the second major structural unit or the "Announcement Proper."

The first major structural subunit of 2:2–4:6 is the announcement concerning the ideal Zion in 2:2-4. This passage is characterized by its 3rd-person objective announcement language that distinguishes it from the 2nd-person address forms that dominate the balance of the unit in 2:5–4:6. No particular audience is indicated here, in contrast to 2:5–4:6, which addresses explicitly the "house of Jacob" (2:5; cf. 2:10, 22). As noted above, this passage emphasizes the height of the ideal Zion over against the depths from which the people must be raised in 2:5–4:6.

The second major structural subunit of 2:2–4:6 is 2:5–4:6, which announces the cleansing of Zion. Although this material contains a variety of announcement and address forms, it is dominated by the 2nd-person address forms in 2:5, 10, and 22. V. 5 identifies its audience as the "house of Jacob" by employing the masculine plural imperative verb *lĕkû*, "come," and a vocative *bêt ya'ăqōb,* "O house of Jacob." V. 10 employs the masculine singular imperatives *bô',* "enter," and *hiṭṭāmēn,* "hide," with no explicit indication of the addressee. Likewise, v. 22 employs the masculine plural imperative *hidlû,* "desist," with no indication of the addressee. Despite the minor difference in the form of the imperative verbs, the general context concerning humankind, including the emphasis on worshiping the work of human hands (2:20; cf. 2:8), and the repeated refrains concerning the debasement and fall of humankind (2:11, 17; cf. 2:9), v. 10 and v. 22 are structurally subsumed under v. 6. Thus they are also addressed to the "house of Jacob."

Each address is followed by explanatory material that clarifies its meaning in relation to the central concern for the cleansing of Zion.

The address to the "house of Jacob" in 2:5 was clearly composed as an invitation to join the nations' procession to "the mountain of the house of YHWH," as indicated by the lexical associations between 2:5 and 2:3 (Scott, "Isaiah 1–39," 182; Sweeney, *Isaiah 1–4,* 135-36, 174). It is connected to vv. 6-9, however, by the adversative *kî* at the beginning of v. 6 and the following appositional specification of *ʿamměkā,* "my people," by *bêt yaʿăqōb,* "house of Jacob." Although the texts of v. 6a and v. 9b have frequently been emended on the basis of the LXX, the MT should stand as is (Sweeney, *Isaiah 1–4,* 139-41). Vv. 6-9 employ 2nd-person masculine singular verbs to address YHWH in an accusation speech that outlines Jacob's associations with foreigners, stores of money and war equipment, and summarizes by characterizing this as idolatry and rejection of YHWH. When read together with v. 5, vv. 6-9 establish Jacob's unfitness to participate in the procession to YHWH's Temple Mount. Consequently, 2:5 serves as the central "thesis" for chs. 2–4 in that it points to the contrast between the ideal Zion and the unfit "house of Jacob" (cf. Wiklander, 183). Isa 2:5-9 therefore establishes the need for the cleansing of Zion.

The second address, in 2:10-21, focuses on the actual process of cleansing Zion by announcing the Day of YHWH. It employs universal language to indicate that the entire land or earth and all humankind are threatened by this manifestation of divine power. Although there is no indication that this passage was written in relation to 2:2-4, it does recall the universal aspect symbolized by all the nations streaming to Zion. The imperative warning statement appears in 2:10-11 followed by a 3rd-person announcement, introduced by an explanatory *kî,* "for, because," which describes the Day of YHWH and thus provides the basis for the warning in 2:12-21.

The third address, in 2:22–4:6, focuses on the process of cleansing as applied to Jerusalem and Judah. It begins with the plea to desist from human self-reliance in 2:22, which facilitates the transition from the focus on humankind in general to Jerusalem and Judah in particular. This plea is illustrated by material focusing on the removal of the symbols of such pride in Jerusalem and Judah: the leaders of the community (3:1-15) and the finery of the women (3:16–4:1). Because 2:22 is missing from the LXX, it is frequently considered to be a very late addition to this text. But its appearance in all other MS traditions, including 1QIs[a] and 1QS 5:17, indicates that it was part of the text of Isaiah by the 2nd or early 1st century B.C.E. at the latest. It was likely omitted from the LXX because of its lack of explicit connection to its context.

Isaiah 2:22 is followed by 3:1–4:6, which is connected to 2:22 by the explanatory *kî,* "for, because," in 3:1 and to the preceding material by the references to the Day of YHWH (3:7, 18; 4:1, 2) and the continued concern with the process for cleansing Zion. This material is governed by 3rd-person objective announcement language focusing specifically on Jerusalem and Judah in contrast to the universal language of 2:10-21 and 2:22. The juxtaposition of 3:1–4:6 with 2:22 and 2:10-21 indicates the editor's concern to demonstrate Jerusalem's and Judah's central role in relation to the earth and humankind, so that 3:1–4:6 serves as an explication to 2:22 and thus to 2:10-21 as well. Isa 3:1–4:6 also demonstrates that the purpose of the Day of YHWH is not merely destructive; it is designed to cleanse Zion as the holy site for the temple. The judgment speech in 3:1–4:1 includes two major sections: 3:1-15 condemns the (male) leaders of Jerusalem and Judah for abusing their responsibilities, and 3:16–4:1 condemns the women or "daughters of Zion" for excessive vanity. The announcement of salvation in 4:2-6 shifts the concern to the aftermath of punishment. The result of the Day of YHWH will be the establishment of a purified remnant of Israel in Jerusalem around the site of the temple. In this respect, the ideal portrayal of Zion in 2:2-4 can now be achieved.

Genre

As noted already, the basic generic character of Isaiah 2–4 is PROPHETIC AN-NOUNCEMENT. As such, it has no fixed structure or form other than the announcement of future events, the character of which is determined by the contents of the unit. It appears to have some affinity to the (→) PROPHECY OF SALVATION insofar as its ultimate concern is to announce the purification of Zion and the salvation of the remnant of Israel in Zion, but the extensive use of judgment material in these chapters indicates that the prophecy of salvation does not fully constitute the generic pattern of this text. The use of the judgment material demonstrates that the basic character of this unit is not only to announce salvation but also to explain the purifying function of the punishment that leads to that salvation. In this respect, there are also some affinities with the (→) prophetic explanation of punishment, although the future form of chs. 2–4 precludes a precise analogy with this genre as well. One should note that a hortatory element is present here, insofar as the invitation to the "house of Jacob" (2:5) and the vivid portrayal of punishment and blessing are designed to prompt the audience to identify with the remnant that will be saved. But no specific instructions are given other than the implicit avoidance of that which increases human pride and self-reliance.

As noted above, chs. 2–4 are a composite unit. Although its present form is a PROPHETIC ANNOUNCEMENT concerning the cleansing of Zion, it employs a number of generic entities to achieve its purpose. The passage begins with the ANNOUNCEMENT concerning the future establishment of Zion as the center for YHWH's world rule (2:2-4), which sets forth the ideal goal toward which the rest of the text is directed. The ADDRESSES to the "house of Jacob" that follow are designed to explain how Jacob will attain this goal. The invitation to Jacob (2:5) and the attached ACCUSATION against Jacob (2:6-9) determine the basic explanatory character of this passage in that they highlight the discrepancy between the announced ideal of 2:2-4 and the reality of Jacob's unfitness to meet this ideal. The ADDRESSES in 2:10-21 and 2:22–4:6 employ a combination of judgment-oriented SPEECHES (2:10-21, 22; 3:1-15; and 3:16–4:1) together with the PROPHETIC ANNOUNCEMENT OF SALVATION in 4:2-6 to demonstrate how Jacob/Israel, and thus Zion, will be made fit for the ideal announced in 2:2-4.

Setting

Although a great deal of the material in chs. 2–4 derives from Isaiah ben Amoz, the present form of this text is not the product of the 8th-century prophet. Instead, the structural and conceptual coherence that characterizes this text derives from its editors, who assembled, arranged, and supplemented this material according to their understanding of its contents in relation to later historical situations.

A number of tensions within chs. 2–4 indicate that its constituent subunits were not composed in relation to each other according to a consistent purpose or for their present literary context. The textual subunits of this passage were composed for a number of different purposes in a variety of settings and were only secondarily placed together in their present form.

The most important of these tensions concerns the identity of the people or nation that is the central concern of the passage. According to the SUPER-SCRIPTION in 2:1, the text is concerned with Judah and Jerusalem. Although this is the overall perspective of chs. 2–4, the subunits betray different views. Isa 2:2-4 focuses entirely on Zion and the nations with no mention of Judah whatsoever. The mention of the "house of the God of Jacob" in v. 3 may well refer to Judah as part of all Israel centered around Zion (cf. Wildberger, "Völkerwallfahrt," 66-67), but this is hardly clear. The mention of the "house of Jacob" in 2:5 and 6 raises similar problems in that the referent has often been taken as the northern kingdom of Israel, or more correctly, all Israel. Despite the mention of "house of Jacob" in 2:6, the balance of 2:6-22 employs universal language such as *'ādām*, "humankind," *'ănāšîm*, "people," and *'ereṣ*, "land, earth." Isa 3:1-15 refers explicitly to Jerusalem and Judah, but 3:16–4:1 reverts to the "daughters of Zion" with no Judean reference whatsoever. Finally, the reference to Israel in 4:2-6 contrasts with the "house of Jacob" in 2:5 and 2:6, and the references to Zion and Jerusalem show no awareness of Judah except perhaps through the enigmatic *miqrā'ehā*, "its environs," in 4:5.

Another source of tension within chs. 2–4 stems from the fact that the constitutive subunits show little awareness of each other. For example, 2:2-4 focuses entirely on the nations' pilgrimage to Mt. Zion with no mention of Israel or Judah, both of which figure prominently in the following sections. Likewise, 4:2-6 presents the resolution of Jacob's unfitness to join in the pilgrimage within the structure of the entire passage, but shows no awareness of the nations, YHWH's torah from Zion, or the scenario of world peace. Instead, 4:2-6 focuses on the remnant of Israel in Jerusalem and the protection of the Temple Mount from the elements. The shift from Israel to Jerusalem in 4:2-6 may reflect the general arrangement of 2:5–4:1, but the absence of the "house of Jacob" and an explicit reference to Judah adds to the tension. Furthermore, 4:2-6 appears to place the blame for Jerusalem's past impurity on the "daughters of Zion" who are condemned in 3:16–4:1. But 4:2-6 fails to mention the male leaders who were condemned in 3:1-15. Another example concerns the "Day of YHWH" theme that permeates 2:10–4:6, but only through the general formula *bayyôm hahû'*, "in that day," which appears throughout the rest of chs. 1–39 and prophetic literature in general. Otherwise, there is no evidence that 3:1-15; 3:16–4:1; or 4:2-6 have anything to do with the announcement of the Day of

YHWH in 2:10-21 other than the general theme of punishment by YHWH. Finally, the invitation to the "house of Jacob" and the plea to desist from self-reliance in 2:22 use plural imperative verbs to address the people, but the warning statement in 2:10 uses singular imperative verbs.

Not only is there tension within chs. 2–4, but the key texts that determine the structure and general conceptual development of this text, 2:1; 2:2-4; 2:5; and 4:2-6, date to the exilic and early Persian periods.

As noted above, the designation "Judah and Jerusalem" is the common designation for the Jewish community centered around Jerusalem following the return from Babylonian exile. The appearance of this formula in 2:1 together with the indications discussed above that this superscription is structurally subsumed to that in 1:1 indicates a mid- to late-5th-century date for this verse.

Although Wildberger points to similarities between 2:2-4 on the one hand and both the Zion psalms and texts from Isaiah on the other hand to argue that Isaiah adapted Zion themes in composing this passage ("Völkerwallfahrt"; cf. Cazelles, "Isaïe II 2-5"; Roberts, "Isaiah 2"; and Wiklander), the evidence indicates that 2:2-4 dates to the late 6th century (Sweeney, "Isaiah 2–4"). First of all, whereas both the Zion psalms (Psalms 2; 46; 48; 76) and the Isaiah texts (Isa 8:9-10; 29:1-4; 31:4-5) emphasize YHWH's defeat of the nations and the breaking of their weapons prior to peace and their acknowledgment of YHWH, Isa 2:2-4 portrays the nations as voluntarily submitting to YHWH, seeking torah, and refashioning their weapons into agricultural implements. Second, such peaceful submission to YHWH and pilgrimage to Zion by the nations does not appear in biblical texts until the exilic or early postexilic periods (Jer 3:17-18; 16:19-21; Isa 60:1-7; Hag 2:6-9; Zech 2:8-12; 8:20-23). Third, a number of explicitly postexilic texts (e.g., Joel 4:9-12 [*RSV* 3:9-12]; Zech 8:20-23) as well as some whose late dates are established in critical discussion (Mic 4:1-4; Isa 37:20-32/2 Kgs 19:29-31; see Sweeney, "Isaiah 2–4"; idem, *Isaiah 1–4*, 164-74, for references) employ Isa 2:2-4 as a model in their composition. Otherwise, 51:4, "torah [*RSV* 'a law'] goes forth from me and my justice for a light to the peoples," serves as a model for the composition of 2:2-4 as indicated by its similar vocabulary and syntactical construction as well as its perspective of sending torah to the nations who will then return the exiles to Zion and submit to YHWH in shame. Trito-Isaiah (60:1-7) and Zechariah (Zech 2:8-12; 8:20-23) present the nations' voluntary pilgrimage to Zion not in shame but to recognize YHWH. The portrayal of the nations' voluntary pilgrimage to Zion to receive torah in Isa 2:2-4 stands in the middle of this line of development from Deutero-Isaiah to Trito-Isaiah and Zechariah insofar as it employs Isa 51:4 as its compositional model and serves as such for Zech 8:20-23. Finally, the vision of universal peace corresponds well to the expectations of Jews during the reign of Cyrus (539-530), whose peaceful conquest of Babylon and whose permission for the return of the Jewish exiles to Jerusalem and the rebuilding of the temple contributed to a general feeling of optimism. The political unrest that followed the death of Cyrus makes it unlikely that the passage was written later than the beginning of the reign of Darius I (522-486) and the building of the Second Temple (520-515).

Isaiah 2:5 plays a particularly important role in that it establishes the transition between 2:2-4 and the rest of the passages. In doing so, it establishes the basic character of this text, which explains the punishment of Israel as the means to purify Zion for its role as the center for YHWH's world rule. Isa 2:5 provides the only explicit connection between 2:2-4 and the balance of the text, in that it employs the language of 2:2-4 and provides a link to the following material by its use of the designation "house of Jacob," which also appears in 2:6. Indeed, 2:5 appears to have been deliberately composed to provide such a link (Sweeney, "Isaiah 2–4"). Scott ("Isaiah 1–39," 182) and Vermeylen (*Du prophète,* 131) note that 2:5 is a textual variant of 2:3, which employs similar vocabulary and grammatical forms. Furthermore, the appearance of *bêt ya'ăqōb* in v. 6 is awkward and appears to be an addition to a passage that never mentions the "house of Jacob" again but refers consistently to "humankind." This addition, of course, enables 2:5 to make the transition between 2:2-4 and 2:6ff. The composition of this verse would have to postdate that of 2:2-4.

Isaiah 4:2-6 depicts the future establishment of the remnant of Israel in a purified Zion with its protective Temple Mount. In this respect, it provides the climax for chs. 2–4, since it resolves the discrepancy between the ideal Zion portrayed in 2:2-4 and Jacob's less than ideal state in the following material. Scholars have already noted the shift in this passage between v. 2 and vv. 3-6 that indicates that vv. 3-6 were composed later than v. 2 and change the concern from the survivors of Israel to the remnant in Jerusalem. In its description of the restoration v. 2 employs the term *gā'ôn,* "pride, excellence," which corresponds to the terminology (*gē'eh,* "proud, exalted," 2:12) of 2:6-21 while providing a contrast to the concern with human pride and self-reliance. Nevertheless, the lack of correspondence between the vocabulary and concepts of 4:2, particularly its agricultural imagery, which appears nowhere else in chs. 2–4, indicates that it was not composed for its present position at the end of these chapters, but that it was drawn from some other context. The term *ṣemaḥ yhwh,* "shoot of YHWH," has been identified as a technical term for a messianic figure in the Prophets (J. G. Baldwin, "*Ṣemaḥ* as a Technical Term in the Prophets," *VT* 14 [1964] 93-97). It first appears as such in the exilic and early Persian periods. In its earliest forms it appears to describe a royal figure (Jer 23:3-5; 33:14-26), but later it is applied to priestly figures as well (Zech 3:8; 6:9-15). In its present context, it has been defined along priestly lines by vv. 3-6, which emphasize priestly concerns of holiness (v. 3), purification (v. 4), and the Temple Mount (vv. 5-6). Nevertheless, one cannot rule out an originally royal association for v. 2, and vv. 3-6 appear to have been added in part to remove any potential royal understanding in the aftermath of Zerubbabel's decline at the expense of the priesthood (cf. Hag 2:20-23; Zech 6:9-15). Furthermore, the emphasis on the survivors of Israel in v. 2, in contrast to the remnant in Zion in vv. 3-6, corresponds to Second Isaiah's concerns for the return of Israel or Jacob to Jerusalem. These considerations indicate that 4:2 was written in the 6th century prior to the building of the Second Temple and the decline of Zerubbabel. Vv. 3-6 stem from the mid- to late 5th century and represent the final redaction of the book (see below on 4:2-6).

Because 2:1 and 4:3-6 are late additions that pertain to the final redaction of the book, 2:2–4:2 is the basic compositional stratum of these chapters. Isa 2:5 is obviously the key text in determining the setting of this composition because it links the parts into a coherent whole. It presupposes 2:2-4, which were composed during the general peace of the reign of Cyrus (539-530), but adds material that indicates general upheaval in the form of the Day of YHWH and continued suffering for the people prior to the realization of peace. This material and the emphasis on the role of the Temple Mount in establishing peace among the nations suggest that the early years of Darius I (522-486) are the historical setting for the composition of this unit. The building of the Second Temple, the revolts and general upheaval that took place in the Persian empire at this time, and the view that the establishment of the temple would lead to recognition among the nations and general peace (Hag 1:6-9; Zech 8:20-23) are all presupposed by this text. But projection of Isa 2:2-4 as an ideal yet to be realized, and only after considerably more upheaval, indicates that the composition of this passage took place after the completion of the temple when the prophecies of Haggai and Zechariah failed to materialize. In this respect, Isaiah 2–4 represents a case of cognitive dissonance in which the postexilic Jewish community projected its unrealized expectations for the Second Temple into the future (cf. Carroll, *When Prophecy Failed*).

Intention

The structure and contents of chs. 2–4 demonstrate that its intention is to explain why the projected ideal of world peace and the nations' recognition of YHWH at Zion in 2:2-4 have not yet been realized and how the suffering of Israel will lead to this goal. In the context of its late-6th- or early-5th-century setting, this text provides a theological rationale for the disasters that Israel has endured at the hands of Babylonia: destruction and invasion (2:6-22), exile and poverty (3:1-15), and humiliation (3:16–4:1). Such disasters are the work of YHWH, who is punishing the people for their pride, self-reliance, and rejection of YHWH, and who is thereby preparing Zion for its intended role by reducing the people to a purified remnant centered around Jerusalem. An important aspect of this text, however, is its future orientation. In this respect, it also provides a rationale for future suffering and the fact that the ideal Jerusalem had not been attained with the building of the Second Temple and the restoration of Jerusalem. There is also a hortatory aspect, since the focus on the people's pride as the cause for punishment and the fact that the ideal Zion has not materialized suggest that the problem still persists. Although no specific call for a change of action appears in this text, the emphasis on human pride provides a subtle reminder of the people's responsibilities as part of a projected purified remnant. Furthermore, the emphasis on the nations in 2:2-4 and the use of universal language in 2:10-21 in reference to the Day of YHWH (cf. 2:22) place the concern with Zion in a worldwide context that accounts for the upheavals of the reign of Darius I (522-486).

This perspective holds true even in the context of the mid- to late 5th century when the final form of the book was produced. The addition of 2:1 and 4:3-6 does not significantly change the basic intention of this text. Nonetheless, several new elements appear with the addition of 4:3-6. One is the emphasis on a priestly understanding of the "shoot of YHWH," rather than on a royal figure, in 4:2. This emphasis legitimizes the priestly administration of Judah and Jerusalem under Ezra and Nehemiah. In addition, the emphasis on the pillar of cloud and flame over the Temple Mount emphasizes the motif that symbolized YHWH's leadership of the people in the exodus and wilderness traditions, and corresponds to Ezra's understanding of his return to Jerusalem as a new exodus and entry into the promised land (cf. Koch, "Ezra"). Finally, the focus on the daughters of Zion as the primary cause of Zion's pollution is striking. It appears that the author of this passage derived this view from the structure of this chapter, which places the women last and appears to assign them blame for the actions of the men (cf. 3:12 and the discussion below). Again, Ezra's focus on foreign women as the source for the pollution of the "holy seed" or "remnant" in Jerusalem (cf. Ezra 9–10, esp. 9:11, 14, 15) may well stand behind this assertion.

As noted in the discussion of the structure of the book as whole, Isaiah 2–4 serves as a programmatic introduction to chs. 5–27 and 28–35. In this respect, it introduces the Day of YHWH theme to which the *bayyôm hahû'*, "in that day," passages refer.

Bibliography

K. Budde, "Zu Jesaja 1–5," *ZAW* 49 (1931) 16-40, 182-211; 50 (1932) 38-72; H. Cazelles, "Qui aurait visé, à l'origine, Isaïe II 2-5?" *VT* 30 (1980) 409-20; H. Junker, "Sancta Civitas, Jerusalem Nova: Eine formkritische und überlieferungsgeschichtliche Studie zu Is 2," *TThSt* 15 (1962) 17-33; Koch, "Ezra" (→ "Introduction to the Book of Isaiah"); J. Magonet, "Isaiah 2:1–4:6, Some Poetic Structures and Tactics," *Amsterdamse Cahiers* 3 (1982) 71-85; J. J. M. Roberts, "Isaiah 2 and the Prophet's Message to the North," *JQR* 75 (1984-85) 290-308; M. A. Sweeney, "Structure and Redaction in Isaiah 2–4," *HAR* 11 (1987) 407-22; idem, *Isaiah 1–4* (→ "Introduction to the Book of Isaiah"), 35-36, 134-84; Tucker, "Prophetic Superscriptions" (→ "Introduction to the Prophetic Literature"); B. Wiklander, *Prophecy as Literature: A Text-Linguistic and Rhetorical Approach to Isaiah 2–4* (ConBOT 22; Uppsala: Gleerup, 1984); H. Wildberger, "Die Völkerwallfahrt zum Zion, Jes. II 1-5," *VT* 7 (1957) 62-81.

SUPERSCRIPTION, 2:1

Structure

Unlike 1:1, which clearly contains a superscription, 2:1 gives no indication of including a well-defined title. Its present form is simply a single statement.

Genre

This verse is clearly a SUPERSCRIPTION that defines the character of the following material as "the word that Isaiah ben Amoz saw concerning Judah and Jerusalem."

Setting

As noted above, this verse is clearly correlated with the superscription in 1:1 by its use of the qualification "that Isaiah ben Amoz saw" and the reference to "Judah and Jerusalem." The correlation with 1:1 and the appearance of the designation "Judah and Jerusalem" establish a mid- to late-5th-century setting for the verse in its present form. It is entirely possible that the verse was composed during the late 6th century as a superscription for 2:2–4:2, but there is no secure evidence for this claim.

Intention

The purpose of this verse is to identify all of chs. 2–4 as "the word that Isaiah ben Amoz saw concerning Judah and Jerusalem." Ackroyd's argument ("Note") that this verse was composed to identify only 2:2-4(5) as the work of Isaiah and not Micah (cf. Mic 4:1-5) must be rejected. Isa 2:2-4 focuses on Zion, with no mention of Judah. As noted above, the references to Jacob in 2:3 and 2:5 include all of Israel, not just Judah. In contrast to 2:2-4(5), chs. 2–4 as a whole focus specifically on Judah and Jerusalem as the remnant that will emerge from the punishment of Israel in a purified Zion.

Bibliography

P. R. Ackroyd, "A Note on Isaiah 2,1," *ZAW* 75 (1963) 320-21; Tucker, "Prophetic Superscriptions" (→ "Introduction to the Prophetic Literature"), 56-70.

PROPHETIC ANNOUNCEMENT CONCERNING ZION'S ROLE AS CENTER FOR YHWH'S WORLD RULE, 2:2-4

Structure

I. Concerning the fact of Zion's establishment	2-3a
A. Cosmological dimension: elevation of Zion	2a
B. Social/political dimension: nations' pilgrimage to Zion	2b-3a
II. Concerning reason for Zion's establishment	3b-4
A. Reason proper: YHWH's torah	3b-4bα
B. Consequences/results: world peace under YHWH's rule at Zion	4bβ

The boundaries of this unit are determined by its future orientation, its focus on Zion and the nations, the 3rd-person descriptive language employed throughout the passage, and the absence of any specific indication of its addressee. Although many scholars maintain that 2:5 is part of this unit because of its lexical similarities and its idyllic contents, this view must be rejected. The lack of a syntactical link between vv. 4 and 5, the use of an imperative address to the "house of Jacob," and the explanatory *kî* in v. 6 (which links vv. 5 and 6ff. together) demonstrate that v. 5 introduces a new structural subunit within chs. 2–4.

The structure of the passage is constituted by a combination of its syntactical features and its contents, particularly the imagery of ascent and descent. Vv. 2-3a constitute a *wāw*-consecutive verbal formation in which the imperfect verbal statement *nākôn yihyeh*, "shall be established," governs the following converted perfect verbs. The converted perfect verbs then describe the primary action of the statement, which is directed toward ascending the mountain. Two perspectives are evident within vv. 2-3a: the cosmological dimension, which describes the elevation of Zion in v. 2a, and the social and political dimension, which describes the nations' ascent of the mountain in vv. 2b-3a.

Verses 3b-4 begin with a causal *kî* that links this section to vv. 2-3b and defines YHWH's torah as the reason for Zion's establishment. Again, the section is constituted by a *wāw*-consecutive verbal formation beginning with the imperfect *tēṣē'*, "shall go forth," in v. 3b and extending through the converted perfects in v. 4a-bα that describe YHWH's judging the nations and the reworking of their weapons into agricultural tools. V. 4bβ is syntactically independent of vv. 3b-4bα, but provides a summary statement of the peace that results from YHWH's dispensing torah among the nations. Vv. 3b-4 provide a chiastic contrast to vv. 2-3a by emphasizing the torah that descends from Zion to the nations (see Magonet).

Genre

The genre of this passage is frequently defined as a (→) description of salvation (Kaiser, *Isaiah 1–12,* 49) or a word of promise (Fohrer, *Jesaja,* 1:47; Wildberger, *Jesaja,* 78) on the basis of its contents. But the absence of a fixed generic form and the nature of the contents of this passage indicate that it is simply a PROPHETIC ANNOUNCEMENT stating the future establishment of Zion as the center for YHWH's world rule.

Setting

As noted above, a number of factors indicate that the reign of King Cyrus (539-530 B.C.E.) provides the historical setting for this passage. Its differences from Isaiah's use of the Zion tradition (cf. 8:9-10; 29:1-4; 31:4-5), its dependence on 51:4, its influence on early postexilic texts such as Zech 8:20-23 and Isa 37:20-32/2 Kgs 19:29-31, and its general vision of peace and the nations' voluntary recognition of YHWH all support this setting.

The passage also appears in Mic 4:1-5 in a somewhat different form. The relationship between the two passages has been thoroughly discussed (cf. Kilian, *Jesaja 1–39,* 86-91; B. Renaud, *La formation du livre de Michée* [EBib; Paris:

Gabalda, 1977] 160-63; Wildberger, *Jesaja,* 78-80). The addition of material in Isa 2:4-5 presupposes 2:2-3 and 1 Kgs 5:5 and appears to be the result of the editor's attempt to universalize Mic 4:1-5 (cf. B. Renaud, *Michée-Sophonie-Nahum* [SB; Paris: Gabalda, 1987] 72-73).

Intention

The purpose of this passage is clearly to portray Zion as the center for YHWH's rule of the nations in an era of world peace. The passage is frequently described as eschatological because of the opening statement, *wĕhāyâ bĕ'aḥărît hayyāmîm,* "and it shall come to pass in the latter days," and its rendering in the LXX as *hoti estai en tais eschatais hēmerais,* "and it shall come to pass in the final days." But as semantic studies of the phrase have shown, particularly in relation to the Akkadian *ina aḥrat umi,* "in future days," it refers merely to a time in the future, not to the eschatological end of time (Wildberger, *Jesaja,* 81-82; cf. S. J. De Vries, *Yesterday, Today, and Tomorrow* [Grand Rapids: Eerdmans, 1975] 50). The historical setting of this passage in the reign of King Cyrus is particularly important because of Cyrus's lenient treatment of Jews, including his permission to return to Jerusalem and rebuild the temple (2 Chr 36:22-23; Ezra 1:1-4; 6:3-5; cf. *ANET,* 316). Although this policy was selectively applied (cf. A. Kuhrt, "The Cyrus Cylinder and Achaemenid Imperial Policy," *JSOT* 25 [1983] 83-97), its application to Judah and the Judean exiles prompted great optimism for the reestablishment of Jerusalem and an ensuing era of peace. His assumption of the Babylonian throne and the traditions of Babylon's ziggurat Entemenaki as the center for divine rule and peace for the earth (cf. Enuma Elish, *ANET,* 60-72) were apparently influential in this respect. At this point, Babylon, the symbol of the nations and their threat to Judah, emerged as Judah's benefactor under Cyrus. Cyrus had already been identified as YHWH's anointed and the builder of the temple in Isa 44:28 and 45:1. Because Cyrus was sometimes understood as the earthly agent through whom YHWH worked, the author of 2:2-4 presented YHWH as the true ruler of the world and Zion as the true location of YHWH's rule of the nations and the source for world peace. The reestablishment of Jerusalem and the temple would be understood as a sign that this era of peace had been realized.

Bibliography

K. Budde, "Verfasser und Stelle von Mi. 4,1-4 (Jes. 2,2-4)," *ZDMG* 81 (1927) 152-58; M. Delcor, "Sion, centre universel," in *Études bibliques et orientales des religions comparées* (Leiden: Brill, 1979) 92-97; J. Magonet, "Isaiah's Mountain or the Shape of Things to Come," *Prooftexts* 11 (1991) 175-81; G. von Rad, "The City on the Hill," in *The Problem of the Hexateuch and Other Essays* (tr. E. W. Trueman Dicken; New York: McGraw-Hill, 1966) 232-42; J. J. M. Roberts, "Double Entendre in First Isaiah," *CBQ* 54 (1992) 39-48; S. Talmon, "Prophetic Rhetoric and Agricultural Metaphor," in *Storia e tradizioni di Israele* (Fest. J. A. Soggin; ed. D. Garrone and F. Israel; Brescia: Paideia,

1991) 267-79; H. W. Wolff, "Schwerter zu Pflugscharen — Missbrauch eines Prophetenwortes? Praktische Fragen und exegetische Klärungen zu Joël 4,9-12, Jes 2,2-5 und Mic 4,1-5," *EvT* 44 (1984) 280-92.

PROPHETIC ANNOUNCEMENT CONCERNING THE PUNISHMENT OF JACOB/HUMANKIND: THE DAY OF YHWH, 2:5-21

Structure

Discussion of the structure of this passage is complicated by its association with 2:22 and 3:1–4:6 in the final edited form of the text. The juxtaposition of these passages is clearly the result of editorial activity that sought to focus on Judah and Jerusalem (3:1–4:6) in the context of a general announcement of the Day of YHWH against Jacob or humankind, thereby preparing the reader for the notion that the remnant in Jerusalem constitutes the survivors of Israel (4:2-6). The issue is further complicated by the redactional addition of the invitation to the house of Jacob in 2:5 and the reference to the house of Jacob in 2:6. When considered apart from 2:22 and 3:1–4:6, the structure of 2:5-21 is constituted by its imperative addresses to its audience in 2:5 and 2:10. The unit is demarcated by its imperative address form, its concern with the house of Jacob and humankind, and its overall focus on the Day of YHWH.

The structure of the first address in 2:5-9 is defined by the imperative invitation to the house of Jacob in v. 5 and the following material in vv. 6-9 that is attached to v. 5 by an explanatory *kî*. The 2nd-person address forms in v. 6aα and v. 9b have presented problems to interpreters because of the use of 3rd-person forms throughout the rest of the passage. Although many scholars have followed the LXX and other versions in emending these passages to make them more consistent with the 3rd-person forms in vv. 6aβ-9a, a thorough examination of the readings preserved in the VSS demonstrates that they represent the translator's or scribe's attempts to make sense out of a confusing text (Sweeney, *Isaiah 1–4*, 139-41). The discrepancy in form is due to the author's attempt to cast vv. 6-9 as an accusation speeech against Jacob addressed to YHWH. In this respect, the two 2nd-person addresses to YHWH in v. 6aα and v. 9b constitute the basic structure of this address. Vv. 6aβ-9a are attached to v. 6aα by *kî* and serve as an explanation of the reasons for YHWH's rejection of Jacob. The syntactical break between v. 8a and 8b indicates two basic reasons for the rejection: the land is corrupted with false gods (vv. 6aβ-8a) and the people are corrupted with false gods (vv. 8b-9a). Consequently, vv. 6-9a constitute the accusation speech proper and v. 9b is a petition to YHWH not to pardon the people.

The structure of the second announcement in vv. 10-21 is likewise defined by its imperative address in vv. 10-11 and the explanatory material introduced by *kî* in vv. 12-21. The subunit is constituted as an address to the people and focuses entirely on describing the Day of YHWH and its consequences. The imperative address in vv. 10-11 functions as a warning insofar as it includes a command to hide (v. 10) and a statement that the fall of human pride and the exaltation of YHWH (v. 11) are the reasons for the command to hide. The basis for this warning is then spelled out in vv. 12-21 in the form of an announcement of the Day of YHWH. Vv. 12-19 describe the Day of YHWH and its consequences in a series of statements that are all linked by copulative *wāw*s. The basic statement in v. 12 explains that the Day of YHWH is directed against all that it is high, uplifted, etc. (v. 12a-bα), and that such symbols of human pride will fall as a consequence (v. 12bβ). This is specified in vv. 13-19. Vv. 13-16 contain a catalog of common symbols of pride including trees (v. 13), mountains (v. 14), fortifications (v. 15), and ships (v. 16). The consequences are then spelled out in vv. 17-19. In general they include the humiliation of humankind and the exaltation of YHWH, recapping the theme of the warning in vv. 10-11. Specifically they include humankind's rejection of the false gods in the face of

YHWH's splendor. This last point is particularly important because the reference to the false gods links vv. 10-19 with vv. 6-9, which prominently mention the false gods. Vv. 20-21 are syntactically independent of vv. 12-19, but they are linked by their introductory reference to the Day of YHWH with the formula *bayyôm hahû'*, "in that day." In this respect, they summarize the results of the Day of YHWH for humankind: rejection of the false gods (v. 20) in order to hide from YHWH's splendor (v. 21).

Genre

Discussion of the generic character of 2:5-21 is likewise complicated by its redactional association with 2:22 and 3:1–4:6, as well as by the additions made to the original material in 2:5, 6, and 20-21. As noted in the discussion of the final form of chs. 2–4, 2:5–4:6 constitute a PROPHETIC ANNOUNCEMENT of the cleansing of Zion. With the elimination of the plea to desist from self-reliance in 2:22 and the material concerning Judah and Jerusalem in 3:1–4:6, the character of this material changes to a PROPHETIC ANNOUNCEMENT concerning the punishment of Jacob or humankind.

As noted above, 2:5 is an editorial addition to this text designed to link it to 2:2-4. Generically, this verse constitutes an INVITATION and influences the overall understanding of the passage by focusing on the "house of Jacob" in particular rather than humankind in general and by emphasizing the contrast between Jacob's present state and the ideal put forward in 2:2-4. In this respect, 2:5 and the addition of "house of Jacob" in 2:6 transform the concern of this text to the cleansing of Jacob as a preparation for its role in the ideal Zion.

When one considers 2:6-21 apart from 2:5 and the addition of the "house of Jacob" in 2:6, its generic character changes somewhat. It is no longer concerned with the preparation of Jacob for a role in the ideal Zion but with the general punishment of humankind on the Day of YHWH. Although its basic genre is still that of PROPHETIC ANNOUNCEMENT, insofar as the unit is constituted as a proclamation of the Day of YHWH, the text appears to be based on a modified form of the PROPHECY OF PUNISHMENT over the people. The ACCUSATION SPEECH is presented in the form of an ADDRESS by the prophet to YHWH rather than the people in vv. 6-9. Vv. 10-21 clearly constitute the ANNOUNCEMENT of the intervention of God (punishment) in the form of the Day of YHWH, albeit without the usual (→) messenger formula or *lākēn*, "therefore," that characterize the PROPHECY OF PUNISHMENT genre.

Even this characterization is influenced by additional material in vv. 20-21. These verses were added to explain the somewhat enigmatic vv. 18-19 (see below). But in attempting to clarify vv. 18-19, vv. 20-21 change the character of the passage from one that focuses on the Day of YHWH as a purge of the *'ĕlîlîm*, "false gods," to one that focuses on the punishment of the people themselves.

Setting

Apart from the redactional additions in 2:5 and 2:6, the bulk of the remaining material in 2:6-21 derives from the prophet Isaiah. An exception to this, however, appears in vv. 20-21. These verses borrow a great deal of their language from other parts of the oracle, including *bayyôm hahû'*, "in that day" (cf. vv. 12, 17); *'ĕlîlê kaspô*, "false gods of silver," and *'ĕlîlê zĕhābô*, "false gods of gold" (cf. vv. 7a, 8a, 18); *'ăšer 'āśû-lô lĕhištaḥăwōt*, "which they made for themselves to worship" (cf. v. 8b); *lābô' bĕniqrôt haṣṣurîm ûbisʿipê hasselāʿîm*, "to enter the cracks of the stones and the crevices of the rocks" (cf. vv. 10a, 19a); and *mippĕnê paḥad yhwh ûmēhădar gĕʾônô bĕqûmô laʿărōṣ hāʾāreṣ*, "because of [*RSV* 'from before'] the fear of YHWH and because of [*RSV* 'from before'] his glorious splendor when he arises to terrify the earth" (cf. vv. 10b, 19b).

In addition, vv. 20-21 are parallel to the enigmatic vv. 18-19 and appear to be designed to clarify their meaning. The text of v. 18 is uncertain (see Sweeney, *Isaiah 1–4*, 176) but it clearly indicates that the "false gods" are the object of punishment who will hide from YHWH's wrath. According to vv. 20-21, humankind will cast off its false gods in order to hide from YHWH. The effect of vv. 20-21 is to shift responsibility for the Day of YHWH to the people, since they, rather than the false gods, are now portrayed as the object of YHWH's anger. Vv. 20-21 refer only to 2:6-19 and show no awareness of the text in its larger redactional context. Consequently, this addition must date to the period before the redactional addition of 2:2-4 and 2:5-6*. These verses give no indication of a specific historical setting or organizational role in the larger structure of chs. 2–4 and can be placed any time from the late 8th to the late 6th century. Although the unity of the remaining material in 2:6-19 is frequently questioned on the grounds that these verses vary in form (cf. Wildberger, *Jesaja*, 95-96), they should be considered a unified composition. Wildberger's four original units, vv. 6, 7-9a(18), 12-17, and 19, are unable to stand alone. The refrains in vv. 9a, 11, and 17 bind this material together, and vv. 18-19 combine the two primary themes of vv. 6-9 (*'ĕlîlîm*, "false gods") and vv. 10-17 (hiding from the splendor of YHWH) in a summarizing statement of the results of the Day of YHWH.

The historical setting for 2:6-19 appears to be during the reign of Hezekiah, prior to Sennacherib's invasion. Hezekiah was known for his political alliances with foreign nations in an effort to oppose Assyrian hegemony. Principal allies included Egypt, Philistia, and Phoenicia. Hezekiah subdued Philistia early in his reign (cf. 2 Kgs 18:8) and appears to have placed an ally on the throne of Ekron (cf. *ANET*, 287) to guarantee support (cf. v. 6). Egypt was well known for producing chariots (cf. v. 7b), and the *śĕkîyôt*, "water crafts," of v. 16 have been identified as a type of Egyptian vessel (Clements, *Isaiah 1–39*, 46). The mention of *qedem*, "east," has been taken as a reference to Aram and together with the mention of Jacob in v. 6 as an indication that this oracle refers to the northern kingdom of Israel during the Syro-Ephraimite War (Cazelles, "Isaïe II 2-5," 413). As noted above, "Jacob" refers to all Israel centered at Zion in this context. Although the use of *qedem* may be associated with upper Retinu or north Canaan in the Egyptian story of Sinuhe (cf. *ANET*, 19 n. 10), the term is commonly used as a general reference to territory east of Egypt, with no indication of Aram as a special referent (cf. KB, s.v. *qedem;* contra Roberts, "Isaiah 2," 301). Furthermore, *qedem* is used in relation to Aram in 9:11 and in relation to Edom, Moab, and Ammon in 11:14-15, indicating that it is simply a general term for the east. In this respect, Hezekiah's alliances with eastern countries, such as Babylon (cf. 39:1-8) or possibly Moab, Edom, and Ammon, would be presupposed here. Finally, Hezekiah's attempts to fortify the city (cf. v. 15), his relations with Phoenicia (cf. vv. 13, 16a), and his financial preparations for the revolt (v. 7a) are all attested elsewhere (2 Chr 32:27-31; on Phoenicia, see *ANET,* 287-88). Isaiah's opposition to Hezekiah's alliances (Isa 19:1-3; 30:1-7; cf. 18:1-7) is entirely consistent with the perspective of this passage. Consequently, its date must be sometime between 715 and 701.

Intention

In view of the above remarks, it is clear that the intention of this passage is to express Isaiah's opposition to Hezekiah's preparations for revolt against Assyria. Like Amos (cf. Amos 5:18-20), Isaiah employs the motif of the Day of YHWH to express his opposition. The Day of YHWH was apparently drawn from ancient Israel's holy war traditions, which portrayed YHWH as fighting on behalf of Israel's enemies (cf. G. von Rad, *Old Testament Theology* [tr. D. M. G. Stalker; 2 vols.; New York: Harper & Row, 1962-65] 2:119-25). Here the motif has been reversed so that it appears as a threat against the people and thus enhances both the prophet's emphasis on YHWH's opposition to Hezekiah's actions and the impact of the oracle on its audience. The use of universal language is hardly surprising here, since the Day of YHWH was generally directed against other nations. A shift to language referring directly to Jerusalem and Judah, such as that of 3:1–4:1, would likewise enhance the impact of the prophet's words. The technique was previously used by Amos in his oracles against the nations and their climactic critique of Israel (Amos 1:3–2:16). Isaiah is likewise well acquainted with such rhetorical strategies (cf. Isa 5:1-7).

Bibliography

J. Blenkinsopp, "Fragments of Ancient Exegesis in an Isaian Poem (Jes 2,6-22)," *ZAW* 93 (1981) 51-62; Cazelles, "Isaïe II 2-5?" (→ 2:1–4:6); R. Davidson, "The Interpretation of Isaiah II 6ff.," *VT* 16 (1966) 1-7; A. Marx, "Esaïe ii 20, une signature karaïte?" *VT* (1990) 232-37; L. Neveu, "Isaïe 2,6-22: le Jour de YHWH," in *La vie de la Parole: De l'Ancien au Nouveau Testament* (*Fest.* P. Grelot; Paris: Desclée, 1987) 129-38; B. C. Ollenburger, *Zion, City of the Great King: A Theological Symbol of the Jerusalem Cult* (JSOTSup 41; Sheffield: JSOT Press, 1987) 110-12; Roberts, "Isaiah 2" (→ 2:1–4:6); J. S. Rogers, "An Allusion to Coronation in Isaiah 2:6," *CBQ* 51 (1989) 232-36; K. Seybold, "Die anthropologischen Beiträge aus Jesaja 2," *ZTK* 74 (1977) 401-15.

ADDRESS CONCERNING THE PROCESS OF CLEANSING: APPLICATION TO JERUSALEM AND JUDAH, 2:22–4:6

Structure

Discussion of the structure of 2:22–4:6 is complicated by its composite nature. Although its present form displays a coherent structure and intent within the larger context of chs. 2–4, it contains a number of disparate texts composed for different purposes and in different historical settings.

The major division within this unit is between 2:22 and 3:1–4:6. The plea to desist from human self-reliance clearly relates to the preceding material in 2:5-21, as indicated by its universal perspective concerning *hā'ādām,* "humankind," and its imperative address form that corresponds to 2:5 and 2:10. By contrast, 3:1–4:6 employs 3rd-person announcement language and focuses entirely on Jerusalem and Judah. This section is connected to 2:22 by the explanatory *kî* in 3:1. In the context of chs. 2–4, 2:22 provides the transition from the universal concerns of the Day of YHWH in 2:10-21 to a specific concern with Jerusalem and Judah. Isa 3:1–4:6 explains the fate of Jerusalem and Judah on the Day of YHWH.

Within 3:1–4:6, 3:1–4:1 focuses on the punishment of Jerusalem and Judah, and 4:2-6 focuses on the salvation of the remnant of the people in Zion. Although there is no syntactical connection between these two units, they are nonetheless bound together by the common references to "that day" (4:2; cf. 3:7, 18; 4:1), the overall concern with the punishment of Jerusalem, the dominant 3rd-person announcement language, and the focus on the daughters of Zion (4:4; cf. 3:16-17).

The prophetic explanation of punishment in 3:1-11 constitutes the first major structural subunit of 3:1–4:1. Although 3:1-11 and 3:12-15 are frequently grouped together because of their similar focus on the leaders of the people, there are compelling grounds for associating 3:1-11 more closely with 3:16–4:1 (see below). The structure of 3:1-11 is determined by the interest in presenting an explanation for the deportation of the leaders of Jerusalem and Judah. Vv. 1-7 begin by describing the removal of the leaders in catalog fashion with a single sentence (vv. 1-3) and the chaos that will result from the absence of persons capable of exercising authority (vv. 4-7). The explanation for this disastrous state of affairs appears in vv. 8-11, introduced by an explanatory *kî*. Vv. 8-9 maintain that the cause for this calamity is the people's rebellious nature. The explanatory statement is expanded by vv. 10-11, which appear to be modeled on the "woe" statement in v. 9b ("Woe to them, for they have accomplished evil for themselves") and attempt to comment on its sentiments. The first (v. 10) asserts that such a calamity is justified because the people are eating the fruit of their deeds, but the second laments the fate of the wicked, who will suffer the consequences of their own actions (v. 11).

Isaiah 3:12–4:1 constitutes a prophetic announcement of judgment against the leaders and the women of Jerusalem. Vv. 12-15 are commonly associated with vv. 1-11 because of their focus on YHWH's judgment against the leaders, but several considerations indicate that they should be associated with 3:16–4:1

instead. First, there is no syntactical connection between vv. 12-15 and the preceding material. Second, the *waw*-consecutive statement at the beginning of v. 16 establishes a syntactical connection between 3:16–4:1 and 3:12-15. Finally, v. 12a maintains that women rule over the people. Although the original reading of *wĕnāšîm*, "and women," may well have been *wĕnōšîm*, "and creditors" (cf. LXX, TJ), the statement associates these verses with 3:16–4:1 by pointing to the interrelationship between the leaders and the women of Jerusalem. The juxtaposition of these sections indicates that the position and thus the wardrobes of the women are gained by the leaders' oppression of the poor (3:14b-15a). Although the women are emphasized in 3:16–4:1, their suffering is linked to the death of the men (3:25). When considered in relation to each other, 3:12-15 and 3:16–4:1 constitute a prophetic judgment speech. When considered individually, 3:12-15 presents the accusation speech against the leaders and 3:16–4:1 presents the announcement of judgment against the women.

The accusation speech in 3:12-15 includes a syntactically independent lament in v. 12 that decries the corruption of the people by incompetent leaders. The trial scene in vv. 13-15 portrays YHWH's confrontation with the leaders. Within this scene, vv. 13-14a state YHWH's actions to initiate the lawsuit and vv. 14b-15 contain an oracular report of YHWH's court speech, including YHWH's rhetorical questions as to why they oppress the people.

The structure of the announcement of judgment against the women in 3:16–4:1 is constituted by the report of YHWH's judgment speech in 3:16-17 and an elaboration of the consequences in 3:18–4:1. Although 3:16-17 is frequently understood as a combination of accusation and judgment, the word-play in v. 16 concerning chained feet indicates that the passage can be understood both in relation to the fashionable walk of the Jerusalem women and to the chained procession of captives (cf. Sweeney, *Isaiah 1–4*, 155-56). The consequences of judgment appear in 3:18–4:1 introduced by *bayyôm hahû'*, "in that day." Vv. 18-23 describe YHWH's removal of the women's finery in catalog fashion, and 3:24–4:1 describe the resulting degradation. The structure of 3:24–4:1 is defined as a series of contrasts between the former dress of the women and their present destitute state. Specific examples occur in v. 24a, and the general summation follows in 3:24b–4:1. V. 24b has presented a problem to text critics because no obvious contrast is presented for the statement "for instead of beauty," as in v. 24a. Although the LXX and Vulgate delete the statement and 1QIs^a adds *bšt*, "shame," the MT appears to be correct. The contrast is provided by the following oracle in 3:25–4:1, which graphically depicts the desperate state of the women (Wiklander, 80-81; Sweeney, *Isaiah 1–4*, 154). The form of this oracle is an announcement of punishment that includes the announcement of the death of the city's men (3:25) and the consequent humiliation of the women (3:26–4:1).

The prophetic announcement of salvation in 4:2-6 concludes the unit and counterbalances the judgment material in 3:1–4:1. With its introductory *bayyôm hahû'*, "in that day," it indicates that there will be a positive outcome to the previously announced punishment of Jerusalem and Judah. It begins with a statement announcing the restoration of the survivors of Israel in v. 2. This is followed in vv. 3-6 by a specification that the remnant in Jerusalem will be sanctified for life (v. 3) and that YHWH will protect Zion and the Temple Mount (vv. 4-6). The references to washing away the "filth of the daughters of Zion" and "bloodstains of Jerusalem" indicate that the previously announced punishment is understood as a cleansing of the city in preparation for its holy status and protection by YHWH.

Genre

The composite nature of this unit also complicates the discussion of its generic character. Although it contains a variety of generic entities, the imperative statement in 2:22 defines the generic character of the entire unit as an ADDRESS. Isa 2:22 is a WISDOM SAYING (cf. Ps 118:8-9; Isa 31:1-3), the primary function of which is to instruct its audience. In this case the content of the instruction is to desist from human self-reliance, which is illustrated in the following explication (3:1–4:6) by a demonstration that all symbols of human pride, including the leadership of Judah and Jerusalem and the status of the women, are to be removed by YHWH and replaced with an exalted remnant in a purified Jerusalem. Although the addressee is not named here, the context defines "house of Jacob" (2:5) as the addressee. The contents of the unit define it as an ADDRESS concerning the process of cleansing Judah and Jerusalem.

The first generic element of the explication is the PROPHETIC EXPLANATION OF PUNISHMENT in 3:1-9 that introduces the section concerned with the punishment of Jerusalem and Judah. Although this genre is obviously related to the (→) prophetic announcement of punishment, it reverses the normal sequence of accusation and punishment by beginning with a DESCRIPTION OF PUNISHMENT in vv. 1-7. This is followed by material of an accusatory nature in vv. 8-9 that functions as a PROPHETIC EXPLANATION OF PUNISHMENT. Instead of condemning an accused party, this text inquires into the cause of punishment. The appended material in vv. 10-11 constitutes two WISDOM STATEMENTS. Although *'imrû*, "say," in v. 10 is frequently emended to *'ašrê*, "happy," on the basis of the parallel to *'ôy*, "woe," in v. 11, this is unjustified. The VSS offer no textual basis for this emendation, and the parallel appears to be unduly influenced by Luke 6:20-26 (cf. Holladay, 484). In their present context, they comment on the meaning of the WOE STATEMENT in v. 9b. The imperative in v. 10 affirms the righteousness of retribution for one's deeds, and v. 11 expresses regret for the wicked who suffer this punishment. This is followed by a PROPHETIC ANNOUNCEMENT OF JUDGMENT against the leaders and women in 3:12–4:1. Vv. 3:12-15 include a LAMENT concerning the corruption of the people by the leaders and women (v. 12) and a REPORT of YHWH's ACCUSATION SPEECH against the leaders. Together, vv. 12-15 constitute the ACCUSATION against the leaders. The ANNOUNCEMENT OF PUNISHMENT appears in 3:16–4:1 and encompasses both the women and the men. Although the section is initially directed against the women with a report of YHWH's judgment speech against the women (3:16-17) and a CATALOG of the women's finery that is to be removed (3:18-23), the JUDGMENT SPEECH in 3:25–4:1 includes the death of the men as the cause for the degradation of the women. The effect is to tie punishment of the women together with that of the men, just as the present text of 3:12-15 includes the women in the accusation against the leaders.

Finally, 4:2-6 constitutes a DESCRIPTION OF SALVATION. It derives from the (→) prophetic announcement of salvation but lacks the usual messenger formulation of that genre. Instead, it focuses on the effects of YHWH's intervention.

Setting

Obviously, the setting of the final form of chs. 2–4 determines the historical setting of 2:22–4:6. But the composite nature of this text and the Isaianic origin of much of its material complicate the issue. Two texts deserve special attention because of their determinative roles in placing this material within the larger framework of chs. 2–4. Isa 2:22 provides the transition between the two addresses to the "house of Jacob" in 2:5-9 and 2:10-21 concerning the Day of YHWH, on the one hand, and material relating to Jerusalem and Judah in 3:1–4:6, on the other hand. Isa 4:2-6 provides the climactic conclusion to the process of cleansing Zion and relates back to the initial portrayal of an ideal Zion in 2:2-4. The balance of the material in 3:1–4:1 does not directly constitute the structure of the larger context.

Isaiah 2:22 is a notoriously difficult text to date. Although it plays a determinative role in the structure of chs. 2–4, it does not appear to have been composed for that role in that its vocabulary shows no special awareness or connection with either the preceding or the following material, other than the use of hāʾādām, "humankind," which echoes the language of 2:6-21. Its absence in the LXX has suggested to many scholars that it is a late gloss to the text, but it could only have been added to relate to 2:6-21 and not to 3:1ff. Its wisdom character makes it a potential candidate for Isaianic authorship, since the prophet frequently employs wisdom forms. Unfortunately, there is no other clear evidence to date this text. Its date of composition could be any time from the late 8th century to the late 6th or early 5th century when the basic structure of chs. 2–4 was established.

Isaiah 3:1-9 appears to presuppose the deportation of leading figures in Jerusalemite and Judean society, including military leaders, administrative personnel, and skilled craftspersons. The deportation of such figures was a common element of Assyrian policy in dealing with rebellious provinces and vassal states, and is attested as part of Sennacherib's sanctions against Judah in the aftermath of Hezekiah's revolt in 701 (ANET, 288). The participial formation of this section (cf. v. 1) and its character as a prophetic explanation of punishment indicate that the deportation was taking place when the passage was composed. One can conclude, therefore, that it was composed in the immediate aftermath of Hezekiah's revolt in 701.

The wisdom sayings in vv. 10-11 clearly presuppose v. 9b in that they comment on the meaning of this verse. Furthermore, they borrow vocabulary from vv. 8-9, including maʿallêhem, "their actions" (v. 10; cf. maʿallêhem in v. 8); rāʿ, "evil" (v. 11; cf. rāʿâ, "evil," in v. 9); gĕmûl, "deed" (v. 11; cf.

gāmĕlû, "they have done," in v. 9); and *'ôy,* "woe" (v. 11; cf. *'ôy* in v. 9b). Again, a precise date is difficult to determine, but the wisdom character of these sayings makes Isaianic authorship at least a possibility. Consequently, these verses, like v. 22, can be dated anytime between the late 8th century and the late 6th or early 5th century.

Although 3:12–4:1 constitutes a prophetic announcement of judgment, its constituent parts do not appear to have been composed in relation to each other. The accusation against the leaders does not appear to have included the women originally, in that the LXX and TJ understood *wĕnāšîm,* "and women," in v. 12 as *wĕnōšîm,* "and creditors." The reference to "creditors" better fits the context, which stresses the oppression of the people and the taking of spoil from them. The reference to "women" apparently reflects the association of this passage with 3:16–4:1. Likewise, the reference to men in 3:25 does not explicitly presuppose the leaders of 3:12-15, but constitutes only a secondary association.

Isaiah 3:12 is a key text in understanding the composition of this passage, since it provides the transition between 3:1-9 (10-11) and 3:12–4:1. It borrows a great deal of its vocabulary from vv. 1-9, including *nōgĕśāw,* "its oppressors" (cf. *wĕniggaś,* "and he shall oppress," in v. 5); *mĕ'ôlēl,* "wantonness" (cf. *wĕta'ălûlîm,* "mischiefs," in v. 4); and *māšĕlû bô,* "ruled it" (cf. *yimšĕlû-bām,* "shall rule them," in v. 4). Furthermore, the situation described in vv. 13-15 does not exactly correspond to vv. 1-9, in that vv. 8-9 presuppose that the people are corrupt, not oppressed as in vv. 13-15. Furthermore, vv. 13-15 mention only elders and commanders, not the comprehensive catalog of vv. 1-3. The general charge of injustice against leaders in vv. 13-15 could have been composed at any time during Isaiah's career, and it appears that v. 12 was composed by the prophet to link vv. 13-15 to vv. 1-9(10-11). The original association of vv. 12-15 with vv. 1-9(10-11) is indicated not only by the interest in relating an earlier condemnation of the leaders by the prophet to their deportation in 701, but also by the *inclusio* formed between the oracular formula *nĕ'um 'ădōnāy yhwh ṣĕbā'ôt,* "oracle of the Lord YHWH of hosts," in v. 15b and *hā'ādôn yhwh ṣĕbā'ôt,* "the Lord YHWH of hosts," in v. 1.

The 2nd-person feminine address form of 3:25–4:1 indicates that these verses were originally addressed to a city, most probably Jerusalem, and that they were originally composed for a context other than 3:16–4:1. Their presupposition that the city will be devastated indicates that they were composed in relation to Hezekiah's revolt, when such an event was a distinct possibility. Furthermore, the incomplete nature of v. 24b indicates that 3:25–4:1 was deliberately worked into the structure of 3:16–4:1. The material in 3:16-24 could have been composed at any time, but the emphasis on fine clothing indicates a time of prosperity, such as during the reign of Hezekiah. Again, the association of this material with 3:1-15 indicates an interest in confirming earlier statements by the prophet in the aftermath of Hezekiah's revolt.

Isaiah 4:2-6 appears to be a composite text. Whereas v. 2 focuses on the survivors of *Israel,* vv. 3-6 focus exclusively on the remnant in *Jerusalem.* Elsewhere, Isaiah never focuses on the remnant from Jerusalem, but he does refer to the remnant of Jacob (10:21), or Israel (10:21), or "his [YHWH's] people" (11:11, 16; 28:5). The only exception appears to be 37:32, which derives from a much later period (see below). Furthermore, a number of features of vv. 3-6 indicate a postexilic setting for these verses. The "cloud by day and smoke and flaming fire by night" (v. 5) is a direct reference to the exodus and wilderness traditions, in which a pillar of cloud by day and a pillar of fire by night symbolized YHWH's protective presence (cf. J. Vollmer, *Geschichtliche Rückblicke und Motive in der Prophetie des Amos, Hosea und Jesaja* [BZAW 119; Berlin: de Gruyter, 1971] 176-77). The exodus and wilderness traditions do not appear to play any role in the work of Isaiah, but they are constitutive for that of Second Isaiah (cf. B. W. Anderson, "Exodus Typology in Second Isaiah," in *Israel's Prophetic Heritage* [*Fest.* J. Muilenburg; ed. B. W. Anderson and W. Harrelson; London: SCM, 1962] 177-95; idem, "Exodus and Covenant in Second Isaiah and Prophetic Tradition," in *Magnalia Dei: The Mighty Acts of God* [*Fest.* G. E. Wright; ed. F. M. Cross Jr. et al.; Garden City: Doubleday, 1976] 339-60; K. Kiesow, *Exodustexte im Jesajabuch* [OBO 24; Freiburg: Universitätsverlag; Göttingen: Vandenhoeck & Ruprecht, 1979]), as is the use of creation language such as *bārā'* in v. 5 (C. Stuhlmueller, *Creative Redemption in Deutero-Isaiah* [AnBib 43; Rome: Pontifical Biblical Institute, 1970] 60-61). These verses also demonstrate a marked interest in priestly matters, such as purification following menstruation, the holiness of the people, and designation of the environs of the Temple Mount as *miqrā'ehā* (cf. Sweeney, *Isaiah 1–4*, 179-80). The concern with priestly matters, as well as the exodus and wilderness tradition, must be set in the period of Ezra's and Nehemiah's reforms during the mid- to late 5th century when the return to Jerusalem was conceived as a new exodus and entry into the promised land to build a community based on torah and priestly purity (cf. Koch, "Ezra").

Isaiah 4:2 does not fit this pattern. As noted above in the discussion of chs. 2–4, its concern with the restoration of the survivors of Israel and its use of the technical term *ṣemaḥ*, "shoot," indicate a setting in the 6th century when exiles were first returning to Jerusalem to reestablish the temple and the city of Jerusalem (cf. Roberts, "Meaning of *ṣemaḥ haššem*"). Although it does not appear to have been composed for its present position, its focus on Israel corresponds to the designation "house of Jacob" in 2:5 and reflects the concern of Deutero-Isaiah to see Jacob/Israel restored to Zion in the late 6th century. It was only later, in the time of Ezra and Nehemiah, that interest would focus on Jerusalem as the remnant of Israel.

Intention

As noted above, the intention of the final form of this text is to explain the significance of the Day of YHWH in relation to Jerusalem and Judah. In the late-6th/early-5th-century edition of 2:2–4:2, 2:22–4:2 explains the punishment of Jacob/Israel as a preparation for its role in the ideal Zion. The expansion of this material in 4:3-6 in the mid- to late 5th century focuses on the remnant in Jerusalem and the Temple Mount to portray a purified and holy Zion in the time of Ezra and Nehemiah as the result of the suffering Israel has endured.

Material from the prophet Isaiah appears in 3:1–4:1. As noted above, the editorial work that assembled this material may well have been completed as early as the late 8th century, either by the prophet or by his followers. Although this unit contains material from various settings, the prophetic explanation of punishment in 3:1-9 clearly sets the interpretative agenda for this material. It presupposes Sennacherib's deportation of officials and leading citizens from Jerusalem and Judah (*ANET,* 288), and attempts to explain this as an act of YHWH designed to punish the people for their rebelliousness. The precise nature of the rebelliousness is not stated. Rather, the focus is on the chaos that will result from the absence of leadership. A number of earlier oracles were then edited and attached to 3:1-9 in order to explain the nature of the people's rebelliousness and also to confirm the prophet's previous criticisms of the people. Vv. 10-11 are of uncertain origin, but affirm the righteousness of the punishment while lamenting its need. Vv. 12-15 appear to relate primarily to 3:1-9(10-11) insofar as they condemn the leaders for leading the people astray as well as for robbing them and oppressing the poor. Obviously, the original form of vv. 13-15 did not focus so much on the people's corruption as on the leaders taking economic advantage of them. Vv. 12-15 also serve as the means for introducing 3:16–4:1 by mentioning the women among the people's oppressors. This passage focuses on the high status of the women by emphasizing the loss of their fine wardrobes. The editorial association of this passage with 3:12-15 indicates that the finery of the women comes to be viewed as the product of the people's oppression by their leaders. Finally, 3:25–4:1 clearly renders judgment against both the women and the men by pointing to the destitute state of the women after the men have been killed. This oracle was apparently composed for another context concerning the defeat of the city, but in the present context it provides the climax of Isaiah's condemnation of the leaders and the women.

Bibliography

W. L. Holladay, "Isa. III 10-11: An Archaic Wisdom Passage," *VT* 18 (1968) 481-87; Koch, "Ezra" (→ "Introduction to the Book of Isaiah"); E. E. Platt, "Jewelry of Bible Times and the Catalog of Isa 3:18-23," *AUSS* 17 (1979) 71-84, 189-201; J. J. M. Roberts, "The Meaning of *ṣemaḥ haššem* in Isaiah 4:2," in *Haim M. I. Gevaryahu Memorial Volume* (ed. J. J. Adler; Jerusalem: World Jewish Bible Center, 1990) 110-18; B. Stade, "Zu Jes. 3,1.17.24. 5,1. 8,1f.12-14.16. 9,7-20. 10,26," *ZAW* 26 (1906) 129-41; H.-M. Weil, "Exégèse d'Isaie, III,1-15," *RB* 39 (1940) 76-85.

PROPHETIC INSTRUCTION CONCERNING THE SIGNIFICANCE OF ASSYRIAN JUDGMENT AGAINST ISRAEL: RESTORATION OF THE DAVIDIC EMPIRE, 5:1–12:6

Structure

I. Announcement of judgment against Israel and Judah	5:1-30
A. Allegorical statement: judicial allegory	1-7

The demarcation of Isaiah 5–12 is determined by a combination of formal and thematic factors. In contrast to chs. 2–4, which focus specifically on Jerusalem and Judah, chs. 5–12 focus on Israel in general, its punishment by the Assyrian empire, and the projected outcome of that punishment in the restoration of the Davidic empire. The unit begins with Isaiah's "Song of the Vineyard" in 5:1-7. This song is formulated in 1st-person address language and discusses the fate of Israel. It is syntactically unrelated to the preceding section, which is formulated in 3rd-person announcement language and which discusses the future of Jerusalem. The following material in 5:8-30 specifies the punishment for Israel announced by the Song of the Vineyard. The common use of the woe oracle form (5:8, 11, 18, 20, 21, 22; cf. 10:1) and the "outstretched hand" formula (5:25; cf. 9:11, 16, 20 [RSV 12, 17, 21]; 10:4) indicate that 5:1-30 and 9:7 (RSV 8)–10:4 form a literary envelope around the so-called *Denkschrift* ("memoir") of Isaiah in 6:1–9:6 (RSV 7). The woe oracle form and the references to YHWH's "anger" in 10:5 establish a link to 5:1-30 and 9:7 (RSV 8)–10:4, and 10:20-26 makes specific allusions to 7:1–9:6 (RSV 7), especially 9:1-6 (RSV 2-7). Likewise, the imagery of a pruned tree sending out new shoots in 10:5–12:6 relates to the imagery of a the stripped stump that serves as the basis for the "holy seed" in 6:1-13. Isa 10:5–12:6, which is also held together syntactically by conjunctive *waws* (10:20, 27; 11:1, 10, 11; 12:1), *lākēns* (10:16, 24), and the formulation *wĕhāyâ bayyôm hahû'*, "and it shall come to pass in that day" (10:20, 27; 11:10, 11; cf. 12:1, 4), round out the unit. Finally, the superscription in 13:1 clearly introduces the oracles against the nations in chs. 13–23.

The structure of this block is determined by its instructional or explanatory character insofar as it announces judgment against Israel and Judah in 5:1-30 and then proceeds to explain the significance, cause, and outcome of that judgment throughout the balance of the unit in 6:1–12:6.

The first major section of this block, then, is the announcement of judgment against Israel and Judah in 5:1-30. The details of the structure of this unit are fully discussed below. This judgment is expressed allegorically in vv. 1-7 and concretely in vv. 8-30, which include an indictment (vv. 8-24) and a prophetic announcement of punishment introduced by *'al-kēn*, "therefore" (vv. 25-30).

The second major section of this block is the explanation of the judgment against Israel and Judah in 6:1–12:6, which takes up both the causes of the judgment as well as its projected outcome in the reestablishment of the Davidic empire. The causes are discussed in the narratives of 6:1–8:15. Isaiah's vocation account appears in 6:1-13 and sets the themes of impending judgment and a surviving remnant as the basis for renewal. The narratives concerning YHWH's signs in 7:1–8:15 are linked syntactically to 6:1-13 by the introductory *wayĕhî*, "and it came to pass," as well as by the general concern with illustrating how the judgment announced in 6:1-13 came to pass. These narratives take up the house of David in 7:1•25 and Judah in 8:1-15.

Although 8:16–9:6 (RSV 7) is related to 7:1–8:15 by its content, the imperatives that introduce this section in 8:16 signal the introduction of a new, syntactically independent subunit. That is, 8:16–9:6 (RSV 7) constitutes a prophetic instruction concerning YHWH's signs to Israel and the house of David.

It indicates that although Israel is currently undergoing a period of punishment that requires patience and the willingness to wait (8:16-17), those who understand Isaiah's signs will realize that ultimately a new Davidic monarch will emerge to usher in a reign of peace (8:18–9:6 [*RSV* 7]). The fulfillment of this scenario of judgment followed by restoration is illustrated by 9:7 (*RSV* 8)–12:6, which is structurally juxtaposed over against 8:16–9:6 (*RSV* 7) by its parallel thematic structure. Isa 9:7 (*RSV* 8)–10:4 announces judgment against Israel/Jacob by means of a historical review of Israel's rejection of YHWH culminating in an announcement of judgment. Isa 10:5–12:6 then takes up the "woe" form employed against the leaders of Israel in 10:1-4 to shift to a condemnation of Assyria for overstepping its role as YHWH's agent of punishment by threatening Jerusalem. Overall, 10:5–12:6 is concerned with the restoration of the Davidic empire in that the woe oracle against Assyria in 10:5-11 introduces a general announcement of Assyria's fall and the subsequent rise of the Davidic monarchy in 10:12–12:6. As noted in the detailed discussion of 10:5–12:6 below, this announcement is characterized by its future perspective (10:12), including the use of the formula *wĕhāyâ bayyôm hahû'*, "and it shall come to pass in that day" (10:20, 27; 11:10, 11; cf. 12:1, 4), to present a scenario whereby the fall of the Assyrian monarch leads directly to the rise of the Davidic monarch and the restoration of Israel. Consequently, the announcement of punishment of the Assyrian monarch in 10:12-19 leads to an announcement concerning the relief of the remnant of Israel from Assyrian oppression in 10:20-26. This in turn leads to an announcement concerning the fall of the Assyrian monarch, pictured as an overgrown tree that is pruned, and the subsequent rise of the Davidic monarch, portrayed as a shoot growing from the remaining stem in 10:27–11:9. Isa 11:10 then announces the nations' recognition of the monarch, and 11:11-16 announces the return of the remnant of Israel from foreign exile and the reestablishment of Israel using language that portrays this process as a second exodus. Finally, the hymn of thanksgiving in 12:1-6 concludes the unit with its hymnic reprise of the exodus theme.

Genre

Because chs. 5–12 are a composite unit, they clearly were not written according to a single generic pattern but include a number of generic entities that were worked into their present positions by redaction. Nevertheless, one must recognize that redaction is not a random or haphazard activity but takes place with specific goals in mind that influence the final shape of the literature at hand. The present form of chs. 5–12 is shaped according to the generic pattern of liturgical INSTRUCTION or INSTRUCTION of the community. This is clear from the structure of the passage, which is designed to explain the meaning of the Assyrian judgment of Israel. In this case, the Assyrian invasion of Israel and Judah is portrayed as a judgment by YHWH that was brought about by lack of trust in YHWH's promises of protection on the part of both Israel and Judah on the one hand, and on the part of the house of David on the other. At the same time, the passage indicates that this punishment will ultimately lead to the restoration of the Davidic empire insofar as it envisions a reunited Israel, which includes the lands of the Philistines, Moabites, Edomites, and Ammonites, under the leadership of a new Davidic monarch.

That the purpose of this block is not simply to announce but also to convince is clear from the fact that the block as a whole is cast as a projection of the future on the basis of past events. The material announcing the reestablishment of a united Israel under a Davidic monarch employs the formulaic expression *wĕhāyâ bayyôm hahû'*, "and it shall come to pass in that day." The intent of this block is to convince its audience that a renewed Davidic empire will be the outcome of the Assyrian punishment. Consequently, the block has a parenetic character that supports its role as community INSTRUCTION.

Finally, the concluding hymn of thanksgiving in 12:1-6 points to a liturgical role for this block. INSTRUCTION of the community typically takes place in a liturgical setting as indicated by the many psalms that share this generic identification (Psalms 34; 37; 50; 52; 58; 78; 95; 105). As noted below in the discussion of setting, Isaiah 5–12 likely had a place in the liturgy of King Josiah's Passover festival, which celebrated his program of religious reform and national restoration. In this respect, chs. 5–12 play a major role in presenting the Josianic view of Israel's history of Assyrian subjugation and Israel's prospects after Assyria's fall.

Setting

Isaiah 5–12 clearly functions as part of the final edition of the book of Isaiah produced in the late 5th century B.C.E. But as the discussion of the individual units of this block demonstrates, none of this material was composed in the 5th century or even in the 6th. Instead, several portions of the text, including 7:1-9, ch. 10, and 11:1–12:6, appear to have been composed during the reign of King Josiah (639-609), in order to support his program of religious reform and national restoration for Israel, while the balance was composed by Isaiah at various periods during the late 8th century. Because of the crucial role the Josianic texts play in organizing the material and determining its essential message, chs. 5–12 appear to be a redactional block edited into its present form during the reign of King Josiah.

Isaiah 11:1–12:6 is clearly the most influential block of material in this regard. As noted in the detailed discussion of this unit below, several of its features indicate its Josianic origin. Its use of the imagery of a new shoot growing out of an old stem to depict the new Davidic monarch (11:1) relates the near destruction of the Davidic dynasty to the assassination of Amon in 640, and its recovery to the installation of the eight-year-old Josiah by those who put down the revolt. The reference to a small boy's leadership role in a new period of peace for Zion (11:6-9) likewise presupposes the installation of the young Josiah. Furthermore, the projected reunification of Ephraim and Judah, their conquest of Philistia, Moab, Edom, and Ammon, and the return of the exiled remnant of Israel from Egypt and Assyria all correspond to Josiah's program for reestablishing a Davidic empire centered around Jerusalem. Finally, the use of exodus

116

imagery to portray this restoration corresponds to Josiah's use of the Passover celebration in support of his program (2 Kgs 23:21-23; 2 Chr 35:1-19).

The use of the exodus imagery in 11:1–12:6 is particularly important. It not only points to Josiah's Passover celebration as the setting for this text, but it also demonstrates how the Josianic redaction drew on the Isaianic material of chs. 5–12 and related it to the traditions of the exodus and wilderness wanderings. Isa 11:1–12:6 thereby presents the restoration of Israel in Josiah's time as the new exodus and the culmination of the process of history that began in the late 8th century with the Syro-Ephraimite War and the Assyrian invasions of Israel and Judah.

The clearest indication of the use of exodus imagery in this material is the portrayal of YHWH's hand that redeems the remnant of Israel from exile in Egypt and Assyria (11:11) and smites the Red Sea of Egypt and the Euphrates to provide a highway for the exiles to return home. This portrayal obviously draws on traditions of the exodus that describe the parting of the Reed Sea under the extended hand of Moses (Exod 14:16, 21, 26-27), but it also depends on several features of the Isaianic material in Isaiah 5–10. For example, 10:20-26 refers to the return of the remnant of Israel and YHWH's "rod" *(maṭṭeh)* and "staff" *(šēbeṭ)* extended over the sea. Likewise, the "hand" of YHWH draws on the formula "in all this his anger has not turned and his hand is still stretched out" (5:25; 9:11, 16, 20 [*RSV* 12, 17, 21]; 10:4) and its association with the "staff/rod" *(šēbeṭ/maṭṭeh)* of punishment in 10:5, 15, and 24-26.

Another indication of the use of exodus and wilderness traditions in this text appears in the mention of the "ensign of the peoples" *(lěnēs 'ammîm)* in 11:10 and the "ensign for the nations" *(nēs laggôyîm)* in 11:12. The expression here refers to the Davidic monarch who will be recognized by the nations and signal the return of the exiles and restoration of Israel. This expression clearly draws on the "ensign" that YHWH uses to summon the Assyrians in 5:26, where it appears in association with the formula "in all this his anger has not turned and his hand is still stretched out" in 5:25. In this context, it expresses YHWH's anger against the people who have rejected "the torah of YHWH of hosts" and whose "root" will be rotten in 5:24 (cf. 11:1 on "root"). In the context of ch. 11, it expresses the end of the process of punishment begun with the Assyrian invasion. Interestingly, *nēs,* "ensign," appears in only one other biblical context in association with the imagery of the "outstretched hand," the narrative of the war with Amalek in Exod 17:8-16. Israel defeats Amalek when Moses' hand, holding the "rod of God" *(maṭṭeh hā'ĕlōhîm),* is held up. After the battle, an altar is built to commemorate the victory that Moses names *yhwh nissî,* "YHWH is my ensign," signifying YHWH's defeat of Israel's enemies. Amalek also appears in Balaam's final oracle concerning Israel in Num 24:14-24, where it is the first of a series of nations to be destroyed in association with the rise of a royal figure and the future glory of Israel. The series of nations concludes with Assyria and Eber. Whatever the specific references to the "ensign" and Assyria may signify, it is clear that Isa 11:1-16 draws on these traditions and previous material from chs. 5–10 to formulate its own view of history extending from the Assyrian invasions to the rise of King Josiah.

Finally, the hymn of thanksgiving in 12:1-6 establishes the liturgical setting for this text. It, too, draws on exodus traditions in that v. 2b quotes a slightly altered version of Exod 15:2a (cf. Ps 118:14), "[For] YHWH [God] is my strength and song, he has become my salvation." Likewise, v. 5a, "Sing to YHWH, for he has done gloriously," corresponds to Exod 15:1b. Isa 12:1-6 relates to general hymnic phraseology as well, as indicated by the correspondence between v. 4a and Ps 105:1. Nevertheless, the correspondence of this psalm to phraseology from Exodus 15 and the context of Isaiah 11, both of which clearly employ Exodus imagery, shows the redaction's intention to present this psalm as a thanksgiving hymn for the new "exodus" of King Josiah's time.

The interest in presenting King Josiah's program of reform and national restoration in terms of a new exodus also has implications for understanding the role and function of Isa 7:1. As noted in the detailed discussion of 7:1-25, v. 1 is a later addition to this text that was reworked during the reign of King Josiah. It was taken from its original context in 2 Kgs 16:5 and reworked for its present context. It is not necessary to the narrative of Isa 7:2-25; it stands outside the sequence of events presented therein. Its primary function appears to be to provide a transition between the account of Isaiah's commission in 6:1-13 and the following narratives concerning Isaiah's signs in 7:2–8:15. In this respect, the introductory *wayĕhî*, "and it came to pass," in 7:1 presents 7:1–8:15 as the consequence and fulfillment of the message of judgment in 6:1-13.

Although scholars generally regard 6:1-13 as the introduction to the so-called Isaiah memoir in 6:1–9:6 (*RSV* 7), there appears to be little basis to maintain, as Budde did, that this text constitutes an autobiographical account of the prophet's experience during the Syro-Ephraimite War (for a critique of the *Denkschrift* hypothesis that differs somewhat from the following, see Irvine). It is striking that Isaiah's vocation account shows little relation to the following material except on the most general level. Isa 7:1–9:6 (*RSV* 7) is generally viewed as the fulfillment of the message of judgment in 6:1-13, but despite the fact that the vocation account was written by the prophet, no evidence suggests that 6:1-13 forms part of the same composition as 7:1–8:15. The 1st-person formulation of 8:1–9:6 (*RSV* 7) and the proposed original 1st-person formulation for 7:2-25 constitute the only potential link, but key themes and motifs from 7:1–9:6 (*RSV* 7) are absent in 6:1-13 and vice versa. Isa 6:11-12 describes the land emptied of its inhabitants, which corresponds to the portrayal of 5:9-10, but this motif appears nowhere in 7:1–9:6 (*RSV* 7). As noted in the discussion of ch. 5, 5:9-10 does associate its emptied land imagery with that of the destroyed vineyard, which is taken up in 7:23-25. Isa 6:1-13 does not employ such vineyard imagery, however, but focuses instead on the image of Israel as a stripped stump that provides a potential source of new growth (v. 13). Although this imagery does not correspond to 7:1–9:6 (*RSV* 7) or 5:1-30, it does correspond to 11:1–12:6, which employs the imagery of a stripped stem and the new shoots that grow from it to represent the new Davidic monarch and the restoration of Israel. Likewise, the reference to the "tenth" that remains (v. 13a) relates to the concern with the remnant in 10:20-26 and 11:11-16. Finally, 7:1–9:6 (*RSV* 7) places great emphasis on the dichotomy of light and darkness, which corresponds to 5:30 but does not appear in 6:1-13.

The relationship between 6:1-13 and 11:1–12:6 becomes particularly important when considered within the context of the Josianic interest in the exodus tradition. Although 6:1-13 makes no explicit mention of the exodus and wilderness traditions, a number of its themes and motifs do correspond to those of the exodus and wilderness traditions. Most important is Isaiah's commission to make the heart of the people fat, their ears heavy, and their eyes closed so that they will be unable to repent and be saved (vv. 9-10). This corresponds to YHWH's hardening of Pharaoh's heart throughout the Exodus narrative so that the divine plans could be carried out. The appearance of seraphim is significant in that their only other appearance outside Isaiah (cf. 14:29; 30:6) is in connection with the wilderness wandering (Num 21:4-9; Deut 8:15), where they torment the rebellious people at YHWH's command. Likewise, Isaiah's question "How long?" (*'ad-mātay*) calls to mind YHWH's question to Moses: "How long will this wicked congregation murmur against me?" (Num 14:27) prior to YHWH's decision to punish Israel with forty years of wilderness wandering. Finally, Isaiah's lament that he is a man of unclean lips corresponds to Moses' objections that he is slow of speech (Exod 4:10) and a man of uncircumcised lips (Exod 6:12, 30). The response that YHWH makes people dumb, deaf, seeing, and blind (Exod 4:11) prior to sending Moses on his task likewise relates to Isaiah's commission. Although Isaiah's vocation account does not appear to be written with the exodus and wilderness traditions in mind, it certainly provides adequate stimulation for a redaction that intends to associate the two.

Consequently, Isa 6:1-13 appears to have been introduced into its present context by the Josianic redaction of chs. 5–12. Apart from a general concern with the judgment of Israel, it has little apparent relationship to its immediate context in chs. 5–10, but it relates directly to 11:1–12:6 by virtue of its exodus associations and its use of stump imagery to portray the potential new growth of Israel following its punishment. It is worked into the present context by the addition of Isa 7:1, which presents the narratives concerning the invasion of Israel by Assyria in 7:2–8:15 as the consequence or fulfillment of Isaiah's vocation account. Isa 6:1-13 thereby functions as a means for legitimizing the message of judgment and restoration that permeates chs. 5–12. As such, it also functions in support of the overall portrayal in chs. 5–12 of Josiah's program as the fulfillment of YHWH's plans to punish and to rebuild Israel by means of the Assyrian empire. The concluding thanksgiving hymn in 12:1-6 suggests that chs. 5–12 may have played a role in the liturgy for Passover that Josiah celebrated in connection with his reform (2 Kgs 23:21-23; 2 Chr 35:1-19).

Intention

Although the present form of chs. 5–12 stems from the 7th-century Josianic redaction of Isaiah, these chapters clearly function as part of the 5th- and 6th-century editions of the book. In both of these contexts, chs. 5–12 point to the rule of a righteous monarch who will restore the unity of the people following the period of their oppression. In relation to the 5th-century context of chs. 1–66 as a whole, chs. 5–12 point to the rule of YHWH as sovereign of the earth insofar as they emphasize YHWH's role as monarch of the entire world (cf. 2:2-4; 66:1-2). Likewise, the exodus imagery of these chapters points to the return to Jerusalem led by Ezra (cf. Koch, "Ezra," who argues that Ezra's return is presented as a new exodus). When read in relation to the 6th-century edition of the book, chs. 5–12 likewise point to YHWH's world rule (cf. 2:2-4) manifested through the rule of Cyrus (44:28; 45:1; cf. R. G. Kratz, *Kyros im Deuterojesaja-Buch: Redaktionsgeschichtliche Untersuchungen zu Entstehung und Theologie von Jes 40–55* [FAT 1; Tübingen: Mohr [Siebeck], 1991]; and O. H. Steck, *Gottesknecht und Zion: Gesammelte Aufsätze zu Deuterojesaja* [FAT 4; Tübingen: Mohr [Siebeck], 1992] 155-60, both of whom argue that the so-called Cyrus layer [*Kyros-Ergänzungs-Schicht*] of Deutero-Isaiah portrays Cyrus as the manifestation of YHWH's world rule). The exodus imagery of this passage would relate to the exodus imagery of Deutero-Isaiah, which portrays the return of Jews to Jerusalem from Babylonian exile in the late 6th century. In both editions of the book, the image of Assyria as YHWH's tool of punishment would be understood in relation to the Babylonian empire.

Nevertheless, it is clear from the preceding discussion that the present form of chs. 5–12 was composed during the reign of King Josiah. The intention of the Josianic edition of these chapters is to portray King Josiah's program of religious reform and national restoration as the culmination of YHWH's plans to punish and restore Israel by means of the Assyrian empire. It begins with an announcement of judgment against Israel in 5:1-30 and then explains the significance of that judgment by portraying the events that led to the Assyrian invasion of Israel, the ultimate collapse of the Assyrian empire because of its monarch's threats against YHWH and Jerusalem, the subsequent rise of a new Davidic monarch, and the return of Israel's exiles to a reestablished and reunited Davidic empire.

Two key points are made in the scenario presented here. First, it is a theological view of history in that YHWH is always presented as the one who is in complete control of historical events. Israel is punished because of its rebellion against YHWH, which rebellion necessitates the introduction of the Assyrian empire as YHWH's tool of punishment. When the Assyrian monarch oversteps his bounds by refusing to acknowledge YHWH's power and by threatening Jerusalem, YHWH makes the decision to punish the Assyrian empire as well. The result is YHWH's action to restore the Davidic monarch and Israel. The second major point is that this process is viewed as a means for reuniting Israel under the Davidic monarchy. From the time of Jeroboam's revolt against the house of David, Israel had been split into two kingdoms. This division is presupposed at the beginning of this unit in that the entire scenario is engendered by Israel's and Syria's attack against Jerusalem and the house of David. The introduction of the Assyrian empire prepares for the destruction of the northern kingdom. This prepares the way for the remnant of Israel, portrayed in 10:20-23 as the survivors of the northern kingdom of Israel, to return to the Davidic dynasty (note *'ēl gibbôr* as the Davidic monarch in 10:21 and 9:5 [*RSV* 6]). The reunification of Israel and Judah was one of the primary objectives of Josiah's reform program, as indicated by his destruction of the altar at Bethel (2 Kgs 23:15-20), which had stood as the symbol of northern Israel's rejection of the house of David from the time of Jeroboam (1 Kgs 12:25-33; cf. 13:1-32, esp. vv. 2-3).

Bibliography

B. W. Anderson, " 'God with Us' — in Judgment and in Mercy: The Editorial Structure of Isaiah 5–10(11)," in *Canon, Theology, and Old Testament Interpretation* (*Fest.* B. S. Childs; ed. G. M. Tucker, D. L. Petersen, and R. R. Wilson; Philadelphia: Fortress, 1988) 230-45; K. Budde, *Jesaja's Erleben: Eine gemeinverständliche Auslegung der Denkschrift des Propheten (Kap. 6,1–9,6)* (Gotha: L. Klotz, 1928); S. A. Irvine, "The Isaianic *Denkschrift:* Reconsidering an Old Hypothesis," *ZAW* 104 (1992) 216-31; Koch, "Ezra" (→ "Introduction to the Book of Isaiah"); T. Leskow, "Jesajas Denkschrift aus der Zeit des syrisch-ephraimitischen Krieges," *ZAW* 85 (1973) 315-31; C. E. L'Heureux, "The Redactional History of Isaiah 5.1–10.4," in *In the Shelter of Elyon: Essays on Ancient Palestinian Life and Literature in Honor of G. W. Ahlström* (ed. W. B. Barrick and J. R. Spencer; JSOTSup 31; Sheffield: JSOT Press, 1984) 99-119; J. Lindblom, *A Study on the Immanuel Section in Isaiah: Isa. vii,1–ix,6* (Lund: Gleerup, 1958); K. Marti, "Die jesajanische Kern in Jes 6,1–9,6," *Karl Budde zum siebzigsten Geburtstag* (BZAW 34; ed. K. Marti; Giessen: A. Töpelmann, 1920) 113-21; H.-P. Müller, "Glauben und Bleiben: Zur Denkschrift Jesajas Kapitel vi 1–viii 18," *Studies on Prophecy* (VTSup 26; Leiden: Brill, 1974) 25-55; K. Nielsen, "Is 6:1–8:18 as Dramatic Writing," *ST* 40 (1986) 1-16; H. G. Reventlow, "Das Ende der sog. 'Denkschrift' Jesajas," *BN* 38/39 (1987) 62-67; W. Werner, "Vom Prophetenwort zur Prophetentheologie: Ein redaktionskritischer Versuch zu Jes 6,1–8,18," *BZ* 29 (1985) 1-30.

ANNOUNCEMENT OF JUDGMENT AGAINST ISRAEL AND JUDAH, 5:1-30

Structure

I. Allegorical statement: juridical allegory	1-7
A. Prophet's introduction	1a
B. Prophet's statement of owner's actions and expectations concerning vineyard	1b-2
1. Concerning friend's ownership of choice vineyard	1b
2. Concerning owner's actions on behalf of vineyard to produce choice grapes	2a
3. Concerning owner's disappointed expectations: vineyard produces sour grapes	2b
C. Owner's first address to audience: appeal for judgment	3-4
1. Appeal for judgment proper addressed to people of Jerusalem/Judah	3
2. Twofold rhetorical question establishing propriety of owner's actions	4
a. What more can be done?	4a
b. Why wait for choice grapes and receive sour grapes?	4b

D. Owner's second address to audience:
announcement of vineyard's destruction   5-6
    1. Introduction to announcement   5a
    2. Owner's proposed actions against vineyard   5b-6
       a. Break down its protective fences   5b
       b. Leave it untended to become a waste   6a
       c. Prevent rain from watering it   6b
E. Prophet's explanation: YHWH's judgment
against Israel and Judah   7
    1. Vineyard of YHWH is house of Israel   7aα
    2. Men of Judah are YHWH's plantings   7aβ
    3. Failed expectations   7b
II. Specific statement: prophetic announcement
of punishment   8-30
A. Indictment: woe series   8-24
    1. First woe series   8-17
       a. Woe statements   8-12
          1) Concerning property foreclosure   8-10
             a) Woe exclamation concerning
property foreclosure   8
             b) Prophet's report of YHWH's
vow to punish   9-10
                (1) Auditory report formula   9a
                (2) YHWH's vow   9b-10
                   (a) Vow proper: houses
will be abandoned   9b
                   (b) Cause: diminished produce   10
          2) Concerning drunkenness/lack of perception   11-12
             a) Woe exclamation concerning drunkenness   11
             b) Elaboration concerning failure
to perceive YHWH's deeds   12
       b. Consequences   13-17
          1) Exile of people   13
          2) Abasement of people   14-17
             a) Sheol opens mouth   14a
             b) Nobility goes down to Sheol   14b
             c) Humankind is abased   15
             d) YHWH is exalted   16
             e) Lambs will graze   17
    2. Second woe series   18-24
       a. Woe statements   18-23
          1) Concerning pursuit of falsehood   18-19
             a) Woe exclamation concerning
those who practice falsehood   18
             b) Specification concerning those
who mock YHWH's actions   19
          2) Concerning deceit   20

The basic structure of this passage is determined by the distinction between the allegorical language in vv. 1-7 and the specific language in vv. 8-30. Both units are influenced by juridical trial patterns in that both attempt to establish the guilt of Israel and Judah as the basis for the announcements of judgment against them. The two parts of the passage work together insofar as the allegorical language and rhetorical appeal for judgment in vv. 1-7 lure the audience into self-condemnation. The specific language of vv. 8-30 likewise reinforces the message of judgment by linking internal social and judicial abuse to the approach of the Assyrian army. Both parts are further linked by the prophet's 1st-person address in vv. 1 and 9.

The structure of the juridical allegory in vv. 1-7 is determined by a combination of the contents and the identity of the speaker. The prophet employs a 1st-person address form in v. 1a to introduce the song with a statement that he will sing of his friend's love for a vineyard. The prophet continues with a combination of 1st- and 3rd-person descriptive language in vv. 1b-2 to describe his friend's (i.e., the owner's) preparation of the vineyard and his failed expectations. V. 1b states that his friend owns a choice vineyard; v. 2a states the owner's actions to insure that the vineyard will produce choice grapes; and v. 2b states that the vineyard produced only sour grapes instead of the expected choice grapes. Vv. 3-4 continue to employ 1st-person forms, but the addition of the imperative address to the audience (v. 3) and the references to "my vineyard" indicate that the owner/YHWH is the speaker here who appeals to the people of Jerusalem and Judah for their judgment of the situation. V. 3 contains the owner's appeal to the people of Jerusalem/Judah for judgment. V. 4 contains two RHETORICAL QUESTIONS that establish the owner's proper action in tending the vineyard: v. 4a asks what more can be done, and v. 4b asks why the owner should expect sour grapes. The combination of 1st- and 2nd-person perspectives continues in vv. 5-6, but the focus shifts to the owner's/YHWH's announcement that the vineyard will be destroyed. V. 5a introduces the announcement, which specifies YHWH's actions in vv. 5b-6. These actions include breaking down the vineyard's protective barriers in v. 5b, leaving it untended to become a waste in v. 6a, and preventing rain from watering it in v. 6b. Finally, v. 7 shifts to 3rd-person descriptive language which indicates that the prophet is explaining the meaning of the parable in relation to YHWH's condemnation of Israel and Judah. The explanation includes statements that the vineyard of YHWH is the house of Israel in v. 7aα, that the men of Judah are YHWH's plantings, and that YHWH's failed expectations in v. 7b include "murder" *(miśpāḥ)* instead of "justice" *(mišpāṭ)* and "outcry" *(ṣěʿāqâ)* instead of "righteousness" *(ṣědāqâ)*.

The structure of vv. 8-30 is determined by the juridical pattern of indictment followed by an announcement of punishment. In addition, vv. 8-24 are constituted by a series of *hôy* ("woe") oracles that condemn the guilty among the people, combined with statements of consequences beginning with *lākēn,* "therefore," in vv. 13, 14, and 24. On the one hand, although vv. 8-24 contain statements of consequences that might disrupt the pattern of indictment/consequence, the concluding statement that "they have rejected the torah [*RSV* 'law'] of YHWH Sabaoth and the word of the Holy One of Israel they have rejected [*RSV* 'despised']" establishes the basic character of vv. 8-24 as indictment. On the other hand, vv. 25-30 begin with *ʿal-kēn,* "therefore," which breaks the *hôy/lākēn* pattern and serves as a general summation of consequences for vv. 8-24. Vv. 26-30 illustrate these general consequences with a description of the Assyrian army's approach.

The structure of vv. 8-24 is determined by its *hôy/lākēn* ("woe/therefore") pattern, which appears twice in vv. 8-17 and 18-24. The first series (vv. 8-17) begins with two woe statements that decry property foreclosure (vv. 8-10) and drunkenness, indicating a failure to perceive YHWH's actions (vv. 11-12). Vv. 8-10 include the basic woe exclamation in v. 8, which specifies those who foreclose on property as the objects of the prophet's condemnation. This is followed by the prophet's report of YHWH's vow to punish those who foreclose in vv. 9-10. An auditory report formula, "In my ears [swore] YHWH Sabaoth" *(běʾoznāy yhwh ṣěbāʾôt),* appears in v. 9a followed by YHWH's vow in vv.

9b-10. The vow is identified by its characteristic *'im-lō'* ("indeed"), which introduces YHWH's statement that houses will be abandoned. V. 10, introduced by causative *kî*, "because," states that the cause of this abandonment will be the diminished produce of the vineyards. The woe oracle in vv. 11-12 focuses on drunkenness and the inability to perceive correctly. The woe exclamation concerning those who drink to excess appears in v. 11. V. 12 then elaborates by describing the drunks' inability to perceive YHWH's deeds. Two statements introduced by *lākēn*, "therefore," correspond to each woe statement. V. 13 describes the exile of the people and corresponds to the empty homes mentioned in vv. 8-10. Vv. 14-17 describe the abasement of the people by employing the imagery of Sheol swallowing the people, much like a drunk swallows wine (cf. Hab 2:4-5). The imagery is developed as a sequence of actions: v. 14a describes Sheol's open mouth; v. 14b describes the nobility descending into Sheol; v. 15 describes the abasement of humankind; v. 16 describes YHWH's exaltation; and v. 17 describes lambs grazing among the ruins (presumably of the houses mentioned in vv. 8-10). Vv. 14-17 recap both oracles in that the imagery of drunkenness corresponds to vv. 11-12, but the imagery of lambs grazing in the ruins takes up the imagery of destroyed houses in vv. 8-10.

The second series (vv. 18-24) begins with four woe oracles in vv. 18-23 followed by a statement of the consequences in v. 24. The first woe oracle appears in vv. 18-19, which condemn the pursuit of falsehood. The woe exclamation proper appears in v. 18, and v. 19 specifies this statement by identifying those who mock YHWH's actions by demanding proof. The second appears in v. 20, which focuses on deceit. The woe exclamation appears in v. 20a, and the specification in v. 20b focuses on those who attempt to misrepresent reality by deliberately confusing light and darkness (v. 20bα) and bitter and sweet (v. 20bβ). The third appears in v. 21 as a basic woe exclamation concerning self-aggrandizement. The fourth appears in vv. 22-23, which recap the theme of drunkenness in order to portray the perversion of justice. The woe exclamation in v. 22 condemns drunkenness, and the specification in v. 23 relates this theme to judicial impropriety. Finally, the *lākēn* statement in v. 24 describes the resulting destruction of the people (v. 24a), and it supplies the reason for their punishment insofar as they have rejected YHWH's torah (v. 24b).

The announcement of punishment in vv. 25-30 portrays YHWH's summons of an unnamed enemy army. By employing formulaic language to describe YHWH's wrath against the people in terms of the "outstretched arm" motif (cf. 9:11, 16, 20 [*RSV* 12, 17, 21]; 10:4; Jer 21:5), v. 25 provides the basic statement of YHWH's intention to punish. Vv. 26-30 then present a detailed description of the army as it marches toward its next victim. An announcement of YHWH's summons of the army appears in v. 26a, followed by a description of the army's swift response in vv. 26b-30. This is basically stated in v. 26b and specified in vv. 27-30 by employing a sequence of images. V. 27 describes the troops who are not weary (v. 27a) and whose clothing is completely in order, indicating that they are ready for action (v. 27b). V. 28a states that their weapons are sharp. V. 28b describes their horses with hooves like flint and their chariot wheels like the whirlwind. Vv. 29-30 provide the climax of this portrayal of a dangerous enemy by focusing on the motif of roaring. The enemy roars like a lion seizing prey in v. 29, and v. 30 elaborates on this metaphor by comparing their roaring to the mythological image of the sea (v. 30a) and then portraying the land plunged into darkness (v. 30b).

Genre

Isaiah 5:1-30 is a composite unit whose generic character is determined by the redactional arrangement of its constituent subunits. In its present form, this chapter displays two generic patterns. The first is that of an ALLEGORY and its explanation. Vv. 1-7 employ an ALLEGORY to announce judgment against Israel and Judah, and vv. 8-30 employ specific language to explain the meaning of that judgment. The second is that of the PROPHETIC JUDGMENT SPEECH. Both vv. 1-7 and vv. 8-30 contain the standard elements of this genre: (1) a statement of the reasons for judgment (vv. 1b-2, 8-24); (2) a logical connector (*wĕʿattâ*, "and now," in vv. 3 and 5; *ʿal-kēn*, "therefore," in v. 25); and (3) an announcement of judgment (vv. 5-6, 25-30). Consequently, the generic character of the final form of 5:1-30 may be described as "allegorical prophetic judgment speech."

In addition to its overarching generic character, ch. 5 contains a number of constituent generic entities. The first is the juridical ALLEGORY in vv. 1-7. The passage is based on the imagery of a vineyard and describes the owner's care in tending it to produce good grapes. When the vineyard produces unsuitable grapes, two RHETORICAL QUESTIONS directed to the audience ask them to judge the situation. Although the form of the questions presupposes an answer, the content indicates that no answer is possible. In fact, the questions do not seek an answer but intend to establish that the owner has exhausted all possible alternatives and should expect good grapes for his efforts. As a result, the owner announces that the vineyard is to be destroyed. The final verse explains the meaning of the ALLEGORY by identifying YHWH as the owner, Israel as the vineyard, Judah as the "choice plantings," and YHWH's expectations of justice and righteousness and the resulting murder and outcry.

The generic character of this passage has been the subject of extensive discussion, which Willis has surveyed. The current consensus views it as a juridical parable on the basis of its juridical intent and parabolic form (Willis; Yee), but this is not entirely accurate. Strictly speaking, a parable employs metaphorical language to convey a moral or maxim, much like the rabbinic parables of talmudic literature or Jesus' parables in the NT. Isa 5:1-7 conveys no such moral or maxim, but simply announces judgment against Israel and Judah. Such use of metaphorical language is more properly described as ALLEGORY (Bjørndalen).

The second constituent generic entity is the PROPHETIC JUDGMENT SPEECH pattern in vv. 8-24. Although this generic pattern defines the character of the chapter as a whole, it is based in the series of WOE ORACLES and consequences found in these verses. In this instance, the statements concerning the reasons for judgment are cast in the form of WOE ORACLES or woe exclamations in vv. 8, 11-12, 18-19, 20, 21, and 22-23. Each is introduced by *hôy,* "woe!" and employs a 3rd-person description of the crimes committed by the addressees of the woe statements. In one case, in vv. 8-10, the woe statement (v. 8) is supplemented by a prophetic AUDITION REPORT concerning a vow by YHWH (vv. 9-10). As noted above, the vow is easily identified by the IMPRECATION FORMULA *'im-lō',* "surely," which emphasizes YHWH's intent to destroy the houses, thereby reinforcing the WOE ORACLE in v. 8. The consequences for the crimes mentioned in the WOE ORACLES appear in vv. 13, 14-17, and 24. Each is introduced by the connector *lākēn,* "therefore," and constitutes the ANNOUNCEMENT OF JUDGMENT of the PROPHETIC JUDGMENT SPEECH. When considered in relation to the final form of this chapter, v. 24b plays a transitional role by reinforcing the accusatory character of vv. 8-24 so that these verses constitute the INDICTMENT SPEECH prior to the ANNOUNCEMENT OF JUDGMENT in vv. 25-30. But when the verse is considered solely in relation to vv. 8-24, it serves as a concluding summary of the accusations made in these verses (Jensen, *Use of tôrâ,* 95-104).

The final generic entity is the description of an enemy nation in vv. 26-30. This is not an independent genre, but an expansion and reinforcement of the ANNOUNCEMENT OF JUDGMENT. It focuses on the element of description, and it is designed to evoke a reaction of fear, awe, or repentance on the part of the audience by portraying the invincibility of the enemy.

Setting

Although the final form of Isa 5:1-30 relates to its present position as part of the framework for the so-called Isaianic memoir or *Denkschrift* in the larger literary context of the Josianic redaction of chs. 5–12, discussion of the setting of this text must account for its composite nature and complex history of composition. On the basis of its different generic forms, scholars have argued that ch. 5 includes three separate texts that stem from originally independent contexts. These include the vineyard ALLEGORY in vv. 1-7; the woe series in vv. 8-24, which is grouped together with 10:1-4 to constitute an originally independent woe series; and the description of the Assyrian army in vv. 25-30, which employs the "outstretched hand" formula and constitutes an element of the "outstretched hand" oracle series in 9:7-20. According to Barth (*Jesaja-Worte,* 110-17, 192-94; cf. Clements, *Isaiah 1–39,* 55-58, 66-67; L'Heureux; Vermeylen, *Du prophète,* 159-86), these previously independent texts were combined as part of the larger late-7th-century Assyrian redaction that constitutes the bulk of chs. 5–11 and other portions of chs. 1–39. Although the overall hypothesis of a late-7th-century Assyrian or Josianic redaction in chs. 5–11 provides a cogent model for the formation of this material, there are indications that particular modifications are necessary to explain adequately the process of composition, the settings of the various units that comprise this material, and their relationship to the larger literary context. Such considerations have an important impact on understanding the setting of the texts that make up ch. 5.

The first involves the relationship between the vineyard ALLEGORY in 5:1-7 and the woe series in 5:8-24. Although scholars generally regard these texts as originally independent, a number of features demonstrate their interdependence and indicate that they were composed to function together as two parts of a larger unit. Despite the vineyard allegory's coherent structure, generic character, and intent, it is dependent on vv. 8-24 to spell out the full meaning of its message. The allegory does identify its major referents as YHWH, Israel, and Judah, and clearly demonstrates its intent to argue that Israel and Judah are being punished by YHWH for failing to meet the required standards of justice and righteousness. Nevertheless, the allegory does not specify these failings or the means and nature of the punishment that YHWH intends to impose, and thus leaves the audience with only a general impression of the prophet's message. Vv. 8-24 provide this specific information. These verses charge the leadership of the country with excessive land appropriation (vv. 8-10) and perversion of justice (vv. 20-23), which are linked to the leadership's drunkenness and lack of perception (vv. 11-12, 18-19, 22). They also specify the punishment of the people in terms of exile, hunger, and thirst (v. 13; cf. vv. 9-10, 17), as well as in terms of general destruction (vv. 14-17, 24). Furthermore, vv. 1-7 are linked to vv. 8-24 by a number of features that emphasize the vineyard imagery in particular and the agricultural context in general (cf. L'Heureux, 117-18, n. 24). These include the catchword reference to *kerem,* "vineyard," in v. 10, the frequent references to drunkenness and wine (vv. 11-12, 14, 22), which is the product of a vineyard, and the references to agricultural ruin (vv. 9-10, 17, 24), which reflect the fate of the vineyard. An additional feature concerns the perversion of justice (vv. 8, 20-23) that provides the climax for each text and thus defines their basic concern and the reason for punishment. Finally, although the authenticity of v. 24b has been questioned on the grounds that it contains no specific connection to vv. 22-24a (Barth, *Jesaja-Worte,* 115-16), it provides an ideal concluding summary for vv. 1-24a. By asserting that the people have rejected YHWH's torah and the word of the Holy One of Israel, v. 24b relates well to the themes of wisdom and justice that appear in vv. 18-24a, as well as to the theme of failed justice and righteousness that appears at the conclusion of the vineyard allegory in v. 7.

The second concerns the relationship of vv. 25-30 to vv. 1-24. In their present context, these verses are clearly attached to the preceding material by the introductory *'al-kēn,* "therefore," so that they specify the means for the punishment of Israel and Judah in terms of YHWH's summons of the enemy army. Nevertheless, there is no indication that this unit was originally related to the preceding material. The woe series in vv. 8-25 already has adequate conclusions in the *lākēn* ("therefore") clauses (vv. 13, 14-17, 24) following each woe statement. Furthermore, vv. 25-30 display no awareness of the vineyard or agricultural imagery employed throughout vv. 1-24, nor do they relate to their basic theme of perversion of justice in any appreciable manner. Their major images of the "outstretched hand" (v. 25), the "ensign to the nations" (v. 26), and the contrast of light and darkness (v. 30) have no basis or connection to vv. 1-24.

Indeed, one should not overlook the significance of the "outstretched hand" formula in v. 25. Because this formula is the characteristic refrain of the oracle series in 9:7 (*RSV* 8)–10:4, many scholars maintain that vv. 25-30 were originally part of the series in 9:7 (*RSV* 8)–10:4 (Clements, *Isaiah 1–39*, 66-70; Vermeylen, *Du prophète*, 174-85). Yet this formula always serves as a concluding refrain. Insofar as the formula appears at the beginning of vv. 25-30, it is impossible for this unit to have originally formed another uniform element of the series in 9:7 (*RSV* 8)–10:4. Because vv. 25-30 function as the conclusion for the preceding woe series in the present form of the text, scholars have overlooked the introductory character of the refrain in v. 25 in relation to the "outstretched hand" series in 9:7 (*RSV* 8)–10:4. V. 25 is not simply another occurrence of the formula. It begins in v. 25a with a statement that places YHWH's stretching of his hand in the context of divine wrath, natural upheaval, and punishment of the people. The standard form of the refrain appears only in v. 25b prior to the announcement that YHWH has summoned the Assyrian army. Because it provides the context and explains the meaning of the refrain, and because it introduces the Assyrian army as YHWH's agent of punishment against Israel, v. 25 constitutes the introductory statement of the refrain that provides the point of reference for the following occurrences in 9:7 (*RSV* 8)–10:4. Although the series is interrupted by the so-called Isaianic memoir in 6:1–9:6 (*RSV* 7), each occurrence of the "outstretched hand" formula in 9:7 (*RSV* 8)–10:4 relates back to the initial appearance of the refrain in 5:25. In this respect, the approach of the enemy army explains the suffering of Israel portrayed throughout 9:7 (*RSV* 8)–10:4. The lasting consequences of the Assyrian invasion explain why YHWH's hand is still "stretched out" against the people. Clearly, the placement of 5:25-30 at the conclusion of 5:1-24, and perhaps even the formulation of v. 25 with the introductory *ʿal-kēn*, is the result of redactional activity responsible for forming the larger unit of which ch. 5 is now a part. In its original form, however, 5:25-30 constituted the introduction to the "outstretched hand" oracle series in 9:7 (*RSV* 8)–10:4.

Although the present form of 5:1-24 clearly functions together with 5:25-30 and 9:7 (*RSV* 8)–10:4 to provide a literary framework for the so-called Isaiah memoir in 6:1–9:6 (*RSV* 7), it appears to derive from an originally oral setting. The use of the allegory at the beginning of the chapter, the appeal to the audience in vv. 3-4, and the formulaic "woe" language all demonstrate that this text was composed to function as a public announcement of the prophet's views concerning the ultimate significance of the Syro-Ephraimite War and its consequences for Israel and Judah. The vineyard imagery suggests a potential setting in relation to the temple Sukkot (Booths) festival, when the grape harvest was brought in and the winter rains were about to begin (cf. v. 6). At this time, a large audience would have been available in the temple courtyard to hear Isaiah's condemnation of the northern kingdom of Israel and its leadership for its failure to maintain justice and righteousness in relation to the southern kingdom of Judah. Because the punishment is described in somewhat general terms relative to the specific imagery of destruction and punishment in 9:7-20 (*RSV* 8-21), it is likely that this oracle stems from the period prior to the Assyrian invasion of Israel during the Syro-Ephraimite War (735-732). The setting of 5:25-30 must be considered in relation to 9:7 (*RSV* 8)–10:4, but it appears to stem from the period following the Assyrian attack when the full impact of Assyrian military might was realized.

Intention

The intention of 5:1-24 is clearly to convince the people of Jerusalem and Judah that the Assyrian invasion of Israel during the Syro-Ephraimite War is an act of YHWH to punish the country for its failure to maintain its standards of justice and righteousness. By employing the metaphorical language of the vineyard in vv. 1-7, Isaiah lures his audience into accepting his basic premise that Israel deserves to be punished for failing to meet YHWH's expectations. Once the audience has agreed with this basic premise, the prophet is then able to make the more specific charges in vv. 8-24 and thereby reinforce his point by citing the crimes and consequences listed therein.

That the people of Jerusalem and Judah are the audience for Isaiah's speech is evident from v. 3, where the audience is invited to participate in the decision concerning the disposal of the vineyard. In contrast, there is no indication that the northern kingdom of Israel and its leadership are the object of Isaiah's condemnation. Scholars are generally accustomed to maintaining that both Israel and Judah are condemned in this oracle, but a close examination of the terminology and images employed in the allegory indicates that only Israel is condemned here, although Judah suffers as well. V. 7 identifies "the house of Israel" as the vineyard but Judah is identified only as "his [YHWH's] choice planting." These identifications are significant when viewed in relation to the rest of the allegory. The reason for the condemnation of the vineyard is that it did not produce the choice grapes that the owner expected of it. Although the vines planted in the vineyard (v. 2) will also suffer, they are not condemned per se. Only the vineyard is the focus of punishment. Furthermore, the terms employed in v. 7 include *mišpāḥ*, "bloodshed, murder," and *ṣěʿāqâ*, "outcry," frequently associated with bloodshed or murder. When considered in relation to the events surrounding the Syro-Ephraimite War, it is quite easy to see how Israel would be condemned, insofar as it joined Aram in mounting an invasion of Judah. But it is not so easy to see Israel's crimes in relation to Judah. Judah was the victim in this case. It suffered as a consequence of Israel's actions, first in relation to Israel's and Aram's invasion of the country and attempt to install ben Tabael as king in place of Jotham or Ahaz, and later as a consequence of Assyria's imposing tribute and other marks of vassalage on Judah in return for saving the country from the Syro-Ephraimite coalition. Although Isaiah condemns Judah in connection with the Syro-Ephraimite War, it is not for bloodshed or violations of justice and righteousness, but for lack of faith in YHWH's guarantee of security for the nation (cf. 7:1–8:15; esp. 7:9).

This interpretation is borne out by the nature of the crimes and consequences listed in 5:8-24. This section portrays a people going off into exile (v. 13), an empty and desolate land (vv. 9-10, 17), and general destruction (v. 24a), and places primary blame on the leadership of the country. Although Judah suffered immensely, it did not go into exile as a result of the war, nor were its leaders removed. But a larger portion of the northern Israelite population was carried off into exile by the Assyrians (2 Kgs 15:29), and the leadership of the country was punished by Hoshea's assassination of King Pekah (2 Kgs 15:30). Furthermore, the crimes listed in this passage fit those of the northern kingdom of Israel. Apart from the charges of drunkenness and lack of perception, the specific crimes are land appropriation (v. 8) and the perversion of truth and justice. Although these crimes are often viewed as references to local social injustice, there is no indication that either Jotham or Ahaz were illegally appropriating land or manipulating the legal system prior to the Syro-Ephraimite War. When these crimes are viewed in an international context, however, land appropriation and perversion of truth and justice were precisely at issue in Israel's invasion of Judah, insofar as it was an attack on the sovereignty of a former ally that was designed to bring it under Israelite control. In this respect, one should keep in mind that prophets commonly refer to international events in terms of localized crimes (cf. Amos 1:3, 11, 13; Isa 10:14; Nah 3:5-7, etc.). Although the vague language and present setting of this text in relation to chs. 5–12 allows for an understanding that sees both Israel and Judah as the objects of YHWH's wrath, it is apparent that the original version of this oracle expressed Isaiah's condemnation of the northern kingdom of Israel and its leaders for the invasion of Judah during the Syro-Ephraimite War (cf. 17:1-14).

Bibliography

K. Beyer, "Althebräische Syntax in Prosa und Poesie," in *Tradition und Glaube: Das frühe Christentum in seiner Umwelt* (*Fest.* K. G. Kuhn; ed. G. Jeremias, H.-W. Kuhn, and H. Stegemann; Göttingen: Vandenhoeck & Ruprecht, 1971) 76-96; Bjørdalen, *Untersuchungen* (→ 1:2-3), 247-343; W. P. Brown, "The So-Called Refrain in Isaiah 5:25-30 and 9:7–10:4," *CBQ* 52 (1990) 432-43; R. B. Chisholm Jr., "Structure, Style, and the Prophetic Message: An Analysis of Isaiah 5:8-30," *BSac* 143 (1986) 46-60; J. L. Crenshaw, "A Liturgy of Wasted Opportunity (Am. 4:6-12; Isa. 9:7–10:4; 5:25-29)," *Semitics* 1 (1970) 27-37; E. W. Davies, *Prophecy and Ethics* (→ 1:2-3), 65-89; J. A. Dearman, *Property Rights in the Eighth-Century Prophets: The Conflict and Its Background* (SBLDS 106; Atlanta: Scholars Press, 1988); J. A. Emerton, "The Translation of Isaiah 5,1," in *The Scriptures and the Scrolls* (*Fest.* A. S. van der Woude; ed. F. García Martínez et al.; VTSup 49; Leiden: Brill, 1992) 18-30; A. Graffy, "The Literary Genre of Isaiah 5,1-7," *Bib* 60 (1979) 400-409; P. Höffken, "Probleme in Jesaja 5,1-7," *ZTK* 79 (1982) 392-410; H. Junker, "Die literarische Art von Is 5,1-7," *Bib* 40 (1959) 259-66; D. Kellermann, "Frevelstricke und Wagenseil: Bemerkungen zu Jesaja V 18," *VT* 37 (1987) 90-97; L'Heureux, "Redactional History" (→ 5:1–12:6); O. Loretz, "Weinberglied und prophetische Deutung," *UF* 7 (1975) 573-76; D. Lys, "La vigne et le double je: Exercice de style sur Esaïe V 1-7," in *Studies on Prophecy* (VTSup 26; Leiden: Brill, 1974) 1-16; H. Niehr, "Zur Gattung von Jes 5,1-7," *BZ* 30 (1986) 99-104; D. N. Premnath, "Latifundialization and Isaiah 5.8-10," *JSOT* 40 (1988) 49-60; W. Schottroff, "Das Weinberglied Jesajas (Jes 5, 1-7): Ein Beitrag zur Geschichte der Parabel," *ZAW* 82 (1970) 68-91; G. T. Sheppard, "More on Isaiah 5:1-7 as a Juridical Parable," *CBQ* 44 (1982) 45-47; G. R. Williams, "Frustrated Expectations in Isaiah V 1-7: A Literary Interpretation," *VT* 35 (1985) 459-65; J. T. Willis, "The Genre of Isaiah 5:1-7," *JBL* 96 (1977) 337-62; G. A. Yee, "A Form-Critical Study of Isaiah 5:1-7 as a Song and a Juridical Parable," *CBQ* 43 (1981) 30-40.

ISAIAH'S COMMISSION ACCOUNT, 6:1-13

Structure

I.	Presence vision report	1-2
	A. Concerning YHWH	1
	B. Concerning seraphim	2
II.	Audition report: doxology by seraphim	3-4
	A. Concerning doxology by seraphim	3
	B. Concerning effects of doxology in temple	4
III.	Report of Isaiah's reaction: exclamation of distress concerning his impurity	5
IV.	Report of seraph's response: purification	6-7
	A. Concerning its movement	6
	B. Concerning its purification of Isaiah's lips	7
	1. Act of purification	7aα
	2. Statement of purification	7aβ-b
V.	Report of YHWH's question and Isaiah's response	8
	A. YHWH's questions: who will go?	8a
	B. Isaiah's response: send me	8b
VI.	Commission report	9-10
	A. Speech formula	9aα
	B. Commission speech	9aβ-10
	1. Content of commission: what to say	9aβ-b
	a. Commission formula: go and say	9aβ
	b. Statement to people	9b
	2. Explanation of commission	10
	a. Effect of commission on people	10a
	b. Purpose of commission	10b
VII.	Report of Isaiah's question and YHWH's response	11-13
	A. Report of Isaiah's question: how long?	11a
	B. Prophet's report of YHWH's response	11b-13
	1. Report proper	11b
	2. Prophet's elaboration	12-13

Although ch. 6 is part of several larger units in the various layers of the structure of the book, several of its features indicate that it constitutes a coherent structural subunit. First, its narrative formulation distinguishes it from the poetic oracular material in ch. 5. Second, its narrative 1st-person singular form as an account by Isaiah distinguishes it from the following narratives in 7:1-25, which are formulated as 3rd-person accounts about Isaiah. Finally, the concern with Isaiah's vision of YHWH and the events that take place during this vision pervades the entire chapter and distinguishes it from the surrounding material.

The structure of this text is determined by several features, including its syntactical structure, which is determined by the verbs that govern each section, the shifts in subject that take place from section to section, and the sequence of speeches that appear in each section.

The first unit is the presence vision report in vv. 1-2. This unit sets the stage for the entire account by describing Isaiah's vision of YHWH's presence in the temple. The unit is governed by the *wāw*-consecutive verb, *wā'er'eh*, "and I saw," which follows a subordinate temporal clause stating that the vision took place "in the year of the death of King Uzziah" (742 B.C.E.). Whereas *wā'er'eh* identifies Isaiah's "seeing" as the primary action of the section, the remaining verbs describe the objects of Isaiah's vision. The participles relate the static situation of YHWH (*yōšēb*, "was sitting") and YHWH's train (*mělē'îm*, "was filling") in v. 1 and of the seraphim (*'ōmĕdîm*, "were standing") in v. 2. The imperfect verbs of v. 2, *yĕkasseh*, "it would cover" (bis), and *yĕ'ôpēp*, "it would fly," express the continuous action of the seraphim. This vision provides the context for the speeches and activities that appear in the following verses.

The audition report in vv. 3-4 includes the report of the doxology uttered by the seraphim in v. 3 and the effects of this utterance on the temple in v. 4. At this point, the subject shifts from the 1st-person singular reference to Isaiah in vv. 1-2 to 3rd-person singular references to the seraphim. The syntax of this passage is governed by the two copulative perfect verbs that describe the utterance by the seraphim: *wĕqārā'*, "and it called," and *wĕ'āmar*, "and it said." Together, the two verbs form a hendiadys in which they refer to the same act of speaking. Following the quotation of the doxology, the *wāw*-consecutive imperfect verb *wayyānu'û*, "and they moved," depends syntactically on *wĕqārā'/wĕ'āmar* and relates the movement of the doorposts as the consequence of the utterance by the seraphim. The imperfect verb *yĕmmālē'*, "it would fill," expresses the continuous action of the smoke filling the temple.

For the report of Isaiah's reaction in v. 5, the subject shifts back to a 1st-person singular reference to Isaiah. After seeing the vision of YHWH described in vv. 1-2 and hearing the doxology of the seraphim in vv. 3-4, Isaiah utters an exclamation of distress concerning his state of impurity. The passage is governed by the *wāw*-consecutive verb *wā'ōmar*, "and I said," which provides the narrative context for that exclamation. All other verbs are part of the exclamation itself.

Verses 6-7 report the seraph's response to Isaiah's exclamation. Again, the subject of the verbs shifts from Isaiah to the seraph. The governing verbs of this section are all *wāw*-consecutive imperfects and express a sequence of action that leads to Isaiah's purification. The seraph approaches (*wayyā'āp*, "and it flew") Isaiah with a coal taken from the altar, and then touches (*wayyagga'*, "and it touched") the coal to Isaiah's lips and says (*wayyō'mer*, "and it said") that Isaiah's sins have been removed. The remaining verbs are part of the seraph's statement.

The dominant 1st-person verbs of v. 8 indicate that the subject has shifted back again to Isaiah for a report of YHWH's question and Isaiah's response. The structure of this section is determined by the question-and-response pattern expressed through two *wāw*-consecutive imperfect verbs. The verb *wā'ešma'*, "and I heard," governs the syntax of the report of YHWH's question, which is introduced by the participle *'ōmēr*, "saying." Following YHWH's question, "Whom shall I send and who shall go for us?" the verb *wā'ōmar*, "and I said," introduces Isaiah's response, "Here I am, send me."

133

The subject shifts to YHWH as indicated by the 3rd-person verb for the commission report in vv. 9-10. The syntax of this passage is governed by the speech formula *wayyō'mer,* "and he said," in v. 9aα, and the rest of the passage constitutes the commission speech by YHWH to Isaiah. The speech itself is governed by its imperative and 2nd-person singular address style directed to the prophet. It concentrates first on what the prophet should say in v. 9aβ-b, including a typical commissioning formula, "go and say to this people" (v. 9aβ), and a quotation of what the prophet should say (v. 9b). This statement is explained by another imperative in v. 10 expressing the intended effect of Isaiah's commission on the people, which is to close their hearts, ears, and eyes (v. 10a), so as to prevent them from understanding and repenting and thereby being healed (v. 10b).

Finally, the subject shifts back to Isaiah for the final section, which reports Isaiah's question to YHWH and YHWH's response. The structure of this passage is governed by a question-and-answer pattern as determined by its two dominant verbs. The *wāw*-consecutive imperfect verb *wā'ōmar,* "and I said," introduces Isaiah's question to YHWH, "How long, my Lord?" YHWH's answer is introduced by the *wāw*-consecutive imperfect verb *wayyō'mer,* "and he said." YHWH's response is basically stated through a wordplay on the verbal root *š'h,* "to be destroyed." YHWH responds, "Until cities are destroyed [*šā'û*] without inhabitant and houses without a person, and the land shall be destroyed [*tiššā'eh*] as a desolation." The interaction of the Qal perfect form and the Niphal imperfect form of the verb indicates that although the destruction is impending (imperfect), its realization is an established fact (perfect). In their present position, vv. 12-13 further describe the process of destruction mentioned in v. 11b. The 3rd-person reference to YHWH in v. 12 indicates that the prophet is speaking as in v. 11b, where he reported YHWH's response. Vv. 12-13 therefore constitute the prophet's elaboration of YHWH's statement in v. 11b insofar as its converted perfect verbs depend syntactically on the *wāw*-consecutive imperfect *wayyō'mer* of v. 11b.

Genre

The genre of this passage has provoked considerable disagreement among scholars. It is often understood as the call narrative (i.e., → vocation account) of the prophet insofar as the vision is dated to the year of the death of King Uzziah, which would be a likely date for the beginning of Isaiah's career, and insofar as it portrays Isaiah's commission to carry out YHWH's instructions concerning the judgment of the people. In this respect, Habel (pp. 309-12) argues that ch. 6 contains five of the six elements typically found in prophetic call narratives, including the divine confrontation (vv. 1-2), the introductory word (vv. 3-7), the commission (vv. 8-10), the objection (v. 11a), and the assurance (vv. 11-13). Although the sixth element, a sign to confirm the prophetic call, does not appear in this chapter, Habel speculates that the Immanuel sign of ch. 7 may well complete the call narrative sequence.

But there are problems with the identification of ch. 6 as a typical prophetic call narrative. Habel has already noted that the chapter deviates from the standard form, not only because it does not include all the requisite elements but also because of its similarities to Micaiah ben Imlah's vision reported in 1 Kgs 22:19-21. Like Isaiah, Micaiah stands in the heavenly assembly or temple, but there is no indication that Micaiah is called to be a prophet in this setting. Rather, his presence in the heavenly council suggests that he already had standing as a prophet and that he simply reports his experiences in the council in order to explain his statements concerning impending disaster to King Ahaz and King Jehoshaphat in the war with Aram. Furthermore, just as Micaiah is never addressed, so Isaiah is never directly addressed until he responds to YHWH's question, "Whom shall I send and who shall go for us?" Isaiah's presence before YHWH indicates that he was not called to become a prophet at this point, but was simply present at a time when a specific task was to be performed. On the basis of the comparison with 1 Kgs 22:19-21, Wildberger (*Jesaja,* 236) argues that Isaiah 6 is not a prophetic call narrative but a "throne council vision" *(Thronratsvision).* Hurowitz likewise identifies it as a "throne vision" (p. 41; citing Y. Kaufmann, *Toledot Ha-Emunah Ha-Yisre'elit* [Jerusalem and Tel Aviv: Mosad Bialik, 5727 = 1957], 3:206-8; ET: *The Religion of Israel* [tr. M. Greenberg; Chicago: University of Chicago, 1960] 388). Steck (p. 191) compares Isaiah 6 to the "receipt of a commission in a heavenly scene" found in Zech 1:7ff. and Job 1:6-12, and identifies the chapter as an example of the "granting of an extraordinary commission in the heavenly throne assembly."

In addition to the form, the contents of Isaiah 6 present problems in identifying it as an example of a prophetic call narrative. Isaiah's COMMISSION to harden the hearts of the people so that they will not repent contradicts the essential thrust of his activity, particularly in relation to his audience with King Ahaz in the following chapter. Because of the difficulties in reconciling the COMMISSION in ch. 6 with the prophet's prophetic activity, Kaplan suggests that ch. 6 does not represent a call narrative at all, but the prophet's despairing reflection on the failure of his attempts to convince the people to repent, written after he had been active for some time. Likewise, Knierim (p. 59) notes the imagery of YHWH's throne and the associated motif of judgment in order to argue that the chapter is a combination of two different genres of the (→) vision report, including a vision of judgment together with a vision of call (cf. Wagner). Finally, Kaiser (*Isaiah 1–12,* 123) points to the literary function of ch. 6 as the introduction to the so-called memoir or *Denkschrift* and notes that biblical narrators are not interested in biographical facts as such but in their significance for the message. On the basis of the initiatory character of Isaiah's purification and the association of Ezekiel's call with a throne scene, Kaiser maintains that Isaiah 6 can be considered a call scene written by later narrators concerned with using the past as a mirror for later times.

I take up the question of dating below, but Kaiser's understanding of the literary function of this chapter is significant insofar as it provides a basis for understanding its generic character. Scholars have long noted the association of this chapter with the Isaianic "memoir" and consequently with the Syro-Ephraimite War. Whether the chapter reflects an actual experience of the prophet or is the product of later reflection, it provides a rationale for Isaiah's failure to convince Ahaz and the people to repent in the Syro-Ephraimite War. But this chapter does not function only in relation to the Syro-Ephraimite War. As noted in the discussion of chs. 5–12, the "memoir" is embedded in a context that presupposes Judah's experience in relation to Assyria's invasions of the late 8th century. Consequently, chs. 5–12 portray the Assyrian invasions as the fulfillment of Isaiah's warning of impending disaster for Judah. When considered in relation to chs. 1–39 as a whole, or even chs. 1–66 in light of the later Babylonian destruction, ch. 6 becomes a paradigm for Isaiah's entire prophetic career (on the significance of ch. 6 in the context of the book as a whole, see R. F. Melugin, *The Formation of Isaiah 40–55* [BZAW 141; Berlin and New York: de Gruyter, 1976] 82-86; cf. Seitz, "Divine Council"). Both deliverance and restoration of the nation are predicated on the punishment of Israel and Judah in the book of Isaiah, both in chs. 1–39 and in chs. 1–66. The people were to experience disaster and judgment so that YHWH's power would be recognized. Consequently, ch. 6 sums up the essential activity or vocation of the prophet in terms of preparing the people for judgment. In this respect, ch. 6 functions as the call narrative or VOCATION ACCOUNT of the prophet. Whether it represents an authentic account of his experience at the beginning of his career or is the result of later reflection is irrelevant. In its present context, it is meant to be understood as the prophet's call or commission to his vocation. Because its primary purpose is to convey the prophet's commission, it is properly understood as a VOCATION ACCOUNT.

In addition to the overarching generic pattern, several other generic elements appear in this passage. First is the VISION REPORT, which conveys the prophet's encounter with YHWH in this chapter. The VISION REPORT is constituted by the prophet's description of what he experiences in his vision of YHWH, including both the presence vision in vv. 1-2 and the AUDITION REPORT in vv. 3-4. The AUDITION REPORT includes a DOXOLOGY uttered by the seraphim, which is typically a pithy, lyrical affirmation of divine glory. In this case, the DOXOLOGY extols the holiness of YHWH.

The report of Isaiah's reaction to the vision includes the prophet's EXCLAMATION OF DISTRESS. The exclamation begins with the typical formula *'ôy lî,* "woe is me." This distinguishes it from the WOE ORACLE, which begins with the similar-sounding warning cry *hôy,* "woe!" Generally, *'ôy* is a simple exclamation whereas *hôy* appears in a number of specialized contexts including funeral laments, vocative APPEALS, ADDRESSES, warnings, and prophetic indictments (cf. Janzen, *Mourning Cry,* 19-20).

Finally, the REPORT of the COMMISSION appears in vv. 9-10. It begins with the typical COMMISSIONING FORMULA, *lēk wĕ'āmartā,* "go and say," followed by an indication of the addressee, "to this people." The COMMISSION itself conveys YHWH's charge to Isaiah and consists of the commands concerning what Isaiah is to say to the people and its effect. Because the COMMISSION is the central feature of this passage, it influences the generic character of the whole as an ACCOUNT OF A COMMISSION.

Setting

According to the initial statement of this passage, Isaiah's vision takes place in the year of the death of King Uzziah (ca. 742). The message of judgment that appears in this chapter makes sense in the light of the international situation at this time. Tiglath-pileser III had recently ascended the throne of Assyria (745) and had made clear his intentions to expand westward into Aram and Israel. One year prior to Uzziah's death (cf. 2 Kgs 15:32), the Gileadite general Pekah ben Remaliah had assassinated Pekahiah, the ruling monarch of the northern kingdom of Israel, as part of an overall plan to form an alliance with King Rezin of Damascus and other kingdoms in the Syro-Israelite region to oppose the Assyrian incursions. Pekah's Gileadite background and the repeated attempts by Aram to conquer this region during the 9th and 8th centuries may well have suggested to many that Aram had finally succeeded in bringing Israel under its sway (see Irvine), but one must recall that Gilead was frequently the center for intense Israelite nationalism and fidelity to Mosaic YHWHism, as indicated by the activities of Elijah and Elisha among others. Regardless of the motives, however, the following narratives in chs. 7–8 and the oracles in chs. 5, 9–10, and 17 make clear that Isaiah was adamantly opposed to the Syro-Ephraimite coalition and its attempts to oppose Assyrian expansion. Although Israel and Judah formed two separate kingdoms, Isaiah tended to see their fate bound together, as indicated by his references to Israel and Judah in his vineyard allegory in 5:1-7 and subsequent use of "Israel" as a designation including Judah after 722 (cf. Høgenhaven, 10). In this case, the statements of impending judgment in Isaiah's vision would indicate his view that Israel and Judah would suffer serious consequences from any attempt to oppose Tiglath-pileser III. That the prophet was capable of making such political predictions at the death of an old king and the beginning of the reign of his successor is indicated by his forecast of disaster for the Philistines at the death of King Ahaz in 715 (14:28-32). Isaiah was likely well aware of Philistine plans to revolt against Assyria in 712, and his statements can be understood to express his opinion concerning the futility of such a revolt and to warn the new king, Hezekiah, against participating in it. In this respect, one should note that Micaiah ben Imlah's vision of YHWH's court also provided the authority for his advice to Ahab and Jehoshaphat to avoid battle with Aram. Isaiah's vision appears to have a similar function insofar as it predicts judgment in a context of potential confrontation with the Assyrian empire.

There are two major problems concerning the historical setting of this chapter. The first is that Isaiah's commission to harden the hearts of the people and thereby to prevent their repentance does not appear to be consistent with Isaiah's attempts to persuade King Ahaz that reliance on YHWH alone, and not on the Assyrians, will deliver Judah from the Syro-Ephraimite coalition and preserve his throne. On this basis, many scholars have followed Kaplan in maintaining that Isaiah 6 was written after the Syro-Ephraimite War and reflected Isaiah's frustration after failing to dissuade Ahaz and Judah from turning to the Assyrians for aid. Judah's subsequent submission to Assyrian suzerainty (cf. 2 Kgs 16:7-18) and Isaiah's withdrawal from public debate (Isa 8:16-18) appear to support such a view. But one must keep in mind that Isaiah's approach to Ahaz and Judah in 7:1–8:15 took place long after the northern kingdom of Israel had initiated its policy and attacked Judah in an attempt to bring it into the coalition with Aram. At this point, in Isaiah's view, the northern kingdom had sealed its fate (cf. 7:7-9), but Judah still had the opportunity to avoid the consequences of submission to the Assyrians. In this respect, the judgment mentioned in Isaiah's vision would be carried out when Assyria retaliated against the northern kingdom; and even if Judah did not join the Syro-Ephraimite coalition, it had suffered the consequences of invasion by the coalition partners.

The second problem concerns the authenticity of vv. 12-13. These verses are frequently viewed as postexilic additions to 6:1-11 because of the 3rd-person reference to YHWH in v. 12a in a context where YHWH is supposed to be the speaker, and because the concept of the remnant with its associated reference to the *zer'a qōdeš,* "holy seed," in v. 13 is believed to be a postexilic development (cf. the reference to *zera' haqqōdeš,* "holy race," in Ezra 9:2; Hausmann, 159-62). Although the above discussion of the structure of this passage demonstrates that there is no disruption of the speech by YHWH in v. 11, insofar as the prophet resumes speaking in the present form of the passage, there are other indications that vv. 12-13 are later additions. The converted perfect *wĕriḥaq,* "and he will remove far away," does not relate well syntactically to the prophet's statement *wayyō'mer,* "and he said," in v. 11b, but does relate well to the imperfect *tiššā'eh,* "it will be destroyed," in the speech by YHWH. Furthermore, the reference to *hā'ādām,* "human beings," in v. 12 takes up the reference to *mē'ên 'ādām,* "without human beings," in YHWH's speech in v. 11b, and *hā'āreṣ,* "the land," in v. 12 relates similarly to *wĕhā'ădāmâ,* "and the land," in v. 11b.

Although YHWH's speech presents a well-constructed example of chiastic parallelism, involving the verbal root *š'h* and the phrases *mē'ên yōšēb/mē'ên 'ādām* and *'ādām/wĕhā'ădāmâ,* vv. 12-13 fall well outside this poetic structure and appear to be an attempt to take up key words and concepts in order to interpret the meaning of YHWH's statement in terms of a remnant, expressed as a "tenth" or a "stump" that will be subject to continued punishment. The remnant is frequently understood as Judah, the tenth or the stump that remains of the whole of Israel after the Assyrian invasion. Nonetheless, although vv. 12-13 appear to be an addition that attempts to explain the meaning of YHWH's speech in terms of continued punishment of Judah, there is no evidence that this addition is postexilic. A fully developed remnant theology does not appear here, either in terms of the typical vocabulary (i.e., *šĕ'ār, niš'ār, pĕlêṭâ,* etc.), or in terms of a returning remnant. Furthermore, the reference to "holy seed" in Ezra 9:2 does not indicate a postexilic context for the similar reference in Isa 6:13. The concept of Israel as a distinct people appears throughout its history, and Ezra's reform was as much influenced by the book of Isaiah as it was influential in its composition (Koch, "Ezra").

Insofar as vv. 12-13 discuss a continued punishment of Judah after an initial punishment of all Israel, they can be easily understood in relation to Sennacherib's invasion of Judah in 701. As demonstrated above, the so-called Isaianic memoir was expanded by material that related directly to later Assyrian invasions of Judah, especially the threats made against Jerusalem by the Assyrian monarch in 10:5-19, which can be understood only in relation to Sargon II's attempts to blockade Jerusalem. Insofar as the following narratives spell out the meaning of ch. 6, and insofar as they ultimately take up the issue of the Assyrian invasions as the fulfillment of Isaiah's threats against Judah (7:10-25), vv. 12-13 must be viewed as added material that connects the report of Isaiah's vision to the following material and relates to the situation of the later Assyrian invasions of Judah. Moreover, insofar as Isaiah later expressed his opposition to Hezekiah's revolt as an analogy to the failed revolts of the northern kingdom, the addition of vv. 12-13 may well have been composed by the prophet himself sometime between the beginning of Hezekiah's reign in 715 and the Assyrian attack of 701 in an attempt to apply the vision to a later situation and to dissuade Hezekiah from a confrontation with the Assyrians (cf. K. Nielsen, *Tree,* 144-58).

With regard to its social setting, the vision clearly takes place in the Jerusalem temple. The imagery associated with YHWH is that of the *děbîr,* "inner sanctuary" or "Holy of Holies," where the ark resides. The ark is consistently portrayed as the "footstool" of YHWH (Ps 132:7) or the place where YHWH is "enthroned on the cherubim" (Ps 99:1; 1 Sam 4:4; 2 Sam 6:2; 2 Kgs 19:15; Isa 37:16; 1 Chr 13:6). Likewise, although the terminology differs, the seraphim appear to correspond to the winged cherubim that stand above the ark in the Holy of Holies (1 Kgs 6:23-28; 8:6-7). Studies by Joines and Keel *(Visionen)* have pointed to the Egyptian portrayal of winged serpent figures around the throne of Pharaoh in analogy to the cherubim; and Görg has demonstrated that the Egyptian terms *srrf* and *sfr,* "serpent, dragon, etc.," are cognates of Heb. *śārāp,* "seraph," indicating an even closer analogy to the Egyptian imagery discussed by Joines and Keel. Finally, smoke and cloud are associated with appearances by YHWH in the Holy of Holies and symbolize the divine presence in the temple (see 1 Kgs 8:9-13; cf. Exod 40:34-38; Lev 16:2).

Engnell's study points to a number of royal motifs that can be associated with the portrayal of YHWH in Isaiah's vision. The throne with its guardian winged creatures is a typical motif in the Egyptian royal court (so Joines and Keel above) as well as in Mesopotamian throne rooms. Furthermore, when the Egyptian pharaoh is seated on his throne in the "Morning House," the high priest steps forward and utters the formula, "Pure, pure [*w'b w'b*] is the King of the South and the North; thy purity is the purity of Horus, Seth, Thoth, and Sopou" (Engnell, p. 36), which corresponds to the doxology uttered by the seraphim in Isa 6:3. Engnell also cites Mesoptamian analogies such as the mouth purification rites of the Akkadian royal *kuppuru* ritual and the Egyptian royal *pr dw3.t* ritual, both of which preceded an audience with the king (cf. Isa 6:5-7; cf. Hurowitz). The Akkadian *Maqlu* incantation series includes a statement by Anu, the Royal Sky God of Heaven, to the *ashipu*-priest "sent out" by Anu asking *mannu lushpur,* "whom shall I send?" in analogy to YHWH's question in Isa 6:8. Finally, Knierim points out that judgment is a typical activity of the king seated on his throne. Clearly, these features indicate that YHWH is portrayed as a king enthroned in the Holy of Holies of the Jerusalem temple.

Yet it would be a mistake to follow Engnell or Cazelles ("La vocation") in maintaining that this scene represents an enthronement ceremony that would take place on New Year's Day. There is no evidence in the Hebrew Bible indicating that kings were enthroned at the New Year. The examples of coronation ceremonies, including those of Saul (1 Sam 9:22–10:8; cf. 11:12-15), Solomon (1 Kgs 1:38-40), and Jehoash (2 Kgs 11:9-14), indicate that kings were anointed and enthroned as the occasion required, not at the New Year. Instead of enthronement, the element of judgment should be emphasized (Knierim). In this respect, the occasion for Isaiah's vision must be identified with the Day of Atonement (Yom Kippur) on the 10th day of the 7th month. Not only is this considered to be the time when YHWH passes judgment on the people, but it is also the only time of the year when YHWH appears in the Holy of Holies in the cloud above the mercy seat (Lev 16:14, 30-34). Only the high priest is allowed to appear before YHWH in the Holy of Holies with the appropriate offerings, but he does so on behalf of the people who are gathered at the temple for the holiday. Although there is no indication that Isaiah filled a priestly role, his presence at the temple during the Yom Kippur ceremonies appears to be the most likely setting for his vision. In this regard, Hurowitz's observations concerning the role of mouth purification in Mesopotamian ritual contexts supports a cultic setting for the activities portrayed in this text.

Intention

The primary intention of this passage is clearly to legitimize Isaiah's prophetic activity in relation to the disasters that befell Israel and Judah at the hands of the Assyrian empire. Insofar as both kingdoms suffered Assyrian invasion in the late 8th century, Isaiah's task is defined as hardening the people's hearts so that judgment can be carried out. Ch. 6 portrays this task as the result of a decision by YHWH in the heavenly council or throne room, thereby explaining Israel's and Judah's suffering as the result of YHWH's judgment. Such council scenes or commission accounts are typically used to legitimize a prophet's activity in the Hebrew Bible.

The problem presented by this chapter is whether it represents the prophet's actual purpose, his self-understanding from the time of his commission, or a reflection on his task after failing to persuade Ahaz to avoid reliance on the Assyrian empire during the Syro-Ephraimite War. The question depends on whether Isaiah actively sought to deceive the people and thereby to bring about their judgment or whether he retrojected the judgment of Israel and Judah into his understanding of his initial commission. Obviously, this question has important hermeneutical implications for the understanding of Isaiah and his prophetic role. If the former is true, Isaiah did not act in accordance with his commission insofar as he tried to warn Ahaz and thereby avoid punishment for Judah. If the latter is true, then the veracity of Isaiah's commission account is undermined.

Yet the presentation of the issue in terms of such diametrically opposed choices may well represent a failure to differentiate between the present literary setting of this passage and its original life setting in establishing its intent. First of all, ch. 6 clearly functions as the literary introduction to the so-called memoir in 6:1–9:6 (*RSV* 7) (cf. Kaiser, *Isaiah 1–12,* 121). In this respect its function is to legitimize the judgment that is projected for Judah (and Israel). Yet the literary function of this chapter is not limited to that of a "memoir" alone. As part of the larger unit in chs. 5–12, ch. 6 not only legitimizes the message of judgment in these chapters but also indicates the necessary prelude of disaster that will eventually result in the restoration portrayed in chs. 10–12. In this respect, chs. 10–12 define the purpose of YHWH's harsh decree of unavoidable judgment by presenting the purge that will result in a new Davidic monarch, a second exodus, and the restoration of Israel and Judah. Indeed, such a role underlies not only ch. 6 but the entire book as well, with its pattern of judgment and subsequent restoration for Israel as a testimony to YHWH's universal rule.

Yet the literary association between ch. 6 and the rest of the "memoir" may well run a risk of failing to understand the original intention of this passage. In the present literary context, the report of Isaiah's encounter with Ahaz in chs. 7–8 is understood as the illustration of the judgment mentioned in the prophet's commission, since it presents Isaiah's predictions of Assyrian invasion as the fulfillment of that judgment. As literary analysis of the "memoir" indicates, however, it is an edited text that associates the 3rd-person report of Isaiah's encounter with Ahaz in 7:1-25 with the 1st-person report of Isaiah's vision in 6:1-13. Insofar as ch. 6 relates to the time of the death of King Uzziah (742), and insofar as 7:1-25 relates to the Syro-Ephraimite War some seven to ten years later (735-732), it is clear that ch. 6 was not composed in relation to ch. 7, but was associated with it only some time after the initial composition. This means that the original intent of ch. 6 must be defined apart from its relationship to ch. 7 and the "memoir" as a whole.

When one considers ch. 6 apart from its context, vv. 12-13 take on special significance. As noted above, these verses are apparently a later addition to vv. 1-11 which indicate that the remaining "tenth" of the people, generally under-stood as Judah, will be subject to judgment a second time. The use of the term *ăśirîyâ*, "tenth," for Judah apparently relates to the practice of dedicating or sanctifying one-tenth or a tithe of one's income and belongings for use in the temple (cf. Lev 27:30-33; Num 18:21-24; Deut 14:22-29; 26:12-15). Con-sequently, Judah as the surviving "tenth" of Israel is the portion that is dedicated to YHWH and thereby sanctified (cf. v. 13bβ). Therefore, the judgment men-tioned in vv. 1-11 is directed to all Israel of which Judah is to be the surviving remnant. Such a perspective is consistent with Isaiah's critique of the northern kingdom of Israel and his view that all Israel includes both the northern kingdom of Israel and the southern kingdom of Judah (cf. Høgenhaven, 10). Isaiah's statements concerning the northern kingdom consistently portray its judgment as already decided. It is his statements to the southern kingdom that fail to produce an appropriate response. In this respect, the addition of vv. 12-13 to 6:1-11 paves the way for the introduction of the narratives in chs. 7–8, which illustrate the punishment of the remaining "tenth" (Judah). Consequently, the original intent of 6:1-11 was to express condemnation of the northern kingdom of Israel, but the addition of vv. 12-13 expressed the judgment of the southern kingdom of Judah and enabled the editors to combine ch. 6 with the narratives concerning Isaiah's confrontation with Ahaz in the balance of the "memoir" (7:1–9:6 [*RSV* 7]).

Bibliography

A. Auret, "Jesaja 6:1aα meer as 'n historiese nota?" *NGTT* 32 (1991) 368-77; G. K. Beale, "Isaiah vi 9-13: A Retributive Taunt Against Idolatry," *VT* 41 (1991) 257-78; H. Cazelles, "La vocation d'Isaïe (ch. 6) et les rites royaux," in *Homenaje a Juan Prado* (ed. L. Alvarez Verdes and E. J. Alonzo Hernandez; Madrid: Consejo Superior de Investigaciones Cientificios, 1975) 89-108; J. Day, "Echoes of Baal's Seven Thunders and Lightnings in Psalm XXIX and Habakkuk III 9 and the Identity of the Seraphim in Isaiah VI," *VT* 29 (1979) 143-51; I. Engnell, *The Call of Isaiah: An Exegetical and Comparative Study* (UUÅ 4; Uppsala: A.-B. Lundequistska; Leipzig: Harrassowitz, 1949); M. Görg, "Die Funktion der Serafen bei Jesaja," *BN* 5 (1978) 28-39; B. Gosse, "Isaïe 52,13–53,12 et Isaïe 6," *RB* 98 (1991) 537-43; N. Habel, "The Form and Significance of the Call Narratives," *ZAW* 77 (1965) 297-323; C. Hardmeier, "Jesajas Verkündigungsabsicht und Jahwes Verstockungsauftrag in Jes 6," in *Die Botschaft und die Boten* (*Fest.* H. W. Wolff; ed. J. Jeremias and L. Perlitt; Neukirchen-Vluyn: Neukirchener, 1981) 235-51; J. Hausmann, *Israels Rest: Studien zum Selbstverständnis der nachexilischen Gemeinde* (BWANT 124; Stuttgart, Berlin, Cologne, and Mainz: Kohlhammer, 1987) 159-62; F. Horst, "Die Visionsschilderungen der alttestamentlichen Propheten," *EvT* 20 (1960) 193-205; V. Hurowitz, "Isaiah's Impure Lips and Their Purification in Light of Akkadian Sources," *HUCA* 60 (1989) 39-89; E. Jenni, "Jesajas Berufung in der neueren Forschung," *TZ* 15 (1959) 321-39; K. R. Joines, "Winged Serpents in Isaiah's Inaugural Vision," *JBL* 86 (1967) 410-15; idem, *Serpent Symbolism in the Old Testament* (Haddonfield: Haddonfield House, 1974); idem, "Seraphim," *BibIll* 15/1 (1988) 12-15; M. Kaplan, "Isaiah 6:1-11," *JBL* 45 (1926) 251-59; O. Keel, *JHWH-Visionen und Siegelkunst: Eine neue Deutung der Majestätsschilderungen in Jes 6, Ez 1 und 10 und Sach 4* (SBS 84/85; Stuttgart: Katholisches Bibelwerk, 1977) 46-124; A. F. Key, "The Magical Background of Isaiah 6:9-13," *JBL* 86 (1967) 198-204; Kilian, *Jesaja 1–39,* 112-30; idem, "Der Verstockungsauftrag Jesajas" (→ "Introduction to the Book of Isaiah"); E. C. Kingsbury, "The Prophets and the Council of YHWH," *JBL* 83 (1964) 279-86; R. Knierim, "The Vocation of Isaiah," *VT* 18 (1968) 47-68; L. J. Liebreich, "The Position of Chapter Six in the Book of Isaiah," *HUCA* 25 (1954) 37-40; Long, "Reports of Visions" (→ "Introduction to the Prophetic Literature"); H. Niehr, "Zur Intention von Jes 6,1-9," *BN* 21 (1983) 59-65; M. Nobile, "Jes 6 und Ez 1,1–3,15: Vergleich und Funktion im jeweiligen redaktionellen Kontext," in *The Book of Isaiah/Le Livre d'Isaïe* (ed. J. Vermeylen; BETL 81; Leuven: Leuven University Press and Peeters, 1989) 209-16; R. Rendtorff, "Jesaja 6 im Rahmen der Komposition des Jesajabuches," in ibid., 73-82; J. De Savignac, "Les 'Seraphim,' " *VT* 22 (1972) 320-25; J. M. Schmidt, "Gedanken zum Verstockungsauftrag Jesajas (Is. VI)," *VT* 21 (1971) 68-90; J. Schreiner, "Zur Textgestalt von Jes 6 und 7,1-17," *BZ* 22 (1978) 92-97; J.-P. Sonnet, "Le motif de l'endurcissement (Is 6,9-10) et la lecture d' 'Isaïe,' " *Bib* 73 (1992) 208-39; O. H. Steck, "Bemerkungen zu Jesaja 6," *BZ* 16 (1972) 188-206; M. E. W. Thompson, *Situation and Theology: Old Testament Interpretations of the Syro-Ephraimite War* (Prophets and Historians Series 1; Sheffield: Almond, 1982) 48-53; W. Vogels, "Les récits de vocation des prophètes," *NRT* 95 (1973) 3-24; R. Wagner, *Textexegese als Strukturanalyse: Sprachwissenschaftliche Methode zur Erschliessung althebräischer Texte am Beispiel des Visionsberichtes Jes 6,1-11* (ATSAT 32; St. Ottilien: EOS, 1989); C. F. Whitley, "The Call and Mission of Isaiah," *JNES* 18 (1959) 38-48; A. Zeron, "Die Anmassung des Königs Usia im Lichte von Jesajas Berufung," *TZ* 33 (1977) 65-68.

ACCOUNT CONCERNING YHWH'S JUDGMENT AGAINST JUDAH: ISAIAH'S SIGNS TO THE HOUSE OF DAVID AND JUDAH, 7:1–8:15

Structure

I. Concerning Ahaz: dialogue report	7:1-25
II. Concerning Judah: autobiographical report concerning the Maher-shalal-hash-baz sign and its significance	8:1-15

Because of the size and complexity of Isa 7:1–8:15, I have divided the discussion into two parts. Part one focuses on 7:1-25, part two on 8:1-15.

The demarcation of 7:1–8:15 is determined by a combination of its formal features and contents. Following the autobiographical narrative concerning the prophet's vision of YHWH in 6:1-13, 7:1 introduces a narrative report with a chronological formula that relates the unit to the reign of Ahaz during the Syro-Ephraimite War rather than to the reign of Uzziah (cf. 6:1). Although 7:1-9 is presented in the form of a 3rd-person objective report, the balance of the unit in 7:10–8:15 is presented in autobiographical form, as indicated by the 1st-person references to the prophet throughout this material. Below I explain the reasons for this shift.

Despite the shift in form, it is clear that 7:10-25 and 8:1-15 depend on 7:1-9 in the present form of the narrative. The relationship between 7:10-25 and 7:1-9 is established by the introductory speech formula, *wayyôsep yhwh dabbēr 'el-'āḥāz lē'mōr,* "and YHWH again spoke to Ahaz saying," the reference to the "house of David" in v. 13 (cf. v. 2), and the general setting of the prophet's dialogue with Ahaz. Likewise, 8:1-15 depends on 7:1-9 and 7:10-25. This is clear from its references to Assyrian intervention in relation to the Syro-Ephraimite crisis in 8:4 and 7 (cf. 7:17, 20), its references to Immanuel in 8:8 and 10 (cf. 7:14), and the general context of the use of Isaiah's children as signs. The narrative continues until 8:16, where imperative forms, directed to the prophet's followers, mark the shift from reporting past events to announcing future plans.

The passage falls into two basic parts, which are demarcated primarily by their contents and secondarily by their respective forms. Isa 7:1-25 takes up the prophet's signs to Ahaz in the form of a dialogue report, whereas 8:1-15 takes up Isaiah's signs for Judah in the form of an instruction or commission report.

I. CONCERNING AHAZ: DIALOGUE REPORT, 7:1-25

Structure

A. Narrative report concerning circumstances of dialogue		1-9
	1. Concerning the attempted Syro-Ephraimite attack against Jerusalem	1

143

Within the dialogue report of 7:1-25, vv. 1-9 constitute a narrative report concerning the circumstances of the dialogue. Although these verses are frequently understood as the first stage in the encounter between Isaiah and Ahaz, the present form of the passage indicates that it narrates the circumstances in which the dialogue between Isaiah and Ahaz took place. This is clear not only from the chronological notice concerning the attempted Syro-Ephraimite attack against Jerusalem and the report of that attempt to Ahaz in vv. 1-2, but also from the report of YHWH's instructions to Isaiah prior to the dialogue in vv. 3-9. The dialogue report proper appears only in vv. 10-25, where it is clear that the situation is no longer of YHWH's instruction to the prophet, but a report of YHWH's or Isaiah's conversation with Ahaz.

The structure of vv. 1-9 is governed by its *wāw*-consecutive imperfect verbs in vv. 1-3, which establish the narrative sequence of the passage and convey its three essential subjects. V. 1 reports the attempted attack by the Syro-Ephraimite coalition against Judah and includes a chronological statement concerning the fact of the attempted attack in the days of Ahaz (v. 1a) and its subsequent failure (v. 1b). V. 2 narrates the report of this attempted attack to Ahaz, here referred to as "the house of David" (v. 2a), and his fearful reaction to this report (v. 2b). Vv. 3-9 report YHWH's commission or instructions to Isaiah to meet with Ahaz and convey YHWH's reassurance that the Syro-Ephraimite threat will not succeed. Following the YHWH speech formula in v. 3aα, the speech itself follows in vv. 3aβ-9. Its present form is that of a commissioning speech whereby YHWH commissions the prophet to meet with

Ahaz and deliver YHWH's message of reassurance. It falls into two basic instructions as defined by its imperative and 2nd-person verbal clauses. The imperative *ṣē'-nā' liqra't*, "go please to meet," introduces the instruction to meet Ahaz in v. 3abβ-b, and the 2nd-person *wĕ'āmartā 'ēlāyw*, "and you shall say to him," introduces the instruction to speak in vv. 4-9. The instruction to speak begins with the command to speak in v. 4a followed by the content of the command in vv. 4b-9, which takes the form of a reassurance speech to Ahaz. The speech begins with a typical reassurance formula, including the statement *'al-tîrā'*, "do not fear," in v. 4b and the basis for the reassurance in vv. 5-9.

The structure of vv. 5-9 presents a particular problem because of the difficulties in interpreting the preposition *ya'an kî*, "because," in v. 5 and the resulting syntactical structure. Although some scholars understand vv. 5-6 as the basis for v. 4 so that vv. 5-6 explain Ahaz's fear of Rezin and ben Remaliah (cf. Sæbo), the preposition *ya'an kî* typically introduces the *Begründung* or "basis" for a following consequence in Isaiah (3:16-17; 8:6-7; 29:13-14). Sæbo correctly cites Num 11:19-20 as an example where *ya'an kî* appears in the middle of the statement it modifies, but he fails to note that the basic issue in understanding the use of this preposition is not its position in the sentence but its use to introduce the basis or *Begründung* of a consequence. In this respect, *ya'an kî* precedes the statement that the people had rejected YHWH in Num 11:20b as the basis for the consequence that they would eat meat until they became sick of it in Num 11:19-20a. With regard to Isaiah 7, on the one hand vv. 5-6 do not constitute the basis for a consequence stated in v. 4. V. 4 is a statement of reassurance, as noted above. On the other hand, vv. 7-9 do state a consequence for which vv. 5-6 serve as the basis insofar as they announce that the *rā'â*, "evil," that Rezin and ben Remaliah "planned" *(yā'aṣ)* "will neither stand nor come to be" (v. 7; *lō' tāqûm wĕlō' tihyeh*). Although Sæbo objects that vv. 8-9 constitute the *Begründung* to v. 7 on account of the introductory *kî*, "because," in v. 8, he fails to note that this *kî* is explanatory insofar as it explains why Rezin's and ben Remaliah's plans will not come to pass. As the discussion of the intention of this passage will demonstrate, Rezin and ben Remaliah are only kings of Aram and Ephraim, and, as such, they are not capable of resisting YHWH's intentions. Following the introductory messenger formula in v. 7a, the message from YHWH appears in the form of a reassurance oracle proper in vv. 7b-9a and an admonition to the "house of David" to rely on YHWH in v. 9b.

The report of the dialogue between YHWH/Isaiah and Ahaz appears in vv. 10-25. YHWH is identified as the speaker in v. 10, but the combination of 1st-person perspective with 3rd-person references to YHWH throughout the so-called YHWH speeches in this passage (vv. 13, 14, 20; cf. vv. 11, 12, 17, 18) demonstrates that Isaiah is here portrayed as speaking on YHWH's behalf. Vv. 18-25 are frequently considered as secondary additions to this passage insofar as they lack the speech formulas, 2nd-person address perspective, or other explicit indications that they are part of the preceding dialogue. The absence of a suitable literary context other than the speech reports of 7:10-17 (cf. 8:1) and the neutral 3rd-person form of these verses indicates that they are subsumed under the dialogue report of vv. 10-17 in the present form of the passage. In this context, they develop the threat of Assyrian intervention in v. 17 (cf. vv. 18-20) and the imagery of curds and honey associated with the Immanuel sign in vv. 14-16 (cf. vv. 21-25).

The structure of this passage is determined by the sequence of conversation between YHWH/Isaiah and Ahaz, and by the speech formulas that designate the speakers. Consequently, the passage includes three major subunits: the report of YHWH's/Isaiah's first address to Ahaz (vv. 10-11); the report of Ahaz's response (v. 12); and the report of YHWH's/Isaiah's second address to Ahaz (vv. 13-25). Each speech report is constituted by its respective speech formula followed by the speech proper. Consequently, the report of YHWH's/Isaiah's first address to Ahaz (vv. 10-11) includes the narrative speech formula in v. 10 and the speech proper in the form of a command to Ahaz to ask YHWH for a sign. The report of Ahaz's response includes the speech formula in v. 12a and the response proper in v. 12b in the form of his refusal to test YHWH. The report of YHWH's/Isaiah's second address to Ahaz likewise includes the speech formula in v. 13aα and the speech proper in vv. 13aβ-25 in the form of an announcement of the Immanuel sign and an explanation of its consequences.

The second speech by YHWH/Isaiah begins with the announcement of the Immanuel sign in vv. 13aβ-17, which is defined not only by its concern for announcing the sign but also by its 2nd-person address perspective directed to Ahaz. It begins with a rhetorical question to Ahaz concerning his trying of YHWH's patience (v. 13aβ-b), followed by the announcement of the sign (vv. 14-17). The introductory *lākēn*, "therefore," indicates that the sign is presented here as a consequence of Ahaz trying YHWH. It begins with a statement of consequence in v. 14a followed by the announcement of the sign proper in vv. 14b-17. The announcement consists of an annunciation of the birth of Immanuel in v. 15 followed by an elaboration on the sign in vv. 15-17. This includes a description of the food that Immanuel will eat until he is weaned (v. 15) and an explanation that YHWH will bring the Assyrians onto the scene before Immanuel is weaned (vv. 16-17). V. 16 constitutes the protasis of this explanation, which defines the chronological framework. V. 17 constitutes the apodosis, which states the resulting consequence of Assyrian intervention.

The second part of this speech consists of an explanation of the consequences of the Immanuel sign in vv. 18-25. This section is defined by its use of the formula *bayyôm hahû'*, "in that day," in vv. 18, 20, 21, and 23, its 3rd-person announcement perspective, and its contents, which presuppose and elaborate on the meanings of various features of the preceding Immanuel sign. Of the four *bayyôm hahû'* statements that appear in this passage, three begin with the formula *wĕhāyâ bayyôm hahû'*, "and it shall come to pass in that day" (vv. 18-19, 21-22, and 23-25), and one begins with the formula *bayyôm hahû'*, "in that day" (v. 20).

These formal features have several implications for the structure of this passage. First, the initial *wĕhāyâ bayyôm hahû'* formula in v. 18 begins with a conjunctive *wāw* that ties the entire passage to the preceding speech in vv. 13aβ-17. Second, the conjunctive *wāw*s of the same formulas in vv. 21 and 23 indicate that vv. 21-22 and 23-25 are tied structurally to v. 20. Third, the absence of a conjunctive *wāw* in the introductory *bayyôm hahû'* formula of v. 20 indicates a structural distinction between vv. 18-19 and 20-25. This distinction is borne out by the contents of the respective passages. Whereas vv. 18-19 contain a general statement announcing YHWH's summons of the "fly" (Egypt) and the "bee" (Assyria) and their consequent settling on the land, vv. 20-25 describe specific consequences of this intervention. These include the shaving of hair, typical of the treatment of captives, in v. 20; the reliance on milk and honey as the only food available in the land following this intervention (vv. 21-22); and the consequent desolation of the land (vv. 23-25).

Genre

The predominantly narrative form of 7:1–8:15 identifies its genre as REPORT or, more precisely, ACCOUNT. ACCOUNT and REPORT are virtually synonymous, except that ACCOUNT tends to be used in instances where the narrative is explanatory in nature. In this case, the relation of this passage to the preceding COMMISSION in ch. 6 defines the genre of 7:1–8:15, since this narrative explains how Isaiah's commission to "harden the heart" of the people (6:10) comes to pass. As many scholars have noted, Isaiah attempts to offer Ahaz a sign of salvation or reassurance in this passage, and Ahaz's rejection of the offer results in the condemnation of the monarch and people. As noted in the section on intention below, Isaiah's presentation of his son Shear-jashub, whose name means "a remnant shall return," provokes Ahaz's rejection of YHWH's offer. The contents of the passage define it as an ACCOUNT of YHWH's judgment against Judah and an ACCOUNT of YHWH's signs to the "house of David" (Ahaz) and Judah.

There is a problem, however, in the generic identification of this passage in that 7:1-9 appears as a 3rd-person narrative REPORT whereas 8:1-15 appears as a 1st-person autobiographical ACCOUNT. The middle section in 7:10-25 is somewhat ambiguous. Although YHWH is designated as the speaker in v. 10, the 1st-person form and 3rd-person references to YHWH throughout the speeches attributed to YHWH indicate that Isaiah is in fact the speaker. One should note, however, that the reference to YHWH as speaker in v. 10 is entirely consistent with the prophet's perspective of his role as YHWH's mouthpiece, so that 7:10-25 fits easily into the context of an autobiographical REPORT by the prophet. In this respect, one should note that TJ renders v. 10 as wĕʾôsîp nĕbîyāʾ daywy lĕmalālāʾ ʿim ʾāḥāz lĕmêmār, "And the prophet of YHWH again spoke to Ahaz saying." Nevertheless, the objective form of this passage eases the transition between the 3rd-person narrative of 7:1-9 and the 1st-person narrative of 8:1-15. The reasons for this discrepancy are bound up with the process of the literary composition of this passage in the context of the Josianic redaction of chs. 5–12 and will be discussed below.

In addition to the overarching genre of ACCOUNT, a number of subordinate genres also appear in this passage. The first is the commissioning SPEECH that YHWH is reported to have made to Isaiah in 7:3-9. The speech begins with a modified form of the typical COMMISSIONING FORMULA, lēk wĕʾāmartā, "go and say" (cf. 6:9) in vv. 3-4: ṣēʾ-nāʾ liqraʾt ʾāḥāz . . . wĕʾāmartā ʾēlāyw, "go out please to meet Ahaz . . . and you shall say to him." The balance of the COM-

MISSIONING speech relates the speech that Isaiah is to make to Ahaz according to YHWH's instructions. This speech includes the typical REASSURANCE FORMULA, *'al-tîrā'*, "do not fear," as one of its initial elements. This formula commonly appears in the priestly ORACLE OF SALVATION as a means of reassuring the addressee that YHWH will provide protection, salvation, etc., in a time of crisis. In this case, the reassurance is provided in the form of a MESSENGER SPEECH, introduced by the MESSENGER FORMULA in v. 7a, which maintains that YHWH will not allow the evil plans of Rezin and ben Remaliah to be achieved. The concluding admonition statement in v. 9b is designed to dissuade Ahaz from turning to other means of support in this crisis, presumably the Assyrian empire, and to maintain faith in YHWH, who will provide protection against the Syro-Ephraimite threat.

The second subordinate genre is the PROPHETIC ANNOUNCEMENT OF A SIGN, which appears in the context of the REPORT OF A DIALOGUE of 7:1-25. In its present form, the passage includes the *bayyôm hahû'* statements of vv. 18-25, although these statements lack the 2nd-person address perspective of the speech in vv. 13aβ-17. Although these verses clearly build upon the speech in vv. 13aβ-17, they should not be included as part of the genre PROPHETIC ANNOUNCEMENT OF A SIGN. The announcement is presented as a consequence of Ahaz trying YHWH's patience, and follows a RHETORICAL QUESTION in v. 13aβ-b. The announcement contains the elements that are typically found in the genre. The declaration of an event as a sign from YHWH appears in the form of the ANNUNCIATION of the birth of Immanuel in v. 14b. The description of the event to be taken as a sign appears in v. 15 with reference to Immanuel's diet of curds and honey until he is weaned. Finally, vv. 16-17 constitute the subordinate clause that explains the significance of the sign, namely, that YHWH will bring the Assyrians into the region prior to Immanuel's weaning. Although the *bayyôm hahû'* passages further explain the significance of the sign, they appear to be an expansion of the genre that develops several of its images.

Setting

Despite the presence of the 1st-person autobiographical narrative in 7:1–8:15, the appearance of 3rd-person narrative about the prophet in 7:1-9 indicates that Isaiah is not the author of the present form of this text. As demonstrated in the discussion of the structure of this passage, the entire unit is tied together by various literary and thematic elements so that it focuses on Isaiah's signs to Ahaz and Judah in connection with the Syro-Ephraimite crisis. But literary discrepancies between its constituent subunits indicate that it is an edited text. Isa 7:1-9 appears in 3rd-person narrative form that discusses the prophet in objective terms, whereas 8:1-15 appears in 1st-person autobiographical narrative form. Isa 7:10-17 is a somewhat ambiguous case insofar as it appears in 3rd-person narrative form, which identifies YHWH as the speaker, but the 1st-person perspective of its speeches and the 3rd-person references to YHWH in those speeches indicate that Isaiah is actually the speaker. Because the prophet can portray himself as YHWH's mouthpiece, this passage can be considered either as autobiographical material or as 3rd-person narrative. Finally, the absence of 2nd-person address forms directed to Ahaz in 7:18-25 raises questions as to whether this section was originally part of the speech to Ahaz in vv. 13aβ-17. These discrepancies indicate that although Isaiah appears to be responsible for a great deal of material in this unit, a Josianic writer employed Isaiah's work in producing the final form of this text.

Any attempt to trace the redaction history of this passage must account for both the literary and thematic factors that unite this text as well as the discrepancies that indicate its composite character. An analysis of these factors indicates that although the present form of 7:1-25 is the product of the Josianic redaction that produced the final form of chs. 5–12, the underlying form of the passage in 7:2–9:6 (*RSV* 7) stems from the prophet who produced this text in the aftermath of Ahaz's submission to Assyria in the Syro-Ephraimite War. The Isaianic form of this text was an autobiographical account of the prophet's encounter with Ahaz and the conclusions that he drew from that encounter. The Isaianic form of 7:2-17 and 20 emphasized the promises of YHWH's protection that Isaiah conveyed to Ahaz, and 8:1-15 emphasized the consequences that Isaiah projected once Ahaz rejected YHWH's protection. Finally, 8:16–9:6 (*RSV* 7) projected Isaiah's belief that a Davidic monarch would eventually preside over the land in peace. The purpose of Isaiah's account was to point to the consequences of Ahaz's actions in an attempt to persuade King Hezekiah that YHWH would restore Davidic rule over the former northern kingdom of Israel. Rather than resist the Assyrians, Hezekiah must accept them as YHWH's agents for action and must recognize the opportunity that the downfall of Israel presents for the Davidic dynasty to restore its rule over a united people Israel. In contrast, the Josianic form of this text gives far greater attention to Ahaz's shortcomings and the consequences that would result from his lack of trust in YHWH.

Three primary lines of evidence support this contention. The first involves the literary character of 7:1-17, including its objective narrative form and evidence that this form is the product of a later writer who reworked an originally autobiographical narrative. The second involves the secondary literary character of 7:18-25, including its objective announcement form and its interpretative function, which resignifies the meaning of the Immanuel sign in 7:10-17 as a threat of Assyrian and Egyptian invasion. The third involves the relationship of this material to 8:16–9:6 (*RSV* 7), which projects an ideal Davidic ruler who contrasts sharply with the portrayal of Ahaz and Judah in 7:1–8:15. These lines of evidence demonstrate the presence of a Josianic redaction of this text in 7:1, 3-4, 17, 18-19, 20, and 21-25. The redaction transformed an autobiographical account of Isaiah's promises of deliverance to Ahaz during the Syro-Ephraimite War into a 3rd-person report of that encounter emphasizing Ahaz's rejection of the prophet's promises. It thereby produced a text that served as a structural parallel to 8:1-15, that provided the premises for 8:1–9:6 (*RSV* 7), and that tied the entire narrative into the overarching framework of chs. 5–12 as well as to the Josianic version of chs. 36–37.

It is clear that 7:1 derives from the Josianic redaction that produced the final form of chs. 5–12. Many scholars have noted that this verse is nearly identical to 2 Kgs 16:5, which describes the attempted attack by Rezin and Pekah against Jerusalem. Although some have argued that Isa 7:1-17 originally formed part of the Kings narrative (e.g., Kraeling), Isa 7:1 includes several minor variations from 2 Kgs 16:5 that indicate that the verse was drawn from its original place in the Kings narrative and adapted to the present context in Isaiah. First, Isa 7:1 adds the chronological statement, "And it came to pass in the days of Ahaz ben Jotham ben Uzziah, king of Judah, that Rezin, king of Aram [*RSV* 'Syria'], and Pekah ben Remaliah, king of Israel, came up to Jerusalem for war against it, but they were not able to fight against it," which replaces the text at 2 Kgs 16:5, "Then Rezin, king of Aram, and Pekah ben Remaliah, king of Israel, came up to Jerusalem for war and they besieged Ahaz, but they were not able to fight." Although the reference to the father (Jotham) is common in such annalistic reports, the reference to the grandfather (Uzziah) is exceptional. The reason for the reference to Uzziah is clear from the context, however, insofar as it ties this narrative to the preceding vision report in Isaiah 6 that takes place "in the year of the death of the King Uzziah" (6:1). The change in verb forms from *'az ya'ăleh*, "then . . . came up," in 2 Kgs 16:5 to *'ālâ*, "came up," in Isa 7:1 merely accommodates the addition of the chronological statement. Second, the statement *wayyāṣurû 'al-'āḥāz*, "and they besieged Ahaz," in 2 Kgs 16:5 is replaced by *lammilḥāmâ 'ālêhā*, "for [the] war against it," in Isa 7:1. This modification relates to the dynastic interests of the following narrative insofar as it shifts attention away from Ahaz as an individual and allows for the focus on the "house of David" (cf. v. 2) as a whole. This interest is continued in v. 2 not only by the mention of the "house of David" but also by the notice that "his heart and the heart of his people shook like the shaking of the trees of the forest before the wind." In this respect, it is noteworthy that the Davidic royal palace in Jerusalem was called "the House of the Forest of Lebanon" (1 Kgs 7:2; 10:17, 21; 2 Chr 9:16, 20). For further discussion of this issue, see the section on the Intention of this passage below.

A primary reason for Josianic interest in this passage is the location of Isaiah's meeting with Ahaz "at the end of the conduit of the upper pool by the highway of [*RSV* 'to'] the fullers' field" (Isa 7:3). This is where the Assyrian Rabshakeh demanded unconditional surrender from King Hezekiah during Sennacherib's invasion of Judah in 701 (cf. Isa 36:2; 2 Kgs 18:17), and it serves as one of several important points of comparison between the portrayal of Ahaz's response to foreign invasion in Isa 7:1–9:6 (*RSV* 7) and Hezekiah's response to similar circumstances in chs. 36–39 (cf. Ackroyd, "Isaiah 36–39"). As Clements shows, the Hezekiah narratives in chs. 36–37 are the product of the Josianic redaction (*Isaiah and the Deliverance of Jerusalem* [JSOTSup 13; Sheffield: JSOT Press, 1980]; see the commentary to Isaiah 36–37 below). Furthermore, studies of the DtrH argue for a Josianic edition of the book of Kings (F. M. Cross Jr., *Canaanite Myth and Hebrew Epic* [Cambridge: Harvard University Press, 1973] 274-89; R. Nelson, *The Double Redaction of the Deuteronomistic History* [JSOTSup 18; Sheffield: JSOT Press, 1981]), and that the Hezekiah narratives in 2 Kings 18–20 represent the climax of the Josianic edition of Kings (I. A. Provan, *Hezekiah and the Books of Kings* [BZAW 172; Berlin and New York: de Gruyter, 1988]). My own study (*Isaiah 1–4*, 12-17; contra Seitz, *Destiny*) shows that the Hezekiah narratives in Isaiah 36–39 were deliberately drawn from their original context in 2 Kings 18–20 and modified to present an ideal portrayal of the faithful Hezekiah in contrast to the faithless Ahaz. Within the context of the Josianic redaction of Isaiah, then, the primary function of this location is to tie the Ahaz narrative to the Hezekiah narratives in Isaiah 36–39.

Despite the role that the location of Isaiah's confrontation with Ahaz plays within the context of the Josianic redaction, the core of the following narrative in 7:2–8:15 appears not to have been composed as part of that redaction. Rather, it is an earlier narrative that was employed and reworked by the Josianic redaction in the present form of the text. Although 7:1 provides the historical context for the narrative that follows, this function is duplicated in 7:2 by the mention of Aram's alliance with Ephraim and the resulting fear of the "house of David," albeit without the chronological specificity of 7:1. Furthermore, it is clear that the narrative beginning in 7:2 follows awkwardly from 7:1. Isa 7:1 reports the failed attempt of the Syro-Ephraimite coalition to attack Jerusalem, but the narrative in 7:2-25 describes a situation prior to that attack when Ahaz was inspecting his water system — a vital element in the defense of the city — in anticipation of such an attack. Although the present form of 7:2–8:15 explains why the Syro-Ephraimite coalition was unable to attack Jerusalem successfully (i.e., YHWH's plans to bring the Assyrians would thwart their plans), 7:1 plays no essential role in 7:2–8:15, but serves merely to provide the general setting, which is partially replicated in 7:2. Its primary functions are threefold. First, within the immediate context, it informs the reader that the Syro-Ephraimite coalition was unable to take Jerusalem, and thereby undermines Ahaz's resistance to YHWH's promise of salvation through Isaiah. Second, within the context of 6:1–9:6 (*RSV* 7), it connects the following narrative to Isaiah's vision report in ch. 6. Finally, within the larger context of the book of Isaiah, it plays a role in connecting this material with the Hezekiah narratives of chs. 36–39. Consequently, 7:2–8:15 must be considered apart from 7:1.

As noted in the discussion of the structure of this passage, in the present form of the text, 7:10-25 clearly depends on 7:1-9, and 8:1-15 depends on 7:1-25, especially vv. 10-25. Because 8:1-15 and possibly 7:10-25 appear in autobiographical form, the 3rd-person narrative form of 7:2-9 appears as somewhat of an anomaly. Obviously, Isaiah did not write this section in contrast to the explicitly autobiographical material in 8:1-15 and perhaps also the implicitly autobiographical material in 7:10-25. Yet the passage as it now stands depends heavily on these verses insofar as they present the setting that the following material presupposes. Nevertheless, there are indications that the present form of 7:2-9 derives from a later author. The passage must have appeared originally as a 1st-person autobiographical account of the initial stage of Isaiah's encounter with Ahaz, but the present 3rd-person report form of this passage indicates that it was written some time after the death of the prophet. Although the present form of 7:2-9 appears to derive from the Josianic redaction, it is based on an earlier autobiographical form of this text that stems from Isaiah. The reasons for this conclusion require further elaboration.

The first line of evidence, mentioned already, involves the 3rd-person instructional perspective of vv. 3-9. Because of the autobiographical context of

6:1–8:15, scholars frequently propose that the 3rd-person references to Isaiah in 7:3 should be emended to 1st-person references to Isaiah so that the entire narrative will be consistent (*BHS;* cf. on 7:10). Unfortunately, this is not a fully adequate explanation, not only because no such reading appears in any text or version of Isaiah, but also because it does not resolve the problem of the instructional perspective of these verses. Obviously, this perspective conflicts with the 3rd-person reporting perspective of vv. 10-25 insofar as there is an abrupt transition from YHWH's instruction of Isaiah concerning his meeting with Ahaz to the report of the conversation that took place at that meeting in vv. 10-17. As 8:1-4 shows, Isaiah is fully capable of providing a consistent narrative framework in relation to his reports of instructions by YHWH, but such consistency does not appear here.

Despite this tension, the introductory statement in 7:10, *wayyôsep yhwh dabbēr 'el-'āḥāz lē'mōr,* "and again YHWH spoke to Ahaz saying," links 7:10-25 to 7:1-9. There is no indication that 7:10-25 presupposes the instructional format of vv. 3-9, since the statement that *YHWH* again spoke to Ahaz indicates a shift in perspective from YHWH's instruction of the prophet to YHWH's speech to Ahaz. Nevertheless, 7:10-25 does presuppose the reassurance speech that Isaiah is instructed to speak to Ahaz, insofar as the command to request a sign in v. 11 relates to the reassurance oracle in vv. 3-9, and insofar as the mention of the two kings in v. 16 relates to the statements concerning Rezin and ben Remaliah in vv. 3-9. The fact that 7:10-25 presupposes the reassurance oracle in vv. 3-9 indicates that these verses belong together with 7:10-25.

The problem appears to lie in the formulation of 7:3-4 and 7:10. Not only is there tension between the two texts in that the former reports YHWH's instructions to the prophet whereas the latter reports YHWH's speech to Ahaz, presumably through the prophet, but also they stand in contrast to the autobiographical form of 6:1–9:6 (*RSV* 7). It is noteworthy that the 3rd-person form of both of these statements corresponds to the perspective of 7:1. To complicate things further, they also appear to be formulated as parallels to Isaiah's autobiographical statements in 8:1, "and YHWH said unto me, 'Take for yourself a large tablet and write on it," and 8:5, "and YHWH again spoke to me [*wayyōsep yhwh dabbēr 'ēlay;* cf. 7:10] saying."

Furthermore, 7:3-4 convey two important pieces of information that aid in determining their setting and perspective. First, vv. 3-4 include mention of Isaiah's son Shear-jashub, who appears to serve as a symbol of the remnant of Judah that will survive the Syro-Ephraimite War in the present context of 7:1–8:15. Interestingly, this contrasts with the portrayal of Shear-jashub as a symbol for the remnant of *Israel* that will survive the Assyrian invasion in 10:20-23. The reinterpretation of this symbol in relation to the inhabitants of Jerusalem in 10:24-26 indicates that the figure of Shear-jashub has been similarly resignified in 7:3-4. This is reinforced by the fact that 8:16–9:6 (*RSV* 7) will argue that the Assyrian invasion of Israel presents an opportunity to reestablish its rule over the former northern kingdom of Israel, presumably the remnant of Israel that will return to the Davidic monarch here called *'ēl gibbôr* (10:21; cf. 9:6 [*RSV* 7]; see the commentary to these passages below). As I argue in the commentary to 10:24-26, this passage stems from the Josianic redaction of

Isaiah. Second, 7:3-4 specifies the location of the encounter between Isaiah and Ahaz as "the end of the conduit of the upper pool by the Fuller's Field," which happens to be the location of the Rabshakeh's speech to Hezekiah in 36:2. This setting plays a major role in relating the narrative concerning Ahaz's reaction to YHWH's promises in a time of crisis to the narrative concerning Hezekiah's reaction in a similar crisis (cf. Ackroyd, "Isaiah 36–39"). Whereas Ahaz rejects YHWH's promise and leads the nation to disaster, Hezekiah accepts the promise and sees the deliverance of Jerusalem. As I argue in the commentary to chs. 36–37, this narrative likewise stems from the Josianic court.

Consequently, 7:3-4 and 7:10 appear to reflect the hand of the Josianic redaction of Isaiah, as does 7:1. Although 7:1-25 does not appear to be composed ad hoc by this redaction, evidence of Josianic reworking of an earlier narrative, based on the autobiographical forms in 8:1 and 8:5, appears in 7:1, 3-4, and 10. The narrative was originally autobiographical in form itself, but it was reformulated in order to focus on Shear-jashub as a symbol of the remnant of Judah and to contrast the faithless Ahaz with the faithful Hezekiah. Such concerns stem from the Josianic redaction, which focused on the restoration of Judah in the aftermath of the Assyrian collapse, and which employed Hezekiah, in contrast to Ahaz, as the ideal Davidic model for the reign of King Josiah.

The second line of evidence involves the literary character and interpretative function of 7:18-25. This unit presents interpreters with numerous problems on account of its differences in form from the preceding speech by the prophet to Ahaz in vv. 13aβ-17, its references to Egypt and Assyria in v. 18, and its interpretative character with regard to the image of "curds and honey" from the preceding Immanuel sign. Because of these problems, scholars frequently maintain that the entire passage is secondary or that parts of it, such as vv. 18-20, are Isaianic but that these parts have been glossed and expanded into their present form.

The form of these verses is quite distinct from the preceding material. Whereas the form of the speech to Ahaz is that of 1st-person address to a 2nd-person addressee, vv. 18-19 and 21-25 are formulated in 3rd-person announcement language preceded by the formula wĕhāyâ bayyôm hahû'. V. 20 employs similar announcement language, but the perspective of its speaker is 1st person ('ădōnāy, "my Lord") and it begins with a different introductory formula, bayyôm hahû'. The wĕhāyâ bayyôm hahû' and bayyôm hahû' formulas are frequently understood as editorial introductions to secondary additions in biblical texts. Nevertheless, the previous discussion of the structure of the text noted that 7:18-25 can be incorporated into the speech to Ahaz in vv. 13aβ-17 in that this section can be understood as an announcement of the consequences of the Immanuel sign. Vv. 18-19 and 20 take up the concern with Assyrian intervention from v. 17, and vv. 21-22 interpret the "curds and honey" mentioned in connection with the Immanuel sign. Consequently, the secondary character of this passage cannot be established solely on the basis of its difference in form.

Other features of 7:18-25 indicate its literary relationship to the preceding speech to Ahaz. This evidence includes variations of form within 7:18-25 (in that v. 20 differs from the rest of this text), the interpretative character of vv.

18-19 and 21-25, and the transitional function of the passage as a whole. As the following discussion will demonstrate, v. 20 is the original conclusion to the speech to Ahaz, whereas vv. 18-19 and 21-25 are the product of the Josianic redaction of Isaiah.

In its present form, 7:18-25 not only elaborates on the threat of Assyrian intervention mentioned in relation to the Immanuel sign in vv. 13aβ-17, but also provides a transition to the material in ch. 8. By focusing on the Assyrian invasion of the land and its consequent devastation, 7:18-25 shifts attention away from Ahaz and the "house of David" in 7:10-17 and focuses on the land and people of Judah, which are the concern of 8:1-15. In making this transition, it aids in uniting two formally distinct units, insofar as 8:1-15 is explicitly formulated in 1st-person autobiographical narrative while 7:10-17 is formulated as 3rd-person narrative with a potentially autobiographical character.

Questions arise, however, concerning the transitional character of this section. There is evidence that 7:10-17 and 20 transform 7:3-9, an original reassurance to Ahaz that he would be delivered from the Syro-Ephraimite coalition, into a threat of Assyrian intervention. Several factors support this view. First, the name Immanuel is in itself an implicit statement of reassurance. The Heb. *'immānû 'ēl* means "God is with us," and the statement that God is with someone is a common means of divine assurance throughout biblical tradition, both in general (cf. Exod 3:12; Judg 6:12; 1 Kgs 8:57; Jer 1:8; Ps 46:7) and in relation to David in particular (1 Sam 16:18; 18:12, 14; 2 Sam 5:10). Second, the "curds and honey" that Immanuel will eat also sustained David and his men in the wilderness during Absalom's revolt (2 Sam 17:29), and frequently serve as a symbol of plenty, as in the "land flowing with milk and honey" (Exod 3:8, 17; 13:5; Num 13:27; 16:13; Deut 31:20; Jer 11:5; Ezek 20:6, 15; etc.). In the present context, this expression is used to define the period of time in which the Syro-Ephraimite coalition will be removed from the land (vv. 15-16). Finally, the mention of "the king of Assyria" *('ēt melek 'aššûr),* which defines v. 17 as a threat, seems to be a gloss. The phrase appears as an appositional definition of "days that have not come since Ephraim turned aside from Judah." Insofar as the Ephraimite revolt introduced a period of decline for Judah and the Davidic dynasty, the "days that have not come since the departure of Ephraim" refers to the former glorious days of the Davidic dynasty under David and Solomon when the kingdom was united. The addition of "the king of Assyria" to this statement provides a sense of irony, in that it changes a reassurance into a threat, for Assyrian domination will be worse than any reverses suffered since the Ephraimite revolt. Isa 7:18-25 builds upon this change by focusing on the threat posed by Assyrian intervention.

Isaiah 7:18-19 is a somewhat enigmatic case. The reference to YHWH's summons of the "fly" and the "bee" apparently presupposes the "curds and honey" of the Immanuel sign, since flies and bees would be attracted to these items. Furthermore, the passage continues to focus on the threat of Assyrian invasion but now includes Egypt as well. The mention of both Egypt and Assyria in this context is particularly perplexing because the Egyptians play no other role whatsoever in 7:1–8:15, nor is there evidence that Egypt was involved in the region during the Syro-Ephraimite crisis. Only after the Assyrians had secured a position in the region did the Egyptians back a revolt by the Philistines against the Assyrians in 713-712. Because of these problems, and because Egypt and Assyria are mentioned in relative clauses that modify the primary images of the "fly" and the "bee" that YHWH will summon, the references to Egypt and Assyria are often considered as secondary additions designed to update the passage to the later period when Egypt was actively involved in the region (Barth, 199-200). In this view, the "fly" and the "bee" of vv. 18-19 originally referred only to Assyria.

There are two problems with this understanding. First, that Egypt and Assyria appear in relative clauses is no basis for excising them from the text. Second, there is no reason why Egypt should be introduced simply to "update" a passage that refers to Assyria when no mention of Egypt appears elsewhere in 7:1–8:15. Indeed, Dietrich (*Politik*, 97, 121-22) argues that the appearance of Egypt together with Assyria as a threat to Judah indicates that the historical background of these verses lies in the early reign of Hezekiah. After the Assyrian defeat of the Syro-Ephraimite coalition in 732, Assyria established itself as the dominant power in the region. This posed an obvious threat to Egypt in that it removed the minor kingdoms of this area as a buffer between Egypt and the Assyrians. Consequently, Egypt attempted to foment a revolt against Assyria by Philistia and Judah. But Dietrich's arguments do not account fully for Isaiah's perspectives on Egypt. Isaiah opposed an alliance with Egypt just as he opposed an alliance with Assyria against the Syro-Ephraimite coalition (cf. chs. 18–20). According to Isaiah, Egypt's leadership was unstable — the country had just concluded a bloody civil war (cf. 19:1-15) and would not constitute a reliable ally for Judah. Probably, a war that pitted Egypt against Assyria would be fought in Judah and would result in the devastation of Judah's land. Isaiah's oracles concerning Egypt never focus on the Egyptians as a threat to Judah; rather they focus on Egypt's unreliability and maintain that Egypt will never be able to come to Judah's aid (cf. 18:1-7; 19:1-15; 30:1-5; 31:1-3). Although Isaiah would have plenty of grounds to see Assyria as a threat, it seems unlikely that the prophet would perceive Egypt as a threat as well. Egypt does, however, emerge as a threat against Judah during the reign of Josiah in the late 7th century. Furthermore, the reference to Egypt in v. 18 anticipates the references to the return of exiles from Egypt and Assyria in 11:11-16, another Josianic passage.

At this point, one should note that there is a disruption in the form of 7:18-25. As already mentioned, 7:20 differs from the other statements in 7:18-25 in that it begins with the formula *bayyôm hahû'* rather than the *wĕhāyâ bayyôm hahû'* that introduces vv. 18-19, 21-22, and 23-25. Normally, one would expect that an initial *bayyôm hahû'* or another reference to "day" would be followed in the next occurence by the conjunctive *wĕhāyâ bayyôm hahû'* (10:12–11:16; 27:2-23; Zeph 1:7-11; cf. Isa 3:18–4:1; 4:2-3; 14:1-3; 19:16-17, 19-22). In the present text, the conjunctive formula in vv. 18-19 disrupts such a sequence. Furthermore, in contrast to the 3rd-person formulation of vv. 18-19, v. 20 is formulated as a 1st-person announcement, as indicated by its use of *'ădōnāy*, "my Lord." Although the conjunctive formulas in vv. 21-22 and 23-25 follow naturally from the *bayyôm hahû'* in v. 20, vv. 21-25 are also formulated in the 3rd person. Finally, v. 20 announces only the intervention of the king of Assyria, whereas vv. 18-19 mention both Egypt and Assyria. Vv. 21-25 provide no clue as to whether they envision Egypt and Assyria or only Assyria as the cause of devastation, but their 3rd-person formulation and the introductory *wĕhāyâ bayôm hahû'* associate them with vv. 18-19 more than with v. 20. These considerations suggest that vv. 18-19, 21-25 are intrusive in the context of vv. 18-25 and that v. 20 originally stood as the concluding statements to the speech to Ahaz in 7:13aβ-17. V. 20 shares the 1st-person formulation of the speech to Ahaz, and it takes up the concern with the king of Assyria that appears at the end of the speech in v. 17. The reference in v. 20 to the shaving of hair, typical of the treatment of war captives (cf. Deut 21:10-13), amplifies the threatening nature of the appearance of the king of Assyria in v. 17.

In this regard, one should note that vv. 18-19 represent an attempt at inner-biblical exegesis in that they employ language from 5:26 for the summoning of a foreign army, including the verb *yišrōq lě*, "he will whistle for," i.e., "summon" (cf. *wĕšāraq lô*, "and he will whistle for it," in 5:26), and the reference to Egypt: *'ăšer biqsēh yĕ'ōrê misrāyim*, "which is at the end of the Nile of Egypt" (cf. *miqsēh hā'āres*, "from the end of the earth," in 5:26). Thus vv. 18-19 employ language that was earlier used to describe the threat posed to Israel by Assyria in order to describe a potential threat by both Egypt and Assyria. A similar instance of inner-biblical exegesis appears in the reference to curds and honey in vv. 21-25 and their relation to the address to Ahaz in 7:13aβ-17. This image, however, is understood differently within the two passages. Vv. 15-17 employ the curds and honey as a symbol for the time that will pass before the threat of the Syro-Ephraimite coalition is removed. In contrast, vv. 21-22 employ the curds and honey as a symbol for the deprivation of those people left in the land who survive the Assyrian invasion, insofar as they will have only dairy products and honey to eat after the land has been ravaged. In this respect, the honey and curd imagery of vv. 21-22 is tied up with that of vv. 23-25, which describe the devastation of the land as a result of Assyrian invasion and the consequent use of the land for pasturing cattle and sheep rather than agriculture. Interestingly, the imagery and language of this passage derive from the vineyard oracle of 5:1-7. Thus "a thousand vines worth a thousand shekels" are overgrown with "thorns and briars" (*šāmîr wāšayit;* cf. 5:6), and the mountains that were cultivated with a weeding hook (*bamma'dēr yē'ādērûn;* cf. *yē'ādēr* in 5:6) are left unprotected to be trampled by sheep (*lěmirmas śeh;* cf. *lěmirmās* in 5:5). The writer of vv. 21-25 apparently employed the vineyard allegory of 5:1-7 to reinterpret the curds and honey of the Immanuel sign as a symbol for the devastation of the land by the Assyrians rather than as a symbol for the removal of the Syro-Ephraimite threat. Furthermore, the mention of "with arrows and with bows" in v. 24 takes up language that also appears in 5:28. Thus vv. 21-25 share a characteristic with vv. 18-19 in that both employ language from ch. 5. Furthermore, they share an identical form with vv. 18-19, employ a perspective of threat by outside invaders, and nowhere identify only Assyria as the source of the threat. Consequently, they were written together with vv. 18-19 as part of the Josianic redaction of Isaiah. As such, they tie this passage to the overall framework of chs. 5–12.

Further correspondence between vv. 10-17 and v. 20 appears in relation to the specification of "the king of Assyria" in vv. 17 and 20. As in v. 17, the appearance of *běmelek 'aššûr,* "with the king of Assyria," likewise changes v. 20 from a statement of reassurance to one of threat. Scholars generally understand this phrase as an appositional definition of the phrase *bě'ebrê nāhār,* "across the river," which is frequently understood as a designation for Mesopotamia, the location of Assyria. This view is mistaken, however, in that *'ebrê nāhār* refers to Aram, not to Mesopotamia, as indicated by the appearance of the variant form *'ēber hannāhār* in 1 Kgs 5:4; Ezra 8:26; Neh 2:7, 9; and 3:7. Wildberger (*Jesaja,* 305) claims that the term depends on the perspective of the speaker since in Josh 24:2 and 14 the term refers to Mesopotamia. He fails to note, however, that the references in Joshua to Abraham's dwelling in *'ēber hannāhār* are not to Ur of the Chaldees but to Haran in Aram. Consequently, *běmelek 'aššûr* is not an appositional definition of *bě'ebrê nāhār* but of the entire phrase *běta'ar haśśěkîrâ bě'ebrê nāhār,* "with the hired razor in *'ebrê nāhār* [i.e., Aram]." The original form of v. 20 therefore contained a statement of threat not against Judah but against Aram, the leader of the Syro-Ephraimite coalition (cf. 7:2). When considered in relation to the reassurance speech to Ahaz in the earlier form of vv. 13aβ-17, v. 20 specifies the deliverance of Judah by YHWH's promise to punish Aram. The addition of the references to "the king of Assyria" in both v. 17 and v. 20 in the context of the threatening material in 7:18-25 changes the character of this text from promise to threat.

From these arguments, it is clear that the final form of 7:18-25 is the product of a redaction dating to the reign of Josiah. In supplying vv. 18-19 and 21-25, this redaction accomplished several goals. First, by removing v. 20 from its original context and adding the glosses concerning the king of Assyria in vv. 17 and 20, it presented a reinterpretation of the Immanuel sign. Whereas the original understanding of this sign was one of reassurance to Ahaz that he would be delivered from the Syro-Ephraimite coalition, its present form announces the threat of Assyrian intervention in the land. Vv. 18-25 reinforce this threat by portraying the devastation that the land will suffer. Second, it provides a transition between the material concerning the encounter with Ahaz in ch. 7 and that concerning Isaiah's signs to Judah in ch. 8. In this respect, it not only provides a transition from concern with the monarchy to concern for the people and land of Judah, but it also associates 7:2-25 with material that presupposes Ahaz's rejection of Isaiah's advice to rely on YHWH alone and his subsequent request for Assyrian assistance (8:6-7; cf. 2 Kgs 16:5-9). This provides the historical perspective for the reinterpretation of the Immanuel sign evident in Isa 7:18-25. Third, by adding the reference to Egypt in vv. 18-19, it emphasizes a concern of the Josianic period when Egypt posed a threat to Judah's newly acquired independence. Fourth, it emphasizes Ahaz's lack of trust in YHWH's promises to defend Jerusalem and the Davidic dynasty, and thereby presents Ahaz as a foil to Hezekiah, who serves as the model of Josianic rule.

The third line of evidence involves the relationship of 7:2–8:15 to 8:16–9:6 (*RSV* 7). The latter passage announces Isaiah's plans to withdraw from the scene and to wait for a new ideal Davidic monarch who will preside over all Israel in a period of peace. It is this passage that defines the purpose of the pre-Josianic narratives in 7:2–8:15 in relation to the historical background in the early years of Hezekiah. It also provides the basis for Josianic interest in the text, insofar as it projects Davidic rule over all Israel in the wake of the Assyrian downfall. This passage presents an ideal picture of the Davidic king and may well have served as part of Hezekiah's coronation liturgy. Furthermore, it presents this ideal king as a hope for the people after a period of confusion. The narratives in 7:1–8:15 must be understood against this ideal in that they present an account of how Ahaz's decisions to ignore Isaiah's advice and request aid from Assyria led to catastrophe. Furthermore, the redaction of this material, which focuses on the dynastic implications of this incident and reinterprets the Immanuel sign from one of reassurance to one of threat, presupposes Ahaz's decision and its consequences. It presents Ahaz as a contrast to the ideal monarch of 8:23–9:6 (*RSV* 7). Ahaz abandoned reliance on YHWH and brought Judah to disaster, but it is YHWH who guarantees the throne of the ideal monarch of 8:23–9:6 (*RSV* 7) (see esp. 9:6 [*RSV* 7]). Insofar as it incorporates the autobiographical material of 7:2-17, 20, and 8:1-15 concerning Ahaz's refusal to accept YHWH's promises of security for Jerusalem, this passage may be understood as an attempt to dissuade Hezekiah from bringing the country to ruin by joining an alliance against Assyria, as his father Ahaz did by joining an alliance with Assyria against the Syro-Ephraimite coalition.

Intention

Although 7:1–9:6 (*RSV* 7) constitutes a major element of the Josianic redaction of Isaiah, the previous discussion demonstrates that apart from modifications in 7:1, 3-4, 10, 17, 18-19, and 21-25, which tie this text to the larger context of the Josianic redaction, the underlying form was apparently produced by the prophet at the beginning of Hezekiah's reign. Consequently, a discussion of the intention of 7:1-25 must account for both settings.

As a product of the Josianic redaction of Isaiah, 7:1-25 presents Ahaz as an example of a faithless Davidic monarch who rejects the promises of YHWH's protection to the dynasty and the city of Jerusalem. The result is disaster for Jerusalem and Judah insofar as YHWH will bring the Assyrian empire to punish the land until a faithful Davidic monarch, presumably Josiah, shall arise and bring peace.

The intention of the Isaianic narrative differs somewhat in that its purpose is to dissuade the new king, Hezekiah, from undertaking any alliances with other nations to oppose the Assyrians. To achieve this purpose, the narrative portrays Ahaz's rejection of YHWH's guarantee of security to the Davidic dynasty and Judah during the Syro-Ephraimite crisis in favor of a political alliance with the Assyrian empire. Two essential points are made. First, Judah will suffer the consequences of devastation of its land as well as Assyrian oppression and domination (8:5-8, 11-15) as a result of Assyrian intervention in the conflict. Second, the Assyrians are brought to the country by YHWH as a punishment for Ahaz's and the people's lack of faith in the divine guarantee of security offered to Ahaz (7:2-17, 20; 8:6-7). The narratives concerning the "house of David" (7:1-25) and the people and land of Judah (8:1-15) serve as a backdrop for the expectations of faithfulness and security expressed for the new Davidic king in 8:16–9:6 (*RSV* 7) that appear in both recensions of the narrative, i.e., for Josiah in the Josianic redaction and for Hezekiah in the Isaianic version of the narrative. Various elements in each of the three major components of both versions of this narrative demonstrate their individual perspectives.

Both versions of the narrative in 7:1-25 focus on the failure of Ahaz, as a representative of the Davidic dynasty, to trust in YHWH's assurances of security during the Syro-Ephraimite crisis. The dynastic implications of this failure are indicated from the outset by the reference to "the house of David" in v. 2 (cf. v. 13) and the notice that "his heart and the heart of his people shook like the shaking of the trees of the forest before the wind." Not only does his fear demonstrate a failure to accept the assurances of divine protection for Jerusalem and the Davidic dynasty that stand at the very basis of Judean royal ideology (2 Samuel 7; 23; 1 Kings 8; Psalms 2; 46; 48; 76; 89; 110; 132; etc.), but the mention of the "forest" calls to mind the name of the Davidic royal palace, "the House of the Forest of Lebanon" (1 Kgs 7:2; 10:17, 21; 2 Chr 9:16, 20; cf. von Rad, *Old Testament Theology*, 2:155-75).

The focus on the issue of dynastic security is evident from several other elements of this narrative as well. The first is Isaiah's son Shear-jashub, who appears in the Josianic version. The name means "a remnant will return," and it is frequently taken as a reference to the return or repentance of part of the Judean population following the Assyrian invasion, based on its context in relation to 8:1-15. That Shear-jashub apparently plays no further role in this narrative raises questions about this interpretation, however; one would expect some development or explanation of this image or sign later in a narrative that concerns itself with Judah's fate. On the contrary, Shear-jashub appears to function in relation to the Josianic version of the narrative in vv. 2-9 as a means to assure Ahaz that a remnant of Judah will survive the crisis. But the name would have functioned very differently in relation to the Isaiah version of the narrative. The only other mention of Shear-jashub appears in 10:20-23, where the name signifies the return of the people of the northern kingdom of Israel, here identified as "the remnant of Israel," "the escaped of the house of Jacob," and "the remnant of Jacob," to reliance on YHWH. This is in keeping with Davidic ideology in general and with the perspective of 8:23–9:6 (*RSV* 7), which ideally claims rule over all of Israel (cf. Irvine, *Crisis*, 138-77). When viewed against this background, it is clear that Shear-jashub functioned originally as a sign of reassurance to Ahaz in keeping with the reassurance offered in vv. 4-9. Not only does the oracle promise Ahaz deliverance from the Syro-Ephraimite coalition, but the presence of Shear-jashub also assures Ahaz of Israel's return to YHWH, and consequently, to the Davidic dynasty. The Josianic form of the narrative, however, changes the significance of this sign in order to demonstrate Ahaz's lack of faith that YHWH will protect Jerusalem.

Second, the initial description of the Syro-Ephraimite crisis in both versions of this passage emphasizes that it is a threat to Ahaz and thus to the Davidic dynasty. According to 7:6, the goal of the Syro-Ephraimite attack was to replace the ruling Davidic monarch with a man identified only as "ben Tabeel." Vanel has proposed that he was a member of the Tyrian royal house on the basis of an Assyrian tributary list dating to 738 that mentions Tubail, king of Tyre. This understanding is problematic, however, in that Phoenicians do not seem to be involved in the attack on Judah. It is unlikely that the Israelite Pekah would support Phoenician control of Judah, given past attempts by Phoenicia to control the northern kingdom during the reign of Ahab and his Phoenician queen, Jezebel. Opposition to Phoenician influence in Israel was led by the prophet Elijah of Tishbe, in the territory of Gilead (1 Kgs 17:1). It is more likely that Pekah was an Aramaean sympathizer who represented an attempt by Aram (Syria) to take control of both Israel and Judah in its preparations for confrontation with the Assyrians (cf. Irvine, *Crisis,* 101-9). This is in keeping with Pekah's origin in Gilead (2 Kgs 15:25), a region that frequently came under Aramaean influence, and with the statement in Isa 7:2 that "Aram had settled [*nāḥâ;* RSV 'is in league with'] on Ephraim." The term *nāḥâ,* "had settled," is somewhat enigmatic. Its literal meaning is "to cause to rest." In the present context, however, it refers to Aram's settling on, and thereby dominating, Israel. Regardless of ben Tabeel's origin, it is clear that he is not of the "house of David" and that he therefore represents a threat to the continuation of the Davidic dynasty.

Third, the statement "if you will not believe, surely you will not be secure," draws on the language of the Davidic covenant tradition in which YHWH guarantees the throne of David forever. The statement is based on a wordplay of the verb *'mn,* "to be faithful, secure, firm." It generally conveys a sense of constancy, reliability, or steadfastness, and appears frequently in the guarantees for the security and permanence of the Davidic royal house (1 Sam 25:28; 2 Sam 7:16; 1 Kgs 8:26; Isa 55:3; Ps 89:29; 1 Chr 17:23; 2 Chr 1:9; 6:17; etc.). In the present context, it reminds Ahaz of YHWH's guarantee to the Davidic dynasty and admonishes him not to give up faith in YHWH. Insofar as Ahaz's alternative is to turn to the Assyrian monarch for assistance, Isaiah here advises Ahaz to trust in YHWH and not in foreign alliances. Although this advice may seem naive, it presupposes that the Assyrian monarch would find reason to enter the region anyway and that Jerusalem could withstand a siege until an Assyrian attack against the exposed northern flanks of Aram and Israel forces the Syro-Ephraimite coalition to withdraw. Ahaz's request for assistance would only obligate Judah to Assyria as a vassal unnecessarily. Ahaz's subsequent submission to Tiglath-pileser following his requested assistance in the Syro-Ephraimite War bears this out (cf. 2 Kgs 16:5-18). In effect, such a move would cost Judah its independence and compromise the integrity of the Davidic dynasty.

The final indication that this narrative focuses on the issue of the security and integrity of the Davidic dynasty appears in the sign of Immanuel. Because of the importance of the Immanuel figure in the NT accounts of the virgin birth of Jesus (Matt 1:23), scholars have devoted an extraordinary amount of attention to the interpretation of this passage (for summaries of the discussion, see Kilian, *Verheissung;* idem, *Jesaja 1–39,* 12-26). Scholars agree that Heb. *'almâ,* understood in the NT as "virgin" based on LXX *parthenos,* refers to a woman of childbearing age but has nothing to do with whether she is a virgin. Numerous identifications of Immanuel have been proposed, the most important of which are a royal child of the Davidic line, often identified specifically as Hezekiah, or a son of the prophet Isaiah. As Stamm shows in his studies of this material, chronological problems stand in the way of identifying the child as Hezekiah, in that Hezekiah was born well before the Syro-Ephraimite War. Despite the fact that the context refers only to Isaiah's children as "signs and portents" (Isa 8:18), there are likewise difficulties in identifying Immanuel as a son of Isaiah in that the prophet already has one son, Shear-jashub, and ʿalmâ is taken by many to refer to a woman who has not yet borne a child. Because the identity of the ʿalmâ is never made clear, it is impossible to identify Immanuel with certainty. In any case, the significance of the Immanuel sign lies not in the identity of the child but in the meaning of its name and its role in defining the period of time before the Syro-Ephraimite threat is removed. The statement "YHWH is with him" is frequently applied to David (1 Sam 16:18; 18:12, 14; 2 Sam 5:10) as well as to Hezekiah (2 Kgs 18:7), indicating its significance as a sign of security for the Davidic dynasty. Furthermore, the reference to the child eating curds and honey, "until he knows to reject the bad and choose the good," refers to the period of time in which Immanuel will be weaned from soft food suitable for an infant and defines the period of time before the Syro-Ephraimite coalition will be removed from the land, thereby guaranteeing the security of Ahaz and the "house of David."

As indicated by its association with Isa 8:1-15, which discusses the consequences that will befall Judah for its rejection of YHWH's protection, the present form of this narrative presupposes Ahaz's subsequent appeal to the Assyrian monarch for assistance (cf. 2 Kgs 16:5-18). In the discussion of the setting of this unit I noted that the original understanding of Isaiah's message to Ahaz as one of reassurance has been modified and reinterpreted in the Josianic version to signify the emergence of the threat of Assyrian intervention in Judah. Evidence for the reinterpretation of this passage includes the removal of v. 20 from its original location immediately following v. 17, the additions of the glosses referring to the "king of Assyria" in vv. 17 and 20, the addition of material referring to the threat posed by foreign invasion in vv. 18-19 and 21-25, and the juxtaposition of 7:1-25 with 8:1-15. In this respect, the period of time in which Immanuel will be weaned signifies not only the removal of the Syro-Ephraimite threat but also its replacement with the even greater threat of Assyrian (and Egyptian) invasion. Not only do the curds and honey define the time when Assyria will intervene: they also become a symbol of the devastation of the land in the wake of Assyrian invasion. Those who remain in the land will have only curds and honey to eat since all the agricultural areas will be overgrown with thorns and thistles and overrun with enemy archers. As such, they are fit only for grazing by the few cattle and sheep that are left to the survivors to provide the milk.

It is with this reinterpretation of Isaiah's signs to Ahaz from reassurance to threat that the ultimate intent of 7:2-25 within the context of the Josianic version of 7:1–9:6 (*RSV* 7) becomes clear. As noted in the discussion of the setting of this passage, the reference to the invasion of the land by both Egypt and Assyria indicates the period in which this narrative was assembled and the purpose it was to serve. Egypt did not pose a threat to Judah during the Syro-Ephraimite War and subsequent Assyrian invasion. It did attempt to become active on the scene after Assyria had established itself in the region, but Isaiah's oracles concerning Egypt focus not on any threat it may pose but on its unreliability as an ally. Egypt did become a threat to Judah in the late 7th century, however, following the collapse of Assyria. The inclusion of Egypt with Assyria as threats in this passage clearly serves as a basis for portraying the new Davidic king in 9:1-6 (*RSV* 2-7) and 11:1-16 as one who will bring peace to the kingdom and restore its captives from both Assyria and Egypt. Obviously, such a portrayal points to Josiah as the Davidic king. In this regard, Ahaz is presented as a foil to Josiah. Ahaz's lack of faith led to disaster for the Davidic dynasty and for Judah and Jerusalem. A faithful Davidic monarch will bring restoration and peace.

With regard to the Isaianic version of this narrative, Ahaz again serves as a foil, but in this case the narrative places its emphasis on the positive aspects of the promise to Ahaz in 7:2-17 and 20; i.e., if Ahaz shows faith, YHWH will deliver the dynasty and the land. Ahaz's refusal of the sign serves as the premise for disaster in 8:1-15 and as antithetical to the faithful monarch portrayed in 8:16–9:6 (*RSV* 7). The new monarch will see the possibility of restoration and peace if he avoids the mistakes of his predecessor Ahaz. Just as Ahaz's alliance with Assyria led to the Assyrian invasion of the region, so will Hezekiah's proposed alliances threaten similar consequences. When considered in relation to 8:23–9:6 (*RSV* 7), which envisions peace, security, and rule over all the land of Israel and Judah for the new Davidic monarch, it becomes clear that the Isaianic form of 7:2–9:6 (*RSV* 7) is designed to dissuade the new monarch Hezekiah from pursuing a policy of confrontation with Assyria.

Bibliography

Ackroyd, "Isaiah 36–39" (→ "Introduction to the Book of Isaiah"); A. Auret, "Hiskia — die oorspronklike Immanuel en messias van Jesaja 7:14: 'n Bron van heil en onheil," *NGTT* 32 (1991) 5-18; R. Bartelmus, "Jes 7,1-17 und das Stilprinzip des Kontrastes Syntaktisch-stilistische und traditionsgeschichtliche Anmerkungen zur 'Immanuel-Perikope,' " *ZAW* 96 (1984) 50-66; J. Begrich, "Der Syrisch-Ephraimitische Krieg und seine weltpolitischen Zusammenhänge," *ZDMG* 83 (1920) 213-37; R. Bickert, "König Ahas und der Prophet Jesaja: Ein Beitrag zum Problem des syrisch-ephraimitischen Krieges," *ZAW* 99 (1987) 361-84; A. J. Bjørndalen, "Zur Einordnung und Funktion von Jes 7,5f," *ZAW* 95 (1983) 260-63; K. Budde, "Jesaja und Ahaz," *ZDMG* 84 (1930) 125-38; idem, "Das Immanuelzeichen und die Ahaz-Begegnung Jesaja 7," *JBL* 52 (1933) 22-54; D. L. Christensen, *Prophecy and War in Ancient Israel: Studies in the Oracles against the Nations in Old Testament Prophecy* (BMS 3; Berkeley: BIBAL, 1989) 127-29; R. E. Clements, "The Immanuel Prophecy of Isa. 7:10-17 and Its Messianic Interpretation," in *Die Hebräische Bibel und Ihre Zweifache Nachgeschichte* (*Fest.* R. Rendtorff; ed. E. Blum, C. Macholz, and E. E. Stegemann; Neukirchen-Vluyn: Neukirchener, 1990) 225-40; C. Dohmen, "Verstockungsvollzug und prophetische Legitimation: Literar-kritische Beobachtungen zu Jes 7,1-17," *BN* 31 (1986) 37-55; Donner, *Israel unter den Völkern* (→ 1:4-9), 7-18, 140-41; G. Fohrer, "Zu Jes 7,14 im Zusammenhang von Jes 7,10-22," *ZAW* 68 (1956) 54-56; M. Görg, "Hiskija als Immanuel: Plädoyer für eine typologische Identifikation," *BN* 22 (1983) 107-25; W. C. Graham, "Isaiah's Part in the Syro-Ephraimitic Crisis," *AJSL* 50 (1933-34) 201-16; A. H. J. Gunneweg, "Heils- und Unheilsverkundigung in Jes. VII," *VT* 15 (1965) 27-34; E. Hammershaimb, "The Immanuel Sign," *ST* 4 (1949) 124-42; P. Höffken, "Notizen zum Textcharakter von Jesaja 7,1-17," *TZ* 36 (1980) 321-37; idem, "Grundfragen von Jesaja 7,1-17 im Spiegel neuerer Literatur," *BZ* 33 (1989) 25-42; J. Høgenhaven, "The Prophet Isaiah and Judaean Foreign Policy under Ahaz and Hezekiah," *JNES* 49 (1990) 351-54; idem, "Die symbolischen Namen in Jesaja 7 und 8 im Rahmen der sogenannten 'Denkschrift' des Propheten," in *The Book of Isaiah/Le Livre d'Isaïe* (ed. J. Vermeylen; BETL 81; Leuven: Leuven University Press and Peeters, 1989) 231-35; F. D. Hubman, "Randbemerkungen zu Jes 7,1-17," *BN* 26 (1985) 27-46; H. Irsigler, "Zeichen und Bezeichnetes in Jes 7,1-17: Notizen zum Immanueltext," *BN* 29 (1985) 75-114; S. Irvine, "Isaiah's She'ar-Yashub and the Davidic House," *BZ* 37 (1993) 78-88; J. Jensen, "The Age of Immanuel," *CBQ* 41 (1979) 220-39; R. Kilian, *Die Verheissung Immanuels Jes 7,14* (SBS 35; Stuttgart: Katholisches Bibelwerk, 1968); E. G. Kraeling, "The Immanuel Prophecy," *JBL* 50 (1931) 277-97; J. Lindblom, *A Study of the Immanuel Section in Isaiah (Isa. vii,1–ix,6)* (Lund: Gleerup, 1958); W. McKane, "The Interpretation of Isaiah VII 14-25," *VT* 17 (1967) 208-19; M. Rehm, *Der königliche Messias im Licht der Immanuel-Weissagungen des Buches Jesaja* (Kevelaer: Butzon & Bercker, 1968) 30-121; G. Rice, "A Neglected Interpretation of the Immanuel Prophecy," *ZAW* 90 (1978) 220-27; L. G. Rignell, "Das Immanuelszeichen: Einige Gesichtspunkte zu Jes. 7," *ST* 11 (1957) 99-119; J. J. M. Roberts, "Isaiah and His Children," in *Biblical and Related Studies Presented to Samuel Iwry* (ed. A. Kort and S. Morschauser; Winona Lake: Eisenbrauns, 1985) 193-203; M. Sæbo, "Formgeschichtliche Erwägungen zu Jes. 7:3-9," *ST* 14 (1960) 54-69; J. J. Scullion, "An Approach to the Understanding of Isaiah 7:10-17," *JBL* 87 (1968) 288-300; Seybold, *Das davidische Königtum* (→ "Introduction to the Prophetic Literature"), 66-79; Stacey, *Prophetic Drama* (→ "Introduction to the Prophetic Literature"), 113-20; J. J. Stamm, "La Prophétie d'Emmanuel," *RHPR* 23 (1943) 1-25; idem, "Die Immanuel-Weissagung: Ein Gespräch mit E. Hammershaimb," *VT* 4 (1954) 20-33; idem, "Die Immanuel-Weissagung und die Eschatologie des Jesaja," *TZ* 16 (1960) 439-55; idem, "Die Immanuel-Perikope: Eine Nachlese," *TZ* 30 (1974) 11-22; O. H. Steck, "Rettung und Verstockung: Exegetische Bemerkungen zu Jesaja 7,3-9," *EvT* 33 (1973) 77-90; idem, "Beiträge zum Verständnis von Jesaja 7,10-17 und 8,1-4," *TZ* 29 (1973) 161-78; Tångberg, *Mahnrede* (→ "Introduction to the Prophetic Literature"), 66-75; A. Vanel, "Tâbe'él en Is. VII 6 et le roi Tubail de Tyr," *Studies on Prophecy* (VTSup 26; Leiden: Brill, 1974) 17-24; J. H. Walton, "Isa 7:14: What's in a Name?" *JETS* 30 (1987) 289-306; J. Werlitz, *Studien zur literarkritischen Methode: Gericht und Heil in Jesaja 7,1-17 und 29,1-8* (BZAW 204; Berlin and New York: de Gruyter, 1992) 95-250; H. M. Wolf, "A Solution to the Immanuel Prophecy in Isaiah 7:14–8:22," *JBL* 91 (1972) 449-56; H. W. Wolff, *Frieden ohne Ende: Jesaja 7,1-17 und 9,1-6 ausgelegt* (BibS[N] 35; Neukirchen: Neukirchener, 1962); E. Würthwein, "Jesaja 7,1-9," in *Wort und Existenz: Studien zum Alten Testament* (Göttingen: Vandenhoeck & Ruprecht, 1970) 127-43; F. Zimmermann, "The Immanuel Prophecy," *JQR* 52 (1961-62) 154-59.

II. CONCERNING JUDAH: AUTOBIOGRAPHICAL REPORT CONCERNING THE MAHER-SHALAL-HASH-BAZ SIGN AND ITS SIGNIFICANCE, 8:1-15

Structure

As noted in the discussion of ch. 7 in part one of this unit, 8:1-15 is related to ch. 7 insofar as it provides a parallel account concerning the significance of Isaiah's children. Whereas ch. 7 relates the significance of Shear-jashub and Immanuel for the Davidic dynasty, 8:1-15 relates the significance of Maher-shalal-hash-baz for Judah. Both 8:1-15 and 7:1-25 have parallel structures including YHWH's instructions to the prophet (8:1-4; 7:2-9) followed by a section in which YHWH speaks again, introduced by the formula *wayyôsep yhwh dabbēr,* "and YHWH again spoke" (8:5; 7:10). Furthermore, the references to Immanuel in 8:8 and 9 and the reinterpretation of the name from an assurance of security to a threat recalls the Immanuel sign of ch. 7 and its similar resignification. Finally, the allegorical portrayal of Assyria as a river associates 8:1-15 with 7:1-25 on account of the mention of Ahaz's inspection of the water system in 7:2. Ahaz's concern with his water system indicates his concern that the city will not be able to withstand siege and is apparently a factor prompting him to turn to Assyria for assistance. Because Ahaz and Judah reject YHWH's guarantee of security, as symbolized by the city's water system, the land will be inundated by the Assyrian army.

Although 8:1-15 is clearly linked to 7:1-25 as a parallel account, there are a number of indications that it forms a distinct subunit vis-à-vis ch. 7. Isa 8:1-15 is written in a clear 1st-person autobiographical style in contrast to 7:1-25, which contains 3rd-person objective reporting language in vv. 1-9, the ambiguous reporting language of vv. 10-17, and the largely objective announcement language of vv. 18-25. Furthermore, 8:1-15 introduces a new child, Maher-shalal-hash-baz, which is understood as a sign for Judah in contrast to the signs of ch. 7, which were directed to the Davidic dynasty. Isa 8:1-15 is written from the perspective of the aftermath of Ahaz's decision to request aid from the Assyrians, whereas ch. 7 presupposes a situation prior to the king's request. Finally, 8:1-15 focuses on the threat posed by Assyria, whereas ch. 7 concentrates on the threat posed by the Syro-Ephraimite coalition.

The structure of this unit includes two basic sections that are defined by the concern to report the sign of Maher-shalal-hash-baz (vv. 1-4) and to explain its significance (vv. 5-15). The two sections are demarcated formally by the YHWH speech formulas that appear at the beginning of each section. Although

166

a third YHWH speech formula appears in v. 11, it is subordinated to vv. 9-10 by its introductory *kî*, and vv. 9-10 are linked in turn to the preceding material by the reference to *ʿimmānû ʾēl*.

The structure of the report concerning the birth of Maher-shalal-hash-baz in vv. 1-4 is determined by the narrative sequence of events and the *wāw*-consecutive imperfect verbs that govern the statement concerning each event. V. 1 reports YHWH's instructions to the prophet to write the name Maher-shalal-hash-baz on a large tablet. It is governed by the verb *wayyōʾmer*, "and he said," and includes the speech formula in v. 1aα and the instruction speech itself in v. 1aβ-b. The instructions include imperative commands to "take" *(qaḥ)* the tablet (v. 1aβ) and to "write" *(kětōb)* the name on it (v. 1b). The verb *wěʾāʿîdâ*, "and I caused to witness," in v. 2 introduces the report of Isaiah's compliance with these instructions by securing two reliable witnesses. The verb *wāʾeqrab*, "and I drew near," introduces a further statement of Isaiah's compliance by fathering the child with the "prophetess." The verbs *wattahar wattēled*, "and she became pregnant and gave birth," are a hendiadys that merely reports the results of Isaiah's "approach" to the prophetess. Finally, the verb *wayyōʾmer*, "and he said," introduces YHWH's instructions concerning the naming of this child in vv. 3b-4. Following the speech formula in v. 3bα, the instruction speech in vv. 3bβ-4 includes the basic instruction to name the child Maher-shalal-hash-baz (v. 3bβ) and an explanation introduced by *kî běṭerem*, "Because before," which defines the time in which the Syro-Ephraimite threat will be removed from the land.

The structure of the section concerning the significance of the sign is determined by the use of disputation language to challenge the popular conception that YHWH will protect Judah. Instead, it announces disaster against Judah and then explains that YHWH is the cause of that disaster. The structure is indicated formally by Isaiah's presentation of YHWH's judgment speech against Judah in vv. 5-8, which announces that the Assyrians will take control of the land. The refutation of the common understanding that Immanuel signifies YHWH's protection in vv. 9-15 reinforces the point of the preceding judgment speech.

Verses 5-8 contain Isaiah's presentation of YHWH's judgment speech against Judah. As noted in the previous section (part one), although the passage includes Isaiah's quotation of YHWH's statement concerning the reasons for judgment in v. 6, the appearance of the title *ʾǎdōnāy*, "my Lord," in v. 7 indicates that Isaiah announces the consequences. Consequently, vv. 5-6 report YHWH's statement of the reasons for judgment including the speech formula in v. 5 and the speech itself in v. 6. The conjunction *yaʿan kî*, "because," normally introduces the basis for a following consequence. As the example in 3:16 shows, the basis can be stated by YHWH and the consequences by the prophet so that the statement by YHWH resembles an oath that does not explicitly state consequences but presupposes them. Isaiah's statement of the consequences in vv. 7-8 employs the allegory of Assyria as a great river. Following the basic statement that YHWH will bring the river, i.e., the king of Assyria, against the people (v. 7a), the *wāw*-consecutive perfect verbs appear in paired statements that portray the river overflowing its banks (v. 7b), flooding Judah (v. 8a), and filling the land of Immanuel (v. 8b).

The disputation proper appears in vv. 9-15 with Isaiah's refutation of the popular understanding of Immanuel. Its role in the present structure is to confirm the preceding judgment speech. It begins with the prophet's quotation summoning the nations to defeat because "God is with us." The slogan is defined by its plural imperative verbs that are addressed to the nations. It includes three basic commands including a call to attention that summons the nations to hear and be crushed (v. 9a), a command to gird and be crushed (v. 9b), and a command to take counsel and fail that includes the basis for the nations' defeat (i.e., "God is with us," v. 10). The refutation proper in vv. 11-15 is connected to this slogan by the introductory *kî*, "because." These verses indicate that in fact YHWH is not with us but against us as the ultimate cause of the Assyrian invasion. The refutation begins with Isaiah's report of YHWH's instruction not to follow the people in considering the Syro-Ephraimite coalition to be a threat, including the prophet's explanatory messenger formula (v. 11) and YHWH's instruction statement proper (v. 12). Vv. 13-15 contain Isaiah's instructions to sanctify or fear YHWH as the one who poses the real threat to Judah. This section contains the prophet's instruction statement proper (v. 13) and his elaboration on the reasons that the people should fear YHWH (vv. 14-15), including YHWH's role as a *miqdāš* (lit. "sanctuary," but see the discussion of the Intention of this passage below) or "threat" to the two houses of Israel and Jerusalem in v. 14 and the resulting casualties among the people in v. 15.

Genre

The overarching genre of 8:1-15 is autobiographical ACCOUNT concerning the Maher-shalal-hash-baz sign and its significance. This is indicated formally by the narrative style of the passage, which is governed by *wāw*-consecutive imperfect verbs, and its consistent 1st-person singular perspective that indicates that the prophet is the speaker. The contents of the passage define the subject of this autobiographical ACCOUNT.

A number of subordinate genres also appear in this text. The REPORT concerning the birth of Maher-shalal-hash-baz is built around two INSTRUCTIONS by YHWH to the prophet in vv. 1 and 3b-4. Each is introduced by a SPEECH FORMULA indicating that Isaiah is reporting a SPEECH by YHWH. The INSTRUCTIONS themselves are characterized by masculine singular imperative verbs directed to the prophet and convey YHWH's basic commands concerning this sign, the attestation of the name in v. 1aβ-b, and the naming of the child in vv. 3bβ-4. The 1st-person statements in vv. 2-3a merely indicate Isaiah's compliance with YHWH's instructions.

The PROPHETIC JUDGMENT SPEECH genre stands behind Isaiah's presentation of YHWH's judgment against Judah in vv. 5-8. The basis or reasons for judgment are presented in vv. 5-6 in the form of Isaiah's quotation of a speech by YHWH (v. 6). The introductory *ya'an kî*, "because," normally presupposes a consequence, but the end of YHWH's speech in v. 6 precludes this. Instead, Isaiah supplies the consequences in vv. 7-8 with a statement introduced by *wĕlākēn*, "and therefore." An analogous example appears in 3:16-17, where

Isaiah also announces the consequences to a statement of reasons for punishment spoken by YHWH. Consequently, this is a modified form of the PROPHETIC JUDGMENT SPEECH.

Verses 9-15 constitute a DISPUTATION in which the prophet attempts to refute the common understanding of Immanuel as a symbol for YHWH's guarantee of protection to Jerusalem and Judah. In keeping with the standard DISPUTATION form (see Graffy, 15-29; cf. D. F. Murray, "Rhetoric"), the passage contains a quotation to be refuted (vv. 9-10) and the refutation itself (vv. 11-15). Insofar as the announcement of judgment in vv. 5-8 is directed to Immanuel (v. 8), this DISPUTATION is designed to confirm the announcement of judgment.

The prophet begins with a quotation of a common slogan that expresses the belief in Immanuel as a guarantee of security. Sæbo identifies this slogan as an "invitation to battle" stemming from the holy war tradition, but it is more properly designated as a "summons to defeat" insofar as it is directed to Jerusalem's enemies and projects their defeat. In keeping with the standard SUMMONS TO WAR form, it does include the summons proper, as indicated by its imperative forms calling the nations to prepare themselves for battle, as well as a motivating statement, *kî ʿimmānû ʾēl,* "for God is with us." It differs, however, in that the summons also includes imperative forms that call the nations to defeat. Consequently, it appears to be a modified form of the standard SUMMONS TO WAR (cf. Judg 3:28; 4:6-7, 14; 7:9). Because it calls the nations to defeat, it thereby expresses the common understanding of Immanuel as a guarantee of YHWH's protection. As Sæbo points out (p. 138), its holy war background has been combined with the Zion and Davidic traditions of Jerusalem's inviolability (cf. 1 Kgs 8:57; Ps 46:8, 12 [*RSV* 7, 11]; 2 Chr 32:8). In its present position, it appears as a sort of rhetorical straw dog insofar as the prophet's purpose is to refute it in the following verses.

The refutation appears in vv. 11-15. It begins with an expanded MESSENGER FORMULA in v. 11, which states YHWH's intention to keep him from following the people and introduces YHWH's instruction to him, expressed as a prohibition, not to fear the Syro-Ephraimite conspiracy. The prophet then concludes in his own words by warning the people to sanctify and fear YHWH as the one who is bringing disaster on the two houses of Judah and on the inhabitants of Jerusalem (vv. 13-15). According to Graffy (p. 109), the addressees of disputation speeches commonly include "the house of Israel" (cf. v. 14), "the inhabitants of Jerusalem" (cf. v. 14), and "this people" (cf. vv. 6, 11). In this manner, Isaiah intends to refute the understanding that "God is with us" by demonstrating that God is against us.

Setting

Although the compositional unity of 8:1-15 is frequently questioned on various grounds, its consistent 1st-person autobiographical perspective and the interrelationship of the report concerning Maher-shalal-hash-baz in vv. 1-4 with the disputational material in vv. 5-15 suggest that it is a compositional unity. The issue is further complicated by two additional factors. The first involves the failure to recognize the literary implications of the structural parallel between 8:1-15 and 7:1-25 and the temporal perspective of 8:1-15; the second involves the failure to recognize the disputational character of 8:5-8.

As noted in the discussion of the structure of this passage, 8:1-15 has a literary structure parallel to that of 7:1-25. Both narratives begin with a report of YHWH's instructions to the prophet concerning the use of one of his sons as a sign in relation to the Syro-Ephraimite War (7:2-9; 8:1-4), and both narratives include sections that employ the same introductory YHWH speech formula, *wayyôsep yhwh dabbēr,* "and again YHWH spoke," to introduce sections elaborating the meaning of their respective signs (7:10-17; 8:5-8). In addition, both the Immanuel sign of 7:10-17 and the Maher-shalal-hash-baz sign of 8:1-4 function primarily as means for defining the time in which the Syro-Ephraimite coalition will be removed from the land on account of the appearance of the Assyrian king (7:16-17; 8:4). The narratives differ in that 8:1-15 has a consistent 1st-person autobiographical narrative perspective, whereas 7:1-25 shifts from 3rd-person objective report in vv. 1-9, to an ambiguous 3rd-person narrative that may well be autobiographical in vv. 10-17, to proclamation language that in turn shifts from 3rd person (vv. 18-19), to 1st person (v. 20), and finally back to 3rd person again (vv. 21-25).

Although it is commonly assumed that ch. 8 is modeled on ch. 7, the composite nature of ch. 7 and its parallels to ch. 8 suggest that precisely the opposite is the case: ch. 7 was composed after the pattern of ch. 8. This is supported by three considerations. First, although ch. 7 contains some 1st-person materials from the prophet, it is composed in a predominantly 3rd-person style, indicating that someone other than the prophet was responsible for its final form. As indicated by the discussion of ch. 7, it appears that the Josianic redaction edited the prophet's originally autobiographical text to create this narrative. Second, the appearance of the YHWH speech formula in 7:10 is awkward and leads to a difficult transition between vv. 2-9 and vv. 10-17. Its presence in a context where Isaiah is clearly the speaker suggests an interest that stems from outside the present context. A desire to pattern this material after that of 8:1-15 provides such an interest. Third and finally, the condemnatory nature of the Maher-shalal-hash-baz sign indicates that 8:1-15 presupposes the situation following Ahaz's decision to seek Assyrian aid. As indicated by the discussion of 7:1-25, the material concerning the Shear-jashub and Immanuel signs was reworked to change them from promises of security to threats of the consequences of Assyrian intervention. The perspective of 7:1-17 presupposes an encounter with Ahaz prior to his decision, but the present form of 7:1-25 reflects the situation following his decision. The edited Josianic form of ch. 7 thereby presents a perspective on Immanuel similar to that of 8:5-15, insofar as it signifies an Assyrian threat. But curiously, ch. 8 never alludes to Immanuel as a child or as a sign to Ahaz. This evidence suggests that 7:1-25 draws its understanding of Immanuel from 8:1-15, not vice versa.

These considerations have implications for the composition of 8:1-15 as well as for that of 7:1-25. Scholars have frequently argued that 8:1-4 is an independent unit and that the material beginning in v. 5 is a secondary addition to this text (Wildberger, *Jesaja*, 313-14, 322). This is based on the fact that Maher-shalal-hash-baz does not appear again after v. 4, that vv. 1-4 are the only unit of this passage consistently formulated as a 1st-person report, v. 5 being a redactional addition, and that the reference to the king of Assyria in v. 4 is a gloss. There are problems with this argument, however. First, Maher-shalal-hash-baz does not need to appear in this narrative again, any more than Shear-jashub and Immanuel needed to be mentioned again after their initial introductions. The only role that this child plays is to define the time in which the Assyrian king appears to remove the Syro-Ephraimite coalition. Once the Assyrian monarch is mentioned, he, not Maher-shalal-hash-baz, becomes a primary focus of attention throughout the rest of the unit. Second, vv. 5-15 are formulated in a consistent 1st-person autobiographical form. The 1st-person forms are most conspicuous in the framework verses, 5 and 11, which precede the quotations of speeches by YHWH in vv. 6 and 12. Of the discourses that follow, the title *'ădōnāy,* "my Lord," in v. 7 indicates that vv. 7-8 share the 1st-person perspective of vv. 1-4 and 5. Vv. 13-15 do not require a 1st-person form since they are formulated as the prophet's 2nd-person plural address to the two houses of Israel and the people of Jerusalem. Third, unlike the appositional reference to the Assyrian king in 7:17, the reference to the Assyrian monarch fits smoothly into the syntax of 8:4. Furthermore, the threatening character of the name Maher-shalal-hash-baz contrasts with the assuring character of Immanuel. This point suggests that this sign was understood as a threat to Judah from the outset, insofar as the removal of the Syro-Ephraimite coalition would lead to the introduction of an even greater threat in the form of the Assyrian king. The material in vv. 5-15 simply elaborates on the meaning of that threat.

The references to "Rezin and ben Remaliah" in v. 6 and "the king of Assyria and all his glory" in v. 7 are frequently viewed as glosses introduced to specify the water allegory that appears in this text (see *BHS*). The appositional character of these identifications disrupts the allegorical contexts, and together with the difficulties caused by the reading *ûmĕśôś,* "and the joy" (see the discussion of Intention below), suggests that they are indeed glosses. The removal of these references does not, however, change the essential character of vv. 6-8 as an allegorical description of Assyria's overrunning Judah.

Because of the imperative perspective of vv. 9-10 and the difficulties involved in defining its function in relation to its present context, scholars have frequently identified this text as an independent composition derived from the holy war and Zion traditions (so Sæbo). Debate continues as to whether the present form of this text was composed for a cultic context or by the prophet for the present context (see Kilian, *Jesaja 1–39,* 47-49, for a summary of the debate), but the key issue is its function in the present context. As the discussion of the structure and genre of this passage demonstrates, vv. 9-15 constitute a disputation genre in which the prophet attempts to refute the common understanding of Immanuel held by the people. Insofar as he quotes vv. 9-10 as an example of the belief that Immanuel signifies YHWH's protection, and then refutes it by claiming that YHWH is responsible for the people's present troubles, it is an integral part of this text.

Clearly, this text was written by Isaiah in the aftermath of Ahaz's decision to appeal to Assyria for assistance in the Syro-Ephraimite crisis. When considered in relation to its original conclusion in 8:16-18 (see below), it reflects his frustration with the king's decision and his belief that the Assyrians would simply take control of the country. It may also reflect the suppression of his views in the aftermath of the Assyrian intervention and the reduction of Judah to vassal status. Although it was later taken up as part of the Josianic redaction of 7:1–9:6 (*RSV* 7), the earliest form of this text apparently dates to the early reign of Hezekiah.

Intention

The intention of this passage clearly centers around the Maher-shalal-hash-baz sign and Isaiah's interpretation of its significance in relation to the Syro-Ephraimite War. Like the present form of the Immanuel sign in 7:14-17, it functions as a means for specifying the period of time in which the army of the Syro-Ephraimite coalition will be removed from Judah, namely, before the child is able to speak its first words, "my father and my mother." It also specifies the time in which the Assyrian empire will appear in the region, since the Assyrians will be the cause for the removal of the Syro-Ephraimite army. The balance of the passage in vv. 5-15 focuses on the consequences of the Assyrian intervention for Judah. The intervention of the Assyrians is here interpreted as punishment of Judah for its refusal to trust in YHWH's protection.

Several interpretative problems remain, however, before one can fully understand the intention of this passage. The first involves the reading *ûmĕśôś* in v. 6, and the appositional specifications *'et-rĕṣîn ûben-rĕmalyāhû,* "Rezin and the son of Remaliah," in v. 6 and *'et-melek 'aššûr wĕ'et-kol-kĕbôdô,* "the king of Assyria and all his glory," in v. 7 (for full discussion, see Sweeney, "On *ûmĕśôś*"). *Māśôś* is a noun that means "joy, exultation," and clearly does not fit the present context when considered in relation to the following specification concerning "Rezin and the son of Remaliah." The direct object indicator *'et* at the beginning of this clause requires a verb to precede it. The preceding statement that the people "rejected" *(mā'as)* the waters of Shiloah does not provide an appropriate antecedent in that the people's rejection of Rezin and ben Remaliah is hardly a subject for the prophet's condemnation. *Māśôś* is frequently emended to the infinitive form *mĕsōs,* "dissolve, melt," on the basis of Isa 10:18 (cf. *BHS*) and their similar pronunciations. The resulting understanding is that the people "dissolve" or "melt in fear" before Rezin and ben Remaliah because of their failure to trust in YHWH. This reading also creates problems, however, in that the infinitive construction *mĕsōs* results in awkward syntax. Consequently, many commentators have argued that all of v. 6b and the similar appositional phrase in v. 7aα are glosses that have been introduced to specify the allegorical references of this passage (cf. *BHS*). The addition of these glosses resulted in the confused reading of v. 6b.

Despite its difficulties, *ûmĕśôś* appears to be the original reading in this passage in that 66:10-14 associates the "waters of Shiloah" in 8:6 with the *māśôś* of Jerusalem. This passage from Trito-Isaiah employs similar vocabulary and water imagery to describe the rejoicing associated with YHWH's planting of the "glory of the nations" (*kěbôd gôyîm;* cf. v. 7 and the "glory" of the Assyrian king) in Jerusalem. The use of *měśôś* in 8:6 was apparently intended as an adjective to describe the waters of Shiloah "that run gently and rejoice," but the result was the present awkward syntax of the verse. In this case, the awkward reading calls attention to sexual imagery employed in 8:7-8, including the images of "overflowing waters" and the "outspread skirt" as means to portray the Assyrian king's "rape" of the land of Judah (see Sweeney, "On *ûměśôś*"). This interpretation would confirm that vv. 5-9 referred originally to the Assyrian threat against Judah and not against Aram and Israel (contra Rignell). In this context, the extension of the "wings" or "skirts" that will fill Immanuel's land in v. 8b refers to the extension of Assyrian power throughout Judah. Likewise, the vocative address *'immānû 'ēl* here symbolizes Judah and not the child mentioned in 7:14.

In the discussions of structure and genre I have already noted the role of 8:9-10 in relation to the disputation genre. Here these verses function as a representation of the popular understanding of Immanuel as a symbol for YHWH's protection of Jerusalem. The following material is designed to refute this understanding and show that YHWH stands behind the threat posed by the Assyrian empire.

One problem in this connection is YHWH's statement to Isaiah not to say *qešer* for all that this people will say *qešer* in v. 12. The noun *qešer* generally refers to a conspiracy or internal revolt. On this basis, Rignell questions the common understanding that this verse refers to YHWH's instructions not to feel threatened by the Syro-Ephraimite coalition, and postulates that the term refers to an internal Judean conspiracy against Ahaz following his decision to appeal to Assyria. But this view overlooks the fact that Pekah ben Remaliah's assassination of the ruling king Pekahiah and his subsequent ascension to the throne was likely an Aramean-backed conspiracy to gain control of Israel and align it with Aram (cf. Irvine, *Crisis,* esp. 101-7). Likewise, the plan to depose Ahaz with ben Tabeel represented an attempt to topple the ruling house of David and replace it with a figure who would likewise bring Judah into the Aramean camp. When viewed from this perspective, it is quite easy to understand the use of the term *qešer* in this passage. When read in relation to its context, it represents YHWH's instructing Isaiah not to fear the plans of the Syro-Ephraimite coalition.

A second problem centers on the appearance of the terms *taqdîšû,* "you shall sanctify," in v. 13 and *lěmiqdāš,* "for a sanctuary," in v. 14. Because of the difficulties involved in understanding these terms in the context of statements that speak about the threat posed by YHWH to the two houses of Israel and the inhabitants of Jerusalem, they are frequently emended to *taqšîrû,* "you shall bind," and *lěmaqšîr,* "for a binding" (cf. *BHS*). These statements would therefore instruct the people to bind themselves with YHWH instead of to the above-mentioned conspiracy. Unfortunately, such emendations fail to consider the threatening aspects of sanctity in ancient Israelite thought. Sanctity or holiness can be a threat against the people when not properly respected or approached. Examples include YHWH's killing of Korah and his people for violating YHWH's sanctity by making inappropriate incense offerings (Numbers 16), and

YHWH's killing of Uzzah for touching the ark in an inappropriate manner (2 Samuel 6). The same logic applies here in that the people have treated YHWH's sanctity inappropriately by not trusting in the divine promise of protection for Jerusalem. Consequently, YHWH turns against the people to punish them for this breach of divine sanctity.

In the larger context of 7:1–9:6 (*RSV* 7), 8:1-15 describes the consequences of Ahaz's decision to reject the divine guarantee of security and appeal to the Assyrian monarch for assistance during the Syro-Ephraimite War. It is a parallel narrative to 7:1-25, which focuses on the dynastic consequences of Ahaz's rejection of YHWH's protection as represented by the Immanuel sign. Isa 8:1-15 focuses on Maher-shalal-hash-baz as a sign for the consequences that the land and people of Judah will suffer as a result of this failure to trust YHWH. In this respect, the water imagery of vv. 6-8 is crucial to the Josianic version of this text. Just as Ahaz refuses to trust his city's water system (cf. 7:2) and YHWH's guarantee of security, so the Assyrian army is portrayed as a flood that will inundate the land of Judah. Isa 8:1-15 therefore serves the purposes of the Josianic version of 7:1–9:6 (*RSV* 7) by showing the consequences of Ahaz's previous failure to trust YHWH. As noted above, such an argument was designed to contrast the faithless Ahaz with an ideal future monarch, namely, Josiah, by demonstrating the consequences of faithless action in relation to the benefits of trust in YHWH.

One must also consider 8:1-15 in relation to its original Isaianic context, including the autobiographical narrative that apparently stands behind the present form of 7:2-17, 20 and the conclusion in 8:16–9:6 (*RSV* 7). Here it portrays Judah's rejection of YHWH's promise of security and the resulting consequences of Assyrian domination of the land. When read in relation to the prophet's statements to "bind up the testimony, seal the instruction among my disciples," wait for YHWH, etc., in vv. 16-18, it reflects the defeat of Isaiah's position and his frustration in the aftermath of Ahaz's decision to appeal for Assyrian assistance. The purpose of this text would therefore be to record the sign and confirm the validity of its interpretation. At this point, Isaiah was compelled to withdraw from public debate on the issue and await a more propitious time to resume his participation in the discussion of Judean affairs. Such a propitious time apparently came at the beginning of the reign of Hezekiah when the prophet attempted to convince the new monarch to avoid new alliances that would lead inevitably to a confrontation with Assyria.

Bibliography

J. Boehmer, " 'Dieses Volk,' " *JBL* 45 (1926) 134-48; K. Budde, "Zu Jesaja 8, vers 9 und 10," *JBL* 49 (1930) 423-28; C. A. Evans, "An Interpretation of Isa 8,11-15 Unemended," *ZAW* 97 (1985) 112-13; K. Fullerton, "The Interpretation of Isaiah 8 5-10," *JBL* 43 (1924) 253-89; Gonçalves, *L'expédition de Sennachérib* (→ 1:4-9), 309-13; Høgenhaven, "Prophet Isaiah" (→ 7:1-25); idem, "Die symbolischen Namen" (→ 7:1-25); Irvine, *Crisis* (→ "Introduction to the Book of Isaiah"), 179-213; H. Klein, "Freude an Rezin," *VT* 30 (1980) 229-34; A. Laato, *Who Is Immanuel? The Rise and the Founder-*

ing of Isaiah's Messianic Expectations (Åbo: Åbo Academy Press, 1988) 163-73; N. Lohfink, "Isaias 8,12-14," *BZ* 7 (1963) 98-104; L. G. Rignell, "Das Orakel 'Maher-salal Has-bas': Jesaja 8," *ST* 10 (1956) 40-52; M. Sæbo, "Zur Traditionsgeschichte von Jesaia 8,9-10," *ZAW* 76 (1964) 132-44; O. H. Steck, "Beiträge zum Verständnis von Jesaja 7,10-17 und 8,1-4," *TZ* 29 (1973) 161-78; M. A. Sweeney, "On *ûmᵉśôś* in Isaiah 8.6," in *Among the Prophets: Language, Image and Structure in the Prophetic Writings* (ed. D. J. A. Clines and P. R. Davies; JSOTSup 144; Sheffield: JSOT Press, 1993) 42-54.

PROPHETIC INSTRUCTION CONCERNING YHWH'S SIGNS TO ISRAEL AND THE HOUSE OF DAVID, 8:16–9:6 (*RSV* 7)

Structure

I. Announcement of intention to wait for YHWH		8:16-17
A. Command to seal testimony/torah		16
1. Bind testimony		16a
2. Seal torah		16b
B. Explanation: wait for YHWH		17
II. Basis for announcement: instruction concerning the significance of YHWH's signs to Israel and "house of David"		8:18–9:6
A. Opening assertion: Isaiah and his children are signs in Israel from YHWH		8:18
B. Disputation concerning significance of signs: deliverance for Israel and "house of David"		8:19–9:6
1. Quotation of the opposing position: reliance on mediums and sorcerers		8:19
a. Conditional speech formula		19aα
b. Speech proper		19aβ-b
1) Command to inquire from mediums and sorcerers		19aβ
2) Rhetorical question asserting need to inquire from mediums and sorcerers		19b
2. Refutation: inefficacy of reliance on mediums and sorcerers versus reliance on YHWH's testimony/torah		8:20–9:6
a. Basic instruction: to torah and testimony		8:20a
b. Concerning results of people's failure to rely on YHWH's torah and testimony: failure, rebellion, and darkness		20b-22
1) Introductory statement: oath/conditional statement concerning failure of people's reliance on mediums and sorcerers		20b
2) Elaboration concerning failure of people's position		21-22

The interpretation of this passage has been severely hampered by difficulties in establishing the meaning of many of its words, their referents, and their interrelationships in the larger syntactical structure of the text. Consequently, a full discussion of the philological basis for the interpretation of this text appears in the discussion of its intention.

Isaiah 8:16–9:6 is demarcated by a combination of its grammatical features and an interest in contrasting the positions of those who rely on YHWH's testimony and torah as opposed to those who rely on mediums and sorcerers. Although the 1st-person perspective of vv. 16-18, the references to the torah and testimony in v. 16, and Isaiah's children as signs and portents in v. 18 all indicate that these verses originally formed the conclusion to 8:1-15, the imperative verbs of v. 16 interrupt the narrative perspective of 8:1-15 and indicate the beginning of a new subunit within the larger context. Furthermore, the material in 8:19–9:6 is syntactically connected to 8:16-18 by the introductory *wĕkî,* "and if," as well as by the references to testimony and torah that appear in v. 20. V. 23aβ-b continues to draw out the contrast that begins in vv. 20-23b between those who rely on mediums and sorcerers as opposed to those who rely on YHWH, and the royal psalm of thanksgiving illustrates the success of those who rely on YHWH's signs. The word of judgment against Israel in 9:7 clearly begins a new unit.

The first major subunit of this passage is 8:16-17, which announces Isaiah's intention to withdraw from public debate on the Syro-Ephraimite War and to wait for YHWH's actions to materialize. Although v. 18 is commonly included with vv. 16-17, the introductory *hinnēh,* "behold," suggests that v. 18 introduces a new section. This is confirmed by the absence of a syntactical connection between vv. 18 and 17 and the presence of the conjunctive *wĕkî,* "and if," at the beginning of v. 19, which connects the following material to v. 18. Vv. 16-17 begin with a two-part command as defined by the imperative verbs in v. 17, "bind up [*ṣôr*] the testimony, seal [*ḥătôm*] the torah among my teachings." The two commands apparently form a hendiadys in that both convey the same basic meaning. V. 17 is linked to v. 16 by its introductory conjunctive *wāw* and by its continuation of the 1st-person singular speaker's perspective. It explains the reason for Isaiah's commands in that the prophet announces his intention to wait for YHWH.

The second major section of this unit appears in 8:18–9:6. These verses are linked by a combination of factors, including syntax and content. They continue the 1st-person singular perspective of vv. 16-17 and explain the basis for the preceding announcement by providing instruction concerning the significance of YHWH's signs for Israel and the house of David. The section begins with Isaiah's assertion in v. 18 that he and the children that YHWH has given him are "signs" and "portents" in Israel. Although the balance of the subunit in 8:19–9:6 abandons the 1st-person form of v. 18, 8:19–9:6 provides instruction concerning the significance of these signs as indicators of YHWH's deliverance of Israel and the house of David.

Isaiah 8:19–9:6 begins with a disputation concerning the people's reliance on mediums and sorcerers in v. 19. The disputation contains a quotation (note the conditional speech formula in v. 19aα) of the people's command to inquire from the sorcerers and mediums in v. 19aβ and their rhetorical question in v. 19b that asserts the need to inquire from these sources (see the discussion of Intention below for the philological discussion of the passage as a whole, which justifies this interpretation).

Isaiah 8:20–9:6 then refutes this point with an instruction that contrasts the inefficacy of the people's reliance on mediums and sorcerers against the efficacy of reliance on YHWH's torah and testimony. It begins with the basic instruction in v. 20a, "To the torah [*RSV* 'teaching'] and to the testimony." Although this statement lacks an imperative verb, the preposition *lĕ,* "to," lends the statement imperative force as a command to rely on the torah/testimony. Vv. 20b-22 then focus on the failure of the people's lack of reliance on the torah/testimony with a series of statements that are linked with conjunctive *wāws*. This subunit begins with an oath or conditional statement concerning the inefficacy of the people's view: "Indeed, if they will say a thing like this which is inefficacious" (for a discussion of the *'im-lō'* formula, see Y. Thorion, *Studien zur klassischen hebräischen Syntax* [Berlin: Reimer, 1984] 56-57; see the section below on Intention for a discussion of the word *šaḥar,* "dawn," "efficacy"). Vv. 21-22 then describe the consequences of the people's position. They shall "pass by/neglect it" (i.e., torah/testimony; see below on Intention), oppressed and hungry (v. 21a). As a result, "they shall hunger, become incensed, curse their king and God, and turn to rebellion [*RSV* 'turn their faces upward]" (v. 21b). When they look at the earth they will see darkness, into which they will be thrust (v. 22).

The asseverative *kî,* "but," introduces the next subunit (8:23–9:6), which discusses the success of those who rely on Isaiah's torah and testimony. It begins in v. 23aα with a counterstatement to the experience of those who neglect the torah and testimony, "But there will be no gloom to the one who is secure in it" (i.e., the torah and testimony; see the discussion of Intention below). This is followed by an explanatory statement in v. 23aβ-b, introduced by *kā'ēt,* "now," that contrasts the experience of those who do not rely on YHWH with those who do. It begins with v. 23aβ-b, which explains the contrasting views of each group concerning the significance of the Assyrian annexation of northern Israelite territory during the Syro-Ephraimite War (cf. 2 Kgs 15:29). The first group "disparages" *(hēqal)* or sees no value in the annexation of the land of Zebulun and the land of Naphtali (v. 23aβ; see discussion of Intention below), whereas the second group "gives honor" *(hikbîd)* or welcomes the annexation of the "Way of the Sea," "Transjordan," and "Galilee," employing Hebrew versions of the new names given to the three Assyrians provinces carved out of the former lands (see below on Intention). This sentiment is then reinforced by the following royal psalm of thanksgiving for YHWH's deliverance of the people from oppression and the establishment of a new Davidic king (9:1-6). As the discussion of the intention of this passage indicates, Isaiah saw Tiglath-pileser's annexation of this territory and the defeat of the Syro-Ephraimite coalition as an opportunity for the house of David to reassert its rule over the remnant of the northern kingdom of Israel.

The royal psalm of thanksgiving in 9:1-6 builds on the contrast of light and darkness imagery from the preceding material. This psalm begins with the introductory statement in v. 1, which employs perfect verbs to describe the people's perception of a great light from the midst of their darkness. The verbs shift to 2nd-person perfect forms directed to YHWH in v. 2 to introduce a new section (vv. 2-5) concerning the joy of the people. V. 2 addresses YHWH and basically states that God has "increased the joy [read *haggîlâ* for *haggôy lō';* see below on Intention] and made great the celebration." Vv. 3-5 then elaborate on the reasons for this celebration in a series of three statements, each of which is introduced by an explanatory *kî,* "because," which provides the basis for the preceding statement. Thus v. 3 addresses YHWH with 2nd-person verbs that explain that God has crushed the oppressor of the people. V. 4 explains v. 3 by referring to the destruction of military garments as a signal of the end of war.

V. 5 then announces the "birth" or enthronement of a new Davidic king as the reason for the new era of peace. V. 6 differs from the preceding material by employing an imperfect verbal form *(ta'ăśeh)* to announce YHWH's guarantee that the new monarch's reign will experience "peace without end" and justice and righteousness forever.

Genre

The overarching genre of 8:16–9:6 is prophetic INSTRUCTION concerning YHWH's signs to Israel and the house of David. The primary criterion for identifying the INSTRUCTION genre in this passage is the content, insofar as the passage is designed to explain the significance of the "signs" (i.e., Isaiah and his children) to an unspecified audience. Formal criteria also indicate that this is an example of the INSTRUCTION genre in that the various subgenres of this passage are typical elements of instruction speech.

The announcement of Isaiah's intention to wait for YHWH in 8:16-17 begins with the imperative COMMANDS to "bind the torah, seal the testimony" in 8:16. These COMMANDS are not only typical examples of instructional language, but their concern with torah, "instruction," and testimony identifies the basic concern with the signs that YHWH has given to Israel (cf. 8:17). That torah and testimony refer to these signs is evident from the fact that they are here understood as a document that can be bound and sealed in the manner typical of the ancient world. In their present context, they refer to the *gillāyôn gādôl,* "large scroll," that Isaiah was commanded to write in 8:1. This scroll contains YHWH's instructions concerning the Maher-shalal-hash-baz sign, and it is here treated as a legal document insofar as two witnesses are required to verify its contents (Deut 19:15; cf. Num 35:30; Deut 17:6; on the use of *tĕ'ûdâ,* "testimony," as a legal document, cf. Ruth 4:17 and the legal process outlined in Ruth 4:7-12). Insofar as this document contains the record of YHWH's signs to Israel, the command to bind and seal it and the announcement that Isaiah will wait for YHWH indicate the prophet's interest in preserving it until the sign is confirmed.

The basis for the announcement in 8:18–9:6 comprises the essential instructional material of this passage. It begins with an assertion that Isaiah and his children are "signs" and "portents" in Israel (8:18). Not only does this assertion indicate the focus of the passage on explaining the significance of the signs, but it also serves a rhetorical function as a proposition whose validity must be confirmed or denied. The following material in 8:19–9:6 functions accordingly in that its purpose is to invalidate the competing claim that reliance should be placed in mediums and sorcerers rather than in YHWH and the signs. Consequently, the DISPUTATION quotes the people's contention in v. 19 that mediums and sorcerers should be consulted in the current situation of crisis (cf. 1 Samuel 28, where Saul consults the spirit of the dead prophet Samuel by means of the witch of Endor prior to his final battle with the Philistines).

The balance of the unit in 8:20–9:6 then refutes the relative merits of the

179

competing claims. It begins in v. 20a with an implicit COMMAND to rely on the torah and testimony and hence on YHWH's signs. The OATH or conditional statement in v. 20b, introduced by the *'im-lō'*, "if not," challenges the validity of those who rely on the mediums and sorcerers to understand the meaning of the present situation. Those who reject or neglect the torah/testimony will see only the negative side of the situation, i.e., the oppression and hunger caused by the invasion of the land, and this will cause them to rebel against their king and God (cf. Exod 22:28). When they gaze at the land, they will see darkness, an image used elsewhere to describe the invading Assyrian army (Isa 5:30). Following the evaluation of this popular position, vv. 22bβ-23aα state that there will be no darkness for those who rely on the torah/testimony, which indicates that such persons will realize YHWH's saving action in bringing about the Assyrian invasion. This becomes clear in v. 23aβ-b, which contrasts the two positions with regard to their evaluation of the Assyrian annexation of northern Israelite territory during the Syro-Ephraimite War (2 Kgs 15:29). The former, i.e., those who do not rely on YHWH's signs, will see this action as a disaster insofar as they will despise the lands of Zebulun and Naphtali. The latter, however, will welcome it insofar as they give honor to the "Way of the Sea," "Transjordan," and "Galilee of the nations," employing Hebrew equivalents for the names of the three Assyrian provinces that were created out of the lands of Zebulun and Naphtali.

The validity of this view is then reinforced by the ROYAL PSALM OF THANKSGIVING that concludes the passage in 9:1-6. This psalm celebrates the enthronement of a new Davidic monarch against the background of thanksgiving to YHWH for relieving the country from oppression by its enemies. This indicates the ultimate significance of the signs, especially Maher-shalal-hash-baz, "the spoil speeds, the prey hastens." Not only will the Assyrian invasion bring hardship to the country; it will also relieve Israel and the Davidic dynasty from the threat posed by the Syro-Ephraimite coalition. The annexation of the northern district and the removal of Pekah ben Remaliah from the throne open the way for the Davidic monarch to reassert authority over the northern kingdom of Israel and finally to bring peace to the land. For Isaiah, a proper understanding of the signs that he has recorded entails acceptance of the suffering caused by the Assyrian invasion as the price to be paid for the return of the northern kingdom to the Davidic dynasty. This is indicated by the Shear-jashub ("a remnant will return") sign and the Immanuel ("God is with us") sign.

Setting

Although 8:16–9:6 clearly constitutes the conclusion to the so-called Isaiah memoir in the present form of 7:1–9:6, insofar as it focuses on the significance of the prophet's children as "signs" and "portents," various features of this text indicate its composite character. Isa 8:16-18 appears to function as the conclusion to the narrative concerning Isaiah's recording of the Maher-shalal-hash-baz sign in 8:1-15, as well as to the original autobiographical account that appears to stand behind the present form of 7:2-17 and 20. As noted in the discussion of 8:1-15, this material was composed during the early reign of Hezekiah, and it reflects the period after Ahaz's decision to appeal to the Assyrian empire for assistance. It expresses the prophet's opposition to that decision in an attempt to convince the new monarch to avoid alliance with Egypt against Assyria by pointing to the disastrous consequences of Ahaz's alliance with Assyria. This conclusion is based on grounds of form, content, and the historical presuppositions of this material.

Although 8:16-18 and 8:19–9:6 are formally part of the same discourse by the prophet, it is noteworthy that 8:16-18 is formulated in 1st-person singular announcement language whereas 8:19–9:6 is formulated in 3rd-person announcement language. Furthermore, 8:16-18 uses masculine singular imperative verbs, ṣôr, "bind," and ḥătôm, "seal," whereas 8:19–9:6 uses 2nd-person masculine plural references, including the preposition with pronominal suffix 'ălêkem, "unto you," and the imperative diršû, "inquire," in v. 19. The 1st-person perspective of 8:16-18 corresponds to that of 8:1-15. Likewise, the 3rd-person perspective of 8:19–9:6 corresponds to that of 7:2-25. In each case, the shift to 2nd-person forms of address indicates the concluding function of both 8:16-18 and 8:16–9:6 in relation to their respective contexts by directing the respective narratives to particular audiences. The concluding 2nd-person addresses indicate that some conclusion is to be drawn from the narrative material. In the case of 8:16-18, it expresses Isaiah's frustration with and opposition to Ahaz's decision to appeal to Assyria for help in the Syro-Ephraimite crisis as related in the preceding narratives. In the case of 8:16–9:6, it attempts to explain the significance of the signs related in the preceding narratives in terms of YHWH's deliverance of Israel and the house of David.

With respect to content, 8:16-18 relates directly to 8:1-15 since the torah and testimony of v. 16 identify the character of the document that Isaiah is instructed to write in 8:1-4. As noted in the discussion of genre above, tĕ'ûdâ, "testimony," designates a document of a legal character (cf. Ruth 4:7), and the document mentioned in 8:1-4 is clearly a legal document as indicated by the presence of the two witnesses, Uriah the priest and Zechariah ben Berechiah. Although the precise nature of the legal act recorded in the document is unclear, it appears to relate to the naming of the child Maher-shalal-hash-baz. Furthermore, the mention of Isaiah and his children as "signs" and "portents" also relates to this narrative as well as to the autobiographical account that stands behind 7:2-17 and 20. Interestingly, 8:19–9:6 never mentions the children or refers to the "signs" and "portents" explicitly. Instead, this passage concentrates on the torah and testimony of 8:16 in what appears to be a deliberate attempt to focus attention on the significance of these terms. In this respect, 8:19–9:6 appears to shift the meaning of these terms somewhat. Whereas 8:16-18 presupposes that these terms refer to the document that Isaiah wrote concerning Maher-shalal-hash-baz, 8:19–9:6 presupposes that these terms refer to reliance on YHWH in general as opposed to reliance on the mediums and sorcerers. Isa 8:19–9:6 therefore relates these terms to the entire account of YHWH's signs to the people in 7:1–8:15, insofar as these narratives provide the basis for the conclusion in 8:19–9:6 that YHWH will deliver Israel and the house of David.

With respect to historical allusions, in the discussion of 8:1-15 above I noted that this passage presupposes the aftermath of Ahaz's decision to appeal to Assyria for assistance in the Syro-Ephraimite crisis. Isa 8:16-18 reflects Isaiah's decision to withdraw from public debate on the issue and to await the outcome of events. Although 8:1-18 announces disaster for the people, there is no indication that the expected catastrophe has actually taken place — it is only anticipated. Consequently, it presupposes a situation prior to the actual Assyrian intervention. But 8:19–9:6 clearly presupposes actual Assyrian intervention insofar as 8:23 alludes specifically to Tiglath-pileser's annexation of the northern Israelite territories as a result of the Syro-Ephraimite War (2 Kgs 15:29; cf. *ANET*, 283-84).

Furthermore, the ROYAL PSALM OF THANKSGIVING in 9:1-6 presupposes the enthronement of a new Davidic king, specifically Hezekiah. Although the interpretation and historical setting of this psalm have been extensively debated among scholars (cf. Kilian, *Isaiah 1–39*, 5-10, for a summary of the discussion), there are indications that it is intended as a psalm to celebrate the enthronement of a Davidic king. First, the reference to the "child that is born to us, a son has been given to us" in v. 5 presupposes not the actual birth of a child but Jerusalemite royal ideology that saw the Davidic monarch as the "son" of YHWH (cf. 2 Sam 7:14; Pss 2:7; 89:26-27). Second, the reference to the government being set upon his shoulder indicates the inauguration of his authority. As Alt points out, Egyptian enthronement liturgies likewise grant the new king throne names that refer to qualities desired of the new monarch similar to those names appearing in v. 5. That the Egyptians employ five such names whereas the present text employs only four does not provide sufficient reason to negate the analogy or to emend the present text. Finally, although the psalm refers to YHWH's victory over the oppressors as a past event in vv. 1-4, the perspective of this psalm is future-oriented as indicated by the statement "the zeal of YHWH Sabaoth will do this" in v. 6. YHWH's defeat of the new king's enemies in conjunction with the establishment of his kingship is a common motif in Jerusalemite royal ideology (2 Sam 7:1; Psalm 2; 89:19-29; 132:17-18), and the concluding statement guarantees YHWH's support to the new ruler. There is no indication, however, that this psalm was written for any specific king, much less Hezekiah. Alt's argument that 8:23aβ-b is an integral part of the psalm must be rejected in view of the formal shift that takes place at 9:1 and the absence of any historical reference in the psalm itself. It may well be that it was a regular feature of the enthronement liturgy for the Judean kings. Whether it was written specifically for Hezekiah or not, it now appears in the context of literature that was written in conjunction with the Syro-Ephraimite War and the years that followed. Consequently, the new king presupposed in the present context must be Hezekiah. Some might object that the absence of any reference to the destruction of Samaria in 722-721 precludes identification of this king as Hezekiah. However, although the chronology of this period is extremely problematic, one should keep in mind that 2 Kgs 18:1 places the beginning of Hezekiah's reign in the third year of Hoshea, approximately eight years prior to the fall of Samaria.

The above arguments lead to the conclusion that Isa 8:16-18 should be dated in relation to 8:1-15, which was written in the early reign of Hezekiah and which reflects Ahaz's decision to appeal to Assyria for assistance. This passage concludes 8:1-15 (and perhaps an early autobiographical form of 7:2-17 and 20 as well). The document appears to reflect Isaiah's withdrawal in frustration from public debate on the issue and his decision to wait for a more propitious time before attempting to speak out again. The additional material in 8:19–9:6 demonstrates that the document dates to the early years of Hezekiah's reign at a time when the Egyptians were attempting to stir up revolt against the Assyrians. It was written to convince the new king to avoid alliances with Egypt since Ahaz's previous alliance with Assyria is identified as the cause of the country's present troubles. In this respect, it suggests the opportunity to reassert Davidic authority over the northern kingdom of Israel insofar as the Assyrians are understood here to act on YHWH's behalf. Isaiah's advice to rely on YHWH's signs would finally heal the rift between Israel and Judah that had existed since the northern tribes revolted against the house of David.

Intention

The intention of 8:16–9:6 is determined by a number of factors, including: (1) its relation to the preceding material in 7:1–8:15 concerning Isaiah's children and their function as signs concerning the Syro-Ephraimite War; (2) its relation to the historical background of the Syro-Ephraimite War and the aftermath of that war, including Egyptian overtures, first to Israel before 724 (2 Kgs 17:4) and later to Philistia (Isaiah 20) in 715-713, to revolt against Assyria; (3) its relation to the enthronement of King Hezekiah as indicated by 9:1-6; (4) its instructional genre; and (5) its contents, which focus on the distinction between those who rely on mediums and sorcerers to determine the meaning of the Assyrian intervention in the Syro-Ephraimite War and those who rely on YHWH's torah and testimony.

Although the interpretation of this passage is frequently based on differentiating between the credibility of the mediums and sorcerers as opposed to the prophet and his followers, the underlying issue appears to be two contrasting views concerning the significance of the Assyrian intervention in the region during the Syro-Ephraimite War and its implications for the future of Judah and the Davidic dynasty. As noted in the discussions of structure, genre, and setting above, the interpretation of this passage centers primarily on vv. 19-23, which outline the two contrasting positions. Scholarly discussion of this passage indicates a great deal of confusion. Although scholars have noted the contrast between the mediums and sorcerers on the one hand and the prophet and his followers on the other, the contrasting images of light and darkness in this passage have defied adequate explanation. This is due to the failure to understand much of the terminology employed in this passage on the one hand, and the relation of 8:19–9:6 to 8:16-18 and to the larger context of 7:1–9:6 on the other. Consequently, a philological basis is required to support the interpretation offered here.

The first problem appears in the oath or conditional statement in v. 20b, "Surely for this word that they speak there is no dawn." As noted in the discussion of the structure of this passage, this statement challenges the people's reliance on the mediums and sorcerers mentioned in v. 19. The Heb. *šāḥar* is generally translated "dawn," but the root *šḥr* on which it is based appears to have a variety of connotations. The basic root means "to be black" and appears to extend its meaning to dawn on the basis of the blackness of night that immediately precedes dawn. The root connotes a sense of efficacy insofar as dawn represents the beginning of a new day and the renewed act of creation that is associated with the rising of the sun and the overcoming of night in ancient thought. The use of *šaḥrût*, "blackness," refers to the "prime/dawn of life" in Qoh 11:10, and *šaḥôr*, "black," refers to the woman's beauty in Cant 1:5 ("I am dark and comely"). This sense of efficacy appears in the use of *šaḥrāh*, "its dawn/enchantment/atonement," in Isa 47:11, "But evil shall come on you, for which you cannot atone." Here the parallel with *kaprāh*, "its expiation," indicates the use of the term in a context of sorcery (cf. 47:12) and suggests the action of correcting or enchanting away evil (cf. Clements, *Isaiah 1–39*, 122). Likewise, the root frequently means "to look early" or "to seek diligently" (cf. 26:9; Ps 63:2), and commonly parallels the verb *drš*, "to seek/inquire" of God (Hos 5:15; Ps 78:34; Job 8:5; cf. Prov 11:27). In the present context, *drš* describes the alternatives of "inquiring" either from the mediums and sorcerers or from God (v. 19). When considered in relation to such inquiry, *šāḥar* must be understood not only as "dawn" but also in the sense of the efficacy of inquiring from the sorcerers and mediums. V. 20b should therefore be read: "Surely for this word that they speak there is no efficacy," i.e., consulting the mediums and sorcerers is fruitless. As noted in the discussion of the structure of this passage, this statement is then illustrated by the following demonstration of the consequences that will result from the actions of those who follow the advice of the mediums and sorcerers.

Verse 21 contains a number of problems. The first concerns the subject of the verbs, which are 3rd-person masculine singular forms as opposed to the plural forms of vv. 19-20. As many scholars have noted, the antecedent for these verbs is *ʿam*, "people," in v. 19b, which employs a 3rd-person singular verb *yidraš*, "it shall inquire," in that context as well.

The more difficult problem involves the 3rd-person feminine pronoun suffix in the phrase *wĕʿābar bāh*, "and it shall pass by/through it." There is no evident feminine singular noun that serves as the antecedent for this pronoun in the present context. Scholars consequently have concluded that *ʾereṣ*, "land," should be implied from the general context so that the verse translates, "and they shall pass through the land greatly distressed and hungry" (cf. *BHS*). The term "land" appears only after this verse, however, which indicates that it cannot be the antecedent. Here one should note that the only feminine singular nouns that appear prior to *wĕʿābar bāh* in the present context are *tôrâ* and *tĕʿûdâ*, "instruction" and "testimony." Insofar as these nouns form a hendiadys (cf. 8:16, 20), they not only provide an adequate antecedent for *wĕʿābar bāh* but are indeed the only antecedent in the present context. The meaning of the verb *ʿabar* as "transgress" or "neglect" results in a statement that describes the experience of those who "transgress" or "neglect" YHWH's torah and testimony: "and they [the people] shall transgress/neglect it, oppressed and hungry." As a result of such hunger and suffering, the people will become incensed and curse its king and God.

The statement "and they shall turn their faces upward" *(RSV)* appears to derive from a contrast with the following statement that they will look to the earth, but it makes little sense in the present context of the people cursing its king and God. The word *lĕmā 'ēlâ* is generally translated "upward," but the noun *ma'al* can also mean "unfaithful, treacherous act." It is commonly used for treachery against God (Josh 22:22; 1 Chr 9:1; 2 Chr 29:19; 33:19; Ezra 9:2, 4; 10:6) and provides a better conclusion to the statement that "they will curse their king and their God and turn to rebellion." In this case, the *he* accusative has been added to *ma'al* to reinforce the sense of turning *toward* rebellion.

The first part of v. 22 describes the people looking at the land and seeing "distress and darkness" *(ṣārâ wĕḥāšēkâ)* and "the gloom of anguish" *(mĕ'ûp ṣûqâ)*, which produces a chiastic word arrangement insofar as both *ḥāšēkâ* and *mĕ'ûp* refer to darkness and both *ṣārâ* and *ṣûqâ* refer to distress. The verse ends with the statement *wa'ăpēlâ mĕnuddāḥ*, "and they will be thrust into thick darkness," which takes *'am*, "people," as the subject of the verb *mĕnuddāḥ*, "is thrust into."

As noted in the discussion of the structure of this passage, the imagery begins to shift with v. 23aα. The statement is commonly translated, "but there will be no gloom [*mû'āp*] for her that was in anguish [*mûṣāq lāh*]," but this translation assumes parallel meanings for *mû'āp*, "gloom," in v. 23 and *mĕ'ûp*, "gloom," in v. 22 on the one hand, and for *mûṣāq*, "anguish," in v. 23 and *ṣûqâ*, "anguish," in v. 22 on the other. But this is clearly incorrect for *mûṣāq/ṣûqâ*. Whereas *ṣûqâ* is a feminine noun derived from the root *ṣwq*, "to be distressed," *mûṣāq* is a Hophal participle derived from the root *yṣq*, "to pour, cast, flow." In its Hophal form, this verb means "to be firmly established," as indicated by its use in Job 11:15, where it parallels *wĕlō' tîrā'*, thus, "you will be secure and will not fear." Likewise, *mĕ'ûp* is a masculine noun that means "darkness" or "gloom," but *mû'āp* is a Hophal participle from the root *y'p*, which means "weariness." As such, it forms a grammatical parallel to *mûṣāq*. A further problem concerns the referent for the 3rd-person feminine pronoun of this passage *(lāh)*, here rendered simply as "her." As noted above, the similar pronoun in v. 21 referred to the hendiadys *tôrâ wĕtĕ'ûdâ*, "torah and testimony," which appears in v. 20 (cf. v. 16). Consequently, the verse should be rendered, "but there is no weariness for whoever is firmly established to it," i.e., for whoever is secure with the torah and testimony that explains the meaning of Isaiah's signs as opposed to the mediums and sorcerers.

The balance of v. 23 should be translated, "In the former time [*kā'ēt hāri'šôn*] he brought into contempt [*hēqal*] the land of Zebulun and the land of Naphtali, but in the latter time [*wĕhā'aḥărôn*] he will make glorious [*hikbîd*] the Way of the Sea, the land beyond the Jordan, Galilee of the nations." Scholars have been correct to see a contrast of images in this verse based on the parallel statements that employ *hēqal*, "to bring into contempt, despise," and *hikbîd*, "to make glorious, honor," on the one hand, and *hāri'šôn*, "the former," and *wĕhā'aḥărôn*, "and the latter" on the other. But there are several problems (for a full discussion, see Emerton, esp. 158-60). First, the verbs *hēqal* and *hikbîd* are perfect forms and therefore both refer to past events. This undermines the *RSV* translation that distinguishes between events pertaining to the past and those pertaining to the future. Second, 'ēt, "time," is a feminine noun, whereas both hāri'šôn and hā'aḥărôn are masculine, which renders them incapable of serving as adjectives for "time." Furthermore, the term kā'ēt must be taken as the equivalent of kĕ'attâ, but in pausal form, and translated "now" (cf. Emerton, 158-60). This means that "the former" and "the latter" should be understood personally as the subjects of the verbs. Emerton (pp. 168-69) understands "the former" and "the latter," when taken together, to be a reference to "totality" so that the two terms refer to "everyone, from first to last." Others have understood them as references to kings of Israel (Ginsberg; Eshel) or Assyria (G. R. Driver).

Unfortunately, each of these solutions is inadequate in that each ignores the larger context of the passage. The "former" and the "latter" refer to the two contrasting positions that have been noted in this context. The "former" designates the position of the mediums and sorcerers whose views lead to "darkness" and rebellion against king and God (vv. 20b-22). The "latter" refers to those who rely on the torah and testimony that explain the meaning of Isaiah's signs (v. 23aα). One should note that Alt (pp. 210-11) has correctly argued that "the land of Zebulun and the land of Naphtali" is equivalent to "the Way of the Sea, the land beyond the Jordan, Galilee of the nations" in that the former terms refer to the Israelite names for the northern part of the kingdom of Israel and the latter refer to the names that the Assyrians gave to the three provinces they created out of this territory after Tiglath-pileser annexed it. Consequently, "the Way of the Sea" refers to Dulru (Dor), "Galilee of the nations" refers to Magidu (Megiddo), and "the land beyond the Jordan" refers to Gal'azu (Gilead). This interpretation has important implications when considered in relation to the following psalm that celebrates YHWH's defeat of enemies and enthronement of the new Davidic king, as well as in relation to the larger context of 7:1–9:6, which maintains that the Assyrians were brought by YHWH to remove Pekah and Rezin. The "former one," who follows the view of the mediums and sorcerers, will see the Assyrian annexation of this territory as a tragedy and will likely turn against king and God for leading the country into such a disaster. The "latter one," who properly understands Isaiah's signs, however, will recognize that YHWH has brought the Assyrians to remove the threat posed to the house of David by Rezin and Pekah, and that the defeat of the Syro-Ephraimite coalition opens the way for the Davidic monarchy to reassert its control over the northern kingdom of Israel and thereby to repair a long-standing breach within the twelve tribes.

Overall, one must understand the passage in relation to the enthronement of the new Davidic king, Hezekiah. It functions in relation to 7:1–8:15 as an attempt to convince Hezekiah to avoid an alliance with Egypt that would bring him into confrontation with the Assyrian empire. It employs instructional language in an attempt to explain the significance of Isaiah's signs concerning the Syro-Ephraimite War in relation to the kingdom of Judah in general and the royal house of David in particular. As noted above, Ahaz's rejection of Isaiah's signs resulted in Judah's suffering of the consequences of Assyria's intervention. Although Judah was not subject to attack as Israel was, it was reduced to vassal status as a result of Tiglath-pileser's invasion (2 Kgs 16:7-18) and undoubtedly suffered the hardships that would result from the presence of the Assyrian army in the region. Isaiah presents the Assyrian intervention as an opportunity for the

Davidic dynasty. He notes that those who see the Assyrian annexation of Zebulun and Naphtali as a tragedy constitute a threat to his rule in that they will end up cursing king and God in rebellion. But if the Assyrian intervention is viewed as an act of YHWH that removed the threat posed by Pekah and Rezin to Judah and the house of David, it would indicate that YHWH had provided the opportunity to reassert Davidic control over the northern kingdom of Israel. Not only would such a view fend off potential revolt in a time of national crisis, but it would also preclude joining an alliance with Egypt that would only result in Assyrian retaliation and greater tragedy for the land. Isaiah's advice here remains consistent with his overall position to rely solely on YHWH.

Bibliography

A. Alt, "Jesaja 8,23–9,6: Befreiungsnacht und Krönungstag," in *Kleine Schriften zur Geschichte des Volkes Israel* (Munich: Beck, 1953) 2:206-25; R. A. Carlson, "The Anti-Assyrian Character of the Oracle in Is. ix 1-6," *VT* 24 (1974) 130-35; R. P. Carroll, "Translation and Attribution in Isaiah 8.19f," *BT* 31 (1980) 126-34; M. B. Crook, "A Suggested Occasion for Isaiah 9,2-7 and 11,1-9," *JBL* 68 (1949) 213-24; G. R. Driver, "Isaianic Problems," in *Festschrift Wilhelm Eilers* (ed. G. Wiessner; Wiesbaden: Harrassowitz, 1967) 43-49; J. A. Emerton, "Some Linguistic and Historical Problems in Isaiah VIII.23," *JSS* 14 (1969) 151-75; H. Eshel, "Isaiah viii 23: An Historical-Geographical Analogy," *VT* 40 (1990) 104-9; H. L. Ginsberg, "An Unrecognized Allusion to Kings Pekah and Hoshea of Israel," *ErIs* 5 (1958) 61*-66*; B. Greger, "Das '*galyl* der Völker' — Jes 8,23," *BN* 51 (1990) 11-12; J. Høgenhaven, "On the Structure and Meaning of Isaiah VIII 23B," *VT* 37 (1987) 218-21; idem, "Prophet Isaiah" (→ 7:1-25); K. Jeppesen, "Call and Frustration: A New Understanding of Isaiah viii 21-22," *VT* 32 (1982) 145-57; Kilian, *Jesaja 1–39*, 5-10; M. H. O. Kloppers, "Jesaja 8:23–9:6 en advent," *NGTT* 32 (1991) 378-86; T. J. Lewis, *Cults of the Dead in Ancient Israel and Ugarit* (HSM 39; Atlanta: Scholars Press, 1989) 128-32; Z. Meshel, "Was There a 'Via Maris'?" *IEJ* 23 (1973) 162-66; H.-P. Müller, "Uns ist ein Kind geboren . . . Jes. 9,1-6 in traditionsgeschichtlicher Sicht," *EvT* 21 (1961) 408-19; idem, "Das Wort von den Totengeistern Jes. 8,19f," *WO* 8 (1975-76) 65-76; G. von Rad, "The Royal Ritual in Judah," in *The Problem of the Hexateuch and Other Essays* (tr. E. W. Trueman Dicken; Edinburgh and London: Oliver & Boyd, 1966) 222-31; B. Renaud, "La Forme Poetique d'Is 9,1-6," in *Mélanges bibliques et orientaux en l'honneur de M. Mathias Delcor* (AOAT 215; eds. A. Caquot, S. Légasse. and M. Tardieu; Kevelaer: Butzon & Bercker; Neukirchen-Vluyn: Neukirchener, 1985) 331-48; H. G. Reventlow, "A Syncretistic Enthronement Hymn in Is. 9,1-6," *UF* 3 (1971) 321-25; E. Robertson, "Some Obscure Passages in Isaiah," *AJSL* 49 (1932-33) 313-24; G. Schwarz, ". . . zugunsten der Lebenden an die Toten?" *ZAW* 86 (1974) 218-20; J. J. Staub, "A Review of the History of the Interpretations of Isaiah 8:11–9:6," in *Jewish Civilization: Essays and Studies* (ed. R. A. Brauner; Philadelphia: Reconstructionist Rabbinical College, 1979) 1:89-107; M. A. Sweeney, "A Philological and Form-Critical Reevaluation of Isaiah 8:16–9:6," *HAR* 14 (1994) 215-31; M. E. W. Thompson, "Isaiah's Ideal King," *JSOT* 24 (1982) 79-88; K. A. Van Der Jagt, "Wonderfull Counsellor . . . (Isaiah 9.6)," *BT* 40 (1989) 441-45; D. Vieweger, " 'Das Volk, das durch das Dunkel zieht . . .' Neue Überlegungen zu Jes (8,23aβb) 9,1-6," *BZ* 36 (1992)

77-86; J. Vollmer, "Zur Sprache von Jesaja 9,1-6," *ZAW* 80 (1968) 343-50; idem, "Jesajanische Begrifflichkeit?" *ZAW* 83 (1971) 389-91; P. Wegner, "Another Look at Isaiah viii 23b," *VT* 41 (1991) 481-84; idem, "A Re-examination of Isaiah ix 1-6," *VT* 42 (1992) 103-12; C. F. Whitley, "The Language and Exegesis of Isaiah 8,16-23," *ZAW* 90 (1978) 28-42; H. Wildberger, "Die Thronnamen des Messias, Jes. 9,5b," *TZ* 16 (1960) 314-32.

PROPHETIC WARNING TO ISRAEL'S LEADERS: HISTORICAL REVIEW OF ISRAEL'S REJECTION OF YHWH AND ANNOUNCEMENT OF JUDGMENT, 9:7 (*RSV* 8)–10:4

Structure

I. Concerning YHWH's word against Jacob/Israel		9:7-11
A. Basic statement		7
B. People's response: arrogance and defiance		8-9
C. YHWH's raising enemies of Rezin to devour Israel		10-11a
D. Concluding refrain concerning YHWH's anger		11b
II. Concerning people's failure to turn to YHWH		12-16
A. Basic statement		12
B. YHWH's cutting off leadership		13-14
C. Prophetic judgment speech		15-16a
1. Motivation for judgment: people corrupted by corrupt leaders		15
2. Announcement of punishment against people		16a
D. Concluding refrain concerning YHWH's anger		16b
III. Concerning consequences for people		17-20
A. For land: scorched by fire		17-18a
B. For people: internal conflict		18b-20a
C. Concluding refrain concerning YHWH's anger		20b
IV. Condemnation of leadership: woe oracle		10:1-4
A. Woe oracle proper		10:1-2
1. Woe address to leadership		10:1
2. Specifications concerning injustice		10:2
B. Condemnation to captivity and death: rhetorical questions and answers		10:3-4a
C. Concluding refrain concerning YHWH's anger		10:4b

As noted in the discussion of chs. 5–12 as a whole, this passage plays an important role in the superstructure of these chapters on account of its links to 5:1-30 and 10:5–12:6. Nevertheless, it constitutes a coherent subunit within the larger framework, as indicated by its distinctive concluding refrain, "in all this, his anger has not turned and his hand is still stretched out," in vv. 11b, 16b, 20b, and 10:4b. The introductory statement, "My Lord has sent a word against Jacob and it has fallen upon Israel," lacks any grammatical or syntactical connection with the preceding Isaianic "memoir" in 7:1–9:6 and focuses on the punishment of the northern kingdom of Israel as opposed to the deliverance of the kingdom of Judah and the Davidic dynasty. As noted in the discussion of the superstructure of chs. 5–12, 10:1-4 plays a transitional role in that its woe oracle form, the absence of a specific addressee, the general concern with the punishment of those who plunder the weak, and the forward-looking perspective of its concluding refrain introduce the extended woe oracle against Assyria in 10:5-34. Nevertheless, the concluding refrain binds 9:7-20 to 10:1-4 so that this entire unit comes to form an introduction to the following material, and thus YHWH's anger and punishment against the northern kingdom of Israel are extended to the Assyrians.

The four appearances of the concluding refrain define the structure of this passage. This results in a four-part sequence that displays a coherent pattern of conceptual development.

The first subunit takes up the fact of judgment against Israel (9:7-11). Its internal structure is constituted by a series of verbal statements that are linked by conjunctive wāws but shift the subjects of the verbs to define a sequence of action and response. The first is the basic statement of the passage in v. 7 that "my Lord ['ǎdōnāy] has sent a word against Jacob and it has fallen on Israel." This is followed in vv. 8-9 by a statement concerning the people's arrogant and defiant response to this situation that quotes them as saying, "Bricks have fallen but we will build with dressed stones. Sycamores are cut down but we will replace them with cedars." Vv. 10-11a then describe YHWH raising the enemies of Rezin, who will then proceed to devour Israel. The characteristic refrain of the passage then concludes the subunit in v. 11b.

The second section, 9:12-16, takes up the people's failure to turn to YHWH. Again, its internal structure is constituted by a series of verbal statements with shifting subjects linked by wāws. The first in v. 12 constitutes the basic statement of the subunit that the people have not turned to YHWH. The second in vv. 13-14 takes up YHWH's removal of the leadership of Israel, here described metaphorically as "head and tail, palm branch and reed." The third in vv. 15-16a is a prophetic judgment speech against the people that includes the motivation for judgment (i.e., that corrupt leaders have corrupted the people, v. 15), followed by the announcement of judgment against the people (v. 16a). The characteristic refrain again concludes the subunit (v. 16b).

The third subunit, 9:17-20, takes up the consequences of the people's failure to turn to YHWH. It employs the metaphor of fire to describe the consequences suffered by the land on account of the people's wickedness (vv. 17-18a). The metaphor is then applied to the people (vv. 18b-20a), who are portrayed as fuel for the fire in that their internal dissension causes them to devour each other in their attempt to survive. Again, the refrain concludes the subunit (v. 20b).

The fourth subunit differs from the preceding three in that it is no longer descriptive but addresses the leadership of the people who are ultimately responsible for this state of affairs (10:1-4). This subunit employs a WOE ORACLE to address the leaders, including the basic "woe" statement addressed to the leaders, here described as "those who decree iniquitous decrees and the writers who have written oppression" (v. 1), and a specification of their unjust acts against the weak of society (v. 2). Vv. 3-4a contain a series of rhetorical questions to the leaders that ask what they will do at the time of punishment, etc. (v. 3), and their answers, which indicate that they will be taken captive or killed (v. 4a). Again, the characteristic refrain concludes the subunit (v. 4b).

Genre

Discussion of the genre of 9:7–10:4 has been complicated by two major issues. On the one hand, formal similarities have led many scholars to conclude that 9:7–10:4 constitutes a secondary editorial assemblage and that the original texts were 9:7-20 + 5:25-30, characterized by the refrain "in all this, his anger has not turned and his hand is stretched out still," and 5:8-24 + 10:1-4, characterized by the "woe" form. Although there is some justification for this view, the result of this complication has been a failure to assess adequately the formal and generic characteristics of the present form of this text. On the other hand, the appearance of the refrain in this passage has led many scholars to conclude that this is a liturgical text that the prophet employed in its original form as part of some ritual activity. Although objections have been raised against this view, it merits closer examination in the present context.

Repeated refrains are frequently characteristic of liturgical poetry. Perhaps the best-known example of such refrains and their use in the Hebrew Bible is the formula *kî lě'ōlām ḥasdô*, "for his mercy endures forever," which appears throughout Psalm 136 and is employed to characterize the people's praise of YHWH at the building of the Second Temple in Ezra 3:10-11. On this basis, scholars have argued that prophetic texts that employ such refrains functioned in a cultic context. Examples include Amos 1:3–2:16 and 4:6-11, which have been identified as examples of covenant curse liturgies (H. Graf Reventlow, *Das Amt des Propheten bei Amos* [FRLANT 80; Göttingen: Vandenhoeck & Ruprecht, 1962] 56-90; W. Brueggemann, "Amos IV 4-13 and Israel's Covenant Worship," *VT* 15 [1965] 1-15; cf. A. Bentzen, "The Ritual Background of Amos i 2–ii 16," *OTS* 8 [1950] 85-99), and Isa 9:7-20 and 5:25-30, which have been identified as "historical parenesis" (Wildberger, *Jesaja,* 209) or a "liturgy of wasted opportunity" (Crenshaw). Objections have been raised against this liturgical understanding in that it is notoriously difficult to demonstrate either that the prophets played a well-defined role in the ancient Israelite and Judean temple liturgies on the one hand or that the statements found in Amos 4:6-12 and Isa 9:7–10:4; 5:25-30 are linked to any ritual tradition of covenant cursing on the other (for a full discussion of objections to the liturgical understanding of the Amos material, see H. W. Wolff, *Joel and Amos* [tr. W. Janzen, S. Dean McBride Jr., and C. A. Muenchow; Hermeneia; Philadelphia: Fortress, 1977] 144-52). Furthermore, 9:7–10:4 appears to contain specific historical references that would undermine a stereotypical cultic function (cf. Høgenhaven, *Gott und Volk,* 44-53). Finally, biblical narratives contain examples of prophets who employed ritual practices against opponents, such as Balaam (Numbers 23–24) or Elijah (1 Kings 18), but in no case do refrains play a role in the prophetic oracles or statements that accompany these actions. Such refrains are likewise absent in narratives concerning prophetic utterances about enemies apart from ritual action, such as in Micaiah ben Imlah (1 Kings 22) and Isaiah (Isaiah 37/2 Kings 19).

One should note that although refrains do appear in some prophetic texts, they apparently function as rhetorical devices designed to reinforce the prophet's message. Whereas liturgical texts employ their respective refrains to reinforce the praise of the deity (e.g., Psalms 118; 136; 146–150), prophetic texts such as Amos 1:3–2:16 and 4:4-13 employ refrains to reinforce the notion of YHWH's punishment of Israel or Israel's failure to repent. In the case of Amos 1:3–2:16, the repetition of the formula "for three transgression of PN and for four, I will not turn it aside," functions as a means for reinforcing the audience's acceptance of YHWH's judgment against each of the nations mentioned, and leads them to accept the final oracle that condemns Israel. The repetition of the refrain "yet you did not return to me," in relation to Amos's catalog of YHWH's punishments inflicted on Israel, appears to constitute a parody of liturgical forms in the context of condemning northern Israelite cultic practice at Bethel and Gilgal.

Isaiah 9:7–10:4 likewise appears to use the refrain "in all this, his anger has not turned and his hand is stretched out still," as a rhetorical device to reinforce the prophet's message. It appears in a context that employs a HISTORI-CAL REVIEW of Israel's arrogance and consequent suffering in connection with the Syro-Ephraimite War (9:7-20 [*RSV* 8-21]) as a prelude to condemning the leadership of the country (10:1-4). The repetition of the refrain in each subunit of this passage reinforces the notion of YHWH's anger against Israel. In this respect, it reinforces the prophet's essential point that YHWH will punish Israel for its actions in relation to the Syro-Ephraimite War. But one should also note that the refrain indicates YHWH's continuing anger and thereby leads the hearer or reader from one subunit of this text to the next until the condemnation of the leadership of the country appears in 10:1-4. This understanding indicates that the condemnation of those who are ultimately responsible for the current situation is the major goal of the prophet in this oracle.

Yet the appearance of the refrain at the end of this passage raises questions about its relationship to the following material. Insofar as the refrain indicates YHWH's continuing anger, the reader or hearer expects something more. In this case, the following material contains a WOE ORACLE directed against Assyria. When it becomes evident that Assyria is condemned for the same crimes as northern Israel, including arrogance (10:12-15) and plundering of the weak (10:6-11), and that it will suffer the same fate of burning (10:16-19), it is clear that the refrain in 9:7–10:4 is intended to lead the reader or hearer not only to the condemnation of the leadership of the northern kingdom of Israel but ulti-mately to the condemnation of Assyria as well.

Other features of this passage indicate that it constitutes a transition to the material beginning in 10:5. The "woe" form of 10:1-4 anticipates the WOE ORACLE beginning in 10:5; and the absence of a specific identification of the leaders in 10:1-4 as Israelite, in contrast to the specific Israelite identifications found in each of the previous three subunits of the passage, likewise indicates the relationship of 9:7–10:4 to the following material. Furthermore, 14:24-27 makes an explicit statement that the fall of Assyria represents YHWH's out-stretched hand. When this is considered together with the relation of 9:7–10:4 to 5:1-30, which employs a "woe" series in vv. 8-24 and the "outstretched hand" formula in v. 25, it becomes clear that there is a progression of thought throughout these chapters that presents northern Israel's punishment for abusing Judah as the prelude to YHWH's punishment of Assyria on the same grounds. Just as YHWH's hand is stretched out against Israel, so is it stretched out against Assyria, which was brought to punish Israel but which overstepped its bounds and became subject to the same punishment. Insofar as the refrain facilitates this transition, it serves not a liturgical function but a literary and rhetorical one. While 9:7–10:4 appears to be modeled on a liturgical form, as indicated by its use of a refrain and a variation of the formula *ûbĕyād ḥăzāqâ ûbizrôaʿ nĕṭûyâ*, "and with a strong hand and with an outstretched arm" (Deut 4:34; 7:19; Jer 21:5; 32:21; cf. Exod 6:6; Deut 5:15; 9:29; 11:2; 26:8; 1 Kgs 8:42; 2 Kgs 17:36; Jer 27:5; 32:17; Ezek 20:33, 34; Ps 136:12; 1 Chr 6:32), in its present literary form and context it does not constitute a (→) liturgy.

In considering the generic character of 9:7–10:4, one must note two important features. The first is the HISTORICAL REVIEW that appears in 9:7-20. As the discussion of the intention of this passage will indicate, these verses allude to Israel's experience in connection with the Syro-Ephraimite War as a means for addressing northern Israelite leadership in the postwar period. Vv. 7-11 take up Israel's attempt to rebuild and to prepare for revolt against Assyria following its defeat. Vv. 12-16 take up Israel's refusal to turn to YHWH despite the loss of the leaders who led the country into the Syro-Ephraimite conflict in the first place. Vv. 17-20 take up the conflict between Gilead and the Ephraimite hill country that led to Pekah's murder of Pekahiah, his usurpation of the Israelite throne, and the subsequent invasion of Judah. This HISTORICAL REVIEW serves as the background for the condemnation of the leadership in 10:1-4. Just as Israel suffered the consequences of Pekah's policies that led to the Syro-Ephraimite confrontation, so Israel in the postwar period will suffer the consequences of an attempt to confront Assyria a second time. This interpretation indicates that 9:7–10:4 constitutes a warning to the leadership of northern Israel in the postwar period to learn from the mistakes of the past. As the HISTORICAL REVIEW in 9:7-20 indicates, Israel has already suffered. The WOE ORACLE in 10:1-4 (on the warning function of the "woe" form, see Zech 2:10-11) and the refrain that announces YHWH's continuing anger indicate that Israel will suffer again.

Setting

Scholars generally view 9:7–10:4 as a redactional combination of material from independent contexts. On the basis of the formal similarity of the "outstretched hand" formula in 9:11, 16, 20 and 5:25, 9:7-20 and 5:25-30 are believed to have originally formed an independent unit (Wildberger, *Jesaja*, 207-12). Likewise, the "woe" form of 5:8-24 and 10:1-4 serves as the basis for the common view that these materials formed another original independent unit (Wildberger, *Jesaja*, 180-83). As noted above, however, there has been little discussion of

the interrelationship of these materials in the present form of the text. Consideration of these interrelationships points to a number of problems and issues that
are relevant for establishing the setting of this text.

On the one hand, scholars have correctly noted that 10:1-4 clearly corresponds to 5:8-24. It shares not only the "woe" oracle form of 5:8-24 but also
the concern in 5:8-24 with the abuse of justice and plundering of the poor. On
the other hand, 10:1-4 differs in several respects from 9:7-20. Isa 10:1-4 employs
an explicit 2nd-person plural address in contrast to the 3rd-person announcement
perspective of 9:7-20. It lacks the specific identifications of Israel, Jacob,
Samaria, and Manasseh and the references to specific historical events found
throughout 9:7-20. Finally, 10:1-4 anticipates punishment as does 5:8-24 but
contains no indication that any punishment has already taken place as in 9:7-20
(esp. vv. 7-11).

One must also consider a number of discrepancies between 10:1-4 and
5:8-24. Isa 10:1-4 includes a 2nd-person plural address perspective that does
not appear in 5:8-24. It also lacks the concern with wine and drunkenness that
appears throughout 5:8-24 and that links the woe series to the song of the
vineyard in 5:1-7. Furthermore, 10:2 makes explicit reference to widows and
orphans who appear in 9:16 but are absent in 5:8-24 despite the emphasis on
justice and dispossession of property. Finally, although the "outstretched hand"
formula in 10:4b is frequently dismissed as a later addition (Wildberger, *Jesaja*,
200-201), it establishes a literary relationship between 10:1-4 and 9:7-20. In this
respect, one should note that scholars have faced tremendous difficulties in
placing 10:1-4 together with 5:8-24. Not only does the 2nd-person plural address
form complicate the issue, but the well-defined concluding statements introduced by *lākēn* in 5:13-14 and 24 preclude attaching 10:1-4 at the end of the
series (e.g., Wildberger, *Jesaja*, 181-82). Likewise, placing 10:1-4 at the head
of the series does not provide a solution (Barth, 111; Clements, *Isaiah 1–39*,
60-62). Not only does the 2nd-person address form of 10:1-4 conflict with the
following material in 5:8-24, but it also disrupts the concern with wine, drunkenness, and vineyards that permeates the entire series from the beginning and
provides the connection with the vineyard song in 5:1-7.

In short, on the one hand 10:1-4 has no clear place in the context of 5:8-24.
On the other hand its mixture of forms and content from both 9:7-20 and 5:8-24
indicates that it presupposes both passages. Furthermore, its rhetorical questions
and 2nd-person plural address form announcing captivity and death for Israel's
leaders make it an ideal conclusion for 5:8-24 + 9:7-20.

This conclusion is particularly important in that 9:7-20 does not appear to
be designed to stand independently from 10:1-4. As noted above, these verses
constitute a historical review of the experience of the northern kingdom of Israel
in relation to the Syro-Ephraimite War. Rather than present a progressive historical sequence of events, 9:7-20 begins with the most recent situation and
works backward through history to earlier events. Thus vv. 7-11 presuppose the
period following the war. This section employs perfect verbs to refer to YHWH's
word against Israel as a past event and presupposes a situation in which the
people have been punished once but are prepared to rebuild and try again in the
face of opposition from territories under Assyrian control (see below on Inten-

tion). Vv. 12-16 presuppose the time of the Assyrian attack itself, when Israel suffered a coup d'état against Pekah resulting in a change of leadership. One should note that Tiglath-pileser III mentions the deportation of "inhabitants" from Israel in connection with his invasion and the coup by Hoshea (*ANET*, 283-84). Vv. 17-20 clearly allude to the internal conflicts of Israel and Judah prior to the Assyrian invasion. The conflict between Manasseh and Ephraim refers to Gileadite attempts to take control of the throne in Samaria, attempts that were finally realized when the Gileadite Pekah assassinated Pekahiah and ruled in his place. Here "Manasseh" refers to the territory of Gilead across the Jordan River and "Ephraim" refers to the central hill country of Israel west of the Jordan. Once Pekah had control of the throne, Israel then attacked Judah to spark the Syro-Ephraimite War. Such a historical review is obviously intended to serve some purpose. But if these verses stand independently, the absence of following material that would define this purpose renders the passage unintelligible. Simply to announce Israel's punishment in this manner after the fact makes little sense.

As noted above, many scholars maintain that 5:25-30 serves as the original conclusion to 9:7-20 on the basis of the "outstretched hand" formula in 5:25. Consequently, the announcement of the approach of the Assyrian army in 5:26-30 would serve as a fitting climax for a series of oracles announcing YHWH's continuing anger at northern Israel. But there are problems with this association. The "outstretched hand" formula appears at the beginning of 5:25-30, not at the end as in the subunits of 9:7-20, so that the passage does not fit neatly into sequence. Furthermore, 9:7-11 indicates that punishment has already come. The appearance of the "outstretched hand" formula supports this perspective in that it refers to continuing anger and thereby indicates that punishment can come again. Although the Assyrian army would clearly constitute YHWH's instrument of punishment in this context, the announcement that they are coming is hardly a fitting conclusion to a passage that presupposes that the Assyrians have already come once. Something is obviously required to follow here, but 5:25-30 does not appear to be the appropriate text.

Instead, 5:25-30 appears to be designed as a conclusion for 5:8-24. Although the statements introduced by *lākēn* in 5:13-14 and 24 announce punishment and provide appropriate conclusions to the woe oracles in 5:8-12 and 15-23, 5:25-30 specifies these announcements of punishment in terms of the approach of the Assyrian army and thereby gives substance to the general statements of punishment that appear in 5:13-14 and 24. At the same time, 5:25-30 appears to serve as an introduction to 9:7-20. The "outstretched hand" formula clearly ties 5:25-30 to 9:7-20, and the attack of the Assyrian army is clearly presupposed as the instrument of punishment in 9:7-20.

By contrast, 10:1-4 does appear to be an appropriate conclusion for 9:7-20. Following on a reversed historical review that presupposes the people's defiance in the face of adversity and their willingness to rebuild and try again after having lost their previous leadership, 10:1-4 stands as a warning to the present leaders not to repeat the mistakes of the past. Israel was already punished once in the Syro-Ephraimite War. YHWH's continuing anger will insure further punishment if the present leadership continues the policies of the past.

This interpretation has important implications for understanding the literary character and setting of 9:7–10:4 in relation to 5:1-30. As noted above in the discussion of 5:1-24, the "woe" series in vv. 8-24 builds on the imagery and concepts of the vineyard allegory in vv. 1-7 so that 5:1-24 forms a well-defined unit. Furthermore, the *lākēn* statements in 5:13-14 and 24 indicate that 5:25-30 is not necessary to the interpretation of 5:1-24 insofar as these statements provide appropriate conclusions to the woe oracles of this passage. Instead, 5:25-30 appears to play a transitional function, since it ties 5:1-24 and 9:7–10:4 together. By this means, 5:1-24 provides the background for 9:7–10:4. That is, the woe oracles explain the initial punishment suffered by Israel. Isa 10:1-4 not only provides a rhetorical envelope that binds 9:7–10:4 to 5:1-24(30); it also defines the purpose of the entire passage of 5:1-30 + 9:7–10:4 as a warning to the leadership of Israel in the period following the Syro-Ephraimite War to refrain from following past policies. YHWH's anger and capacity to punish is still in force. Just as Israel and its previous leadership suffered punishment in connection with Assyria's invasion during the Syro-Ephraimite War, so might Israel under its present leadership suffer a similar fate. As noted above, 5:1-24 dates to the period prior to the Syro-Ephraimite War in 735-732. Isa 9:7–10:4 presupposes the postwar situation but appears to predate the final Assyrian assault against Israel in 724-721. Insofar as 5:25-30 serves as a transitional subunit between 5:1-24 and 9:7–10:4, it, too, appears to date to 732-724.

Intention

As noted above, the intention of 9:7–10:4 is to serve as a warning to the leadership of the northern kingdom of Israel concerning YHWH's continuing anger and capacity to punish in the aftermath of the Syro-Ephraimite War. Given the historical background of the period and the Assyrian reaction to Israel's revolt in 724, the passage appears to be a warning to northern Israel not to attempt to confront the Assyrians. This intention is evident from various features of this text.

First of all is the repeated refrain, "in all this his anger has not turned and his hand is stretched out still," in 9:11b, 16b, 20b; and 10:4b. Not only does it convey YHWH's anger and capacity for punishment, but it also indicates that this is a continuing state of affairs. As such, it indicates that YHWH's anger and punishment have already been realized and that they can be realized again.

Second, the historical review in 9:7-20 rehearses Israel's punishment in the Syro-Ephraimite War but presents the events in reverse historical sequence. By working back from the present situation to prior events, it explains the background to the present situation of Israel in terms of YHWH's punishment of the country. By this means, the passage intends to impress on its audience that YHWH is responsible for the present plight of the northern kingdom and that YHWH is capable of continuing to act against Israel if necessary. Furthermore, the historical review indicates that the people have not yet understood this essential point. Vv. 7-11 clearly presuppose the period following the Assyrian invasion when the people were beginning to rebuild. Their defiant attitude is expressed in their statements that they will replace fallen brick with dressed stone and fallen sycamores with cedar. Furthermore, the reference to "Rezin's enemies" as Aram and the Philistines indicates the postwar period when Assyria could rely on these territories for support. Tiglath-pileser's annals indicate that he invaded both of these territories in the course of the Syro-Ephraimite crisis, and that he replaced their rulers, Rezin of Aram and Hanno of Gaza, with puppets (*ANET*, 283-84). Vv. 12-16 allude to the removal of Israel's leadership in relation to Hoshea's coup, which had resulted in Pekah's assassination and Israel's surrender to Tiglath-pileser. As Tiglath-pileser notes in his annals, he carried away a number of Israelite "inhabitants" to captivity in keeping with standard Assyrian practice of deporting leading figures of defeated countries (*ANET*, 284). Vv. 17-20 refer to the prewar period when the Gileadite Pekah assassinated the ruling king Pekahiah and assumed the throne. Gilead, or the region east of the Jordan River, was the location of the tribe of Manasseh, and Samaria, the capital of the northern kingdom, was situated in the center of the hill country of Ephraim. Once Pekah had secured the throne and imposed Gileadite rule over all of Israel, he was able to attack Judah in an attempt to force it into the Syro-Ephraimite coalition. By pointing to Pekah's usurpation of the Ephraimite throne and his subsequent attack on Judah, the passage points to the root cause of the people's difficulties in the postwar period. One should keep in mind that Pekah's basic motivation for his actions was to organize resistance to the Assyrian empire. By warning the present leadership that its policies are unjust (10:1-4), the passage points to similar results for its efforts to rebuild in an attempt to resist Assyria.

Bibliography

W. P. Brown, "The So-Called Refrain in Isaiah 5:25-30 and 9:7–10:4," *CBQ* 52 (1990) 432-43; Crenshaw, "Liturgy" (→ 5:1-30); K. Fullerton, "Isaiah's Earliest Prophecy against Ephraim," *AJSL* 33 (1916) 9-39; P. A. Kruger, "Another Look at Isa 9:7-20," *JNSL* 15 (1989) 127-41; B. Stade, "Zu Jes. 3,1.17.24. 5,1. 8,1f.12-14.16. 9,7-20. 10,26," *ZAW* 26 (1906) 129-41.

PROPHETIC ANNOUNCEMENT OF
A ROYAL SAVIOR, 10:5–12:6

Structure

I. Woe oracle against Assyria		10:5-11
A. Woe statement		5
B. Basis: Assyria's destructive intent		6-11
1. Concerning YHWH's intention to punish		6
2. Concerning Assyria's intention to destroy		7-11
a. Basic statement		7
b. Elaboration: quotation of Assyria		8-11

Although 10:5–12:6 is generally considered to consist of several originally independent units, a number of its features indicate that this material constitutes a structural unity in the present form of the text. The unit begins with the introductory *hôy* against Assyria that distinguishes the following material from the "outstretched hand" oracles of 9:7 (*RSV* 8)–10:4 that are directed against Israel. Various syntactical features of the passage bind its subunits together, including the conjunctive *wāw*s in 10:12; 11:1; and 12:1, the conjunctive *lākēn*s of 10:16 and 24, and the formula *wĕhāyâ bayyôm hahû'*, "and it shall come to pass on that day," in 10:20, 27; 11:10 and 11 (cf. 12:1, 4), which relates back to the statement concerning YHWH's work on Mt. Zion and the intention to punish Assyria introduced by *wĕhāyâ kî-yĕbaṣṣa' 'ădōnāy*, "and it shall come to pass when my Lord accomplishes." Thematic features, such as the use of tree-trimming imagery and the contrast between the Assyrian and Davidic monarchs, also indicate the unity of the section. Because of the Assyrian monarch's boasts, 10:12 portrays him as a large overgrown tree in need of trimming. Isa 10:15-19 employs similar imagery to portray Assyria as a rebellious axe or saw as well as a forest that will suffer YHWH's burning. Likewise, 10:27 points to Assyria's fullness or fatness (see the discussion of Intention) as a basis for the statement that Assyria will be trimmed or cut down in 10:33-34. The result will be the new shoot of the house of David in 11:1-9, which contrasts the peace and absence of destruction on Mt. Zion under the Davidic monarch (cf. esp. 11:9) with the destructive purpose of the Assyrian monarch (cf. 10:7) and his threats against Zion (10:10-11, 32). The passage concludes with a portrayal of the restoration of Israel and a hymn of thanksgiving. The superscription in 13:1 introduces an entirely new section of oracles against the nations in the book of Isaiah.

The structure of the passage is determined by an interest in announcing the punishment of the Assyrians and the future consequences of that punishment, including the fall of the Assyrian monarch and the rise of the Davidic monarch. Consequently, the passage includes two major sections. The woe oracle in 10:5-11 announces Assyria's punishment, and 10:12–12:6, characterized by its future-oriented language in 10:12, 20, 27; 11:10, 11; 12:1 and 4, announces the consequences of that punishment for both Assyria and Israel.

The woe oracle against Assyria in 10:5-11 is characterized not only by its distinctive *hôy* form but also by the 1st-person perspective of vv. 5-6 that indicates that YHWH is the speaker. This is in contrast to v. 12, which introduces a speech by the prophet. The "woe" statement proper appears in v. 5 followed by the basis for this condemnation of Assyria in vv. 6-11, which focus on Assyria's destructive intent. V. 6 states YHWH's intention to use Assyria as a means for despoiling or punishing Israel, but vv. 7-11 make clear that Assyria's intention is not merely to punish but also to destroy. This intention is basically stated in v. 7, and vv. 8-11 elaborate with a quotation that establishes the Assyrians' intent. Following the speech formula in v. 8b, the speech itself appears in vv. 8b-11. It is constituted by three rhetorical questions that are in fact assertions. The first (v. 8b) asserts that all the Assyrian commanders are kings themselves, apparently reflecting the Assyrians' use of client armies as part of their invasion force. The second (v. 9) compares various cities that have already fallen to Assyrian arms in order to assert that all cities are alike. The third (vv. 10-11) compares the experience of pagan cities with Samaria and Jerusalem as a means for asserting that the Assyrians will destroy Jerusalem just like the others. The references to Samaria's "images" and Jerusalem's "idols" reinforce the Assyrian perspective that these cities are no different from any of the others. This perspective of course proves to be the root of the problem in that Jerusalem is YHWH's city, and YHWH is the one who sent the Assyrians in the first place.

In contrast to 10:5-11, 10:12–12:6 is presented as the words of the prophet that project the future consequences of YHWH's judgment against the Assyrians, including the downfall of the Assyrian monarch and the rise of the Davidic monarchy. The structure of the passage is determined by its future-oriented statements beginning with the verb *wĕhāyâ*, "and it shall come to pass," in 10:12, 20, 27; 11:10 and 11. Following the initial statement of the passage in 10:12, which introduces the announcement of punishment against Assyria in 10:12-19, subsequent passages are introduced by the formula *wĕhāyâ bayyôm hahû'*, "and it shall come to pass on that day." Each of these passages, including 10:20-26; 10:27–11:9; 11:10; and 11:11-16, elaborates and builds on the previous one to present a scenario of Assyrian downfall leading to the reestablishment of the Davidic monarchy. The passage is concluded by a hymn of thanksgiving in 12:1-16, which also employs *bayyôm hahû'* formulaic language in vv. 1 and 4.

Isaiah 10:12-19 constitutes a PROPHETIC ANNOUNCEMENT OF PUNISHMENT against Assyria. The passage begins with an announcement of Assyria's future punishment in v. 12 that employs the imagery of an overladen fruit tree in need of pruning to depict Assyria's arrogance. The basis for this announcement appears in vv. 13-19 in the form of a prophecy of judgment. The motivation for the punishment appears in vv. 13-14 in a quotation of the Assyrian king's boast that his victories are the result of his own power and prudence. This boast of course contradicts the prophet's perspective on the issue, which attributes the Assyrian's accomplishments to YHWH. Consequently, the announcement of judgment in vv. 15-19 begins with rhetorical questions that establish that the Assyrian king is merely a tool in YHWH's hand. Just as an ax or a saw has no right to aggrandize itself over the one who wields it, so the Assyrian king has no right to claim credit for what YHWH has given him. These questions thereby establish the basis for the announcement of judgment proper, which appears in vv. 16-19 introduced by the conjunctive *lākēn,* "therefore." V. 16 basically states that the punishment will include the depletion of the Assyrian king's warriors and the consumption of his glory, and vv. 17-19 elaborate by portraying the Assyrian king as a forest destroyed by YHWH's fire.

The first elaboration, introduced by the formula "and it shall come to pass in that day," appears in 10:20-26, where it announces the future relief of the remnant of Israel from Assyrian oppression. The first subunit of this passage announces the return of the remnant of Israel to YHWH in vv. 20-23. V. 20 contains the basic statement of this concept, and vv. 21-23 elaborate with two syntactically independent statements with their respective explanatory clauses. Vv. 21-22a state that the remnant will return to *ʾēl gibbôr,* an apparent reference to the Davidic monarch as indicated by the appearance of the term in 9:5 (*RSV* 6). The reason for this return is explained in a subordinate clause introduced by *kî ʾim,* "for if," which alludes to the promise to Jacob that Israel's people will be like the sand of the sea (Gen 32:13 [*RSV* 12]; cf. Gen 22:17; Hos 2:1 [*RSV* 1:10]). Vv. 22b-23 state that the decreed destruction will result in righteousness. The explanatory statement introduced by *kî,* "because," indicates that this is YHWH's intention for the entire land. The second part of this passage (vv. 24-26) is introduced by a conjunctive *lākēn,* "therefore," and takes up the consequences of this return in terms of an oracle of reassurance to the people living in Zion. The announcement of reassurance proper appears in v. 24. Vv. 25-26 contain the basis for the reassurance, i.e., YHWH's anger against them will cease (v. 25), and Assyria will be punished like Midian and Egypt in the past (v. 26).

The second elaboration appears in 10:27–11:9 and announces the impending fall of the Assyrian monarch and the subsequent rise of the Davidic monarch. The passage employs the imagery of pruning a tree that has become too "full" or "fat" (cf. *šemen* in 10:27), and that results in the new "shoot from the stem" (*ḥōṭer miggēzaʿ* in 11:1), here identified as the new Davidic monarch. The fall of the Assyrian monarch due to "fullness/fatness" is announced in 10:27-32. This is basically stated in 10:27. The basis for this statement then appears in vv. 28-32 in a list of cities along the northern approach to Jerusalem that are terrorized by the approaching Assyrian army. The list culminates in v. 32 with the Assyrian monarch standing at Nob and threatening Jerusalem. Following a syntactic break indicated by the introductory *hinnēh,* "behold," of v. 33, 10:33–11:9 then announces the rise of the Davidic monarch. It begins with an announcement of YHWH's "trimming" of the Assyrian monarch and his subsequent fall (10:33-34). This is followed by an announcement of a royal savior in 11:1-9, which presents the emergence of a new Davidic monarch as the direct result of the Assyrian's fall. In keeping with the genre, vv. 1-9 begin in vv. 1-3a with an announcement of the new monarch employing the allegorical imagery of a new shoot. It then follows with portrayals of the new king's justice (vv. 3b-5) and the peace brought about by the monarch's rule (vv. 6-8). The passage is summed up in a statement that there will be no destruction in this monarch's reign (contra 10:7) because the whole land is filled with the knowledge of YHWH.

The third elaboration appears in 11:10. This short passage focuses on the nations' future recognition of the new Davidic monarch.

The fourth elaboration in 11:11-16 announces the future restoration of Israel when the remnant of the people return from exile. The structure of this passage is defined by an initial statement, which sets the basic theme of the passage, followed by a series of five additional statements explaining how the initial statement is achieved. Thus v. 11 states that YHWH will redeem the remnant of the people from Assyria, Egypt, etc. V. 12 focuses on the gathering of the exiles. V. 13 takes up the removal of enmity between Ephraim and Judah so that the two can be reunited. V. 14 portrays the restoration of the lost Philistine and Transjordanian territories that were once part of the Davidic empire. V. 15 takes up the smiting of Egypt and the "River" (i.e., the Euphrates = Assyria), and v. 16 portrays the emergence of the "highway" so that the remnant can return home from exile in Assyria as in the exodus from Egypt.

Finally, the passage concludes with a hymn of thanksgiving in 12:1-6. The hymn includes two parts as indicated by the shifting forms of address. Vv. 1-2 are characterized by 2nd-person singular address in the form of an instruction to thank YHWH. Vv. 4-6 are characterized by 2nd-person plural address that includes instructions to draw the water from the springs of salvation (v. 3) and to praise YHWH (vv. 4-6).

Genre

Because of the composite nature of this unit, 10:5–12:6 incorporates a number of generic entities. Overall, the generic character of this text is simply that of prophetic ANNOUNCEMENT OF A ROYAL SAVIOR. This genre has no fixed form, but appears to be a special subcategory of the (→) announcement of salvation that focuses on the rule of a righteous king. In the present instance, the characterization of the entire passage as an ANNOUNCEMENT OF A ROYAL SAVIOR is based on 11:1-9, which announces the rule of a righteous Davidic monarch. All other elements of 10:5–12:6 appear to support this announcement either by providing its basis or by explaining its results.

The present text is oriented toward the future, insofar as it frequently employs the formula *wĕhāyâ bayyôm hahû'*, "and it shall come to pass in that day," to project a number of consequences or results from the condemnation of Assyria that introduces the passage. In this case, the consequences and results comprise the fall of the Assyrian monarchy and the rise of the Davidic monarchy. Particular attention should be paid to the role of the RHETORICAL QUESTIONS in 10:8b-11 and 10:15, as well as to the future orientation of the passage. The RHETORICAL QUESTIONS are initially introduced as the basis for the Assyrian king's speech in 10:8b-11 as a means to establish the reason for his condemnation, i.e., his intent to destroy Jerusalem like other pagan cities. They appear again in 10:15 to establish the basis for the Assyrian monarch's condemnation. RHETORICAL QUESTIONS are essentially a wisdom device employed to prompt an audience to come to the conclusion that the speaker desires. In this case, they are designed to prompt the audience to the conclusion that the Assyrian monarch will be subject to punishment by YHWH. When this role is considered in relation to the future orientation of the passage, an important aspect of 10:5–12:6 as PARENESIS emerges. The perspective of the passage begins in the present situation of threat to Jerusalem caused by the Assyrians. But from this perspective, the passage shifts to the future and effectively asks the audience to accept that YHWH will remove this threat. In doing so, the Assyrian monarchy will collapse and the Davidic monarchy will reemerge in the aftermath. If this passage is presented at the beginning of this process, it essentially asks the audience to have faith in YHWH's promises of protection for Israel, the Davidic monarchy, and Jerusalem. If the passage is presented from the conclusion of this process, it asks the audience to accept that the collapse of the Assyrians and the reemergence of the Davidic monarchy is the work of YHWH. In either case, it indicates the parenetic character of this passage.

The first major generic entity to appear within this unit is the WOE ORACLE against Assyria in 10:5-11. This particular example is not formulated as a direct address to the object of the oracle — a fact indicated by the 3rd-person references to Assyria throughout the passage — but as a condemnation of Assyria directed to another party, in this case Isaiah's Jerusalemite audience. The wisdom background of this form is evident in the use of the RHETORICAL QUESTIONS that constitute the Assyrian's speech in vv. 8b-11 and that assert his intention to destroy Jerusalem just as other pagan cities have been destroyed by Assyrian arms. Not only do these RHETORICAL QUESTIONS establish the intent of the Assyrian, but they also contrast with the RHETORICAL QUESTIONS of v. 15, which precede the ANNOUNCEMENT OF JUDGMENT against the Assyrian monarch and establish the basis for judgment. As noted above, this feature serves the parenetic purposes of the passage as a whole. It is particularly important to note that this oracle is presented as a speech by YHWH, in contrast to 10:12–12:6, which is presented as a speech by the prophet. In this respect, the WOE ORACLE serves as the premise for the balance of the prophet's presentation concerning the coming fall of Assyria and rise of Israel.

The second major generic entity of this passage is the ANNOUNCEMENT OF JUDGMENT against the Assyrian king in 10:12-19. This passage is based in the PROPHETIC ANNOUNCEMENT OF PUNISHMENT in vv. 13-19, which includes the standard motivation for punishment in vv. 13-14, here presented in the form of the Assyrian monarch's boast, and the ANNOUNCEMENT OF JUDGMENT in vv. 16-19 introduced by the particle lākēn, "therefore." The passage varies from the standard form, however, in that it begins with a statement predicting Assyria's judgment in v. 12 and includes the RHETORICAL QUESTIONS in v. 15. These variations serve the parenetic character of the passage as a whole. The prediction alerts the audience to a major aspect of the basic intent of this passage, YHWH's future (note *wĕhāyâ kî,* "and it shall come to pass that") punishment of Assyria. As noted above, the RHETORICAL QUESTIONS in v. 15 establish the basis for the Assyrian monarch's punishment by YHWH, and draw the audience to conclude that YHWH is in fact responsible for Assyria's downfall.

The balance of the passage is characterized by its future announcement language as indicated by the use of the formula *wĕhāyâ bayyôm hahû',* "and it shall come to pass in that day," in 10:20, 27; 11:10 and 11. Nevertheless, several of these "elaborations" are based in alternative generic forms.

Isaiah 10:20-26 is based in the ORACLE of reassurance vv. 24-26. The ORACLE is introduced by its typical formula *'al-tîrā',* "do not fear," in v. 24. Although this form is frequently identified with the priestly ORACLE OF SALVATION, there is no indication of a priestly context here, although one should note that the oracle draws on the traditions of the exodus and Gideon's defeat of Midian to reassure the people of Jerusalem that YHWH will deliver them.

Isaiah 10:27–11:9 is based in the ANNOUNCEMENT OF A ROYAL SAVIOR that appears in 11:1-9. This is a typical form used throughout the ancient Near East to announce the inauguration of the reign of a new king. Its setting is in the royal court, and it focuses on a description of the positive attributes of the new king's rule with special emphasis on the justice of the king's decisions and the peace that the kingdom will enjoy as a result of his rule. As such, it is a variant of the standard PROPHETIC ANNOUNCEMENT OF SALVATION.

The announcements in 11:10 concerning the nations' recognition of the new Davidic monarch and in 11:11-16 concerning the restoration of Israel are likewise examples of the PROPHETIC ANNOUNCEMENT OF SALVATION.

The concluding psalm in 12:1-6 appears to be a mixed genre based largely on the THANKSGIVING SONG (Wildberger, *Jesaja,* 478-79). It includes standard elements, such as the THANKSGIVING FORMULA *'ôdĕkā,* "I thank you," and the reference to YHWH's turning away anger in v. 1. Elements of the HYMN OF PRAISE appear in the call to worship or the imperative summons to praise, give thanks, etc., in vv. 4-6. The HYMN OF PRAISE generally appears in a ceremony for a recent intervention by YHWH on behalf of the people. The collapse of Assyria's threat to Jerusalem might well serve as the appropriate occasion for this psalm. That this psalm has been composed for its present context is clear from the introduction by heralds (Crüsemann, 50-55), and the use of *wĕ'āmartā,* "and you shall say," in combination with the *bayyôm hahû'* formula, which ties the psalm to the preceding material. A further element is the reference to the exodus tradition that appears in vv. 2 and 5 and that ties this psalm to 10:20-26 and 11:10-16 in particular (see also the discussion of Intention below).

Setting

Although the basic setting of 10:5–12:6 is the period of King Josiah's reforms in keeping with that of chs. 5–12 (see the discussion of the overview for these chapters), evidence of historical tension within this unit suggests its composite nature. Whereas 11:1–12:6 focuses especially on the rise of the Davidic monarchy in the overall context of the restoration of Israel, 10:5-34 focuses on YHWH's defense of Zion and the punishment of Assyria. Although both sections share an interest in the restoration of Israel and the centrality of Zion, 10:5-34 shows no interest in the Davidic monarchy and focuses on YHWH's authority as the essential antithesis to Assyrian claims of hegemony. As the following discussion will show, 11:1–12:6 stems from the period of King Josiah's reform but 10:5-34 (+ 14:24-27) stems from the period of Sargon II's invasion of the region to put down the Philistine revolt in 711 B.C.E. Isa 10:5-34 + 14:24-27 was then reworked at the time of the Josianic redaction of chs. 5–12.

A number of factors indicate the Josianic background of 11:1–12:6 (cf. Vermeylen, *Du prophète,* 269-75). First, many scholars have noted that the passage presupposes a threat to the Davidic dynasty, as indicated by its use of "stump" *(gēzaʿ)* and "root" *(šōrēš),* from which a new "shoot" *(ḥōṭer)* or "sprout" *(nēṣer)* must grow. Such imagery indicates that the threat almost succeeded in that it portrays a tree that has nearly been destroyed but is still capable of rejuvenating itself. Although the Davidic dynasty was certainly threatened by the Syro-Ephraimite coalition in 735-732, the threat never reached the point where a ruling monarch was killed or removed from the throne. Instead, the arrival of the Assyrian army put an end to the threat before Ahaz could be replaced by ben Tabeel. Likewise, Hezekiah's position does not appear to have been seriously threatened. Although the country suffered defeat and invasion during his rule, there is no indication that removing him or the dynasty in general was ever seriously considered. But such a scenario fits well with Josiah (639-609). His father Amon was assassinated in a coup by his "servants," a coup apparently motivated by an interest in reversing Manasseh's policy of subservience to the weakening Assyrian empire (2 Kgs 22:19-26; 2 Chr 33:21-25). Nevertheless, the "people of the land" put down the conspiracy and restored the eight-year-old Josiah to the throne. Josiah's age at the time and the fact that no uncle or other Davidic figure exercised authority during his minority suggest that Josiah was the only Davidic heir to survive the coup. Furthermore, the imagery of a new growth signified by "shoot" or "sprout" apparently alludes to the young monarch.

Second, the passage makes specific mention of "a small boy leading them" (v. 6b). The imagery of normally antagonistic wild animals resting harmlessly together is typically used to convey the peace to be realized by the new king's reign and is in keeping with the genre of announcement of a royal savior. Nevertheless, the portrayal of a small boy and his leading role is striking in this context and suggests an allusion to the boy-king Josiah, one of the youngest ruling monarchs of the Davidic dynasty (note the 7-year-old Jehoash; 2 Kgs 12:1).

Third, the emphasis on the new king's justice and wisdom is certainly not remarkable in a text concerned with the reign of any new Near Eastern monarch. But one should note that one of the major features of Josiah's reform was the establishment of a newly found book of law as its basis (2 Kgs 22:8-20; 2 Chr 34:8-33).

Fourth, Isa 11:11-16 emphasizes the cessation of enmity between Ephraim and Judah, their reunification, and the reestablishment of authority over Philistia to the west and Edom, Moab, and Ammon to the east. These verses further emphasize the punishment of Egypt and Assyria in the context of the return of the exiles from these countries. This scenario corresponds precisely to Josiah's attempt to rebuild the Davidic empire in the face of opposition from Egypt and Assyria in the late 7th century. His dismantling of the altar at Bethel indicates his interest in reclaiming the territory and population of the former northern kingdom of Israel (2 Kgs 23:15-20). His marriage to Hamutal of Libnah (2 Kgs 23:31; 24:18) indicates an interest in securing support in the Philistine region, and his marriage to Zebidah of Rumah (2 Kgs 23:36) indicates his interest in support in the north and the Transjordan. Furthermore, as Assyrian power weakened during the course of the late 7th century, Egypt emerged as the major obstacle to Josiah's ambitions and eventually caused his death at Megiddo (2 Kgs 23:28-30).

Finally, the interest in exodus traditions apparent in both 11:11-16 and 12:1-6 is particularly noteworthy in the context of the Josianic redaction. As 2 Kgs 23:21-23 and 2 Chr 35:1-19 indicate, the celebration of Passover served as the festival basis for Josiah's reform. Insofar as Passover celebrates the exodus of Hebrews from Egypt and their return to the land of Israel, this holiday would be particularly important to the ideology of Josiah's program of reform and national restoration. The liturgical character of the psalm in 12:1-6 indicates that this passage may well have played a role in Josiah's Passover celebration.

Although 11:1–12:6 stems from the period of King Josiah's program of reform and national restoration, 10:5-34 appears to derive from the prophet Isaiah and reflects Sargon II's western campaign of 720, in which he put down the revolt of a Syro-Palestinian coalition led by Ilu-bidi (Iau-bidi) of Hamath and defeated the Egyptians at Raphia. Accordingly, the Assyrian king's threat against Jerusalem in 10:27-32 represents Sargon's efforts to intimidate the city and thereby keep Judah out of the conflict. Several factors support such a view.

The first is the itinerary of terrified cities mentioned in 10:28-32. These verses describe an unnamed enemy army that approaches Jerusalem from the north by way of Shechem/Bethel highway. The sites mentioned include Aiath, Migron, Michmash, Geba, Ramah, Gibeah, Gallim, Laishah, Anathoth, Madmenah, and Nob. Not all of these sites can be identified positively, but scholars have concluded that the army deviated from the main highway between Bethel and Jerusalem in order to avoid the Judean fortress at Mizpah while approaching Jerusalem from the north (for the details of this route, see Dalman).

Various attempts have been made to explain this itinerary, but each has failed. Although these verses have often been related to Sennacherib's 701 campaign (Fohrer, *Jesaja,* 1:162-63; Auvray, *Isaïe 1–39,* 138-41; Kaiser, *Isaiah 1–12,* 245-51), that he conducted his campaign from Lachish and the Philistine plain militates against the march of an army along the Shechem/Bethel highway to Jerusalem. Donner's (pp. 30-38) and Irvine's (*Crisis,* pp. 274-79) attempts to claim that this represents the invasion of the Syro-Ephraimite coalition in 735 likewise cannot be sustained in that the context indicates an Assyrian invader. Procksch (*Jesaja I–XXXIX,* 175), Wildberger (*Jesaja,* 427), Clements (*Isaiah*

1–39, 117-19), and Vermeylen (*Du prophète,* 267) maintain that this passage describes Sargon's approach to the city in the course of his campaign to put down the Ashdod revolt in 712-711. But Tadmor's analysis of the Assyrian eponym list demonstrates that Sargon remained at home during this campaign, which eliminates it from consideration (H. Tadmor, "The Campaigns of Sargon II of Assur: A Chronological-Historical Study," *JCS* 12 [1958] 22-40, 77-100, esp. 92-94). Sargon's other campaigns to Philistia during the years 716-711 must be eliminated from consideration in that they were designed to open trade relations with Egypt rather than to put down revolt (see Tadmor, ibid., 77-78; M. Elat, "The Economic Relations of the Neo-Assyrian Empire with Egypt," *JAOS* 98 [1978] 20-34). Furthermore, Assyrian records make no mention of a campaign to Judah at this time. Finally, a number of scholars maintain that the passage represents a projected prophetic vision of enemy invasion, not an actual event (e.g., Dalman; Christensen, "March"; Barth, 65-66).

The present analysis of Isa 10:27-32 and the Assyrian records indicates that Sargon's western campaign of 720 provides the best setting for the approach to Jerusalem described in the present text. After putting down the Syrian and Israelite coalition led by Ilu-bidi at Qarqar (*ARAB,* II, §5; *ANET,* 285), Sargon marched quickly south to face the Egyptians, who supported the rebellious Hanno of Gaza. His defeat of the Egyptian army under Sib'u, his destruction of Raphia on the Egyptian border, and his capture of Hanno secured the region, enabling him to begin the resettlement of Samaria. Sargon would likely have passed by Jerusalem on his way to Egypt in order to intimidate the city, gather supplies and support, and thereby prevent Judah from joining with Egypt and Philistia. If he were to march down the coastal route as Sennacherib did during his 701 campaign, Sargon would arrive in Philistia much more quickly, but he would run the risk of Judean aid being supplied to Ashdod unmolested. It was imperative to move quickly, but Sargon could not afford to leave his rear exposed to Judean attack while facing the Egyptians and Philistines. Consequently, a forced march by way of Jerusalem in order to remove Judah from the conflict would best serve his military situation. The route indicated in 10:27-32 avoids the fortress at Mizpah and thereby indicates Sargon's need for haste. Likewise, Sargon's Nimrud Inscription identifies him as the "Subduer of the Land of Judah" (*musaknis [matu] Iaudu;* see F. E. Peiser, *Sammlung von assyrischen und babylonischen Texten* [ed. E. Schrader; Berlin: H. Reuther, 1890] 2:34-39; *ARAB,* II, §137) in the context of his 720 campaigns against Humbanigash of Elam at Der and Ilu-bidi of Hamath at Qarqar. Isa 10:27-32 gives no indication that Jerusalem was actually attacked, and the location of the Assyrian's presence at Nob, present-day Mt. Scopus, is logical in that it provides a commanding view of the city and the best possible means to display the full strength of the Assyrian army. Once Jerusalem was cowed, Sargon could then proceed toward Philistia with his rear secured and quickly crush Egyptian and Philistine opposition.

The second factor involves the speeches by the Assyrian monarch quoted in 10:8-11 and 10:13-14 that make references to a number of cities taken by the Assyrian army during the late 8th century. With the exception of Jerusalem, the cities referred to were taken by 717 at the latest. Thus the Hittite city of Carchemish was taken by Sargon in 717, and the north Syrian city of Calno was taken by Tiglath-pileser in 738. Hamath, on the Orontes River in Syria, was taken by Sargon in 720, and Arpad, in north Syria, fell to Tiglath-pileser in 738 and again to Sargon in 720. Damascus fell to Tiglath-pileser in 734, and Samaria was taken by Tiglath-pileser or Sargon in 722/721. Although Carchemish did not fall to Sargon II until 717, both Carchemish and Calno had been subjugated by Tiglath-pileser as early as 742. This circumstance indicates that the cities mentioned by the Assyrian king in Isa 10:8-11 and 13-14 were not necessarily conquered by Sargon in 720, but were already subject to him at that time.

The arguments articulated above would account for 10:5-19, 27-34 as an oracle of judgment by Isaiah against Sargon for his threat against Jerusalem. The use of forest imagery and the rhetorical questions to persuade an audience are typical of the prophet, and the oracle would be in keeping with Isaiah's views that YHWH guarantees the security of Zion.

Isaiah 10:20-23 and 10:24-26 present a special case. These passages are frequently considered as later postexilic additions because of the introductory *wĕhāyâ bayyôm hahû'* formula and their intrusive character. A promise to protect the remnant of Israel and the inhabitants of Zion fits well in a passage that focuses on YHWH's defense of Jerusalem against the threat of the Assyrian monarch. But the intrusive character of these verses seems clear from the catchword connections that tie these verses to their larger literary context, and thereby develop the meanings of themes and key words in relation to an overall scenario that looks forward to the fall of Assyria and the return of Israel to Jerusalem and the Davidic monarchy. The first example appears in the contrast between *šĕ'ār yiśrā'ēl,* "the remnant of Israel," in v. 20 that YHWH will deliver, and *šĕ'ār 'ēṣ ya'rô,* "the remnant of the trees of his forest," in v. 19 that refers to the decimated ranks of the Assyrian army following its punishment by YHWH (vv. 16-19). Likewise, the "rod" *(šebeṭ)* and "staff" *(maṭṭeh)* used by Assyria to smite the inhabitants of Jerusalem in "anger" *(za'am)* in vv. 24-25 correspond to the terminology employed in 10:5 to describe Assyria's role as YHWH's agent of punishment, but v. 26 reverses the imagery to portray the smiting of Assyria as a punishment similar to YHWH's smiting of Egypt at the Reed Sea (cf. Exodus 14–15).

Both Isa 10:20-23 and 10:24-26 relate to the larger literary context of 7:1–9:6 (*RSV* 7). Isa 10:20-23 takes up *šĕ'ār yāšûb,* "a remnant shall return," in reference to Isaiah's son who accompanied him in his meeting with Ahaz during the Syro-Ephraimite crisis (7:3). It is noteworthy, however, that the present context does not refer to *šĕ'ār yāšûb* as Isaiah's son, but only as the remnant of northern Israel that will return to *'ēl gibbôr.* As noted in the discussion of ch. 7 above, the reference to Shear-jashub as the son of Isaiah is the product of the Josianic redaction of 7:1-9. Isa 10:20-23 refers to the return of the northern kingdom to YHWH and the Davidic dynasty; the passage alludes to the northern kingdom as the "house of Jacob" and "remnant of Israel," and it refers to the promise of descendants "like the sand of the sea," all of which are linked to the traditions of the northern kingdom. Furthermore, v. 21 calls for their return to *'ēl gibbôr,* which appears in 9:5 (*RSV* 6) as a name for the Davidic monarch. Isa 10:24-26 contains similar references, including the reference to Midian's defeat at the Rock of Oreb (cf. 9:3 [*RSV* 4]) and the reassurance formula "do not fear" (cf. 7:4). In each case, these associations tie 10:5-34 to 7:1–9:6 (*RSV*

7) and develop the theme of the return of the northern kingdom to the Davidic dynasty following the defeat of Assyria.

In considering the function of 10:20-23 and 24-26 as passages that tie vv. 5-19 and 27-34 to a larger literary context, one should keep in mind observations that were made in relation to 9:7 (*RSV* 8)–10:4. The initial *hôy* of 10:5 facilitates a link between this material and 10:1-4, which employs a similar *hôy* form. Likewise, the reference to YHWH's "anger" (*'ap*) relates to the characteristic formula of 9:7 (*RSV* 8)–10:4, *běkol-zō't lō'-šāb 'appô*, "in all this his anger has not turned." As noted in the discussion of 9:7 (*RSV* 8)–10:4, the continuing anger of YHWH is extended from the northern kingdom of Israel to include Assyria for overstepping its bounds. Such a perspective would account for 10:20-23, which calls for the return of the northern kingdom to YHWH, thus ending divine anger against them (10:22b-23; cf. 10:25-26). When one considers that 9:7 (*RSV* 8)–10:4 together with 5:1-30 forms the literary framework for 7:1–9:6 (*RSV* 7), it becomes clear that while 10:20-23 takes up the concern with the northern kingdom in its attempt to tie the anti-Assyrian oracle to the larger context, 10:24-26 takes up the general theme of reassurance to Jerusalem that also dominates this material.

One can draw four conclusions from these observations. First, these passages illustrate an early form of midrashic exegesis that is designed to draw on and develop the images, terminology, and meanings of earlier texts. Second, the role of these passages is to link 10:5-19 and 27-34 to the larger literary context of chs. 5–12. Third, the perspectives of these passages, the return of the northern kingdom to the house of David and YHWH's defense of Jerusalem, are entirely in keeping with the perspective of 7:1–9:6 (*RSV* 7). Fourth, the allusion to the exodus tradition in the form of Egyptian oppression in 10:24-26 associates these passages with 11:1–12:6, which looks to the restoration of all Israel to the Davidic dynasty; but the midrashic exegesis characteristic of 10:20-26 does not appear in 11:1–12:6. It would therefore appear that 10:20-26 is deliberately designed to bind material in chs. 5–10 together, but not chs. 5–12. These considerations indicate that 10:20-26 stems from a hand that attempted to associate material from the Syro-Ephraimite War in 5:1–9:6 (*RSV* 7) with material that presupposes the fall of Samaria and Sargon's threat against Jerusalem in 9:7 (*RSV* 8)–10:34. The result is the application of the prophet's views concerning YHWH's role in the Syro-Ephraimite War to the situation of the fall of Samaria: YHWH will return the northern tribes of Israel to the Davidic dynasty, but Assyria will be destroyed first for overstepping its bounds as YHWH's agent of punishment. The setting for such work would be in Isaiah's attempts to convince Hezekiah of YHWH's intentions to protect Jerusalem and the Davidic house during the aftermath of the fall of Samaria. Sargon's arrogance was disturbing and would lead to his downfall in Isaiah's eyes, but the defeat of the northern kingdom of Israel allows for the reunification of northern Israel and southern Judah under the rule of the Davidic dynasty. Just as an earlier literary context presented 9:1-6 (*RSV* 2-7) as an attempt to convince Ahaz of such a scenario in the aftermath of Tiglath-pileser's decimation of the northern kingdom, so would the later literary context of 9:1-6 (*RSV* 2-7) serve as a means to convince Hezekiah of the same reality in the aftermath of Sargon's western campaign of 720. The same goal would be accomplished in relation to King

Josiah's plans for reunification of Israel and Judah under Davidic rule during the 7th century, when 9:1-6 (*RSV* 2-7) was read together with 11:1-16 in the context of the Josianic redaction of chs. 5–12. The exodus imagery of 11:1–12:6 would then build on the reference to YHWH's smiting of Assyria in analogy to the smiting of Egypt at the Reed Sea in 10:26.

One element is still missing in this reconstruction. If 11:1–12:6 stems from the Josianic redaction of a previous Isaianic text, then 10:27-34 appears to provide a somewhat anticlimactic and disappointing conclusion to an earlier Isaianic layer of material in 5:1–10:34. One should note, however, that 14:24-27 includes a number of features that indicate its role as the original conclusion to chs. 5–10. First, its appearance after the Babylonian oracle in 13:1–14:23 is enigmatic in that it seems to have little relation to its present context. Second, its use of the "outstretched hand" formula and its allusion to the "return" of YHWH's hand in the context of a summary-appraisal form indicates that it was designed as the concluding statement to the series in 9:7 (*RSV* 8)–10:4. Third, its concern with YHWH's defeat of Assyria indicates that it linked 10:5-34 to 9:7 (*RSV* 8)–10:4. This is supported by its concern to defeat Assyria "in my land/on my mountain" (cf. 10:12, 32). It is likewise supported by the similar formulation of YHWH's statement against Assyria in 14:24b-25 and the Assyrian king's statement in 10:8b-11. Both use the oath formula *'im-lō'*, "if not," and the comparative formulation *ka'ăšer . . . kēn*, "just as . . . so," to describe the realization of their respective intentions. Furthermore, the reference to YHWH's removal *(sar/yāsûr)* of the Assyrian "yoke" *('ōl)* and "burden" *(subbāl)* from the "shoulder" *(šekem)* ties this passage midrashically to similar formulations in both 10:27 and 9:3 (*RSV* 4). The enigmatic "from upon them" *(mē'ălêhem)* in 14:25 refers to "my mountains" and "my land" in the same verse.

Isaiah 14:24-27 provides an appropriate conclusion to chs. 5–10. It takes up the "outstretched hand" formula from 9:7 (*RSV* 8)–10:4 and the removal of Assyria's "yoke" and "burden" from 9:3 (*RSV* 4) and 10:27. Its summary-appraisal formulation, which announces YHWH's judgment against Assyria, provides an ideal conclusion to the sequence of images in chs. 5–10 that calls for punishment of the northern kingdom for threatening Jerusalem and leads naturally to a call for punishment of Assyria for the same offense. It thereby testifies to YHWH's sovereignty and pledge to protect Jerusalem in keeping with the perspective of this material. The setting for 10:5-34 + 14:24-27 in the larger context of chs. 5–10 would therefore be in the period following Sargon's campaign to put down the Philistine revolt in 713-711 but prior to Sennacherib's campaign of 705. It appears to have been delivered by the prophet as part of his campaign to dissuade Hezekiah and Judah from attempting a military confrontation with the Assyrians.

On the basis of these arguments, it is possible to reconstruct three settings for 10:5–12:6. The original form, 10:5-19, 27-34, would have been delivered in the context of Sargon's threats to Jerusalem from Nob prior to marching on to Ashdod. The expanded form, 10:5-34 + 14:24-27, appears to be the conclusion of an early form of chs. 5–10 that was designed to dissuade Hezekiah and Judah from considering rash action that might lead to an ill-considered revolt against Assyria in the period following Sargon's invasion by pointing out that YHWH will bring about the Assyrians' downfall. The final form, 10:5–12:6, appears to be the conclusion of the present form of chs. 5–12, which probably functioned as a liturgical text in support of King Josiah's program of religious reform and national restoration in the late 7th century. The most likely setting for this text would be the Passover celebration held to support the reform.

Intention

The intention of 10:5–12:6 must be considered in relation to the three text forms and settings identified in the previous discussion. The earliest form of this text is 10:5-19, 27-34, which stems from the period of Sargon's western campaign of 720. The passage presupposes Sargon's march against Jerusalem following his defeat of the Syrian-Israelite coalition led by Ilu-bidi at Qarqar and prior to his advance against the Egyptians and Philistines at Raphia. Sargon's purpose was to intimidate Hezekiah and to remove Judah as a potential ally to Egypt and Philistia. Isaiah's condemnation of the Assyria monarch for this action reflects his view that the Assyrian monarch had overstepped his role as YHWH's tool for punishing the people of Israel. By threatening Jerusalem, the location of YHWH's temple and the recipient of YHWH's guarantee of protection, Sargon challenged the authority of the deity who sent him against Israel in the first place. In Isaiah's view, such an affront provides the grounds for Assyria's and Sargon's punishment. In the present situation, Isaiah attempts to persuade the population (and probably the king) that Jerusalem will be safe despite the Assyrian threat. There is no evidence that Jerusalem was assaulted or damaged, but Isaiah's extensive use of imagery pertaining to the felling of trees and the destruction of natural growth probably reflects the Assyrian army's denuding of the landscape to provide food and building materials for themselves. As such, it demonstrates Assyria's capacity for destruction to Judah.

The second stage in the formation of this text is 10:5-34 + 14:24-27. As noted above, this passage served as the conclusion to chs. 5–10, which dates to the period following Sargon's western campaign and prior to the Judean revolt of 701. In this capacity, it appears to function as part of a larger text that is designed to dissuade Hezekiah from attempting to confront the Assyrian empire by claiming that YHWH will punish the Assyrians. By employing the "woe" forms and the "outstretched hand" formula from previous sections, it attempts to argue that YHWH's anger will shift from Israel to Assyria on account of the Assyrian monarch's affront to YHWH's sovereignty. It advises patience and the need to wait a while longer before YHWH's action will be realized (10:25-26). By referring back to 7:1–9:6 (*RSV* 7), it emphasizes YHWH's promise that the Assyrian attacks against the northern kingdom of Israel present the opportunity for the Davidic dynasty to extend its power over the former northern kingdom and thereby reunite the tribes of Israel. It therefore presupposes the need to avoid foreign alliances and direct confrontation of the Assyrian empire. A cautious wait rather than direct military action is advised.

The final stage in the composition of this text is represented by 10:5–12:6. This text serves as the conclusion to chs. 5–12 that was edited into its present form in relation to King Josiah's program of religious reform and national restoration. It differs from the previous stages of composition in that it does not look forward to a coming Assyrian collapse but looks to a collapse that is now being realized. In this respect, it is an attempt to persuade its audience, the people of Judah in the late 7th century, that YHWH brought about the fall of Assyria. By appending this material to the entire block of chs. 5–12, the editors attempted to establish continuity with the historical events of the late 8th century, when Assyria's invasion of Israel resulted in the destruction of the northern kingdom but also laid the foundation for Assyria's ultimate collapse. The impending fall of the Assyrian empire and the corresponding resurgence of the Davidic dynasty are the work of YHWH, and fulfill Isaiah's prophecies against Assyria made a century earlier. By projecting the restoration of the monarchy and the return of the exiles, this passage attempts to convince the people that the restoration of the Davidic empire will be the natural consequence of Assyria's collapse and Josiah's rise, since Ephraim and Judah will be reunited, Egypt and Assyria will be defeated, and the Philistines, Edomites, Moabites, and Ammonites will be brought under Davidic rule. In this respect, the primary purpose of this passage is to garner support among the Judean population for Josiah's program of religious reform and national restoration by presenting it as the fulfillment of Isaiah's prophecies of the late 8th century. The portrayal of the Assyrian king as an overripe olive tree ready for harvest in 10:27 and 33-34 relates to the Assyrian empire's use of Israelite labor in Philistia, especially in Ekron (= Tel Miqne), the empire's center for the production of olive oil during the 7th century (for a full discussion cf. S. Gitin, "Tel Miqne-Ekron: A Type-Site for the Inner Coastal Plain in the Iron Age II Period," in *Recent Excavations in Israel: Studies in Iron Age Archaeology* [ed. S. Gitin and W. G. Dever; AASOR 49; Winona Lake: Eisenbrauns, 1989] 23-58).

Bibliography

→ bibliography at "Introduction to the Book of Isaiah." W. F. Albright, "The Assyrian March on Jerusalem, Isa. X,28-32," *AASOR* 4 (1924) 134-40; R. P. Carroll, "Eschatological Delay in the Prophetic Tradition," *ZAW* 94 (1982) 47-58; Childs, *Assyrian Crisis*, 39-44, 61-63; D. L. Christensen, "The March of Conquest in Isaiah X 27c-34," *VT* 26 (1976) 385-99; Crüsemann, *Studien zur Formgeschichte* (→ 1:4-9), 50-56, 227-29; G. Dalman, "Palästinische Wege und die Bedrohung Jerusalems nach Jesaja 10," *PJ* 12 (1916) 37-57; Donner, *Israel unter den Völkern* (→ 1:4-9), 30-38, 142-45; idem, "Der Feind aus dem Norden: Topographische und archäologische Erwägungen zu Jes. 10,27b-34," *ZDPV* 84 (1968) 46-54; K. Fullerton, "The Problem of Isaiah, Chapter 10," *AJSL* 34 (1917-18) 170-84; G. B. Gray, "The Strophic Division of Isaiah 21,1-10 and Isaiah 11,1-8," *ZAW* 32 (1912) 190-98; P. R. Koch, "Der Gottesgeist und der Messias," *Bib* 27 (1946) 241-68; S. Mittmann, " 'Wehe! Assur, Stab meines Zorns' (Jes 10,5–9.13aβ-15)," in *Prophet und Prophetenbuch* (*Fest.* O. Kaiser; ed. V. Fritz, K.-F. Pohlmann, and H.-C. Schmitt; Berlin and New York: de Gruyter, 1989) 111-33; J. P. Peters, "Notes on Isaiah," *JBL* 38 (1919) 77-93; J. T. A. G. M. van Ruiten, "The Intertextual Relationship between Isaiah 65,25 and Isaiah 11,6-9," in *The Scriptures and the Scrolls* (*Fest.* A. S. van der Woude; ed. F. García Martínez et al.; VTSup 49; Leiden: Brill, 1992) 31-42; Steck, "Beobachtungen"; M. A. Sweeney, "Sargon's Threat Against Jerusalem in Isaiah 10,27-32," *Bib* 75 (1994) 457-70.

PRONOUNCEMENTS CONCERNING
THE NATIONS, 13:1–23:18

Structure

I. Pronouncement concerning Babylon	13:1–14:32
II. Pronouncement concerning Moab	15:1–16:14
III. Pronouncement concerning Damascus	17:1–18:7
IV. Pronouncement concerning Egypt	19:1–20:6
V. Pronouncement concerning the Wilderness of the Sea	21:1-10
VI. Pronouncement concerning Dumah	21:11-12
VII. Pronouncement concerning Arabia	21:13-17
VIII. Pronouncement concerning Valley of Vision	22:1-25
IX. Pronouncement concerning Tyre	23:1-18

The prophetic pronouncements concerning the nations in chs. 13–23 are clearly demarcated by the common form of their introductory superscriptions, *maśśā'* PN, "Pronouncement concerning PN" (13:1; 15:1; 17:1; 19:1; 21:1; 21:11; 21:13; 22:1; and 23:1), and the concern of the overall unit with the fate of the various nations identified therein. A new textual unit begins in 24:1, which lacks a superscription and focuses on the fate of the "land" or "earth" at large rather than on a specific nation. The initial superscription concerning Babylon in 13:1, *maśśā' bābel 'ăšer ḥāzâ yěša'yāhû ben-'āmôṣ*, "the pronouncement concerning Babylon that Isaiah ben Amoz saw," is parallel to the superscriptions in 1:1 and 2:1 in that it contains a subordinate clause ("that Isaiah ben Amoz saw") following the generic title of the text ("pronouncement concerning Baby-lon"), which identifies Isaiah as the one "who saw" the following material. This clause identifies 13:1 as the initial superscription of the block of material in chs. 13–23 just as 1:1 and 2:1 introduce chs. 1–66 and chs. 2–4, respectively.

The nine superscriptions in chs. 13–23 constitute the basic structural markers of this unit (see Wildberger, *Jesaja,* 497). Others identify the differ-entiation of the nations as the basic structural principle (Kaiser, *Isaiah 13–39,* 1-2; Kissane, *Isaiah,* 1:xxiv-xxv; Clements, *Isaiah 1–39,* 129-30), or argue that an original collection of oracles with the title "*maśśā'* PN" was supplemented with oracles that lacked such a title (Fohrer, *Jesaja I–XXXIX,* 177-78; Wildberger, *Jesaja,* 498; Gray, *Isaiah I–XXVII,* li; cf. Vermeylen, *Du prophète,* 286). Although chs. 13–23 contain some material that appears to stand outside the standard form of the pronouncements, this extraneous material is subordi-nated structurally to the pronouncement forms (for full discussions of the fol-lowing, see the commentary to the individual subunits below). Thus the sum-mary-appraisal in 14:24-27 demonstrates that the pronouncement concerning Babylon in 13:1–14:23 fulfills Isaiah's prophecies concerning Assyria. Likewise, the pronouncement concerning the Philistines in 14:28-32, which includes a variant form of the *maśśā'* superscription, stands as an appendix to the pro-nouncement concerning Babylon that declares that YHWH's purpose in punish-ing the nations is to assert divine sovereignty in Zion, thereby relating the Babylon pronouncement to the overall concerns of the book of Isaiah. Isa

17:12-14 serves a similar purpose in relation to the pronouncement concerning Damascus in that it announces YHWH's rebuke of the nations who threaten Zion. Isa 18:1-7 then follows up with a focus on the nations' recognition of YHWH (cf. vv. 3, 7). Isa 20:1-6 provides the basis for the pronouncement concerning Egypt in 19:1-25 in that the fall of Ashdod to Assyria legitimizes the condemnation of Egypt, which would likewise fall to Assyria. The pronouncement concerning the "Valley of Vision" (i.e., the Kidron Valley along the eastern edge of Jerusalem) in 22:1-14 demonstrates that Jerusalem, too, must be cleansed in preparation for YHWH's sovereignty, and the oracle against Shebna in 22:15-25 confirms the need for such cleansing by condemning him for erecting a monument to himself on the eastern slopes of the Kidron.

In each case, the *maśśā'* or prophetic pronouncement form determines the overall perspective of the subunits of chs. 13–23. Both collectively and individually, they focus on an explanation of the events announced therein as acts of YHWH that are designed to anticipate YHWH's sovereignty over the world. Such consistency of form and purpose confirms that the *maśśā'* superscriptions stand as the basic structural markers for chs. 13–23. Each introduces one of the nine major subunits of the passage (see the outline above). No discernible order for the nations is evident in chs. 13–23, but the discussion of the setting of these chapters below will demonstrate that the nations included here are those that were brought under Persian rule during the late 6th century.

Genre

The overarching genre of chs. 13–23 is a collection of PROPHECIES CONCERNING FOREIGN NATIONS. The PROPHECY CONCERNING A FOREIGN NATION has no fixed form, but it is identified by its content, which announces the destruction or defeat of a nation, either by an enemy nation or by forces assembled by YHWH. In general, no reason is given for the destruction of a nation so that the genre cannot be identified as a variation of the (→) prophecy of punishment. Rather, the purpose of the genre is to identify the destruction of the nation as an act of YHWH. Apart from chs. 13–23, collections of PROPHECIES CONCERNING FOREIGN NATIONS appear in Jeremiah 46–51; Ezekiel 25–32; Amos 1:3–2:16; and Zeph 2:4-15. Individual examples appear in Isaiah 34; Obadiah; and Nahum.

Isaiah 13–23 is a typical example of the form. Each of the individual subunits in these chapters is formulated as a PROPHETIC PRONOUNCEMENT *(maśśā'),* which is designed to explain events in human affairs as acts of YHWH. It seems clear from the literary setting that the condemned nations are not the intended audience of the prophecies; rather, the oracles are directed to Israel, or, more specifically, to a Judean audience. Hambourg identifies several reasons for the punishment of the nations in chs. 13–23, including Judah's reliance on or alliance with the nation (14:28-32; 15–16; 19:1-15; 18:1-6), hubris on the part of the nation (15–16; 23:1-12; cf. 10:5-19; 37:22-29; 13:1–14:23), or an attempt to take action against Judah (14:25b; 17:1-6, 9-11). This interpretation indicates that the purpose of YHWH's actions is not to punish the nations for some sort of crime or wrongdoing. Rather, the references to YHWH's leadership of the enemy forces and defeat of the nations (13:2-22; 17:12-14; 19:1-15), YHWH's announcements of the time of punishment (16:13-14; 21:16-17; 23:17-18), and YHWH's rule over the nations (18:7; 19:16-25; 23:18) indicate that the purpose of the collection of PROPHECIES CONCERNING FOREIGN NATIONS is to announce the imposition of YHWH's rule in the world.

Setting

The prophecies concerning the foreign nations in chs. 13–23 clearly function in relation to the final 5th-century form of the book of Isaiah insofar as it announces YHWH's punishment of the nations in preparation for the manifestation of divine sovereignty over the world (cf. 2:2-4; 65–66). When viewed in relation to its immediate literary setting as part of the structural block in chs. 5–27, the prophecies concerning the foreign nations in chs. 13–23 follow upon the prophecies concerning Israel in chs. 5–12 and precede the prophecies concerning worldwide upheaval at the inauguration of YHWH's world rule in chs. 24–27. Here it is noteworthy that the nations listed in chs. 13–23 — Babylon (and Philistia), Moab, Aram (and northern Israel), Egypt, Midbar Yam, Dumah, Arabia, Jerusalem, and Tyre — do not constitute a comprehensive catalog of all the world's nations; rather, they constitute the nations that were brought under Persian control in the latter part of the 6th century B.C.E. Insofar as the prophecies concerning foreign nations in chs. 13–23 are designed to announce YHWH's sovereignty over the world, the unit appears to equate YHWH's rule with that of Persia, that is, the establishment of Persian rule over these nations constitutes the establishment of YHWH's rule (cf. Kratz, *Kyros,* passim, who argues that the establishment of Cyrus's rule over the Babylonian empire in 539 manifests YHWH's sovereignty in Deutero-Isaiah). The announcement of the punishment of the nations in chs. 13–23 would presuppose the fall of Egypt to Cambyses in 525 and the internal instability that racked the Persian empire during the early years of Darius from 522 through the end of the 5th century. From the perspective of the final form of the book of Isaiah, such upheaval in the international arena would precede the final revelation of YHWH's sovereignty throughout the world.

Isaiah 13–23 appears to play a similar role in relation to the 6th-century edition of the book of Isaiah. As the following analyses of the individual subunits of these chapters will demonstrate, the pronouncement concerning Babylon in chs. 13–14 was the last of the *maśśā'ôt* to be completed in the late 6th century. All the others were completed earlier. The 6th-century composition of chs. 13–14 and the correlation of the superscriptions in 13:1 and 2:1 demonstrate that the present form of the pronouncement concerning Babylon was composed to be the head of the collection of prophecies concerning foreign nations for the 6th-century edition of the book of Isaiah. As the former international tyrant and leading symbol of opposition to YHWH's will, Babylon is properly placed at the head of the collection and followed by the other nations that submitted to Persia in the late 6th century. As in the 5th-century edition of the book, the imposition of Persian rule over these nations is equated with the establishment of YHWH's sovereignty in the world.

With the exception of the pronouncement concerning Babylon in chs. 13–14, all the prophecies concerning foreign nations in chs. 13–23 were composed in relation to the 7th-century Josianic edition of the book of Isaiah (chs. 15–16; 17–18; 19–20; 23) or in the late 8th or early 7th century (21:1-10, 11-12, 13-17; 22:1-25). This understanding would suggest that a collection of prophecies concerning foreign nations, including those concerning Moab, Damascus, Egypt, Midbar Yam, Dumah, Arabia, Jerusalem, and Tyre, constituted a component of the Josianic edition of Isaiah. As the following discussion of chs. 13–14 will demonstrate, the taunt song concerning the fall of the tyrant in 14:3-23 was originally written in reference to the death of the Assyrian monarch Sargon II in 705. It is difficult to say whether this song and the Philistine oracle in 14:28-32 were included in the Josianic collection. It seems likely that the oracle concerning Sargon was not included in this position since an oracle concerning the downfall of the Assyrian monarch appeared in 10:5-34 in the context of the Josianic edition of 10:5–12:6. The pronouncement concerning Philistia may well have introduced the Josianic collection, however, since its distinctive superscription, "in the year of the death of King Ahaz was this pronouncement," would distinguish it from the following pronouncements and set the collection in relation to the reign of King Ahaz, which appears to be the historical setting presupposed in the Josianic edition of chs. 5–12. As such, the superscription in 14:28 would correlate with the notice in 6:1, "in the year of the death of King Uzziah." Thus the collection would include nations that Josiah intended to subjugate (Philistia, Moab, Damascus, and northern Israel), a nation that constituted Josiah's major obstacle to his ambitions (Egypt), and a projected trading partner as in the days of David and Solomon (Tyre). Midbar Yam, Dumah, and Arabia would be included since these areas were among the first to be taken from the Assyrians in the mid-7th century, and Jerusalem would be included because it, too, had undergone the punishment of Assyrian occupation like all the other nations listed in the collection.

Although the pronouncements concerning Midbar Yam (21:1-10), Dumah (21:11-12), Arabia (21:13-17), and the Valley of Vision (ch. 22), along with major elements of the other pronouncements, appear to have been composed in the late 8th and early 7th century by Isaiah ben Amoz, there is no clear evidence that a collection of prophecies concerning foreign nations constituted a collection earlier than that of the Josianic edition of the book. The material was obviously available in some form, but that form cannot be specified with the evidence at hand.

Finally, scholars generally agree that the social setting of the prophecies concerning foreign nations appears to be in relation to war traditions in ancient Judah (for a summary of the discussion, see Petersen). Such oracles were apparently delivered prior to a battle either to encourage the Israelite/Judean warriors and the king that YHWH had delivered their enemies into their hands (Deut 20:1-4; 1 Kings 21) or as a means to curse enemies and to ensure their defeat (see Numbers 22–24; cf. A. Bentzen, "The Ritual Background of Amos i.2–ii.16," *OTS* 8 [1950] 85-99). With regard to the 8th-century setting of this material, it seems clear that Isaiah did not envision direct confrontations between Judah and nations such as Philistia, Moab, and Tyre. Rather, it seems that such oracles would function in relation to a confrontation between the nation in question and the Assyrian empire. Thus Isaiah likely delivered such oracles as a means to present the Judean monarch with his views of the likely fate of the nations that stood to be invaded by the Assyrians. In this regard, Isaiah likely used the individual prophecies concerning foreign nations as a means to advise the Judean monarch in international affairs. Such oracles would clearly have been employed to discourage alliance with foreign nations and confrontation with Assyria in keeping with Isaiah's isolationist views on Judean foreign policy (see Høgenhaven, "Prophet Isaiah").

Intention

Although it is frequently assumed that the prophecies concerning foreign nations in prophetic books represent YHWH's eschatological and universal world judgment (see Jenkins, esp. 250-51), a survey of the various collections of prophecies concerning foreign nations in the prophetic books indicates that they do not envision universal judgment. Rather, they are quite selective in their choice of nations and are governed by an underlying political agenda. Thus the oracles against the nations in Ezekiel 25–32 include those nations that were projected to be subjugated to the Babylonian empire in the 6th century, including Amon (Ezek 25:1-7), Moab (25:8-11), Edom (25:12-14), Philistia (25:15-17), Tyre (26:1–28:19), Sidon (28:20-23), Israel (28:24-26), and Egypt (29:1–32:32). The oracles in Jeremiah 46–51 include those that were anticipated to be conquered by Babylon, including Egypt (Jer 46:2-28), Philistia (47:1-7), Moab (48:1-47), Ammon (49:1-6), Edom (49:7-22), Damascus (49:23-27), Kedar and Hazor (49:28-33), and Elam (49:34-39), and culminate in the punishment of Babylon itself (50:1–51:64). Amos 1:3–2:16 includes those nations that were the enemies of or subject to the Jehu dynasty, culminating in a condemnation of Jeroboam II's kingdom of northern Israel itself. The list includes Aram (Amos 1:3-5), Philistia (1:6-8), Tyre (Amos 1:9-10), Edom (1:11-12), Ammon (1:13-15), Moab (2:1-3), Judah (2:4-5), and Israel (2:6-16). Zeph 2:4-15 includes those nations that were Josiah's major enemies or that Josiah intended to subjugate (see M. A. Sweeney, "A Form-Critical Reassessment of the Book of Zephaniah," *CBQ* 53 [1991] 388-408), including Philistia (Zeph 2:4-7), Moab and Ammon (2:8-11), Cush (2:12), and Assyria (2:13-15). Finally, Nahum does not represent universal judgment but presupposes the fall of Nineveh (see M. A. Sweeney, "Concerning the Structure and Generic Character of the Book of Nahum," *ZAW* 104 [1992] 364-77), and Obadiah apparently presupposes the fall of Edom in the 6th century. In each case, the punishment of the nations is portrayed as an act of YHWH for some particular political purpose.

When viewed in relation to their respective literary and historical settings in the book of Isaiah, the intentions of the various forms of the collections of prophecies concerning foreign nations become clear. As noted in the previous discussion of the setting of chs. 13–23, the 5th-century edition of these chapters clearly identifies the hegemony of the Persian empire over these nations with the realization of YHWH's sovereignty over the world from Zion. The manifestation of YHWH's rule is identified with that of the Persian empire and points to the eventual realization of YHWH's universal rule once the upheaval of 5th-century Persia has come to an end (cf. 2:2-4; 65–66).

As noted above, the 6th-century edition of the book of Isaiah provides a similar context for understanding the prophecies concerning foreign nations in relation to the emergence of the Persian empire under Cyrus and his early successors in the late 6th century. Persia's subjugation of the listed nations is identified with YHWH's rule and points to a similar scenario of divine sovereignty in the world.

Finally, the late-7th-century Josianic edition of the prophecies concerning foreign nations in 14:28–23:18 presupposes Josiah's political agenda and identifies it with YHWH's plans for the nations. Thus the collection looks forward to Josiah's subjugation of Philistia (14:28-32), Moab (chs. 15–16), and Aram and the territory of the former northern kingdom of Israel (chs. 17–18). It also looks forward to the defeat of Josiah's enemies, including Egypt (chs. 19–20) and Assyria, which suffered defeat in its eastern territories including Midbar Yam (21:1-10), Dumah (21:11-12), and Arabia (21:13-17). It anticipates trade relations with Tyre (ch. 23) as in the days of the early Davidic dynasty, and it presupposes punishment against the city of Jerusalem itself (ch. 22) as a necessary prelude to the realization of YHWH's (and Josiah's) plans. In short, the collection includes the nations that were subjected to Assyria during the 8th and 7th centuries. The Assyrian conquest of these nations is identified with YHWH's will to punish the nations and to prepare for the restoration of a new Davidic empire under Josiah.

Bibliography

→ bibliography at "Introduction to the Prophetic Literature" for Hayes, "Usage of Oracles"; Hoffmann, *Prophecies,* 75-107; and Petersen, "Oracles." P. C. Beentjes, "Oracles against the Nations: A Central Issue in the 'Latter Prophets,' " *BTFT* 50 (1989) 203-9; S. Erlandsson, *The Burden of Babylon: A Study of Isaiah 13:2–14:23* (ConBOT 4; Lund: Gleerup, 1970); J. B. Geyer, "Mythology and Culture in the Oracles Against the Nations," *VT* 36 (1986) 129-45; B. Gosse, "Oracles contre les nations et structures comparées des livres d'Isaïe et d'Ezéchiel," *BN* 54 (1990) 19-21; G. R. Hamborg, "Reasons for Judgement in the Oracles Against the Nations of the Prophet Isaiah," *VT* 31 (1981) 145-59; A. K. Jenkins, "The Development of the Isaiah Tradition in Isaiah 13–23," in *The Book of Isaiah/Le livre d'Isaïe* (ed. J. Vermeylen; BETL 81; Leuven: Leuven University Press and Peeters, 1989) 237-51.

PRONOUNCEMENT CONCERNING BABYLON WITH APPENDIX CONCERNING PHILISTIA, 13:1–14:32

Structure

I. Superscription	13:1
A. Title: pronouncement on Babylon	1a
B. Qualification	1b
II. Prophetic pronouncement *(maśśā')* proper	13:2–14:27
A. Prophetic summons to war	13:2-5
1. Summons proper	2
2. Motivation	3-5
a. Statement by YHWH concerning summons of warriors	3
b. Prophetic explanation: description of YHWH's army gathered to ravage the earth	4-5
B. Prophetic announcement of Day of YHWH with application to Babylon and Israel	13:6–14:23
1. Command to wail	13:6-8
a. Command proper with reason: coming of Day of YHWH	6
b. Consequences of Day of YHWH: basic statement	7-8
1) Weakening of hands and heart	7
2) Comparison to birth pangs	8a
3) Astonishment of people	8b
2. Announcement of Day of YHWH	9-16
a. Announcement proper by prophet	9
1) Concerning the character of coming Day of YHWH: wrath	9a
2) Concerning the purpose of coming Day of YHWH: destruction	9b
a) Of land	9bα
b) Of sinners	9bβ
b. Statement by YHWH concerning actions	10-12
1) Concerning celestial bodies: cessation of light	10
2) Concerning the earth: punishment of wicked and proud	11
3) Concerning human beings: decimation	12
c. Prophetic elaboration concerning consequences of YHWH's actions	13-16
1) Basic statement: shaking of cosmos	13
2) Specific statement: suffering of human beings	14-16
a) Comparison to frightened gazelle and straying sheep	14a
b) Attempted flight by humans	14b
c) Slaughter of humans	15-16

As noted in the overview discussion of chs. 13–23, the structure of these chapters is determined by the repeated use of the formula *maśśā'* PN, "Pronouncement of PN," which introduces each of the constituent subunits of the oracles against the nations in this section. Consequently, this subunit begins with the superscription "The pronouncement concerning Babylon that Isaiah the son of Amoz perceived" in 13:1 and ends with the superscription "The pronouncement of Moab" in 15:1, which introduces the next subunit. The appearance of the superscription "In the year of the death of the King Ahaz, there was this pronouncement" in 14:28 does not indicate the beginning of a new subunit independent from the preceding material. Although it refers to a prophetic pronouncement *(maśśā')*, it does not correspond to the standard form of the title in chs. 13–23 (cf. 13:1; 15:1; 17:1; 19:1; 21:1, 11, 13; 22:1; 23:1). Instead, its formulation with an introductory temporal clause corresponds to that of the introductory temporal statement in 20:1 (cf. 6:1; 7:1) and indicates that 14:28-32 is to be subsumed into the structure of the preceding material. Although the pronouncement contained in 14:28-32 pertains to Philistia and not to Babylon, the discussion of the intent of this passage will demonstrate that 14:28-32 was included as an appendix to the pronouncement of Babylon to demonstrate the assertion that YHWH's intention to punish Assyria is applied to all the nations (14:26) and to demonstrate that YHWH alone will protect Zion (14:32; cf. 14:25). Consequently, the present unit comprises 13:1–14:32.

The first major subunit of this text is the superscription in 13:1. Although the balance of the text following a superscription normally constitutes the second major structural subunit, the present case is exceptional because of the presence of the subordinate superscription in 14:28. Consequently, there are two further structural subunits in this text: the pronouncement proper in 13:2–14:27 and the appendix concerning Philistia in 14:28-32.

This text is an example of the *maśśā'* or pronouncement genre, which has no prescribed structure. As Weis's study of the genre indicates, the *maśśā'* is a specific type of prophetic discourse that employs a variety of literary elements to explain how YHWH's intentions are manifested in human affairs. Consequently, the genre's explanatory function greatly influences the structure and presentation of its individual examples. The problem in interpreting such texts concerns how to identify what conclusion one is to draw from the material presented. Weis's study of this text (pp. 105-9) presupposes that its intention is to assert that the Median attack against Babylon is an act of YHWH. This may be true in a general sense, particularly in relation to the Babylonian material in 13:1–14:23 or even its supposed "original form" in 13:1-22, but Weis's exclusion of 14:24-27 and 28-32 in the present form of this text misses some important points. Not only is the Median invasion of Babylon an act of YHWH in human affairs, but it is predicated on YHWH's promise to destroy the enemy Assyria in YHWH's own land (vv. 24-25) and the application of this promise to the entire earth and all nations in it (v. 26). Furthermore, the implementation of this promise demonstrates YHWH's sovereignty over the entire world, as indicated by both vv. 24-27 (esp. vv. 26-27) and vv. 28-32 (esp. v. 32). In this respect, 13:1–14:32 is analogous to the example of the *maśśā'* genre in Habakkuk 1–2, which employs quotations by YHWH interspersed with prophetic explanations (Hab 1:2–2:5), a taunt song (against the king of Babylon, Hab 2:6-17), and a conclusion in order to point not only to YHWH's efficacy in the world but also to YHWH's sovereignty over the entire earth (Hab 2:18-20; cf. M. A. Sweeney, "Structure, Genre, and Intent in the Book of Habakkuk," *VT* 41 [1991] 63-83).

In the present case, the intention to demonstrate YHWH's world sovereignty is accomplished by the use of the Day of YHWH motif as a means for announcing the Median assault against Babylon as an act of YHWH. Consequently, the structure of the *maśśā'* proper in 13:2–14:27 is influenced by both its explanatory function and the announcement of the Day of YHWH.

The first major subunit of 13:2–14:27 is the prophetic summons to war in 13:2-5. This unit is distinguished by its introductory masculine plural imperative verbs in v. 2 that call for signals to an unidentified party that is to be admitted into the "noble gates." Although the verses that constitute this unit lack syntactical connections and shift speakers, the contents indicate that vv. 3-5 should be grouped together with v. 2, since they identify the unnamed party that is to be admitted into the "noble gates." Although the identity of the "noble gates" is not made clear in this passage, the following material in vv. 3-5 identifies the party to be admitted as YHWH's army that is being mustered for war against the entire earth. That they are being signaled for admission into the noble gates indicates that the addressee of the plural imperative verbs is a group that is to benefit from the presence of this army. This identification is in contrast to the addressees of the masculine plural imperative verb in v. 6 who are commanded to wail. They are thereby identified as the victims of YHWH's army, indicating the beginning of a new subunit.

The structure of vv. 2-5 falls into two primary parts. V. 2 constitutes the summons proper as indicated by its imperative formulation. Neither speaker nor addressee is identified, although it seems likely that either YHWH or the prophet speaks in imitation of a typical summons to sentries to signal and to admit an approaching friendly army. Vv. 3-5 provide the motivation for the enigmatic summons and explain its meaning. V. 3 contains a 1st-person statement by YHWH indicating that YHWH has summoned warriors. Vv. 4-5 contain an explanation by the prophet describing the approaching party as a gathering of nations assembled by YHWH for war against the entire earth.

The second major subunit of the *maśśā'* proper is 13:6–14:23, which constitutes the prophetic announcement of the Day of YHWH with application to Babylon and Israel. The unit is held together by a combination of thematic and formal features. It is concerned throughout with the Day of YHWH (13:6, 9; 14:3) and that Day's effects on Babylon (13:17-22; 14:3-23) and Israel (14:1-2). Furthermore, the introductory *kî*, "but," in 14:2 and the formula *wĕhāyâ bĕyôm*, "and it shall come to pass in the day that," in 14:3 provide a syntactical connection between 14:1-2 and 14:3-23 and the preceding material. The structure of the passage indicates its purpose, which is both to announce the Day of YHWH and to explain its significance for Babylon and, to a lesser extent, for Israel.

The first part of the subunit 13:6–14:23 is the command to wail in 13:6-8. The imperative verb *hêlîlû*, "wail," in v. 6 marks its beginning, and the introductory *hinnēh* of v. 9 marks the beginning of the next part. V. 6 contains the command proper together with the reason for the command: that the Day of YHWH is coming. Vv. 7-8 then describe the consequences of the Day of YHWH as indicated by their introductory *'al-kēn*, "therefore." The consequences are described in general terms in comparison to the following detailed description and include the weakening of hands and heart, indicating fear (v. 7); a comparison to birth pangs, indicating pain (v. 8a); and a statement concerning the astonishment of the people, indicating distress (v. 8b).

The second part of the subunit 13:6–14:23 is the prophetic announcement of the Day of YHWH in 13:9-16. The introductory *hinnēh*, "behold," marks the beginning of this section, and the introductory *hinnēnî* in v. 17 marks the beginning of the next. Isa 13:9-16 falls into three parts. The announcement proper appears in v. 9, which characterizes the Day of YHWH as a day of wrath (v. 9a) and defines its purpose as destruction (v. 9b) for both the land (v. 9bα) and its sinners (v. 9bβ). This serves as the basis for the second part, vv. 10-12, which contains a statement by YHWH concerning action against the world and human beings. This section is introduced by the conjunctive and causative *kî*, "for, because," and includes YHWH's statements concerning the celestial bodies, i.e., the cessation of light (v. 10); the world, i.e., the punishment of the wicked and proud (v. 11); and human beings, who are to be decimated (v. 12). Although the character of v. 10 as a speech by YHWH is not immediately clear, the following converted perfect 1st-person verb *ûpāqadtî*, "and I shall visit/punish," in v. 11 identifies it as such. Consequently, YHWH's statement in vv. 10-12 specifies v. 9 in that it encompasses the punishment of the entire world and the human beings who dwell therein. Vv. 13-16 then contain the prophet's elaboration on the consequences of YHWH's actions as indicated by the introductory *'al-kēn*, "therefore." V. 13 contains the basic statement that heaven and earth will shake because of YHWH's wrath. Vv. 14-16 then specify this statement in relation to the suffering that will take place, as indicated by the introductory *wĕhāyâ*, "and it shall be." First, v. 14a compares the situation of the people to that of a frightened gazelle or straying sheep. V. 14b then describes the people's attempt to flee. Finally, vv. 15-16 describe the slaughter of the people, including that of the men (v. 15) and the fate of their children, homes, and wives (v. 16).

The third major section of the subunit 13:6–14:23 is the prophet's application of the Day of YHWH to Babylon and Israel in 13:17–14:23. The section is introduced by the introductory *hinnēnî*, "behold, I," in 3:17. As noted above, 14:1-2 is joined syntactically by its introductory *kî*, and 14:3-23 is joined by the introductory formula *wĕhāyâ bĕyôm*. Altogether, this material explains the implications of the Day of YHWH for both Babylon and Israel.

The application proper appears in 13:17–14:2. Isa 13:17-22 focuses on Babylon first by describing the Median invasion that the city will suffer. This section begins with YHWH's announcement that "I am arousing the Medes against them" (vv. 17-18). This announcement contains both YHWH's basic statement in v. 17a and the specification of the Medes' qualities in vv. 17b-18, including their disregard for wealth (v. 17b) and their disregard for human life (v. 18). The prophet's explanatory announcement concerning the consequences for Babylon then appears in vv. 19-22, introduced by the formula *wĕhāyĕtâ bābel*, "and Babylon shall become." The pun on v. 19, "and Babylon, splendor [*ṣĕbî*] of the kingdoms, shall be . . . like God's overthrowing . . . ," in the prophet's speech in v. 14, "and it shall be like a frightened gazelle [*ṣĕbî*]," establishes that the prophet is the speaker here. The prophet begins with the basic statement that Babylon shall become like Sodom and Gomorrah in v. 19 and continues with specifications in vv. 20-22. Babylon will no longer exist (v. 20a); bedouin and shepherds will not even stay there (v. 20b); wild beasts and owls will stay there (v. 21a); ostriches and goats will stay there (v. 21b); jackals and serpents will announce themselves in the palaces (v. 22a); and finally, Babylon's time has come (v. 22b). In 14:1-2, the prophet then turns to the consequences for Israel. This 3rd-person statement about YHWH's actions is joined to the preceding material by an explanatory *kî*, "for, but," which here contrasts Israel's experience to that of Babylon. These verses are constituted as a *wāw*-consecutive series of statements concerning Israel's future. They project YHWH's restoration of Israel and its resident aliens to the land of Israel (14:1), and Israel's rule over the nations that formerly oppressed it.

The prophetic instruction to utter a taunt song against the king of Babylon in 14:3-23 is clearly marked by its narrative introduction in vv. 3-4a. It is related to the preceding material in 13:17–14:2 by the conjunctive *wĕhāyâ bĕyôm hānîaḥ yhwh,* "and it shall come to pass in the day that YHWH gives rest," but it is distinguished by its 2nd-person singular address form, apparently directed to Israel. The end of the unit is somewhat difficult to specify due to the shift to the imperative plural address in 14:21 and the oracular statements by YHWH in vv. 22-23, which appear to disrupt the taunt song addressed to the king of Babylon in 2nd-person singular form. Nevertheless, the references to the sons of the king of Babylon in v. 21 and v. 22 tie this material to the taunt song, especially to v. 20b, which pertains to the king's posterity. Furthermore, although vv. 22-23 may well be a later addition (see below on Setting), the references to Babylon (as opposed to the king) and its ruin relate the taunt to the material in 13:17-22. These concluding verses reinforce the character of the song as a taunt, despite its formulation as a dirge.

Following the narrative introduction in 14:3-4a, the taunt song proper appears in vv. 4b-23. The structure of the song is thematically defined by a progression of images that focus on the cessation of the oppressor and culminate in the slaughter of his sons and the ruin of Babylon.

The first subsection of this taunt song is vv. 4b-6, which present a dirge for the end of the oppressor. It is formulated with an introductory *'êk,* "how," which is typical of dirges in ancient Israelite literature. The unit includes the dirge statement proper in v. 4b and a specification in vv. 5-6, which concerns YHWH's breaking the rod of the oppressor (v. 5) and an identification of the rod with the oppressive qualities of the king who wielded it (v. 6).

The imagery shifts to the earth in vv. 7-8, which report the reaction of the trees. This imagery is particularly apt since both the Assyrian and the Babylonian kings were known for their policies of felling trees to send back to the homeland for building purposes (*ANET,* 276, 307). V. 7a portrays the earth at rest now that the oppressor is gone, and vv. 7b-8 portray the rejoicing of the trees. Vv. 7b-8a report the trees' rejoicing, and v. 8b quotes their statement of relief that the cutter will not come now that the king is dead.

Verses 9-17 report the scene that takes place in Sheol in reaction to the arrival of the king. V. 9 reports Sheol's rousing of the dead kings, and vv. 10-15 report their address to the Babylonian king. Following the address formula in v. 10a, the address proper follows in vv. 10b-15 in the form of a taunt. It begins with a statement concerning the Babylonian king's entry into Sheol, which indicates that he is no different from the dead kings despite his former glory (vv. 10b-11). A mocking comparison then follows in vv. 12-14, which employ a dirge statement, introduced by *'êk,* that contrasts the current low state of the Babylonian king (v. 12) with a quotation of his pretensions to set himself higher than God (vv. 13-14). V. 15 reiterates and emphasizes his entry into Sheol by contrasting his present situation in "the furthest reaches of the pit" (*yarkĕtê bôr*) against his pretension to ascend to "the furthest reaches of the north" (*bĕyarkĕtê ṣāpôn,* v. 13b). The north was the mythological home of the gods in ancient Near Eastern thought. Vv. 16-17 return to the portrayal of the scene in Sheol and summarize the encounter by referring to the staring of those who see the king (v. 16a) and their rhetorical question, which reinforces the low state to which he has descended.

Verses 18-20 shift images to focus on the denial of the Babylonian king's legacy. This section begins with vv. 18-19, which are linked by a conjunctive *waw* and contrast the image of the kings of the nations in their tombs (v. 18) against that of the Babylonian king expelled from his grave. This is followed by statements that he shall not be united with the other kings in the grave (v. 20a) and that he will be eternally denied a name (i.e., remembrance) on account of his "corrupt seed."

The final section in vv. 21-23 seizes on this last statement, which it understands as a reference to the king's descendants, in order to present a command to prepare a sacrifice for his sons. The imperative plural form of this command is clearly not addressed to the king, but one must keep in mind that the beginning of the taunt is likewise addressed to a party other than the king. In its present position, this command provides an apt conclusion to the taunt, in that it assures that the king will lack posterity, thus returning to the introductory statement that the oppressor has ceased *(šābat)* in v. 4b. It further reinforces the mocking character of this dirge by culminating in a call for the slaughter of his sons rather than a call to mourn for his loss. The command appears in v. 21, which includes the command proper (v. 21a) and defines its purpose as the prevention of his sons' establishment in the world (v. 21b). Three oracular utterances by YHWH are appended by conversive *wāw*s in vv. 22-23, each of which is defined by the oracular formula *nĕ'um yhwh,* "utterance of YHWH." They include 1st-person statements that YHWH will rise against them (v. 22a), cut off posterity for Babylon (v. 22b), and make Babylon a ruin (v. 23). The imagery of these statements and the focus on Babylon relate the taunt song to the previous material concerning Babylon in 13:17-22.

The concluding section of the *maśśā'* proper in 13:2–14:27 is the summary-appraisal in 14:24-27. This subunit is clearly demarcated by its introductory IMPRECATION FORMULA, which is syntactically independent from the preceding material, and its focus on Assyria, not Babylon. The importance of this section is realized in its relation to the preceding *maśśā'* concerning Babylon that emphasizes the final conclusion to be drawn from YHWH's action in history, namely, that YHWH's oath against Assyria has been applied to all the nations. The invasion against Babylon, "the splendor of the kingdoms" (13:19), demonstrates YHWH's activity just as the overthrow of Sodom and Gomorrah testified to YHWH's actions long before. The section falls into two major parts. Vv. 24-25 constitute the report of YHWH's oath concerning the overthrow of Assyria, including an oath report formula in v. 24a and the oath proper in vv. 24b-25 (which include the oath formula in v. 24b and the content of the oath in v. 25). Vv. 26-27 constitute the second major section, the summary-appraisal, which applies YHWH's oath against Assyria to all the nations. The summary-appraisal proper appears in v. 26, which states that YHWH's decision is fixed for the entire earth (v. 26a) and that YHWH's hand is stretched out against all the nations (v. 26b). The basis appears in v. 27 with a causative *kî* and indicates that YHWH's decision is set and cannot be challenged.

The final section of this unit is the appendix in 14:28-32, which contains the *maśśā'* concerning Philistia. Although this *maśśā'* was clearly originally independent from the present context, its placement here is due not so much to concern for Philistia as to concern with the essential conclusion of this oracle, i.e., that YHWH will establish Zion. Following on the material concerning the destruction of Babylon and the oath against Assyria, the Philistine *maśśā'* emphasizes that YHWH's purpose in destroying these nations is to establish Zion as the home for YHWH's people.

The unit begins with the superscription in 14:28, followed by the *maśśā'* proper in 14:29-32. The *maśśā'* is cast in the form of an order concerning Philistine rejoicing at the fall of an oppressor. The order includes both negative and positive formulations that have the same purpose. The negative formulation appears in vv. 29-30 as a prohibition against rejoicing. The prohibition proper appears in v. 29a as a negative imperative addressed to Philistia not to rejoice over the fall of the oppressor. The reason appears in vv. 29b-30 in that another oppressor will follow the first. The positive formulation appears in vv. 31-32 as a call for communal complaint together with a consequential instruction concerning the gentile embassy. The call for communal complaint proper in v. 32 includes the typical elements of the form: a series of imperatives in v. 31a constitutes the command to wail addressed to the Philistines, and the causal statement introduced by *kî* in v. 31b provides the reason for wailing in that an enemy approaches from the north. V. 32 is connected by a *wāw* that expresses the consequence of this call, i.e., the answer that is to be given to the gentile embassy. A rhetorical question in v. 32a precedes the answer in v. 32b. YHWH will establish Zion so that the people may take refuge there. The meaning of this enigmatic oracle will be discussed in detail below.

Genre

As the discussion of setting demonstrates, chs. 13–14 are clearly a composite unit that was edited into its present form in the latter part of the 6th century. Nevertheless, it has been shaped according to a consistent generic pattern known as the *maśśā'* or PROPHETIC PRONOUNCEMENT. The identification of the entire unit as a *maśśā'* is reinforced by the SUPERSCRIPTION in 13:1, which stands apart from the following material in 13:2–14:32 and characterizes it as such (on superscriptions, see Tucker, "Prophetic Superscriptions").

In his thorough discussion of the *maśśā'*, Weis argues that it is a specific type of prophetic discourse designed to identify YHWH's intentions manifested in human affairs. It is based in and presupposes a revelatory experience of a prophet, such as a vision or audition. It has no fixed structure and may be composed of a number of diverse generic elements. Inasmuch as the genre is founded on a revelatory experience and attempts to explain manifestations of YHWH's activity in human affairs based on that experience, examples of the genre frequently contain a mixture of statements by YHWH and explanatory or elaborative material by the prophet.

In their present form, chs. 13–14 conform to the general characteristics of the *maśśā'* genre. Statements by YHWH appear in 13:3, 10-12, 17-18; 14:22-23 and 24-25, together with the prophet's explanations of the meanings of these statements. Furthermore, the structure of the unit is designed to facilitate its explanatory purpose. The announcement of the Day of YHWH and its implications for the destruction of Babylon and the restoration of Israel, together with the TAUNT SONG against the king of Babylon, lead to the final conclusions to be drawn from this material in 14:24-27 and 28-32. Vv. 24-27 state that YHWH's OATH concerning the overthrow of Assyria is applied to all the nations of which Babylon was perceived as the leader. Vv. 28-32 state that YHWH will found Zion as the refuge for the people.

A number of additional generic entities are subordinated to this overarching generic pattern in the present form of the text. Although the *maśśā'* defines the genre of the entirety of the present form of chs. 13–14, it appears to have grown out of an original *maśśā'* in 13:2-22 to which additional texts have been added. Isa 13:2-22 displays the basic characteristics of the *maśśā'* in its mixture of statements by YHWH and explanatory material by the prophet concerning the significance of the Day of YHWH against Babylon. In this more limited context, the purpose of the *maśśā'* appears to differ somewhat from that of 13:1–14:32. Whereas the larger text focuses on the application of the Assyrian model to Babylon and the foundation of Zion, 13:2-22 focuses strictly on the Median invasion of Babylon as an act of YHWH. The structure of the unit is designed to heighten the dramatic tension, and thus the impact, of this assertion on the reader or hearer by withholding the identification of the Medes and Babylon until the last portion of the oracle in 13:17-22.

The constituent elements of vv. 2-22 appear to be designed to function in relation to its *maśśā'* pattern. Prior to vv. 17-22, the oracle employs very general language and several other generic forms to prepare the reader for its climactic conclusion. The prophetic SUMMONS TO WAR appears to be a prophetic imitation of the standard SUMMONS TO WAR genre. It employs a form of mobilization call in v. 2, and the motivation in vv. 3-5 certainly contains an element of an (→) announcement of judgment. The mobilization call is directed not to the warriors but to an unidentified audience that is instructed to admit the warriors into "the noble gates," presumably a reference to the city of the addressees. Likewise, the motivation itself (vv. 3-5) appears in the form of a description to the same addressees, not to the warriors themselves, in that it is designed to explain that YHWH's army has been gathered to punish the entire earth. Likewise, the announcement concerning the Day of YHWH is expressed in very general terms that portray destruction against the entire earth/land (*hā'āreṣ*, v. 9), world (*tēbēl*, v. 11), or even cosmos (*šamayim/hā'āreṣ*, v. 13; cf. v. 10). The COMMAND to wail in v. 6 appears to be based in the typical CALL TO A PUBLIC COMPLAINT SERVICE, in that it includes the imperative *hêlîlî*, "wail," and the motivation, but it lacks the specific addressee typical of the form.

The INSTRUCTION to utter a TAUNT SONG over the king of Babylon in 14:3-23 reinforces the overall interest in restoration for Israel and the overthrow of Babylon as an act of YHWH. The TAUNT SONG itself in vv. 4b-23 is cast in the form of a DIRGE, the ostensible purpose of which is to mourn the death of the Babylonian king. In this respect, the TAUNT SONG displays a number of characteristic features of the DIRGE, including the particle *'êk*, "how, alas" (vv. 4b, 12), the 3/2 *qînâ* meter, and comparisons of the past glory of the monarch with his present tragedy. Nevertheless, a number of deviations from the (→) dirge form demonstrate that the song's intention is to mock or taunt the Babylonian king. The song does not present the merits of the deceased, but instead focuses on his crimes and failures as a monarch insofar as he abused his land and people (v. 20). Furthermore, the song lacks the imperatives for mourning that are typical of the genre. In fact, the song does not call for mourning at all, although there may be an intentional pun between the name given to the monarch in v. 12, *hêlēl*, "shining one," and the imperative form for "wail," *hêlîlû* or *hêlîlî* (cf. 13:6; 14:31). An imperative does appear toward the end of the song (*hākînû*, "prepare," v. 21), but this refers to the preparation of the slaughter of his sons. The concluding images of the king cast out of his tomb with no posterity express the intention of the TAUNT to portray the king as less than those who are dead. Finally, the oracular speeches by YHWH in vv. 22-23 remind the reader of the relation of the TAUNT SONG to the overall *maśśā'* by emphasizing Babylon and not the king alone as the object of YHWH's actions.

As noted above, the SUMMARY-APPRAISAL in 14:24-27 points to the essential conclusion that is to be drawn from the preceding material, namely, that YHWH's OATH against Assyria has been applied to the nations at large and Babylon in particular. The passage begins with a quotation of YHWH's OATH to destroy Assyria, introduced with the characteristic IMPRECATION FORMULA, *'im-lō'*, "if not, certainly." The SUMMARY-APPRAISAL proper appears in vv. 26-27, introduced by the demonstrative *zō't*, "this," which is typical of the form. The didactic character and wisdom background of the SUMMARY-APPRAISAL are evident in the use of the demonstrative to point to YHWH's OATH as the essential lesson to be drawn with regard to YHWH's activities among the nations.

Finally, the subordinate *maśśā'* concerning Philistia in 14:28-32 contributes to the overall *maśśā'* pattern by pointing to YHWH's foundation of Zion as an essential lesson to be drawn from YHWH's activities in relation to Babylon. The ORACLE is introduced by a SUPERSCRIPTION in v. 28 that characterizes the following as a *maśśā'* and employs a date formula to place it at the time of the death of Ahaz. The *maśśā'* itself in vv. 29-32 is cast in the form of an ORDER that includes both a PROHIBITION against rejoicing at the downfall of an unnamed oppressor (vv. 29-30) and a COMMAND to wail (v. 31). The latter is an example of a CALL TO A PUBLIC COMPLAINT SERVICE and presupposes the formalized lamentation of the community at the approach of an invader. It contains the typical elements of the form, including imperatives to wail, cry out, etc., an identification of the addressee, "all of you, Philistia," and the motivation for lamentation. The essential point of the *maśśā'* is expressed as the answer to a RHETORICAL QUESTION in v. 32, thus "for YHWH will found [*RSV* 'has founded'] Zion and his humble people will take refuge in it." This statement likely presupposes the revelatory experience of the prophet. The formulation *ûmah-ya'ăneh*, "and what shall he answer," is typically associated with prophetic *maśśā'ôt* (Jer 23:35, 37; Hab 2:1; cf. Weis, 111) to indicate YHWH's message.

Setting

Isaiah 13:1–14:32 is clearly a composite text. The present form of the text contains a number of tensions indicating that these chapters were not composed at the same time and on a single occasion. Rather, they contain a number of texts that were composed in relation to settings other than the present context and were later edited into their present form.

Tension within 13:1–14:32 appears first of all in the relationship between 13:1-22 and the balance of the unit. Isa 13:1-22 focuses on the Median invasion of Babylon in relation to the Day of YHWH and YHWH's punishment of the entire earth. This material does not address the situation of Israel, yet 14:1-2 breaks in with a rather awkward transition introduced by *kî,* "but," which focuses on YHWH's mercy to Israel and promise to restore Israel to the land with the nations as its servants. Although the restoration of Israel is a fitting consequence for the destruction of Babylon in biblical literature, it is striking that this concern appears immediately following a text that speaks only of world destruction and in no way raises the issue of Israel's fate, much less YHWH's mercy to Israel. Instead, 14:1-2 appears to be a transitional text that provides a basis for the following instruction to utter a taunt song for the king of Babylon. The mention of Israel in vv. 1-2 provides an identification for the anonymous "you" to whom the instruction in vv. 3-4a is addressed, and YHWH's mercy to Israel provides an occasion for the temporal reference that introduces the passage.

Second, tension also appears in relation to the taunt song passage in 14:3-23. The taunt song itself in vv. 4b-23 employs 2nd-person masculine singular forms to address the "oppressor," the king of Babylon (cf. v. 4a). Although the condemnation of the Babylonian king should occasion no surprise in relation to the threats against Babylon expressed in 13:1-22, it is again striking that the Babylonian king is nowhere mentioned in the preceding material, especially when one considers the transitional material in 14:1-2. The taunt song returns to the subject of Babylon itself in the concluding verses (22-23), but this material is somewhat awkward in the present context. The oracular speeches by YHWH in vv. 22-23 disrupt the taunt by making threats rather than focusing on the king's present low state. Furthermore, they are concerned not so much with the king of Babylon as with his sons and with Babylon itself. The latter point is especially curious when one considers that one of the king's main crimes was to bring his land low and to slay his people (v. 20). It appears somewhat odd that these verses would focus on the ruin of Babylon until one observes that the images used for Babylon's ruin in vv. 22-23 (the death of posterity, the habitation of hedgehogs, pools of water, etc.) correspond to the images of Babylon's destruction in 13:17-22. It would seem, then, that 14:22-23 were added to the taunt song in order to relate it to the general context of the destruction of Babylon in 13:1-22.

A third indication of tension appears in relation to 14:24-27, which is directed against Assyria and makes no mention of Babylon at all. Not only does the focus of attention center on Assyria, but YHWH's oath includes a promise to destroy Assyria "in my land" and "on my mountains" (v. 25). These phrases presumably refer to the land of Israel. The preceding material portrays the destruction of Babylon as the result of a foreign invasion of Babylon itself, not in relation to Babylonian incursions into the land of Israel.

Finally, the *maśśā'* concerning Philistia in vv. 28-32 has no overt connection to the preceding material on Babylon or Assyria. It is even demarcated by its own superscription in v. 28.

These tensions indicate that 13:1–14:32 is composed of texts that were originally independent of their present context: 13:2-22; 14:3-21; 14:24-27; and 14:28-32. Transitional material appears in 14:1-2 and 14:22-23. Each of these texts will need to be examined in order to determine the respective setting of its composition.

Isaiah 13:2-22 is frequently considered as a series of prophetic fragments (e.g., Clements, *Isaiah 1–39*, 132-38), but there is little basis for dividing the passage in this fashion. The *maśśā'* genre here presents a progressive series of images that lead to the final conclusion that the Median invasion of Babylon represents an act of YHWH identified with the Day of YHWH tradition. The decisive criterion for dating this passage is the mention of the Medes' attack against Babylon in v. 17. Although scholars frequently appeal to the role of the Assyrian monarchs as kings of Babylon in attempts to assign this passage to the general period of the prophet Isaiah (e.g., Erlandsson, 164-65), there is little reason for the prophet to disguise his condemnation of an Assyrian monarch in this fashion. The passage betrays no indication that Babylon is ruled by an Assyrian monarch and suggests that Babylon itself is to be punished as a perpetrator of sins, not the victim of Assyrian aggression (v. 9). Furthermore, on no occasion in the late 8th or even the 7th century did the Medes invade Babylon, even when the Assyrian monarchs controlled the region. Rather, Media was frequently Babylon's ally throughout this period in Babylonian attempts to resist or overthrow Assyrian power. Indeed, the Medes aided Babylon in the attack and eventual conquest of Assyria in the late 7th century. Babylon and Media became enemies only after the beginning of the 6th century, when Nebuchadrezzar established the Neo-Babylonian empire as the major power of the region, thereby becoming a threat to the Medes. Only after Cyrus established Achaemenid rule over both Media and Persia did a Median invasion of Babylonia begin, in the mid-6th century. The oracle does not consider the overthrow of Babylon to be an established fact (contra Gosse, *Isaïe 13,1–14,23,* 13), but it anticipates the Median victory over Babylon. The portrayal of bloodthirsty Medes (vv. 17-18) certainly contrasts with Achaemenid policy concerning Babylon following Cyrus's ascension to the Babylonian throne in 539 (see the Cyrus Cylinder, *ANET,* 315-16; cf. A. Kuhrt, "The Cyrus Cylinder and Achaemenid Imperial Policy," *JSOT* 25 [1983] 83-97). Consequently, Isa 13:2-22 must date to the period after Cyrus's invasion of Babylonia in 545 but prior to his peaceful occupation of the city in 539. This *maśśā'* was apparently the product of a prophet who interpreted the significance of the Median invasion for his contemporaries. The similarities to 2:6-21 indicate that this prophet was part of the Isaianic circle that continued to transmit and to develop Isaiah's prophecies in relation to contemporary events.

The transitional function of 14:1-2 indicates that this text presupposes both 13:2-22 and 14:3-23. Its portrayal of Israel's restoration corresponds most closely to that of texts dating to the late 6th century, during the period of the initial return from Babylonian exile and the building of the Second Temple. Thus the image of gentiles returning Israel to its homeland and becoming subject to Israel corresponds to 49:22-26 and particularly to the material in chs. 60–62 (esp. 60:10-14; 61:5-6). The concern with resident aliens joining Israel likewise corresponds to Zech 8:20-23. Thus this text may be assigned to redactional activity in the late 6th century.

The last two verses of Isa 14:3-23 are clearly designed to link the taunt song against the king of Babylon to the *maśśā'* concerning Babylon in 13:2-22. Isa 14:22-23 presupposes both 13:2-22 and 14:3-21 and, like 14:1-2, assists in joining the taunt song to 13:2-22. Nevertheless, these verses appear to relate more closely to 13:2-22 than to 14:1-2, inasmuch as they call for the destruction of Babylon rather than the restoration of Israel. Consequently, while the redactional activity that placed them at the end of the taunt song dates to the late 6th century, they appear to have been composed in relation to 13:2-22 and may even have formed part of the *maśśā'* against Babylon. They therefore date to the mid-6th century.

The primary issue in the dating of 14:3-21 is to identify the king addressed in the taunt song. The problem has been exacerbated by the anonymity of the song and has resulted in a wide variety of identifications, including not only the kings of Babylon but also those of Assyria and even Alexander the Great (cf. Wildberger, *Jesaja,* 543). Although the introduction to the song clearly identifies the addressee as a king of Babylon, scholars have been unable to agree on a suitable Babylonian candidate. Of the Babylonian kings, only Nebuchadrezzar achieved the greatness and power that would stand behind the arrogant boasting portrayed in vv. 13-14, but he is rejected because his son Amel-Merodach succeeded him to the throne after his death in 562. Furthermore, there is no indication that his body was ever desecrated in the manner described in vv. 18-19. A number of scholars have noted that the song itself in vv. 4b-21 never mentions the king of Babylon, and that the only reference to the monarch appears in the song's introduction (vv. 3-4a). Consequently, vv. 3-4a are identified as an editorial addition designed to link the song to its present literary context. Once vv. 3-4a are dismissed, the way becomes clear to identify the subject of the song as an Assyrian monarch and thereby to ascribe the song to Isaiah.

The most cogent proposal is to identify the monarch as Sargon II, whose body apparently was abandoned after he was killed in battle (Ginsberg, "Reflexes," 50; Barth, 136-40). One difficulty with this proposal is that it seems to require that vv. 3-4a be an editorial addition. Although vv. 3-4a clearly relate to the relief from oppression mentioned in vv. 1-2, the transition from 3rd-person report in vv. 1-2 to 2nd-person address is rather abrupt, indicating that these verses are not well integrated into the present context. Nevertheless, the identification with Sargon presents the most satisfactory solution to the problem possible. Sargon's arrogant boasting is well attested and appears to stand behind the description of the Assyrian king in 10:5-34. Like many Mesopotamian monarchs, he was known for stripping Lebanon of its trees for lumber to be sent back to his homeland. The use of tree imagery is particularly apt in relation to Sargon in the book of Isaiah. As noted in the discussion of 10:5-34, the arrogant Sargon is portrayed as a tree that YHWH is about to cut down. The use of the verb *nigda'tā,* "you are hewed down" (v. 12; cf. 9:9 [*RSV* 10]), is certainly appropriate in this respect. His death in battle and the abandonment of his corpse on the battlefield is echoed in the statement "Sargon . . . was not buried in his house," which his son Sennacherib addressed to soothsayers in an attempt to explain his father's fate (cf. Ginsberg, "Reflexes," 50). This corresponds to the description of the king's shrouded corpse, pierced with a sword and cast into the stones of an open pit in vv. 18-19. That Sargon's son Sennacherib maintained the throne after his death does not undermine this interpretation. The taunt song does not report the death of the king's sons as an established fact, but anticipates such an outcome. Sennacherib gained the throne only after fighting a number of rivals who tried to supplant him. Consequently, 14:4b-21 may be dated to approximately 705 B.C.E. It appears to be Isaiah's public response to the death of Sargon, whom he had condemned for his arrogant boasting in 10:5-34.

The application of a taunt song originally directed against an Assyrian monarch to the anticipated fall of the king of Babylon may help to explain the appearance of the summary-appraisal concerning Assyria in 14:24-27. As noted above, this text establishes the analogy between the fate of Babylon and that of Assyria in the present context. Nevertheless, it does not appear to have been composed for the present context in that it makes no reference to Babylon and gives no hint at an awareness of its present literary setting. Instead, the phraseology echoes that of 10:5-34. Thus the statement "Just as I intended so it has happened, just as I determined so shall it stand" (v. 24b), contrasts with the Assyrian monarch's statement in 10:10-11, "Just as my hand reached for the pagan kingdoms . . . so shall I do to Jerusalem and its idols." Likewise, YHWH's statement, "the removal of his yoke from upon them and his burden from upon his shoulder shall depart," corresponds closely to the statement concerning the projected removal of the Assyrian yoke in 10:27, "his burden shall depart from on your shoulder and his yoke from on your neck."

As argued in the discussion of 10:5-12:6, 14:24-27 forms the original conclusion to 10:5-34 that was displaced by the addition in 11:1-12:6 in relation to the Josianic redaction. Clearly, YHWH's oath to destroy the Assyrians "in my land and upon my mountains" (14:25a) corresponds to the situation of 10:5-34 where the Assyrian monarch invades Judah and threatens Jerusalem itself from Nob (Mt. Scopus). Consequently, this text dates to 720 when Sargon marched through Judah on his way to Philistia following his defeat of Ilu-bidi in Syria. The placement of this passage in the present context would of course be later. The summary-appraisal in vv. 26-27 may well stem from this later period and testifies to the fact that Isaiah's prophecies were studied by later tradents so that conclusions could be drawn from them. The appearance of v. 27, with its statement concerning YHWH's "outstretched hand," demonstrates that the writer of this verse made an analogy with 9:7 (RSV 8)-10:4, where the formula concerning YHWH's outstretched hand appears repeatedly. The appearance of this formula in this position reinforces the conclusion that 14:24-27 formed the original ending for the prophecies in chs. 5–10.

The relationship of 14:24-27 and 14:4b-21 to Sargon II and his expedition to Philistia in 720 may help to explain part of the reason for the appearance of the maśśā' concerning Philistia in 14:28-32. The passage has no explicit relation to the present context other than the principle of YHWH's foundation of Zion discussed above. The superscription indicates that the passage is to be dated to the death of King Ahaz. This dating presents interpreters with problems in that the threat uttered against Philistia appears to stem from Assyria, here portrayed as smoke coming from the north (v. 31). Consequently a number of interpreters attempt to relate this passage to the death of Tiglath-pileser III in 727, shortly before the death of Ahaz if 725 is accepted as the correct date (cf. Begrich). Others have proposed the death of Shalmanezer V (Donner, 112-13) or Sargon II (G. R. Driver; Bewer; cf. Clements, *Isaiah 1–39,* 148). The problem may be resolved, however, when one considers that Ahaz was a loyal vassal to the Assyrians, especially Tiglath-pileser, to whom he owed his life and throne (cf. 2 Kgs 16:5-9). The Philistines were among the nations that Tiglath-pileser subdued during the Syro-Ephraimite War (*ANET,* 283). As a loyal vassal to Assyria, Ahaz would have had some responsibility for maintaining Assyrian interests in the region, even if they extended only as far as turning over renegades who passed through his territory to the Assyrian authorities. As Ahaz was isolated during the Syro-Ephraimite War and thus was responsible for calling in the Assyrians to defend him, one could expect that he had few friends in the region and pursued Assyrian interests. His death would have been the signal for the Philistines to make overtures to his successor, Hezekiah. Whether Hezekiah came to the throne in 725 or 715 is immaterial. The Philistines supported Hoshea's revolt in 724 and later started their own in 714-713. In either case, therefore, they could be expected to approach Hezekiah for support. Isaiah's opposition to any form of political alliance is clear, and the present *maśśā'* appears to be his statement concerning the response to be made to the Philistine embassy, i.e., that Hezekiah should not join a coalition with the Philistines because YHWH is perfectly capable of securing Jerusalem. In any case, the Philistines could expect disaster at the hands of the Assyrians if they attempted a revolt, which is precisely what happened when Sargon invaded Philistia in 713 (cf. *ANET,* 286-87). Such an oracle reinforces the prophet's role as a political advisor to the king.

With the dates established for the individual texts that constitute 13:1–14:32, it now remains to determine the setting of the text as a whole. A number of factors indicate that these chapters were edited into their present form in the mid- to late 6th century, in that they anticipate the fall of Babylon to the Medes and the end of the Babylonian ruling house.

Obviously, the date of the present form of the text cannot be earlier than its latest components. As noted above, 13:2-22 dates to the mid-6th century during the time of the Median-Persian invasion of Babylonia but prior to Cyrus's ascension to the Babylonian throne in 539. Likewise, 14:1-2 dates to a period shortly after this time, since it presupposes 13:2-22 and provides a literary transition to the other texts that constitute this unit. The portrayal of the nations restoring Israel to its land and becoming servants corresponds to a number of texts that stem from the latter part of the 6th century, approximately at the time of the building of the Second Temple, including 49:22-26; 60–62; Hag 2:1-9; Zech 2:10-16; and 8:20-23. Insofar as Isa 14:1-2 is the key organizing text of this passage, and insofar as it links texts pertaining to the fall of Babylon and the Babylonian ruling house, the redaction that shaped these chapters into their present form must date to the latter part of the 6th century, about the time of Cyrus's ascension to the Babylonian throne and the beginning of the process of the building of the Second Temple. The redaction of this text marks the fall of

Babylon not only as a momentous political event but also as an event anticipated by Isaiah's prophecies insofar as Babylon's demise appears to be the fulfillment of Isaiah's prophecies concerning Assyria's downfall (14:24-27). Babylon's fall thereby testifies to his message of YHWH's continuing presence on and defense of Zion (14:28-32).

In addition, several features of chs. 13–14 indicate that their redaction took place in relation to the late-6th-century redaction of chs. 2–4. Both of these passages appear at the beginning of major sections of the book of Isaiah. Chs. 2–4 precede the material pertaining to Israel and Judah in chs. 5–12, and chs. 13–14 appear at the head of the oracles against the nations in chs. 13–23. Isa 13:1 reads, "The pronouncement concerning Babylon that Isaiah the son of Amoz saw"; and 2:1 reads, "The word that Isaiah the son of Amoz saw concerning Judah and Jerusalem." Furthermore, both sections focus on the "Day of YHWH" as an expression of YHWH's punishment of evil in the world (13:6, 9 and 2:12). Both passages employ variations of the verb *šāpēl,* "to bring down" (13:11; and 2:9, 11, 12, 17), to emphasize that the day of YHWH is directed against the proud and arrogant in the world (13:11 and 2:10, 11, 12, 17, 19, 21). Likewise both passages focus on humanity (*'ādām/'ănāšîm;* 13:12 and 2:9, 11, 17, 20, 22). They differ in that chs. 2–4 focus on the Day of YHWH in relation to the punishment of Jerusalem/Judah, whereas ch. 13 focuses on Babylon. But whereas ch. 13 is designed to bring down Babylon, the "glory [*ṣĕbî*] of the kingdoms" and "the splendor [*tip'eret*] and pride [*gā'ôn*] of the Chaldeans" (13:19), chs. 2–4 are directed to the reestablishment of Jerusalem as the place where "the branch of YHWH will be beautiful [*liṣbî*] and glorious, and the fruit of the land shall be the pride [*lĕgā'ôn*] and glory [*lĕtip'eret*] of the survivors of Israel" (4:2). Finally, the superscriptions for both sections are formulated similarly, indicating their respective roles in introducing major structural components of the book. Consequently, both chs. 2–4 and chs. 13–14 appear to be the products of the same redaction that produced the late-6th century edition of the book of Isaiah.

Intention

The intention of the final edited form of chs. 13–14 is defined in relation to the explanatory character of the *maśśā'* genre and its historical context in the latter part of the 6th century. As noted above, an important aspect of the *maśśā'* genre is that the prophet observes phenomena taking place in the world and, based on a revelatory experience, draws conclusions concerning the manifestation of YHWH's actions in the world. In this instance, the explanatory function of the *maśśā'* in chs. 13–14 is not limited to presenting the Median invasion of Babylonia as YHWH's action on the Day of YHWH. Rather, the presentation of the Day of YHWH against Babylon in 13:2-22 serves as the basis for what follows. The inclusion of additional material in 14:1-23, 24-27, and 28-32 brings out several other important conclusions concerning the Day of YHWH against Babylon.

In its present context, 14:1-23 points to the anticipated restoration of the Israelite exiles to the land of Israel and the fall of the Babylonian ruling house. The conjunction of these two events and the emphasis on Israel's suffering associated with the king points to Nebuchadrezzar as the object of the taunt song in this unit. Although Nabonidus was the last ruling monarch of Babylonia, he was not a descendant of Nebuchadrezzar, who was responsible for the destruction of Jerusalem, the exile of the people, and their consequent suffering under Babylonian rule. Following his death in 562, however, Nebuchadrezzar's son Amel-Marduk was murdered by his brother-in-law, Nergal-shar-usar, who then succeeded him on the throne. Nergal-shar-usar died in 556 after having been defeated in Cilicia in an apparent effort to counteract Median attempts to move against Asia Minor. His son, Labashi-Marduk, was removed from the throne and replaced by Nabonidus, who ruled until Cyrus of Persia-Media deposed him in 539 and ascended the throne. Consequently, the ruling house of Nabopolassar and Nebuchadrezzar fell from power as the Medes and Persians began to assert themselves against the Babylonians. The mocking character of the taunt expresses satisfaction at the just reward represented by the fall of this ruling house that had done so much to oppress the people of Judah. Wildberger (*Jesaja,* 542) notes that there may be a wordplay on the Hebrew spelling of the name Nebuchadnezzar in the phrase *kĕnēṣer niṭʿāb,* "like a despised branch" (14:19), but rightly concludes that there are insufficient grounds to confirm such a speculation.

Isaiah 14:24-27 presents the fall of Babylon and the Babylonian ruling dynasty as the fulfillment of YHWH's promise to destroy Assyria. Although these verses say nothing about Babylon, they point to YHWH's oath as a decision made concerning the entire world and all nations. Babylon, as the head of the nations in the mid-6th century, would provide a natural target for such an oath in this period and an analogy for the world-dominating Assyrian empire of the late 8th century. Not only does this present the *maśśāʾ* against Babylon as a fitting introduction for the oracles against the nations in chs. 13–23, but it also provides some insight into the transmission process of Isaiah's oracles and the way in which they were interpreted and applied to contemporary events in later periods. The summary-appraisal, with its wisdom background, indicates that Isaiah's work was studied. The placement of this passage in the present context indicates that, on the basis of such study, conclusions were drawn from his oracles concerning the meaning of contemporary events.

Although the subordinate Philistine *maśśāʾ* in 14:28-32 has no overt connection to the preceding material, its primary conclusion that YHWH founds Zion for the protection of the people reinforces several points made above. First, it points to YHWH's intentions to protect the people and to restore them to their homeland (cf. 14:1-2). But it also points to YHWH's sovereignty in the world and emphasizes that YHWH has no need to enter into alliances with other nations because YHWH is fully capable of controlling their destinies (14:24-27). Such an assertion stands at the basis for all of chs. 13–14 in that the Day of YHWH against Babylon simply represents the manifestation of YHWH's activities in human events.

Apart from their context in the present edited form of the text, each of the individual texts on which chs. 13–14 are built displays a unique intention in relation to its respective earlier historical context.

The intention of 13:2-22 is likewise apparent in relation to the explanatory function of the *maśśā'* genre. As noted in the discussion of the structure of this passage, it begins with rather general statements and images concerning the gathering of an army, its role in punishing the earth, and the character of this punishment as a manifestation of the Day of YHWH, but then leads the reader to the specific identification of the event that stands behind these images, i.e., the Median invasion of Babylon. In this respect, the phenomenon on which the prophet's revelatory experience is based is made known only at the end of the passage. This increases the dramatic effect of the conclusion that the Median invasion of Babylon is an act of YHWH and thereby testifies to YHWH's power to control human events in the world.

As noted above, the taunt song in 14:4b-21 is directed against the Assyrian monarch Sargon II (721-705), who was killed in battle and whose body was abandoned on the battlefield without proper burial. Sargon has a special notoriety due to his taking credit for the destruction of Samaria and the deportation of the population of the northern kingdom of Israel in 721, and due to his threats against Jerusalem during his western campaign of 720. Isaiah apparently composed and publicly spoke the present taunt song after news of Sargon's death reached Jerusalem in 705. As noted above, it is cast in the form of a dirge but lacks any attempt to mourn for the dead monarch. Instead, it contrasts his arrogant boasting and claims for world dominion with his ignominious death without so much as a proper burial. In the end, it calls for the death of his sons and the end of his dynasty as a consequence for his oppressive policies.

A key element in the song is the description of the dead king's experience in Sheol and the mocking he endures at the hands of the dead kings of the nations. Here the song borrows ancient Near Eastern mythological motifs relating to the morning star, Venus, which is apparently behind the king's designation as *hêlēl ben-šāḥar*, "the shining one, son of the dawn." Scholars have been unable to agree upon a specific myth that stands behind this designation and the experiences portrayed in the song, but three major possibilities have been put forward (cf. Wildberger, *Jesaja*, 551-52). Grelot has attempted to identify this passage with the Greek myth of Phaethon (from *phaetos*, "to shine"), the son of the dawn, Eos, according to some accounts, and the son of the sun god Helios according to others. Phaethon ignores his father's warnings and drives his chariot too close to the sun, threatening to set the earth afire. The result is that Zeus throws a thunderbolt at him causing him to fall to his death. In Canaanite mythology, the morning star is identified with the god Athtar. According to the Ugaritic Baal cycle (*ANET*, 129-42), the fertility god Baal is defeated by Mot, the god of death, and descends into the netherworld. This causes extensive mourning and lack of fertility among the Canaanite gods and the world at large. Following Baal's death, Athtar attempts to take Baal's place as ruler of the gods, but when he attempts to sit on Baal's throne, he finds that it is much too large for him. He consequently abandons the throne and descends to rule in El's earth, apparently a much lesser realm than that of Baal (cf. J. Gray, "The Canaanite God Horon," *JNES* 8 [1949] 27-34).

Another possibility is the Babylonian-Assyrian myth, "Ishtar's Descent to the Underworld" (*ANET*, 106-9), which is based on the old Sumerian myth, "Inanna's Descent to the Underworld" (*ANET*, 52-57). Ishtar is the queen of heaven in Akkadian mythology and is identified with the morning star, Venus. According to the myth, Ishtar determines to journey to the underworld for unknown reasons. As she descends through each of the seven gates leading to the depths of the underworld, she is progressively stripped of ornaments and clothing that testify to her exalted status until she stands naked before her sister, Ereshkigal, ruler of the underworld. The sixty miseries are then unleashed against her, resulting in the absence of fertility in the world of the living. Unable to save herself, Ishtar must be rescued by the chief god Ea, who creates the eunuch Asushunamir, who in turn descends to the underworld to retrieve her. Like the Canaanite Baal, Ishtar's return from the underworld is preceded by mourning rites that mark the end of the dry season and the beginning of the rainy season. Thus she is called back to the land of the living in order to bring the rains that sustain life. It would appear that Isaiah's taunt song and use of motifs from the myths that accompany the mourning rites for the dead fertility god in the ancient Near Eastern world is an attempt to satirize the death of Sargon II in relation to one of the most fundamental patterns of ancient Near Eastern religiosity: the death and rebirth of the fertility god or goddess, which governs the dry and rainy seasons of the land, and thus determines the seasons of fertility and lack thereof. Here one should also note that the Latin Vulgate translated *hêlēl* as "Lucifer" so that this passage is frequently associated with the fall of Satan from heaven.

Likewise, 14:24-27 presupposes Sargon II in its original role as the conclusion of 10:5-34 in particular and chs. 5–10 in general. The passage sums up YHWH's intentions to punish the arrogant boasting and threats against Jerusalem of the Assyrian monarch recorded in 10:5-34. By alluding to the "outstretched hand" formula of 5:25-30 and 9:7 (*RSV* 8)–10:4, it also testifies to YHWH's power, which brought the Assyrians as a means for punishing Israel and is now used to punish the Assyrian monarch for overstepping his bounds.

Finally, 14:28-32 relates to the period when the Philistines were preparing for their revolt against Sargon and the Assyrian empire in 715-713. The death of Ahaz is significant here, because Ahaz was a loyal vassal to Assyria, which loyalty saved both his throne and his life during the Syro-Ephraimite War. Consequently, Ahaz would have little reason to ally with the Philistines, who also suffered during the Assyrian invasion that put an end to the war. But at the death of Ahaz, the Philistines apparently saw their opportunity to approach his son and successor Hezekiah in order to persuade him to join the revolt. Isaiah's *maśśā'* apparently represents the prophet's council to the monarch on how to answer the Philistine delegation. The response that "YHWH has founded Zion that his people will find refuge in it" (v. 32) indicates Isaiah's consistent belief that Judah should avoid all political alliances against Assyria and depend on YHWH alone to defend Zion. The reference to the smoke coming from the north (v. 31) apparently refers to the prophet's belief that the Assyrians would surely come to put down this revolt and that the Philistines would have no chance. In such a situation, why should Judah join the Philistines, who did not come to the aid of Hezekiah's father during the Syro-Ephraimite War? To oppose Assyria would be to oppose the one power that had secured the Judean dynasty's — and thus Hezekiah's — position on the throne. To Isaiah, such a revolt would spell disaster not only for the Philistines, but for Hezekiah and Judah as well.

Bibliography

→ bibliography at "Introduction to the Prophetic Literature" and "Introduction to the Book of Isaiah." B. Alfrink, "Der Versammlungsberg im äussersten Norden (Is. 14)," *Bib* 14 (1933) 41-67; L. R. Bailey, "Isaiah 14:24-27," *Int* 36 (1982) 171-76; J. Begrich, "Jesaja 14,28-32," *ZDMG* 86 (1933) 66-79 (repr. in *Gesammelte Studien zum alten Testament* [TB 21; Munich: Kaiser, 1964] 121-31); H. Bost, "Le chant sur la chute d'un tyran en Ésaïe 14," *ETR* 59 (1984) 3-14; K. Budde, "Jesaja 13," in *Abhandlungen zur semitischen Religionskunde und Sprachwissenschaft, Wolf Wilhelm Grafen von Baudissin zum 26. September 1917* (ed. W. Frankenberg and F. Küchler; BZAW 33; Giessen: Töpelmann, 1918) 55-70; J. B. Burns, "Does Helel 'Go to Hell'?" *PEGLMBS* 9 (1989) 89-97; idem, "*Hôlēš ʿal* in Isaiah 14:12: A New Proposal," *ZAH* 2 (1989) 199-204; R. E. Clements, "Isaiah 14,22-27: A Central Passage Reconsidered," in *The Book of Isaiah/Le Livre d'Isaïe* (ed. J. Vermeylen; BETL 81; Leuven: Leuven University Press and Peeters, 1989) 253-62; P. C. Craigie, "Helel, Athtar and Phaethon (Jes 14,12-15)," *ZAW* 85 (1973) 223-25; Donner, *Israel unter den Völkern* (→ 1:4-9), 110-13, 145-46; V. O. Eareckson III, "The Originality of Isaiah XIV 27," *VT* 20 (1970) 490-91; Erlandsson, *Burden of Babylon* (→ 13:1–23:18); D. V. Etz, "Is Isaiah XIV 12-15 a Reference to Comet Halley?" *VT* 36 (1986) 289-301; K. Fullerton, "Isaiah 14:28-32," *AJSL* 42 (1925-26) 86-109; J. B. Geyer, "Twisting Tiamat's Tail: A Mythological Interpretation of Isaiah XIII 5 and 8," *VT* 37 (1987) 164-79; H. L. Ginsberg, " 'Roots Below and Fruit Above' and Related Matters," in *Hebrew and Semitic Studies Presented to Godfrey Rolles Driver* (ed. D. W. Thomas and W. D. McHardy; Oxford: Clarendon, 1963) 72-76; idem, "Reflexes of Sargon in Isaiah after 715 B.C.E.," *JAOS* 88 (1968) 47-53 (= *Essays in Memory of E. A. Speiser* [ed. W. Hallo; New Haven: American Oriental Society, 1968] 47-53); B. Gosse, "Un text pré-apocalyptique du règne de Darius: Isaïe XIII,1–XIV,23," *RB* 92 (1985) 200-222; idem, "Isaïe 14,28-32 et les traditions sur Isaïe d'Isaïe 36–39 et Isaïe 20,1-6," *BZ* 35 (1991) 97-98; P. Grelot, "Isaïe XIV 12-15 et son arrière-plan mythologique," *RHR* 149 (1956) 18-48; W. A. Irwin, "The Exposition of Isaiah 14:28-32," *AJSL* 44 (1927-28) 73-87; H. Jahnow, *Das hebräische Leichenlied im Rahmen der Völkerdichtung* (BZAW 36; Giessen: Töpelmann, 1923) 239-53; O. Loretz, "Der kanaanäisch-biblische Mythos vom Sturz des Sahar-Sohnes Helel," *UF* 8 (1976) 133-36; J. W. McKay, "Helel and the Dawn-Goddess: A Re-examination of the myth in Isaiah XIV 12-15," *VT* 20 (1970) 451-64; R. H. O'Connel, "Isaiah xiv 4b-23: Ironic Reversal Through Concentric Structure and Mythic Allusion," *VT* 38 (1988) 407-18; U. Oldenburg, "Above the Stars of El: El in Ancient South Arabic Religion," *ZAW* 82 (1970) 187-208; W. S. Prinsloo, "Isaiah 14,12-15 — Humiliation, Hubris, Humiliation," *ZAW* 93 (1981) 432-38; G. Quell, "Jesaja 14,1-23," in *Festschrift Friedrich Baumgärtel zum 70. Geburtstag 14. Januar 1958* (ed. L. Rost; Erlangen: Erlanger Forschungen, 1959) 131-57; F. Vanderburgh, "The Ode on the King of Babylon, Isaiah XIV 4b-21," *AJSL* 29 (1912-13) 111-21; Weis, 76-77, 105-24; G. A. Yee, "The Anatomy of Biblical Parody: The Dirge Form in 2 Samuel 1 and Isaiah 14," *CBQ* 50 (1988) 565-86.

PRONOUNCEMENT CONCERNING MOAB, 15:1–16:14

Structure

In keeping with the formulation of the oracles against the nations in chs. 13–23, this passage is introduced by the superscription *maśśā' mô'āb,* "Pronouncement concerning Moab." As indicated by the concluding material in 16:13-14, the passage is concerned with Moab throughout so that the superscription "Pronouncement concerning Damascus" in 17:1 marks the beginning of the next unit.

As Tucker notes ("Prophetic Superscriptions," 57-58), superscriptions stand apart from the material they introduce so that the basic structure of this passage falls into two parts: the superscription in 15:1a and the body of the unit in 15:1b–16:14. The superscription provides a generic identification of the following material as a *maśśā'* or prophetic pronouncement. As noted in the previous section, the prophetic *maśśā'* has no specific literary structure, but employs various generic elements to explain how YHWH's intentions are manifested in human affairs. The explanatory concern of the *maśśā'* is evident in the concluding verses of this passage (16:13-14), which explain not only that the preceding material concerning Moab's suffering is a word of YHWH concerning Moab, but also that it will take effect in three years. In this manner, the passage presents Moab's projected suffering as an act of YHWH. The introductory formula of 16:13-14, "This is the word that YHWH spoke unto Moab previously," indicates that 16:13-14 is a summary-appraisal and that these verses stand apart from the rest of the passage and summarize their essential character. Consequently, the basic structure of 15:1b–16:14 falls into two parts: 15:1b–16:12 and the summary-appraisal in 16:13-14.

The contents of 15:1b–16:12 and the predominant 3/2 *qînâ* meter (cf. Kaiser, *Isaiah 13–39,* 65) indicate that this passage is a prophetic lamentation over the destruction of Moab. The unit is cast largely in 1st-person descriptive language, which indicates that the prophet is the speaker, but the imperative forms concerning a proposed embassy to Bat-Zion (Jerusalem) or Judah interrupts this literary style. This indicates that the passage includes three basic subunits. Isa 15:1b-9 contains the lamentation proper, 16:1-5 contains the prophet's proposal to appeal to Judah for shelter, and 16:6-12 contains the prophet's renewed lament over Moab.

The prophet's lamentation proper in 15:1b-9 is characterized by its descriptive language concerning the mourning of the Moabites over the invasion of their land and its 1st-person perspective (vv. 5a, 9), which indicates that the prophet is the speaker. The passage presents a scenario of suffering throughout the entire country in that vv. 2-4 focus on locations north of the Arnon River and vv. 5-7 focus on locations south of the Arnon. Vv. 8-9 present problems in that Eglaim is located south of the Arnon at modern *Rugm el-Gilime* and Beer-elim is located north of the Arnon near modern *Wadi at-Tamad* (Wildberger, *Jesaja,* 617; for a survey of sites in Moab, see J. M. Miller, "Moab and the Moabites," in *Studies in the Mesha Inscription and Moab* [ed. A. Dearman; ABS 2; Atlanta: Scholars Press, 1989] 1-40; J. M. Miller, ed., *Archaeological Survey of the Kerak Plateau* [ASOR Archaeological Reports 1; Atlanta: Scholars Press, 1991]). This geographical discrepancy and the asseverative nature of the particle *kî,* "indeed," which introduces both v. 8 and v. 9, parallel to those uses of *kî* in v. 1b, has prompted both Petersen ("Oracles") and Weis (p. 114) to argue that 15:8-9 introduces a new unit that continues through ch. 16.

This position is incorrect on several grounds. First, the reference to "the outcry that encompasses the border of [*RSV* 'has gone round the land of'] Moab" indicates that v. 8 is concerned with the entire country, not just specific locations within Moab (Kaiser, *Isaiah 13–39,* 69). Second, by choosing locations in both the northern and southern parts of the country, the author indicates that the disaster overtakes the entire land. Furthermore, the choice of cities located in both north and south corresponds to vv. 2-4, which focus on northern locations, and vv. 5-7, which focus on southern locales. Third, the comprehensive concern of vv. 8-9 corresponds to that of v. 1b, where "Ar Moab" and "Kir Moab" refer to the populated territory of Moab rather than to specific cities. In addition, vv. 1b and 8-9 correspond by their formal similarity in that each is constituted by two statements introduced by asseverative *kî.* Likewise, vv. 2-4 and 5-7 focus on the northern and southern parts of the country, respectively, but both conclude with summary statements in v. 4b and in v. 7 that are introduced by *'al-kēn,* "therefore." The result is a ring composition in which the introductory (v. 1b) and concluding (vv. 8-9) sections are parallel in terms of both form and content, and the middle sections (vv. 2-4 and 5-7) are formally similar while focusing on the two major parts of the country.

The structure of 15:1b-9 is constituted by these four text blocks. V. 1b constitutes the introduction to the prophet's lamentation in that it proclaims the devastation of the territory of Moab in parallel statements introduced by asseverative *kî.* Ar Moab is sometimes identified as a specific city in Moab, but its location has never been confirmed. In a number of passages (e.g., Deut 2:18, 29), it functions as a general designation for the territory of Moab. Kir Moab likewise has never been securely identified as a specific site and appears to be another territorial designation parallel to Ar Moab. Vv. 2-4 comprise a series of statements concerning Moab's mourning for its stricken cities. The statements are defined by their focus on specific cities, all of which are located north of the Arnon River. Thus v. 2a takes up weeping by *habbayit,* perhaps the royal house of Moab, and Dibon on the high places. V. 2b takes up Moab's weeping over Nebo and Medeba. Vv. 3-4a focus on wailing by Heshbon and Elealeh. Finally, v. 4b contains a summary statement introduced by *ʿal-kēn,* "therefore," which portrays Moab's warriors crying out, presumably in their defeat at the hands of the invading enemy. Vv. 5-7 comprise a series of statements that focus on the prophet's lament concerning Moab's refugees who are fleeing to the south, away from the stricken northern cities. This section begins with a 1st-person statement by the prophet concerning his own crying out for Moab. Following the initial statement concerning the refugees fleeing to Zoar in v. 5a is a series of statements concerning southern localities, each introduced by *kî.* V. 5bα takes up the weeping on the ascent of Luhith, v. 5bβ takes up the outcry on the Horonayim road, v. 6a focuses on the devastation at the Waters of Nimrim, and v. 6b focuses on the withering of grass and vegetation. Finally, v. 7 contains a summary statement, introduced by *ʿal-kēn,* "therefore," which portrays the refugees carrying their possessions toward the Wadi of Willows at the border of Edom. Vv. 8-9 contain the prophet's summation of the lament in two statements introduced by asseverative *kî.* As noted above, v. 8 relates the outcry that encompasses the entire land of Moab, including Eglaim in the south and Beer-elim in the north. V. 9 relates the prophet's weeping for the survivors or remnant of Moab (see below on Intention).

As noted above, the masculine plural imperative verb *šilḥû,* "send," interrupts the 1st-person descriptive language of 15:1-9. Imperative verbs also appear in vv. 3-4 in a context that projects a future situation of Moab's flight and appeal to Bat-Zion to protect the fugitives. Whereas the imperative verbs and the projecting language appear in 16:1-5, the 1st-person descriptive language similar to that of 15:1-9 resumes in 16:6. Consequently, 16:1-5 forms a separate subunit within the passage. Although many take the 1st-person pronoun suffix in v. 4, *niddāḥay mô'āb,* "my fugitives, Moab," as an indication that YHWH is the speaker here, the following discussion will demonstrate that vv. 3aβ-4 constitute the contents of a petition to Judah by the ruler of Moab to protect his people. Consequently, the 1st-person pronoun suffix refers to the ruler of Moab. Insofar as the masculine plural imperative in v. 1 is addressed to the ruler of Moab, the speaker of the entire passage is the prophet, who quotes the petition to be made by the ruler of Moab.

Isaiah 16:1-5 comprises the prophet's proposal, directed to the ruler of Moab, to seek shelter from Judah on account of the invasion described in 15:1b-9. The structure of the passage is determined by the masculine plural imperative verbs found in vv. 1 and 3aα. Although the Qere reading indicates that the Masoretes have corrected the masculine plural imperative *hābî'û,* "bring," to the feminine singular imperative *hābî'î,* that the masculine plural imperative *ʿăśû,* "make," was not similarly changed indicates that the Ketiv form should be retained. The Qere reading apparently reflects an attempt to conform the verb to the following feminine singular imperatives in vv. 3aβ-4, but this indicates that the Masoretes did not understand that these verses quote the ruler of Moab's petition to Bat-Zion.

Isaiah 16:1-2 contains the command to send a peace offering to Bat-Zion or Judah. 2 Kgs 3:4 provides a ready example of the Moabite practice of sending lambs *(kārîm)* to the Davidic monarch in Jerusalem as a sign of submission. The command is addressed to the *mōšēl 'ereṣ*, "ruler of the land," and it employs a masculine plural imperative that is commonly used in deference to royalty. The command proper appears in v. 1. V. 2, introduced by *wĕhāyâ,* "and it shall come to pass," then describes Moab's projected situation of flight across the fords of the Arnon River. Isa 16:3-5 contains a second command addressed to the ruler of Moab as indicated by the masculine plural formulation of the imperatives in v. 3aα. The prophet commands the ruler to call a counsel and to make a petition. The term *pĕlîlâ* is frequently translated "justice" or "decision," but the term derives from the verbal root *pll,* which means "to pray" or "to request intercession," and is commonly used in post-Biblical Hebrew to refer to "argument" or "plea" as well as "decision" or "judgment" (M. Jastrow, *Dictionary of the Targumim, the Talmud Babli and Yerushalmi, and the Midrashic Literature* [repr. Brooklyn: P. Shalom, 1967] 1182). In this instance, the term refers to the petition or plea made to Bat-Zion or Judah, requesting asylum for Moab's refugees. This is clear from vv. 3bβ-4, which contain the contents of the petition. The feminine singular imperative verbs are addressed to Bat-Zion (v. 1). The structure of the petition is determined by its three imperative verbs, which function here as appeals. They include an appeal for protection (v. 3bβ), an appeal for the concealment of the fugitives (v. 3b), and an appeal for refuge that *(kî)* the oppression may stop (v. 4). Consequently, 16:3-4 contains the prophet's command for counsel/petition, in which v. 3aα contains the command proper and vv. 3bβ-4 contain the contents of the command. This is followed by a statement concerning the projected results of the petition, introduced by the converted perfect *wĕhûkan,* "and it shall be established," in v. 5. This statement indicates that the Davidic throne or rule will be established over Moab as a result of the petition.

Isaiah 16:6-12 resumes the 1st-person descriptive language found in 15:1b-9 so that these verses constitute a renewed prophetic lament over Moab. The structure of the passage is determined by the 1st-person plural statement in v. 6, addressed by the prophet to his audience, and by the two 1st-person singular statements introduced by *'al-kēn,* "therefore," in vv. 9-10 and 11-12 in which the prophet describes his reactions to the situation described in vv. 6-8. Vv. 6-8 are concerned with the reception of the report of Moab's downfall. The prophet's acknowledgment of this report to his unspecified audience appears in v. 6. Vv. 7-8, introduced by the conjunctive *lākēn,* "therefore," employs both objective language (v. 7a) and 2nd-plural address (v. 7b) to describe Moab's wailing as the consequence of Moab's downfall. V. 7 expresses this in terms of Moab's longing for the raisin cakes of Kir-hareseth, and v. 8, introduced by causative *kî,* builds on this image with an allegorical description of the demise of the people as a ruined vineyard that has been devastated by the "lords of the nations." The prophet's following two statements of his reaction to this situation likewise build on the allegory. Vv. 9-10 describe his weeping for the loss of the vintage and harvest. Vv. 11-12 describe his grieving for the suffering of the people.

Isaiah 16:13-14 constitutes the second major structural subunit of the *maśśā'* in 15:1b–16:14. These verses constitute a summary-appraisal form as indicated by the characteristic introduction, *zeh haddābār*, "this is the word," in v. 13 and its didactic or evaluative character. V. 13 identifies the preceding material in 15:1b–16:12 as "the word that YHWH spoke to Moab formerly [*mē'āz*]." V. 14 presents the situation of the present (*wĕ'attâ*, "and now") by reporting YHWH's statement that projects the decimation of Moab in three years. The didactic function of these verses is evident in that YHWH's statement indicates the time when the prior word of YHWH to Moab will finally be realized or applied.

Genre

The overarching genre of chs. 15–16 is the prophetic *maśśā'* or PROPHETIC PRONOUNCEMENT. As noted above, the *maśśā'* is a type of prophetic discourse that attempts to explain how YHWH's intentions are manifested in human affairs. Although the genre lacks a characteristic literary form, the identification of this text as an example of the *maśśā'* genre is evident from several of its features. First is the SUPERSCRIPTION in 15:1a, which identifies the following text as a *maśśā'*. Additional features include the structure of the passage as a whole and the explanatory function of the SUMMARY-APPRAISAL in 16:13-14. As noted above, the structure of this text falls into two basic parts: the prophetic LAMENT over the destruction of Moab in 15:1b–16:12, and the SUMMARY-APPRAISAL in 16:13-14. Curiously, the prophetic LAMENT makes no mention of YHWH, nor does it give any indication that the invasion of Moab is to be understood as an act of YHWH. Only in the SUMMARY-APPRAISAL of 16:13-14 are such issues taken up. Isa 16:13-14 explicitly identifies the preceding material as a word of YHWH and transmits YHWH's statement that this word will take effect in three years. In this respect, 16:13-14 identifies the projected invasion of Moab as an act of YHWH, thus characterizing chs. 15–16 in their entirety as a prophetic *maśśā'*. Nevertheless, that 15:1b–16:12 contains no identifying characteristics of the *maśśā'* genre, along with the secondary nature of 16:13-14, indicates that the presentation of this text as a *maśśā'* is the result of later redaction (see below on Setting).

The bulk of this text is constituted as a prophetic LAMENT over the destruction of a nation (15:1b–16:12). This identification is evident from the contents of the text and from the traces of the 3/2 *qînâ* or dirge meter that are apparent in 15:1b-9 (Kaiser, *Isaiah 13-39*, 65). Van Zyl (pp. 20-21) challenges the common interpretation of this material as an elegy on Moab and instead maintains that the text is a mocking song sung by the enemies of Moab, probably the bedouin who invaded the country. He points to the replacement of the typical *'êk*, "how," by *kî* and observes "a certain triumphant note throughout the poem" (p. 21). This is certainly evident in 16:6, which states that Moab's pride, arrogance, and haughtiness are not "in proportion to him [*badāyw*]," i.e., not justified by Moab's capabilities. Nevertheless, the expressions of the prophet's empathy for Moab (15:5, 9; 16:9-10, 11-12) cannot be dismissed as mere sarcasm. Rather, they are designed to support the prophet's proposal in 16:1-5 that Moab petition Judah for refuge from the invader. In this respect, the prophet's statements of empathy with Moab are based on a realistic assessment of Moab's desperate situation and need to turn to an outside power for support. Van Zyl's observations that the poem does not represent a pure form of an elegy are correct, but his conclusion that this is a mocking song sung by enemies must be rejected. Rather, the form has been adapted to a context that encourages Moab to turn to Judah and the house of David. The song is therefore not that of an enemy but that of a potential ally or even quasi-suzerain.

The prophet's proposal to seek shelter from Judah is not a generic classification per se, in that "proposal" is more a functional definition of 16:1-15. It includes two primary generic elements that define its essential character. The text is based in two sets of COMMANDS in v. 1 and v. 3aα that define its propositional character. The context of Moab's suffering indicates that the imperative forms here convey the prophet's intent to persuade the ruler of Moab to act on his proposal. After all, the calling of counsel (v. 3aα) and the decision to submit to Judah (v. 1) are the prerogatives not of the prophet but of the Moabite king. The PETITION in vv. 3aβ-4 is identified by its character as a request or plea from one party to another asking for some definite response. In this instance, Moab addresses Judah in order to request asylum or protection for its people. The imperative forms convey the sense of an appeal in that Moab is in no position to dictate the Judean decision but must put itself at the mercy of Judah in a situation of crisis. Also included here (vv. 7-12) is a vineyard ALLEGORY, which is typical of Isaiah.

Finally, the SUMMARY-APPRAISAL in 16:13-14 is easily identified by its use of the demonstrative pronoun *zeh*, "this," and its didactic function. In this instance, it identifies the preceding material as the word of YHWH and maintains that this word will be fulfilled in three years. As noted above, the SUMMARY-APPRAISAL establishes the character of the text as a whole as a *maśśā'*, inasmuch as it identifies the suffering of Moab as an act of YHWH.

Setting

As noted above, the summary-appraisal in 6:13-14 clearly stands apart from the preceding material and identifies that material as the "word of YHWH that he spoke to Moab previously." Inasmuch as this statement contrasts the previous word of YHWH with its own present circumstances, as indicated by the introductory *wě'attâ*, "and now," in v. 14, one must identify 16:13-14 as a later addition to this text. Furthermore, 16:13-14 establishes the character of this text as a *maśśā'* in that it identifies the suffering of Moab as an act of YHWH. The superscription in 15:1a, which identifies this text as a *maśśā'*, must have been added at the same time as 16:13-14. The date and situation of these additions will be discussed following that of 15:1b–16:12.

Isaiah 15:1b–16:12 clearly presupposes an invasion of Moab. The question of its historical setting obviously depends on establishing the time of the invasion and the identity of the attackers. This has proved quite problematic in the history of exegesis in that the text lacks clear historical data that might establish such a setting, and extrabiblical evidence for an invasion of Moab in the late 8th century is wanting. The issue is further complicated by the fact that Jer 48:29-38 nearly duplicates large portions of this text, especially Isa 16:6-12, although Wildberger (*Jesaja,* 605-9) has shown that the deviations in the Jeremiah text and its sporadic use of material from Isa 15:1b-9 indicate that the Jeremiah text is dependent on that of Isaiah.

A number of proposals for the historical background of this material have been made, but all have proved inadequate (cf. Kaiser, *Isaiah 13–39,* 60-65; Wildberger, *Jesaja,* 595-98). Rudolph revived portions of Hitzig's old hypothesis by arguing that the attack against Moab was that of the Israelite king Jeroboam II (786-746) as reported in 2 Kgs 14:25, but there is no evidence that Isaiah used the words of earlier prophets (Wildberger, *Jesaja,* 604). Furthermore, the vineyard allegory in 16:7-12 is typical of Isaiah. Others have followed Donner ("Neue Quellen," esp. 173-78), who identifies the attacker as a bedouin tribe called the Gidariya, who are mentioned in Nimrud Letter XIV as attacking Moab in the late 8th century (cf. H. W. F. Saggs, "The Nimrud Letters, 1952 — Part II," *Iraq* 17 [1955] 126-60, esp. 131-33). This hypothesis fails, however, because Isaiah 15–16 portrays the northern regions of Moab, previously inhabited by Israel, as the area of attack rather than the southern regions, which would be open to bedouin incursions (see further below). Scholars have likewise failed to identify an Assyrian invasion of Moab in the 8th century; Moab appears customarily on Assyrian tribute lists with no indication that the country was invaded. Although attacks against Moab were recorded in the mid-7th century by Arab tribes opposed to the Assyrians, and in the early 6th century by the Babylonians who destroyed the country (cf. Kaiser, *Isaiah 13–39,* 63-64), these later dates must be ruled out in that they would provide no occasion to appeal to Jerusalem for assistance while Moab's refugees fled to the south.

In order to posit an appropriate setting for 15:1b–16:12, one must consider two essential features of this material. First, the attack against Moab centers on its northern territories, specifically on the cities of Nebo, Medeba, Heshbon, Elealeh, and Jazer. Other northern cities, such as Dibon and Jahaz, are listed as witnesses to the attack but not as its direct victims. Furthermore, the southern locations listed in 15:5-7 are portrayed as the scene of refugees in flight, not as cities that have borne the brunt of enemy invasion. Consequently, the attacker comes from the north and drives Moabite refugees to the south. This is particularly striking when one considers that the northern cities that were attacked were all cities situated in the territory that Israel previously settled and that King Mesha of Moab brought under Moabite authority in the 9th century (see "Moabite Stone," *ANET,* 320-21; and the essays on the Moabite Stone in A. Dearman, ed., *Studies in the Mesha Inscription and Moab* [ABS 2; Atlanta: Scholars Press, 1989]; cf. 2 Kings 3). Isaiah 15–16 portrays Moab as being pushed out of former Israelite territory and back to its home territory just north of the Arnon River.

Second, the petition to Bat-Zion or Jerusalem for refuge in 16:1-5 limits the potential historical settings of this text. Jerusalem was certainly in no position to offer refuge in 582 when Moab was attacked by the Babylonians and destroyed. Likewise, such an appeal would make little sense in the period following Hezekiah's failed revolt against Assyria, since the establishment of Davidic authority over Moab would hardly be expected from Jerusalem as an Assyrian vassal. Even when Judah was free from Assyrian control under Josiah, Judah could be expected to be the cause of Moab's suffering rather than its refuge, as Josiah apparently viewed Moab as a potential target for expansion. Hezekiah's revolt in 701 and the Philistine revolt in 715-713 likewise do not provide appropriate occasions for this oracle in that Moab submitted to Assyria on both occasions before an Assyrian attack against the country materialized. Shalmanezer V's invasion in 724-722 focused on the remnant of northern Israel and did not include campaigns east of the Jordan; this region had already been annexed by Tiglath-pileser III following the Syro-Ephraimite War.

These two considerations point to Tiglath-pileser's invasion of Aram and Israel during the Syro-Ephraimite War of 734-732 as the most appropriate occasion for this oracle. Tiglath-pileser's forces concentrated their activities along the major trade routes running along the outer regions of northern Israel, including the King's Highway in Transjordan, the routes through the Jezreel Valley, and the coastal plain route leading to Philistia. Gilead was one of the regions annexed by Tiglath-pileser following this campaign, and it stands to reason that the Assyrian assault would include territories formerly occupied by Israel since the Arnon River forms the natural boundary for northern Moab. It is noteworthy that 1 Chr 5:23-26 reports that Tiglath-pileser exiled the Reubenites, the Gadites, and the half-tribe of Manasseh, inasmuch as the former Israelite cities mentioned in Isaiah 15–16 were included in the territory of Reuben and Gad (cf. Numbers 32). Likewise, King Mesha's inscription on the Moabite Stone mentions his capture of territory formerly occupied by the men of Gad (*ANET*, 320-21).

An appeal by Moab to Jerusalem for sanctuary makes perfect sense in this situation. The Assyrians entered the region at the request of King Ahaz of Judah, who found himself surrounded by enemies in the Syro-Ephraimite War. Consequently, Jerusalem might have some influence with the Assyrians, however limited, to call off the Assyrian army from a country that did not pose a threat either to Judah or to the Assyrians. Such an interpretation is supported by the fact that Moab is not listed as one of the countries that attacked Judah during the Syro-Ephraimite crisis. Furthermore, it is listed together with Ammon, Ashkelon, Judah, Edom, and Gaza as tributaries to Tiglath-pileser III (*ANET*, 282), whereas the primary combatants, Aram and Israel, are not listed at all. Although Tiglath-pileser apparently concentrated on destroying Aram and Israel, his demonstration of power seems to have convinced other kingdoms in the region to submit to his authority. An Assyrian assault against former Israelite territories occupied by Moab would certainly provide an appropriate demonstration of power to Moab, while adding ostensibly Israelite territory to Assyria's borders.

The social setting of this oracle appears to lie in prophetic advice to the Judean king concerning the situation of Moab. Although one cannot entirely rule out an address to Moab in an attempt to convince the Moabites to accept Davidic authority, the comments concerning Moab's unwarranted pride (16:6) and the righteous authority of the Davidic monarch (16:5) would hardly appeal to Moab's monarch even in a situation of crisis. It seems much more likely that Isaiah's oracle was directed to King Ahaz in an effort to convince him to grant asylum to the Moabite refugees and perhaps to intercede with Tiglath-pileser on Moab's behalf. Although Isaiah rejected Ahaz's submission to Assyria, he did favor the extension of Davidic authority over the northern kingdom of Israel. Inasmuch as Moab was formerly part of the Davidic empire, one could expect that he would welcome the extension of Davidic authority over Moab as well. Such an argument would likely appeal to Ahaz's ambitions. It would also explain why southward-fleeing Moabites would be expected to rely on Jerusalem to the west for safety.

Finally, the summary-appraisal in 16:13-14 clearly presupposes 15:1b–16:12 as older material that must be applied to the present. Unlike the preceding material, these verses look forward to the destruction of Moab in three years. Consequently, one must rule out the 8th century and the first half of the 7th century, for there would be little Judean interest in the decimation of Moab during the period of Assyrian rule. Likewise, one must rule out the Babylonian destruction of Moab in 582, for there would be little point in looking forward to the submission of Moab to Judah following the destruction of Jerusalem by the Babylonians. The most appropriate setting for 16:13-14 appears to be during the reign of King Josiah of Judah (639-609). Josiah's reform program included his desire to reestablish the old Davidic empire following the decline of the Assyrian empire in the late 7th century. His ambitions to expand into Moab are evident in Zeph 2:8-11 (cf. Sweeney, "Zephaniah"; Christensen, "Zephaniah 2:4-15") and Isa 11:14 (see the discussion of this verse above; and Sweeney, "Jesse's New Shoot"). Likewise, Deut 23:4-7 indicates the low regard in which the Moabites were held during the Josianic period and beyond. In this instance, the addition of Isa 16:1a and 13-14 to 15:1b–16:12 would be to apply Isaiah's earlier lamentation for Moab to the situation of the late 7th century and thereby to support Josiah's intentions to expand his authority into Moab. The transformation of Isaiah's lamentation into a *maśśā'* indicates that the destruction of Moab and its submission to Davidic authority represent the will of YHWH. The passage thereby provides prophetic legitimization to Josiah's political ambitions regarding Moab. As such, it shows an effort to study earlier prophetic material and to apply it to contemporary situations. One may assume that such an oracle would be made public in order to build support for Josiah's policies. Josiah's early death, however, prevented the realization of these plans.

Intention

The intention of Isaiah 15–16 is manifested in relation to the historical contexts of the respective editions of this text. As noted in the overview of chs. 13–23, the pronouncement concerning Moab functions as one of the oracles against the nations designed to demonstrate YHWH's sovereignty over the entire world. Although Moab had ceased to exist by the mid-6th century, it continued to function as a symbol for nations that would suffer YHWH's punishment at the time of Israel's restoration (cf. 25:10b-12).

The intention of the Josianic edition of this text derives from its formulation as a prophetic *maśśā'*. As noted above, the *maśśā'* is a type of prophetic discourse designed to elucidate how YHWH's intentions are manifested in human affairs. In the case of chs. 15–16, this generic characterization is evident not only in the superscription in 15:1a, which identifies the text as "the pronouncement of Moab," but also through the concluding summary-appraisal in 16:13-14. These verses identify the preceding material as "the word of YHWH that he spoke to Moab previously" and project the fulfillment of this word in three years. As such, they indicate that the downfall of Moab represents YHWH's intentions for the country and thereby identify the demise of Moab as an act of YHWH.

This claim is particularly significant when considered in relation to King Josiah's religious and political reforms of the late 7th century. Following the collapse of Assyrian authority in the Syro-Israelite region, Josiah saw his opportunity to reestablish the old Davidic empire. Together with his attempts to centralize the religious and political activity of the country in Jerusalem, Josiah shut down the former sanctuary of the northern kingdom of Israel at Bethel (2 Kgs 23:15-20). In addition, as already noted, his marriages indicate his political ambitions to expand both northward and westward. His marriage to Zebidah, daughter of Pedaiah of Rumah (2 Kgs 23:36), secured his hold on the Jezreel Valley and the northern Galilee region, and his marriage to Hamutal, the daughter of Jeremiah of Libnah, provided a toehold in the region of Philistia (2 Kgs 23:31; 24:18; cf. J. A. Wilcoxen, "The Political Background of Jeremiah's Temple Sermon," in *Scripture in History and Theology* [*Fest.* J. C. Rylaarsdam; ed. A. L. Merrill and T. W. Overholt; Pittsburgh: Pickwick, 1977] 151-66). In addition, prophetic statements from the period, such as Zeph 2:8-11 and Isa 11:14, indicate his interest in expanding across the Jordan as well, although this ambition never seems to have been realized (cf. Christensen, "Zephaniah 2:4-15"; Sweeney, "Zephaniah"; idem, "Jesse's New Shoot"). As noted above, Josiah's removal of the high place for Chemosh of Moab receives special mention in the account of his reforms (2 Kgs 23:13), and Deut 23:4-7 indicates special animosity against both the Ammonites and the Moabites.

In this situation, the *maśśā'* concerning Moab provides prophetic legitimization for Josiah's intentions to extend his authority over the country. By presenting the material concerning Moab as YHWH's past word concerning the fate of the country, the summary-appraisal in Isa 16:13-14 indicates a reliance on its authority as a prophetic utterance of Isaiah. By projecting the fulfillment of this word in three years, it provides authorization for action against Moab as an act of YHWH. The projected extension of Davidic authority over Moab in 16:5 takes on special significance in this context in that the oracle becomes a warrant for Josiah to attack Moab and bring it under his rule.

The intention of the Isaianic edition of 15:1b–16:12 is evident in the interplay of the two sections containing lamentations for Moab (15:1b-9; 16:6-12) and the section proposing a Moabite petition to Judah for security (16:1-5).

The first lament focuses on an invasion of Moab that affects the entire country. The initial statements concerning Ar Moab and Kir Moab indicate a comprehensive perspective on the entire territory of Moab. As noted above, the

250

term *Ar Moab* is often translated as the "city of Moab," but its usage indicates that it refers to Moabite territory in general (Deut 2:18, 29). Likewise, Kir Moab means "wall of Moab" or "walled city of Moab," and it is frequently identified with Kir-hareseth, although this identification is unwarranted given the explicit mention of Kir-hareseth in 16:7, 11. Like its parallel, Ar Moab, Kir Moab refers to the populated territory of Moab. Isa 15:8 likewise identifies the comprehensive nature of the catastrophe by referring to the outcry that encompasses the border of Moab. A closer look at the oracle, however, indicates that the center of the attack is against the northern regions of Moab (15:2-4) while the south is the scene of refugees fleeing from the invaders (15:5-7; see the discussion above). The passage identifies several cities as the victims of the invaders, including Nebo, Medeba, Heshbon, Elealeh, and Jazer, while other cities are listed as witnesses to the disaster or sites for fleeing refugees. Furthermore, the concluding statement of vv. 2-4, which mention the northern cities, refers to the outcry of Moab's warriors (v. 4b), whereas the concluding statement of vv. 5-7, which mentions the southern locations, refers to Moab's fleeing refugees (v. 7). Clearly, the attack centers on the north, not on the south. It is noteworthy that the cities that were attacked lay in the region once occupied by the northern Israelite tribe of Reuben, and that Moab had expanded into this area north of its traditional border around the Arnon River only in the mid-9th century during the reign of the Moabite king Mesha (cf. *ANET*, 320-21; 2 Kings 3). As argued above, this evidence indicates that the attacking forces were Tiglath-pileser III's Assyrian troops, who invaded the Gilead region during the Syro-Ephraimite War (735-732). The Assyrian troops apparently occupied former territories of Israel and drove the Moabites back to their traditional borders just north of the Arnon.

The prophet's proposal that Moab submit to Bat-Zion or Judah in Isa 16:1-5 takes on special significance in this situation. King Ahaz of Judah was the one who called on the Assyrians for assistance in the Syro-Ephraimite War in the first place. One might therefore expect that Ahaz could have some influence with the Assyrians to prevent them from attacking one of the few countries in the region that did not actively participate in the Syro-Ephraimite attack against Jerusalem (cf. 2 Kgs 16:5-6, which lists Syria, Israel, and Edom as the attackers, but not Moab). Although the passage appears to be directed to Moab, as indicated by the imperatives in 16:1 and 3, and by the 2nd-person forms of address in 16:7 and 9, it is not certain that Moab is the intended audience of this text. It lacks any indication of a communication transmitted to the Moabites, and its references to Moab's unwarranted pride (16:6) and ineffective supplication to its deities (16:12) would not necessarily encourage Moabite acquiescence. Rather, the interest in extending Davidic authority over Moab indicates that this oracle was addressed to the Davidic monarch Ahaz in order to convince him to accept Moab's petition for refuge. The prophet maintains that Davidic rule will thereby be extended over Moab and corresponds well to his own view concerning the reestablishment of Davidic authority over the territories that formerly belonged to the Davidic empire.

Bibliography

→ bibliography at "Introduction to the Prophetic Literature." C. Bonnet, "Échos d'un rituel de type Adonidien dans l'oracle contre Moab d'Isaïe (Isaïe, 15)," *Studi Epigrafici e Linguistici* 4 (1987) 101-19; D. Christensen, "Zephaniah 2:4-15: A Theological Basis for Josiah's Program of Political Expansion," *CBQ* 46 (1984) 669-82; H. Donner, "Neue Quellen zur Geschichte des Staates Moab in der zweiten Hälfte des 8. Jahrh. v. Chr.," *MIOF* 5 (1957) 155-84; E. Easterly, "Is Mesha's *qrhh* Mentioned in Isaiah xv 2?" *VT* 41 (1991) 215-19; E. Power, "The Prophecy of Isaias against Moab," *Bib* 13 (1932) 435-51; R. Rendtorff, "Zur Lage von Jaeser," *ZDPV* 76 (1960) 124-35; W. Rudolph, "Jesaja XV–XVI," in *Hebrew and Semitic Studies Presented to Godfrey Rolles Driver* (ed. D. W. Thomas and W. D. McHardy; Oxford: Clarendon, 1963) 130-43; W. Schottroff, "Horonaim, Nimrim, Luhith und Westrand des 'Landes Ataroth': Ein Beitrag zur historischen Topographie des Landes Moab," *ZDPV* 82 (1966) 163-208; Sweeney, "Jesse's New Shoot" (→ 10:5–12:6); Talmon, "Prophetic Rhetoric" (→ 2:2-4); A. H. Van Zyl, *The Moabites* (POS 3; Leiden: Brill, 1960) 20-23; Weis, 113-27, 477-79; U. Worschech and E. A. Knauf, "Dimon und Horonaim," *BN* 31 (1986) 70-95; V. Zapletal, "Der Spruch über Moab: Is. 15 und 16," in *Alttestamentliches* (Freiburg: Universitæts-Buchhandlung, 1903) 163-83.

PRONOUNCEMENT CONCERNING DAMASCUS, 17:1–18:7

Structure

I. Superscription	17:1a
II. Prophetic pronouncement *(maśśā')* proper	17:1b–18:7
A. Oracular reports concerning YHWH's announcement of judgment against Israel	17:1b-6
1. First report: announcement of judgment against Damascus/Aram and Ephraim/Israel	1b-3
a. Announcement of judgment proper	1b-3bα
1) Statement concerning ruin of Damascus	1b
2) Statement concerning abandonment of cities of Aroer	2a
3) Announcement of consequences	2b-3bα
a) Places for cattle	2b
b) Cessation of defenses of Ephraim and sovereignty of Damascus	3a
c) Remnant of Aram will be like glory of Israel	3bα
b. Oracular formula	3bβ
2. Second report: announcement of judgment against glory of Jacob	4-6
a. Announcement of judgment proper	4-6bα
1) Introductory statement concerning diminishing of glory of Jacob	4

The demarcation of this unit is particularly problematic in that the superscription, "Pronouncement concerning Damascus," in 17:1a appears to apply only to 17:1b-3, which mention Damascus. Not only does concern shift to Israel, the nations, and especially Cush in the following material, but formal distinctions, such as the appearance of an introductory *hôy* in 17:12 and 18:1, have prompted many scholars to maintain that the passage consists of a collection of independent units (e.g., Wildberger, *Jesaja,* 633-97).

Nevertheless, there are several indications that the unit comprises 17:1–18:7. First, the unit is demarcated at the beginning by the superscription "Pronouncement concerning Damascus" in 17:1a. The next superscription, "Pronouncement concerning Egypt," does not appear until 19:1a. Second, agricultural imagery of the harvest and gleaning of the fields ties the passage together thematically (see Talmon). This theme appears initially in 17:4-6, which describes the punishment of Israel by a comparison to harvesting the fields of Emeq (*RSV* Valley of) Rephaim. The image continues in 17:10-11, which describes the planting of Adonis gardens and their failure; in 17:13, which describes the rebuke of the nations in terms of threshing grain at the harvest; and in 18:3-6, which describes YHWH's trimming of the shoots at harvest time as the means by which the nations recognize YHWH's action in the world. Third, the identification of this text as a *maśśā'* presupposes an explanatory function that identifies the manifestation of YHWH's actions in human affairs. No text within this unit identifies YHWH as an active agent in human affairs until 18:3-6, in which YHWH's trimming of the shoots is identified as the cause for the nations' recognition of YHWH. Although scholars frequently interpret this as a reference to the punishment of Cush (e.g., Clements, *Isaiah 1–39,* 165-66), there is no indication in 18:1-7 that the oracle is directed against the messengers of Cush. Instead, it is directed against Israelite messengers sent to Cush (cf. 18:2 and the discussion of the intention of this passage below). The context of this passage within 17:1–18:7 identifies the trimmed shoots as YHWH's punishment of Israel, not Cush. Fourth, although the superscription identifies Damascus as the object of concern, it is evident that Damascus serves only as an initial means to introduce other concerns. The passage quickly shifts from a focus on Damascus and Israel in 17:1b-3 to an exclusive concern with Israel in 17:4-6. From there, it shifts to YHWH as the God of Israel in 17:7-8 and then to Israel's failure to recognize YHWH in 17:9-11. YHWH's rebuke of the nations in 17:12-14 precedes 18:1-7, in which the nations of the earth (cf. 18:3), exemplified by Cush (cf. 18:7), recognize YHWH. Consequently, the concern with recognition of YHWH emerges as the major interest defining this passage.

The structure of 17:1–18:7 is defined by its interest, on the one hand, in focusing on the present situation of the ruin of Damascus and the abandonment of the cities of Aroer, and on the other hand, in projecting the future consequences of this situation for Israel, which is sending messengers to Cush to request support for its planned revolt against Assyria in 724 B.C.E. (cf. 2 Kgs 17:4 and the discussion of setting below). Following the initial division between the superscription in 17:1a and the body of the text in 17:1b–18:7, the text falls into three main parts. Isa 17:1b-6 comprises the oracular reports concerning YHWH's coming judgment of Israel, demarcated by the oracular report formulas in 17:3bβ and 17:6bβ and the syntactic connection constituted by the formula *wĕhāyâ bayyôm hahû'*, "and it shall come to pass on that day," in 17:4. Isa 17:7-8 comprises a prophetic announcement that humanity will recognize YHWH, introduced by the syntactically independent formula *bayyôm hahû'*, "in that day," which builds on the preceding formula in 17:4. Isa 17:9–18:7 comprises a prophetic announcement concerning YHWH's future punishment of Israel and recognition by the nations, again introduced by the formula *bayyôm hahû'*. This subunit is also held together by its imagery of YHWH's trimming of the shoots (18:3-6) planted by Israel (17:10-11), the contrast between Israel forgetting YHWH (17:10) and the nations' recognition of YHWH (18:3, 7), and YHWH's capacity to punish nations (17:12-14; cf. 17:9 and 18:4-6).

Isaiah 17:1b-6 contains two oracular reports concerning YHWH's announcement of judgment against Israel. Although they are linked by the conjunctive formula *wĕhāyâ bayyôm hahû'*, "and it shall come to pass in that day," each is defined by a concluding oracle formula (v. 3bβ and v. 6bβ). The first report in vv. 1b-3 focuses on the announcement of judgment against Damascus/Aram and Ephraim/Israel. It includes the announcement proper in vv. 1b-3bα and the oracle formula in v. 3bβ. The announcement consists of three syntactically independent statements. The first in v. 1b employs a participle to describe the present ruined state of Damascus. The second in v. 2a employs a nonverbal statement to describe the present abandonment of the cities of Aroer on the northern Moabite border in the Transjordan region. Both of these statements prepare for an announcement of the projected consequences for Israel in vv. 2b-3bα. This statement is based on the imperfect verb *tihyeynâ*, "they shall be," and the subsequent converted perfect verbs describing Israel's future. V. 2b states that they (Damascus and Aroer) shall be for cattle and that no one shall frighten the cattle away. V. 3a states that Israel's defense (*mibṣār*, "fortress") shall cease together with Damascus's sovereignty (*mamlākâ*, "government"). Finally, v. 3bα states that Israel's glory shall be like the remnant of Aram.

The second oracular report (vv. 4-6) contains an announcement of judgment against the glory of Jacob. Like the preceding report, it contains the announcement proper in vv. 4-6bα and the oracle formula in v. 6bβ. It clearly builds on the first report by focusing on the fate of the "glory of *Israel*," which appeared in the climactic statement of the first report and in the oracle formula that emphasizes the "utterance of YHWH, *the God of Israel*," as opposed to the previous "utterance of YHWH Sabaoth." The announcement consists of three statements introduced by the verb *wĕhāyâ*, "and it shall be," followed by a fourth that describes the results of the previous three. V. 4 contains the introductory statement concerning the diminishing of the "glory of Israel." V. 5a contains a simile comparing this diminishing of Israel to the harvest of grain, and the simile in v. 5b compares it to the gleaning of ears in Emeq Rephaim. The concluding statement in v. 6a-bα describes the result of Israel's diminishing in terms of the few gleanings left after harvest.

The prophetic announcement that humanity will recognize YHWH in 17:7-8 is based on a simple two-part structure that contrasts a positive statement of what humanity will do to a negative statement of what it will not do. V. 7 states that humanity will look to its Maker, the Holy One of Israel. V. 8 states that it will not look to the idolatrous objects of pagan worship that people build with their own hands. Its focus on humanity's recognition of YHWH and its central location within the passage (at the head of the statements concerning the future consequences of Israel's punishment) indicate that this passage expresses the primary concern of 17:1–18:7.

The prophetic announcement concerning YHWH's punishment of Israel and recognition by the nations in 17:9–18:7 is designed to demonstrate that YHWH's punishment of Israel, expressed here in terms of the agricultural metaphor of trimming the shoots at harvesttime, will result in the nations' recognition of YHWH's power. It includes three major sections, defined by the introductory exclamation *hôy* in 17:12 and 18:1.

Isaiah 17:9-11 constitutes an announcement of judgment against Israel. It is based on the case-consequence pattern of Israelite case law that calls for an indictment followed by a consequence or announcement of punishment. Vv. 9-10a comprise the indictment that Israel has abandoned YHWH. The indictment begins with a 3rd-person objective statement in v. 9 that the future ruin of Israel will be like the ruined cities of the Amorites and Hivites that they abandoned on account of the Israelite conquest under Joshua (cf. Deut 7:1). The mention of the Amorites and Hivites is particularly significant here, in that the previously mentioned cities of Aroer (Isa 17:2, *RSV* margin) were on the border of the Amorite kingdom (Deut 4:47-48; Josh 12:2) conquered by the Reubenites (Josh 13:16). The passage clearly intends to use the abandoned Amorite cities of Aroer as a paradigm for Israel's coming punishment. The indictment proper appears in v. 10a. Its introductory causal *kî,* "because," indicates that Israel's forgetting of YHWH is the cause of the coming punishment. Furthermore, the formulation of the indictment in 2nd-person feminine address form, like the announcement of consequences that follows, heightens the accusatory nature of the passage. The consequences or announcement of punishment proper follows in vv. 10b-11, introduced by ʿal-kēn, "therefore." V. 10b begins with the statement of the case that the people will plant foreign shoots, here identified as the Phoenician and Syrian precursors to the Hellenistic Adonis gardens that were planted to mark the onset of the summer season when the god would die (Kaiser, *Isaiah 13–39,* 83; cf. Delcor). The prophet's statement of consequences in v. 11 presupposes the rapid demise of these shoots, which usually withered in a day's time, to indicate Israel's rapid "harvest" or painful punishment.

The announcement concerning (YHWH's) rebuke of the nations/sea in 17:12-14 employs themes and language from mythological traditions concerning YHWH's subduing of the sea at creation to express the defeat of the nations. Although YHWH is not explicitly mentioned here, the deity is presupposed as the subject. This announcement comprises four syntactically independent statements that describe the basic sequence of events pertaining to YHWH's rebuke of the nations/sea. V. 12 contains the introductory statement that compares the multitude of nations to the roaring of the sea. V. 13 takes up the rebuke of the nations, whose scattering is expressed metaphorically in terms of the grain that is thrown into the wind in order to be threshed at harvesttime. V. 14a describes the resulting death or demise of the nations by morning. V. 14b concludes with a summary-appraisal statement maintaining that such a fate awaits "those who hate [*RSV* 'despoil'] us" and "those who despoil [*RSV* 'plunder'] us." The identity of "us" is not made clear, but the setting of this mythical motif in the context of the Jerusalem cult tradition indicates that it refers to Jerusalem or Judah (see below on Setting).

The announcement concerning YHWH's recognition by the nations in 18:1-7 is demarcated by its introductory exclamation *hôy* and its focus on Cush or Ethiopia. It begins with a syntactically independent statement concerning the land of Cush in vv. 1-2a. Although the introductory *hôy* is frequently taken as a threatening cry against Cush, typical of prophetic woe oracles (cf. Janzen, *Mourning Cry*, 60-61), the absence of a threat against Cush and the identity of the messengers in v. 2 as Israelite messengers sent to Cush indicates that the *hôy* is nothing more than an opening interjection of recognition (cf. *RSV*). V. 2b is formulated with the imperative verb *lĕkû,* "go," which introduces a command to messengers to go to the land of Cush. Clearly one cannot identify the messengers described here with those sent by Cush along its rivers, as the latter messengers are sent to a nation described with the characteristics of the land of Cush, "a nation tall and smooth, to a people feared near and far, a nation mighty and conquering, whose land the rivers divide." Although these messengers are frequently identified as Ethiopian messengers received in the Judean court, the use of the imperative *lĕkû,* "go," indicates that these messengers are sent, not received. As Judah undoubtedly carried on diplomatic relations with Egypt, ruled by an Ethiopian dynasty in this period, the overall concern of 17:1–18:7 with Israel suggests that this statement refers to the embassy sent by King Hoshea of Israel to King So of Egypt in preparation for the revolt against Assyria in 724 B.C.E. (2 Kgs 17:4).

Isaiah 18:3-6 shifts to an announcement that the nations of the earth will recognize YHWH. The announcement proper appears in v. 3, expressed in terms of the nations "seeing" and "hearing" (contra 6:9). The basis for this recognition, introduced by a causal *kî,* appears in vv. 4-6, which express it in terms of YHWH's trimming the shoots at the time of harvest. V. 4 contains the prophet's report of YHWH's statement, including the messenger formula in v. 4aα and the statement proper in v. 4aβ-b. YHWH's 1st-person statement, "I will be at rest and I will look about in my habitation," corresponds to that of a homeowner relaxing in the garden and contemplating the trimming of decorative plants. In the present context, these verses indicate that YHWH is the one who performs the following actions. The prophet's explanation appears in vv. 5-6, introduced by a causal *kî.* V. 5 states that he (i.e., YHWH) will trim the shoots. Although v. 6 is syntactically independent, the subject of the sentence is the trimmed shoots of v. 5 that will be left for the birds and the beasts. In the context of 17:1–18:7, this trimming of the shoots must be understood as YHWH's punishment of Israel (cf. 17:4-6, 10b-11; 18:2b).

The concluding statement of the subunit appears in v. 7, which reprises the description of Cush in v. 2b and indicates that Cush will present a tribute-gift *(šay)* to YHWH at Mt. Zion. Such a gift indicates tribute due to a conqueror (Ps 68:30 [*RSV* 29]) or to YHWH as sovereign lord (Ps 76:12 [*RSV* 11]). The presentation of this gift "at that time" associates it with YHWH's "trimming of the shoots" and indicates that it is the result of the Ethiopians' witness of YHWH's punishment of Israel.

Genre

The overarching genre of chs. 17–18 is the prophetic *maśśā'* or PROPHETIC PRONOUNCEMENT. As noted above, the genre has no set structure or literary form, but it is constituted by its function as a prophetic discourse that attempts to identify how YHWH's intentions are manifested in human affairs. Consequently, the explanatory function, designed to demonstrate YHWH's activity in the realm of human events, is the key criterion for identifying this genre.

In the case of chs. 17–18, the explanatory function is evident from the fact that the text begins with observations of a present state of affairs. It extrapolates projected consequences that are identified as an act of YHWH. Here the *maśśā'* begins with an observation of the present ruined state of the city of Damascus and the abandonment of the cities of Aroer. In both cases, the governing verb is a passive participial formation (*mûsār,* "removed," for Damascus in 17:1, and *'ăzubôt,* "abandoned," for the cities of Aroer in v. 2), indicating their present situation. The language then shifts to the imperfect as the text projects future consequences that will apply to Israel. Key among them are the agricultural metaphor by which Israel is portrayed as a harvested or gleaned field (17:4-6) and the comparison with the abandoned cities of the Amorites and Hivites (cf. the abandoned cities of Aroer in v. 2; biblical tradition identifies these cities as Amorite; Num 32:33-34; Deut 3:12-13; 4:47-48; Josh 12:2-3). Both prepare the reader/hearer for the conclusion that YHWH is the active agent behind these events in that YHWH is responsible for the fertility of the land and for driving out the previous inhabitants so that Israel could take possession of it (cf. Deut 26:5-15). The rebuke of the nations in Isa 17:12-14 reinforces the notion of YHWH's activity in this text even though it does not explicitly mention YHWH. Finally, Cush's recognition of YHWH is set in a context that makes clear that YHWH is responsible for "trimming of the shoots," i.e., for the ruin projected for Israel in the earlier part of this text. In this respect, the *maśśā'* in chs. 17–18 does not identify YHWH's action in an event that has already taken place. Rather, it employs observations of present phenomena, together with an understanding of YHWH's active role in nature and history, to project a future act of YHWH in the human realm.

The *maśśā',* or PROPHETIC PRONOUNCEMENT, in chs. 17–18 employs a number of generic elements in presenting its explanation of YHWH's involvement in human affairs. The most important of these is the prophetic ANNOUNCEMENT OF JUDGMENT. This genre is already apparent in the two oracular reports of 17:1b-3 and 17:4-6, which employ the ORACULAR FORMULA to convey simple announcements of judgment by YHWH. These announcements contain no indictment but simply proclaim the misfortune that is about to fall on Israel.

The full pattern of the prophetic ANNOUNCEMENT OF JUDGMENT appears in 17:9–18:7. Isa 17:9-11 provides the basis of this section, including both the indictment and the announcement of consequences or punishment typical of the legal background of this genre. Nevertheless, the form is modified here to meet the explanatory needs of the overarching *maśśā'* genre. The indictment in 17:7-10a begins with a focus on the phenomenon of Israel's soon-to-be abandoned cities, calling to mind the abandoned cities of Aroer in 17:2, and then presents the indictment proper as the cause for such a phenomenon. By beginning with such an explicit comparison with the abandoned Amorite cities, the indictment thereby causes the reader/hearer to focus on YHWH's expulsion of the Amorites and leads to the conclusion that YHWH will likewise be responsible for Israel's similar fate. The ANNOUNCEMENT OF JUDGMENT proper in 17:10b-11 expresses Israel's punishment by means of agricultural harvest imagery, in analogy with 17:4-6, and again points to YHWH as the cause of punishment in that YHWH provides the harvests of the land that the people reap. The focus on the people's planting of Adonis gardens points to the ultimate cause of the problem: the people have failed to recognize YHWH's role in creating the fertility of the land. They will therefore suffer historical consequences since YHWH both provides fertility and protects from outside invaders on the condition of Israel's adherence to its covenant with YHWH (cf. Deuteronomy 28).

The balance of the passage likewise employs additional generic elements to support the explanatory function of the *maśśā'* and its attempt to demonstrate the need to recognize YHWH as the ultimate cause of events in the land. The introductory *hôy* of Isa 17:12-14 is frequently interpreted as the standard opening of the prophetic (→) woe oracle, but no accusation of wrongdoing is leveled against the nations in this *hôy* statement. Rather, the fate of the nations is presented in 3rd-person objective terms, indicating that the *hôy* is addressed to the prophet's audience and functions merely as an exclamation designed to draw the audience's attention to the discourse. This is supported by the 1st-person common plural formulation of the SUMMARY-APPRAISAL in v. 14b, which indicates that the party addressed is not the nations but an unidentified "us." The SUMMARY-APPRAISAL, identified by its opening demonstrative *zeh*, "this," and by its didactic function, is apparently designed to demonstrate to Isaiah's audience that YHWH guarantees protection against enemies. Consequently, there is no need to send messengers to propose a foreign alliance, as portrayed in 18:7. The didactic thrust of the SUMMARY-APPRAISAL is that such action is uncalled for.

Finally, one should recognize that the introductory *hôy* of 18:1-7 likewise does not function as the introduction to a prophetic (→) woe oracle. No accusation is leveled against Cush, which merely functions as an example of the nations that will recognize YHWH. Again, the *hôy* functions merely as an exclamation that draws the reader's/hearer's attention to the issue at hand, i.e., that even far-off Cush will recognize YHWH, whereas northern Israel, which sends messengers to Cush to procure the protection that YHWH guarantees, does not. The *maśśā'* thereby identifies the cause of YHWH's action against Israel.

Setting

Scholars generally question the unity of chs. 17–18 based on its variety of forms and its shifting concerns with Damascus, Israel, the nations, and Cush. Wildberger concedes that 17:1-11 constitutes a "kerygmatic unity" (*Jesaja*, 638-39) in that these verses have been edited under the influence of a polemical attitude against idolatry characteristic of Deutero-Isaiah (p. 655). Yet the above analysis of the structure and genre of this passage demonstrates that the unity of chs. 17–18 does not lie in its shifting forms and the identity of the nations that appear within this text. Rather, it lies in the agricultural imagery, especially that of the harvest, which permeates the various subunits, and in the overall concern with the recognition of YHWH, specifically the failure to recognize YHWH on the part of northern Israel and the projected recognition of YHWH by Cush and the other nations of the world. The concern with idolatry in 17:7-8 stems from the overall concern with the harvest and with recognition of YHWH. Such a concern in turn grows out of the concern with the Adonis cults associated with the harvest and the people's adherence to a deity associated with Phoenicia and Syria. Israel's political alliance with Syria during the Syro-Ephraimite War comes into play here as the oracle begins with a description of the ruined state of Damascus and the loss of sovereignty in Syria as a means for projecting the fate of Israel if it continues on its present course. The need to recognize YHWH must be conceived in both religious and political terms. YHWH guarantees the security of the people; there is therefore no need to turn to alliances with foreign powers. Just as the Syro-Ephraimite coalition led to disaster for Damascus and the Transjordan, so will an alliance with Cush or Egypt lead to disaster for Israel.

Isaiah 17:12-14 and 18:1-7 have proved to be particularly key texts in the discussion of the unity of this passage. Many scholars trace 17:12-14 to the Jerusalem cult tradition, based on its affinities with Psalm 46 and the motif of YHWH's rebuke of the nations that threaten Zion (see Kilian, *Jesaja 1–39*, 49-51, for a summary of the discussion). Important elements of the Jerusalem tradition appear here, including use of the combat myth in which the nations are portrayed in terms of the primordial sea, the rebuke of the nations just as the sea was defeated at the time of creation, and the motif of relief in the morning after a night of threatening chaos. Nevertheless, the inclusion of the harvest motif, in which the defeat of the nations is expressed in terms of the separation of chaff from grain, demonstrates that this passage was intentionally designed for its present context, and that the prophet merely employed language and motifs from the Jerusalem tradition to meet the needs of the present text. Likewise, 18:1-7 is frequently challenged in that its concern with Cush causes many scholars to associate it with the Egyptian material in chs. 19–20. But the above discussion demonstrates that there is no threat against Cush in this passage. Rather, the threat is against the messengers that are sent to Cush. This text employs the harvest metaphor to illustrate the calamity that will overcome the land of the source of the messengers as a means to facilitate their nations' recognition of YHWH. In this context, Cush is representative of the nations at large.

The historical background of this passage must be placed after the Syro-Ephraimite War and prior to northern Israel's revolt against Assyria in 724 B.C.E. The passage employs participial forms to point to the ruin of Damascus and the abandonment of the cities of Aroer as a present fact. Tiglath-pileser III's campaigns of 734-732 ruined Damascus and cost Syria its sovereignty (cf. 17:3; for a discussion of Damascus's demise, see W. T. Pitard, *Ancient Damascus: A Historical Study of the Syrian City-State from Earliest Times until Its Fall to the*

Assyrians in 732 B.C.E. [Winona Lake: Eisenbrauns, 1986] 179-89). Likewise, his troops took control of the Gilead region, including the territory north of the traditional boundary of Moab at the Arnon River (cf. Isaiah 15–16). This territory corresponds to the region of Aroer (cf. Num 32:34; Deut 2:36; 3:12; 4:48; Josh 12:2; 13:9, 16; 2 Sam 24:5; 2 Kgs 10:33; 1 Chr 5:8). The loss of the Transjordan stripped Israel of a major buffer zone and thus impaired its defensive capability (cf. Isa 17:3). The passage points to the ruin of Damascus and the abandonment of the region of Aroer as a means to project future catastrophe for Israel — the same catastrophe that the Amorites, who previously inhabited the region of Aroer, suffered when the Israelites entered the country. Insofar as 18:1-7 describes messengers sent to Cush, King Hoshea's embassy to King So of Egypt prior to the revolt of 724 appears to be the appropriate setting for this warning of impending destruction for Israel (2 Kgs 17:4). Isaiah is clearly opposed to Hoshea's move and sees in it only disaster for Israel, which had already suffered as a result of its alliance with Damascus in the Syro-Ephraimite War.

The social setting for this passage appears to be the Judean royal court. The projection of Cushite tribute to YHWH at Mt. Zion in 18:7 and the use of rebuke of the nations motif common to the Jerusalem cult tradition confirm this setting. Judah and other countries in the region were undoubtedly approached by Hoshea for support in his bid for independence. The present oracle would therefore have been produced in reaction to northern Israelite plans to obtain the backing of Egypt or Cush in an attempted revolt. In this respect, chs. 17–18 point to Isaiah's role as advisor to the king of Judah (cf. chs. 7; 36–39), although whether this role is official or self-appointed is not clear. The oracle states Isaiah's objections to involvement in such a scheme. The Syro-Ephraimite alliance failed to resist Assyria and resulted in the ruin of Syria and the loss of Gilead. An Egyptian alliance with Israel will result in Israel's ruin. Instead, Judah should trust in YHWH's guarantee of security and avoid any association with this ill-fated plan.

Intention

Isaiah 17–18 presupposes the historical situation of Hoshea's embassy to King So of Egypt to gain support for his revolt against the Assyrian empire in 724 (2 Kgs 17:4). As noted above, the passage points to the results of the Syro-Ephraimite War, the ruin of Damascus and the loss of the Transjordan region, as a means to project similar disastrous consequences for Israel if it joins with Egypt in an attempt to throw off Assyrian hegemony.

The structure of this text indicates that the recognition of YHWH, as opposed to foreign deities, is the key issue. Isa 17:7-8 assumes the central position in this text at the head of the projected consequences of Israel's actions. Although it follows 17:4-6, which is introduced by the *wĕhāyâ bayyôm hahû'* formula, the absence of the syntactical connection in the opening formula *bayyôm hahû'* in 17:7 marks this passage off from what precedes it, and indicates to the reader that an important transition has taken place in the text. From 17:7-8, the text focuses primarily on this issue. The people of Israel do not recognize the rock of their security (17:10). YHWH repulses the nations that attempt to despoil the land (17:12-14), and the nations in their turn will recognize YHWH (18:3-7). The agricultural harvest metaphor lends itself to this concern insofar as YHWH is conceived as the owner of the land and the ultimate guarantor of its fertility and security (cf. Leviticus 26; Deuteronomy 28). Just as the farmer reaps the harvest and leaves only a few gleanings as the remnant of the field's produce, so YHWH will harvest Israel, leaving only a few survivors as the remnant of the deity's sweep through the country.

The interest in Adonis cult practices likewise lends itself to the concern with the recognition of YHWH. As noted above, the onset of the dry summer season was marked by the planting of Adonis gardens in small dishes of water where the shoots would sprout and then die in a period of eight days to mark the death of the fertility deity Adonis (cf. de Vaux). The Adonis cult was widely practiced in Phoenicia and Syria and is thereby identified with Damascus and the Syro-Ephraimite coalition. Here the prophet seizes on the short life of the Adonis shoots to demonstrate the transitory nature of reliance on foreign powers. The owner of the land is YHWH, not Adonis, not the Syrians, and certainly not Cush. YHWH therefore guarantees both the fertility of the land and its safety from foreign invaders. When it comes time to reap the harvest, it will be YHWH's, and YHWH will be the one who takes action against the people for failing to recognize the deity's role in the land's welfare. As a result of YHWH's actions, the prophet maintains that Cush and the nations at large will recognize YHWH's power even if Israel does not.

The Jerusalem setting is particularly important here, in that it indicates that this text is addressed to a Judean audience, not the least of which is the Davidic king. Chs. 17–18 thereby function as the prophet's warning to avoid involvement with Israel in its attempted alliance with Egypt. The result can only be disaster. Judah must rely on its tradition of YHWH's promise of security to the land, thereby recognizing YHWH, not foreign deities or powers, as its ultimate source of security.

Bibliography

J. Day, *God's Conflict with the Dragon and the Sea: Echoes of a Canaanite Myth in the Old Testament* (Cambridge: Cambridge University Press, 1985) 101-3; M. Delcor, "Le problème des jardins d'Adonis dan Isaïe 17,9-11 à la lumière de la civilisation Syro-Phénicienne," *Syria* 55 (1978) 371-94; B. Gosse, "Isaïe 17,12-14 dans la rédaction du livre d'Isaïe," *BN* 58 (1991) 20-23; H. P. Müller, *Ursprunge und Strukturen alttestament-licher Eschatologie* (BZAW 109; Berlin: Töpelmann, 1969) 86-101; F. Stolz, *Strukturen und Figuren im Kult von Jerusalem* (BZAW 118; Berlin: de Gruyter, 1970) 214-15; Talmon, "Prophetic Rhetoric" (→ 2:2-4); R. de Vaux, "The Cults of Adonis and Osiris: A Comparative Study," in *The Bible and the Ancient Near East* (tr. D. McHugh; London: Darton, Longman & Todd, 1966) 210-37; H. Winckler, "Das Land Kus und Jes. 18," in *Alttestamentliche Untersuchungen* (Leipzig: E. Pfeiffer, 1892) 146-56.

PRONOUNCEMENT CONCERNING EGYPT, 19:1–20:6

Structure

The unit begins with the superscription *maśśā' miṣrāyîm,* "Pronouncement of Egypt," in 19:1a and continues through 20:6, where the superscription *maśśā' midbar-yām,* "Pronouncement of the Wilderness of the Sea," introduces the following unit. Although 20:1-6 focuses on Isaiah's symbolic action at the time of the Assyrian siege of Ashdod, the prophet's sign is interpreted in relation to the anticipated conquest of Egypt by the Assyrians. Isa 20:1-6 must therefore be included with the material concerning Egypt in 19:1-25. Consequently, the first structural subdivision in this unit is between the superscription in 19:1a and the *maśśā'* proper in 19:1b–20:6.

As noted above, the *maśśā'* genre has no set structure or other formal identifying characteristics other than its contents, which attempt to identify the manifestation of YHWH's intentions in the realm of human events. Here the basic structural division in the *maśśā'* proper is between 19:1b-25, which focuses on YHWH's future plans for Egypt, and 20:1-6, a report of a symbolic action, which focuses on a past event as a basis for the prophecy concerning Egypt. In this instance, Isaiah's symbolic action in relation to the siege of Ashdod is presented as a prophecy that anticipates Assyria's conquest of Egypt. Consequently, the report of Isaiah's symbolic action legitimizes the preceding material by demonstrating that YHWH's intentions concerning Egypt's upcoming punishment and exaltation were made known in the past.

The prophecy concerning Egypt in 19:1b-25 consists of three basic subdivisions, including the theophanic announcement of YHWH's punishment of Egypt in 19:1b-10, a taunt against Pharaoh and his officials in 19:11-15, and the announcement of future consequences for Egypt in 19:16-25. Although these three subsections are held together by their common concern with YHWH's upcoming actions in relation to Egypt, each is generically distinct and syntactically independent.

The theophanic announcement concerning YHWH's punishment of Egypt in 19:1b-10 is syntactically unified by its conjunctive *wāws* throughout the passage and its generic basis in the theophany report. In keeping with the typical two-part theophanic form, vv. 1b-4 focus on YHWH's coming to Egypt and vv. 5-10 focus on the consequences of YHWH's coming as manifested in the natural world. Theophanic reports are commonly cast as prophetic announcements of punishment. Consequently, vv. 1b-4, demarcated by the oracular report formula in v. 4bα, present a prophetic announcement of punishment against Egypt in relation to YHWH's theophany. The prophet is the speaker throughout, as indicated by the objective 3rd-person references to YHWH in vv. 1b and 4. V. 1b is an introductory statement that announces YHWH's approach to Egypt (v. 1bα) and Egypt's terrified reaction (v. 1bα). The prophet then reports YHWH's oracular threat against Egypt in vv. 2-4. YHWH's speech in vv. 2-4bα includes three statements, each involving a 1st-person singular verb. It includes statements that YHWH will stir up civil war in Egypt (v. 2), that YHWH will swallow or destroy Egypt's counsel (v. 3a), and that YHWH will hand Egypt over to a harsh ruler (vv. 3b-4bα).

Verses 5-10 are frequently considered as a unit separate from vv. 1b-4 because they focus on the drying up of the Nile River rather than on Egypt's political situation (Wildberger, *Jesaja,* 703-4). But the conjunctive *wāw*-consecutive verbal form of *wĕniššĕtû-mayim,* "and waters will dry up," which introduces the passage in v. 5, and the relation of natural upheaval to YHWH's approach in the theophanic report genre demonstrate the structural link between vv. 1b-4 and vv. 5-10. The passage focuses on the consequences of YHWH's approach to Egypt by depicting the natural disaster of the drying up of the Nile, the primary support for life in Egypt, and its effects on the people's livelihood. The passage is constituted by a series of statements, each introduced by a *wāw*-consecutive perfect verb, which presents a sequence of events leading from natural disaster to human suffering. V. 5 focuses on the drying up of the waters of the Nile. Vv. 6-7 focuses on the stench caused by the death of plant life around the dried Nile. V. 8 focuses on the languishing fishermen. V. 9 focuses on the confounding of the textile workers. Finally, v. 10 summarizes the entire situation by pointing to the failure of those in Egypt who depend on the Nile to provide a living.

The taunt against Pharaoh and his officers and counselors in 19:11-15 is syntactically independent from the preceding material. It is demarcated by its initial exclamation, introduced by *'ak,* "how!" and by its contents, which focus on the Egyptians' inability to fathom YHWH's intentions for Egypt. It is constituted by four syntactically independent statements. The first is the exclamation in v. 11a that focuses on the foolishness of the officials of Zoan and the advisors of Pharaoh. The second is a rhetorical question in v. 12, cast in 2nd-person plural address form directed to Pharaoh's officials, which emphasizes their incompetence. The third is also a rhetorical question, this time in 2nd-person singular address form apparently directed to Pharaoh, which questions the competence of his counselors, who are unable to declare what YHWH plans for Egypt. Finally, the prophet summarizes his views of the Egyptians' incompetence in vv. 13-15 by pointing out their foolishness (v. 13) and by pointing to YHWH as the cause of their confusion (vv. 14-15). Accordingly, he states that YHWH introduces confusion in Egypt in v. 14a and then describes the results in vv. 14b-15 in terms of Egypt's going astray with its leaders unable to act.

The announcement of the future consequences and results for Egypt is clearly demarcated by its characteristic introductory *bayyôm hahû'* ("in that day") formula in vv. 16, 18, 19, 23, and 24. Although the passage is syntactically independent, it is linked to the preceding material by its references to "that day," which can refer only to the previously mentioned theophanic appearance of YHWH in Egypt. The passage is constituted by a series of statements, each introduced by the *bayyôm hahû'* formula, which project the successive stages of YHWH's plan to punish and then bless Egypt. The first is vv. 16-17, which focus on the Egyptians' fear of YHWH's actions, here expressed as his "moving hand," and of the land of Judah, which apparently figures in YHWH's plan. The second is v. 18, which refers to five cities in the land of Egypt that speak the language of Canaan and are sworn to YHWH. The third is vv. 19-22, which refer to an altar in Egypt and a stele on the border of Egypt that are presented as signs of Egypt's coming distress and healing. The four sentences that constitute this section introduce the altar and stele in Egypt (v. 19), present them as a sign (v. 20), indicate the Egyptians' acknowledgment of YHWH (v. 21), and describe YHWH's punishment and subsequent healing of Egypt (v. 22). The fourth is v. 23, which announces a highway from Assyria to Egypt and Egypt's serving of Assyria. The fifth is vv. 24-25, which focus on YHWH's blessing of the land, including Israel, Egypt, and Assyria.

Isaiah 20:1-6 is distinguished by its narrative form, which relates Isaiah's symbolic action to the Assyrian siege of Ashdod as a past event. As noted above, it provides a basis for the preceding material concerning the future of Egypt by pointing to Isaiah's action as a past announcement of YHWH's intention to have the Assyrians conquer Egypt. The narrative begins with a temporal statement in 20:1 based on an invasion report formula that sets the action in relation to the Assyrian conquest of Ashdod in the reign of Sargon II. The report of a symbolic action proper appears in vv. 2-6, introduced by the formula *bā'ēt hahî'*, "in that time." The narrative follows the typical form of the report of a symbolic action by presenting YHWH's instruction to Isaiah to perform the symbolic act together with Isaiah's compliance in v. 2. Vv. 3-6 then present the explanation of the act. First, vv. 3-4 state the analogy between Isaiah walking naked and barefoot for three years and the coming captivity of the Egyptians, who will be naked and barefoot when the Assyrians lead them away captive. Vv. 5-6 then state the consequences for the Philistines, who will be dismayed by this prediction of Egypt's fall, their main hope for relief from the Assyrians.

Genre

The SUPERSCRIPTION in 19:1a identifies this passage as a prophetic *maśśā'* or PROPHETIC PRONOUNCEMENT concerning Egypt. Again, the *maśśā'* has no formal structure or literary characteristics but is constituted by its explanatory function to identify YHWH's intentions as manifested in the realm of human events. This function is evident throughout chs. 19–20, which project the conquest of Egypt as an act of YHWH. Isa 19:1b-25 contrasts YHWH with the counselors of Egypt by focusing on the Egyptians' inability to fathom YHWH's plans for Egypt. Vv. 1b-4 describe YHWH's actions against Egypt with statements that declare YHWH's intention to deliver Egypt into the hands of a harsh ruler. V. 3 makes explicit reference to "swallowing" or "destroying" Egypt's "counsel." Vv. 11-15 emphasize the incompetence of the Egyptian officials by highlighting their "stupid counsel" (v. 11) and their inability to fathom "what YHWH Sabaoth has decided concerning Egypt" (v. 12). Likewise, v. 14 emphasizes YHWH's role in confusing Pharaoh's officials, resulting in Egypt's confusion and inability to act. Whereas 19:1b-15 present YHWH's plan concerning Egypt as an event that is taking place in the present, as indicated by the participial verb forms employed in v. 1b, vv. 16-25 project the realization of YHWH's intentions in the future with the eventual blessing of the land, including Israel, Egypt, and Assyria. Vv. 16-17 in particular refer to YHWH's actions as "the shaking of the hand of YHWH Sabaoth [*těnûpat yad-yhwh ṣěbā'ôt*] that he shakes against him [i.e., Egypt]" and "the plan of YHWH Sabaoth [*'ăṣat yhwh ṣěbā'ôt*] that he decides [*yô'ēṣ*] against him [i.e., Egypt]." Isa 20:1-6 then identifies the Assyrian conquest of Ashdod as the basis for this projection by pointing to Isaiah's symbolic actions in relation to the siege of the city. Here the prophet portrays himself walking naked and barefoot for three years as a sign and portent that predicts the Assyrian conquest of Egypt as an act of YHWH.

The prophetic *maśśā'* in chs. 19–20 is constituted by a number of subordinate generic elements. The first is the PROPHECY CONCERNING A FOREIGN NATION in 19:1b-25. Like the prophetic *maśśā'*, the PROPHECY CONCERNING A FOREIGN NATION has no specific formal identifying characteristics. Instead, it is constituted on the basis of its focus on the destruction of a foreign nation by an enemy. In many respects, it is compatible with the *maśśā'* genre in that its intention is to identify the destruction of a foreign nation as an act of YHWH, God of Israel. The destruction is generally identified as an event in progress, which corresponds to the use of the participles describing YHWH's approach to Egypt at the beginning of the passage.

The second is the theophany announcement in 19:1b-10. It is based in the (→) theophany report, which describes a theophany of YHWH, but differs from that genre in that it does not merely describe YHWH's coming but projects the results of that coming in the natural world, as indicated by the *wāw*-consecutive perfect verbs in vv. 5-10. The two typical elements of the (→) theophany report, YHWH's coming and manifestations of YHWH's coming in terms of natural upheaval, appear here in vv. 1b-4 and vv. 5-10, respectively. Together, they correlate sociopolitical and cosmological events by portraying the internal political struggle in Egypt (see below on Setting) and the drying up of the Nile and its consequences for Egyptian society as parallel aspects of YHWH's activity and plans for Egypt.

The PROPHETIC ANNOUNCEMENT OF PUNISHMENT in vv. 1b-4 is frequently a constituent generic element of the (→) theophany report. It is generally the essential element of the PROPHECY OF PUNISHMENT, and it is identified here by its characteristic introductory *hinnēh,* "behold," along with its 1st-person address in which YHWH announces punishment against Egypt. The ORACULAR FORMULA in v. 4bα identifies YHWH as the speaker in the report of an oracle in vv. 2-4.

Isaiah 19:11-15 presents the consequences of YHWH's coming to Egypt and, as such, relates to the PROPHETIC ANNOUNCEMENT OF PUNISHMENT. But these verses are cast in the form of a TAUNT against Pharaoh and his counselors, and thereby serve the purposes of the *maśśā'* by pointing out the inability of the Egyptians to understand YHWH's intentions. They contrast YHWH's power with Pharaoh's lack of power and thus highlight the difference between the God of Israel and the God of Egypt. The RHETORICAL QUESTIONS in vv. 11-12 emphasize the effect of the TAUNT by confronting the Egyptians directly with their inadequacy and incompetence in the face of YHWH's power.

The ANNOUNCEMENTS of future events in vv. 16-25 are identified by their characteristic *bayyôm hahû'* formulas. Here they project the full realization of YHWH's intentions into the future, thereby providing direction for understanding the purpose of the current chaos in Egypt. As such, they indicate that Egyptian internal conflict is not only caused by YHWH but serves YHWH's intention to realize blessing in the land involving Israel, Egypt, and Assyria.

Finally, a REPORT OF A SYMBOLIC ACTION appears in 20:1-6. It is introduced by the INVASION REPORT in v. 1, which establishes the historical context of the report in relation to Sargon II's conquest of Ashdod in 712. The report itself appears in vv. 2-6 and includes the standard elements of the genre: the instruction to perform the act in v. 2a, the report of compliance in v. 2b, and the interpretation of the act in vv. 3-6. This REPORT OF A SYMBOLIC ACTION confirms and legitimizes the main intent of the *maśśā'* by pointing to the fall of Ashdod as a prelude to the fall of Egypt, and by indicating that these events are sanctioned and planned by YHWH.

Setting

Although chs. 19–20 focus on the upcoming punishment of Egypt, scholarly consensus maintains that these chapters do not constitute an original literary unity. Rather, chs. 19–20 are a composite text made up of three constituent textual subunits, which are defined on grounds of both form and content. Isa 19:1-15 is a prophetic ORACLE that announces YHWH's coming punishment of Egypt. Isa 19:16-25 contains a series of prose statements, each introduced by the formula *bayyôm hahû',* that project blessing for Egypt, Israel, and Assyria following a period of punishment against Egypt. Finally, 20:1-6 is a prose historical NARRATIVE concerning Isaiah's symbolic action in relation to the Assyrian siege of Ashdod and projecting punishment against Egypt.

The issue is further complicated by the view of many scholars that both 19:1-15 and 19:16-25 are composite texts in and of themselves. For example, Wildberger (*Jesaja*, 703-4) notes the appearance of the oracular formula at the end of v. 4 and the thematic shift in v. 5 in order to argue that only vv. 1b-4 and vv. 11-14 constitute the original oracle of the prophet predicting political chaos in Egypt. In contrast, vv. 5-10 focus on the natural disaster of a dried-up Nile River. Vv. 5-10 are therefore a secondary insertion into this text, and v. 15, identified as a prose expansion by Wildberger (*Jesaja*, 703), is merely a gloss (p. 707). Isa 19:16-25 is generally dated to the postexilic period due to the appearance of the *bayyôm hahû'* formula throughout the passage (vv. 16, 18, 19, 21, 23, 24) and its so-called universalist perspective. The *bayyôm hahû'* formula is generally taken as a formal indicator of a late redactional addition to prophetic texts, and the "universalist" perspective is generally believed to be the product of a postexilic setting. The appearance of the *bayyôm hahû'* formula at the beginning of statements in vv. 16, 18, 19, 23, and 24 serves as the basis for the view that 19:16-25 comprises a series of four or five additions made successively by separate hands in the postexilic period (Clements, *Isaiah 1–39*, 169-70; Kaiser, *Isaiah 13–39*, 105; Wildberger, *Jesaja*, 729-31).

The view that 20:1-6 was not composed by the same author(s) as 19:1-15 and 19:16-25 is justified by the fact that 20:1-6 is presented as a historical narrative about the prophet, whereas 19:1-15 and 19:16-25 are presented as statements by the prophet. But a number of questionable assumptions in the scholarly discussion of this material indicates that this consensus needs to be reconsidered.

As noted in the discussions of structure and genre above, 19:1-15 comprises an announcement of a theophany. The text is based in the theophany report genre, which typically combines an announcement of YHWH's approach together with a portrayal of natural upheaval. This generic identification undermines the contention that vv. 5-10 should be excised from this text because of the shift in theme between vv. 1b-4 and the appearance of the oracular formula in v. 4b. Rather, their portrayal of the drying up of the Nile River and the consequences for those who depend on the Nile for their living is the cosmological counterpart to the political chaos announced in vv. 1b-4 and 11-14. The theophany report genre combines both political and natural consequences of YHWH's appearance to suggest a comprehensive reaction to YHWH as ruler of both the social and natural realms. Likewise, the view that v. 15 is a prose expansion is based on the view that it is dependent on 9:13 (*RSV* 14), which likewise refers to "head and tail, palm branch and reed." Although these terms refer to leaders in both instances, 9:13 (*RSV* 14) is part of a larger passage directed against the northern kingdom of Israel. The lack of any reference to Egypt in 9:7 (*RSV* 8)–10:4 or to northern Israel in 19:1-15 indicates that Isaiah is merely using the same terminology to refer to leadership in two quite different contexts. The similar use of such terminology does not justify the view that the two passages are dependent in any way. Consequently, 19:1-15 stands as a literary unity.

A number of scholars have noted the close connection between vv. 23 and 24-25 (e.g., Wildberger, *Jesaja*, 730; Clements, *Isaiah 1–39*, 170), which suggests that they are written by the same hand. But this raises questions concerning the general view that vv. 16-25 must be constituted by separate units, especially since these verses describe a relatively coherent sequence of events that traces the eventual outcome of Egypt's punishment in blessing for Egypt, Israel, and Assyria. A number of assumptions have contributed to this view. The first is that the appearance of the *bayyôm hahû'* formula necessarily indicates a late redactional addition to the text. Nothing inherent in the formula requires such a view and, as demonstrated above, it appears in various Isaianic texts, such as 7:20 and 3:7. Likewise, the appearance of such a formula does not indicate a literarily independent statement, as the series in 7:18-25 demonstrates. Finally, the view that the supposed "universalism" of this text stems from a late postexilic setting must be rejected on the grounds that blessing for Egypt and Assyria hardly constitutes universalism, especially since Egypt is to be subservient to Assyria and Israel is clearly identified as a third party in this arrangement. Furthermore, contrary to the view of many scholars that no suitable preexilic setting can be postulated for this text, the following discussion will demonstrate that the scenario of a cooperative relationship between Egypt, Israel, and Assyria stems from the mid-7th century B.C.E., when the Assyrian monarch Esarhaddon conquered Egypt in 671 and his successor Assurbanipal installed the 26th Egyptian Dynasty (Saite) to rule the country. During this period, King Manasseh of Judah proved himself a loyal ally of Assyria, as Assurbanipal's annals indicate that Manasseh sent troops to support Assurbanipal's Egyptian campaign (*ANET,* 294).

A number of features suggest that only two stages of textual development stand behind 19:16-25. Indeed, the theme of judgment against Egypt does not begin to shift to one of salvation for Egypt at v. 16. Rather, the shift is evident only in vv. 19-22. Vv. 16-17 build on the imagery of 19:1-15 not only by emphasizing the coming judgment against Egypt and Egypt's fearful reaction to YHWH's action, but also by focusing on YHWH's "purpose/counsel" (*'ăṣat yhwh*) that he is "purposing/deciding" (*yô'ēṣ*) against Egypt. This terminology corresponds to earlier references in 19:1-15 that mock the "wise counselors of Pharaoh" (*yō'ăṣê par'ōh*) who "give stupid counsel" (*'ēṣâ nib'ārâ;* v. 11) and who are unable to declare "what YHWH Sabaoth has purposed [*yā'aṣ*] against Egypt" (v. 12). There is also a grammatical distinction in that vv. 16-17 consistently employ singular verbs (*yihyeh,* "will be"; *wěḥārad ûpāḥad,* "and he will tremble with fear/tremble and fear") and singular pronouns (*'ēlāyw,* "unto him," and *'ālāyw,* "against him") in reference to Egypt, whereas vv. 19-25 employ plural verbs (*yiṣ'ăqû,* "they cry"; *wěyādě'û,* "and they will know"; *wě'ābědû,* "and they will worship"; *wěnāděrû,* "and they will make vows"; *wěšillěmû,* "and they will perform them/repay"; *wěsābû,* "and they will return"; *wě'ābědû,* "and they will worship") and plural pronouns (*lāhem,* "for them"; *wěhiṣṣîlām,* "and deliver them"; *lāhem,* "their [supplications]"; *ûrěpā'ām,* "and heal them"). Finally, vv. 16-17 refer to "the land of Judah" but vv. 19-25 refer to "Israel."

These considerations suggest different authorship for vv. 16-17 and 19-25. On the one hand, vv. 16-17, which focus on Egypt's fear of YHWH's actions, clearly constitute the original conclusion to vv. 1-15. On the other hand, vv. 19-25 must be regarded as a later expansion of this text that projects the restoration of Egypt. V. 18 is somewhat ambiguous since it contains none of the criteria that indicate a division between vv. 16-17 and 19-25. A discussion of the historical background of the two text blocks demonstrates that v. 18 belongs with vv. 19-25.

The references to YHWH's stirring up Egyptians against Egyptians in 19:2 clearly presupposes the period of internal political instability Egypt suffered during the late 8th century. No less than four Egyptian dynasties were competing for power during this period, and not until approximately 715 did the 25th Dynasty, under the leadership of Pharaoh Shabaka, established its rule over all Egypt (J. Bright, *A History of Israel* [3rd ed.; Philadelphia: Westminster, 1981] 280-82; W. W. Hallo and W. K. Simpson, *The Ancient Near East: A History* [New York: Harcourt, Brace, Jovanovich, 1971] 287-92; J. H. Hayes and J. M. Miller, eds., *Israelite and Judaean History* [OTL; Philadelphia: Westminster, 1977] 415-16). The oracle is clearly intended to undermine confidence in Egypt, which is presented as internally divided, undecided, and weak.

This presents two potential settings for the oracle. The first is the revolt of the northern kingdom of Israel against Assyria in 724-721. According to 2 Kgs 17:4, King Hoshea of Israel sent messengers to So, king of Egypt, which suggests Egyptian backing for the support. Unfortunately, no Pharaoh So is known, although attempts have been made to see this as a reference either to Sais, capital of the 24th Dynasty, or to Osorkon IV, the last ruler of the 23rd Dynasty (Miller and Hayes, *History,* 234-36). Despite this difficulty, it seems clear that Israel's revolt was predicated on an expectation of Egyptian aid. In such an instance, Isaiah's oracle would have been designed to convince Hezekiah to stay out of the revolt since Egypt was an unstable and unreliable ally that would fear even tiny Judah. Sargon II's annals indicate that the Egyptians attempted to send a relief force in 720, but this force was defeated at Raphia (*ANET,* 284-85).

The second possible historical setting for this oracle is the Philistine revolt against Assyria in 713-711. Clear evidence of Egyptian involvement in this revolt is indicated by Sargon's annals (*ANET,* 285-87), although the Egyptians proved to be ineffective allies. Again, Isaiah's oracle would have been designed to warn Hezekiah against participating in this revolt. Although Shabaka had united Egypt by this time, Egypt's past history of inner division and its failure to aid Israel effectively would support Isaiah's advice to avoid confronting Assyria.

Several arguments speak in favor of a setting in relation to Israel's revolt. First, the internal division of Egypt was much more pronounced during the years 724-720 than during 713-711. Second, the oracle aligns YHWH's purposes with those of Assyria, and fits well with the prophet's condemnation of the northern kingdom of Israel (cf. 5:1-30; 9:7 [*RSV* 8]–10:4). Third, the Egyptians were defeated by Assyria at Raphia in 720 as mentioned above, but the oracle focuses only on internal Egyptian divisions, rather than past defeats, as the grounds for discounting Egypt. Furthermore, Sargon made no attempt to confront Egypt after 720, which conflicts with the oracle's portrayal of YHWH's advance against Egypt. In fact, although Sargon was clearly prepared to defend himself against Egyptian interference in Philistia, he attempted to establish trade relations with Egypt (cf. M. Elat, "The Economic Relations of the Neo-Assyrian Empire with Egypt," *JAOS* 98 [1978] 20-34, esp. 27-30; N. Na'aman, "The Brook of Egypt and Assyrian Policy on the Border of Egypt," *TA* 6 [1979] 68-90).

Isaiah 19:18-25 clearly does not date to the time of Isaiah. It conflicts directly with Isaiah's view of punishment against Egypt so clearly articulated in 18:1-7; 19:1-17; 30:1-7; and 31:1-3. Furthermore, a cooperative arrangement between Egypt, Israel, and Assyria, with Assyria as the dominant partner, flatly contradicts Isaiah's well-known opposition to Israelite or Judean alliances with foreign powers. Rather, the historical setting for this section must be placed in the reign of King Manasseh of Judah (687/6-642). During Manasseh's reign, Esarhaddon was able to bring Egypt under Assyrian control (671), and his successor, Assurbanipal, installed the 26th Dynasty, initially led by Necho and later by Psammetichus I (= Psamtik I), as the rulers of the country under Assyrian protection. During this period, Manasseh sent troops to support Assurbanipal's Egyptian campaigns (*ANET,* 294), and later sources, such as Letter of Aristeas 13, indicate that Jews began to settle in Egypt during the reign of Psammetichus, although it is uncertain whether Psammetichus I or Psammetichus II is intended here.

Verse 18 is particularly important in this regard because of its reference to five cities speaking the language of Canaan and swearing allegiance to YHWH. A number of foreign military colonies were established by the Assyrians and the Egyptian Saite (26th) Dynasty in Egypt during this period to defend Egyptian borders. A great deal of evidence suggests that the Jewish military colony at Elephantine at the southern border of Egypt was established at this time, and Jeremiah makes reference to Jewish colonies at Memphis, Pathros, Tahpanhes-Daphnae, and Migdol (Jer 44:1). The Jewish colony at Elephantine built its own temple for the worship of YHWH. Indeed, many VSS and 1QIsa^a read *haḥeres,* "the sun," in place of *haheres,* "the destruction," which suggests an original reference to the Egyptian city of On or Heliopolis, "City of the Sun," that was replaced by later scribes attempting to blot out a reference to a heretical temple that may have been located there (for full discussion of the Elephantine material, see B. Porten, *Archives from Elephantine* [Berkeley: University of California, 1968] esp. 8-16; idem, "The Jews in Egypt," in *Cambridge History of Judaism,* vol. 1: *Introduction: The Persian Period* [ed. W. D. Davies and L. Finkelstein; Cambridge: Cambridge University Press, 1984] 372-400). The vision of Assyrian domination in a cooperative relationship with Egypt and Israel corresponds well to Manasseh's policy of cooperation with Assyria. Isa 19:18-25 appears to be designed to relate Isaiah's oracle against Egypt to this policy by portraying it as the projected outcome of Isaiah's condemnation of the country.

Isaiah 20:1-6 is the key to establishing the setting of the entire passage. This narrative was clearly written to portray Isaiah's symbolic actions in relation to the Assyrian siege of Ashdod in 713-711. As such, it is directed against Egypt, which evidently encouraged the Philistines to revolt (cf. *ANET,* 285-87). The descriptive form of the narrative demonstrates that it was composed not by Isaiah but by another who was writing about him. The proper setting for such a composition would have evidently been a circle of disciples who intended to preserve a record about the prophet. Although it is difficult to establish exactly when this narrative was composed, it is clear that its placement in the present text, if not its composition, serves the interests of the Josianic redaction of the book of Isaiah.

It seems odd that this narrative functions as a confirmation or legitimization of the previous material concerning Egypt in the present form of the text.

It also seems odd that it returns to the theme of punishment against Egypt after 19:18-25, which projects a future of blessing for Egypt in association with Israel and Assyria. Yet a condemnation of Egypt in association with a siege of Ashdod is especially important during the reign of King Josiah. With the death of Assurbanipal in 627, it became increasingly clear that Assyria would no longer be able to dominate Judah. In fact, Josiah's program of national and religious reform began during the twelfth year of Josiah's reign according to 2 Chr 34:3 (i.e., 627), the time of Assurbanipal's death. Egypt was evidently an ally of Assyria at this time and stepped in to take control of territories previously controlled by Assyria. It is noteworthy that Psammetichus conducted a twenty-nine-year siege against the city of Ashdod (Herodotus 2.157). Consequently, Egypt presented the most formidable obstacle to Josiah's plans for reestablishing the Davidic empire (for discussion of this period, see Miller and Hayes, *History,* 383-85, although their theory that Egypt controlled Judah at this time must be rejected).

The placement of 20:1-6 in its present position reinforces the condemnation of Egypt that appears at the beginning of this passage, despite the scenario of blessing in 19:18-25, and it associates that condemnation with a siege of the city of Ashdod. In view of Egypt's alliance with Assyria at this time, the oracle demonstrates the results of Egypt's restoration; i.e., Egypt acts as Assyria's agent to carry captives who previously looked to Egypt for deliverance away from Ashdod and the Philistine coastland (cf. v. 6). Consequently, one must understand chs. 19–20 as a Josianic diatribe against Egypt in the late 7th century.

Intention

The overall intention of chs. 19–20 is governed by their characterization as a prophetic *maśśā'* and their focus on Egypt, in that they attempt to explain YHWH's intentions with regard to Egypt as manifested in human events. The specific details of this intention vary for each stage of the text's redaction.

In the present setting of the 5th-century edition of the book of Isaiah, chs. 19–20 function as a component of the oracles against the nations in chs. 13–23. These oracles are designed to announce YHWH's judgment against the nations prior to establishing sovereignty in Jerusalem, and concern those nations that came under Persian suzerainty in the late 6th century. Insofar as Persian activities were identified as acts of YHWH, the conquest of Egypt by Cambyses in 525 would be seen as a fulfillment of this oracle, demonstrating YHWH's intention to subdue the nations while establishing sovereignty throughout the world. For further discussion, see the introductory overview of chs. 13–23.

As the discussion of the setting of this text indicates, the present form of chs. 19–20 is the product of the late-7th-century Josianic redaction of Isaiah. Again, the explanatory function of the *maśśā'* genre defines the intention of this text as attempting to delineate YHWH's purpose concerning Egypt. During the latter part of the 7th century, Assyrian influence in the region waned, and Egypt reemerged as a major power in the Syro-Palestinian corridor. Egyptian activity in the region suggests that Egypt established control of much of the coastal plain with its trade route running toward the Jezreel Valley and Damascus as well as north to Phoenicia (see Miller and Hayes, *History,* 387-90). Although it is doubtful that Judah became a vassal to Egypt prior to the death of Josiah in 609, a reemergent Egypt would have posed the greatest threat to Josiah's program of national restoration. Chs. 19–20, with their focus on the condemnation of Egypt, serve Josiah's interests in this regard.

The arrangement of this section is somewhat odd in that it shifts from condemnation of Egypt (19:1-17), to blessing for Egypt (19:18-25), and finally back to a second condemnation (20:1-6). This alternation presupposes Egypt's experience throughout the period of Assyrian influence in the region. Egypt was initially threatened and conquered by Assyria, but the 26th (Saite) Dynasty emerged as a cooperative ally of Assyria after Assurbanipal relinquished direct control of the country. By returning to the theme of the condemnation of Egypt in 20:1-6 following the blessing outlined in 19:18-25, chs. 19–20 emphasize the original intent of Isaiah's condemnation of Egypt in 19:1-17. The focus on the Assyrian siege of Ashdod in 20:1-6 calls to mind the Egyptian siege of the city during the reign of Josiah. Likewise, Isaiah's symbolic action, which predicts the demise of Egypt, demonstrates Josiah's and Judah's hopes for the downfall of Egypt in this period.

As noted above in the discussion of setting, 19:1-25 represents an edition of this text that stems from the reign of King Manasseh of Judah (687/6-642). The text promotes Manasseh's policy of cooperation with Assyria and Egypt by presenting blessing for Egypt as the ultimate outcome of Isaiah's diatribes against the country. Following the condemnation of Egypt in the first part of the passage, 19:18-25 describes the process by which Egypt's fortunes will be reversed so that the country will eventually emerge as a partner who will share blessings with Assyria and Israel.

Several features of this text are noteworthy in this regard. V. 18 describes the establishment of five cities in Egypt that speak the language of Canaan (i.e., Hebrew or Aramaic) and that swear loyalty to YHWH. Vv. 19-22 describe an altar to YHWH in Egypt and a stele dedicated to YHWH on the border of Egypt, together with a projection of Egypt's turning to YHWH and YHWH's deliverance of the country. V. 23 describes the highway between Assyria and Egypt together with Egypt's serving of Assyria. Vv. 24-25 describe Israel as the third partner in this consortium and affirm general blessing for Israel, Egypt, and Assyria. As noted above, Manasseh sent troops to support Assurbanipal's campaigns in Egypt and later to support the 26th (Saite) Dynasty installed by Assurbanipal. Likewise, the Jewish military colony at Elephantine, with its own temple to YHWH, was established at the southern border of Egypt to defend the Egyptian frontier. Nevertheless, Egypt remained subservient to Assyria throughout this period and supported Assyrian interests, as did Israel under Manasseh. The 7th-century edition of this text in 19:1-25 attempts to justify Manasseh's policies with relation to Egypt by portraying them as the true intention of Isaiah's initial condemnation; that is, Egypt will suffer at YHWH's/Assyria's hands only to emerge as a partner in a coalition led by Assyria. Israel's role in this coalition, clearly as a third and subservient partner, is presented as a blessing for Israel in keeping with the will of YHWH. As such,

Isaiah's oracle in 19:1-17 legitimizes the restoration of Egypt and the formation of this three-partner coalition, dominated by Assyria, in 19:18-25.

Isaiah 19:1-17 is clearly a condemnation of Egypt. As noted above, this oracle must be understood in relation to Egyptian attempts to foment revolt against Assyria by the northern kingdom of Israel. The portrayal of YHWH's advance against Egypt is clearly to be identified with a threatened Assyrian advance against the Egyptians when they moved to put down the revolt in 724. That the Assyrians mounted no full-scale attack against Egypt, limiting themselves to a defensive victory against a relief force at Raphia in 720, is immaterial. At the outset of the revolt, the prophet taunts Egypt for the foolishness of its pharaoh and his counselors, who are unable to discern the intentions of YHWH. When portrayed against the internal conflicts that racked Egypt prior to the emergence of the 25th Dynasty in 710-709, such incompetence could bring only disaster to Egypt. It is important to note that the oracle presupposes that YHWH's purpose is to allow the northern kingdom to be taken and punished by the Assyrian empire, which would contradict the normal expectation that YHWH would protect a country bound to YHWH in covenant. Indeed, Isaiah refers to the leadership of Egypt in 19:15 with the same terminology employed for the leadership of the northern kingdom in 9:13 (*RSV* 14) ("head and tail, palm branch and reed"), which demonstrates the prophet's association of, and opposition against, both Egypt and northern Israel.

Finally, 20:1-6 is clearly designed to explain the significance of Isaiah's symbolic act of walking naked and barefoot during the Assyrian siege of Ashdod in 713-711. Here the action is understood not as a condemnation of Ashdod per se but as a demonstration of the fate of Egypt and of those who rely on Egypt in the coastal plain (for a discussion of the function of symbolic acts in general and the present text in particular, see Stacey, esp. 122-26). Isaiah's action thereby condemns Egypt for its failure to support Ashdod in the very revolt that Egypt fomented. Although the historical background of this passage is uncertain, ranging from the immediate disciples of the prophet in the 8th century to Josianic redaction in the late 7th century, it is clearly the product of anti-Egyptian circles in Judah and may well stem from opponents to Manasseh's policy of cooperation with Assyria and Egypt.

Bibliography

T. K. Cheyne, "The Nineteenth Chapter of Isaiah," *ZAW* 13 (1893) 125-28; A. Condamin, "Interpolations ou transpositions accidentelles? (Michée, II,12, 13; Osée, II,1-3, 8, 9; Isaïe, V,24, 25; XIX,21, 22)," *RB* 11 (1902) 379-97; A. Feuillet, "Un sommet religieux de l'ancien testament: L'oracle d'Isaïe XIX (vv. 16-25) sur la conversion de l'Egypte," *RSR* 39 (1951) 65-87; Fohrer, "Die Gattung der Berichte" (→ "Introduction to the Prophetic Literature"), 92-112; B. Gosse, "Isaïe 14,28-32" (→ 13:1–14:32); A. van Hoonacker, "Deux passages obscurs dans le chapitre XIX d'Isaïe (versets 11, 18)," *Revue Benedictine* 36 (1924) 297-306; A. van der Kooij, "The Old Greek of Isaiah 19:16-25: Translation and Interpretation," in *VI Congress of the International Organization for Septuagint and Cognate Studies, Jerusalem 1986* (ed. C. E. Cox; SBLSCS 23; Atlanta: Scholars Press, 1987) 127-66; O. Loretz, "Der ugaritische Topos *b'l rkb* und die 'Sprache Kanaans' in Jes 19,1-25," *UF* 19 (1987) 101-12; J. M. Miller and J. H. Hayes, *A History of Ancient Israel and Judah* (Philadelphia: Westminster, 1986); L. Monsengwo-Pasinya, "Isaïe XIX 16-25 et universalisme dans la LXX," *Congress Volume, Salamanca 1983* (ed. J. A. Emerton; VTSup 36; Leiden: Brill, 1985) 192-207; J. F. A. Sawyer, " 'Blessed Be My People Egypt' (Isaiah 19.25): The Context and Meaning of a Remarkable Passage," in *A Word in Season* (*Fest.* W. McKane; ed. J. D. Martin and P. R. Davies; JSOTSup 42; Sheffield: JSOT Press, 1986) 57-71; A. Spalinger, "The Year 712 B.C. and its Implications for Egyptian History," *JARCE* 10 (1973) 95-101; Stacey, *Prophetic Drama* (→ "Introduction to the Prophetic Literature"); W. Vogels, "L'Égypte mon peuple — l'universalisme d'Is 19,16-25," *Bib* 57 (1976) 494-514.

PRONOUNCEMENT CONCERNING THE WILDERNESS OF THE SEA, 21:1-10

Structure

I. Superscription	1a
II. Prophetic pronouncement *(maśśā')* proper	1b-10
A. Report of prophetic audition and reaction	1b-4
1. Audition report	1b-2
a. Metaphorical description of approaching invader	1b
b. Audition report proper	2
2. Report of prophet's reaction to audition	3-4
a. Anguish in loins/pains like childbirth	3a
b. Writhing from hearing/terrified from seeing	3b
c. Straying heart/terror overtakes	4a
d. Summation: twilight of desire has become anguish	4b
B. Confirmation of audition: command to go to battle stations at approach of messenger	5-10
1. Command to go to stations	5
a. Description of situation: feast	5a
b. Command proper	5b
2. Basis for command: prophet's announcement of watchman's report	6-10
a. Report of YHWH's command to set watchman	6
b. Announcement of watchman's report	7-9
1) Concerning his observation of approaching riders	7
2) Concerning his report of riders' announcement	8-9
a) Announcement formula	8a
b) Watchman's announcement proper: Babylon has fallen	8b-9
c. Confirmation of report to audience that announcement was from YHWH	10

Although 21:1-10 clearly formed an original unit with 21:11-12 and 21:13-17 (see below on Setting), the appearance of the superscription *maśśā'* PN, "pronouncement concerning PN," in vv. 1a, 11a, and 13a indicates that each text constitutes a distinct textual subunit within the larger structure of chs. 13–23. Consequently, 21:1-10 is demarcated by the appearance of the superscription *maśśā' midbar-yām,* "pronouncement concerning the Wilderness of the Sea," in v. 1a and the appearance of the superscription *maśśā' dûmâ,* "pronouncement concerning Dumah," in v. 11a, which introduces the following subunit. Consequently, the passage comprises two basic subunits: the superscription in v. 1a and the *maśśā'* proper in vv. 1b-10.

The dominant perspective of the *maśśā'* proper in vv. 1b-10 is that of the 1st-person singular, which indicates that the prophet is the speaker. The passage contains two major subunits. The prophet's 1st-person description of an audition and his reaction to it appear in vv. 1b-4. This perspective changes in v. 5, where infinitive absolute verbs are employed to describe a scene of feasting that is disrupted by 2nd-person plural imperative commands to prepare for battle. The following material concerning the prophet's announcement of the watchman's report resumes the 1st-person form, and the introductory *kî,* "for, because," indicates that vv. 6-10 function as the basis for the command in v. 5. Consequently, vv. 5-10 form the second major subunit of this text in that the announcement of the watchman's report concerning the fall of Babylon explains the prophet's audition experience and confirms it as a word from YHWH.

The structure of vv. 1b-4, in turn, falls into two major parts based on form and content. Vv. 1b-2 report the prophet's experience of an audition concerning an enemy that is approaching the "Land of the Sea" (i.e., Merodach-baladan's home territory; see the discussion of Setting). V. 1b contains a metaphorical description of the enemy's approach that employs the imagery of a whirlwind passing through the wilderness. The audition report proper appears in v. 2, introduced by a reporting formula in v. 2a. The audition contains three elements. The statement "the plunderer plunders and the destroyer destroys" employs language typically used in the book of Isaiah to describe the approach of an enemy bent on destruction (cf. 16:4; 24:16; 33:1). The feminine singular commands, "Go up, O Elam, lay siege, O Media," refer to commands given to the defenders to resist the invaders (cf. Nah 2:2; MacIntosh, 111-12; for further discussion, see below on Setting). The 1st-person statement by the prophet, "all her sighing/lamentation [*RSV* adds 'she has caused'] I have brought to an end," apparently indicates the loss of all hope for the victim's survival. Vv. 3-4 begin with an introductory *'al-kēn,* "therefore," which indicates the prophet's reaction to the bad news of the fall of the "Wilderness of the Sea" (cf. Hillers). This section is constituted by three paired statements and a concluding summary statement concerning the prophet's anguish. V. 3a focuses on the pain in the prophet's loins, which is compared to the pains of childbirth. V. 3b focuses on the physical reaction of the prophet who is writhing from what he has heard and terrified by what he has seen. V. 4a employs the imagery of a lost party overtaken by a predator in the wilderness to describe the prophet's straying heart and the terror that overtakes him. Finally, the summation in v. 4b describes the prophet's hopes that have turned to anguish.

The meaning of the prophet's audition is made clear in vv. 5-10, which contain an announcement of the fall of Babylon and state that YHWH is the ultimate source of this message. The passage begins with a command directed to military officers to take up their stations and prepare for battle. V. 5a employs infinitive absolute verbs to describe a scene of feasting that introduced the command proper in v. 5b. The basis for the command appears in vv. 6-10, introduced by *kî,* "because, for," and relates the report of a watchman who spots an approaching rider with news of the fall of Babylonia. V. 6 reports YHWH's command to the prophet to station a watchman, including the statement, "what he will see, he will declare." Vv. 7-9 convey the watchman's report: his observation of approaching riders in v. 7 and his report of the riders' announcement, including the announcement formula in v. 8a and the watchman's report in vv. 8b-9. The riders' report is: "fallen, fallen is Babylon; and all the images of her gods he has shattered to the ground." V. 10 is a 1st-person statement by the prophet addressed to "my threshed and winnowed one," an apparent reference to the prophet's audience, which will suffer the wrath of the Assyrian empire. Here he states, "what I have heard from YHWH Sabaoth, the God of Israel, I have declared to you." The introductory *'ăšer,* "what," and the use of the Hiphil verb *higgîd,* "to declare," correspond to the formulation of the watchman's statement in v. 6 and indicate that the statements in vv. 6 and 10 are meant to form an *inclusio* for the prophet's announcement of the watchman's report.

Genre

The SUPERSCRIPTION of this unit indicates its generic character as a *maśśā'* or PROPHETIC PRONOUNCEMENT, which has no specific structural or literary characteristics, but is constituted by its interest in explaining YHWH's intentions as manifested in human affairs (Weis). In the present text, the explanatory function is evident in vv. 6-10, which indicate that the announcement of the fall of Babylon is an act of YHWH. This explains the meaning of the prophet's audition in vv. 1b-4, which describe the Assyrian advance against Merodach-baladan's Babylonian-based coalition. The defeat of this coalition is portrayed here as an act of YHWH.

Several generic elements appear within the prophetic *maśśā'* in 21:1-10. The first is the AUDITION REPORT in vv. 1b-4. Here the audition is portrayed as a "hard vision" that is communicated to the prophet, but the content of this vision is conveyed entirely in statements made by the combatants and the prophet. In this respect, vv. 1b-4 constitute an "event vision" in that the prophet employs these statements to present a description of an event that he is privileged to witness. The prophet's reaction in vv. 3-4 constitutes the second typical element of such event visions. In this instance, it is one of anguish and represents a typical response to bad news (cf. Hillers). The prophet's reaction supports the view that this passage refers to the defeat of Merodach-baladan, who was allied with Judah in the late 8th century, and not the fall of Babylon to Cyrus in the late 6th century, when Babylon would be regarded as an oppressor of Judah (see the discussion of Setting below).

The COMMAND to go to battle stations appears in v. 5. As noted above, the infinitive absolute verbs of v. 5a indicate the portrayal of a situation that is interrupted by the masculine plural imperatives in v. 5b. Although the oiling of shields has been explained as an action necessary for their storage (cf. Weis, 133-34), a soft, pliant leather shield would better resist arrows or other projectiles. A hard, brittle shield would crack or shatter on impact and leave its bearer exposed. Such a leather shield would be of use on the walls of a fortified city, where it would protect against projectiles and where the watchman described in this passage would be expected to stand. In any case, such a shield would be useless against swords.

Finally, the prophet's announcement of the watchman's report indicates a typical function of defense in the ancient world. The watchman or lookout observes those who approach a defended city and makes appropriate announcements, such as the call to battle stations in v. 5.

Setting

In its present form as part of the 5th-century edition of the book of Isaiah, 21:1-10 constitutes one of the oracles against the nations in chs. 13–23. Although there is some confusion as to the meaning of the superscription, "Pronouncement concerning the Wilderness of the Sea," the passage is generally taken as an oracle concerning the fall of Babylon, based on the reference to its fall in v. 7.

Scholars attempting to establish the earlier settings of this oracle face a multitude of problems. Many scholars maintain that the oracle dates to the mid-6th century in relation to Cyrus's conquest of the city of Babylon, based on the commands in v. 2, "Go up, O Elam! Lay siege, O Media!" which suggest an Elamite and Median assault against the city (cf. Clements, *Isaiah 1–39,* 176-77; Kaiser, *Isaiah 13–39,* 120-22; Wildberger, *Jesaja,* 770-71; Gosse, *Isaïe 13,1–14,23,* 43-67). But this view raises a number of difficulties. Elam had ceased to exist as an independent entity following Assurbanipal's defeat of the country and the destruction of its capital city Susa in 647-646 B.C.E. Afterward, Elam was simply absorbed into the Median kingdom and later the Persian empire. Furthermore, Babylon never fell to a Median assault, much less one by Elam, but surrendered peacefully and opened its gates to Cyrus in 539, inviting him to become the next Babylonian king. If 21:1-10 stems from the mid-6th century, it is difficult to understand why the author would react to the news of an assault against the oppressor of Judah with pain and sickness (vv. 3-4), and it is difficult to understand why the author would refer to Babylon as "the Wilderness of the Sea." Despite attempts to argue that 21:1-10 anticipates the fall of Babylon (so Wildberger, *Jesaja,* 771), these difficulties rule out the view that 21:1-10 dates originally to the mid-6th century.

Other scholars attempt to relate 21:1-10 to Assyrian campaigns against the Babylonian ruler Merodach-baladan in the late 8th century. Barnes, Dhorme, and Hayes and Irvine (pp. 272-74) all argue that it relates to Sargon II's conquest of Babylon in 710, but Sargon entered Babylon peacefully at this time after Merodach-baladan fled the city (*ARAB* II, §§ 35, 38; Brinkman, esp. 18). Likewise, Sennacherib captured Babylon in 703 only after Merodach-baladan fled the city, which promptly admitted Sennacherib and his forces (Brinkman, esp. 26). Erlands-son (pp. 81-92) prefers Sennacherib's defeat of Merodach-baladan in 700, but this view raises difficulties in that Elam is the chief ally and supporter of Merodach-baladan in this period. Finally, Macintosh attempts to resolve the problem by claiming that the passage is a "palimpsest," i.e., that it was originally written in relation to the Assyrian campaigns against Babylonia in the late 8th century but was reinterpreted and reformulated (i.e., overwritten) in relation to the fall of Babylon in the 6th century. Although promising, Macintosh's argument depends on the acceptance of several textual emendations; e.g., in v. 2 he emends "all lamentation I have ceased [*hišbattî*]" to "cease [*hašbîtû*] all lamentation." Further-more, he argues against Bach that v. 2 does not refer to the prophetic summons to war (R. Bach, *Die Aufforderungen zur Flucht und zum Kampf im alttestamentli-chen Prophetenspruch* [WMANT 9; Neukirchen: Neukirchener, 1962] 58), but to the shouts of the inhabitants of Jerusalem who urge on the Elamites and Medians against the Assyrians (Macintosh, 111-12).

Despite the difficulties in positing a late-8th-century setting for 21:1-10, a number of considerations support this setting or one slightly later, in the early 7th century. Although the passage presupposes Assyrian campaigns against Merodach-baladan, they appear to relate most closely to Sennacherib's cam-paigns against Babylon and against the Arab tribes of the northeastern Arabian desert, just west of Babylonia. These campaigns culminated in the conquest and destruction of Babylon in 689 and the defeat of the Arabian tribes in the northern Syrian and Arabian deserts in 691-689.

The first involves the reference to *midbar-yām*, "Wilderness of the Sea," in the superscription for the oracle. There have been persistent attempts to relate this term to the land ruled by the Babylonian ruler Merodach-baladan, generally referred to as *mat tamti*, "Land of the Sea," in Akkadian records. The region is in the southern part of Babylonia, in the swampy area where the Tigris and Euphrates Rivers empty into the Persian Gulf. Gray (p. 351) has been most influential in objecting to this identification by pointing out that this region is marshy and hardly corresponds to the wilderness portrayed by the Hebrew term *midbār*. But Gray's case is based in part on his emendation of the text, in which he eliminates *yām*, "sea," on the basis of the LXX *to horama tēs erēmou*, "the word concerning the wilderness." Erlandsson (p. 82) points out, however, that *mat tamti* is best translated *'ereṣ yām*, "land of the sea," in Hebrew, although this does not preclude identification of *midbar-yām* with *mat tamti*.

But scholars have apparently overlooked an important document pertaining to the reign of Merodach-baladan designated King List A (cf. Brinkman, 35-36, 41). King List A iv:10 identifies Merodach-baladan as a member of the *bal kur tam(tim)*, "dynasty of the Sealand." The term *kur tam* is especially important here in that *kur* refers to marginal or border areas (i.e., *Kost, Nahmung;* see Brinkman, who cites R. Borger), much as *midbār* refers to areas bordering the settled regions of the land of Judah or Israel in the Hebrew Bible. Contrary to Gray, the term *midbār* does not exclude a marshy region in that it refers not to the absence or presence of water in the land but only to its placement on the borders of settled regions (cf. BDB, 184; Dhorme, 405, notes that *midbār* refers either to desert or to steppe). Merodach-baladan is portrayed as a nomadic tribal leader who rules a semi-inhabited area and ascends the throne in Babylon only when a native Babylonian ruler is unable to do so. Consequently, *midbar-yām* is an appropriate Hebrew designation for the *kur tam* ruled by Merodach-baladan.

Especially noteworthy is Merodach-baladan's alliance with Elam, which proved to be his strongest supporter. King Umbaigas of Elam protected Merodach-baladan's ascension to the Babylonian throne by defeating Sargon II at the battle of Der in 720 (cf. Brinkman, 12-13), a conflict in which Merodach-baladan apparently arrived too late for battle. Later, following Sargon's capture of Babylon in 710 and his invasion of Dur-Jakin in 709, Merodach-baladan fled to Elam for protection. Merodach-baladan again took refuge in Elam following Sennacherib's capture of Babylon in 703 and his campaigns against Dur-Jakin, Merodach-baladan's home city, in 700.

As Macintosh notes (pp. 111-12), one should consider the commands "go up, O Elam; lay siege, O Media" not as war shouts of attacking Elamites and Medians against a besieged Babylon but as shouts of encouragement to Elamites and Medians defending against an attacker. The verb *ṣûr,* translated here as "lay siege," basically means "enclose" and can be used in reference to either offensive warfare in the sense of "besiege" or defensive warfare in the sense of "enclose" or "barricade" (e.g., Judg 9:31). In this respect, it is noteworthy that when the verb *ṣûr,* "to besiege," refers to an offensive siege against a city, it generally employs the preposition *ʿal,* "against," or *ʾel,* "unto" (cf. BDB, 848). Judg 9:31 employs the verb without these prepositions in reference to stirring up the city of Shechem against Abimelech. Alternatively, the verb may derive from *ṣûr* III, "to show hostility, treat as a foe" (cf. BDB, 849), so that the command would be translated, "harass/show hostility, O Media," in reference to an exhortation to resist the invaders. In either case, such meanings for *ṣûrî māday* would be parallel to the meaning of *ʿălî ʿēlām,* "go up, O Elam!" as an exhortation to resist invasion. The object of this call to action would be the approach of the "plunderer" *(bôgēd)* and the "destroyer" *(šôdēd),* terms frequently employed for attackers in the book of Isaiah (16:4; 24:16; 33:1).

Many scholars consider 21:1-10, 11-12, and 13-17 to be originally independent oracles that have been brought together by an editor into their present context. The grounds for this view are the appearance of individual superscriptions for each of these oracles, their concern with different locations or peoples, and the difficulties of relating the oracles concerning Dumah and Arabia/Kedarites to the Babylonian oracle, especially if it is set in the 6th century. Yet once the identification of *midbar-yām* with the Sealand ruled by the nomadic chieftain Merodach-baladan is established, it becomes clear that 21:1-10 formed an original unit, together with vv. 11-12 concerning Dumah and vv. 13-17 concerning Arabia and the Kedarites, that is set in the late 8th and early 7th century.

Ephal (pp. 112-23) notes that the Annals of Sennacherib identify *Ba-as-qa-nu,* the brother of *Ia-ti-ʾ-e,* queen of the Arabs *(A-ri-bi = Ar-ba-a-a),* among the chieftains captured by Sennacherib in his campaign against Merodach-baladan and his Elamite supporters in 703. Furthermore, walled towns such as *Dur A-bi-ia-ta-ʾ* and *Dur U-a-a-it* were conquered and looted by Sennacherib's forces in south Babylonia. Ephal's discussion of the Abiyataʾ and Uait/Uaiteʾ identifies Kedarites *(Qid-ra-a-a)* and Arabs *(A-ri-bi)* as components of these ethnic groups. Sennacherib was able to drive Merodach-baladan out of Babylon in 703 and replace him with a native puppet ruler Bel-Ibni (Brinkman, 26). On his second campaign in the region in 700, Sennacherib forced Merodach-baladan to flee from his native Dur-Jakin to Elam for refuge, after which Merodach-baladan is never heard from again. These records clearly demonstrate Kedarite and Arab, as well as Elamite, support for Merodach-baladan in his attempt to fend off Sennacherib.

Perhaps the most noteworthy of Sennacherib's campaigns in the region are those against Babylon and the Arab tribes of the northeastern Arabian desert west of Babylonia in 691-689. Although Merodach-baladan had left the scene, Sennacherib continued in his attempts to subdue the nomads in the region. Not only did he destroy Babylon in 689, he also conducted a major campaign in the desert west of Babylonia against *Te-'-el — hu-nu*, queen of the Arabs, and Hazael, identified as "King of the Arabs" in the inscriptions of Esarhaddon and Assurbanipal and as "King of the Kedarites" in other inscriptions of Assurbanipal (cf. Ephal, 118-19). The only place name to survive in Sennacherib's inscription concerning the campaign (Berlin, Staatliche Museen tablet VA 3310) is Adummatu, identified by Ephal as the oasis Dumah or Dumat al-Jandal in the Wadi Sirhan (Ephal, 119-21). Adummatu was a fortress and religious center that apparently controlled the major Arab trade routes between Syria and Babylonia through the north Arabian desert. The prefix *A-* is common in Assyrian documents of proper names so that Adummatu is to be equated with Dumah (Ephal, 121-22, n. 415). Inasmuch as Isa 21:1-17 focuses on the fall of Babylon, the loss of Dumah (see below on 21:11-12), and the defeat of the Kedarites in Arabia, the passage apparently presupposes Sennacherib's campaigns against the nomads in western Babylonia and the north Arabian desert in 691-689.

Isaiah's interest in these matters is clear. Merodach-baladan forged an alliance with Hezekiah of Judah as part of a plan to launch a two-sided revolt against Assyria with attacks in the west and the east (cf. Isaiah 39). Unfortunately, Merodach-baladan's reliability was questionable, especially since he failed to show up in time for the battle of Der in 720, allowing his Elamite supporters to defeat Sargon II's forces, while he claimed much of the credit and the Babylonian throne. Furthermore, he consistently failed to stand and fight against the Assyrians but fled to Elam as his standard tactic even when they attacked his home city of Dur-Jakin (cf. J. A. Brinkman, "Elamite Military Aid to Merodach-baladan," *JNES* 24 [1965] 161-66). With such a record, it is clear that Isaiah would have good reasons to oppose Hezekiah's alliance with Babylon and Merodach-baladan, apart from Isaiah's general opposition to Judean alliances with foreign powers as demonstrated in the Syro-Ephraimite War. Although there is little evidence for Isaiah's activity after Sennacherib's invasion of 701, 21:1-10, 11-12, 13-17 all appear to presuppose Sennacherib's 691-689 campaigns in the east when Babylon and Dumah were destroyed and the Kedarites were defeated. These oracles present the defeat of these parties as an act of YHWH and confirm the prophet's opposition to an alliance against Sennacherib.

In this respect, it is noteworthy that ch. 22 presupposes the aftermath of Sennacherib's siege of Jerusalem, and that ch. 23 is directed against Tyre, whose fall to Babylon in 701 caused the collapse of the western alliance and left Hezekiah to face Sennacherib alone. Whether these oracles are written by the prophet Isaiah prior to Sennacherib's campaigns in 691-689 is difficult to say, given the lack of evidence for his activity after 701. But ch. 22 indicates that Isaiah survived Sennacherib's siege of Jerusalem, and the oracles in ch. 21 certainly represent confirmation of his views concerning Hezekiah's alliance with Merodach-baladan against Sennacherib.

Intention

The intent of 21:1-10 is defined primarily by its generic character as a *maśśā'*, or prophetic pronouncement, and by its two-part structure, which includes a report of a prophetic audition in vv. 1b-4 and a confirmation of that audition in vv. 5-10 explaining its significance.

As noted in the discussion of the genre of this passage, the purpose of the prophetic *maśśā'* is to explain how YHWH's intentions are manifested in human affairs. Here the oracle begins with the prophet's audition report concerning an attack from the wilderness by an unnamed party designated only as "treacherous one" and "destroyer" in v. 2. Both the Medes and the Elamites are exhorted to defend themselves prior to the prophet's report of his pain and anguish at the news of the invasion. Clearly, the prophet's anguish indicates his sympathy for the defenders. This reaction precludes an interpretation that identifies 6th-century Babylon as the party under attack, in that Babylon was responsible for the destruction of Jerusalem and the temple of Solomon as well as the Babylonian exile. One would expect a different reaction at Babylon's fall during the 6th century.

The confirmation of the prophet's audition in vv. 5-10 confirms the identity of the invaded party as Babylon and explains the significance of Babylon's fall. Here the prophet reports that YHWH had instructed him to place a watchman who would report what he sees. The prophet states that the watchman reports approaching riders who announce the fall of Babylon and the destruction of its idols. As noted in the discussion of the setting above, the fall of Babylon to Sennacherib in 689 provides the most appropriate background for this oracle, especially since Sennacherib refers to smashing its gods (cf. *ARAB* II, §438). This is especially noteworthy since Babylon, under the leadership of Merodach-baladan, had allied with Hezekiah to revolt against Assyrian rule. The full intent of the passage becomes clear in the last verse as Isaiah announces that the report of the fall of Babylon stems from YHWH. YHWH was clearly responsible for the fall of Babylon and thus for the collapse of Judah's major ally in its attempt to resist Assyrian rule. Such a view corresponds to Isaiah's views that foreign alliances to resist Assyrian rule are futile and that the Assyrians act as YHWH's agents for carrying out the divine will. As such, the oracle confirms Isaiah's opposition to Hezekiah's alliance with Babylon (cf. ch. 39) in that the prophet views such an act as opposition to the will of YHWH.

Bibliography

→ bibliography at "Introduction to the Book of Isaiah." W. E. Barnes, "A Fresh Interpretation of Isaiah XXI 1-10," *JTS* 1 (1900) 583-92; C. Boutflower, "Isaiah XXI in the Light of

Assyrian History I," *JTS* 14 (1913) 501-15; J. A. Brinkman, "Merodach-Baladan II," in *Studies Presented to A. Leo Oppenheim, June 7, 1964* (Chicago: Oriental Institute, 1964) 6-53; F. Buhl, "Jesaja 21,6-10," *ZAW* 8 (1888) 157-67; W. H. Cobb, "Isaiah xxi.1-10 Reexamined," *JBL* 17 (1898) 40-61; E. Dhorme, "Le désert de la mer (Isaïe, XXI)," *RB* 31 (1922) 403-6; I. Ephal, *The Ancient Arabs: Nomads on the Borders of the Fertile Crescent, 9th-5th Centuries B.C.* (Jerusalem: Magnes, 1984); Erlandsson, *Burden of Babylon* (→ 13:1–14:32), 81-92; K. Galling, "Jesaja 21 im Lichte der neuen Nabonidtexte," in *Tradition und Situation: Studien zur alttestamentlichen Prophetie* (*Fest.* A. Weiser; ed. E. Würthwein and O. Kaiser; Göttingen: Vandenhoeck & Ruprecht, 1963) 49-62; B. Gosse, "Le 'moi' prophétique de l'oracle contre Babylone d'Isaïe XXI,1-10," *RB* 93 (1986) 70-84; D. R. Hillers, "A Convention in Hebrew Literature: The Reaction to Bad News," *ZAW* 77 (1965) 86-90; A. A. Macintosh, *Isaiah XXI: A Palimpsest* (Cambridge: Cambridge University Press, 1980); J. Obermann, "YHWH's Victory Over the Babylonian Pantheon: The Archetype of Is. 21 1-10," *JBL* 48 (1929) 307-28; R. B. Y. Scott, "Isaiah XXI 1-10; The Inside of a Prophet's Mind," *VT* 2 (1952) 278-82; E. Sievers, "Zu Jesajas 21 1-10," in *Vom Alten Testament* (*Fest.* K. Marti; ed. K. Budde; Giessen: Töpelmann, 1925) 262-65; Weis, "Definition" (→ "Introduction to the Prophetic Literature"); G. Wilhelmi, "Polster in Babel? Eine Überlegung zu Jesaja XXI 5+8," *VT* 25 (1975) 121-23; H. Winckler, *Alttestamentliche Untersuchungen* (Leipzig: E. Pfeiffer, 1892) 120-25.

PRONOUNCEMENT CONCERNING DUMAH, 21:11-12

Structure

I. Superscription	11a
II. Prophetic pronouncement *(maśśā')* proper	11b-12
A. Report of question from Seir put to watchman/prophet	11b
1. Report formula	11bα
2. Question proper	11bβ
B. Report of watchman's/prophet's response: no news	12
1. Report formula	12aα
2. Response proper	12aα-b

As noted above, 21:11-12 constitutes an original unit together with vv. 1-10 and 13-17 (for further discussion, see the previous discussion of Setting for 21:1-10). In the present context of the prophetic pronouncements in chs. 13–23, this text constitutes a distinct subunit as indicated by its introductory superscription, *maśśā' dûmâ*, "Pronouncement concerning Dumah," in v. 11a. The appearance of the superscription *maśśā' ba'rāb*, "Pronouncement on Arabia," in v. 13a indicates the beginning of a new unit. Consequently the passage falls into two parts: the superscription in v. 11a and the *maśśā'* proper in vv. 11b-12.

The structure of this passage is relatively simple in that it is constituted by the pattern of question and response. V. 11b contains a report of a question from Seir put to a watchman. The 1st-person formulation of the report indicates that the prophet is both speaker and watchman in this passage. The question merely asks if there is news during the night watch. The report formula in v. 12aα precedes the response proper in + v. 12aα-b, which merely states that only morning and night have come. This response indicates that there is no news and that the person from Seir who posed the question should ask again later.

Genre

The SUPERSCRIPTION of this brief passage identifies it as a *maśśā'* or PROPHETIC PRONOUNCEMENT. In this instance, the explanatory function of the genre is indicated by the QUESTION-AND-ANSWER SCHEMA, which defines the structure of the passage. The response indicates that no explanation is forthcoming, but it does suggest the social setting of the prophetic *maśśā'* in inquiries made to a prophet.

Setting

As noted in the discussion of 21:1-10, Sennacherib's campaigns against the nomads inhabiting the desert west of Babylonia in 691-689 B.C.E. mention the capture of the desert oasis Adummatu, identified by Ephal (pp. 119-21) as Dumah. The site is also known as Dumat al-Jandal and is located in the Wadi Sirhan along the main trade route through the north Arabian desert between Babylon and Syria. Although some identify the site with Dumah just southwest of Hebron, in part because of the LXX reading of *idumaea* for *dûmâ*, this is wrongly based on the appearance of the term "Seir" in v. 11 and the fact that Idumean Dumah was still known as late as post-Christian times (see Kaiser, *Isaiah 13–39*, 129-30). Here the reference to Seir indicates the direction that one would look for news from Dumat al-Jandal. As indicated by the watchman's answer, there is no word from Dumah, indicating its loss.

Intention

The intent of this passage is defined by its generic character as a prophetic *maśśā'*, the content of the watchman's report, and the historical background of the passage in relation to that of vv. 1-10 and 13-17. As noted above, the purpose of the prophetic *maśśā'* is to identify the realization of YHWH's intentions in human affairs. Clearly, the watchman's response that only morning and night have come indicates that there is no news from Dumah. Given the historical background in relation to Sennacherib's conquest of Dumah or Dumat al-Jandal in 689, a major oasis and Arab religious center on the caravan routes through the north Arabian desert, it becomes clear that the watchman's report is intended to indicate the fall of Dumah to Sennacherib's forces. The oracle lacks any reference to YHWH's intentions, however, which suggests this oracle's dependence on its literary context, where both 21:1-10 and 21:13-17 identify the fall of Babylon and the defeat of Kedar, respectively, as acts of YHWH.

Bibliography

C. Boutflower, "Isaiah XXI in the Light of Assyrian History II," *JTS* 15 (1914) 1-13; Ephal, *Ancient Arabs* (→ 21:1-10); Galling, "Jesaja 21" (→ 21:1-10); B. Gosse, "Isaïe 21,11-12 et Isaïe 60–62," *BN* 53 (1990) 21-22; P. Lohmann, "Das Wächterlied Jes 21,11-12," *ZAW* 33 (1913) 20-29.

PRONOUNCEMENT ON ARABIA, 21:13-17

Structure

I. Superscription	13a
II. Prophetic pronouncement *(maśśāʾ)* proper	13b-17
A. Report of aid to fugitives in Arabia	13b-15
1. Report of aid proper	13b-14
a. Dedanites bring water to thirsty	13b-14a
b. Temanites bring bread to fugitives	14b
2. Reason for aid: fugitives from battle	15
B. Explanation: report of YHWH speech projecting decimation of Kedar in one year	16-17
1. Report of YHWH speech proper	16
2. Prophet's reiteration	17

As noted above, 21:13-17 forms an original unit with vv. 1-10 and 11-12. In its present context in chs. 13–23, the introductory superscription *maśśāʾ baʿrāb,* "Pronouncement concerning Arabia," identifies it as a distinct unit within the oracles against the nations. The appearance of the superscription *maśśāʾ gêʾ ḥizzāyôn,* "Pronouncement concerning the Valley of Vision," in 22:1a marks the beginning of the new unit. Isa 21:13-17 therefore consists of two basic subunits: the superscription in v. 13a and the *maśśāʾ* proper in vv. 13b-17.

The structure of the *maśśāʾ* proper is determined by the explanatory function of the genre and the character of the language employed. It contains two basic parts. The first is vv. 13b-15, which report that aid is given by Dedanites and Temanites to fugitives in Arabia. Vv. 13b-14 contain the basic report of that aid in which the Dedanites bring water to the thirsty (vv. 13b-14a) and the Temanites bring bread to the fugitives (v. 14b). V. 15, introduced by an explanatory *kî,* "because," states that the fugitives are fleeing from battle. The second part of the *maśśāʾ* proper appears in vv. 16-17, likewise introduced by an explanatory *kî,* which present an explanation for the previous scene in the form of the prophet's report of YHWH's projection of the decimation of Kedar. The prophet reports YHWH's speech in v. 16 that Kedar will be destroyed in a year. He adds his reiteration in v. 17, which stresses that the decimation of Kedar will take place because it is the word of YHWH.

Genre

The SUPERSCRIPTION in v. 13a identifies the genre of this passage as prophetic *maśśā'* or PROPHETIC PRONOUNCEMENT. The *maśśā'* is constituted not by a specific literary structure or characterization but by an intent to demonstrate that YHWH's purposes are manifested in human affairs. This intent is evident in the basic structure of the passage, which presents a report of aid to fugitives from war in the Arabian desert and the explanation for this situation, namely, that it is the result of YHWH's projection that Kedar would be destroyed in a year's time. The prophet's explanation employs a variation of the MESSENGER FORMULA, *kî-kōh 'āmar 'ǎdōnāy 'ēlāy,* "for thus my Lord said unto me," as a means to indicate that the projection of Kedar's demise is a word of YHWH.

Setting

As noted in the discussion of 21:1-10, Sennacherib's campaigns against the nomads of the deserts west of Babylonia in 691-689 B.C.E. included the capture of Dumat al-Jandal and the defeat of various Arab tribes including the Kedarites. The Dedanites and the Temanites who aid the fugitive Kedarites in this passage inhabited the cities of Dedan and Tema and the surrounding region. Their location in the northwestern Saudi Arabian peninsula is just south of Edom or Seir, mentioned in 21:11-12. This locale indicates flight away from Babylon, which Sennacherib also destroyed at this time. Isa 21:13-17 apparently presupposes this defeat.

Intention

The intent of this passage is defined by its character as a prophetic *maśśā'* and its reference to Sennacherib's defeat of Kedar in the north Arabian desert in 689. As noted above, the purpose of the prophetic *maśśā'* is to identify the intention of YHWH in relation to human events. Here the prophet begins with a description of fugitives in the desert aided by Dedanites and Temanites. Vv. 16-17 provide an explanation for this scene indicating that the defeat of Kedar and its decimation fulfills a promise made by YHWH. As such, the prophet points to the defeat of a people allied with Babylon, which in turn was allied with Hezekiah of Judah against Sennacherib, as an act of YHWH. This is in keeping with the prophet's opposition to the alliance (cf. Isaiah 39) and his view that Assyria acted as an agent for carrying out YHWH's purposes.

Bibliography

Boutflower, "History II" (→ 21:11-12); Galling, "Jesaja 21" (→ 21:11-12).

PRONOUNCEMENT CONCERNING THE VALLEY OF VISION, 22:1-25

Structure

     Isaiah 22:1-25 is demarcated by the superscription in v. 1a, *maśśā' gê' ḥizzāyôn,* "Pronouncement concerning the Valley of Vision," and by the superscription in 23:1a, *maśśā' ṣōr,* "Pronouncement concerning Tyre," which introduces the following unit. The passage focuses throughout on the Valley of Kidron, here designated "Valley of Vision" by the prophet (see discussion below of Intention). Its overall concerns include the Assyrian siege of Jerusalem, which would focus on the east side of the city facing the Kidron Valley, and the tomb of Shebna, which would have been located across the Kidron from the eastern wall.

     Following the superscription in v. 1a, the structure of 22:1b-25 is determined by a combination of generic, thematic, and formal features. The introductory YHWH speech formula indicates the basic division of this text, in which vv. 1b-14 focus on the significance of the Assyrian siege of Jerusalem in the Kidron Valley and vv. 15-25 focus on the significance of the removal from office and deportation of the royal steward Shebna. This two-part division facilitates the explanatory function of this text as a *maśśā'* or prophetic pronouncement in that the dismissal and deportation of Shebna confirm the prophet's explanation of the significance of the Assyrian siege of Jerusalem as an act of YHWH. Just as Shebna's removal from office indicates a clear abrogation of YHWH's guarantee of security to the house of David, so the Assyrian siege of Jerusalem represents an abrogation of YHWH's guarantee of security to the city. In Isaiah's view, YHWH's guarantee of security to the house of David indicates that only YHWH could be responsible for the deportation of Shebna. Likewise, YHWH's guarantee of Jerusalem's security indicates that only YHWH could threaten that security. Consequently, the siege is an occasion for mourning, not defiant rejoicing, in that YHWH was the cause of the attack in the first place, not the defense against it.

The structure of vv. 1b-14 is determined by its generic character as a disputation speech in which the prophet disputes the people's rejoicing at the lifting of the Assyrian siege of the city. He presents the counterthesis in vv. 1b-4 that this is an occasion for weeping and lamentation. The refutation appears in vv. 5-14, which assert that the siege represents YHWH's day of attack and confusion directed against the city. Consequently, the people are condemned for their celebration and their failure to recognize YHWH's threatening action.

The statement of the counterthesis in vv. 1b-4 begins with a rhetorical question in vv. 1b-2a. The 2nd-person feminine singular formulation of the question in v. 1b indicates that it is directed to the city of Jerusalem at large, designated by 2nd-person feminine singular noun forms in v. 2a ("you who are full of shoutings, tumultuous city, exultant town"). The question challenges the people's celebration on the rooftops, thereby indicating the thesis to be disputed: that the Assyrian siege is cause for defiant celebration. Vv. 2b-3 contain three statements in 2nd-person feminine singular address form that confront the celebrating city with the reality of its situation, i.e., that its soldiers were defeated. V. 2b asserts that the dead were not killed in battle. V. 3a asserts that the officers were "captured by the bow," i.e., killed while trying to flee, and v. 3b declares that all who were found were captured while trying to flee. Together, vv. 2b-3 constitute a statement of counterevidence against the people's view that there is cause for such defiance. Instead, the city was defeated. Consequently, Isaiah announces his intention to mourn for "the destruction of the daughter of my people" in v. 4. The introductory *'al-kēn,* "therefore," establishes the connection between v. 4 and the preceding material, and provides the means to contrast the prophet's weeping with the people's celebration. The 2nd-person masculine plural formulation of the prophet's address, "Look away from me . . . do not labor to comfort me," contrasts with the 2nd-person feminine singular formulation of vv. 1b-3. This merely indicates that his outcry is not directed specifically to the city of Jerusalem but generally to whoever might happen to hear.

Verses 5-14 constitute the refutation of the people's view that the Assyrian siege is an occasion for defiant rejoicing by asserting that YHWH in fact had intended the siege as an occasion for mourning and lamentation. The introductory *kî,* "because," in v. 5 indicates the explanatory function of vv. 5-14 in relation to the prophet's counterthesis in vv. 1b-4. Specifically, vv. 5-14 announce the Day of YHWH against Jerusalem and Judah as the occasion for mourning. The structure of vv. 5-14 falls into two basic parts. V. 5a is an announcement of the Day of YHWH as a day of "tumult and tramping and confusion." In and of itself, this statement is enigmatic in that one could take it to refer to the defeat of the Assyrians. Vv. 5b-14 make clear that this is a reference to the trauma suffered by Judah at the hands of the invaders. Although v. 5b contains participial verb formations like those of v. 5a, the conjunctive *wāw* at the beginning of v. 6 and those found through v. 14 tie vv. 5b-14 together. Consequently, the lack of a conjunction at the beginning of v. 5b and the participial verb formations facilitate the role of vv. 5b-14 as an appositional specification of v. 5a, but the shift to perfect and converted perfect verb formations throughout the balance of the passage indicate the prophet's retrospective assessment of the current situation announced in v. 5a. Furthermore, the references to "that day" in vv. 8b and 12a tie vv. 5b-14 to the announcement of the Day of YHWH in v. 5a.

The structure of vv. 5b-14 is concentric. The passage begins with a description of the current situation of siege in the Valley of Vision as indicated by the participial verb formation of v. 5b. It ends with the current situation of the people's celebration as indicated by the infinitive verb formations of v. 13. V. 6 is linked to v. 5b by a conjunctive *wāw* and employs perfect verbs to describe Elam's and Kir's deployment against the city as a means for specifying the participial description of siege in v. 5b. Likewise, v. 14 is linked to v. 13 by a conjunctive *wāw* where it draws out the consequences of the people's celebration by announcing YHWH's oath that such transgression will not be forgiven until death.

Sandwiched in between are vv. 7-12, which contain the prophet's retrospective review of the situation. These verses are introduced by *wayĕhî*, "and it was that," and held together by the *wāw*-consecutive formations that introduce its major sections in vv. 7, 8b, and 12. Vv. 7-8a are cast in the form of a 2nd-person feminine singular address to Jerusalem or Judah (cf. v. 8a) focusing on the invasion of Judah. V. 7 describes the enemy horsemen and chariots arrayed in the valley and against the gate of the city. In its present form, the subject of the 3rd-person masculine singular form of *wayĕgal*, "and he has taken away," must be YHWH, but this presents a problem in that it conflicts with the plural formations of v. 7. Although it is possible that this verse is a gloss, it is more likely that the verb was originally plural (cf. LXX) in keeping with the parallel formations in vv. 9 and 10 in which a perfect verb precedes a *wāw*-imperfect formation. It was possibly changed to a singular to emphasize YHWH's role in bringing about the siege. In either case, it refers to the stripped defenses of Judah. The address form shifts abruptly to 2nd-person masculine plural in vv. 8b-11.

Likewise, the phrase *bayyôm hahû'*, "in that day," signals a new subsection within vv. 5-14 and recalls the Day of YHWH announced in v. 5a. Although the initial verb *wattabbēṭ*, "and you looked," is formulated as 2nd-person masculine singular in contrast to the 2nd-person masculine plural formations of the balance of the subunit, it is likely that it was originally plural (cf. LXX). The change to singular may be due to the influence of the singular verb in v. 8a or to an attempt to identify Shebna as the individual addressee of the unit. The reference to "the House of the Forest" in v. 8b may well have justified such an

291

attempt, since it is identified with "the house of David," which had been under Shebna's charge (cf. vv. 15b, 22a; cf. also 1 Kgs 7:2).

Verses 8b-11 focus on the preparations and perceptions of the people and include four statements constituted by 2nd-person masculine plural perfect and *wāw*-consecutive imperfect verbs. V. 8b describes how the people looked to their defenses, v. 9 describes their storing water, v. 10 describes their fortifying the wall, and v. 11 describes the pool that they made between the walls. In addition, v. 11 concludes the series by stating that they did not look *(lō' hibbaṭṭem)* to the one who made it and devised it, thereby returning to the initial statement concerning the people's looking *(wattabbēṭ)* in v. 8b.

Finally, v. 12 shifts its focus to YHWH as indicated by its 3rd-person masculine singular *wāw*-consecutive imperfect report form. As in v. 8b, the *bayyôm hahû'* formula refers back to the announcement of the Day of YHWH in v. 5a. V. 12 reports YHWH's announcement that the day was for mourning and lamentation.

By beginning with the current situation of siege in vv. 5b-6, reviewing the situation in vv. 7-12, and returning to the current situation of rejoicing in vv. 13-14, the prophet establishes the basis for a condemnation of the people who have failed to perceive the significance of YHWH's action. The prophet thereby confirms his view that the Assyrian siege is an occasion for lament, in that it represents YHWH's attack against the city, not YHWH's defense of it.

The structure of the basis for the disputation in vv. 15-25 is constituted by the prophet's address to Shebna in vv. 16-24 together with its introductory and concluding report forms in vv. 15 and 25, respectively.

Verse 15 provides the introduction to the report of the significance of the prophet's announcement of judgment against Shebna. It is a report of YHWH's instruction to the prophet to go to Shebna. This report is constituted by the YHWH speech formula in v. 15a and the instruction proper in v. 15b.

The prophet's address to Shebna is identified by its 2nd-person masculine singular address forms, which appear throughout the passage. The address is based in the genre of prophetic announcement of judgment. It begins with an apparent indictment in the form of a rhetorical question that demands to know why Shebna has constructed a tomb for himself. The announcement of judgment per se then appears in vv. 17-24, which describe Shebna's fate. Vv. 17-18 constitute the prophet's announcement of YHWH's judgment against Shebna in the form of a direct address, including statements that YHWH will cast him away and that YHWH will deport him to a wide land where he will die. Vv. 19-24 then shift to a report of a speech by YHWH to Shebna as indicated by the 1st-person common singular subject and 2nd-person masculine singular address form. V. 19 focuses on Shebna and states that he will be removed from office. Vv. 20-24 then shift to Eliakim ben Hilkiah, who will be installed as Shebna's replacement. These verses are constituted by a series of converted perfect verbal statements, addressed to Shebna, that announce a sequence of events relating to Eliakim's investiture. YHWH will call for Eliakim (v. 20), invest him with authority (v. 21), give him the key to the "house of David" (v. 22), and give him a secure position for his family (v. 23), so that his family will depend on him for its position (v. 24).

Finally, the oracular report in v. 25 that Shebna will be removed from his secure position together with all who depend on him for support provides the concluding summation of vv. 15-25. By employing its metaphorical references to "the peg that was fashioned in a secure place," the passage indicates that YHWH's guarantee of security has been rescinded.

Genre

The genre of 22:1-12 is prophetic *maśśā'* or PROPHETIC PRONOUNCEMENT. This is evident not only from the SUPERSCRIPTION in v. 1a, which identifies the passage as the *"maśśā'* concerning the Valley of Vision," but also from the explanatory function of the entire passage. As noted in the previous pronouncements, the basic function of the prophetic *maśśā'* is to identify the intent or action of YHWH in world events (Weis). Isa 22:1-25 examines two interrelated events, the Assyrian siege of Jerusalem in 701 B.C.E. and the deportation of the royal steward Shebna, in an attempt to establish that both are acts of YHWH. The significance of this identification is heightened by the people's belief that YHWH would defend Jerusalem, which provides the occasion for their defiant celebration. In this instance, Isaiah argues that YHWH was responsible for bringing about the siege in the first place, so that the siege is not an occasion for rejoicing over YHWH's defense of the city but an occasion for mourning over YHWH's punishment.

In addition to citing YHWH's OATH that the people's transgression will not go unpunished, the prophet points to two other factors to support his contention: Jerusalem's defenders were not only defeated but also killed or captured while trying to flee from the enemy (vv. 2b-3), and the royal steward Shebna will be removed from office and deported to Assyria (vv. 17-25). The latter is especially important because Shebna held a "secure position" as steward over the royal house of David. His removal and deportation indicate that YHWH has rescinded the promise of security to Shebna. Furthermore, the terminology for Shebna's "secure position," *māqôm ne'ĕmān* (vv. 23, 25), corresponds to that employed by the prophet for the security of the city of Jerusalem, *qiryâ ne'ĕmānâ* ("secure city," 1:21, 26) and the Davidic king (*'im lō' ta'ămînû kî lō' tē'āmēnû,* "if you are not faithful, you shall not be secure," 7:9). This analogy indicates the prophet's contention that YHWH's guarantee of security to Jerusalem and the Davidic dynasty has been rescinded and that it is YHWH who threatens Jerusalem.

The prophet employs a number of generic entities in 22:1-25 to make his case. The most important of these is the DISPUTATION pattern in vv. 1b-14. The purpose of this genre is to contest the views of an opposing group and to offer a counterthesis. The surface structure of the genre varies according to the specific circumstances of the situation, but it generally includes three underlying elements: thesis, counterthesis, and refutation (D. F. Murray; cf. Graffy, 107-18). In the present passage, the opposing viewpoint is expressed implicitly in the RHETORICAL QUESTION that introduces the DISPUTATION in vv. 1b-2a, that is, that the Assyrian siege of the city is an occasion for defiance. After pointing to the defeat of Jerusalem's defenders, who were killed or captured while trying to flee (vv. 2b-3), the prophet presents his own contention that this is an occasion for lamentation over "the destruction of the daughter of my people," i.e., Jerusalem (v. 4). The refutation appears in vv. 5-14. The prophet begins with an announcement of the Day of YHWH as a "day of tumult and tramping and confusion" (v. 5a). Such a statement is enigmatic in and of itself, but the following elaboration indicates that the tumult, etc., is directed not against the Assyrians but against Judah, whose valleys are filled with enemy troops, whose protection is removed, and whose houses are pulled down to strengthen the fortifications. The prophet concludes his refutation by quoting YHWH's statement that the day is for weeping and lamentation (v. 12), and YHWH's OATH that the people's transgression will not go unpunished (v. 14). The concluding SPEECH FORMULA in v. 14bα emphasizes that YHWH is the speaker of the OATH.

The REPORT concerning the significance of the PROPHETIC ANNOUNCE-MENT OF JUDGMENT against Shebna in vv. 15-25 provides the basis for DISPU-TATION and thus for the prophetic *maśśā'* as a whole since it calls into question YHWH's guarantee for the security of Jerusalem and the house of David. The generic character of this passage as a REPORT is evident from the MESSENGER FORMULA in v. 15a and the concluding ORACULAR FORMULA in v. 25a. Several subordinate generic elements contribute to this REPORT. The COMMISSIONING FORMULA in v. 15b further substantiates the identification of this passage as a REPORT in that it recounts YHWH's commission to Isaiah to deliver the following message. The prophet's statements to Shebna, recorded in vv. 16-24, are based in the PROPHETIC ANNOUNCEMENT OF JUDGMENT. The accusation against Shebna is implied in the RHETORICAL QUESTION that introduces Isaiah's statements in v. 16 challenging Shebna for constructing his tomb. The ANNOUNCE-MENT OF JUDGMENT then follows in vv. 17-24, including the prophet's statements that YHWH will deport Shebna to "a wide land" where he will die (vv. 17-18), and YHWH's address to Shebna that Eliakim ben Hilkiah will replace him in office (vv. 19-24). The concluding ORACULAR REPORT in v. 25 confirms YHWH's intention to remove Shebna and his family from a secure position. The ORACULAR FORMULA in v. 25aα and the legitimation formula in v. 25bα confirm this statement as a word of YHWH.

Setting

Scholars generally agree that ch. 22 contains two separate oracles pertaining to Sennacherib's invasion of Judah in 701 B.C.E. Vv. 1b-14 relate the prophet's disputation and condemnation of the people's defiant celebration during the Assyrian siege of Jerusalem, and vv. 15-25 relate the prophet's condemnation of a high Judean official for pretentiousness in constructing a tomb for himself. Furthermore, there is general agreement that both oracles have been subjected to later redactional expansion (for summaries of the discussion see Wildberger, *Jesaja*, 809-11; and Clements, *Isaiah 1–39*, 182-83, 187-88). Although the two oracles appear to have been written on separate occasions in relation to the Assyrian siege, the above analysis of the structure and genre of 22:1-25 indicates that they function together in their present context, in that vv. 15-25 provide confirmation for the disputation in vv. 1b-14. Furthermore, a reexamination of the literary features and historical background of the two oracles indicates that neither was subjected to later redactional expansion.

Several problems have prompted scholars to conclude that an original Isaianic oracle in vv. 1b-4 and 12-14 has been expanded by later additions in vv. 5-11 (Gray, 363-65; Kaiser, *Isaiah 13–39*, 138-40; Clements, *Isaiah 1–39*, 182-83). These include the references to Elam and Kir as part of the invading army in v. 6, the shift to 2nd-person masculine plural form in vv. (8b)9-11, and the references to a continued Assyrian siege throughout vv. 5-11 when the oracle presupposes the defiant celebration of the city during the siege.

Scholars tend to view the mention of Elam and Kir as references to troops that constituted part of Nebuchadrezzar's army during the siege of Jerusalem in 587 (cf. Clements, *Isaiah 1–39*, 185). The reason for this is that it is unlikely that Elamite troops formed part of Sennacherib's army insofar as Elam supported the Chaldean prince Merodach-baladan, who resisted Assyrian attempts to establish hegemony in Babylon and Elam during the reigns of Sargon II and Sennacherib (cf. Brinkman, "Merodach-Baladan II"; idem, "Elamite Military Aid to Merodach-Baladan," *JNES* 24 [1965] 161-66). Furthermore, Elamite troops fought together with Media and Babylonia against the Assyrians in the late 7th century, even though Elam had ceased to exist as an independent political entity and had been absorbed into the larger Median empire. The exact location of Kir has never been established satisfactorily, but the identification of Kir as the original homeland of the Arameans in Amos 9:7 and the deportation of northern Israelites to Kir under Tiglath-pileser III (2 Kgs 16:9) suggest a location in upper Mesopotamia (cf. C. H. Gordon, "Kir 2," *IDB* 3:36). Consequently, the appearance of Elam is the decisive factor in identifying vv. 5-8a as a description of the Babylonian siege of Jerusalem in that it is unlikely that soldiers from a country allied with Judah during the late 8th century would participate in an Assyrian invasion of the country.

But the appearance of Elamite troops as part of the Assyrian army at this time should occasion no surprise. In his first campaign against Merodach-baladan, ca. 703 (cf. Brinkman, "Merodach-Baladan II," 22-26), Sennacherib reports his defeat of Merodach-baladan and the army of Elam with whom the Chaldean prince was allied (*ARAB* II, 116-17). In addition, Sennacherib reports the capture of a great deal of war material, including chariots, horses, wagons, and mules, as well as thousands of captives. Under these circumstances, it is not surprising that Elamite troops would participate in the Assyrian invasion of Judah in 701 insofar as the Assyrians generally made use of captured war equipment and defeated soldiers to bolster their own armies. By employing Elamite troops against Judah far to the west of Elam, Sennacherib not only enhanced his own military resources but also removed potential enemy soldiers who might oppose him in later campaigns against Elam. Likewise, the presence of troops from Kir should be expected insofar as 2 Kgs 16:9 indicates that Kir had been under Assyrian control since the time of Tiglath-pileser III. As an Assyrian vassal, Kir would be expected to contribute troops to its overlord's army in keeping with the usual terms of Assyrian vassal treaties.

Verses 8b-11 (or 9-11a) are frequently viewed as later additions because they shift from the 2nd-person feminine singular address perspective of vv. 1b-3 and 7 to 2nd-person masucline singular (v. 8b) and 2nd-person masculine plural (vv. 9-11) address forms and because they portray Jerusalem as defeated in contrast to the celebrating city portrayed in vv. 1b-2a and 13. But vv. 8b-11 refer to the preparations for war, including the building of the water system now known as Hezekiah's tunnel in preparation for an Assyrian siege (cf. 2 Kgs 20:20; 2 Chr 32:3-5; *ANET,* 321; cf. Amiran, 75-78). The shift to 2nd-person masculine plural may be explained rhetorically, however, by a shift from an address to the city per se, expressed in singular feminine form (cf. *'îr hômîyâ* and *qiryâ 'allîzâ* in v. 2a), to the inhabitants of the city, expressed in masculine plural form; that is, the city does not perform the defensive tasks described in vv. 8-11, but the inhabitants do (note the references to the "city of David" in v. 9 and "Jerusalem" in v. 10). As noted previously, the 2nd-person masucline singular address form in v. 8b appears to be a later scribal modification from an original 2nd-person masculine plural form (cf. LXX). It seems to depend on a similar change to a 3rd-person masculine singular form (*wayĕgal,* "and he uncovered") from an original 3rd-person masculine plural form that would better fit the context of v. 7. A later scribe apparently changed v. 8a to singular in order to identify YHWH as the subject of "and he has taken away the covering of Judah." This would not only point to YHWH's role in bringing the Assyrians against Judah but would also remove a potentially offensive theological statement. The term *māsāk,* "covering," can be used in a mundane sense (cf. 2 Sam 17:19), but most frequently it appears in reference to the coverings that shielded the entrances and enclosures of the wilderness tabernacle (cf. Exod 26:37; 35:12; 39:34; 40:21; Num 3:25, 26, 31; 4:5, etc.). A shift to 2nd-person masculine singular in v. 8b would not only be consistent with that of v. 8a but would also heighten the identification of Shebna from vv. 15-25 as the one responsible for the people's lack of perspective. The reference to the "House of the Forest," i.e., the royal palace complex (cf. 1 Kgs 7:1-8), would be identified with the "house of your Lord," i.e., the royal palace, in which Shebna served as chief steward (v. 15b).

With respect to the view that vv. 8b-11 (cf. vv. 5-8a) refer to a defeated Judah in contrast to the celebrating city portrayed in vv. 1b-2a and 13, one should note that nowhere does the passage refer to the withdrawal of Assyrian troops. Furthermore, the statement in v. 13b, "Let us eat and drink, for tomorrow we die," indicates that the threat to the city has not been removed, and that vv. 2b-3 refer to the dead and captured defenders of the city. Consequently, the tumultuousness and feasting described in vv. 1b-2a and 13 cannot be interpreted as a celebration of the withdrawal of Assyrian troops. Rather, it refers to the defiance of the city as the Assyrians prepare their siege. One should note that in reporting the siege of Jerusalem, Sennacherib refers to the desertion of Hezekiah's "irregular and elite troops which he had brought into Jerusalem, his royal residence, in order to strengthen [it]" (*ANET,* 288; cf. vv. 2b-3). The setting of 22:1b-14 must be *during* Sennacherib's siege of Jerusalem in 701, not after the siege was lifted.

A number of scholars likewise view the oracle against Shebna in 22:15-25 as a composite text (for a summary of positions, see Kaiser, *Isaiah 13–39,* 149). Vv. 20-25 are sometimes regarded as secondary because of the doubts that Isaiah could have predicted both the rise and downfall of Shebna's replacement at the same time that he was predicting Shebna's removal from office (Gray, 375). Likewise, vv. 20-23 have been interpreted as a Josianic addition because they actually focus on the fall of the Davidic dynasty with which the office of royal steward is identified (Clements, *Isaiah 1–39,* 188). Although the background of the Davidic dynasty is important here, as the discussion of the intention of this passage indicates, the basic issue is the fate of the royal steward Shebna and his replacement by Eliakim ben Hilkiah. The reference to Eliakim ben Hilkiah is quite understandable in this context, since the removal of Shebna from office would be announced in conjunction with the appointment of his replacement. The reference to "the peg that was fastened in a sure place" in v. 25 refers to the removal not of Eliakim ben Hilkiah but of Shebna and his family.

A further problem appears in the identification of Shebna as chief steward (lit. "who is over the house," *ʾăšer ʿal-habbāyit,* v. 15b) and Eliakim ben Hilkiah as his replacement. According to 36:3, 22; and 37:22, Shebna is identified as "the scribe" *(hassōpēr),* whereas Eliakim ben Hilkiah is identified as the chief steward, "who was over the household." Scholars have been at a loss to explain how Eliakim ben Hilkiah could be identified as chief steward in the context of negotiations with the Assyrians during Sennacherib's siege, whereas ch. 22, which is believed to stem from the period of the lifting of the siege, could identify Shebna as chief steward. Some have maintained that the mention of Shebna in v. 15 is a gloss that attempts to harmonize the oracle with the narrative in chs. 36–37 (Clements, *Isaiah 1–39,* 188-89), but this does not account for the identification of Shebna as chief steward rather than scribe. More frequently, scholars maintain that vv. 20-23 represent such an attempt at harmonization with chs. 36–37 (see Kaiser, *Isaiah 13–39,* 149-50; Clements, *Isaiah 1–39,* 188-89).

With respect to these problems, one should keep in mind several major points. First, chs. 36–37 stem from the period of the Assyrian or Josianic redaction of Isaiah. Consequently, it is likely that the mention of Eliakim ben Hilkiah here as chief steward reflects the confusion or distortion of historical facts that characterizes this narrative (see further on chs. 36–37 below).

Second, one must consider the reason for Shebna's condemnation. Scholars generally agree that Isaiah condemns Shebna for his ostentatiousness in building a magnificent tomb for himself. Yet the building of a tomb cannot be the sole issue here. Archaeologists have identified a number of tombs on the present site of the village of Silwan, across the Kidron Valley from the eastern walls of the Iron Age city of Jerusalem (see Ussishkin). Although many of the inscriptions over the tombs have been lost or damaged as the sites were inhabited and robbed, several remain. Included among them is one that reads, "This is [the sepulcher of . . .]yahu who is over the house. There is no silver and no gold here but [his bones] and the bones of his slave-wife with him. Cursed be the man who will open this!" (Ussishkin, 42; for the deciphering of the inscription, see N. Avigad, "The Epitaph of a Royal Steward from Siloam Village," *IEJ* 3 [1953] 137-52; idem, "The Second Tomb Inscription of the Royal Steward," *IEJ* 5 [1955] 163-66). Although it is difficult to assert that this is the tomb of

Shebna, even if the full form of his name might read šĕbānyāhû in accordance with the tomb inscription, it is clear that the slopes of the Kidron opposite the eastern walls of Jerusalem served as the burial site for Jerusalem's high officials during the reign of the Davidic monarchy. Why then should Shebna be condemned simply for building himself a tomb when it was such a common practice?

A third consideration is the reference to Shebna's deportation and death in a wide land in conjunction with his removal from office (vv. 17-19). As argued above, 22:1b-14 stems from the period *during* Sennacherib's siege of Jerusalem, not the period following the withdrawal of Assyrian troops. Inasmuch as Sennacherib took prisoners back to Nineveh (*ANET*, 288), it may well be that Shebna was chief steward prior to the end of the siege but was included among the deportees. Sennacherib states specifically that Hezekiah "sent his personal messenger [*rakabusu*] . . . in order to deliver the tribute and do obeisance as a slave" (*ANET*, 288). The ideal candidate for such a mission would be Shebna, the chief steward, whose deportation to Nineveh (note the reference to Shebna's death in a wide land, v. 18) would leave the office open to another. The decision to capitulate and the decision concerning the terms of that capitulation would have taken place prior to the withdrawal of Assyrian troops. Isaiah's condemnation of Shebna presupposes his deportation, presumably to Assyria.

These factors suggest that the setting for 22:15-25 must be located in the period of Hezekiah's capitulation to Assyria when the decision was made to send tribute to Sennacherib as the price for Assyrian withdrawal. Although it cannot be confirmed that Shebna was the official who delivered the tribute mentioned in Sennacherib's annals, it seems likely that the chief steward, who would have been the senior official in charge of the Davidic house, would have been a likely candidate for such a mission. Naturally, such a deportation would have removed Shebna and his family permanently from a secure position. This would also explain the premise of Isaiah's condemnation of Shebna: he will never use the tomb that he built for himself. Likewise, he will never attain the permanent remembrance among his people that his burial in such a tomb would entail, nor will his family remain in its secure position.

From the above discussion, vv. 1b-14 and 15-25 were clearly two separate oracles composed at different times in relation to the Assyrian siege of Jerusalem in 701. Nevertheless, the analysis of their structure and genre demonstrates that the oracle against Shebna in vv. 15-25 confirms the prophet's disputation against the people and his condemnation of their defiant celebrating during the siege. The removal of Shebna from his secure position undermines the promise by YHWH to guarantee the security of the city of Jerusalem and the Davidic dynasty. Either 22:15-25 was written as an expansion of 22:1b-14 while the negotiations to end the siege were taking place, or the two oracles were combined during this period or shortly thereafter. In either case, the concern with the Assyrian siege and especially the Kidron Valley (see below on Intention) link the two passages together.

The date of the superscription in v. 1a (*maśśā᾽ gê᾽ ḥizzāyôn*, "Pronouncement concerning the Valley of Vision") cannot be ascertained with any certainty, but it appears to derive from the mention of the Valley of Vision (*gê᾽ ḥizzāyôn*) in v. 5 and the reference to the "burden" *(maśśā')* in v. 25. That it is an enigmatic reference to Jerusalem in the midst of a collection of *maśśā'ôt* against foreign nations suggests that it stems from a relatively early date. It may well be the title supplied by the prophet responsible for producing the final form of vv. 1b-25.

Intention

As part of the 5th-century edition of the book of Isaiah, ch. 22 functions as one of the oracles against the nations in chs. 13–23 that signify YHWH's judgment against the nations prior to their recognition of YHWH as ruler of the world. The inclusion of a pronouncement concerning Jerusalem and Judah among the oracles against the nations indicates that YHWH's actions pertain to Judah as well (cf. ch. 17 on Aram and Israel). Although Jerusalem will serve as the seat for YHWH's rule (cf. 2:2-4), Judah and Jerusalem must be cleansed in preparation for that role.

With respect to its late-8th-century setting, the intention of ch. 22 centers around events connected with the Kidron Valley and the Assyrian siege of Jerusalem in 701. It likewise depends on the explanatory function of the *maśśā'* genre to detect the actions of YHWH manifest in human events. In this respect, the Assyrian siege of Jerusalem, along with the removal from office and deportation of the chief steward Shebna, indicates that YHWH is acting to threaten the city of Jerusalem and the Davidic house. Such an assertion would contradict the standard Davidic/Zion theology that undergirded the identity of the city and dynasty as the chosen of YHWH. The prophet asserts that the Assyrian siege against Jerusalem was brought by YHWH. Consequently, there is no reason for the people to celebrate because YHWH will not act to defend the city.

This intention is manifested through the identification of the Valley of Vision with the Kidron Valley and the general two-part structure and generic subelements of the pronouncement. The reference to the Valley of Vision *(gê' ḥizzāyôn;* vv. 1a, 5a) has proved to be enigmatic. The name is not otherwise preserved in any known record, and various attempts to identify it with the Hinnom Valley south of biblical Jerusalem or the Tyropoeon Valley west of the city have not proved convincing (cf. Gray, 366). Likewise, attempts to reinterpret the name as a reference to calamity must be rejected (G. R. Driver).

Despite its designation as the Valley of Vision, two major factors indicate that the valley in question is actually the Kidron Valley east of the biblical city of Jerusalem. First, the focal point of Sennacherib's siege of Jerusalem appears to be the eastern approaches to the city which face the Kidron Valley. This is evident from the biblical accounts, which place the negotiations between the Assyrian Rabshakeh and the Judean officials at "the conduit of the upper pool on the highway to the Fuller's Field" (36:2; 2 Kgs 18:17). This location corresponds to that of the Gihon spring, which opened into the Kidron Valley, Warren's shaft on the eastern slopes of the city of David, and the northern or upper portion of Hezekiah's tunnel that supplied water to Jerusalem in this period (cf. Amiran, 75-78; J. Wilkenson, "Ancient Jerusalem: Its Water Supply and

Population," *PEQ* 106 [1974] 33-51). The focus on this location is deliberate, for the water system proved to be the weak point of the city that enabled David to capture it centuries earlier (2 Sam 5:6-9) and that prompted both Ahaz (Isa 7:3) and Hezekiah (2 Kgs 20:20; 2 Chr 32:1-8, 30-31) to concern themselves especially with defending it.

The focus on Shebna's tomb in vv. 15-25 also points to the Kidron Valley. As noted above, the present-day location of the village of Silwan, across the Kidron Valley from the eastern walls of the city of David, was the burial place of high officials during the reign of the Davidic monarchs (cf. Ussishkin, "Necropolis"; idem, *The Village of Silwan: The Necropolis from the Period of the Judean Kingdom* [Jerusalem: Israel Exploration Society and Yad Izhak Ben-Zvi, 1993] esp. 188-202). One of the tombs found there preserved an inscription indicating that it was the burial place of one of the royal stewards (see above on Setting). Although this tomb cannot be identified positively with that Shebna in Isaiah 22, the finds do indicate that this place served as a burial ground for high officials during the Davidic monarchy and provide information on the nature of the burial of such officials. During the siege of Jerusalem, the tomb that Shebna prepared for himself would have been in the hands of the Assyrian siege forces. It would also have been quite visible from the site of negotiations mentioned in Isa 36:2 and 2 Kgs 18:17.

The problems that scholars have encountered in identifying the Valley of Vision with the Kidron are due to the belief that the Valley of Vision is the actual name of a valley in the vicinity of Jerusalem. But this view fails to account for the above indications of a setting in the Kidron Valley and Isaiah's well-known penchant for wordplay. The term *ḥizzāyôn* means "vision" or "revelation" and corresponds to the general intention of the *maśśā'* genre to "reveal" YHWH's actions manifested in the human realm. In this respect, it appears to be a term that not only serves the purposes of Isaiah's discourse in this passage but also is a play on the word "Kidron" (*qidrôn*). Both terms employ the nominative ending -*ôn* attached to the main root so that they rhyme. Furthermore, the meaning of the verbal root *qdr* is "to be dark" (cf. *qadrût,* "darkness, gloom," BDB, 871). It usually appears in reference to the darkening of the sky (Jer 4:28; Joel 2:10; 4:15 [*RSV* 3:15]) or mourning (2 Sam 19:25; Jer 8:21; 14:2; etc.), but it can also be used figuratively to refer to the lack of revelation from YHWH (e.g., Mic 3:6). Isaiah's use of *ḥizzāyôn,* "vision," in place of *qidrôn,* "darkness," indicates his view that YHWH's actions are manifested in the Assyrian siege in the Kidron Valley. Although the name of the Kidron suggests YHWH's actions are hidden from normal view, the prophet has revealed the true significance of the siege through prophetic vision.

The second major indication of the intent of this passage is its generic character as a prophetic pronouncement and its two-part structure. The purpose of the prophetic pronouncement is to reveal the actions of YHWH in human events (cf. Weis). This intention is evident in the two-part structure of the passage that disputes the people's view that the Assyrian siege is an occasion for defiant celebration (vv. 1b-14) and supports the prophet's contention that the Assyrian siege represents YHWH's abrogation of the promise of security to Jerusalem and the house of David (vv. 15-25).

As noted above, the disputation in vv. 1b-14 presents Isaiah's counter-argument to the people of the city who are on the rooftops celebrating in the face of the Assyrian siege. The basis for this celebration appears to be the belief that the Assyrians will be unable to take the city, which had prepared for assault by strengthening the walls and building a new water system (vv. 8b-11). A further basis would be the Davidic/Zion ideology of the city that maintained that YHWH would defend Jerusalem against enemies (cf. Psalms 46; 48; 76). Such defiance in the face of the enemy calls to mind the Jebusites' taunts against David prior to his conquest of the city (2 Sam 5:6).

In contrast to the people, Isaiah maintains that the Assyrian siege is an occasion for mourning. In support of his contention, he points to the defenders of the city, who were either killed or captured while fleeing (vv. 2b-3), and to the continued presence of besieging soldiers in the Kidron and other valleys around Jerusalem (vv. 5-8a). His statements include reference to the Day of YHWH as a day of tumult, trampling, and confusion against Judah rather than against Judah's enemies (v. 5), thereby reversing the view that the day will be one of deliverance. Likewise, the references to Elam and Kir (v. 6) are significant. The Elamites supported Merodach-baladan, Hezekiah's major ally in the revolt (cf. ch. 39). Although they likely entered Assyrian service as a result of their defeat by Sennacherib in 703, their presence in the besieging army would have been a source of demoralization for the Judean defenders. Kir was the land to which Tiglath-pileser exiled survivors from Damascus, a country that had been allied with the northern kingdom of Israel during the Syro-Ephraimite War (2 Kgs 16:9). Their presence might well call to mind the defeat of northern Israel a generation earlier. The prophet also points to the people's reliance on weapons and defense in contrast to their failure to look to YHWH (vv. 8b-11). Finally, he quotes YHWH's statement that this should be an occasion for mourning and the deity's oath that the people will never be forgiven for their transgression until they die (vv. 12-14).

Yet the disputation alone is insufficient proof of the prophet's contention because it is based on the prophet's assertion of YHWH's statements, which could be contrasted with the assertion that YHWH would defend the city and the dynasty. Consequently, the disputation depends on the oracle against Shebna in vv. 15-25 to provide the basis and final confirmation of the truth of Isaiah's assertion. Shebna is identified as the chief steward of the Davidic house, a position that gives him authority to act on behalf of the king as well as supervision of the royal palace complex (cf. H. J. Katzenstein, "The Royal Steward (Asher 'al ha-Bayith)," *IEJ* 10 [1960] 149-54). It is clear from the passage that such a position provides him not only with personal security but also with a "secure place" for his family. Such security would be expressed through the position of authority in connection with the royal palace complex and by burial in a magnificent tomb such as those found on the site of the present village of Silwan. Consequently, the royal steward shares in the security promised the Davidic dynasty and the city of Jerusalem in that his welfare is bound up with that of the Davidic house.

But Shebna's removal from office and deportation bring to an end the security that his position afforded to him and to his family. In such circumstances, his position and that of his family will no longer be secure and the tomb that would have symbolized his security and preserved the memory of his name will be of no use. Inasmuch as Shebna's security and that of his family are bound up with that of the house of David, what do his removal and deportation say about the security of the Davidic dynasty and the city of Jerusalem? It obviously calls into question YHWH's promises to the house of David and the city of Jerusalem as expressed in Davidic/Zion theology. Consequently, the removal of Shebna from office and his deportation to a wide land where he will die support the prophet's contention that the Assyrian siege was an act of YHWH. In the prophet's view, YHWH is not guaranteeing the security of the city; rather, YHWH is the one who threatens it. In his view, this calls for mourning on the part of the people rather than defiant celebration. After all, the people's defiance would have to be directed against YHWH in the view of the prophet.

Bibliography

R. Amiran, "The Water Supply of Israelite Jerusalem," in *Jerusalem Revealed: Archaeology of the Holy City 1968-1974* (ed. Y. Yadin; Jerusalem and New Haven: Israel Exploration Society, 1976) 75-78; Brinkman, "Merodach-Baladan II" (→ 21:1-10); M. Broshi, "The Expansion of Jerusalem in the Reigns of Hezekiah and Manasseh," *IEJ* 24 (1974) 21-26; R. E. Clements, *Isaiah and the Deliverance of Jerusalem: A Study of the Interpretation of Prophecy in the Old Testament* (JSOTSup 13; Sheffield: JSOT Press, 1980) 33-34; idem, "The Prophecies of Isaiah and the Fall of Jerusalem in 587 B.C.," *VT* 30 (1980) 421-36; J. A. Emerton, "Notes on the Text and Translation of Isaiah xxii 8-11 and lxv 5," *VT* 30 (1980) 437-51; K. Fullerton, "A New Chapter out of the Life of Isaiah," *AJT* 9 (1905) 621-42; A. Kamphausen, "Isaiah's Prophecy Concerning the Major-Domo of King Hezekiah," *AJT* 5 (1901) 43-74; E. Koenig, "Shebna and Eliakim," *AJT* 10 (1906) 675-86; R. Martin-Achard, "L'oracle contre Shebnâ et le pouvoir des clefs, Es. 22,15-25," *TZ* 4 (1968) 241-54; T. N. D. Mettinger, *Solomonic State Officials: A Study of the Civil Government Officials of the Israelite Monarchy* (ConBOT 5; Lund: Gleerup, 1971) 70-110; D. Ussishkin, "The Necropolis from the Time of the Kingdom of Judah at Silwan, Jerusalem," *BA* 33 (1970) 34-46; Weis, "Definition" (→ "Introduction to the Prophetic Literature"), 139-42, 480-81; J. Willis, "Historical Issues in Isaiah 22,15-25," *Bib* 74 (1993) 60-70.

PRONOUNCEMENT CONCERNING TYRE, 23:1-18

Structure

I. Superscription	1a
II. Prophetic pronouncement (*maśśāʾ*) proper	1b-18
A. Call for communal complaint addressed to Phoenicia	1b-14
1. Command to wail addressed to ships of Tarshish	1b
a. Command proper	1bα$_1$

Isaiah 23:1-18 is demarcated by its introductory superscription in v. 1a, *maśśā' ṣōr*, which identifies the passage as a "pronouncement concerning Tyre." The focus on Tyre and the Phoenician reaction to the destruction of Tyre continues through 23:18. Isa 24:1, with its introductory *hinnēh* and its focus on YHWH's overturning the land at large, marks the end of the pronouncements concerning the nations and the beginning of a new section. The superscription in v. 1a constitutes the first major subunit of the passage. The pronouncement proper follows in vv. 1b-18.

The pronouncement proper in vv. 1b-18 includes two basic parts that are identified by their respective forms. Vv. 1b-14, characterized by a series of commands pertaining to lamentation and reaction to the fall of Tyre, constitute a call for a communal complaint. Vv. 15-18, characterized by the future-oriented formulas *wĕhāyâ bayyôm hahû'*, "and it shall come to pass in that day," in v. 15 and *wĕhāyâ*, "and it shall come to pass," in vv. 17 and 18, constitute a prophetic announcement of future events. The contents of vv. 15-18 make it clear that the future events are the seventy-year punishment and subsequent restoration of Tyre.

The structure of the call for a communal complaint in vv. 1b-14 is constituted by a series of six commands in vv. 1b, 2, 4, 6, 10, and 14. Furthermore, each command is followed by the basis for the command. The forms of the commands vary depending on their respective addressees as masculine plural forms (vv. 1b, 2, 6, 14) or feminine singular forms (vv. 4, 10), but all pertain to reactions to the destruction of Tyre. Likewise, although the specific addressees vary, all are components of Phoenicia. Although another imperative command appears in v. 12b, it is subsumed structurally under the preceding material (vv. 10-11) by the *wāw*-consecutive statement concerning YHWH's command to cease exultation in v. 12a.

The six imperatives of the call for a communal complaint outline a sequence of concern that begins in v. 1b with a command to wail for the loss of the harbor directed to the ships of Tarshish and reaches its climax in vv. 8-9 and 10-13 with the identification of YHWH as the cause of the destruction. Afterward, in v. 14, the passage returns to the initial command (v. 1b) with a similar command to wail for the loss of refuge directed to the ships of Tarshish.

The first command appears in v. 1b. The command proper appears in v. 1bα$_1$ as a masculine plural command to wail *(hêlîlû)* directed to the ships of Tarshish. The basis for the command follows in v. 1bα$_2$-b, which describes the ships' inability to return to port from the land of the Kittim (i.e., Cyprus).

The second command appears in vv. 2-3. The command proper appears in v. 2a as a masculine plural command to be silent *(dōmmû)* directed to the coastal inhabitants. The basis for the command follows in vv. 2b-3, which describe the loss of commerce suffered by Sidon.

The third command appears in vv. 4-5. The command proper appears in v. 4aα as a feminine singular command to be ashamed *(bôšî)* directed to Sidon. The basis for the command in vv. 4aα-5 focuses on the destruction of Tyre and consists of two parts. V. 4aα-b focuses on the failure of the sea to provide protection by reporting a statement by the sea that it did not give birth to children, a metaphorical statement that it had no obligation to protect Tyre. V. 5 reports the astonished reaction in Egypt at the news that Tyre had fallen.

The fourth command appears in vv. 6-9. The command proper appears in v. 6 as a twofold masculine plural command directed to the coastal inhabitants to go *('ibrû)* to Tarshish in v. 6a and wail *(hêlîlû)* in v. 6b. The basis for the command follows in vv. 7-9. It is constituted by two rhetorical questions indicating that the disaster is brought about by YHWH. V. 7 asserts that the exile of Tyre to a distant land is no cause for exultation. V. 8 asks who brought about the downfall of Tyre, and v. 9 answers that it was YHWH.

The fifth command appears in vv. 10-13. It is the largest section of the call for a communal complaint and provides the climax in that it identifies YHWH as the cause of the destruction of Tyre. The first part of this section contains the basic command to pass through the land that lacks defenses in vv. 10-11. The command proper appears in v. 10 as a feminine singular command to pass through *('ibrî)* the land directed to the daughter of Tarshish. The basis for the command follows in v. 11 with two statements that indicate that YHWH stretched out a hand to cause the destruction (v. 11a) and that YHWH commanded the destruction (v. 11b). Vv. 12-13 then expand on the passage by focusing on the cessation of exultation. The unit is introduced by a *wāw*-consecutive statement in v. 12a that concerns YHWH's command to cease exulting. V. 12b contains a twofold feminine singular command directed to the daughter of Sidon to arise *(qûmî)* and go *('ăbōrî)* to the land of the Kittim, which will give no rest. The basis for the command follows in v. 13 with a statement concerning Assyria's destruction of Chaldea. This statement is apparently meant to convey the power of the Assyrians and their ability to destroy Tyre and Cyprus as well.

The sixth and final command in the sequence appears in v. 14. It repeats the initial masculine plural command to wail *(hêlîlû)* found in v. 1b. The command proper appears in v. 14a directed to the ships of Tarshish. The basis for the command, the loss of refuge, appears in v. 14b. By repeating the initial command in this fashion, the passage returns full circle to its starting point after having made the point that YHWH is the cause of the catastrophe.

The prophetic announcement of future events in vv. 15-18 focuses on the seventy-year punishment of Tyre and its subsequent restoration. The passage consists of three basic parts identified by their respective introductory *wěhāyâ* statements.

Verses 15-16, introduced by the formula *wěhāyâ bayyôm hahû'*, "and it shall come to pass in that day," state that Tyre will be forgotten for seventy years. V. 15a contains the basic statement of Tyre's period of punishment "like the days of one king." Vv. 15b-16 then provide an analogy with the actions of a forgotten harlot. V. 15b states the analogy and v. 16 contains the harlot's song, who employs the harp to remind her clients that she should be remembered. The analogy with the harlot is made not only because of Tyre's commercial role selling goods to the nations but also because Asherah or Astarte, the Canaanite fertility goddess, was the chief deity of the city (Katzenstein, 9, 20).

The second basic part of this passage appears in v. 17, introduced by the formula *wĕhāyâ*, "and it shall come to pass." The statement focuses on YHWH's visitation of Tyre and the restoration of Tyre's role as merchant or harlot of the nations.

The third and final part of this passage is v. 18, likewise introduced by the formula *wĕhāyâ*. This statement focuses on the dedication of Tyre's commercial profits as holy to YHWH.

Genre

The overarching genre of ch. 23 is PROPHETIC PRONOUNCEMENT *(maśśā')*. This is evident from the introductory SUPERSCRIPTION for the passage in v. 1a, which identifies it as such. It is also evident in the explanatory function of the passage, which identifies the manifestation of YHWH's intentions in human events. This appears most clearly in vv. 15-18, which explain YHWH's plans to restore Tyre and to dedicate its profits as holy to YHWH after the seventy years of punishment have been concluded. YHWH's activities are also evident in vv. 8-9 and 11-12a, which identify YHWH as the party responsible for the destruction of Tyre. Two other major generic entities appear within the PROPHETIC PRONOUNCEMENT.

Verses 1b-14 constitute a CALL FOR A COMMUNAL COMPLAINT (Wolff). This genre is characterized by three elements: (1) the call itself in the form of a sequence of imperatives; (2) the direct address to the parties involved; and (3) the reason or motivation for the complaint. As the preceding discussion of the structure of this passage indicates, all three elements are present. Although the genre stems from a liturgical context of public lamentation, it is frequently adopted for prophetic use. Here one cannot be certain if a liturgical setting is intended, but it suits the prophet's purpose to announce the fall of Tyre as an act of YHWH. This purpose is likewise served by the RHETORICAL QUESTIONS in vv. 7 and 8-9, which identify YHWH as the cause of the catastrophe.

The PROPHETIC ANNOUNCEMENT OF FUTURE EVENTS in vv. 15-18 is identified by the formulas *wĕhāyâ bayyôm hahû'*, "and it shall come to pass in that day," in v. 15 and the following formula *wĕhāyâ*, "and it shall come to pass," in vv. 17 and 18. This section points to YHWH's intentions in bringing about the downfall of Tyre. Accordingly, Tyre is to be restored after seventy years so that its commercial profits can be dedicated as holy to YHWH.

Setting

The final form of the pronouncement concerning Tyre in 23:1-18 is set in the 5th-century edition of the book of Isaiah, where it functions as one of the pronouncements concerning the nations that demonstrate YHWH's sovereignty over the earth. Nevertheless, there is evidence that the present form of this text was composed in the late 7th century as part of the Josianic redaction of First Isaiah and that it is based on an earlier Isaianic call to lament in vv. 1b-14 that dates to the capitulation of Phoenicia to Sennacherib in 701.

There is a clear distinction between the call for a communal complaint in vv. 1b-14 and the announcement of future events in vv. 15-18 that suggests successive stages in the composition of this passage. Whereas vv. 1b-14 focus generally on Phoenicia, Sidon, and Tyre, vv. 15-18 focus exclusively on Tyre. Likewise, vv. 1b-14 presuppose a major disaster against Phoenicia, whereas vv. 15-18 anticipate the restoration of Tyre after seventy years of neglect. Furthermore, the future orientation of vv. 15-18 is somewhat incongruous in relation to the retrospective view of vv. 1b-14. The statement "and it shall come to pass in that day" in v. 15 is unclear when read in relation to the already completed event that stands behind vv. 1b-14. Vv. 15-18 therefore modify vv. 1b-14 from a situation of lamentation over the fall of Phoenicia to one of anticipation of the restoration of Tyre and the sanctification of its commerce to YHWH. These differences suggest that vv. 1b-14 and vv. 15-18 stem from different settings and that they were written for different purposes, although it seems clear that vv. 15-18 were written in relation to vv. 1b-14.

Although Sennacherib's invasion of Phoenicia in 701, which forced King Luli of Sidon to flee (cf. *ANET,* 287), provides a likely setting for vv. 1b-14, only a few scholars support this position (Erlandsson, 97-102; Rudolph; Høgenhaven, 160; Gosse, *Isaïe 13,1–14,23,* 104). The primary problem appears to be that vv. 1b-14 represent a retrospective view of the destruction of Tyre, but Sennacherib did not destroy the city in his invasion. Rather, the cities of the Phoenician seacoast seem to have capitulated at the approach of his army, forcing King Luli of Sidon (and Tyre) to flee to Kition in Cyprus for safety (cf. Katzenstein, 246-51). Likewise, other attempts to place 23:1b-14 in relation to Assyrian campaigns against Tyre in the late 8th century have failed to gain support. These include Cheyne's suggestion (*Introduction,* 144) that the chapter relates to Shalmanezer V's siege of Tyre in 727-722 and Hayes and Irvine's position (pp. 288-90) that the chapter presupposes the submission of Cyprus and Phrygia to Sargon in 709. As a result, scholars tend to place ch. 23 in relation to periods when Sidon or Tyre was destroyed. The various suggestions include Esarhaddon's destruction of Sidon in 678 and siege of Tyre in 672 (Vermeylen, *Du prophète,* 342-43; Lipinski; Clements, *Isaiah 1–39,* 192; Wildberger, *Jesaja,* 863-66; Watts, *Isaiah 1–33,* 304); the capture of Sidon by the Persian monarch Artaxerxes III Ochus in 348 or 343 (Duhm, *Jesaia,* 166; Marti, *Jesaja,* 180-81; Kaiser, *Isaiah 13–39,* 162-63; cf. Werner, 56); and the destruction of Tyre by Alexander the Great in 332 (Procksch, *Jesaja I–XXXIX,* 300; Fohrer, *Jesaja* 1:257-58; Lindblom; Fischer and Rüterswörden; cf. Werner, 56).

Despite the reservations of these scholars, however, three major factors suggest that Phoenicia's capitulation to Sennacherib in 701 does provide the proper setting for 23:1b-14. First, the passage contains no confirmation that Tyre (or Sidon) is destroyed; it speaks only generally of humiliation, downfall, and the lack of protection. The statement in v. 1b that "Tyre is laid waste, without house or haven" *(RSV)* is incorrectly translated. The word "Tyre" does not appear in this passage, which should be translated, "for robbed [*šuddad*] of home, from entering from the land of Cyprus" (cf. v. 14). This statement is addressed to the ships of Tarshish that are unable to return to their home port. The reason is not stated, but Luli's flight to Cyprus and the submission of the region to Sennacherib provide a likely scenario. Second, v. 12b relates a flight to Cyprus in search of sanctuary, which supports this interpretation. Likewise, v. 7b refers to Sidon's dwelling far away. Third, v. 13 relates the Assyrian devastation of Chaldea. Again the verse has been mistranslated in the NRSV and should read, "Behold the land of the Chaldeans, this people is not, Assyria turned it into a desert." Various campaigns were conducted by the Assyrians against the Chaldeans in the late 8th century, but this verse appears to presuppose Sennacherib's campaign against the Chaldean prince Merodach-baladan in 703. This campaign preceded Sennacherib's assault against Phoenicia and the western alliance that revolted against him in 705. It was designed to put down the eastern alliance, centered around Merodach-baladan, so that Sennacherib could secure his throne. Once the Chaldeans were defeated, Sennacherib turned his attention to the west (cf. Brinkman, 22-26). Isa 23:13 presents the Chaldean defeat as an example or prelude to the collapse of Phoenicia.

The principal objections to such a thesis have been summarized by Wildberger (*Jesaja,* 863-64). In general, he cites the opinion of scholars such as Duhm, Eissfeldt, Dillmann-Kittel, and Procksch that the style and ideas of ch. 23 do not correspond to those of Isaiah, but critical examination indicates that this view is unfounded.

We have already dealt in part with his first specific objection, i.e., that this is a retrospective statement that fails to match the historical facts of the late 8th century. Wildberger states that Cyprus and Tarshish (cf. vv. 1b, 6, 10, 12, 14) are not involved in the Phoenician capitulation, but this fails to account for Luli's overseas flight, presumably to Phoenician colonies such as Cyprus or Tarshish that could provide him with sanctuary. That the sea does not claim its sons and daughters, i.e., does not provide sanctuary for the fleeing Phoenicians, indicates merely that the Phoenician navy was unable to defend the country against the Assyrians. Furthermore, Sennacherib's statement that Luli perished (*ANET,* 287) may also be hinted at here.

Second, Wildberger maintains that the mention of Assyria in v. 13 is a late gloss based on a misunderstanding of an original 'ăšer. His case does not hold up, however, as indicated by his elaborate attempt to repoint the rest of the verse following Duhm and Marti. The problem stems from the fact that the statement "this people is not" refers to the previously mentioned Chaldeans, not to the following Assyrians. In the present form of the verse, the statement "Assyria turned it into [lit. 'appointed it for'] a desert," stands in appositional relationship to the statement "this people is not." Altogether, the verse reads, "Behold the land of the Chaldeans, this people is not, Assyria turned it into a desert." As such, the verse refers to the destruction unleashed against Chaldea by Sennacherib's invasion force in 703.

Finally, Wildberger maintains that the language and ideas of the chapter are not those of Isaiah. He cites the use of the verb y's, "to counsel," and the noun 'ēṣâ, "counsel," as terms that are typical of the oracles against the nations (cf. Jer 49:20; 50:45), but the verb appears frequently in Isaiah (Isa 7:5; 14:24,

26, 27; 19:12, 17; 32:7, 8), as does the noun (5:19; 8:10; 11:2; 14:26; 16:3; 19:3, 11, 17; 25:1; 28:29; 29:15; 30:1; 36:5). In fact, ch. 23 is filled with expressions that are characteristic of Isaiah: *hêlîlû*, "wail" (v. 1b; cf. 13:6; 14:31 in Hiphil imperative forms; cf. 15:2, 3; 16:7 [bis]); *wĕlō' giddaltî baḥûrîm rômamtî bĕtûlôt*, "and I did not raise boys, nor did I rear girls" (v. 4b; cf. 1:2 [*giddaltî/rômamtî*]); *mā'ôz*, "refuge" (vv. 4, 11, 14; cf. 17:9, 10; 30:2, 3); *'allîzâ*, "exultation," and *'ālaz*, "to exult" (vv. 7, 12; cf. 13:3; 22:2; 32:13); *lĕhāqēl kol-nikbaddê-'āreṣ*, "to humiliate all the honored of the earth" (v. 9b; cf. 3:5, *wĕhanniqleh bannikbād*, "and the despised with the honored"); *yādô nāṭâ 'al-hayyām*, "his hand he stretched out over the sea" (v. 11; cf. 5:25 [bis]; 9:11, 16, 20 [*RSV* 12, 17, 21]; 10:4; 14:26, 27); *hirgîz mamlākôt*, "he shook kingdoms" (v. 11; cf. 13:13; 14:16; in Qal, 5:25; 14:9; 28:21; 32:10, 11); *lō' tôsîpî 'ôd la'lôz*, "you shall never again exult" (v. 12; cf. 1:5; 8:5; 10:20); and *mappēlâ*, "ruin" (v. 13; cf. 17:1; 25:2; this word appears only in Isaiah).

Not only do the vocabulary and style show close connections with the rest of Isaiah, but so do the ideas. Wildberger states that Isaiah is concerned not with the fate of other nations but only with that of Jerusalem and Judah. But this view ignores Isaiah's perspective that YHWH controls or influences the activities of foreign nations, such as Assyria, the rod of YHWH's anger (10:5), and the fact that vv. 8-9 and 11-12 specifically identify YHWH as the cause of Phoenicia's collapse. Likewise, such a view ignores the role that the pronouncements concerning the nations play in Isaiah's prophecies: to warn Judah and Jerusalem of YHWH's activities on the international scene and the potential for judgment against Israel, Judah, and Jerusalem. The point of the present passage concerning Phoenicia is to demonstrate YHWH's power to Judah and Jerusalem. Such a passage would hardly be directed to Tyre, but presupposes a Jerusalemite/Judean audience.

On the basis of the above considerations, one must conclude that Phoenicia's capitulation to Assyria provides the historical setting for 23:1b-23.

Isaiah 23:15-18 appears to presuppose a different setting, when Tyre was able to return to prosperity and possible service to YHWH. In this respect, it is noteworthy that the text specifies seventy years as the period when Tyre would lie neglected. Likewise, this period is specified as the lifetime of one king. Esarhaddon employs seventy years as the period designated for the desolation of Sumer and Akkad (*ARAB* II, §650, p. 245), which corresponds to a normal human lifespan. The span is significant historically, however, in that it matches the period when Tyre was restricted from engaging in trade relations. This lasted until the collapse of Assyrian authority after the death of Assurbanipal in 627. In this respect, it is noteworthy that seventy years following Phoenicia's capitulation to Sennacherib corresponds to the year 631, the 8th year of the reign of Josiah, which 2 Chr 34:3 identifies as the year that Josiah began to seek YHWH. Although the seventy-year figure can hardly be tied securely to this date, it does indicate that the period saw the general decline of Assyria and the rise in the fortunes of both Judah and Tyre (Katzenstein, 296-97). Insofar as Josiah intended a general restoration with Judah, including trade relations with Tyre like those enjoyed by David and Solomon, it appears that the Josianic period provides the likely historical setting for vv. 15-18. In this case, vv. 15-18 would present the downfall of Tyre as a temporary condition that would be rectified when YHWH restored Judah in the reign of King Josiah. Once Tyre was restored, its commerce would be dedicated as holy to YHWH (v. 18); that is, trade with Judah would resume.

Because of the focus specifically on Tyre in the Josianic period, it appears that the superscription in v. 1a dates to the Josianic period as well.

Intention

The intention of this passage is defined in relation to the various editions of the book of Isaiah of which it was a part. In both the 5th- and 6th-century editions of Isaiah, ch. 23 portrays Tyre as one of the nations that came under YHWH's rule in the context of the establishment of the authority of the Persian empire in the region. In its present form, the chapter projects a period of suffering followed by a general restoration of the fortunes of Tyre and the dedication of its commerce to YHWH. Tyre never achieved the prominence and power it enjoyed in previous periods, but its incorporation into the Persian empire placed it in a relatively favorable position. Although its fortunes would later change in the 4th century, the early period of Persian rule saw Tyre's kings enjoying political status and legal rights greater than those of a governor or satrap (Katzenstein, 346-47). Such a role for Tyre would fit into the general perspective of the 5th-century (and 6th-century) edition of Isaiah that the establishment of Persian rule was to be equated with the establishment of YHWH's sovereignty over all the nations of the world. As a component of YHWH's empire, Tyre's trading activities would then be dedicated to YHWH.

The late-7th-century context of the Josianic restoration of Judah and re-daction of Isaiah presents a similar interpretation for ch. 23. Again the chapter portrays the restoration of Tyre after a period of neglect and suffering. As noted above, the seventy-year period of Tyre's neglect would have ended in 631 if calculated precisely. This would point to the early period of Josiah's reign when Tyre began to emerge not only as a free city following the collapse of Assyrian authority but also as the leading city of the Phoenician coastal states (Katzenstein, 296-97). A combination of shared interests in the collapse of Assyria and geopolitical factors would present Tyre and Judah as potential allies in this period. Josiah was acting to consolidate his authority over the southern part of the Syro-Palestinian corridor, including Philistia, Moab, Edom, and Ammon (11:11-16; cf. Zeph 2:4-14), following the collapse of Assyria and prior to the rise of Egypt. Furthermore, his moves to the north to secure the territory of the former northern kingdom of Israel as far as Naphtali (2 Chr 34:6) would place him on the borders of Phoenician or Tyrian territory. In such a situation, an alliance with Tyre like that enjoyed by David and Solomon would bring trade benefits to Judah as well as secure the northern border. In such a situation, the commerce of Tyre would be considered holy to YHWH.

Finally, the late 8th century presents a different context for interpreting Isaiah's call to lament over the fall of Phoenicia in vv. 1b-14. These verses presuppose the fall not just of Tyre but of all Phoenicia, as indicated by the addressees that appear throughout the poem, including the ships of Tarshish (vv.

310

1b and 14), the inhabitants of the coast and merchants of Sidon (v. 2), Sidon (v. 4; cf. Tyre in v. 5), the inhabitants of the coast (v. 6; cf. Tyre in v. 8), the daughter of Tarshish (v. 10; cf. Canaan in v. 11), and the virgin daughter of Tarshish (v. 12). As noted above, the passage presupposes the flight of Luli, king of Sidon (v. 12b; cf. v. 7b), and the collapse of Phoenician resistance at the approach of Sennacherib in 701 (cf. *ANET,* 287; Katzenstein, 246-51). The prophet's intention here is to point to the desperate situation of Judah, which was a ringleader in the revolt against Sennacherib, following the collapse of one of its major western allies. Following the capitulation of Phoenicia, Sennacherib reports that "all the kings of Amurru," which included most of the western alliance, "brought sumptuous gifts and . . . kissed my feet" (*ANET,* 287). This left Hezekiah of Judah and Sidqia of Philistia as the only kings in the west still opposing Sennacherib. Isaiah portrays a desperate situation for Judah, in which YHWH is identified as the cause of the Phoenician collapse (vv. 8-9, 11-12), and in which Chaldea, Hezekiah's chief eastern ally in the revolt (cf. ch. 39), had already fallen to Sennacherib's forces (v. 13). Consequently, Isaiah presents continued resistance against Sennacherib as contrary to the will of YHWH.

Bibliography

Brinkman, "Merodach-Baladan II" (→ 21:1-10); Erlandsson, *Burden of Babylon* (→ 13:1–14:23), 97-102; T. Fischer and U. Rüdersvörden, "Aufruf zur Volksklage in Kanaan (Jesaja 23)," *WO* 13 (1982) 36-49; P. W. Flint, "The Septuagint Version of Isaiah 23:1-14 and the Massoretic Text," *BIOSCS* 21 (1988) 35-54; Høgenhaven, *Gott und Volk* (→ "Introduction to the Book of Isaiah"), 157-61; H. J. Katzenstein, *The History of Tyre* (Jerusalem: Schocken Institute for Jewish Research, 1973); A. van der Kooij, "A Short Commentary on Some Verses of the Old Greek of Isaiah 23," *BIOSCS* 15 (1982) 36-50; J. Lindblom, "Der Ausspruch über Tyrus in Jes. 23," *ASTI* 4 (1965) 56-73; J. Linder, "Weissagung über Tyrus," *ZKTh* 65 (1941) 217-21; E. Lipinski, "The Elegy on the Fall of Sidon in Isaiah 23," *ErIs* 14 (1978) 79-88; W. Rudolph, "Jesaja 23:1-14," in *Festschrift für Friedrich Baumgärtel* (ed. J. Herrmann; Erlangen: Universitätsbund, 1959) 166-74; Ju. B. Tsirkin, "The Hebrew Bible and the Origin of Tartessian Power," *Aula Orientalis* 4 (1986) 179-85; W. G. E. Watson, "Tribute to Tyre (Is. XXIII 7)," *VT* 26 (1976) 371-74; Werner, *Studien* (→ "Introduction to the Book of Isaiah"), 54-60; H. W. Wolff, "Der Aufruf zur Volksklage," *ZAW* 76 (1964) 48-56.

PROPHETIC ANNOUNCEMENT OF YHWH'S NEW WORLD ORDER: PROPHECY OF SALVATION FOR ZION/ISRAEL, 24:1–27:13

Structure

I. Prophetic announcement of YHWH's punishment
   of the earth   24:1-23

Isaiah 24–27 has long been recognized as a distinct unit within the larger structure of the book of Isaiah. Because of its interest in the resurrection of the dead (26:14, 19) and its general eschatological character, it has often been identified as an apocalypse and one of the latest compositions of Isaiah 1–39 (for the history of research on chs. 24–27, see Millar, 1-22; Wildberger, *Jesaja*, 893-96). More recent studies, however, have challenged this view, arguing that chs. 24–27 at best point to the origins of apocalyptic in the 6th century B.C.E. (Millar; Johnson).

The demarcation of this unit is quite clear. It follows the last of the oracles against the nations in chs. 13–23, shifting its concern from individual nations to the entire earth (*'ereṣ*) and its inhabitants. Introduced by an initial *hinnēh*, "behold," it is syntactically independent from the preceding material. Its perspective is universal, in that it focuses on the punishment of the entire earth followed by its restoration, including a banquet for all the nations held by YHWH on Mt. Zion (25:6-8). It is characterized by an interest in the demise of an unnamed exalted city (24:10, 12; 25:2, 3; 26:5) and the strong city of the speaker (26:1). It is oriented to the future, with continuous references to "that day" (24:21; 25:9; 26:1; 27:1, 2, 6, 12, 13) and to YHWH's mountain (24:23; 25:7, 10; 27:13), which will be the site of the banquet of the nations and the redemption of Israel. It employs fertility or agricultural imagery throughout to describe the punishment of the earth as well as the redemption of Israel, which forms the climax of the unit. With its introductory *hôy*, "woe!" 28:1 introduces an entirely new unit that is concerned with the Ephraimite kingdom and the implications of its experience for Judah.

The structure of the unit is also clear, insofar as it shifts its concern from YHWH's punishment of the earth and its implications to YHWH's blessing of the earth and its implications for both the nations and Israel.

Isaiah 24:1-23 is a prophetic announcement of YHWH's punishment of the earth, and it focuses on the earth's devastation as a consequence of the violation of the "eternal covenant" (*běrît 'ôlām*) by its inhabitants (cf. v. 5). The introductory announcement of YHWH's punishment of the earth appears in vv. 1-2, followed by the prophet's announcement of YHWH's word concerning the basis for the earth's devastation in vv. 3-13. Vv. 14-23 contain the prophet's explanation or interpretation of YHWH's word according to a disputation pattern. Here the prophet challenges the people's rejoicing by pointing out that YHWH intends the overthrow of the earth's kings in order to establish a new world order with YHWH as ruler on Mt. Zion. For a detailed discussion of the structure of this passage, see the discussion of 24:1-23.

A prophetic announcement of YHWH's blessing of the earth, which concludes climactically with the restoration of Israel to Zion, then follows in 25:1–27:13. YHWH's blessing of the earth at Zion is described in 25:1-12, including a song of praise by the prophet to YHWH (vv. 1-5) followed by an announcement of YHWH's banquet for the nations at Zion that concludes with statements concerning the removal of Israel's shame and the overthrow of Moab. The results of this announcement are then proclaimed in 26:1–27:13, which includes three separate subsections, each introduced by the formula *bayyôm hahû'*, "in that day." Isa 26:1-21 announces Judah's song of complaint petitioning YHWH for deliverance from its enemies. Isa 27:1 announces YHWH's defeat of Leviathan, the primordial dragon of chaos, which symbolizes YHWH's acts to restore order in the world. Finally, 27:2-13 announces YHWH's restoration of Israel to Zion in the form of an exhortation designed to convince Israel to accept YHWH's offer of reconciliation.

Altogether, chs. 24–27 constitute a prophecy of salvation for Israel at Zion in the form of a prophetic announcement of YHWH's new world order. As such, these chapters explain the current chaos of the world and Israel's suffering at the hands of the nations as a plan by YHWH to assert divine rule over the world at Zion.

Genre

Scholarly discussion of the genre of chs. 24–27 has run a wide gamut, including preexilic judgment literature, prophetic eschatology, prophetic liturgy, early or proto-apocalyptic, and late postexilic apocalyptic (for a full survey of the discussion concerning the genre and historical background of chs. 24–27, see Redditt, "Isaiah 24–27," 232-68; see also Millar, 1-9).

By far the most important issue has been whether chs. 24–27 constitute an (→) apocalypse. Since early studies by Smend and Duhm (*Jesaia*, 172-94), scholars have pointed to a number of features of chs. 24–27 that suggest their apocalyptic character. Such features include its world judgment and the end of the nations of the earth; YHWH's establishment of world rule at Zion; the use of mythological motifs such as YHWH's defeat of Leviathan or the conquest of death; the reactions of the moon and the sun to YHWH's rule; the eschatological banquet of the nations on Mt. Zion; the interpretation of earlier prophecy; the pseudonymous nature of the composition; and others (for a list of apocalyptic characteristics, see Lindblom, 102). These characteristics have convinced many scholars that chs. 24–27 are an apocalypse, commonly labeled the "Isaiah Apocalypse" or the like (e.g., Clements; Kaiser; Vermeylen, "La composition").

But many scholars have noted that chs. 24–27 lack important characteristics of later apocalyptic literature (e.g., Anderson; Hanson; Johnson, 100;

Y. Kaufman; Millar, 1-9; Redditt, "Isaiah 24-27"; "Once Again"; Rudolph).
The composition gives no indication that the secrets of the cosmos are revealed,
nor is there any semidivine guide who leads the reader through a tour of heaven
or hell. There is no indication of a periodization of history in that the defeat of
the earthly kings does not represent a fundamental transformation of the cosmos
or the end of world history as it is known. No pronounced dualism between the
forces of good and those of evil is evident; the references to the wicked ones in
26:1-21 appear to be nothing more than enemies of Judah rather than representatives of cosmic disruption. Perhaps most importantly, chs. 24–27 lack the
pessimistic worldview that is characteristic of apocalyptic. Chs. 24–27 portray
the coming salvation of Israel and the nations following the downfall of the
oppressive city. Rather than waiting for YHWH to intervene in world affairs to
punish the wicked, chs. 24–27 understand the fall of the city to be an act of
deliverance by YHWH to which Israel and the nations may now respond.
Because of these considerations, many scholars have shied away from identifying chs. 24–27 as a full APOCALYPSE, identifying it instead as prophetic eschatology (Lindblom; Plöger; Rudolph) or early/proto-apocalyptic (Hanson; Johnson; Millar, 1-9; Redditt).

Chapters 24–27 do employ many elements that appear in later apocalyptic
and eschatological texts. But as the absence of many other elements indicates,
these chapters can hardly be characterized as apocalyptic in the fullest sense,
although they may represent an early stage in the development of apocalyptic
literature. Perhaps most telling is that chs. 24–27 interpret the fall of the "city
of chaos" as an act of YHWH in the historical realm. As indicated by the frequent
references to this city throughout the text, it is apparently viewed as an oppressor
of Israel. Although the fall of this city does not resolve all the problems suffered
by Israel and the nations, it presages the establishment of YHWH's rule on Zion
and the resulting benefits for the nations and the restoration of exiled Israel to
Jerusalem. Unlike apocalyptic literature, which is written from a position of
powerlessness and pessimism in which human action is no longer an effective
means to overcome suffering in the world, chs. 24–27 call on their audience to
respond to YHWH's actions. In this respect, chs. 24–27 stand squarely within
the prophetic tradition, which always demanded a response from its audience
to change its actions or to adopt a specific program.

The prophetic character of chs. 24–27 is likewise evident in the generic
entities that constitute the larger structure of this text. As the discussion of the
structure of chs. 24–27 indicates, the text is constituted by two major sections:
24:1-23, which announces YHWH's punishment of the earth, and 25:1–27:13,
which announces YHWH's blessing of the earth and its results. Especially telling
in this regard is the presence of a DISPUTATION SPEECH at the end of each major
section in 24:14-23 and 27:7-13 (for details, see the discussion of the individual
sections below). Isa 24:14-23 challenges the prevailing view of the nations that
the overthrow of the city of chaos is an act that will benefit them. Instead, the
refutation of this view indicates that YHWH will not stop at the overthrow of
the city of chaos. Rather, YHWH intends the overthrow of all the kings of the
earth as well in preparation for establishing divine rule on Mt. Zion. As such,
the DISPUTATION in 24:14-23 qualifies the PROPHETIC ANNOUNCEMENT OF

PUNISHMENT in 24:1-13. YHWH's actions are directed not only against the city of chaos but in fact against the entire earth. That the speaker announces YHWH's word in 24:3-13 reinforces the prophetic character of this section. The DISPUTATION SPEECH in 27:7-13 plays an even more important role insofar as it contributes to the EXHORTATION to the people of Israel in 27:2-13. It is designed to convince the people that YHWH is acting to restore Israel to Zion, now that the punishment of Israel's sins has been completed. As such, it is designed to motivate the people to accept YHWH's offer of reconciliation that appears in the vineyard ALLEGORY of 27:2-6.

Equally important is the generic character of the two major subsections of chs. 24–27. Isa 24:1-23 is identified as a PROPHETIC ANNOUNCEMENT of YHWH's PUNISHMENT of the earth. The prophetic character of this unit is evident through the speaker's conveyance of the word of YHWH in vv. 4-13. These verses in and of themselves constitute a PROPHETIC ANNOUNCEMENT OF PUNISHMENT. The DISPUTATION SPEECH clarifies the implications of this announcement for the nations and YHWH's relationship to them. Likewise, the generic character of 25:1–27:13 is a PROPHETIC ANNOUNCEMENT of YHWH's blessing of the earth and its results for Israel. Again, the prophet speaks, sometimes in song (25:1-5; 26:2-21), sometimes in objective announcement language (25:6-12; 26:1; 27:1, 2-13), but the prophet also conveys the word of YHWH (27:2-6) while interpreting its significance and that of YHWH's actions.

One must consider the two major sections of chs. 24–27 in relation to each other when considering the generic character of the whole. The PROPHETIC ANNOUNCEMENT OF PUNISHMENT against the earth in 24:1-23 provides the premise for the entire composition; the fall of the city of chaos presages the establishment of YHWH's world rule at Zion. The announcement of YHWH's blessing of the earth and its results for Israel in 25:1–27:13 draws out the implications of YHWH's coming world rule; Israel will be redeemed from exile and restored to the worship of YHWH at Mt. Zion. In sum, the generic character of the whole is a PROPHETIC ANNOUNCEMENT OF SALVATION that focuses on the establishment of YHWH's new world order. Once announced, it remains only for the people to accept the reality of YHWH's action and to work for its realization.

A final issue in the discussion of genre in chs. 24–27 is the liturgical character of the composition. A number of scholars have pointed to the presence of hymnic passages, such as the SONG OF THANKSGIVING in 25:1-5 or the SONG OF VICTORY in 26:1-6, in order to argue for the liturgical character of the composition (e.g., Lindblom; Fohrer). The progressive flow of thought and the presence of relatively large structural units militate against Lindblom's contention that chs. 24–27 constitute a prophetic cantata in which the subunits were meant to be sung antiphonally by two prophetic choirs. Nevertheless, the presence of so much hymnic material in chs. 24–27, such as the THANKSGIVING SONG in 25:1-5 and the COMPLAINT SONG in 26:1-21, suggests a liturgical setting for this text. It is noteworthy that prophetic liturgies have no fixed form but employ a variety of independent genres in forming a text for a particular setting and purpose. In this case, one cannot deny that chs. 24–27 may well constitute a PROPHETIC LITURGY designed to commemorate the fall of the "city of chaos" mentioned throughout the text and to interpret the significance of that fall.

Setting

In its present context as part of the 5th-century edition of the final form of the book of Isaiah, chs. 24–27 play an important role in relation to the preceding material. Scholars have already noted that chs. 24–27, with their image of worldwide judgment against all the nations of the earth, follow nicely after the pronouncements concerning the nations in chs. 13–23 (Skinner, *Isaiah I–XXXIX*, lxviii-lxix; Clements, *Isaiah 1–39*, 196-97; Wildberger, *Jesaja*, 892-93; Vermeylen, *Du prophète*, 35). An examination of the textual citations found in chs. 24–27, however, indicates that these chapters relate also to chs. 1–12, in that they cite heavily from these chapters as well as from chs. 13–23. Citations of Isaianic texts include 24:13/17:6; 24:16/21:2 and 33:1; 25:4-5/4:5b-6 and 32:1-2; 25:11b-12/2:9-17; 26:5/2:6-21; 26:17-18/13:8; and 27:1-13/5:1-7 and 11:10-16 (for a full discussion of these citations, see Sweeney, "Textual Citations"). In addition, 27:1-13 alludes heavily to chs. 1 and 17 (see Sweeney, "New Gleanings"). Consequently, chs. 24–27 explain the manifestations of YHWH's world rule at Zion in relation to the judgment against the nations expressed in chs. 13–23 and the punishment and subsequent restoration of Israel and Judah expressed in chs. 1–12. Likewise, 2:2-4 conveys the central role that Zion will play in this scenario.

Attempts to establish the setting and date of composition of chs. 24–27 have been plagued by its mixture of hymnic material, prose, and other forms of poetry, as well as by the lack of specific historical allusions, especially with regard to the exalted city that figures so prominently. Consequently, dates for the composition of chs. 24–27 have ranged all the way from the late 8th century B.C.E. (i.e., the time of the prophet Isaiah) to the 2nd century C.E. Although the discovery of a complete Isaiah scroll (1QIsa^a) dating to the latter part of the 2nd century B.C.E. at Qumran establishes a terminus ad quem, the range of dates continues to be quite wide (for a summary of scholarship, see Wildberger, *Jesaja*, 905-6; Millar, 15-21; Redditt, "Isaiah 24–27," 232-68). Furthermore, the majority of scholars consider these chapters to be a collection of hymnic, prophetic, and eschatological fragments that have grown into their present form over the course of centuries (e.g., see Wildberger, *Jesaja*, 893-905, including his summary of scholarship; cf. Clements, *Isaiah 1–39*, 196-200; Vermeylen, *Du prophète*, 349-81).

Despite the shifts in form or genre that have caused many scholars to conclude that these chapters are fragmentary, the present analysis of the structure and genre of chs. 24–27 demonstrates a high degree of coherence and unity of purpose. Indeed, several lines of evidence support the contention that chs. 24–27 are a relatively unified composition, insofar as 24:1–26:13 appear to have been composed in relation to an earlier 27:1-13. Not only do chs. 24–27 display a coherent literary structure and generic character as a prophetic announcement of salvation, but their worldview is consistently universal insofar as it focuses on YHWH's plans for the "land" or "earth" (*'ereṣ*) in general, including the nations and Israel. Furthermore, the entire work presupposes the overthrow of an anonymous "city of chaos" (24:10), which is further identified as a "fortified city" with a palace of aliens (25:2) and an "exalted city" (26:5) that is cast down. In addition, chs. 24–27 employ a relatively consistent mythological pattern employing motifs of death, life, and agricultural fertility to express its concern with the overthrow of the oppressive ruling city and the renewed life of the oppressed. Chs. 24–27 consistently posit that YHWH's holy mountain at Zion will be the locus for YHWH's blessings of the nations and Israel together with divine world rule (24:23; 25:6-8, 9-10; 26:21; 27:12-13). Finally, citations and allusions to prior prophetic traditions, whether from Isaiah or from other prophets, are employed to demonstrate that this scenario represents a fulfillment of earlier prophecy (see Sweeney, "Textual Citations," esp. 44-45, n. 23; idem, "New Gleanings"; Wildberger, *Jesaja,* 910-11; Day, "Case"; idem, "Prophecy," in *It Is Written: Scripture Citing Scripture [Fest.* B. Lindars; ed. D. A. Carson and H. G. M. Williamson; Cambridge: Cambridge University Press, 1988] 39-55, esp. 48-51).

Nevertheless, there are some indications that 27:1-13 may have a different origin than that of 24:1–26:21, although it has been worked into the overall framework of chs. 24–27. Whereas chs. 24–26 are primarily concerned with the nations at large, ch. 27 focuses especially on Israel. This is all the more striking when it is noted that whereas ch. 27 employs terms such as "Israel" or "Jacob" in reference to the people (27:6, 9, 12), chs. 24–26 use either nonspecific language, such as "his people" (25:8), or clearly specific language, such as "Judah" (26:1), in reference to Jews. Likewise, ch. 27 is distinguished by its concern with a "fortified city" (27:10), but here it refers not to an alien oppressive city but to an Israelite city that has suffered punishment for the sins of Jacob. Even the terminology is different. Whereas chs. 24–26 employ the term *qiryâ,* "city," as the primary designation for the city in every instance (24:10, *qiryat tōhû;* 25:2, *qiryâ bĕṣûrâ;* 26:5, *qiryâ niśgābâ*), 27:10 employs the term *'îr,* "city," i.e., *'îr bĕṣûrâ.*

Furthermore, the use of mythological motifs differs somewhat. Although both share a concern with agricultural fertility, 24:1–26:13 employs the imagery of death and life, whereas 27:1 refers specifically to Leviathan, the mythological chaos monster from Israelite tradition (see Day, *Conflict,* esp. 141-51). Nevertheless, Day points to the relationship between Leviathan and the other mythological themes of chs. 24–27 by reference to Ugaritic myths concerning the enthronement of Baal following his defeat of Yamm, the dragon or sea monster of chaos. That association, together with the shared agricultural imagery and the fact that 27:1-13 forms a fitting climax to chs. 24–27 (cf. 25:9-10a), suggests that 24:1–26:21 may well have been composed as a précis to a preexisting 27:1-13. I will discuss the matter below in relation to the setting of 27:1 and 27:2-13.

Although chs. 24–27 play an important role within the present structure of the 5th-century edition of the final form of the book of Isaiah, the date of the composition of the present form of these chapters appears to be the 6th century, following the destruction of Jerusalem and the Babylonian exile in 587/586, i.e., about the time of the return to Jerusalem in the early Persian period (cf. Anderson; Hanson; Johnson, 100; Millar, 115-20). A number of factors speak in favor of such a date.

First, chs. 24–27 focus on YHWH's actions against the entire earth, but the present analysis notes the central role that the downfall of the anonymous "city of chaos" plays in the composition. Numerous candidates have been suggested for the identity of the city, including Nineveh, Babylon, Carthage, Tyre, a city in Moab, Samaria (see Vermeylen, *Du prophète,* 351), and most recently, Jerusalem (Johnson), but none has commanded general acceptance. As the present analysis demonstrates, however, the city is identified as an exalted oppressive city whose downfall heralds YHWH's punishment of the entire earth, the establishment of YHWH's rule over all nations, and the redemption of Israel from exile. Two cities best fit this role, insofar as they represent the power of the nations to rule the earth and to take Israel into exile: Nineveh and Babylon. The others hardly constituted a significant threat against Israel.

In the present case, Babylon must be chosen as the city presupposed in this composition, because the citations of earlier prophetic literature in chs. 24–27 include Jer 48:43-44a (Isa 24:17-18a), which stems from the period in which Babylon, not Nineveh, constituted a major threat. Although the book of Nahum demonstrates that Nineveh serves well as a paradigm for establishing the significance of the downfall of an oppressive city as an act of YHWH (cf. M. A. Sweeney, "Concerning the Structure and Generic Character of the Book of Nahum," *ZAW* 104 [1992] 364-77), Babylon fits well with the data supplied in Isaiah 24–27.

The designation *qiryat tōhû,* "city of chaos," is especially telling here. Babylon was well known in the ancient world as the city that claimed to be the navel of the earth. Although this was not so unusual among major cities of the ancient world, Babylon was able to press this claim by its conquest of much of the Near East in the 6th century. The city name Babylon, *bab ilu* in Akkadian, means "gateway of the gods," and its ziggurat was known as Entemenanki, "Lord of the Foundation of Heaven and Earth." The Babylonian creation epic, Enuma Elish, celebrated the role of Marduk, the Babylonian city god, as creator of the earth and monarch of the gods. This is particularly significant since Marduk gained this station by his defeat of Tiamat, the dragon goddess of the sea who represented cosmic chaos and whose name *(ti'amatu)* is the Akkadian linguistic equivalent to Heb. *tōhû,* "chaos." Marduk's defeat of Tiamat not only gave Marduk the right to rule the gods according to Babylonian mythology, but also gave Babylon the right to rule the nations since its ziggurat was the center of world order and stability. The designation "city of chaos" in 24:10 is designed as a deliberate pun to call to mind Tiamat and to question the self-proclaimed role of Babylon as the center of world order. Likewise, the references to the "fortified city," the "exalted city," and the "palace of aliens" call to mind Nebuchadrezzar's efforts to build up the city in the 6th century, including three major palaces, the fortifications for which Babylon was well known, and the artistic features, such as the hanging gardens, that made Babylon one of the wonders of the world in its day. In this respect, it is no accident that the pronouncement concerning Babylon in 13:1–14:23 heads the pronouncements concerning the nations in chs. 13–23. Furthermore, the language concerning the downfall of the exalted city in 26:5-6 and the earth in 24:1-13, as well as the pains of childbirth in 26:17-18, corresponds to that of YHWH's attack against Babylon in 13:1-22. Finally, the citation of 21:2 in 24:16 is entirely appropriate since this verse decries the treachery of the Medes and Elamites, who are portrayed as Babylon's enemies in ch. 21. Certainly, this reference hints at the Medes' threat against Babylon under Cyrus in the 6th century.

Second, the universal outlook of chs. 24–27, with their focus on YHWH's rule of the nations and the return of Israel from exile to Zion, corresponds to the ideology of the late 6th century as represented in 2:2-4 and in Deutero-Isaiah. As noted in the discussion of 2:2-4 above, the image of Israel's return and YHWH's universal world rule of the nations from Zion corresponds to expectations recorded in Deutero-Isaiah, Trito-Isaiah (Isaiah 60–62), Haggai, and Zechariah. In each case, the fall of Babylon to Persia and the return of Jews to Jerusalem heralded an era in which the nations would recognize YHWH as the creator of the universe, the author of historical events, and the ruler of the earth.

Isaiah 24–27 shows affinities with Deutero-Isaiah in particular. It draws on past traditions of Noah and the flood (24:5, 18b; cf. Kaiser, *Isaiah 13–39*, 183-84, 190-91) just as Deutero-Isaiah draws on traditions of creation (e.g., 40:12-31), Noah (54:9-10), Abraham (41:8), the exodus crossing of the sea (43:16-21), and David (55:3). Furthermore, the use of hymnic forms corresponds to that of Deutero-Isaiah, where the hymns of praise function as major structural markers within the composition (see now Matheus, *Singt dem Herrn*) and includes similar motifs such as the praise of YHWH from the ends of the earth (24:14-16aα/42:10-13; 48:20; 52:9-10), YHWH as a warrior (26:21/42:10-13), and childbirth (26:17-18/54:1-2). Chs. 24–27 share not only the hope of Deutero-Isaiah but also Haggai's, Zechariah's, and Trito-Isaiah's anticipation of YHWH's establishment of Zion at the center of the nations. Consequently, the disruptions that affected the Persian empire during the reign of Cambyses (530-522) and beyond may well stand behind the expectation that YHWH still must finish with the remaining kings of the earth following the fall of the "city of chaos" in Isaiah 24–27.

Third, the citations of prophetic tradition outside Isaiah testify not only to the universal perspective of the passage but also to a 6th-century setting. The quotations are found in Isa 24:2/Hos 4:9; Isa 24:17-18a/Jer 48:43-44a; Isa 24:20/Amos 5:2; Isa 24:23/Mic 4:7; and Isa 26:21/Mic 1:3 (cf. Wildberger, *Jesaja*, 910). In each case, the quoted text is drawn from a context that deals specifically with the punishment of Israel (or Moab in the case of Isa 24:17-18a/Jer 48:43-44a), but each is universalized in that references to the punishment of Israel are replaced with references to the punishment of the earth. The motivation in each case appears to lie in the contexts from which they were cited. In those contexts, universal language or the implications of Israel's punishment are expressed in relation to the earth at large. The author of chs. 24–27 is apparently applying a hermeneutic that sees the punishment of Israel as a paradigm for the punishment of the entire earth. In the present instance, such a view is legitimized by the application of past prophecy to the present situation (for a discussion of this issue, see Sweeney, "Textual Citations," 44-45, n. 23).

Furthermore, the citation of Jer 48:43-44a in Isa 24:17-18a indicates a 6th-century context. The Jeremiah text is the latest to be cited and would date to the early 6th century.

Fourth, the reference to the downfall of Moab in 25:10b-12 is frequently regarded as a secondary intrusion. The reference to the downfall of a specific nation is especially striking in the context of universal judgment. The motivation for its inclusion seems to be the citation of Jeremiah's oracle against Moab in 24:17-18a (Jer 48:43-44a) in which "inhabitant of Moab" has been replaced by "inhabitant of the earth." Furthermore, the wording of Isa 25:7, "the covering that covers [*hallôṭ hallôṭ*] all the peoples," may provide additional motivation. The term *lôṭ*, "covering/to cover," forms a pun with the Hebrew name for Lot, ancestor of Moab according to Gen 19:36-37, so that the condemnation of Moab in Isa 25:10b-12 may well represent a case of inner-biblical exegesis. This is entirely appropriate in the 6th century when the Babylonian invasion of Moab in 582 may well have put an end to Moab's political existence (see J. A. Dearman, "Moab," *Harper's Bible Dictionary* [ed. P. Achtemeier et al.; San Francisco and New York: Harper & Row, 1985] 643-44). From the perspective of the author of chs. 24–27, Moab's fate presaged that of the nations.

Consequently, it appears that the late 6th century represents the best setting for the composition of the present form of chs. 24–27. The affinities with Deutero-Isaiah, Trito-Isaiah, and Isa 2:2-4 suggest that the circle of exilic prophets who edited the Isaiah traditions in the late 6th century were responsible for the composition of these chapters and their placement after chs. 2–23*. The affinities with Haggai and Zechariah suggest a date after the composition of Deutero-Isaiah, in association with the return to rebuild Jerusalem and the temple in the latter part of the 6th century (cf. Amsler).

Intention

The intention of chs. 24–27 is determined by a combination of external factors, including the redactional position of this material, and internal factors, including structure, genre, and mythological themes pertaining to fertility and kingship. The textual citations from Isaiah and from other prophetic traditions relate both to the redactional placement of chs. 24–27 within the book of Isaiah and to the internal development of their argumentation and themes.

In the final form of the book of Isaiah, chs. 24–27 close a major redactional unit within chs. 2–27 that takes up YHWH's judgment and redemption of Israel (chs. 2–12) and the pronouncements concerning the nations. Chs. 24–27 present the climax and outcome of both of these sections insofar as they describe a worldwide judgment against the earth and the result of that judgment in the establishment of YHWH's kingship at Zion, the redemption of the nations at Zion, and the return of Israel to Zion as the climax of the unit. As such, chs. 24–27 take up the program of chs. 2–27 announced at the outset in 2:2-4. The nations will recognize YHWH's kingship at Zion, and it remains only for Israel to follow suit to complete the new era of peace. Chs. 24–27 project the realization of that ideal, thereby explaining the goal of the judgment and redemption of

Israel in chs. 2–12 and the judgment against the nations in chs. 13–23. Key to this scheme is the downfall of Babylon, the "city of chaos" in 24:10, which stands at the head of the nations in 13:1–14:23 and functions as the exalted and oppressive city in chs. 24–27. It must be brought down to realize YHWH's rule.

In general, this scheme holds true for both the final 5th-century redaction of Isaiah and the 6th-century edition of the book in which chs. 24–27 follow on chs. 2–23*. The 5th-century edition gives greater weight to the punishment of Jerusalem in ch. 1 and the continued delay in the realization of YHWH's plans. In both cases, the Persian empire, which defeated the Babylonians and allowed Jewish exiles to return to Jerusalem to rebuild the temple, is viewed as a provisional tool of YHWH to accomplish divine purposes. The unit anticipates the full revelation of YHWH as the guiding hand behind the Persian empire in the future (cf. R. G. Kratz, *Kyros im Deuterojesaja-Buch*, who argues that YHWH's world rule is manifested in the rule of the Persian empire in Deutero-Isaiah).

The structure and genre of chs. 24–27 are particularly important, since they define the general flow of the argument of this text and its prophetic character. As noted above, the text is a prophetic announcement of salvation that includes two major subunits: the prophetic announcement of punishment for the earth in 24:1-23 and the prophetic announcement of blessing in 25:1–27:13. The identification of this text as a prophetic announcement of salvation accomplishes two major purposes. First, it establishes the divine legitimacy of the program outlined insofar as it presents itself as a prophet's announcement of the word of YHWH. Second, it anticipates a positive outcome to the situation of catastrophe presented at the beginning of the unit, and thereby it provides the Israelite audience with hope for the future realization of YHWH's plans for Israel's redemption at Zion.

The two-part structure of the passage and the presence of disputation texts at the culmination of each section are especially important in this regard. In each case, the disputation passages explain the significance of the preceding material. Isa 24:14-23 establishes that the punishment of the earth does not end with the overthrow of the "city of chaos" (i.e., Babylon), but it will culminate in the overthrow of all the kings of the earth and the establishment of YHWH's rule over the world at Zion. Likewise, 27:8-13 establishes that the punishment of Israel was only that — a punishment. Now that the punishment is complete, YHWH is acting to return Israel from exile to Jerusalem as the climax of the establishment of divine rule of the nations centered at Zion.

The two-part structure contributes to the overall scheme by starting with a situation of chaos and disorder, the fall of Babylon, and projecting that this will lead to the realization of YHWH's blessings in the world, both for the nations and for Israel. As such, the author offers the analysis of the current situation of disorder in order to determine YHWH's intentions behind the world events of the day. Furthermore, the experience of Israel in this passage and in chs. 2–12, punishment followed by redemption, appears to serve as an analogy for the experience of the world at large (punishment in chs. 13–23 followed by redemption in chs. 24–27). From the perspective of the author of chs. 24–27 and in relation to chs. 2–27, YHWH's plans call for the punishment of Israel to initiate the process, followed by the punishment and redemption of the nations, and climaxing finally in the redemption of Israel and establishment of YHWH's kingship over the world at Zion.

Another major element that contributes to the overall intention of chs. 24–27 is their use of mythological themes pertaining to fertility and YHWH's kingship. Agricultural imagery permeates these chapters, including the initial portrayal of a withered land whose grapevines no longer produce (24:1-13), the feast of the nations at Zion with an emphasis on the "fat things full of marrow" and the "wine on the lees well refined" (25:6), the imagery of childbirth and the conquest of death (26:13-19), and the renewed vineyard following a period of desolation (27:2-13). All of these pertain to a general concern with a blessing of fertility in the land and in the lives of its inhabitants. This is a common motif in ancient Near East cultures, which generally portray their gods as champions who attained rule over the land and its fertility by defeating a chaos monster, generally represented as a sea dragon, who stood as an obstacle to the fertility and order of the land and the life of its inhabitants. In Ugarit, Baal attains his position as chief fertility deity, and indeed chief god, by defeating the sea dragon Yamm and the lord of the underworld Mot. Likewise, Babylonian mythology portrays Marduk's rule of the world as the result of his defeat of the sea monster Tiamat, after which Marduk establishes the basic structure of the ordered world of creation.

In this respect, it is no accident that Isaiah 24–27 refers to YHWH's defeat of the "city of chaos" (24:10), the downfall of the Rephaim (26:19), and the defeat of Leviathan (27:1). Each of these figures represents a mythological opponent of YHWH who must be subdued in order to establish order and fertility of the world. "Chaos" *(tōhû)* represents the state of the world prior to YHWH's acts of creation (Gen 1:1), and the state to which it will return if creation is overturned (Jer 4:23). The Rephaim refer to the shades of the dead or the netherworld who threaten the living in Ugaritic mythology (see R. F. Schnell, "Rephaim," *IDB,* 4:35; cf. S. B. Parker, "Rephaim," *IDBSup,* 739). Leviathan represents the sea dragon of chaos that YHWH must subdue in order to establish order in the world (Job 3:8; 41:1; Pss 74:13-14; 104:26; for a full study of this issue, see Day, *Conflict*). As in Near Eastern examples of this mythological pattern, Isaiah 24–27 reports not only the restoration of fertility, life, and order to the world as the result of the deity's victory, but also a victory feast, the construction of a temple for the deity (here presented as Zion, the location of the Jerusalem temple), and the establishment of the deity's kingship over the world (for a full analysis of chs. 24–27 in relation to the Ugaritic Baal myth, see Millar, 65-102).

In the present instance, the citation of the *běrît 'ôlām,* "the eternal covenant," in 24:5 contributes to the imagery of creation. The term *'ôlām* is frequently translated "eternal," but its basic meaning is "world" or "universe." As such it refers to the covenant that establishes the basic order of the world of creation. This is evident in the use of the term *běrît 'ôlām* in reference to the covenant with Noah in Gen 9:16. Although the term is elsewhere employed in relation to specifically Israelite institutions or contexts, it relates these institutions or contexts to the fundamental order of creation in the Israelite worldview. This includes the sabbath (Exod 31:16; Lev 24:8), the Davidic dynasty (2 Sam

23:5; Isa 55:3), YHWH's covenant with Abraham (Gen 17:7, 13, 19), and the promise of the land of Israel to Abraham and Jacob (Ps 105:10; 1 Chr 16:17). In other instances, Davidic/Zion associations are related to the term to express the foundational character of YHWH's promise to return Israelite exiles to Zion (Jer 32:40; 50:5; Ezek 16:60; 37:26; Isa 61:8). One must keep in mind that Zion, by virtue of its identity as the site of YHWH's temple, was conceived as the center of the earth (in competition with Babylon in Babylonian mythology), and thus of the natural order of creation in Israelite tradition. Hence anything associated with Zion, such as the sabbath, David, or the patriarchs and their claim to the land, expressed the fundamental relationship between YHWH and the world established with the Noachic covenant. In the present context, the violation of the *běrît 'ôlām* represents the disruption of world or cosmic order.

The citations of other prophetic traditions likewise serve the overall intention of Isaiah 24–27. Those from the book of Isaiah serve a dual function. On the one hand, they demonstrate the redactional role of chs. 24–27 by citing Isaianic texts that stem predominantly from chs. 2–23. These citations include 24:13/17:6; 24:16/21:2 and 33:1; 25:4-5/4:5b-6 and 32:1-2; 25:11b-12/2:9-17; 26:5/2:6-21; 26:17-18/13:8 and 66:7-9; and 27:1-13/5:1-7 and 11:10-16 (for a full discussion of these citations, see Sweeney, "Textual Citations"). The texts cited from other sections of Isaiah stand at the conclusion of major structural units (32:1-2; 33:1; 66:7-9), indicating their redactional function throughout the rest of the book, and they always duplicate the citation of a text from chs. 2–23. On the other hand, these citations contribute to the overall message of chs. 24–27 that YHWH is establishing divine rule over the entire world at Zion and that Israel's experience serves as a paradigm for that of the world at large. Thus 17:6, which pertains to the punishment of Israel, is applied to the scenario of world-wide punishment in 24:13. Isa 2:9-17, originally directed against Israel, is employed to describe the punishment of Moab in 25:11b-12, and 2:6-21 is employed to describe the punishment of the exalted city in 26:5. Likewise, texts pertaining to the punishment of Babylon in 21:2 and 13:8 are employed to demonstrate the universal significance of Babylon's fall in 24:16 and 26:17, respectively. The vineyard allegory against Israel in 5:1-7 becomes the new vineyard allegory that describes Israel's redemption as the climactic act of YHWH's world plans in 27:2-6, and texts pertaining to the redemption of Israel to Zion in 4:5b-6 and 11:10-16 perform similar roles in 25:4-5 and 27:1-13.

The citations of prophetic texts outside Isaiah likewise contribute to the universalistic perspective of chs. 24–27. The citation of Jer 48:43-44a in Isa 24:17-18a changes the text so that the threat is no longer addressed to the "inhabitant of Moab" but to the "inhabitant of the earth." Likewise, the citations of other prophetic texts that take up the punishment of Israel in their original contexts, including Hos 4:9/Isa 24:2; Amos 5:2/Isa 24:20; Mic 4:7/Isa 24:23; and Mic 1:3/Isa 26:21, are applied to YHWH's punishment of the entire earth in their new context in Isaiah 24–27. In each case, the motivation for such universalization appears to derive from the original text itself. Thus Hos 4:9 stems from YHWH's lawsuit against the "inhabitants of the land" in Hosea 4. The oracle against Israel in Amos 5:1-3 is followed by an announcement of the cosmic consequences for rejecting YHWH in vv. 4-9. Mic 4:6-7 follows the oracle of cosmic peace for the nations in Mic 4:1-5, which appears also in Isa 2:2-4. Finally, Mic 1:2-4 is addressed to the "peoples of the earth" and precedes the condemnation of Israel and Judah in v. 5. It would appear that these citations represent the author's hermeneutical perspective that sees Israel's experience as paradigmatic for that of the earth at large. But in each case, the citation of a prophetic tradition stems from a context in which the condemnation of Israel is accompanied by a statement of its implications for the world at large.

Finally, the use of future-oriented language, such as the *bayyôm hahû'* formulas in 24:21; 25:9; 26:1; 27:1; 27:2; and 27:12-13, and the command to wait for YHWH to act in 26:20, indicate that the scenario outlined here is not yet complete. Likewise, the hymnic language of 25:1-5 and 26:1-21 conveys a sense of anticipation. Although the descriptive language of 24:1-20 indicates that the process is underway with the fall of the "city of chaos," the manifestation of this event as an act of YHWH and the establishment of YHWH's rule on Zion are yet to be realized. In this respect, the fall of the oppressive "city of chaos" and the use of terms *dāl*, "humble" (25:4; 26:6), *'ebyôn*, "needy" (25:4), and *'ānî*, "poor" (26:6), which are commonly employed in psalms to describe the plight of the oppressed nation Israel (cf. J. L. Croft, *The Identity of the Individual in the Psalms* [JSOTSup 44; Sheffield: JSOT Press, 1987] 49-72), provide the background for such expectation in relation to the aftermath of the fall of Babylon to Persia and return of Jews to Jerusalem. In this period and throughout the 5th century, Jews in Jerusalem continued to suffer as the Persian empire underwent serious internal convulsions. Clearly, the promises of greatness made in conjunction with the building of the Second Temple had not yet been realized.

Bibliography

S. Amsler, "Des visions de Zacharie à l'apocalypse d'Esaïe 24-27," in *The Book of Isaiah/Le livre d'Isaïe* (ed. J. Vermeylen; BETL 81; Leuven: Leuven University Press and Peeters, 1989) 263-73; G. W. Anderson, "Isaiah xxiv-xxvi Reconsidered," *Congress Volume, Bonn 1962* (VTSup 9; Leiden: Brill, 1962) 118-26; M. A. Beek, "Ein Erdbeben wird zum prophetischen Erleben (Jesaja 24–27)," *ArOr* 17/1 (1949) 31-40; R. J. Coggins, "The Problems of Isaiah 24–27," *ExpTim* 90 (1979) 328-33; Day, *God's Conflict* (→ 17:1–18:7); idem, "A Case of Inner Scriptural Interpretation: The Dependence of Isaiah xxvi. 13-xxvii. 11 on Hosea xiii. 4-xiv. 10 (Eng. 9) and Its Relevance to Some Theories of the Redaction of the 'Isaiah Apocalypse,' " *JTS* 31 (1980) 309-19; G. Fohrer, "Der Aufbau der Apokalypse des Jesajabuches (Jesaja 24–27)," *CBQ* 25 (1963) 34-45 (repr. in *Studien zur alttestamentlichen Prophetie (1949-1965)* [BZAW 99; Berlin: Töpelmann, 1967] 170-81); M.-L. Henry, *Glaubenskrise und Glaubensbewährung in den Dichtungen der Jesajaapokalypse* (BWANT 86; Stuttgart, Berlin, Cologne, Mainz: Kohlhammer, 1967); D. G. Johnson, *From Chaos to Restoration: An Integrative Reading of Isaiah 24–27* (JSOTSup 61; Sheffield: JSOT Press, 1988); A. Kaminka, "Le développement des idées du prophète Isaïe et l'unité de son livre VIII: L'authenticité des chapîtres xxiv à xxvii," *REJ* 81 (1925) 27-36; M.-J. Lagrange, "L'apocalypse d'Isaïe (24–27), à propose des derniers commentaires," *RB* 3 (1894)

200-231; J. Lindblom, *Die Jesaja Apokalypse: Jes. 24–27* (LUÅ N.F. 1, 34/3; Lund: Gleerup; Leipzig: Harrassowitz, 1938); P. Lohmann, "Die selbständigen lyrischen Abschnitte in Jes 24–27," *ZAW* 37 (1917-18) 1-58; O. Ludwig, *Die Stadt in der Jesaja-Apokalypse. Zur Datierung von Jes. 24-27* (Inaugural Dissertation; Bonn: Rheinischen Friedrich-Wilhelms-Universität, 1961); W. E. March, "A Study of Two Prophetic Compositions in Isaiah 24:1–27:1" (Diss., Union Theological Seminary, 1966); W. R. Millar, *Isaiah 24–27 and the Origin of Apocalyptic* (HSM 11; Missoula: Scholars Press, 1976); B. Otzen, "Traditions and Structures of Isaiah XXIV–XXVII," *VT* 24 (1974) 196-206; S. Pagán, "Apocalyptic Poetry in Isaiah 24–27," *BT* 43 (1992) 314-25; O. Plöger, *Theocracy and Eschatology* (tr. S. Rudman; Oxford: Blackwell, 1968) 53-78; P. L. Lewis Redditt, "Isaiah 24–27: A Form-Critical Analysis" (Diss., Vanderbilt University, 1972); idem, "Once Again, The City in Isaiah 24-27," *HAR* 10 (1986) 317-35; H. Ringgren, "Some Observations on Style and Structure in the Isaiah Apocalypse," *ASTI* 9 (1973) 105-15; W. Rudolph, *Jesaja 24–27* (BWANT 62; Stuttgart: Kohlhammer, 1933); R. Smend, "Anmerkungen zu Jes. 24–27," *ZAW* 4 (1884) 161-224; M. A. Sweeney, "New Gleanings from an Old Vineyard: Isaiah 27 Reconsidered," in *Early Jewish and Christian Exegesis: Studies in Memory of William Hugh Brownlee* (ed. C. A. Evans and W. F. Stinespring; Atlanta: Scholars Press, 1987) 51-66; idem, "Textual Citations" (→ "Introduction to the Book of Isaiah"); A. H. van Zyl, "Isaiah 24–27: Their Date of Origin" OTWSA 5 (1962) 44-57; J. Vermeylen, "La composition de L'apocalypse d'Isaïe (Is. XXIV–XXVII)," *ETL* 50 (1974) 5-38.

PROPHETIC ANNOUNCEMENT OF YHWH'S PUNISHMENT OF THE EARTH, 24:1-23

Structure

Several factors identify 24:1-23 as a distinct unit within the larger structure of chs. 24–27. First, 24:1-23 focuses exclusively on the devastation of the land or earth (*'ereṣ*) and the fall of the "city of chaos" (*qiryat tōhû*, v. 10), whereas the material beginning in 25:1 shifts its attention to YHWH's acts of restoration that will result from the previously described devastation. Second, 24:1-23 primarily employs descriptive language with 3rd-person references to YHWH throughout, whereas 25:1-5 employs a 1st-person perspective for its speaker together with a 2nd-person masculine singular address form directed to YHWH. Although the text shifts back to 3rd-person descriptive language about YHWH in 25:6, this text is connected syntactically to 25:1-5 by its *wāw*-consecutive perfect verb *wĕ'āśâ*, "and he [YHWH] will make," whereas 25:1 lacks any syntactical connection to the preceding text. The 1st-person statement in 24:16, "But I say, 'I pine away, I pine away. Woe is me!'" aids in joining 24:1-23 to the following material by identifying the prophet as the speaker of this text, but the statement is directed to the audience at large, not to YHWH. The 2nd-person masculine singular address form in 24:17 is directed to the "inhabitant of the land," not to YHWH, and derives from Jer 48:43-44a, which is quoted in Isa 24:17-18a. Third, 24:21-23 constitutes a concluding section, introduced by the formula *wĕhāyâ bayyôm hahû'*, "and it shall come to pass in that day," which explains the consequences of the previous material in terms of YHWH's judgment against the earth and its rulers together with YHWH's rule on Zion. Other instances of *bayyôm hahû'* formulas appear in 25:9; 26:1; 27:1; and 27:12-13, but these focus on the positive consequences of the material they follow. In sum, 24:1-23 concentrates on the judgment of the earth, whereas 25:1–27:13 focuses on its restoration.

The first major subunit of 24:1-23 appears in 24:1-2, which constitutes an introductory announcement of YHWH's punishment of the earth. This subunit is identified syntactically by its *wāw*-consecutive perfect verb chain, which begins with the masculine singular active participles *bôqēq*, "lay waste," and *bôlĕqāh*, "make it desolate," in v. 1a, followed by *wĕ'iwwâ*, "and he will twist," and *wĕhēpîṣ*, "and he will scatter," in v. 1b, and *wĕhāyâ*, "and it shall be," in v. 2. V. 1 presents a basic statement of YHWH's devastation of the earth (v. 1a) and its consequences (v. 1b). V. 2 specifies the consequences of this devastation by presenting a series of pairs of persons in Israelite society in which a common or lower-ranked person is contrasted to one of higher social station. By this means, v. 2 emphasizes that the disaster will overtake everyone, regardless of social standing.

The second major subunit of 24:1-23 is vv. 3-13, which provide the basis for the introductory announcement of YHWH's punishment of the earth, here presented as the prophet's announcement of YHWH's word. Although v. 3 is often associated with vv. 1-2 due to their common theme of earthly devastation, several features of v. 3 indicate that it introduces an entirely new subunit. It employs a pair of 3rd-person feminine singular imperfect verbal forms, *hibbôq tibbôq*, "it shall be utterly laid waste," and *hibbôz tibbôz*, "it shall be utterly despoiled," in contrast to the masculine singular participles that introduce vv. 1-2. Not only do these verbs lack any syntactical connection to the preceding material, but the shift in subject from YHWH to the earth (*hā'āreṣ*, v. 3) indicates that the concern of the unit has shifted from YHWH's activity to the situation of the earth. Furthermore, v. 3a provides the reason for the earth's devastated

327

state with a *kî* ("because") that explains this situation as the result of YHWH's word. That word follows in vv. 4-13. Consequently, v. 3 introduces YHWH's word as the cause of the devastation announced in vv. 1-2. V. 3a describes the setting or situation of YHWH's speech in terms of the devastation of the earth, and v. 3b constitutes the YHWH speech formula that identifies YHWH's word as the reason for the devastation.

The quotation of YHWH's word appears in vv. 4-13. Only the speech formula in v. 3b identifies it as such. It functions as an announcement of judgment against the earth and continues until v. 14, which describes the rejoicing over YHWH's deeds by various unnamed people throughout the world. The speech contains two major parts, identified by their parallel structures. They include descriptions of devastation, introduced by the verb pairs *'ăbĕlâ/'umlĕlâ,* "mourns/languishes," in v. 4, and *'ābal/'umlĕlâ,* "mourns/languishes," in v. 7, followed by the reason or basis for the suffering in vv. 5-6 and 13. Vv. 4-6 focus on the mourning and languishing of the land. The reason for the withered state of the land appears in vv. 5-6. These verses maintain that the land's inhabitants have violated the terms of the eternal, or worldwide, covenant *(bĕrît 'ôlām)* that defines the relationship between YHWH and the world. V. 5 states this cause explicitly. V. 6 elaborates on the consequences of this situation with two statements introduced by *'al-kēn,* "therefore." The first, v. 6a, states that there is a curse *('ālâ)* on the land that incriminates its inhabitants, and v. 6b states that the inhabitants of the earth will therefore be diminished. Vv. 7-13 focus on the lack of rejoicing in the land, caused especially by the lack of wine that is due to the withered and unproductive state of the cursed land. The lack of rejoicing is described in vv. 7-12 in a series of statements that take up different aspects of the absence of joy. V. 7 describes the withered vines that diminish the joy of the heart. V. 8 describes the absence of music. V. 9 takes up the absence of song that accompanies the drinking of wine. V. 10 focuses on the closed city of chaos. V. 11 takes up the lack of rejoicing in the streets due to the absence of joy in the land. V. 12 describes the desolation in the city. The basis for this glum picture appears in v. 13, introduced by a causative *kî,* "because," which maintains that this will be the situation of the land. The quotation of 17:6 in v. 13b emphasizes the gleaning of the olives at harvesttime and reinforces the images of a poor harvest in a withered land that leads to the desolate picture described above.

The third major subunit of 24:1-23 is vv. 14-23, which contain the prophet's explanation or interpretation of the preceding material. The subunit is constituted according to the prophetic disputation pattern, which challenges an assertion made by the prophet's opponents and then presents the prophet's counterassertion together with a different interpretation of the situation at hand. The subunit is demarcated not only by the disputation pattern, however, but by its grammatical and syntactical features as well. V. 14 lacks any syntactical link to the preceding material. Furthermore, it clearly does not continue the speech by YHWH in the preceding section, but shifts to new speakers, identified only by emphatic *hēmmâ,* "they," who raise their voices in praise of YHWH. Although the perspective of the passage shifts to 1st-person common singular in

v. 16aβ and to 3rd-person announcement language in v. 21, each section is linked to the preceding section by a conjunctive *wāw*.

The first subunit of the disputation speech appears in vv. 14-16aα, which quote the assertion that the prophet intends to counter. The passage is introduced by a syntactically independent 3rd-person masculine plural imperfect verb, *yiś'û*, "they raise," with the emphatic *hēmmâ*, "they," as subject. The identity of the speakers is never made clear, but the structure and content of these verses suggest that it is the collective inhabitants of the earth (cf. v. 17 et passim). Also note that the speakers are identified with the "islands of the sea" in v. 15. Babylonian maps of the world often identify the outermost regions of the empire as *nagu*, which are portrayed as islands (cf. W. Horowitz, "The Babylonian Map of the World," *Iraq* 50 [1988] 147-65). Vv. 14-16aα comprise four statements, each of which specifies a speaker and statement made in praise of YHWH. Although a specific location is not evident in every statement, it appears that the passage intends to present the praise of YHWH throughout the entire earth by emphasizing major cardinal directions or ends of the earth (cf. v. 16aα). Thus v. 14a introduces the sequence with a general statement that "they lift up their voices, they sing for joy." This is followed by specific quotes. V. 14b contains the statement " 'Over the majesty of YHWH,' they shout from the west" (cf. *RSV*). V. 15a follows, "Therefore in the east, 'Give glory to YHWH!' " V. 15b states, "In the coastlands of the sea, 'To the name of YHWH, God of Israel!' " Finally, v. 16aα concludes, "From the ends of the earth, 'We have heard songs of praise, glory to the Righteous One!' " In each case, YHWH is lauded by the inhabitants of the earth.

That the prophet intends to make a counterassertion against these exclamations of joy is clear from vv. 16aβ-20, which identify the inhabitant of the earth as the victim of YHWH's judgment. This unit is linked to the preceding verses by its conjunctive *wāw*-consecutive *wā'ōmar*, "but I say," which introduces the prophet's contrasting perspective on the situation. V. 16aβ-b includes the prophet's initial statement of woe or mourning (v. 16aβ) followed by his reference to treachery (v. 16b; cf. 21:2); i.e., the speakers of vv. 14-16aα may view the situation as favorable, but it will turn against them. The prophet then quotes the oracle against Moab in Jer 48:43-44a, but alters it so that it refers to the "inhabitants of the earth" rather than the "inhabitants of Moab," thereby universalizing the statement. As such, it presents an introductory warning to the inhabitants of the earth that they are about to be trapped (v. 17). V. 18 then describes the entrapment (v. 18a) together with the reason for the entrapment introduced by causative *kî* (v. 18b). The description of the opening of the heavens and the shaking of the foundations of the earth apparently relates to the cosmic upheaval associated with the Noachic covenant, described as "the eternal covenant" in v. 5. Finally, vv. 19-20 employ a series of statements formulated primarily with Hithpael perfect verbs combined with infinitives absolute to describe the upheaval of the earth (vv. 19-20a). The cause for this upheaval is reiterated in v. 20b in terms of the earth's guilt. Vv. 16aβ-20 therefore indicate that YHWH's actions, praised by the inhabitants of the earth in vv. 14-16aα, will in fact lead to their demise.

Verses 21-23 then provide the prophet's explanation or interpretation of the situation. These verses are constituted as a converted perfect verb chain based on the introductory formula *wĕhāyâ bayyôm hahû'*, "and it shall come to pass on that day," which presents the unit as the projected outcome of YHWH's actions described in the preceding material. Basing one's judgment on syntax and content, one can discern that the passage contains three basic parts. First, v. 21 constitutes the basic statement of the passage that YHWH will punish the armies or hosts of heaven and the kings of the earth, a reference to the pagan rulers of the earth and their gods. Second, v. 22 describes the imprisonment of these kings. Finally, v. 23 describes the cosmic consequences of YHWH's act; the moon and the sun, major deities in the pagan religions of the ancient Near East, will become ashamed because YHWH will rule from Mt. Zion and establish glory for YHWH's elders. In sum, vv. 21-23 indicate that the old world order is about to be overthrown as YHWH establishes rule over the pagan peoples who praised YHWH's acts in vv. 14-16aα.

Genre

The dominant genre of 24:1-23 is PROPHETIC ANNOUNCEMENT OF PUNISHMENT. This is not a pure example of the genre, however, in that the passage is also heavily influenced by the DISPUTATION pattern that appears in vv. 14-23. The author apparently modified the genre according to the needs of the larger literary context by employing elements of the DISPUTATION pattern in the composition as well. Accordingly, the DISPUTATION pattern serves the purposes of the composition by pointing to the true significance of the devastation announced in vv. 1-13.

The PROPHETIC ANNOUNCEMENT OF PUNISHMENT appears primarily in vv. 1-13. As noted in the discussion of the structure of this passage, vv. 1-2 serve as an introduction in which the prophet announces YHWH's punishment of the world in a general fashion. Vv. 3-14 then contain the prophet's announcement of YHWH's word. Following the YHWH SPEECH FORMULA in v. 3, the ANNOUNCEMENT OF PUNISHMENT appears in vv. 4-13 in the form of a SPEECH by YHWH. This is characteristic of the form, although it is usually preceded by a (→) messenger formula rather than by the YHWH SPEECH FORMULA found here. In general, the PROPHETIC ANNOUNCEMENT OF PUNISHMENT is a component of the larger PROPHETIC JUDGMENT SPEECH in which the prophet states the grounds for punishment prior to announcing the punishment itself. Here the form has been modified insofar as it includes a brief statement of the grounds for punishment in v. 5, namely, that the inhabitants of the earth have violated the "eternal covenant." Yet no specific examples of the violation are provided other than the transgression of "instructions" *(tôrōt)* and "statute" *(ḥōq)*. This formulation serves the purposes of the composition, however, in that the condemnation of the inhabitants of the earth is not the main focus of the passage. Rather, the current devastation of the earth is designed to point to an act by YHWH.

The significance of this punishment is made clear in vv. 14-23 in which the prophet provides his interpretation of YHWH's announcement. The author makes use of the DISPUTATION pattern in order to make the point that the punishment of the earth is part of YHWH's plan to establish divine sovereignty over the entire world at Mt. Zion. The DISPUTATION functions specifically to challenge the prevailing opinion of a speaker's audience or opponents, persuading them to abandon their opinion and to adopt that of the speaker. It generally contains three basic elements — the thesis, counterthesis, and dispute — which may be expressed in a variety of ways in the surface structure of the text (for a full discussion of the DISPUTATION pattern, see Graffy; D. F. Murray). The prior ANNOUNCEMENT OF PUNISHMENT was predicated on the fall of an unnamed "city of chaos" (qiryat tōhû) in v. 10. The joyful reaction of people from throughout the earth in vv. 14-16aα suggests that this was an oppressive city that dominated much of the world. In the context of the DISPUTATION pattern, this rejoicing is the thesis that will be challenged. The counterthesis and dispute are apparent in vv. 16aβ-20, where the prophet asserts that this is an occasion for mourning, not rejoicing, in that the entire earth is now in upheaval. The explanation or interpretation of the ANNOUNCEMENT OF PUNISHMENT then appears in vv. 21-23: YHWH is establishing divine rule over the world at Mt. Zion. This will entail the destruction and imprisonment of the kings of the earth and their armies.

The introduction of the DISPUTATION pattern in vv. 14-23 therefore modifies the purpose of the PROPHETIC ANNOUNCEMENT OF PUNISHMENT in vv. 1-13. The passage is not intended to announce punishment in and of itself. Rather, the punishment points to YHWH's assertion of sovereignty in Zion, thereby overthrowing the earthly order and establishing a new world order.

Setting

See the discussion of the setting of chs. 24–27 above.

Intention

The intention of 24:1-23 is defined in relation to its literary context as a component of chs. 24–27, its internal structure, and its use of fertility imagery to portray YHWH's judgment against the earth.

As a component of chs. 24–27, 24:1-23 constitutes the prophetic announcement of punishment against the earth. In this respect, it presents a major world crisis, here the fall of the "city of chaos" (v. 10), as the premise for the entire passage. As noted above, the "city of chaos" must be identified with the city of Babylon, which fell to the Median/Persian army of Cyrus in 539 B.C.E. The structure and imagery of ch. 24 indicate that the anticipated fall of the city serves as the basis for an analysis of the general situation of the world which is designed to show that the current upheaval is an act of YHWH.

The passage begins with a general introduction in vv. 1-2, which describe the general upheaval of the earth, employing language and imagery from Hosea 4 to describe the comprehensive nature of the catastrophe. This is followed by a prophetic announcement of YHWH's word in vv. 3-13, in which the author quotes YHWH's announcement of punishment against the world. Here the cause of the punishment is the violation of the *běrît 'ôlām,* "the eternal covenant" or "the covenant of the world," which was established between YHWH and the world immediately following the flood (Gen 9:16). The purpose of this covenant was to guarantee a stable world order, but the violation of this covenant by the inhabitants of the world has led to the present situation of catastrophe. This is aptly expressed by the designation of the city as *qiryat tōhû,* "city of chaos," which employs the term used to describe the world in Gen 1:2 prior to YHWH's acts of creation. The speech employs the fertility imagery of withered vines and lack of wine and music to describe the general languishing of the earth. The use of this language is not accidental, in view of the appearance of the new vineyard allegory in Isa 27:2-6 that portrays Israel's reestablished fruitfulness as a contrast to the present situation of the earth and as the climax of the entire composition. It is noteworthy that the original song of the vineyard in 5:1-7 introduces a series of woe oracles in 5:8-24 condemning Israel. The second woe oracle in 5:11-17 employs similar images of wine drinking, song, Sheol or death, and YHWH's justice as the cause of the downfall of the arrogant. The allusion to 5:11-17, the use of imagery from Hosea 4, and the citation of Isa 17:6 in v. 13b all point to the author's intention to draw an analogy between the experience of Israel and that of the world. Israel's punishment and redemption serve as a paradigm for the coming experience of the nations.

The disputation speech in 24:14-23 provides the analysis of the current situation in order to present YHWH's intentions. As noted above, vv. 14-16aα present the thesis that the author intends to challenge, i.e., that the unnamed parties, identified only as "they," should rejoice at YHWH's acts. The identity of this group has provoked some debate, but it must refer to the nations of the earth themselves. The contrast of celebration with the prophet's mourning in v. 16aβ-b clearly indicates that it cannot be Israelite exiles, as they are to benefit from YHWH's act. Rather, "they" must refer to the rulers of the earth and the host of heaven identified in vv. 21-23 as the parties that will suffer when YHWH establishes divine rule at Zion. The counterthesis, that these parties have no cause to celebrate, is expressed in vv. 16aβ-20, which describe the continued suffering of the world. The quotations of 21:2 in v. 16b and Jer 48:43-44a in v. 17 point to continued disaster. Likewise, the reference to the open windows of heaven and the shaking foundations of the earth employs imagery and language from the flood tradition to describe the continuing disaster (cf. Gen 7:11; 8:2). The purpose of the disaster is made clear in vv. 21-23: to overthrow the current rulers of the earth so that YHWH's rule will be established on Zion. By this means, the passage anticipates the announcement of blessing that is to follow.

Bibliography

J. P. Floss, "Die Wortstellung des Konjugationssystems in Jes 24: Ein Beitrag zur Formkritik poetischer Texte im Alten Testament," in *Bausteine biblischer Theologie* (*Fest.* G. Johannes

Botterweck; ed. H.-J. Fabry; BBB 50; Cologne and Bonn: P. Hanstein, 1977) 227-44; P. Welten, "Die Vernichtung des Todes und die Königsherrschaft Gottes: Eine traditionsgeschichtliche Studie zu Jes 25,6-8; 24,21-23 und Ex 24,9-11," *TZ* 38 (1982) 129-46.

YHWH'S BLESSING OF THE EARTH AT ZION, 25:1-12

Structure

I.	Communal thanksgiving song for YHWH's defeat of oppressing city	1-5
	A. Introductory call to praise	1
	1. Call proper	1aα-β
	2. Basis: YHWH's miraculous act	1aγ-b
	B. Specific basis: destruction of fortified alien city	2-3
	1. Basis stated	2
	2. Results	3
	a. Praise by strong people	3a
	b. Fear by oppressive nations	3b
	C. Specific basis: protection of poor	4-5
	1. Basis stated	4a-bα
	2. Metaphor explained	4bβ-5
II.	Announcement of YHWH's blessing of peoples and response	6-12
	A. Announcement of blessing	6-8
	1. Basic statement: feast for nations on Mt. Zion and removal of veil	6-7
	a. Feast	6
	b. Removal of veil	7
	2. Appositional explanation	8
	a. Abolish death	8a
	b. Remove shame of his people Israel	8b
	B. Announcement of Israel's response and Moab's demise	9-12
	1. Israel's response: affirmation of YHWH as God	9-10a
	a. Speech formula	9aα
	b. Response proper	9aβ-10a
	2. Moab's demise	10b-12
	a. Trampling of Moab	10b
	b. Analogy to swimmer	11a
	c. Fall of Moab	11b-12

Several factors indicate that 25:1-12 forms a distinct unit within the larger structure of chs. 24–27. Isa 25:1 lacks any syntactical connection to 24:23. Although it shares a 1st-person singular speaker's perspective with 24:1-23 (cf. 24:16aβ), it differs from the 3rd-person masculine singular description of YHWH in 24:1-23 by employing a 2nd-person masculine singular address form directed to YHWH in vv. 1-5. Isa 25:6-12 reverts back to the 3rd-person masculine singular descriptive portrayal of YHWH, but these verses are connected to vv. 1-5 by the conjunctive *wāw* at the beginning of v. 6 (*wĕʿāsâ,* "and he made"). Furthermore, vv. 6-12 elaborate on the blessings resulting from YHWH's actions that are lauded in vv. 1-5. The introductory *bayyôm hahûʾ,* "in that day," in 26:1 indicates clearly that this verse begins a new unit within the larger structure of 25:1–27:13. It is related to 25:1-12 nevertheless, just as 24:21-23 is related to 24:1-20, in that the following material discusses the results of YHWH's blessings announced in 25:1-12. (For further discussion of the interrelationship of these texts within the larger context of chs. 24–27, see the discussion of the super-structure of chs. 24–27 above.)

The first major subunit of 25:1-12 is the communal thanksgiving song in vv. 1-5. This song is characterized by its 1st-person common singular speaker's perspective and by its use of a 2nd-person masculine singular address form directed to YHWH: "O YHWH, you are my God, I praise you, I give thanks to your name" (v. 1aα-β). As noted above, v. 6 shifts to a descriptive portrayal of YHWH that employs 3rd-person masculine singular verbs. The structure of the song is determined by the three causative statements, each of which is introduced by causative *kî* (vv. 1aα, 2, 4). These provide the bases for the initial call to praise in v. 1aα-β. The call to praise is identified by its address to YHWH as well as by its characteristic use of the verbs *ʾărômimkā,* "I praise you," and *ʾôdeh,* "I give thanks." The general basis follows immediately in v. 1aγ-b, "for you have done wonderful things, plans formed of old, faithful and sure." The first of two specific bases appears in vv. 2-3. This basis is stated in v. 2 in reference to the fall of a fortified enemy city that the singer of the song apparently viewed as a threat. The results of the fall of this city appear in v. 3, introduced by *ʿal-kēn,* "therefore." V. 3a announces that an unidentified "strong people" (*ʿam-ʿoz*), presumably the Judean audience of the song (cf. 26:1), will honor YHWH, and v. 3b states that the "community of tyrannical nations" (*qiryat gôyim ʾārîṣîm*) will fear YHWH. The second specific basis for the initial praise of YHWH appears in vv. 4-5, again introduced by causative *kî.* The basis is stated in v. 4a-bα in terms of YHWH giving refuge or protection (*māʿoz*) to the poor and needy. Vv. 4bβ-5, introduced by a causative *kî,* elaborate on this theme metaphorically by portraying YHWH's refuge as a shelter from wind, heat, and rain.

Verses 6-12, linked to the preceding by an initial *wāw,* revert to objective language to announce YHWH's blessings of the nations and Israel together with Israel's response. All the major sections of this subunit are linked by conjunctive *wāw*s. Vv. 6-8 announce YHWH's blessings for both the nations and Israel, here portrayed as "his [YHWH's] people" in v. 8b. The blessings for all the peoples and nations are basically stated in vv. 6-7 in terms of a feast on Mt. Zion (v. 6) and YHWH's removal of the "covering" (*lôṭ*) and "veil" (*massēkâ*) that cover all the peoples (v. 7). The two verses are joined by their parallel *wāw*-consecutive perfect verbs *wĕʿāsâ,* "and he shall make," in v. 6 and *ûbilla',* "and he shall swallow," in v. 7. V. 8 employs the same verb, *billa'* ("he has swallowed"), that introduces v. 7, but without the conjunctive *wāw*-consecutive form. This indi-cates that v. 8 stands as an appositional explanation of the meaning of vv. 6-7 (note the use of *ûmāḥâ*, "and he shall wipe," in v. 8 and *mĕmuḥāyîm*, "smeared," in v. 6). V. 8a states that YHWH has abolished death forever, and v. 8b explains YHWH's actions in specific reference to Israel ("his people") by stating that YHWH will remove their shame from the midst of the earth. The YHWH speech formula at the end of v. 8 closes out vv. 6-8.

Verses 9-12 are attached to vv. 6-8 by a conjunctive *wāw* but clearly begin a new section that focuses on Israel's response to YHWH's blessings announced in vv. 6-8. A modified version of the *bayyôm hahû'* formula introduces the unit in v. 9aα. Israel's response appears in vv. 9aβ-10a, stating that YHWH is their God for whom they have waited for salvation. Now that YHWH has acted, they will rejoice in YHWH's salvation. Appended to the announcement of Israel's response in vv. 9-10a is an announcement of Moab's demise in vv. 10b-12, connected by a conjunctive *wāw*. The announcement comprises three basic parts, each introduced by the *wāw*-consecutive perfect verbs. V. 10b (*wĕnādôš*, "and he shall trample") announces the trampling of Moab. V. 11a (*ûpēraś*, "and he shall spread") employs the analogy of a swimmer spreading his arms to portray Moab's demise. Vv. 11b-12 (*wĕhišpîl*, "and it shall fall") describe the fall of Moab.

Genre

Isaiah 25:1-12 is a component of the larger structural unit, 25:1–27:13, which constitutes a PROPHETIC ANNOUNCEMENT of YHWH's blessing of the earth and its results. As a component of the larger text, the generic character of 25:1-12 is heavily influenced by the PROPHETIC ANNOUNCEMENT of blessing in that it announces that blessing prior to the results that are announced in 26:1–27:13. Nevertheless, this is not a pure example of the genre insofar as the author of 25:1-12 employed modified forms of two major genres in order to serve the overall purposes of the composition.

The first appears in 25:1-5, which constitutes a COMMUNAL THANKSGIVING SONG for YHWH's defeat of an oppressive city. This is typical of the (→) thanksgiving song genre, which is distinguished from the more general (→) hymn of praise insofar as it lauds YHWH for a recent intervention on behalf of the people. In the present case, the city in question is apparently the "city of chaos" mentioned in 24:10. YHWH's defeat of this city is mentioned in v. 1, which employs typical laudatory language, such as *ărômimkā 'ôdeh šimkā*, "I praise you, I give thanks to your name," to praise YHWH prior to stating the reasons for the praise. The reasons for praise then follow in sequence from general to more specific, each of which is introduced by a causative *kî*, "because," in keeping with the typical language of the form. Here a general statement appears in v. 1aα-b, which speaks of YHWH's miraculous deeds. Specific bases appear in vv. 2-3 and 4-5. Vv. 2-3 refer to the destruction of the oppressive city, here described as a "fortified city" and a "palace of aliens." Vv. 4-5 focus on YHWH's protection of the poor and needy, here identified with the audience of the singer, Israel. Although the song follows the typical form of the genre, the reference to the city indicates its relation to the present literary context.

Verses 6-12 constitute an ANNOUNCEMENT of YHWH's blessings and therefore contribute to the generic character of 25:1-12 and the larger context of 25:1–27:13. The text appears to be based in the typical PROPHETIC AN-NOUNCEMENT OF SALVATION, albeit with modifications. The genre typically lacks a basis for YHWH's salvation, in that the attitude of YHWH, not the condition of the people, provides the motivation. Likewise, no specific basis appears here other than YHWH's decision to remove the suffering of the nations and of Israel. The present text varies from the typical form, however, in that YHWH does not speak in the 1st person; rather, objective announcement language is used to present YHWH's act of salvation. Nevertheless, the effects and results of YHWH's act are described in terms of the removal of Israel's ("his people") shame and the downfall of Moab.

When viewed in relation to each other, the COMMUNAL SONG OF THANKS-GIVING in vv. 1-5 and the PROPHETIC ANNOUNCEMENT of blessing in vv. 6-12 present a general ANNOUNCEMENT of YHWH's blessing the earth at Mt. Zion. In this respect, it accounts for the blessing of the nations, who may now rejoice after the fall of the oppressive city, and the blessing of Israel in the midst of the nations. Altogether, these texts serve the larger purpose of announcing YHWH's rule of the world at Mt. Zion.

Setting

See the discussion of the setting of chs. 24–27 above.

Intention

The intention of 25:1-12 is defined by its relation to the literary context of chs. 24–27, its structure and generic character, and its use of mythological themes to describe YHWH's blessing of the world.

Isaiah 25:1-12 stands at the head of the prophetic announcement of salvation in 25:1–27:13. As such, it builds upon the preceding material by pointing to YHWH's blessing of the world as the ultimate outcome of the catastrophe announced in ch. 24. The communal song of thanksgiving in 25:1-5 thanks YHWH for the overthrow of the fortified city and the subsequent relief of the oppressed. The "fortified city" (qiryâ běṣûrâ) corresponds to the "city of chaos" mentioned in 24:10, and therefore is to be identified as Babylon. This is clear not only from the literary context of chs. 24–27 but also from the reference to the "palace of aliens" in 25:2. In the 6th century, Babylon was known for its magnificent palaces, built by Nebuchadrezzar, which symbolized Babylon's domination of the Near East. The references to the protection of the poor in vv. 4-5 employ the imagery of protection from rain and heat, which also appear in the portrayal of YHWH's protection of Zion, the site of the temple, in 4:5b-6. This clarifies the contrast between the Babylonians and the exiled Jews who will benefit from YHWH's actions.

The second part of the passage, 25:6-12, then describes YHWH's blessing of the earth in terms of a great feast to be held on Zion. Again, fertility imagery predominates as the feast will consist of "wine on the lees" and "fat things full of marrow," images for the abundance of food and drink in the now fertile world. Likewise, the defeat of death plays a central role in the banquet (v. 8). Many scholars have noted that the banquet on the mountain and the defeat of death are elements of a common ancient Near Eastern mythological pattern whereby the kingship of the fertility deity is won after defeating opponent gods, including deities of chaos and death. As Delcor notes, the Ugaritic myth of Baal, in which Baal attains kingship by defeating the god of death, Mot, and the sea god of chaos, Yamm, provides a close analogy to the present scene. Although the banquet is held for the nations, the defeat of death is clearly associated with the removal of the shame of YHWH's people (v. 8). Consequently, the restoration of Israel is a central element to YHWH's assumption of kingship in the world. The downfall of Moab appears to acknowledge the demise of Moab at the hands of Babylon in the 6th century. The announcement is apparently motivated by the pun in v. 7 concerning YHWH's removal of "the covering that covers [hallôṭ hallôṭ] all the peoples." Lot (lôṭ) was the father of Moab (Gen 19:30-38), who was born in the midst of natural catastrophe. The use of language concerning the destruction of humankind from Isa 2:6-21 apparently calls to mind the context of similar worldwide catastrophe as the setting for Moab's demise.

Bibliography

M. Delcor, "Le festin d'immortalité sur la montagne de Sion à l'ére eschatologique en Is. 25,6-9, à lumière de la littérature Ugaritique," in *Études bibliques et orientales de religions comparées* (ed. M. Delcor; Leiden: Brill, 1979) 122-31; J. A. Emerton, "A Textual Problem in Isaiah 25,2," *ZAW* 89 (1977) 64-73; R. Martin-Achard, " 'Il engloutit la mort à jamais.' Remarques sur Esaïe 25,8aα," in *Mélanges bibliques et orientaux en l'honneur de M. Mathias Delcor* (ed. A. Caquot, L. Légasse, and M. Tardieu; AOAT 215; Kevelaer: Butzon & Bercker; Neukirchen-Vluyn: Neukirchener, 1985) 283-96; Welten, "Vernichtung" (→ 24:1-23); H. Wildberger, "Das Freudenmahl auf dem Zion: Erwägungen zu Jes. 25,6-8," *TZ* 33 (1977) 373-83; B. Wodecki, S.V.D., "The Religious Universalism of the Pericope Is 25:6-9," in *Goldene Äpfel in silbernen Schalen* (ed. K.-D. Schunck and M. Augustin; BEATAJ 20; Frankfurt am Main, Berlin, and Bern: Lang, 1992) 35-47.

JUDAH'S PETITION TO YHWH FOR DELIVERANCE: ANNOUNCEMENT OF JUDAH'S COMMUNAL COMPLAINT, 26:1-21

Structure

I. Announcement of complaint song   1a
II. Communal complaint song proper: exhortation to
    confidence in YHWH   1b-21

A. Song of praise for YHWH's victory — 1b-6
1. Rejoicing for secure city — 1b
2. Request for admission to city — 2
3. Expression of confidence in YHWH — 3
4. Exhortation to confidence in YHWH — 4-6
  a. Basic statement — 4
    1) Exhortation statement proper — 4a
    2) Basis: YHWH is rock of eternity — 4b
  b. Extended basis: YHWH has defeated
    exalted enemy city — 5-6
B. Affirmation of confidence in YHWH's righteousness:
contrast of righteous and wicked — 7-10
1. YHWH's righteous path — 7
2. Expression of hope in YHWH's righteous laws — 8
3. Psalmist's individual expression of hope — 9
  a. Expression proper — 9a
  b. Basis: inhabitants of world will learn
    YHWH's righteousness — 9b
4. Contrast of wicked who cannot learn righteousness — 10
C. Petition to YHWH to act against wicked — 11-19
1. Blindness of wicked to their own destruction — 11
2. Petition for peace — 12
  a. Petition proper — 12a
  b. Basis: YHWH acts on people's behalf — 12b
3. Extended basis for petition: YHWH's
past actions on people's behalf — 13-15
  a. Description of past rulers — 13-14a
  b. Consequence: YHWH's action to remove them — 14b-15
4. Petition for YHWH to act — 16-19
  a. Petition proper — 16
  b. Metaphor of pregnant woman unable to bear — 17-18
    1) Analogy of pregnant woman to people — 17
    2) Inability to bear — 18
  c. Successful result: cohortative — 19
    1) Success announced — 19a
    2) Reason: YHWH acts — 19b
D. Exhortation to wait for YHWH's intervention — 20-21
1. Exhortation proper — 20
2. Basis: YHWH will act to correct injustice — 21

The first of the units describing the results of the announcement of YHWH's blessing in 25:1-12 is 26:1-21, which announces Judah's petition to YHWH for deliverance in the form of an exhortation based in the communal complaint genre. The demarcation of this text is evident from the introductory *bayyôm hahû'* ("on that day") formula in 26:1 and the identical formula in 27:1, which introduces the second unit of the results (see the discussion of the superstructure of chs. 24–27 above). Isa 26:1-21 is characterized by shifting forms of address, including 2nd-person address forms to YHWH or to an unspecified audience, 1st-person plural and singular speaker's forms, and 3rd-person descriptions of YHWH. The subunit coheres as an example of the communal complaint genre, the key element of which is the plea or petition (vv. 11-19). As is common in this genre, all other elements support the petition. In this specific example, the complaint has been styled as an exhortation designed to motivate the audience to be patient until the petition is granted (vv. 20-21).

The unit opens with an announcement of the complaint song in 26:1a, which functions as an introduction identifying what follows in vv. 1b-21 generically as *šîr,* "song." The song comprises four major subsections, based primarily on thematic grounds.

The first major subsection of the song is the song of praise for YHWH's victory in vv. 1b-6. It is characterized by a 1st-person common plural speaker's style evident in v. 1b, 2nd-person masculine plural forms of address to the gatekeepers in v. 2 and to the audience in vv. 4-6, and a 2nd-person masculine singular address to YHWH in v. 3. Thematically, the song presupposes YHWH's victory over an exalted enemy city (vv. 5-6) and the security enjoyed by the audience of the song in their own city (v. 1b). The thrust of the song is not only to celebrate this victory, but more importantly to convince the audience to trust in YHWH (v. 4) based on YHWH's deeds. The song proceeds through a series of statements with shifting addresses until it reaches its climax in vv. 4-6. V. 1b, characterized by its 1st-person common plural speaker's perspective, conveys the rejoicing of the singers in their secure city. V. 2 employs the masculine plural imperative *pitḥû* ("open!") addressed to the gatekeepers of the city, to open the gates to let a righteous people enter. The righteous people in this case are presumably the Judean audience. V. 3 then employs 2nd-person masculine singular address forms directed to YHWH to express confidence in YHWH's ability to provide peace for the people. Finally, vv. 4-6 provide the climax in that they call on the audience to trust in YHWH. The exhortation to trust in YHWH is basically stated in v. 4, which employs the masculine plural imperative *biṭḥû,* "trust!" (note the assonance with *pitḥû* in v. 2), for the exhortation statement proper in v. 4a, and a causative *kî* ("because") clause to state the basis for the exhortation in v. 4b, i.e., YHWH is the "Rock of Eternity." Vv. 5-6 then present the extended basis for the exhortation in v. 4. Introduced by causative *kî,* vv. 5-6 specify YHWH's destruction of the exalted enemy city so that the feet of the poor and needy could trample its inhabitants.

The second major section of the complaint song appears in vv. 7-10, which affirm confidence in YHWH's righteousness by contrasting the experience of the righteous with that of the wicked. This section is characterized by its use of both 1st-person common plural (v. 8) and 1st-person common singular (v. 9) speaker's perspectives and by its 2nd-person masculine singular address forms directed to YHWH (vv. 7-9). In addition, it employs wisdom sayings in vv. 7a, 9b, and 10a (Kaiser, *Isaiah 13–39,* 210; cf. Clements, *Isaiah 1–39,* 213). These verses are further tied together by their repeated progressive use of vocabulary from verse to verse (cf. Wildberger, *Jesaja,* 986). Thus *'ōraḥ,* "path," appears in vv. 7 and 8; *mišpāṭeykā,* "your laws," and *ta'ăwat-nāpeš/napšî 'iwwîtîkā,* "longing of the soul/my soul longs for you," appear in vv. 8 and 9; and *ṣedeq lāmdû/bal lāmad ṣedeq,* "righteousness they learned"/"he did not learn righteousness," appear in vv. 9 and 10.

The purpose of this subsection is to lay the basis for the petiton that follows in vv. 11-19. It proceeds by presenting a progressive series of statements that build confidence in YHWH's righteousness and the experience of the righteous versus those who are wicked. V. 7 addresses YHWH in 2nd-person masculine singular form, emphasizing that the path of the righteous is straight and that YHWH will smooth the path of the righteous. V. 8 employs a 1st-person common plural speaker's form to express the psalmist's (and thus the community's) desire for the path of YHWH's laws. The psalmist's individual desire for YHWH follows in v. 9. V. 9a contains the expression of hope proper, and v. 9b, connected by a causative *kî,* expresses the basis for that hope in that the inhabitants of the earth will learn YHWH's righteousness. V. 10 concludes the sequence by portraying the wicked as those who are incapable of learning righteousness or perceiving the majesty of YHWH. By mentioning the wicked in this fashion, the psalmist intends to identify himself more closely with YHWH and, at the same time, to alienate the wicked from the deity.

The core of the complaint song appears in the petition for YHWH to act against the wicked in vv. 11-19. This section is characterized throughout by its 2nd-person masculine singular address forms to YHWH and by its 1st-person common plural speaker's perspective. It differs from the preceding material in vv. 7-10 thematically in that it now presents specific requests to YHWH. The structure of the petition is evident on thematic grounds and on the direct address forms that employ the name of YHWH in vv. 11, 12, 13, and 16. The petition begins with a 2nd-person masculine singular address to YHWH, "O YHWH, your hand is lifted up, but they see it not," that reiterates the inability of the wicked to perceive or to learn. The statement concludes with an expression of confidence that the wicked will be consumed. V. 12 employs both 1st-person common plural speaker's perspective and 2nd-person masculine singular address form directed to YHWH to present a preliminary petition that YHWH will grant peace for the people. The petition proper appears in v. 12a, and v. 12b, introduced by a causative *kî,* provides the basis for the petition in that YHWH has always acted on the people's behalf.

Verses 13-15 likewise employ 1st-person common plural speaker's forms and 2nd-person masculine singular address forms directed to YHWH to present an extended basis for the petition in v. 12. Like the initial basis for the petition in v. 12b, the extended basis focuses on YHWH's past actions on the people's behalf. Vv. 13-14a describe YHWH's actions against past rulers, concluding that they are dead as a result of YHWH's intervention. Vv. 14b-15, introduced by *lākēn,* "therefore," present the consequences of YHWH's actions against these rulers; YHWH removed them and in doing so enhanced the nation's and YHWH's own reputation to the ends of the earth.

The petition for YHWH to act appears in vv. 16-19 and constitutes the final and climactic subsection of vv. 11-19. Again, it employs 1st-person common plural speaker's form and 2nd-person masculine plural address form directed to YHWH. The petition proper appears in v. 16, "O YHWH, as an enemy they have visited you, pour out the spell of your chastisement on them!" (cf. *RSV*). The petition presupposes the previous material that distinguished righteous from wicked and called to mind YHWH's past acts of salvation on behalf of the people. The petition is reinforced by vv. 17-18, which employ the metaphor of a pregnant woman, unable to give birth on her own, to describe the situation of the people. V. 17 makes the analogy explicit, and v. 18 states that the people are unable to bring about birth, and thus their own salvation, without assistance. V. 19 then employs cohortative language to convince YHWH to act, thereby bringing about a successful result. V. 19a employs figurative language to announce success, portrayed in terms of the dead coming to life. The meaning of this statement becomes clear in its 2nd-person masculine singular address forms and in v. 19b. The statement is directed to YHWH, as are all the 2nd-person masculine singular address forms of vv. 11-19, and states that "your [i.e., YHWH's] dew of lights" brings down the land of the shades. In other words, YHWH overcomes death and defeat.

The fourth and final section of the communal complaint song appears in vv. 20-21, which exhort the people to wait for YHWH's intervention. The passage is distinguished by its shift in address forms. Here the prophet is speaking to the people, identified as "my people" in v. 20. The exhortation proper appears in v. 20, where the people are asked to shut themselves behind their doors and to wait a little while until the anger is past. The basis for the exhortation appears in v. 21, introduced by a causative *kî hinnēh,* "for behold!" The verse announces that YHWH is coming out to punish the iniquity of the inhabitants of the earth, thereby delivering the people of Judah who presented the petition in the first place.

Genre

As a component of the (→) prophetic announcement of blessing of the earth and its results in 25:1–27:13, 26:1-21 is heavily influenced by that genre insofar as it announces the results of YHWH's blessings. Nevertheless, this text has its own distinct generic character as a COMMUNAL COMPLAINT SONG that announces YHWH's intervention on behalf of Judah while exhorting the people to wait patiently for the intervention to take place. Again, the passage appears to have been composed for the present context, as indicated by the reference to the fall of the exalted city and YHWH's protection of the poor in vv. 5-6, as well as by the exhortational character of the song that will appear again in 27:2-13. Nevertheless, 26:1-21 appears to follow the typical pattern of the COMMUNAL COMPLAINT SONG insofar as the PETITION to YHWH serves as the central element of the song around which all other elements are organized. Following the announcement of the song in v. 1a, four major generic subentities constitute the COMMUNAL COMPLAINT SONG proper in vv. 1b-21.

The first major generic component of the song is a SONG OF PRAISE for YHWH's intervention against enemies in vv. 1b-6. Although this particular song presupposes the fall of the exalted city mentioned in vv. 5-6, the thrust of the song appears to be directed to instilling confidence in YHWH on the part of the audience. This concern indicates that the author of the psalm still anticipates acts by YHWH on behalf of the community. Consequently, v. 1b expresses rejoicing by the people for their strong city, and v. 2 reiterates this theme by demanding admittance of the strong people. But the theme shifts to expressions of confidence in v. 3 and an EXHORTATION to confidence in vv. 4-6 as indicated by the imperative *biṭḥû byhwh 'ădê-'ad,* "trust in YHWH forever!" (v. 4a). This shift suggests that the situation of the community has not yet been completely alleviated even though the exalted city has been defeated.

The second major section of the COMMUNAL COMPLAINT SONG is the affirmation of confidence in YHWH's righteousness in vv. 7-10. This section builds on the motif of trust in YHWH that was introduced in the previous section and indicates that something more is required by the community from YHWH. This concern becomes clear as the affirmations of YHWH's righteousness in vv. 7 and 8 give way to the psalmist's expressions of hope that YHWH's righteousness will be learned by the inhabitants of the world. Specifically, the psalmist contrasts the wicked, who are unable to learn, from the righteous, who long for YHWH's laws. Again, this section indicates that the fundamental problem of the community has not yet been resolved.

The third major section is the PETITION to YHWH to act against the wicked in vv. 11-19, which serves as the focal point of the song. Here the psalmist points out the blindness of the wicked prior to a preliminary PETITION for peace in v. 12. The basis for the PETITION is expressed in terms of YHWH's past actions on behalf of the people, specifically, the removal of past rulers who oppressed the people. The core of the PETITION then appears in vv. 16-19, in which the psalmist points out the wicked have visited trouble on YHWH and then petitions YHWH to "pour out the spell of your chastisement on them!" This PETITION is reinforced by a metaphorical portrayal of the people as a pregnant woman unable to give birth without aid and a cohortative statement concerning YHWH's ability to bring life to the people. Again, the PETITION points to the fact that the community still requires YHWH to act on their behalf.

The final section of the COMPLAINT SONG appears in vv. 20-21 as an EXHORTATION to wait for YHWH's intervention. This is directed by the psalmist to the people, asking them to be patient until YHWH acts on their behalf. Again, the suffering of the community has not been resolved, but relief is anticipated.

Consequently, the COMMUNAL COMPLAINT SONG in 26:1-21 serves the purposes of the larger composition in that it points to the destruction of the oppressive city, but it indicates that the people's situation of suffering has not yet been alleviated. Consideration of this theme will follow in 27:1-13.

Setting

See the discussion of the setting of chs. 24–27 above.

Intention

The intention of 26:1-21 is determined by its literary context as a component of chs. 24–27, its generic character and structure, and the imagery it employs to describe the defeat of the "exalted city" and the restoration of Israel.

Isaiah 26:1-21 is the first of three sections that specify the outcome of YHWH's blessing announced in 25:1-12 (see the introductory discussion of chs. 24–27 as a whole). It focuses specifically on Judah and employs the form of a communal complaint song to call on YHWH to fulfill the blessings that have not yet been achieved. The concluding exhortation calls upon the people to wait for YHWH to act and thereby defines the exhortational character of the communal complaint song. In the present instance, it indicates that the full realization of YHWH's plans for rule of the earth from Zion have not yet been achieved.

The structure of the communal complaint song serves its exhortational purpose by calling on YHWH to act. It therefore provides motivation for the people to remain patient until the time for action comes. As such, it is designed to placate the people in the face of the nonrealization of the promise of blessing. The introductory song of praise in vv. 1b-6 extols YHWH for his defeat of the "exalted city" *(qiryâ nišgābâ)* and employs language from Isaiah's description of the destruction of the land in 2:6-21 to portray the city's downfall. The imagery of the trampling feet of the poor demonstrates clearly that this is an oppressive city, identified with the "city of chaos" (24:10) and the "fortified city" (25:2). The downfall of the city, apparently Babylon, serves as the basis for the calls to trust in YHWH. Vv. 7-10 affirm confidence in YHWH based on divine righteousness. They also prepare the way for the following petition to YHWH by emphasizing the distinction between the desire of the psalmist for YHWH's justice in contrast with the wicked who is unable to perceive YHWH's righteousness and majesty. The sexual metaphor of the psalmist's "desire" *(ta'ăwat,* v. 8; cf. Gen 3:6) heightens the psalmist's attempt to identify with YHWH.

The petition then appears in vv. 11-19. Its structure is determined by four direct addresses to YHWH in vv. 11, 12, 13, and 16, which are designed to gain the deity's attention. This section builds on the distinction of the wicked from the righteous as a further motivation for YHWH to act. The preliminary petition in v. 12 simply asks for a general peace. After reminding YHWH of the destruction of past rulers, the main petition appears in vv. 16-19, calling for YHWH to destroy the present enemy that threatens the people. The need for YHWH to act is expressed in the imagery of childbirth, i.e., the people are unable to act/give birth themselves without assistance. The efficacy of YHWH's actions is expressed with the imagery of death and resurrection, apparently derived from mythological traditions in the ancient Near East concerning the defeat of the deity of death. When YHWH intervenes, Israel will live rather than die as his "heavenly dew" *(ṭal 'ôrōt,* v. 19) sweeps away "the land of the shades." The concluding exhortation in vv. 20-21 asks the people to have patience until YHWH acts to avenge the injustice that has been done to the people.

Bibliography

J. Day, *"ṭal 'ôrōt* in Isaiah 26,19," *ZAW* 90 (1978) 265-69; D. M. Fouts, "A Suggestion for Isaiah xxvi 16," *VT* 41 (1991) 472-75; F. J. Helfmeyer, " 'Deine Toten — Meine Leichen': Heilzusage und Annahme in Jes 26,19," in *Bausteine biblischer Theologie (Fest.* G. Johannes Botterweck; ed. H.-J. Fabry; BBB 50; Cologne and Bonn: P. Hanstein,

1977) 245-58; P. Humbert, "La rosée tombe en Israël," *TZ* 13 (1957) 487-93; J. F. A. Sawyer, "Hebrew Words for the Resurrection of the Dead," *VT* 23 (1973) 218-34.

YHWH'S DEFEAT OF LEVIATHAN, 27:1

Structure

I. YHWH's attack against Leviathan	1a
II. Result: YHWH's slaying of Leviathan	1b

The basis for the demarcation of this brief passage is quite clear. It begins with an introductory *bayyôm hahû'* ("on that day") formula. This formula appears again in 27:2, which introduces the following unit. The structure of this passage is based on its syntax and content. V. 1a contains the 3rd-person masculine singular imperfect verb *yipqōd*, "he will punish," which describes YHWH's attack against Leviathan. V. 1b follows with a *wāw*-consecutive perfect verb, *wĕhārag*, "and he will slay," which describes the results of the attack when YHWH slays the dragon.

Genre

The genre of this passage is simply PROPHETIC ANNOUNCEMENT, insofar as it employs the *bayyôm hahû'* formula to predict a future act of YHWH against Leviathan.

Setting

See the discussions of the setting of chs. 24–27 above and that of 27:2-13 below.

Intention

The intention of 27:1 is determined by its context in chs. 24–27, its use of mythological themes, and its historical setting.

Isaiah 27:1 is the second of three sections describing the future realization of YHWH's blessings announced in 25:1-12. It does so by simply announcing YHWH's defeat of the sea dragon of chaos, Leviathan, known throughout biblical and Ugaritic tradition as the opponent of order prior to the establishment of the created world. In the present case, the defeat of Leviathan presages order not only in the natural world of creation but also in the social world as symbolized by the restoration of Israel to Zion in 27:2-13.

As noted above, 27:1 and 27:2-13 relate to 11:10-16, which employs the same imagery, including the smiting of the Nile into seven streams and a reference to the seven-headed Leviathan, to describe the restoration of Israel to its land. This establishes that the original setting of 27:1 is in the Josianic edition of the book of Isaiah. As such, 27:1 was originally composed to announce the return of the exiles from the northern kingdom of Israel to Zion and the reestablishment of Davidic rule over the whole of the twelve tribes of Israel.

Bibliography

C. F. Burney, "The Three Serpents of Isaiah xxvii 1," *JTS* 11 (1910) 443-47; C. H. Gordon, "Leviathan: Symbol of Evil," in *Biblical Motifs: Origins and Transformations* (ed. A. Altmann; Cambridge: Harvard University Press, 1966) 1-9; C. Rabin, "Bāriah," *JTS* 47 (1946) 38-41.

EXHORTATION TO ISRAEL TO ACCEPT YHWH'S OFFER OF RECONCILIATION: NEW VINEYARD ALLEGORY, 27:2-13

Structure

The demarcation of 27:2-13 is clear. It is introduced by the formula *bayyôm hahû'*, "in that day," which indicates its future orientation. This perspective continues throughout the passage as indicated by the presence of other future-oriented formulas, including *habbā'îm*, "in days to come," in v. 6 and *wĕhāyâ bayyôm hahû'*, "and it shall come to pass in that day," in vv. 12 and 13. Furthermore, agricultural imagery appears throughout the passage, including the new vineyard allegory in vv. 2-6, the term *sa'ssĕ'â*, "measure by measure," in v. 8 (cf. Daiches for the agricultural associations of this term), the references to fruit, harvest, and cattle in vv. 9-11, and the allegorical use of gleaning imagery to portray the return of the exiles to Jerusalem in vv. 12-13 (for a full discussion of the agricultural imagery of 27:2-13, see Sweeney, "New Gleanings," 54-55; cf. Talmon, "Prophetic Rhetoric," 269-70). Finally, the introductory *hôy* and the overall concern with the Ephraimite monarchy in 28:1 mark the beginning of a new unit entirely separate from chs. 24–27.

The structure of this passage is determined by the presentation of the new vineyard allegory in vv. 2-6 and its interpretation in relation to the return of the Israelite exiles to Jerusalem in vv. 7-13. The rhetorical question in v. 7 marks the transition between the two subunits, and each concludes with explicit references to the future in vv. 6 and 12-13.

The structure of the new vineyard allegory is determined by the perspective of its governing verbs and by its content. V. 2 employs the masculine plural imperative *'annû-lāh*, "sing of it!" The speaker is the prophet. Although the addressee is not specified, it is evidently the prophet's audience. The content of the verse merely introduces the subject of the new vineyard and a command to sing about it. V. 2 therefore serves as the introduction to the allegory. Vv. 3-5 contain the allegory proper. These verses are characterized by their use of a 1st-person common singular speaker's perspective that explicitly identifies YHWH (v. 3), not the prophet, as the speaker in the allegory. In v. 3 YHWH states his acts of protection on behalf of the vineyard. V. 3a states YHWH's actions specifically as guarding and watering the vineyard, and v. 3b states that the purpose of YHWH's actions is for the protection of the vineyard against intruders. Vv. 4-5 then shift to YHWH's offer of reconciliation. V. 4a introduces the section by announcing that YHWH is not angry. Vv. 4b-5 then follow by explaining the alternatives open to the people in metaphorical language. On the one hand, v. 4b states that if the people respond with hostility, i.e., if they present obstacles such as thorns and briars (v. 4bα), then YHWH will likewise react with hostility by attacking and kindling them (v. 4bβ). On the other hand, v. 5 states that if the people will accept YHWH's refuge (v. 5a), then YHWH will respond with peace (v. 5b). Following the allegory proper in vv. 3-5, v. 6 then drops the 1st-person common singular speaker's perspective and the language of allegory to form the third major element of vv. 2-6. Here the prophet returns as the speaker to explain the meaning of the allegory in reference to Israel/Jacob's blossoming and growth if it accepts YHWH's offer. V. 6a states that Israel/Jacob will take root and grow, and v. 6b states that they will fill the world with fruit or produce *(tĕnûbâ)*.

The second major section of 27:2-13 appears in vv. 7-13, which interpret the meaning of the allegory in relation to Israel's and Jerusalem's current situation. Although the passage functions as an exhortation to the people to accept YHWH's offer of reconciliation, it is cast in the form of a disputation speech, which attempts to refute the attitudes of the people. As such, the disputation pattern serves the purposes of the exhortation in that it attempts to overcome the pessimistic attitude of the people and to convince them that YHWH is acting to restore them to Jerusalem/Zion.

The first major element of the disputation is the rhetorical question in v. 7 that presupposes the current pessimistic attitude of the people. The passage should be rendered, "Like the smiting of his smiter are they smitten? Or like the slaying of his slain [are they] slain?" The question speaks to the current situation of the people asking if they are as bad off as their oppressors who are now destroyed. Although the people have suffered, the question points to the fact that their oppressors are now completely destroyed whereas the people are not. This concern suggests a basis for hope and thereby leads to the proposition of restoration that follows. As such, the question intends to overcome the people's attitude of despair and to suggest that a better situation is possible.

The refutation of the people's attitude then appears in vv. 8-13, which are syntactically distinct from v. 7 but present YHWH's return of the exiles to Zion as the outcome of the people's suffering. As noted above, the use of agricultural imagery, especially that of gleaning, builds on the imagery of the vineyard allegory to present Israel's suffering as an act of winnowing or gleaning to remove the weeds or chaff and obtain grain or fruit inside. The structure of the passage is determined thematically by the focus on the situation of the people in vv. 8-9 and the focus on the city of Jerusalem in vv. 10-13. The two passages share a similar structure in that each presents the desolate situation of the people or city first, followed by a positive outcome. Likewise, the two passages are linked by an adversative *kî*, "for," in v. 10.

Thus vv. 8-9 focus on the desperate situation of the people. Their current situation, exile, appears in v. 8, expressed explicitly in v. 8a and metaphorically in v. 8b. V. 9 then presents the outcome of this situation as indicated by the introductory *lākēn*, "therefore." The verse focuses on the expiation of the sin of the people, indicating that the exile was a punishment that has now been completed. The purpose of the exile as expiation of sin is stated explicitly in v. 9a. V. 9b states specific evidence of Israel's expiation of sin in reference to the destruction of altars and the removal of Asherim/Hammanim (pillars).

Verses 10-13 then focus on the situation of the city of Jerusalem. Although the city is not explicitly identified in vv. 10-11, vv. 12-13 make clear that Jerusalem is intended here. Vv. 10-11 concentrate on the desolation of the city. Vv. 10-11a portray the city's desolation with a basic statement of its solitary and abandoned state (v. 10a) followed by an elaboration of it situation in terms of the grazing cattle and women gathering tinder that wander about it (vv. 10b-11a). V. 11b, introduced by a causative *kî*, explains the reason for the desolation: the people lack understanding; therefore *(lākēn)* their Maker has no mercy on them and their Creator shows them no favor. Vv. 12-13, linked by conjunctive *wāw*, then portray the favorable outcome of YHWH's actions. As noted above, each verse is introduced by the formula *wĕhāyâ bayyôm hahû'*, "and it shall come to pass on that day." V. 12 announces the recovery of the exiles of Israel from the Euphrates (Mesopotamia) and from Egypt, and v. 13 announces that they will be restored to YHWH's holy mountain in Jerusalem in order to worship YHWH.

Genre

The overarching genre of this passage is EXHORTATION insofar as it is designed to motivate its audience to adopt a specific mode of action. In the present case, the passage attempts to convince its audience to accept the premise that YHWH is acting to restore Israel to Jerusalem. It presents an offer by YHWH in vv. 4-6 that contains a veiled threat against those who might present obstacles to YHWH's intentions, but that also offers reconciliation to those who are willing to accept YHWH's renewed relationship with Israel. From the concluding verses of the passage (vv. 12-13), it appears that the specific action requested of the audience is a return to Zion from exile, or, for those who might already be in Jerusalem, an acceptance of those who are returning as evidence of YHWH's action to restore the Israelite exiles to Zion. Because the EXHORTATION genre has no set textual form, this passage employs a number of subordinate generic entities that contribute to the purposes of the whole.

The first of these is the vineyard ALLEGORY in vv. 2-6. ALLEGORIES have no specific textual structure; rather, they employ metaphorical or figurative language to present a given situation or set of facts in terms of another situation or set of facts. Consequently, the ALLEGORY presupposes a situation of interpretation; that is, the details and images of the ALLEGORY are chosen and presented in relation to the situation that the author intends to discuss. In the present instance, the language and imagery of a vineyard and YHWH's care for it is employed as an allegorical means for discussing YHWH's relationship with Israel. The present ALLEGORY builds on the previous ALLEGORY of 5:1-7, in which the vineyard represents Israel and YHWH's care for the vineyard represents YHWH's protection of Israel. Both images are applied in the present context. But whereas 5:1-7 is designed to present a disruption in the relationship between Israel and YHWH, 27:2-6 is designed to present the restoration of that relationship. Thus YHWH announces that he will care for the vineyard (v. 3) and that he has no anger (v. 4a). The ALLEGORY serves the purposes of the EXHORTATION. Those who present obstacles to YHWH's relationship with Israel, expressed here as those who will place thorns and briars in the vineyard, will be attacked by YHWH. Those who accept YHWH's refuge will have peace. The offer is reinforced by the concluding statement in v. 6 that employs agricultural imagery to announce Israel's renewed growth in the world. As such, v. 6 explains the meaning of the ALLEGORY by explicitly naming Israel/Jacob as the subject of discussion.

The second major generic component of the EXHORTATION in 27:2-13 is the DISPUTATION SPEECH in vv. 7-13. The DISPUTATION SPEECH pattern clearly serves the purposes of the EXHORTATION in that it is designed to challenge a concept or opinion held by the speaker's opponent and to convince the opponent, or the audience, to reject that opinion and to adopt the position of the speaker. The DISPUTATION SPEECH pattern generally comprises three basic elements, which may be expressed in a variety of ways in the surface structure of the text: thesis, counterthesis, and dispute or refutation. In the present case, the thesis is expressed in the form of a RHETORICAL QUESTION in v. 7 that already begins the challenge: "Like the smiting of his smiter is he smitten? Or like the slaying of his slain slaying?" (cf. *RSV*). The question asks whether the audience, here presented as victims of an oppressor, have fared as badly as the oppressor. Because this is a RHETORICAL QUESTION, the answer is obviously negative; the victims have not suffered as greatly as the oppressor who is now dead. In the context of a DISPUTATION SPEECH, this challenges a prevailing opinion that they have suffered so much as to be unable to act on the proposition offered by the speaker in the preceding vineyard ALLEGORY. By pointing out that the people have survived and fared better than their now defunct oppressor, the speaker lays the basis for convincing the audience that a restored relationship with YHWH, and a return of exiled Israel to Jerusalem, is now possible.

The speaker then proceeds with the refutation in vv. 8-13. He points out the fact of Israel's exile in v. 8 and argues that this constitutes a punishment or expiation of Israel's sin of rejecting YHWH for pagan deities in v. 9. The result was the desolation of the city described in vv. 10-11. Vv. 12-13, however, build on the premise that the punishment was an expiation of Israel's sin by announcing that YHWH will now restore Israel to the land that was devastated as a result of the punishment. By employing the same agricultural images of harvest and fruitfulness that appeared in the vineyard ALLEGORY and the subsequent verses, the speaker maintains that YHWH has gleaned the people, removing the chaff from the produce, and that the time has come to gather in the produce, that is, to restore Israel to Zion. As such, the DISPUTATION SPEECH pattern attempts to convince the audience of the reality of YHWH's restoration of Israel to Zion and thereby exhorts the audience to accept YHWH's offer of reconciliation made in vv. 4-5.

Setting

As noted in the discussion of the setting of chs. 24–27 as a whole above, 27:1 and 27:2-13 display several features that distinguish them from the rest of chs. 24–27. These include the exclusive concern with Israel and Jacob in contrast to the world at large or even Judah in particular, the interest in an indigenous fortified city (27:10) that seems to be distinguished from the enemy city vanquished in chs. 24–26, and the use of Leviathan as a mythological symbol that seems to differ from the overall pattern of death-and-life imagery, commonly associated with Mot in Ugaritic mythology. Although ch. 27 is well integrated into the present context of chs. 24–27, and in fact supplies its climax in the redemption of Israel, these factors suggest that ch. 27 was composed at a different time and in a different setting than that of chs. 24–27 as a whole (cf. March, 187-98, who notes the distinction between 27:2-13 and the rest of the composition but assigns this material to a later date). Employing an analogy to Ugaritic myths concerning Baal's kingship following his defeat of Yamm, Day (pp. 145-51) attempts to relate the Leviathan motif to the overall pattern of fertility, feasting, and the kingship of the deity found throughout the rest of chs. 24–27. But chs. 24–26 focus more on the mythology of death, analogous to Mot in Ugaritic mythology. Because the relationship between Baal's defeat of Mot and his defeat of Yamm is not completely clear, it seems best to conclude that the mention of Leviathan in 27:1 aids in tying 27:1-13 to the rest of the unit, but it does not demonstrate that the two sections were composed at the same time.

Rather, the features of 27:1 and 27:2-13 suggest that they were composed in the late 7th century, in conjunction with the Josianic redaction of the book of Isaiah. Several features support this conclusion. First, 27:1-12 refers consistently to sins and to the redemption of Israel and Jacob, but never to Judah or Jerusalem. Although these terms can be used for Israel and Judah as a whole in the exilic or postexilic period, both terms are generally employed for the northern kingdom of Israel at earlier times. This is quite striking, since the previous passage refers specifically to Judah in 26:1. The motif of the return of the northern tribes to Jerusalem (27:12-13) can of course relate to the late 8th century, but it receives special emphasis during the reign of King Josiah, who tried to bring the territory of the former northern kingdom of Israel back to Davidic rule and worship of YHWH at Jerusalem (2 Kings 23).

Second, the references to Egypt and Assyria as locations of the Israelite exiles is particularly striking if one assumes an exilic or postexilic setting for ch. 27. It is certainly possible that such terms could be used to conceal a reference to Babylon, but it is unclear why Babylon's name should be masked in the present literary context. Chs. 24–27 follow immediately after the pronouncements concerning the nations that list Babylon as the first of the nations to be condemned (13:1–14:23). After the fall of the northern kingdom in 722-721, however, Egypt and Assyria were the locations of many Israelite exiles. Again, Josiah's program of national and religious restoration provides a fitting context for the return of exiles from Egypt and Assyria, especially since these countries proved to be Josiah's major enemies at the time. Given his effort to restore the Davidic kingdom and to centralize all worship of YHWH at Jerusalem, the call for the Israelite exiles to return from Egypt and Assyria makes good sense in a late-7th-century Judean context.

Third, ch. 27 cites other Isaianic texts that condemn the northern kingdom of Israel. For example, the new vineyard allegory in 27:2-6 alludes to the original vineyard allegory in 5:1-7 that appears at the head of a context that announces the downfall of the northern kingdom and its implications for Judah. Likewise, ch. 27 alludes to ch. 17, which condemns the Syro-Ephraimite coalition. Specific allusions include the agricultural references to harvest and ears of grain that appear throughout ch. 17 as well, the 'ăšērîm wĕhammānîm, "Asherim and Hammanim (pillars)," in v. 9 which also appear in 17:8, and the mythological motif of Leviathan, the sea dragon of chaos, which corresponds to the motif of the sea as a mythological symbol for chaos in 17:12-14. Most telling is the correspondence to 11:10-16, which likewise employs the motif of the seven-headed sea dragon of chaos, the explicit references to Egypt and Assyria as the place of exile for Israel's captives, and the motif of the rivers that will release the captives to return home. As noted in the discussion of 11:1-16 above, this passage stems from the Josianic redaction of Isaiah. This and the interest in 5:1-7 and 17:1-14 all suggest a Josianic setting for the composition of 27:1-13 as well. In this case, texts speaking to the punishment of Jacob or northern Israel (cf. 27:9) are cited to support the contention of 27:1-13 that Jacob was exiled as punishment for its sins. Now that the punishment is complete, Jacob may return home.

This contention has several implications for understanding ch. 27 in relation to its original setting. First, the destroyed fortified city of v. 10 must be identified as Bethel. The city was apparently destroyed by the Assyrian invasion of the late 8th century (J. A. Dearman, "Bethel," *Harper's Bible Dictionary* [ed. P. Achtemeier et al.; San Francisco: Harper & Row, 1985] 106). According to 2 Kgs 23:15-20, Josiah destroyed the altar at Bethel, but no reference is made to the destruction of the city. Furthermore, 2 Chr 34:4 and 7 refer explicitly to Josiah's destruction of the Asherim/Hammanim in the former northern kingdom of Israel, in association with his destruction of the pagan worship sites of the region. In this respect, it is striking that Isa 27:9 points to the 'ăšērîm wĕhammānîm as manifestations of Israel's guilt prior to its treatment of the abandoned fortified city in v. 10. Likewise, vv. 9-10 point to Israel's sin as the cause for the misfortunes of this city. The reference to a calf roaming about the site in v. 10 (the only animal mentioned in this context) may well allude to the presence of the golden calf for which the site was so notorious in biblical literature.

The original literary setting of this passage cannot be determined with certainty, although the chapter does appear to be closely associated with ch. 17 in particular. It is possible, though speculative, that ch. 27 at one time concluded ch. 17, or a collection of oracles against nations in the Josianic edition of Isaiah (cf. the discussion of the pronouncements concerning the foreign nations in chs. 13–23).

Finally, ch. 27 also has links to ch. 1, especially with regard to the solitary city (v. 10; cf. 1:9) and the people who lack understanding (v. 11; cf. 1:3). Inasmuch as the final form of ch. 1 is the product of a 5th-century redaction,

351

the chapter cannot be used to argue that the city is Jerusalem or the people Judean. Although these statements in ch. 1 apparently derive from the prophet Isaiah, they represent a Josianic attempt to apply Isaianic imagery concerning the punishment of Jerusalem to Bethel.

Intention

The intention of 27:2-13 is determined by its placement in the context of chs. 24–27, its structure and generic character, its relation to previous prophecy from Isaiah, and its historical setting.

Isaiah 27:2-13 is the last of three sections that describe the results of YHWH's blessing of the world in 25:1-12. Insofar as it announces the restoration of Israel to Zion, it presents Israel's redemption as the culmination and confirmation of YHWH's plans to rule the world from Zion. Likewise, it presents the restoration of Israel as the outcome of the world turmoil described in ch. 24.

The character of 27:2-13 is exhortational, insofar as it is designed to convince its audience, the people of Israel, of the reality of YHWH's action to restore the Israelite exiles to Zion. The first part of the passage in vv. 2-6 presents a new vineyard allegory that announces YHWH's renewed protection for Israel. The allegory reverses the previous vineyard allegory in 5:1-7, which announced YHWH's judgment against Israel. In the present case, the agricultural imagery of fertility is employed to describe the new growth that Israel will experience and its influence on the entire world (v. 6). The second part of the passage in vv. 8-13 is designed as a disputation speech, which attempts to refute one thesis and to replace it with another. In the present instance, it attempts to overcome the pessimism of the people by explaining that the suffering of Israel through exile is part of a process that will punish the people for apostasy, but will eventually result in their restoration to Zion. The passage employs the imagery of a deserted city, presumably Jerusalem in the 6th- and 5th-century context of chs. 24–27, to express the function of the exile as a punishment for Israel's apostasy. The passage concludes with a statement that YHWH will restore the exiles to Zion. It employs the agricultural motif of gleaning to express this goal, insofar as gleaning removes the useless chaff to preserve grain. Thus, to preserve the core, part of Israel was lost in the punishment. The final result will be Israel's worship of YHWH at Zion.

As noted in the discussion of setting above, the original setting of 27:1 and 27:2-13 is the Josianic edition of the book of Isaiah. The intention of the passage is similar to the above, except that Israel refers to the former northern kingdom of Israel that Josiah sought to return to Davidic rule. Consequently, the deserted city punished for Israel's sin of apostasy is Bethel, the site of the former royal sanctuary of northern Israel, which Josiah destroyed (2 Kings 23). Again, the function of the passage is to convince the exiled northerners that the return to Zion is an act of YHWH's redemption.

Bibliography

S. Daiches, "An Explanation of Isaiah 27.8," *JQR* 6 (1915-16) 399-404; Day, *Conflict* (→ 17:1–18:7); E. Jacob, "Du premier au deuxième chant de la vigne du prophète Esaïe: Réflexions sur Esaïe 27,2-5," in *Wort — Gebot — Glaube: Beiträge zur Theologie des Alten Testaments* (*Fest.* W. Eichrodt; eds. H.-J. Stoebe et al.; Zurich: Zwingli, 1970) 325-30; March, "Study" (→ 24:1–27:13); E. Robinson, "Isaiah XXVII 2-6," *ZAW* 47 (1929) 197-206; L. Alonso Schökel, "La canción de la viña. Is 27,2-5," *Estudios Eclesiásticos* 34 (1960) 767-74; Sweeney, "New Gleanings" (→ 24:1–27:13).

PROPHETIC INSTRUCTION CONCERNING YHWH'S PLAN/PURPOSE FOR JERUSALEM: ANNOUNCEMENT OF A ROYAL SAVIOR, 28:1–33:24

Structure

I. Prophetic instruction concerning YHWH's purpose in bringing Assyrian hegemony	28:1-29
II. Prophetic instruction concerning YHWH's purpose in bringing about assault against Ariel/Zion	29:1-24
III. Prophetic instruction concerning YHWH's delay in delivering the people from Assyria	30:1-33
IV. Parenesis concerning reliance on Egyptian aid against Assyria	31:1-9
V. Prophetic instruction concerning announcement of royal savior	32:1–33:24
A. Prophetic instruction speech concerning announcement of royal savior	32:1-20
B. Prophetic announcement of royal savior proper	33:1-24

Isaiah 28–33 is demarcated formally by its characteristic *hôy* ("woe") forms in 28:1; 29:1; 29:15; 30:1; 31:1; and 33:1, which distinguish it from the surrounding material, and by its overall concern with the deliverance of Jerusalem from the threat of the Assyrian empire. Following on chs. 24–27, which conclude the literary block in chs. 5–27 by focusing on the significance for Zion of YHWH's punishment of the earth, chs. 28–33 shift to a specific focus on Jerusalem and the threat posed to it by the Assyrian empire. Chs. 28–33 identify YHWH as the cause of the Assyrian threat and present YHWH's plans in a scenario that will see the emergence of a royal savior in Jerusalem together with the downfall of the Assyrian empire. The literary block of chs. 28–33 thereby serves as a fitting conclusion to the first half of the book of Isaiah in chs. 1–33 insofar as it presents the announcement of a royal savior and the downfall of the Assyrian empire as the climax of the message of punishment and restoration in the Assyrian period. As such, it points to the role that Jerusalem will occupy in YHWH's plans for world sovereignty at Zion (cf. chs. 2–4). Ch. 34 then turns

to an address to the nations announcing the coming downfall of Edom. This address opens the second half of the book in chs. 34–66. As noted in the discussion of the structure of the book as a whole, chs. 34–66 take up the realization of YHWH's world sovereignty from Zion that is announced in chs. 1–33.

The structure of chs. 28–33 is relatively simple. It is determined by the introductory *hôy* forms that appear in 28:1; 29:1; 30:1; and 31:1, and by the introductory *hēn* form that appears in 32:1. Although *hôy* forms also appear in 29:15 and 33:1, each of these texts is subsumed structurally by preceding material. As noted in the discussion of ch. 29 (below), the *hôy* form in 29:15 introduces the second half of a prophetic instruction speech concerning YHWH's purpose in bringing an assault against Ariel/Zion. In this context, vv. 15-24 present a resolution to several important points that are raised in vv. 1-14 and thereby present an argument that YHWH's action against Ariel/Zion is designed to lead to Jacob's deliverance. Likewise, the *hôy* form in 33:1 opens a prophetic announcement of a royal savior. Ch. 32 is constituted as a prophetic instruction speech concerning the announcement of a royal savior that prepares the reader for the actual announcement in ch. 33. Insofar as ch. 32 introduces ch. 33, the two chapters form a single unit within the larger structure of chs. 28–33. The introductory *hēn* of 32:1 thereby provides an appropriate introduction to this climactic unit in that it disrupts the preceding sequence of *hôy* forms and points to the positive outcome of YHWH's actions in bringing the Assyrian empire against Jerusalem. The *hēn* in 32:1 likewise provides an appropriate contrast with the *hôy* of 33:1 in that it contrasts the blessing for Jerusalem inherent in the announcement of a royal savior with the downfall of the Assyrian empire.

The resulting structure provides a logical progression of ideas and images that portrays the emergence of a royal savior and the downfall of Assyria as the ultimate purpose or result of YHWH's bringing the Assyrians against Jerusalem. Ch. 28 argues that YHWH brings Assyrian hegemony in order to punish Jerusalem and thereby to cleanse the city of its corrupt leadership. Ch. 29 argues that YHWH is the cause of the assault against Ariel and that YHWH's purpose is the ultimate deliverance of Jacob. Ch. 30 argues that YHWH's deliverance will be delayed, but that the ultimate outcome will be the downfall of Assyria. Ch. 31 argues that it is futile to turn to Egypt for help against Assyria because YHWH is the ultimate cause of the Assyrian threat against Jerusalem. Chs. 32–33 provide the climax to the section by arguing that YHWH will raise a royal savior for Jerusalem at the time of Assyria's coming demise.

Genre

The basic genre of chs. 28–33 is that of prophetic INSTRUCTION. Prophetic INSTRUCTION has no specific structure or formal elements but is identified by its overall concern to give guidance to the people on a specific topic. In the present case, it explains that YHWH has brought the Assyrians against Jerusalem in order to purge the city of its corrupt leadership and to replace it with a royal figure who will inaugurate a reign of righteousness and peace. Chs. 28–33

354

therefore rely heavily on the ANNOUNCEMENT OF A ROYAL SAVIOR in chs. 32–33 as well, in that the emergence of this royal savior figure in Jerusalem constitutes the thematic goal of the unit.

Setting

As the discussion of the individual units that constitute this literary block demonstrates, chs. 28–33 are clearly a composite text. Although these chapters contain a great deal of earlier material from the 8th-century prophet Isaiah ben Amoz, as well as from the 7th-century Josianic edition of Isaiah, the present form of chs. 28–33 stems from the final 5th-century redaction. This is due entirely to the fact that ch. 33, the climactic conclusion to these chapters, was composed during the last stage (see the discussion of the Setting of ch. 33 below). Ch. 33 provides a fitting conclusion to chs. 28–33, in that it presents the royal savior and the fall of the oppressor as the ultimate outcome of Jerusalem's oppression by the Assyrians as portrayed in chs. 28–32. But ch. 33 also provides the conclusion to the first half of the book of Isaiah (chs. 1–33). As the discussion of ch. 33 will demonstrate, this chapter forms a counterpart to the scenario of the purging of Jerusalem presented in ch. 1, in that the emergence of a royal savior and the downfall of the oppressor appears as the result of a process of punishment and deliverance for Jerusalem. Likewise, W. A. M. Beuken's study of ch. 33 ("Jesaja 33 als Spiegeltext im Jesajabuch," *ETL* 67 [1991] 5-35) indicates that ch. 33 is a "mirror text" that contains extensive citations of and allusions to the vocabulary and themes of the two halves of book of Isaiah as a whole (i.e., chs. 1–33 and 34–66). Not only do such citations and allusions enable ch. 33 to present the royal savior and the fall of Jerusalem's oppressor as the ultimate outcome of the message of punishment and restoration directed to Jerusalem in chs. 1–33; they also enable the chapter to present these themes in relation to the scenario that concludes the book of Isaiah in chs. 65–66, in which YHWH announces divine rule over the world from Zion in conjunction with the final defeat of the wicked.

The liturgical character of ch. 33 also comes into play in that it aids in defining the liturgical setting of chs. 28–33 as a block. As the discussion of ch. 33 will demonstrate, this chapter combines elements of the complaint, the royal entrance liturgy, and the announcement of a royal savior. These elements appear to relate to the festival of Sukkot or Booths, which is celebrated at the beginning of the rainy season in Israel, at the dedication of the temple, and at the installation of monarchs. Insofar as ch. 33 presents the appearance of the royal savior as the culmination of chs. 28–33, these chapters would then form a literary block within Isaiah that would best be set in relation to the liturgical celebration of Sukkot. With regard to the 5th-century setting of the book of Isaiah, the connection of these chapters (and of the book as a whole) with the celebration of Sukkot is particularly noteworthy in relation to Ezra's return to Jerusalem. According to Nehemiah 8–10, Ezra read the Torah to the people for the first time at the festival of Sukkot, and the Levites apparently aided in interpreting the Torah to the people (Neh 8:7). Such interpretive activity would likely stand behind the interpretive references to other Isaianic texts in ch. 33. Insofar as Ezra saw his work as a fulfillment of prophecy in the book of Isaiah concerning the return of a "remnant" to Jerusalem (Ezra 9:2, 8; cf. Isa 6:13; see K. Koch, "Ezra and the Origins of Judaism," *JSS* 19 [1974] 173-97), it would appear that the scenario of punishment and restoration for Jerusalem presented in chs. 28–33 would support his program. When read in relation to the literary setting of the book of Isaiah as a whole, the references to a royal savior in chs. 28–33 anticipate YHWH's sovereignty over the world at large in the context of Persian rule (cf. 2:2-4; chs. 65–66; for further discussion, see the comments on ch. 33 below).

Prior to the addition of ch. 33, chs. 28–32 apparently formed an earlier literary unit stemming from the 7th-century redaction of Isaiah during the reign of King Josiah. This is evident from the fact that 30:19-33 and 32:1-20 were composed as part of the Josianic redaction of Isaiah (for details, see the discussions of these texts below). Each of these texts plays an important role in defining the overall character and concerns of chs. 28–32. Isa 30:19-33 builds on an original Isaianic oracle in 30:1-18 in order to present a scenario of delayed salvation in which YHWH will act to destroy the Assyrian empire in answer the pleas of the oppressed people. As in the 5th-century edition of chs. 28–33, the Josianic edition of chs. 28–32 presents the emergence of a royal savior as the ultimate outcome of the process of punishment and oppression that Jerusalem has undergone. In the context of the Josianic edition of Isaiah, these chapters would have been read in relation to the downfall of the Assyrian empire and the reign of King Josiah. It would appear that these chapters formed the final major subunit of the Josianic edition of Isaiah prior to the Hezekiah narrative in chs. 36–37. Whereas chs. 5–12 discuss the downfall of northern Israel and chs. 13–27 discuss the punishment of the nations, chs. 28–32 present Jerusalem's oppression by Assyria in relation to YHWH's plan to purge the city of corrupt leadership and to bring about the righteous reign of the new royal savior. In this matter, the Josianic edition of Isaiah presents the reign of King Josiah as the ultimate fulfillment of Isaiah's prophecies.

Finally, chs. 28–31 appear to have formed a distinct literary block prior to the Josianic edition of the book of Isaiah. The common *hôy* form and instructional character of 28:1-29; 29:1-24; 30:1-18; and 31:1-9 definitely suggest such a possibility, especially since ch. 31 is characterized as a parenetic text. In this instance, ch. 31 could well have formed the climax to an Isaianic series that attempted to dissuade the people, or specifically King Hezekiah, from a policy of alliance with the Egyptian empire in the years prior to the revolt against Sennacherib in 705-701. Ch. 28 makes quite clear that Judah's case is no different than northern Israel's, in that Judah is destined to suffer punishment from YHWH. But the allegory of the farmer in 28:23-29 also makes clear that such punishment is temporary and is designed to purge the people of evil in order that the country can be set right again. Ch. 29 makes clear that the assault against Ariel/Zion is brought about *by YHWH,* and that the purpose of the assault is to bring the people back to YHWH. Isa 30:1-18 expresses YHWH's dissatisfaction with the Judean embassy to Egypt. It maintains that the embassy represents a futile act that will delay deliverance in that it recognizes neither YHWH as the cause of Judah's problems nor YHWH's conditions for the deliverance of the people. Whereas chs. 28–30 are instructional in character, in that they are designed to teach the people that YHWH stands behind Judah's punishment and represents the only means to achieve the country's deliverance, ch. 31 is parenetic in that it attempts to persuade the people to abandon attempts to ally with Egypt and return to YHWH as the means to achieve the deliverance of Judah. Essentially, ch. 31 argues that a return to YHWH and a rejection of reliance on Egypt and its pagan gods will result in the downfall of the Assyrian empire.

Intention

The intention of chs. 28–33 must be determined in relation to the historical and literary setting of each of the compositional stages through which this unit has passed. In every case, the generic character of the unit and the sequence of its subunits also play roles in determining the overall intention of the text.

In the case of the 5th-century edition of chs. 28–33, it is clear that this textual block presents an anticipated royal savior and the downfall of an oppressive tyrant as the ultimate outcome of its prophecies concerning the oppression of Jerusalem by the Assyrian empire. Throughout these chapters, it is clearly YHWH who has brought about the oppressor in the first place in order to remove the corrupt leadership of the country that has turned Judah away from YHWH in order to pursue an alliance with Egypt. The instructional character of these chapters plays a role by arguing consistently that YHWH is the cause of the Assyrian oppression in the first place; it is therefore futile to turn to the Egyptians for aid because, as mortals, they are powerless to do anything to counter YHWH's plans. A return to YHWH will require acknowledgment of YHWH's sovereignty over the city of Jerusalem and will result in its deliverance. At this point, the tyrant will be overthrown and the royal savior will emerge.

It is noteworthy that although chs. 28–32 consistently presuppose that the Assyrian empire is the major enemy that YHWH has brought to punish Jerusalem, ch. 33 does not identify the oppressor or the monarch. This lack of identification reflects the hermeneutical perspective of the final redaction of the book of Isaiah in that it understands the prophet's statements concerning the Assyrian period in relation to the circumstances of the 5th century. Although chs. 28–32 presuppose that Assyria is the major enemy of Judah that will be overthrown when the city is delivered, this obviously cannot apply to a 5th-century setting in which Assyria has disappeared and Persia exercises hegemony over Judah and Jerusalem. Likewise, the 6th-century edition would see Babylon as the major enemy. In such a context, the anonymity of the oppressor in ch. 33 aids in conditioning the portrayal of Assyria throughout the first part of the book; although Isaiah spoke of Assyria as the enemy of Judah and Jerusalem, the prophet's statements apply to later enemies as well, including Babylon in the 6th century and Persia in the 5th. The same applies to the royal savior announced in chs. 32 and 33. Whereas ch. 32 presupposes Josiah as the royal savior, the 6th-century edition of Isaiah presupposes that YHWH fills this role through the agency of Cyrus (cf. 2:2-4; 44:28; 45:1), and the 5th-century edition looks to YHWH alone as the monarch or royal savior (cf. 66:1-2). In this instance, once the oppressor falls and the evil ones are removed from the earth, YHWH's reign will be established (cf. chs. 65–66). The sequence of instructional materials in chs. 28–33 builds toward this conclusion by presenting the downfall of the tyrant and the rise of the royal savior as the logical goal of YHWH's actions to punish Jerusalem with the Assyrians and thereby to purge its corrupt leadership.

As already noted, the Josianic edition of chs. 28–32 appears to have been composed to serve as the conclusion of the 7th-century edition of the book of Isaiah. Again, materials relating to the announcement of a royal savior in ch. 32 appear to form the climax of an instructional sequence that is designed to show that YHWH brought about an oppressor in order to purge Jerusalem of its corrupt leadership. In this instance, the portrayal of Assyria as the major oppressor of Jerusalem and Judah still holds in that the downfall of Assyria could be portrayed as a contemporary event. Thus Isaiah's statements concerning YHWH's plans to purge the city would have been understood in relation to the removal of pro-Assyrian officials and their replacement by supporters of Josiah and his program of national independence from Assyria. The warnings against reliance on Egypt would be particularly pertinent. Apart from Assyria, Egypt formed the only major threat to Judean independence in this period in that Pharaoh Psamtek I (Psammetichus I) emerged as Assyria's primary ally during the latter part of his reign. Again, the reign of King Josiah of Judah is portrayed as the fulfillment of the prophecies of Isaiah ben Amoz.

Finally, the Isaianic edition of chs. 28–31 appears to have been formulated to influence Judean foreign policy toward Egypt in the late 8th century. These chapters make a progressive argument that it is YHWH who brought about the Assyrian oppressors against Jerusalem and that it is therefore useless to turn to the Egyptians for aid. In this case, the goal of the unit is to persuade the audience, perhaps King Hezekiah and his advisors, that reliance on YHWH alone will achieve the desired result of relief from Assyria. This is expressed through the climactic subunit in ch. 31, which is formulated as a parenetic text designed to demonstrate YHWH's role in bringing about the threat against Jerusalem and the need to return to YHWH in order to reverse that threat. Ch. 31 therefore demands that its audience desist from sending embassies to Egypt and relying on foreign gods; the only real deliverance of Jerusalem will come from YHWH.

Bibliography

J. C. Exum, "Isaiah 28–32: A Literary Approach," in *SBL 1979 Seminar Papers,* vol. 2 (ed. P. J. Achtemeier; Missoula: Scholars Press, 1979) 123-51; W. H. Irwin, *Isaiah 28–33: Translation with Philological Notes* (BO 30; Rome: Biblical Institute Press, 1977); M. Löhr, "Jesajas-Studien 3. Schlusswort: Zur Komposition der Kapp. 28–31," *ZAW* 37 (1917-18) 73-76.

PROPHETIC INSTRUCTION CONCERNING YHWH'S PURPOSE IN BRINGING ASSYRIAN HEGEMONY, 28:1-29

Structure

The boundaries of 28:1-29 are demarcated by the introductory *hôy* in v. 1 and by the corresponding *hôy* in 29:1, which introduces the next unit. Although the passage is frequently viewed as a composite unit (e.g., Wildberger, *Jesaja,* 1041-96; Clements, *Isaiah 1–39,* 223-34), it is tied together by its general concern with the approach of Assyria, described metaphorically in terms of destructive hail and water (vv. 2, 16) or as an "overflowing scourge" (vv. 15, 18), and by its focus on the incompetence of Ephraimite and Judean leaders. Likewise, various formal features tie the subunits of this passage together, including the *bayyôm hahû'* formula in vv. 5-6 together with their lexical references to vv. 1-4, the *wĕgam 'ēlleh* in vv. 7-13, and the *lākēn* in vv. 14-22. Although the farmer's allegory in vv. 23-29 is frequently regarded as independent, its introductory call to instruction corresponds to that of v. 14a, and its summary-appraisal form in v. 29 corresponds to the summary in v. 22b, thereby tying the allegory formally to vv. 14-22. Vv. 23-29 therefore serve as the climax for the entire unit, and point to the purpose of YHWH's actions outlined in vv. 1-22.

Isaiah 28:1-29 contains two basic structural units: 28:1-4 constitutes a woe speech to the Ephraimite leaders concerning the Assyrian invader, and 28:5-29 constitutes an instruction speech concerning YHWH's purpose in bringing the Assyrians. The key to this structure lies in the nature of the conjunctions that bind together the various subunits of 28:1-29 and in the position and function of the instruction in vv. 23-29. Although vv. 5-6 are frequently associated with vv. 1-4 because of their correspondences in vocabulary and imagery, the introductory *bayyôm hahû'* formula in v. 5 provides no syntactical connection to vv. 1-4. Rather, syntactical connections are established between vv. 5-6 and 7-13 by the introductory *wĕgam* in v. 7 and between vv. 7-13 and vv. 14-22 by the introductory *lākēn* in v. 14. As noted above, vv. 23-29 and vv. 14-22 lack a syntactical connection, but they are linked by the correspondence between their introductory formulas and by their concluding summary-appraisal forms. In the present context, 28:5-6 therefore introduces the following material and relates it to the preceding woe speech. As such, it portrays the means by which YHWH will become the crown or ruler of the proud drunkards of Ephraim. Thus vv. 5-29 portray the means by which the woe speech in vv. 1-4 will be realized. Vv. 23-29 then define the goal of the entire passage, insofar as they demonstrate that divine intent and instruction stand behind the actions of the farmer; that is, the removal of Ephraimite and Judean leaders together with the emergence of foreign hegemony constitutes YHWH's purpose. Insofar as YHWH is described as one who increases deliverance in v. 29, Assyrian hegemony will not constitute a crushing blow just as cummin and bread are not thoroughly crushed (vv. 23-29). Instead, a positive outcome can be expected in accordance with YHWH's plans.

The woe speech against the Ephraimite leaders in 28:1-4 contains two basic parts. The woe statement in v. 1 includes both the woe statement proper in v. 1a and the relative clause in v. 1b that qualifies "the proud crown of the drunkards of Ephraim," etc., in v. 1a by stating its location in a fertile valley, smitten with wine. Vv. 2-4 lack a syntactical connection to v. 1 but provide the basis for the woe by describing the approach of the Assyrian invader and its consequences for the Ephraimite leadership. V. 2 metaphorically portrays the invader in terms of a destructive storm and overflowing waters. Vv. 3-4 specify the consequences for Ephraim: it will be trampled (v. 3) and devoured like the first blossoming fruit at the beginning of the summer harvest season (v. 4).

Verses 5-29 constitute an instruction speech concerning YHWH's purpose in bringing the Assyrian invader. That purpose is to remove the leadership of Ephraim and Judah. Thematic factors and the syntactical links between vv. 5-6, 7-13, and 14-22 on the one hand, and the formal associations between vv. 14-22 and 23-29 on the other, indicate that there are two basic sections to this subunit. Vv. 5-22 constitute a prophetic announcement concerning the removal of Ephraim's and Judah's leadership. This section includes an announcement that YHWH will assume leadership over the remnant of the people (vv. 5-6), a judgment speech against Ephraim (vv. 5-13), and a judgment speech against Judah (vv. 14-22). Vv. 23-29 constitute an instruction concerning the duration of the punishment and define the didactic character of the whole.

The prophetic announcement concerning the removal of leadership in vv. 5-22 begins with an announcement that YHWH will assume leadership in vv. 5-6. This announcement sets the tone for the entire passage by stating that YHWH's leadership will be the result of the punishments announced throughout the subsequent verses. It consists of three brief statements that define YHWH's new role: YHWH will become the crown of the remnant of the people (v. 5), YHWH will become the spirit of justice (v. 6a), and YHWH will become the strength of the defenders (v. 6b).

The second major part of vv. 5-22 is the prophetic judgment speech against the leaders of Ephraim in vv. 7-13 that delineates the incompetence of the Ephraimite leaders and the consequences of that incompetence. These verses are linked syntactically to vv. 5-6 by the conjunctive *wĕgam 'ēlleh* ("and even/also these") in v. 7a. The indictment appears in vv. 7-8 portraying the leaders of the people, including the priests and prophets, as incompetent and drunkards. The portrayal of the drunken and incompetent leaders appears in v. 7, which includes a general depiction of the priests and prophets staggering around drunk in v. 7a and a specific depiction of the drunken leaders rendering incompetent judgments in v. 7b. V. 8, introduced by a causative *kî* ("because"), provides the basis for the conclusion that the leaders are drunk by pointing to their vomit and filth, intended apparently as both a literal and a metaphorical description of the chaos caused by these leaders.

The consequences of such action are delineated in vv. 9-13, beginning with the rhetorical question in v. 9 that highlights the incompetence of the leadership by stating that only recently weaned babies are available to guide the people. V. 10 states the first consequence by pointing to the immature gibberish of the country's leaders who cannot articulate a coherent policy. Vv. 11-13 build on this description to portray the second consequence in the form of a foreign conqueror who speaks gibberish, i.e., a foreign tongue, to the people. These verses thereby function as a prophetic announcement of punishment against the people. Vv. 11-12 include an announcement of YHWH's address to the people in a foreign tongue. Vv. 11-12a contain the announcement proper, including the basic statement that YHWH will speak in a foreign tongue (v. 11) and the announcement of the content of YHWH's speech, namely, that this is his (YHWH's and the conqueror's) resting place (v. 12a). V. 12b reports the people's reaction: they were unwilling to listen. V. 13 then provides a parallel to vv. 11-12 by announcing that YHWH's word to the people will be gibberish. V. 13a contains the announcement proper, including the word report formula in v. 13aα and the content itself in v. 13aα. V. 13b defines the purpose for YHWH's gibberish by stating that it will result in the judgment and capture of the people.

The third major part of vv. 5-22 is the prophetic judgment speech against the Judean leaders in Jerusalem in vv. 14-22. It is tied to the larger context of vv. 5-22 by the introductory *lākēn,* "therefore," which spells out the implications of Israel's experience for Judah. The subunit begins with an indictment against the Judean leaders in vv. 14-15, which includes a formal call to attention in v. 14 and the basis for the call in v. 15, introduced by a causative *kî*. The basis is that the leaders have made a covenant with "death" that they believe will protect them.

The announcement of punishment, introduced by *lākēn,* follows in vv. 16-22. Vv. 16-20 constitute a messenger speech concerning YHWH's removal of the covenant with "death." Following the messenger formula in v. 16aα, the speech proper in vv. 16aβ-20 is constituted by a *wāw*-consecutive syntactical formation that includes a series of statements concerning YHWH's actions leading to the removal of the covenant with "death." YHWH will establish a secure foundation stone (v. 16aβ-b); YHWH will establish justice (v. 17a); hail and water will remove the false refuge (v. 17b); and the covenant with "death" will end (v. 18a). Vv. 18b-20 are linked appositionally to the previous statements and constitute YHWH's summation of the previous four assertions; they thereby constitute the fifth element in the series. The summation includes two parts directed to a 2nd-person masculine plural audience, presumably the leadership of Judah; v. 18b states that the scourge will pass through or trample "you," and vv. 19-20 state that the scourge will take "you." The latter statement contains three parts: a basic statement in v. 19aα; a qualification in v. 19aβ-b that the scourge will do so repeatedly, causing terror among the people; and a qualification in v. 20 that there will be no place to hide.

The prophet's summation of YHWH's speech appears in vv. 21-22, as indicated by the 3rd-person references to YHWH and the continued references to a 2nd-person masculine plural audience. The prophet's summation includes his statement in v. 21 that YHWH's actions will be analogous to those at Mt. Perazim and the Gibeon Valley, but that they will nonetheless be strange or alien. V. 22 contains his warning not to scoff, which is formulated in 2nd-person masculine plural imperative language and connected to v. 21 by conjunctive *wĕʿattâ*, "and now." The warning proper appears in v. 22a, and the basis for the warning, i.e., the destruction decree by YHWH, appears in v. 22b.

The instruction concerning the duration of the punishment in vv. 23-29 is formulated as an allegory that depicts the actions of a farmer tending his land and crops. By employing such imagery, the instruction attempts to demonstrate that there will be a positive outcome to YHWH's actions, just as the farmer's plowing of land and threshing of grain is of limited duration and designed to produce a positive outcome. The passage contains three major parts. The first is the call to instruction, formulated with 2nd-person masculine plural imperative verbal forms in v. 23. The second is the instruction proper in vv. 24-28. The instruction is introduced by the rhetorical question concerning the farmer's plowing in v. 24. By indicating that the farmer does not plow all day, but only enough to open sufficient ground for his seed, the question asserts that such an act of destruction is of limited duration and serves a constructive purpose. Vv. 25-26, linked by conjunctive *wāw*s, delineate the actions of the farmer in order to point out that in everything he is guided by YHWH. He smooths the land (v. 25aα); he scatters or plants cummin (v. 25aβ); he puts in wheat and barley in order (v. 25bα); he plants spelt on the edges of his land (v. 25bβ); and God guides him in all respects (v. 26). Vv. 27-28 then focus on the proper processing of cummin and bread in order to demonstrate that neither is completely crushed when processed into usable forms. V. 27 states that cummin is not threshed, but beaten with a stick. V. 28 states that bread is crushed, but not thoroughly. Finally, the third major part is v. 29, which constitutes a summary-appraisal form as indicated by the typical *gam-zōʾt,* "also this," formulation. The summary-appraisal emphasizes that all this comes from YHWH and that YHWH brings about salvation. This statement thereby associates the farmer's actions with those of YHWH described in vv. 5-22, and indicates that YHWH's acts of punishment are intended to bring about the restoration of glory to the remnant of the people (v. 5).

Genre

The overarching genre of ch. 28 is the prophetic INSTRUCTION, which is designed to give guidance to its audience. This generic identification is evident from the basic structure of the passage, which begins with a condemnation of the leaders of northern Israel and then proceeds to spell out the ramifications of that condemnation for Judah. In addition, various generic features of the chapter, including the RHETORICAL QUESTIONS in vv. 9, 24, and 25, the CALL TO INSTRUCTION in v. 23 (cf. v. 14), the ALLEGORY of the farmer in vv. 23-29, and the SUMMARY-

APPRAISAL in v. 29, indicate the instructional character of the passage. In keeping with wisdom instruction in general, the prophetic INSTRUCTION in ch. 28 is based on empirical observation of the natural world at large, including the characteristics of rain and storm (vv. 2, 17), the growth of new blossoms and fruit (vv. 1, 4), and the harvest of grain (vv. 23-29). Observation of the social world also plays a role insofar as the speech refers to the drunkenness of the leaders (vv. 1, 7-8), the instruction of people (v. 9), and polemics against the scoffing rejection of instruction (vv. 11-12, 14).

The most important observations, however, pertain to the political realm. The passage presupposes the threat posed by a powerful figure who speaks a foreign tongue (vv. 2, 11-12), presumably the Assyrian monarch, the measures taken to defend against such a threat, including building operations (v. 16) and political alliances (vv. 15, 18), and the implications of the experience of the northern kingdom of Israel for Judah (cf. vv. 1-14 and vv. 14-22). Based on all these observations, the INSTRUCTION draws its conclusions: YHWH is bringing a foreign power to remove the incompetent leadership of the people, but the punishment will be temporary. The ultimate outcome will be positive in that it will lead to the establishment of YHWH's glory and justice over the people.

The prophetic INSTRUCTION in ch. 28 also contains a number of subordinate generic elements that enable it to achieve its aims. The first is the WOE ORACLE in vv. 1-4. This form derives from wisdom circles, which used it to condemn actions that are contrary to the values propagated in wisdom instruction. It is typically used in prophetic contexts to condemn behavior considered by the prophets to be contrary to YHWH's wishes. Here it follows the typical prophetic form, with a woe statement including the exclamation *hôy*, "woe!" followed by participles and noun forms that characterize the leaders of northern Israel as incompetent drunks. A variety of forms can follow the woe statement in prophetic contexts. In this case, vv. 2-4 provide the basis for the woe by describing metaphorically the approach of a powerful enemy, clearly the Assyrian monarch, and the disastrous consequences for Israel. This description sets the stage for the INSTRUCTION that follows in vv. 5-29.

The INSTRUCTION itself comprises a variety of generic elements. It begins with a simple prophetic announcement in vv. 5-6, introduced by a future-oriented *bayyôm hahû'* ("in that day") formula, which projects the restoration of YHWH's glory and justice over the remnant of the people. The core of the INSTRUCTION, however, appears in the two PROPHETIC JUDGMENT SPEECHES in vv. 7-13 and vv. 14-22, and in the ALLEGORY concerning the farmer in vv. 23-29.

The first PROPHETIC JUDGMENT SPEECH appears in vv. 7-13. It is directed against the leaders of the people, here identified only as the prophets and the priests. The context suggests that they are from the northern kingdom of Israel (cf. vv. 1-4), but it will become clear from the subsequent material in vv. 14-22 that the Judean leadership is also included. The speech follows the typical judgment pattern. Vv. 7-8 constitute an indictment against the leaders by portraying them as drunken incompetents who are unable to provide effective leadership for the people. Vv. 9-13 declare that the leaders' incompetence will lead ultimately to the capture and thus the judgment of the people. The RHE-TORICAL QUESTION in v. 9 establishes the lack of effective leadership; v. 10 supports this assertion by describing the leaders' gibberish as the first consequence. Vv. 11-13 then get to the point by describing the second major consequence: the people will be captured and judged when a conqueror who speaks the gibberish of a foreign tongue will take control of the area. The PROPHETIC WORD FORMULA in v. 13aα identifies this as a word of YHWH.

The PROPHETIC JUDGMENT SPEECH against the Judean leaders in vv. 14-22 likewise employs various generic elements to make its point. It is directed against the leaders in Jerusalem who are named in the indictment found in vv. 14-15. The indictment itself is formulated along the general lines of a CALL TO AT-TENTION. It employs only one imperative, šiměʿû, "hear!" but it fulfills the basic function, which is to direct the attention of the audience to the speech that follows. The basis for the call in v. 15 contains the specific indictment that the leaders have concluded a covenant with "death," i.e., they have allied themselves with a foreign power. The announcement of punishment in vv. 16-22 is centered around a MESSENGER SPEECH in vv. 16-20. The MESSENGER FORMULA appears in v. 16aα, and the speech by YHWH appears in vv. 16aβ-20. It conveys YHWH's message that the covenant with "death" will be annulled and that the people will be punished when the foreign conqueror or "scourge" passes through the people, causing terror. The prophet's warning to the people not to scoff concludes the announcement of punishment and contributes to the overall instructional character of the speech.

Finally, the ALLEGORY of the farmer in vv. 23-29 constitutes the climax of the INSTRUCTION SPEECH in vv. 5-29. It is formulated as an ALLEGORY designed to correlate its motifs with the circumstances in the life of the people. Here the activities of the farmer are correlated with the approaching Assyrian monarch who acts on behalf of YHWH. The farmer's activities are essentially destructive, but the destruction is temporary and leads to a positive result. He plows, harrows, and overturns the earth, but it is of limited duration. Because his purpose is to provide food, he plants seeds and orders his land so that cummin and the various grains will grow. Likewise, when he harvests his crops, his actions are essentially destructive, but again they are not thoroughly destructive in that they lead to a positive result. Cummin is not completely threshed with a threshing sledge, but beaten with a stick until it is ready. Grain is not thoroughly crushed, but is only crushed enough to prepare it as food. In this manner, the actions of the farmer are compared to those of the coming invader. There will be destruction and hardship, but the result will be the reestablishment of YHWH's glory and justice once the incompetent leadership is removed. The SUMMARY-APPRAISAL in v. 29, identified by its characteristic gam-zōʾt, "also this," and its references to YHWH's actions make clear that this is an act of YHWH. The positive qualities attributed to YHWH also make clear that there will be a positive outcome to the punishment. The didactic character of the SUMMARY-APPRAISAL form establishes its background in wisdom instruction.

Setting

Isaiah 28 stands at the beginning of a major block of material in chs. 28–33 that focuses on the punishment and cleansing of the city of Jerusalem. Ch. 28 itself presents the punishment of Jerusalem as an analogy to that of the northern kingdom of Israel; but it also makes the point that this punishment is temporary in that it is intended to remove the incompetent leadership of Jerusalem so that the city can be set back on its proper course.

With respect to this literary setting and theme, ch. 28 may be placed in relation to the various editions of the book of Isaiah. In the final 5th-century form of the book as a whole, ch. 28 presupposes the Babylonian exile as the period of Jerusalem's punishment and cleansing prior to its projected restoration as the center of Jewish life. It functions in a similar manner in relation to the 6th-century edition of the book in that it again presupposes the Babylonian exile as the period of Jerusalem's cleansing, but it looks to the reconstruction of the temple in the late 6th century as the time of the city's restoration. In the Josianic edition of the book, it presupposes the period of Assyrian hegemony over Judah during the 7th century as the period of Jerusalem's punishment so that King Josiah's reign will mark the beginning of a new era of just rule. Finally, ch. 28 presupposes the circumstances of the late 8th century in that it looks to the period of the Assyrian invasions as the time of punishment, and anticipates a better future once the Assyrian incursions have run their course.

A number of factors indicate that the present form of ch. 28 stems from the reign of King Hezekiah during the late 8th century while he was making preparations to confront the Assyrian empire. First, the passage presupposes the defeat of the northern kingdom of Israel in 722-721. As the examination of the structure of ch. 28 demonstrates, the condemnation of the leaders of Ephraim in vv. 1-13 provides a paradigm for the fate that is announced for the leadership of Jerusalem in vv. 14-22. That is, the present form of the passage is not directed to announce the fall of the northern kingdom, but to warn the southern kingdom of potential disaster based on the example of the north. Although this in and of itself does not demonstrate that the collapse of the northern kingdom is specifically presupposed, the following factors demonstrate a post-722/721 setting.

Second, the references to the covenant with "death" or Sheol in vv. 15 and 18 relate to Hezekiah's attempts to form an alliance with other powers in order to revolt against the Assyrians. His attempts to ally with Merodach-baladan of Babylon are documented in ch. 39 and 2 Kgs 20:12-19. Likewise, Isaiah's denunciations of the embassies to Egypt in Isaiah 30–31 reflect Hezekiah's attempts to gain Egyptian support. Although attempts have been made to argue that the reference to death refers specifically to the Egyptians (e.g., Clements, *Isaiah 1–39,* 230), the association of death with the institution of the *marzēaḥ* in Canaanite culture (see below) suggests that death functions here as a more general indication of the futility of entering into political alliances against the Assyrians (cf. Kaiser, *Isaiah 13–39,* 250-52).

Third, the setting of a foundation stone in Zion mentioned in v. 16 relates not only to the Davidic tradition, with its promises of eternal security for Zion guaranteed by YHWH, but also to Hezekiah's attempts to fortify the city in preparation for a siege by the Assyrians (cf. Roberts, "YHWH's Foundation"). According to 2 Chr 32:5-6, Hezekiah expanded and strengthened the fortifications of Jerusalem prior to the Assyrian invasion of 701. His building activity has been confirmed by archeological excavations that demonstrate not only the strengthening of the walls of the city during this period but their expansion to enclose the western hill beyond the Tyropoeon Valley as well (for a review of the archeological evidence concerning the fortifications of Jerusalem during the late 8th century, see A. Mazar, *Archaeology of the Land of the Bible* [New York: Doubleday, 1990] 417-24; cf. the papers on the archeology of Jerusalem published in *Biblical Archaeology Today: Proceedings of the International Congress on Biblical Archaeology, Jerusalem, April 1984* [ed. J. Amitai; Jerusalem: Israel Exploration Society, 1985] 435-85). Likewise, the use of water imagery in Isaiah 28, including the portrayal of the invader in terms of a destructive storm and overflowing waters (vv. 2, 15, 17, 18), relates to Hezekiah's attempts to secure Jerusalem's defenses by building the Siloam tunnel as a means to conserve and to protect the city's water supply (2 Kgs 20:20; 2 Chr 32:2-4; Isaiah 22; cf. Mazar, *Archaeology*, 483-85; R. Amiran, "The Water Supply of Israelite Jerusalem," in *Jerusalem Revealed: Archaeology in the Holy City, 1968-74* [ed. Y. Yadin; New Haven and London: Yale University Press and the Israel Exploration Society, 1976] 75-78; for the Siloam inscription, see *ANET*, 321). The references to the foreign invader as *ḥāzāq wĕ'ammiṣ*, "mighty and strong," in v. 2 reflect Hezekiah's speech to the people to "be strong and of good courage" *(ḥizqû wĕ'imṣû)* in the face of the projected Assyrian attack (2 Chr 32:7). Finally, the comparison of YHWH's strange deed to those of Mt. Perazim and the Gibeon Valley (v. 21) refer back to David's defeat of the Philistines by which he secured his rule over all Israel from Jerusalem (cf. 2 Sam 5:17-25; for the relation of Mt. Perazim and the Gibeon Valley to 2 Sam 5:17-25, see Wildberger, *Jesaja*, 1079-80). Inasmuch as Hezekiah intended to reassert Davidic rule over Judah and Israel by defeating Assyria, Isaiah employed these references to support his view that such goals would be better achieved by avoiding a confrontation with the Assyrians and waiting for the crisis to pass. By such strange deeds, Davidic rule could then be secured over the region once the Assyrians passed from the scene.

Although the present form of Isaiah 28 stems from the late 8th century, it appears to be a composite text. Vv. 1-13 deal exclusively with the northern kingdom of Israel, whereas Judah enters the picture only in vv. 14-22. Furthermore, vv. 1-13 are relatively self-contained, insofar as they constitute a condemnation of the leadership of the northern kingdom of Israel based on the prophetic judgment speech pattern and show no dependence on the following material to convey their meaning. But vv. 14-22 are linked to vv. 1-13 by a number of linguistic and thematic connections. The foreign invader is portrayed as an "overflowing scourge" *(šôṭ šôṭēp)* in vv. 15 and 18, which draws on the portrayal of the enemy "like a storm of mighty, overflowing waters" *(kĕzerem mayim kabbîrîm šōṭĕpîm)* in v. 2. The reference to YHWH's placing "justice as the line" *(mišpāṭ lĕqāw)* in v. 17 draws on the references to YHWH acting as "a spirit of justice to him who sits in judgment" *(ûlĕrûaḥ mišpāṭ layyôšēb 'al-ham-mišpaṭ)* in v. 6, as well as on the childish prattle of the incompetent Ephraimite leaders in v. 10 and the incomprehensible gibberish of the foreign speech of the conqueror in v. 13 (*qaw lāqāw qaw lāqāw,* "line upon line, line upon line"). The references to YHWH's stripping away the sanctuary of lies with hail and flood in v. 17 (*wĕyāʿâ bārād maḥsēh kāzāb wĕsēter mayim yišṭōpû,* "and hail will sweep away the refuge of lies and waters will overwhelm the shelter") draws on similar language in v. 2 (*kĕzerem bārād śaʿar qāṭeb kĕzerem mayim kabbîrîm šōṭĕpîm,* "like a storm of hail, a destroying tempest, like a storm of mighty overflowing waters"). The reference to "understanding the message" of terror in v. 19 *(hābîn šĕmûʿâ)* draws on the language of the rhetorical question in v. 9 (*wĕʾet-mî yābîn šĕmûʿâ,* "and to whom will he explain the message?"). Likewise, the references to the "covenant with death" or the "contract with Sheol" mentioned in vv. 15 and 18 relate to the portrayal of the drunken leaders of Ephraim in vv. 7-8, insofar as these verses portray the drinking associated with the *marzēaḥ* institution known in ancient Canaan and Israel.

The *marzēaḥ,* mentioned in various texts from Ugarit, is portrayed as an extended feast of the gods in which El becomes so drunk that he falls into his own excrement. The term also appears in Amos 6:7 and Jer 16:5, where it apparently refers to a banquet or drinking house. Many scholars associate the drinking of the *marzēaḥ* with funerary practices in ancient Canaan, although this does not appear to be the only occasion for the drinking bouts and orgies associated with the *marzēaḥ.* Such drinking can also be associated with the conclusion of a contract, for example. In the present instance, Isaiah associates the funerary character of the *marzēaḥ* with its use by northern Israel to conclude a covenant with an ally (perhaps Egypt?) to oppose the Assyrians (for a full review of discussion associated with the *marzēaḥ,* see T. J. Lewis, *Cults of the Dead in Ancient Israel and Ugarit* [HSM 39; Atlanta: Scholars Press, 1989] 80-94; cf. Jackson). In each of these instances, the references in vv. 14-22 depend on vv. 1-13 to establish their meaning, but vv. 1-13 do not rely on vv. 14-22.

These considerations indicate that vv. 14-22 were composed later than vv. 1-13 in order to apply the experience of the northern kingdom of Israel to a later situation pertaining to the southern kingdom of Judah. As the above discussion indicates, the later situation is that of Hezekiah's preparations for a confrontation with Assyria some time between the fall of northern Israel in 722/721 and Sennacherib's invasion in 701. For their part, vv. 1-13 appear to have been directed against the northern kingdom itself. The setting for such a condemnation obviously predates the fall of Samaria. The portrayal of Israel's leaders as drunken incompetents has appeared before in the oracles of Isaiah (5:11-17; cf. 9:13-17 [*RSV* 14-18]) in conjunction with the prophet's condemnation of Israel for its role in the Syro-Ephraimite War. Although specific historical referents are lacking, the portrayal of Israel is appropriate for the entire period of 735-722/721, during which time Israel concluded agreements with other countries to oppose the Assyrians, and suffered invasion as a result.

Likewise, the allegory of the farmer in vv. 23-29 appears to have little explicit relation to vv. 1-13. Although both passages take up agriculture, vv. 23-29 describe the farmer's labors pertaining to cummin and grain, whereas vv. 1-13 refer to grapes and wine (vv. 1, 4 and 7). The summary-appraisal in v. 29 appears to presuppose the summary in v. 22, but this only indicates an attempt to associate vv. 23-29 with vv. 14-22 on the basis of a formal similarity. Apart from the summary-appraisal in v. 29, vv. 23-29 do not appear to have been composed in direct reference to vv. 1-13 or to vv. 14-22. Because Isaiah is known for his extensive use of wisdom traditions and forms of discourse, one need not doubt that he composed these verses (cf. Whedbee, 51-68). Although the allegory lacks specific indications of the date and setting of its composition, it clearly functions in the present literary setting as the means to demonstrate that the punishment of Judah will be of relatively short duration and that the final result will be YHWH's rule of the remnant of the people. The lack of specific relation to the preceding materials indicates that Isaiah may well have composed this instruction prior to placing the various elements of ch. 28 into their present form.

Intention

The intention of ch. 28 is determined by a variety of factors, including its structure, its generic character as an instruction speech, and its setting in relation to Hezekiah's preparations for a confrontation with the Assyrian empire. Accordingly, ch. 28 represents Isaiah's attempt to persuade Hezekiah to abandon attempts to resist the Assyrians. Like that of northern Israel, a Judean confrontation with the Assyrians could only lead to disaster. Instead, Isaiah counsels that a passive policy will best serve the interests of Jerusalem and the Davidic dynasty. Once the Assyrians pass from the scene, the house of David will be able to assert its rule over all Israel, here described as "the remnant of his [i.e., YHWH's] people" in v. 5.

The woe oracle against the "proud crown of the drunkards of Ephraim" in vv. 1-4 sets the basic themes of the passage by calling attention to the incompetent leadership of the northern kingdom that ultimately led to the destruction of the country. Not only does the oracle sound a note of warning against the Ephraimite leadership, but it also calls to mind the invasion of the country by a mighty and strong figure, i.e., the Assyrian monarch in v. 2, who is portrayed as a destructive storm. Gese's study of the water imagery in this passage and the "overwhelming scourge" of vv. 15 and 18 establishes that it draws upon the imagery applied to the storm god Baal or Hadad throughout Canaan and Aram. This imagery is entirely appropriate since the Assyrian army would have approached Israel from Aram and because Assur, the chief deity of Assyria, appears to have been a storm deity like Baal and Hadad.

The basic concern of the passage becomes clear in vv. 5-6. These verses state the intention of the prophet to project the establishment of YHWH's rule of justice over the people as the ultimate goal of the historical process delineated in this chapter. As such, vv. 5-6 introduce the balance of the unit that describes the failure of the northern Israelite leadership to project the failure of the current attempt by Hezekiah of Judah to resist the Assyrians. Vv. 7-13 present the northern Israelite leaders as incompetent drunks who stagger and reel in the midst of their own vomit. Such a portrayal seems to presuppose the *marzēaḥ* banquet with its excessive drinking as a means to conclude a contract with another party. As a result of such activities, the leaders of northern Israel are reduced to the helpless and ineffective state of children. The leaders who are responsible for the proper guidance and instruction of the people are thereby able to utter only the meaningless syllables *ṣaw lāṣāw, ṣaw lāṣāw, qaw lāqāw, qaw lāqāw*, like a child just learning to speak. As Halpern (p. 119) notes, these syllables are meaningless, but they do correspond to the first letters of the Hebrew words for "vomit" *(qî')* and "excrement" *(ṣō'â)* in v. 8 (contra van der Toorn, who relates these sounds to bird calls associated with the spirits of the dead and uttered by the drunken participants in a necromancy ceremony). Because of their incompetence, the country will be taken by a foreign conqueror, whose strange language will sound just as incomprehensible as the drunken babbling of the country's incompetent leaders.

The experience of Israel serves as the basis for the prophet's warning to the leadership of Judah in vv. 14-22. With its reference to the foundation stone in v. 16, the passage clearly presupposes Hezekiah's building operations designed to strengthen Jerusalem's defense against Assyrian invasion (cf. Roberts, "YHWH's Foundation," and the discussion of setting above). It also presupposes Hezekiah's attempts to conclude alliances with his neighbors in an effort to confront the Assyrians. This is quite clear in vv. 15 and 18, which refer to the "covenant with death" and the "contract with Sheol." The prophet deliberately borrows from the death imagery often associated with the *marzēaḥ* feasting and drinking alluded to in vv. 7-8 to describe the outcome of such alliances. In contrast, YHWH will set the "measuring line" *(qāw*, a deliberate pun on the babbling of vv. 10 and 13) and "measuring scale" or "plummet" in v. 17 so that YHWH, not Hezekiah and his architects, will establish the true security of the city. The passage states that the invader, here described as the "overwhelming scourge," will take the city, and that the "bed" and the "covering," which play roles in the orgies of the *marzēaḥ*, will be unable to protect the people (vv. 18-20). The references to Mt. Perazim and the Gibeon Valley (v. 21) call to mind David's defeat of the Philistines (2 Sam 5:17-25), which established the rule of the Davidic dynasty from Jerusalem over all Israel, but the references to YHWH's strange act indicate that the city will suffer before YHWH reestablishes Davidic rule over the "remnant of his people." The suffering, analogous with the experience of northern Israel, is emphasized by the reference to a "decree of destruction" *(kālâ wĕneḥĕrāṣâ)* for Judah from YHWH (v. 22), the same term used for the decree of destruction for the remnant of Israel in 10:23.

Finally, the allegory of the farmer in vv. 23-29 serves as the climax of the instruction offered to Judah in ch. 28. It portrays the farmer's activities of destruction, plowing and harrowing the earth, prior to planting the seed that will lead to new growth and the production of food. The allegory makes the point that although the farmer's actions are often destructive, they do not result in the full crushing of the harvest; the grain is crushed only as much as is necessary to make it fit for human consumption. Likewise, the cummin and grain are not completely crushed, but beaten with a stick, in much the same way that Israel was beaten with the stick or scourge of Assyria in 10:5-26. Insofar as the farmer's instruction in farming comes from YHWH, the allegory indicates that YHWH's punishment of Judah will not be thorough; rather, it will only be sufficient to chastise the country and to prepare it for the time when YHWH will reestablish just leadership in the land (vv. 5-6). The concluding summary-appraisal, with its references to YHWH's counsel and deliverance, indicates the positive outcome of YHWH's plans for Judah.

Bibliography

K. T. Aitken, "Hearing and Seeing: Metamorphoses of a Motif in Isaiah 1–39," in *Among the Prophets: Language, Image and Structure in the Prophetic Writings* (ed. P. R. Davies and D. J. A. Clines; JSOTSup 144; Sheffield: JSOT Press, 1993) 12-41; J. Boehmer, "Der Glaube und Jesaja: Zu Jes. 7,9 und 28,16," *ZAW* 41 (1923) 84-93; G. R. Driver, "Hebrew Notes," *ZAW* 52 (1934) 51-56; idem, " 'Another Little Drink' — Isaiah 28:1-22," in *Words and Meanings: Essays Presented to David Winton Thomas* (ed. P. R. Ackroyd and B. Lindars; Cambridge: Cambridge University Press, 1968) 47-67; J. C. Exum, " 'Whom Will He Teach Knowledge?': A Literary Approach to Isaiah 28," in *Art and Meaning: Rhetoric in Biblical Literature* (ed. D. J. A. Clines, D. M. Gunn, and A. J. Hauser; JSOTSup 19; Sheffield: JSOT Press, 1982) 108-39; J. P. Floss, "Biblische Theologie als Sprecherin der 'Gefährlichen Erinnerung' dargestellt an Jes 28,7-12," *BN* 54 (1990) 60-80; J. M. Ford, "The Jewel of Discernment (A Study of Stone Symbolism)," *BZ* 11 (1967) 109-16; K. Fullerton, "The Stone of Foundation," *AJSL* 37 (1920-21) 1-50; H. Gese, "Die Strömmende Geissel des Hadad und Jesaja 28,15 und 18," in *Archäologie und altes Testament: Festschrift für Kurt Galling* (ed. A. Kuschke and E. Kutsch; Tübingen: Mohr, 1970) 127-34; M. Görg, "Die Bildsprache in Jes 28,1," *BN* 3 (1977) 17-23; idem, "Jesaja als 'Kinderlehrer'? Beobachtungen zur Sprache und Semantik in Jes 28,10(13)," *BN* 29 (1985) 12-16; W. W. Hallo, "Isaiah 28:9-13 and the Ugaritic Abecedaries," *JBL* 77 (1958) 324-38; B. Halpern, " 'The Excremental Vision': The Doomed Priests of Doom in Isaiah 28," *HAR* 10 (1986) 109-21; J. F. Healey, "Ancient Agriculture and the Old Testament (with Special Reference to Isaiah xxviii 23-29)," *OTS* 23 (1984) 108-19; J. J. Jackson, "Style in Isaiah 28 and a Drinking Bout of the Gods (RS 24.258)," in *Rhetorical Criticism: Essays in Honor of James Muilenburg* (ed. J. J. Jackson and M. Kessler; PTMS 1; Pittsburgh: Pickwick, 1974) 85-98; Janzen, *Mourning Cry* (→ "Introduction to the Prophetic Literature"), 54-55; K. Jeppesen, "The Cornerstone (Isa. 28:16) in Deutero-Isaianic Rereading of the Message of Isaiah," *ST* 38 (1984) 93-99; L. Koehler, "Zu Jes 28,15a und 18b," *ZAW* 48 (1930) 227-28; idem, "Zwei Fachwörter der Bausprache in Jesaja 28,16," *TZ* 3 (1947) 390-93; J. Lindblom, "Der Eckstein in Jes. 28,16," in *Interpretationes ad Vetus Testamentum pertinentes Sigmundo Mowinckel* (Oslo: Land Ogkirke, 1955) 123-32; M. Löhr, "Zwei Beispiele von Kehrvers in den Prophetenschriften des Alten Testaments," *ZDMG* 61 (1907) 1-6; idem, "Jesaias-Studien III," *ZAW* 37 (1917-18) 59-76; O. Loretz, "Das Propehtenwort über das Ende der Königsstadt Samaria (Jes 28,1-4)," *UF* 9 (1977) 361-63; Melugin, "Conventional" (→ "Introduction to the Book of Isaiah"); H. Möller, "Abwägen zweier Übersetzungen von Jes 28,19b," *ZAW* 96 (1984) 272-74; J. A. Montgomery, "Notes on the Old Testament," *JBL* 31 (1912) 140-46; O. Mury and S. Amsler, "YHWH et la Sagesse du Paysan: Quelques remarques sur Esaïe 28,23-29," *RHPR* 53 (1973) 1-5; D. L. Petersen, "Isaiah 28: A Redaction-Critical Study," in *SBL 1979 Seminar Papers*, vol. 2 (ed. P. J. Achtemeier; Missoula: Scholars Press, 1979) 101-22; G. Pfeifer, "Entwöhnung und Entwöhnungsfest im Alten Testament: Der Schlüssel zu Jesaja 28,7-13?" *ZAW* 84 (1972) 341-47; J. J. M.

Roberts, "A Note on Isaiah 28:12," *HTR* 73 (1980) 49-51; idem, "YHWH's Foundation in Zion (Isa 28:16)," *JBL* 106 (1987) 27-45; Scott, "Literary Structure" (→ "Introduction to the Book of Isaiah"); A. Stewart, "The Covenant with Death in Isaiah 28," *ExpTim* 100 (1989) 375-77; S. C. Thexton, "A Note on Isaiah xxviii 25 and 28," *VT* 2 (1952) 81-83; K. van der Toorn, "Echoes of Judaean Necromancy in Isaiah 28,7-22," *ZAW* 100 (1988) 199-217; A. van Selms, "Isaiah 28,9-13: An Attempt to Give a New Interpretation," *ZAW* 85 (1973) 332-39; V. Tanghe, "Dichtung und Ekel in Jesaja xxviii 7-13," *VT* 43 (1993) 235-60; E. Vogt, "Das Prophetenwort Jes 28,1-4 und das Ende der Königsstadt Samaria," in *Hominaje a Juan Prado: Miscelanea de Estudios Biblicos y Hebraicos* (ed. L. Alvarez Verdes and E. J. Alonso Hernandos; Madrid: Consejo Superior de Investigaciones Cientificas, 1975) 109-30.

PROPHETIC INSTRUCTION CONCERNING YHWH'S PURPOSE IN BRINGING ABOUT ASSAULT AGAINST ARIEL/MT. ZION, 29:1-24

Structure

Like the other major units of chs. 28–33, the beginning of 29:1-24 is demarcated by its introductory *hôy* ("woe!"). The appearance of a *hôy* oracle in 29:15 does not indicate the beginning of a new unit that is structurally independent of 29:1-14; rather, there are a number of indications that 29:15-24 is linked to 29:1-14. Although vv. 1-14 present a scenario of assault against Ariel followed by deliverance (vv. 7-8), vv. 9-14 focus only on YHWH's judgment against the people and the inability of the wise to understand YHWH's actions. The motif of YHWH's deliverance reappears only in vv. 15-24, which portray the transformation of the natural world as a prelude to Jacob's sanctification of YHWH for deliverance from oppression.

In addition, several explicit links between the passages indicate that vv. 1-14 and vv. 15-24 are meant to function together. First, the woe oracle in vv. 15-16 builds upon the theme of the lack of wisdom among the wise in v. 14; likewise, v. 24b resolves the issue by pointing to a time when wisdom will be received in Israel. Second, v. 23 resolves the problem of the people's lack of honor for and fear of YHWH presented in v. 13, insofar as v. 23 emphasizes Jacob's sanctification and fear of YHWH. Note also that the verb used for Jacob's fear of YHWH in v. 23, *ya ʿărîṣû*, "they shall stand in awe" (cf. *ʿărîṣ*, "ruthless," in v. 20), corresponds to the reference to Ariel's attackers as *ʿărîṣîm*, "ruthless," in v. 5. By this means, vv. 15-23 indicate that the people's fears should be focused on YHWH, who delivers them from the "ruthless." Finally, v. 18 resolves the issue of the people's blindness and deafness portrayed in vv. 9-12. Likewise, the "spirit of understanding" *(rûaḥ bînâ)* in v. 24 contrasts with the "spirit of deep sleep" *(rûaḥ tardēmâ)* in v. 10, which portrays the people's blindness and deafness. Furthermore, the "words of the book" heard by the deaf in v. 18 corresponds to the book that cannot be understood by the people in vv. 11-12.

Because vv. 15-24 resolve the fundamental issues of vv. 1-14, the two passages constitute a larger structural unit in 29:1-24. Vv. 1-14 focus on YHWH as the cause of the assault against Ariel. Vv. 15-24 focus on the future realization by the people that YHWH's action actually brings about deliverance. Together, vv. 1-14 and vv. 15-24 make up a prophetic instruction speech concerning YHWH's purpose and role in bringing about the assault against Ariel/Mt. Zion. The *hôy* in 30:1 therefore demarcates the beginning of the next major structural unit in chs. 28–33.

The structure of 29:1-14 reflects the fundamental concern of the passage to identify YHWH as the cause of the assault against Ariel. It begins with a portrayal of the threat against Ariel and concludes with an oracle by YHWH that announces judgment against the people for their failure to understand YHWH. The impact of the passage is heightened by the fact that whereas in the

Zion tradition YHWH is the guarantor of Jerusalem's security, here YHWH proves to be the instigator of the assault.

The structure of vv. 1-14 is determined by a variety of syntactical and thematic features. The key to understanding the structure lies in the imperative plural address forms directed to an unspecified audience in vv. 1b and 9. Each serves as the introduction to a subunit that is held together by a series of *wāw*s and other syntactical connectors. Consequently, there are three major subunits in vv. 1-14: vv. 1a, 1b-8, and 9-14.

Verse 1a constitutes a simple woe statement directed to Ariel, otherwise identified as the altar of the temple in Jerusalem (cf. 2 Sam 23:20; Isa 33:7; Ezek 43:15-16). As the initial statement of vv. 1-14, v. 1a sets the tone of threat against Ariel, on which the subsequent subunits build.

The imperative statement, "add year to year" *(sĕpû šānâ ʿal-šānâ),* introduces the first address to the audience in vv. 1b-8, which focus on the attack against Ariel. The imperative perspective does not appear again throughout the rest of the unit, but vv. 2-8 are linked to the imperfect form *ḥaggîm yinqōpû,* "let the feasts run their round," in v. 1b by the *wāw*-consecutive syntactical structure governing the balance of the passage. Vv. 2-8 thereby constitute a series of *wāw*-consecutive statements that progressively build on the initial command to increase or continue the festival observance in the temple by pointing to the threat posed by the assault against Ariel. The perspective of the speaker and the address forms shift throughout these verses. A 1st-person speaker appears in vv. 2-3, followed by an unspecified or 3rd-person perspective in the following verses. Likewise, vv. 3-5a employ a 2nd-person feminine singular address form, but shift to 3rd-person feminine singular in vv. 6-8. Because there is no clear syntactical division that would separate these perspectives within the larger structure of the unit, and because the speaker refers to YHWH in v. 6, the speaker in the passage must be the prophet throughout. The use of the 1st-person forms in vv. 2-3 and the 2nd-person feminine singular address forms in vv. 3-5a provide a sense of irony; for while the instigator of the assault will eventually be identified as YHWH, at this point the prophet identifies only himself as the speaker.

Following the initial command to continue the festivals, the subsequent statements describe the projected assault against Ariel and the sudden deliverance from that assault. In v. 2, the speaker states his intention to oppress Ariel. In v. 3, he specifies his intentions by describing a siege against her in direct address form. In v. 4a he addresses Ariel directly, stating that she will fall and speak from the ground. In v. 4b he tells her that her voice will be like that of a ghost speaking from the ground. In v. 5a-bα, he tells Ariel that her enemies will be numerous like dust or chaff. Vv. 5bβ-6 drop the direct address form to project a brief and sudden punishment of Ariel by YHWH. In v. 7, he compares the assault against Ariel to a dream. Finally, in v. 8, the prophet employs the similes of a starving or thirsting man dreaming of food and drink in order to assert that the threat against Ariel, here called Mt. Zion, will evaporate quickly.

Like vv. 1b-8, vv. 9-14 begin with imperative plural statements that identify the passage as the second address to the audience. It builds on the previous subunit by focusing on YHWH as the cause of the assault against Ariel, but it also emphasizes the people's inability to comprehend the significance of this fact. The three basic structural elements of this subunit, vv. 9-10, 11-12, and 13-14, are identified by their generic characteristics and held together by *wāw*-consecutive formations at the beginning of v. 11 and v. 13. The command to blindness appears in vv. 9-10, identified by its imperative forms that call on the audience to be astonished and blind. The commands proper appear in v. 9, including commands to be astonished and blind in v. 9a and to stagger and reel in comprehension in v. 9b. The basis for the commands, introduced by a causative *kî*, "because," appears in v. 10, which states that YHWH has poured deep sleep on "you" (v. 10a) and that YHWH has blinded the prophets (v. 10b).

The narrative sequence in vv. 11-12 presents the prophet's instruction concerning the people's inability to comprehend. In v. 11 he compares the vision described above to a sealed book that cannot be read. In v. 12 he describes the situation in relation to an illiterate who cannot read the book in the first place, thereby emphasizing his view that the people cannot understand the vision.

The third basic element is the prophet's report of YHWH's judgment speech against the people. Following the speech formula in v. 13aα, the speech proper appears in vv. 13aβ-14. The indictment in v. 13aβ-b, introduced by the typical *ya'an kî*, "because," accuses the people of false honor of YHWH (v. 13aβ-δ) and false fear of YHWH (v. 13b). The consequences, introduced by *lākēn*, "therefore," are announced in v. 14. YHWH will perform miraculous acts (v. 14a), but even the wise among the people will not understand their significance (v. 14b).

The second major component of 29:1-24 appears in vv. 15-24, which make up the prophet's instruction concerning the future revelation or realization that YHWH has delivered Jacob. The structure of the unit is determined by a combination of generic and syntactical features. It comprises three major subunits, vv. 15-16, 17-21, and 22-24, which begin with a focus on the inability of the wise to understand YHWH's purpose and then concentrate on the future when that purpose will be revealed.

The first major subunit is the woe oracle in vv. 15-16, which constitutes a warning to the wise who do not understand YHWH. The woe statement, introduced by *hôy* ("woe!"), appears in v. 15. It consists of the woe statement proper in v. 15a followed by an elaboration in v. 15b, which emphasizes that they believe that their deeds are hidden in darkness (v. 15bα) and that they ask whether anyone knows what they actually do (v. 15bβ). A simile concerning the lack of understanding among the wise then follows in v. 16. The simile itself appears in v. 16a and compares the misconceptions of the wise to that of clay with regard to the potter. The basis for the simile, in v. 16b, maintains that the misconceptions (*hapkĕkem,* lit. "your overturnings") of the wise are like those of a work that says its maker "did not make me," or the creation that says its creator "does not understand." The 2nd-person masculine plural suffix in *hapkĕkem,* "your misconceptions" (v. 16), indicates that this unit is addressed directly to the wise.

The second major subunit of vv. 15-24 is vv. 17-21, which is a prophetic announcement concerning the future demise of the oppressors. The passage is demarcated by its introductory interrogative particle in v. 17 and its syntactical features, including the *wāws* that hold vv. 17-19 together and the causative *kî,* "because," that joins vv. 20-21 to vv. 17-19. Vv. 17-19 constitute a rhetorical question concerning the realization of YHWH's salvation. It comprises three basic parts, based on the shift of subject in each verse, which indicates three different depictions of this realization. V. 17 focuses on the fruitfulness of the natural world, v. 18 focuses on the hearing of the deaf and the seeing of the blind, and v. 19 focuses on the rejoicing over YHWH by the humble and the poor in Israel. Altogether, the rhetorical question indicates that the time of the realization is nearly at hand. The basis for the realization appears in vv. 20-22, which announce the end of oppression. This is basically stated in v. 20, and v. 21 appositionally defines the nature of the oppressors by referring to their deeds that pervert justice.

The third major subunit of vv. 15-24 appears in vv. 22-24, which describe the consequences or results of the end of oppression in the form of a prophetic messenger speech. The unit is introduced by *lākēn,* "therefore," which demonstrates that the speech is announced as a consequence of the preceding subunit. This is important in the overall interpretation of the passage in that it indicates that the following word of YHWH is the conclusion that one should reach. The conclusion is that YHWH has given a word of salvation for Jacob. This demonstrates that the oppression mentioned throughout the passage is intended to lead to a positive outcome. An expanded form of the messenger formula appears in v. 24a followed by the speech by YHWH in vv. 22b-24. The speech begins with the assertion in v. 22b that Jacob will not be ashamed. The basis for this assertion follows in vv. 23-24: Jacob will sanctify YHWH (v. 23) and Jacob will gain understanding (v. 24). This last point resolves one of the primary issues of the entire passage: the people do not comprehend YHWH's actions.

Genre

The overarching genre of 29:1-24 is prophetic INSTRUCTION. This genre typically employs no fixed structure, but may be identified by its use of typical wisdom elements and by its overall intent to examine a specific situation and to draw conclusions about the meaning of that situation.

The basic structure of 29:1-24 demonstrates its fundamental intention to examine a situation of assault against Jerusalem or the Temple Mount, here identified as Ariel. The first major subunit of the passage (vv. 1-14) demonstrates that YHWH is the cause of the assault, which would seem to contradict the standard perspective of the Zion tradition that YHWH guarantees the security of Jerusalem and the temple. The second major subunit of the passage (vv. 15-24) demonstrates that YHWH's intention is actually to bring about salvation for Jacob, despite the initial threat posed to Ariel. The salvation is presented as a miraculous act by YHWH, or specifically as a relief from oppression and attackers. One may infer, therefore, that YHWH's action is intended to demonstrate sovereignty over the entire cosmos and all nations, not only over Judah, insofar as YHWH marshals foreign forces to carry out the assault and then delivers Jerusalem from the threat.

378

Each major subunit of the prophetic instruction in 29:1-24 employs a number of generic elements, including a variety of typical wisdom elements, to achieve its goals.

The prophetic INSTRUCTION that identifies YHWH as the cause of the assault against Ariel in vv. 1-14 is constituted as an inverted PROPHETIC AN-NOUNCEMENT OF JUDGMENT. Whereas the typical prophetic ANNOUNCEMENT OF JUDGMENT presents an accusation followed by an announcement of con-sequences, 29:1-14 presents the consequences in the form of an assault against Ariel, followed by the prophet's report of YHWH's judgment speech that estab-lishes the cause for the punishment. The presence of a number of typical wisdom features indicates that the primary purpose of this text is not to announce judgment; rather, they aid in identifying YHWH as the cause of that judgment.

Isaiah 29:1-14 begins with a woe statement concerning Ariel in v. 1a. Although the woe statement frequently presupposes a situation of mourning (cf. 1 Kgs 13:30; cf. Janzen, *Mourning Cry*, 3-39) and commonly introduces a prophet-ic (→) woe speech of judgment (cf. Westermann, *Basic Forms,* 190-98), the present literary context indicates that v. 1a functions as a warning of impending danger (cf. Zech 2:10-11), insofar as it precedes the first address to the audience in vv. 1b-8 that portrays the assault against Ariel. In this manner, v. 1a sets the general theme of threat or judgment presupposed by the rest of the passage. The first address in v. 1b-8 follows up with a portrayal or ANNOUNCEMENT of that threat in the form of an assault against Ariel. This address is of a somewhat mixed generic character. It appears to be based on the prophetic ANNOUNCEMENT OF JUDGMENT in vv. 2-6, insofar as it describes the assault against Ariel, but shifts to a typical wisdom form of SIMILE in vv. 7-8. SIMILES are commonly used in wisdom literature to demonstrate a particular insight. Here the analogies to the dreams of the starving or parched man are designed to demonstrate that YHWH will relieve Ariel from the assault. Consequently, the SIMILE changes the character of the address and alerts the reader to the fact that a different agenda is at work in this text beyond that of announcing punishment against Ariel.

The second address in vv. 9-14 gets to the main concern of the instruction: YHWH is the cause of the assault against Ariel. It employs a COMMAND to astonishment and blindness in vv. 9-10 that serves as a warning for some impending and startling revelation. By referring to the blinding of the addressee, however, it also employs a typical wisdom element, for wisdom texts commonly begin with an (→) exhortation to open one's ears and heart in order to receive the wisdom that is about to be imparted. (Cf. K. D. F. Römheld, *Wege der Weisheit: Die Lehren Amenemopes und Proverbien 22,17–24,22* [BZAW 184; Berlin and New York: de Gruyter, 1989] 18-27; idem, *Die Weisheitlehre im alten Orient: Elemente einer Formgeschichte* [Biblische Notizen 4; Munich: Biblische Notizen, 1989] passim. Note that although Römheld's surveys indicate that the "ears" and "heart" play the primary roles in such contexts, the "eyes" appear in a few instances. The prominence of the visual metaphor in Isaiah may well be due to a prophetic setting that emphasizes visual experiences rather than audial ones.) The instructional character of the passage is reinforced by the statements pertaining to the people's inability to understand in vv. 11-12, insofar as these verses employ analogy to portray the people or perhaps the wise one who is unable to read a book, and thereby unable to understand YHWH actions. The prophet's report of YHWH's ANNOUNCEMENT OF JUDGMENT in vv. 13-14 makes the point clear: YHWH is the cause of the assault against Ariel. The prophetic ANNOUNCEMENT OF JUDGMENT is formulated in typical fashion with an INDICTMENT or ACCUSATION against the people in v. 13aβ-b and an AN-NOUNCEMENT OF PUNISHMENT or consequences in v. 14. It thereby provides the basis for the prophet's portrayal of the assault against Ariel in vv. 1-8 and brings the reader to the first major conclusion to be drawn in this INSTRUCTION.

The prophetic INSTRUCTION concerning the future realization that YHWH has delivered Jacob is likewise based on the typical PROPHETIC ANNOUNCEMENT OF SALVATION form (cf. Westermann, *Prophetische Heilsspruche;* E.T. *Prophetic Oracles of Salvation*), modified for the present literary context by the inclusion of typical wisdom elements. In this case, the PROPHETIC ANNOUNCEMENT OF SALVA-TION is designed to lead the reader to the conclusion that YHWH's actions, including the oppression of the assault against Ariel, are designed to bring about salvation for the people at large. The WOE ORACLE that introduces the passage in vv. 15-16 serves as a warning to the wise concerning the futility of their attempts to understand YHWH's intentions, but it also highlights the essential point of these verses, which is that YHWH's unfathomed purpose, to bring about the deliverance of Jacob, will ultimately be revealed. Again, the technique of analogy plays an important role. The comparisons of the wise to the manufactured work that claims that its maker did not make it, or to the fashioned work that claims that its creator does not understand, serve as the means to emphasize the inability of the wise to understand YHWH's works. In this manner, the passage prepares for the realization of understanding and good teaching that will appear in v. 24.

Verses 17-21, which contain the prophet's announcement of the future demise of the oppressors, corresponds to the typical PROPHETIC ANNOUNCE-MENT OF SALVATION. But they also contain several wisdom elements, for ex-ample, a RHETORICAL QUESTION, a typical wisdom device to bring the hearer to a desired conclusion, which is designed to announce the imminent rejoicing of the people at the end of the oppression. The analogy to nature in v. 17 is likewise a typical wisdom technique for bringing the student to a desired insight concerning the workings of the human or historical realm. The references to the ability of the deaf to hear and the blind to see (v. 18) employ a typical wisdom motif designed to highlight the obvious nature of the new revelation to all. Finally, the MESSENGER SPEECH that concludes the passage in vv. 22-24 em-phasizes the PROPHETIC ANNOUNCEMENT OF SALVATION as the basic content of the speech, but it also employs references to wisdom insofar as it mentions acquisition of wisdom and teaching by those who previously resisted coming to the proper insight. In this manner, the passage resolves the issue of the wise who are unable to comprehend in vv. 11-12, 14b, and 15-16.

Setting

Isaiah 29 functions as an integral part of the book of Isaiah in its various literary settings. As part of both the 6th- and 5th-century editions of the book, its portrayal of the oppression of Jerusalem, which ultimately leads to the redemption of Jacob, demonstrates a concern to explain the Babylonian destruction of Jerusalem and the temple as part of a larger divine plan for world history. In the case of the 5th-century edition of the book, such a divine plan would point to the manifestation of YHWH's rule over all the nations of the earth. In the 6th-century edition of the book, ch. 29 would presuppose that the restoration of Jerusalem and the building of the Second Temple serve as the major signs demonstrating YHWH's sovereignty over the entire cosmos. In relation to the Josianic edition of Isaiah from the late 7th century, ch. 29 would presuppose Judah's and Jerusalem's affliction by the Assyrians as a prelude to the extension of Davidic sovereignty over the territory of the former northern kingdom of Israel, thereby fulfilling YHWH's miraculous purpose for bringing the Assyrians by reuniting the tribes of Israel under a Davidic monarch.

Despite the fact that ch. 29 manifests a coherent and relatively consistent structure (see the discussion of Structure above), there are indications that the passage is a composite unit. Vv. 1-14 clearly focus on Ariel, which refers to the altar of the temple in Jerusalem (cf. v. 8, which refers to Mt. Zion). Likewise, vv. 1-14 presuppose the ideology of the Zion tradition as an essential element in constructing its message of deliverance for Ariel. But vv. 15-24 say nothing about Jerusalem or the temple; they focus instead on Jacob and Israel, which are to be identified with the northern kingdom of Israel. This observation is reinforced by the references to Lebanon and Carmel in v. 17, both of which are associated with the northern border regions of Israel.

Furthermore, the connections between the two passages are somewhat tenuous in that they are thematic and show no evidence that vv. 1-14 and vv. 15-24 were composed at the same time. Both passages employ the motif of the blind and the deaf, but the only explicit connection between them is the reference to the book in vv. 11-12 and v. 18. Moreover, blindness plays little role in vv. 11-12, and deafness plays no role at all. Blindness is suggested by the reference to YHWH's blinding the prophets in v. 10, but the main issue in vv. 11-12 is the ability to read the book, not blindness per se. Likewise, the lack of wisdom among the people is an important theme in both passages, but there is little in the way of explicit links between the two. The contrast between the "spirit of deep sleep" in v. 10 and the "spirit of understanding" in v. 24 does not provide sufficient basis to maintain the unity of the composition.

Moreover, although vv. 15-24 resolve the tensions of vv. 1-14, they do so by inference. For example, the deliverance of Jacob is the result of the affliction of Ariel, but the passage never makes clear how the affliction of Ariel and its resolution has anything to do with Jacob. Finally, on the one hand, vv. 15-24 appear to be a full-standing unit that resolves its own tensions; that is, the absence of wisdom presented in vv. 15-16 is resolved in v. 24, and the oppression mentioned in v. 20 requires no specific antecedent. On the other hand, vv. 1-14 do not resolve their own tensions, such as the lack of wisdom, the blindness of the prophets, and the meaning of the assault against Ariel. On the basis of these considerations, one may conclude not only that vv. 1-14 and vv. 15-24 presuppose different settings, but that vv. 1-14 may well presuppose vv. 15-24.

Indeed, vv. 15-24 appear to presuppose Tiglath-pileser III's invasion of the northern kingdom of Israel in 734-732. The passage clearly focuses on the eventual deliverance of the northern kingdom of Israel from a situation of oppression. The references to Lebanon and Carmel are especially important at this point because Tiglath-pileser stripped away the northern territories of the northern kingdom of Israel and annexed them into the Assyrian empire (cf. 2 Kgs 15:29). Isaiah apparently saw this as an opportunity for the Davidic dynasty to reassert its control over the northern tribes (cf. Isa 8:16–9:6 [*RSV* 7], esp. 8:23–9:6 [*RSV* 9:1-7]) and thereby to restore the original unity of the Davidic empire.

In this respect, several features of vv. 15-24 are important. First, the formulation and contents of the woe statement in vv. 15-16 correspond to that of the woe oracles directed against the northern kingdom of Israel in 5:8-24, especially the use of *mem*-preformative participles (*hôy hamma'ămîqîm mēyhwh*, "woe to those who make deep from YHWH"; cf. 5:8, 11, 18) and the reference to the absence of wisdom among the people (cf. 5:20, 21). Note also the *mem*-preformative participle in 29:21, which describes those who cause sin, and the following statement concerning the perversion of justice (cf. 5:20, 22-23). Second, the reference to Abraham is especially important insofar as Abraham is generally associated with the Davidic dynasty (cf. Clements, *Abraham and David*). Abraham is closely identified with Hebron, the original capital of the Davidic dynasty, and his covenant is formulated in the same terms as that of David (cf. Genesis 15; 2 Samuel 7–8). These factors indicate that vv. 15-24 were composed in the aftermath of Tiglath-pileser's invasion of the northern kingdom and his incorporation of the northern territories into the Assyrian empire in 732. In this instance, Isaiah presented the catastrophe as an opportunity for Ahaz to restore the original unity of the Davidic empire.

Scholars generally ascribe vv. 1-14 to 705-701 and maintain that the passage is an attack against Hezekiah for his plans to revolt against Sennacherib. Vv. 5-8 are frequently ascribed to a later hand because of their differing form and content (see Clements, *Isaiah 1–39*, 234-35), but this is unjustified. The 1st-person common singular speaker and 2nd-person feminine singular address forms of vv. 1-4 (5a) do not indicate a YHWH speech, but only the speech of the prophet. The shift from the 3rd-person reference to Ariel in v. 2 to 2nd-person feminine singular address forms in vv. 3-4 in the context of the 1st-person common singular speech demonstrates that shifting forms are no criterion for maintaining composite authorship. Likewise, the verb *tippāqēd*, "you/she shall be visited," in v. 6 represents not a 2nd-person masculine singular address form but a 3rd-person feminine singular reference to Ariel and merely resumes the 3rd-person reference form of v. 2, which continues through the end of v. 8. Likewise, the shift to deliverance for Ariel in vv. 7-8 is in keeping with the intent of the entire unit and provides a basis for the incomprehensible purpose of YHWH that forms the basis for the motif of the lack of wisdom among the people. The reference to the short duration of the punishment in v. 5bβ would certainly support the overall concern with the deliverance of Jerusalem. Vv. 7-8 therefore need not be viewed as a later addition. It would appear that the prophet is speaking throughout these verses and perhaps engaging in a symbolic act in which he mimics a siege of Jerusalem like that of Ezekiel in Ezekiel 4 (cf. Isaiah 20).

The positive outcome of the siege against Ariel calls into question the usual assignment of vv. 1-14 to 705-701 and Hezekiah's preparations for revolt against Sennacherib. Little in the Isaiah tradition suggests that the prophet expected a positive outcome from this revolt. Instead, a different setting may better explain the prophet's view that Ariel would be delivered and that Ariel's deliverance would have an impact on Jacob. That setting is the revolt of the northern kingdom of Israel against Assyria in 724-721. Such a scenario would explain the potential threat against Jerusalem/Ariel that would quickly be relieved, since Assyrian troops were present in the region but posed no serious threat to Jerusalem. One must keep in mind that from a Davidic perspective, the territory of the northern kingdom of Israel was part of the Davidic empire, and the presence of Assyrian troops in this area would have represented an attack against Davidic land. This would explain the association between Ariel and Jacob in the final form of the passage as a whole. It would also account for the concern with YHWH's miraculous acts in v. 14; that is, YHWH will use the Assyrians to return the northern kingdom to the rule of the house of David and to restore worship by the whole people at the temple in Jerusalem. This concern suggests that vv. 1-14 were written by the prophet at the time of the revolt of the northern kingdom and that these verses were designed to update the application of vv. 15-24 to the situation of 724-721.

Intention

The intention of ch. 29 varies in relation to its literary setting. In general, the passage portrays the threat of nations assaulting Zion as an act of YHWH and projects a positive outcome for Israel as a result of the dissolution of that threat. In relation to the 6th- and 5th-century editions of the book, ch. 29 therefore anticipates the destruction of Jerusalem as an act of YHWH, and posits that the restoration of the exilic and postexilic periods represents the positive outcome of Jerusalem's suffering. For the 5th-century edition of the book, this would be the anticipated restoration of the Jewish community based around the Jerusalem temple as a center for worldwide recognition of YHWH. For the 6th-century edition of the book, the anticipated return to Jerusalem and the rebuilding of the temple would serve as the focal point for the hopes of the chapter. For the Josianic edition of Isaiah, ch. 29 would portray the period of Assyrian hegemony over the land of Judah as the punishment directed against Ariel. The positive outcome of Ariel's suffering would be the restoration of Jacob, the former northern kingdom of Israel, to Davidic/Josianic control. In all cases, the punishment and subsequent restoration would represent an act of YHWH on behalf of the people.

With regard to the composition of ch. 29, the intention of the passage may be established through consideration of its historical setting in relation to the Assyrian campaigns against northern Israel, its structure and generic character as an instruction speech by the prophet, and its use of the Zion tradition as a means to portray YHWH's intentions in relation to the historical situation.

As noted above, one may relate the historical setting of this passage to two Assyrian campaigns against the northern kingdom of Israel. Vv. 15-24 presuppose Tiglath-pileser's campaigns of 734-732, in which the northern territories of Israel in the Galilee region and Transjordan were stripped away and incorporated into the Assyrian empire. Vv. 1-14 appear to presuppose the Assyrian campaigns of 724-721, in which Shalmaneser V, and later Sargon II, succeeded in conquering the northern kingdom of Israel. The passage as a whole therefore presupposes the Assyrian campaigns as the basis for formulating its message.

The structure and generic character of ch. 29 as a prophetic instruction play an important role insofar as the passage maintains that YHWH is the cause of the assault and that it will ultimately result in deliverance for the people. This somewhat contradictory claim is highlighted by the motif of the wise in Israel, who are unable to comprehend, and by the corresponding emphasis on the blind and deaf, who will understand YHWH's purposes once the deliverance is achieved. Insofar as wisdom texts frequently call on the reader to open the eyes and ears in order to receive instruction, the pedagogical intent of the passage becomes clear. Here the reader is asked to examine a situation of threat and to conclude that deliverance will be the ultimate result. It is not surprising, therefore, that the inability of the wise to understand plays such an important role in this chapter.

Perhaps the most important element in establishing the intent of ch. 29 is its use of the Zion tradition. Here it is noteworthy that the term *Ariel* refers specifically to the altar for burnt offerings at the Jerusalem temple (cf. Akk. *arallu*, "altar hearth"). V. 8 removes any ambiguity by referring to Mt. Zion. In general, the Zion tradition posits YHWH's pledge of eternal security to Jerusalem as the site of the holy temple. Indeed, a particular emphasis of the tradition is YHWH's defense of the city against attacking hordes of nations (cf. Psalms 46; 48; 76). Here the passage turns the Zion tradition on its head, in that YHWH is responsible for mounting the attack of the nations in the first place. This might seem to contradict the tradition, but the passage develops the scenario in order to demonstrate that YHWH really acts in Ariel's interest.

An important element in this development is the portrayal of the dreaming man in vv. 7-8. After presenting the description of the siege against Ariel in vv. 2-6, vv. 7-8 compare the situation to one in which a hungry and thirsty man dreams that he sees food and drink but awakens in each case to find that he is still hungry and thirsty. The meaning of these verses is somewhat enigmatic. Some understand the dream to refer to the situation of Ariel, which imagines that relief, like the food and drink of the dreaming man, is imminent, but then realizes that no relief is in sight. In this case, the dreams portray the demise of Ariel. Such an interpretation must be rejected, however, in that the passage contains no definitive statement that Ariel will be conquered. Instead, the passage as a whole emphasizes the people's inability to comprehend the situation, and vv. 15-24 present a scenario of deliverance for Jacob. Furthermore, the dreams portray a situation of acquisition and denial, not a threat that is realized. This indicates that they portray the situation of the nations who attack Ariel and think they are about to conquer the site, but realize at the last moment that Ariel has escaped their grasp. Such a scenario corresponds well with the statement that Ariel will be afflicted for only a short while (v. 5bβ) and that the ultimate outcome will be deliverance for Jacob. Consequently, the Zion tradition is upheld in ch. 29. Although the people have been indicted by YHWH for insincerity in their acknowledgment of the deity (vv. 13-14), their punishment is only temporary and the security of Zion is preserved.

Nevertheless, as vv. 15-24 demonstrate, YHWH has more in mind than presenting the people of Jerusalem with a temporary scare. The Zion tradition maintains consistently that the Davidic dynasty has the right as YHWH's representative to rule the people and the land. In this regard, the threat to Ariel/Zion and the restoration of Jacob must be seen in relation to each other. "Jacob" normally refers to the northern kingdom of Israel that split away from Davidic rule after the death of Solomon. That Jacob is specified here in the context of the Zion tradition is significant since it indicates the interest of the Davidic dynasty in reestablishing its rule over the northern tribes.

In this regard, several features of vv. 15-24 become significant. First, v. 22 refers to YHWH as God of the "house of Jacob" and as the God "who redeemed Abraham." This latter reference is especially significant insofar as Abraham is frequently associated with the Davidic dynasty. Abraham is closely associated with Hebron, the first capital of the dynasty. Moreover, his covenant in Genesis 15 is formulated in Davidic terms, and his land corresponds to the farthest reaches of the Davidic empire (Gen 15:18-21; cf. 2 Samuel 8; see also Clements, *Abraham and David*). Insofar as Isa 29:15-24 speak of the redemption of Jacob, the reference to Abraham suggests some identification of this redemption with the Davidic dynasty. The return of Lebanon to Carmel (*RSV* "a fruitful field") and of Carmel to forest likewise has implications for understanding this passage in relation to the Davidic dynasty. As noted above, Lebanon and Carmel refer to regions that the Assyrians annexed. The reference to "forest" is somewhat enigmatic, however, in that much of the Syro-Palestinian region was covered by "forest" in the late 8th century. But "forest" has Davidic implications, since the Davidic royal palace in Jerusalem was called "the House of the Forest of Lebanon" (1 Kgs 7:2; cf. Isa 22:8). The return of Lebanon to Carmel and of Carmel to forest signifies not only natural transformation but the return of these regions to Davidic control (cf. 8:16–9:6 [*RSV* 7]).

In sum, Isaiah sees the Assyrian campaigns against the northern kingdom as a potential threat to Jerusalem, but ultimately Jerusalem and the Davidic house will reap the benefits of the Assyrian assaults in that the collapse of the northern kingdom will restore Davidic rule over the entire people of Israel. Not only will Ariel/Zion be saved from the assault of the nations; it will also regain its position as the religious and national center of the people of Israel.

Finally, because ch. 29 emphasizes the inability of the wise to comprehend this message, one may conclude that the chapter was developed to challenge the prevailing opinion of the wise. When placed in an 8th-century context, this suggests that the scenario outlined here, which posits the benefits to the Davidic dynasty that accrue from the Assyrian campaigns against the northern kingdom of Israel, is intended to persuade the king of Judah that the Assyrian campaign serves Davidic and Judean interests. When considered in relation to the prophet's warnings against foreign alliances, ch. 29 is intended to convince the king that patience will be the best policy. Although the Assyrians pose a potential threat,

Judah and the house of David stand to gain from the downfall of Israel, provided that Judah does not antagonize the Assyrians by joining an anti-Assyrian alliance.

Bibliography

W. A. M. Beuken, "Isa 29,15-24: Perversion Reverted," in *The Scriptures and the Scrolls* (*Fest.* A. S. van der Woude; ed. F. García Martínez; Leiden: Brill, 1992) 43-64; R. E. Clements, *Abraham and David: Genesis XV and Its Meaning for Israelite Tradition* (SBT 2/5; London: SCM, 1967); A. H. Godbey, "Ariel, or David Cultus?" *AJSL* 41 (1924) 253-66; Janzen, *Mourning Cry* (→ "Introduction to the Prophetic Literature"), 55-56; R. L. Routledge, "The Siege and Deliverance of the City of David in Isaiah 29:1-8," *TynB* 43 (1992) 181-90; Werlitz, *Studien* (→ 7:1–8:15), 253-320.

PROPHETIC INSTRUCTION SPEECH CONCERNING YHWH'S DELAY IN DELIVERING THE PEOPLE FROM ASSYRIA, 30:1-33

Structure

I. Prophetic instruction speech proper	1-26
A. Oracular report concerning YHWH's dissatisfaction with embassy to Egypt	1-11
1. Oracular report of YHWH's woe speech concerning rebellious sons	1-5
a. Oracular report of woe statement proper	1
b. Specification concerning futile journey to Egypt	2-5
1) Concerning journey to Egypt to request aid	2
2) Consequences: shame	3-4
a) Basic statement	3
b) Cause: association with Zoan and On	4
3) Summation: rebellious sons bring only shame, not aid	5
2. Prophetic announcement *(maśśā')* concerning beasts of Negev/embassy to Egypt	6-7
a. Superscription	6a
b. Prophetic pronouncement *(maśśā')* proper	6b-7
1) Description of caravan	6b
a) Wild beasts of the land	6bα
b) Actions of caravaneers	6bβ
2) Evaluation of embassy: worthless	7
a) Basic statement: Egypt is no help	7a
b) Consequence: Egypt is named "Rahab who sits still"	7b

Isaiah 30 is demarcated by the introductory *hôy* statement, which marks the beginning of a new unit. Although the superscription *maśśā' bahămôt negeb,* "pronouncement of the beasts of the Negev," appears in v. 6, it does not introduce a new structural unit. The pronouncement or *maśśā'* in vv. 6-7 repeats the phrase *'al-'am lō' yô'îlû,* "upon a people that does not profit," from v. 5, thereby indicating that vv. 6-7 are related to vv. 1-5 (see Weis, 248-49, and below). The instructions to write in vv. 8-11 relate to the pronouncement (cf. Habakkuk 1–2, esp. 2:2) and the woe oracle insofar as they define the reason why the people, referred to here as "sons," are so rebellious (esp. v. 9; cf. v. 1). The material in vv. 12-26, introduced by *lākēn,* "therefore," discusses the outcome of this situation in terms of both judgment and delayed deliverance of the people (note the syntactical connections to vv. 12-14 in v. 15, *kî kōh-'āmar 'ădōnāy yhwh qĕdôš yiśrā'ēl,* and in v. 18, *wĕlākēn yĕḥakkeh yhwh laḥănankem;* see further below). The theophanic announcement in vv. 27-33 likewise defines the outcome of this situation by describing YHWH's future deliverance. The *hôy* statement in 31:1 then introduces an entirely new unit.

The basic structure of 30:1-33 is determined by the generic distinction between the prophetic instruction speech in vv. 1-26, in which the prophet announces YHWH's statements in vv. 1-17 and then explains their significance, and the theophanic announcement in vv. 27-33 that describes YHWH's future deliverance of the people.

Within the prophetic instruction speech in vv. 1-26, the oracle formula in v. 1, *nĕ'um-yhwh,* "oracle of YHWH," and the messenger formulas in vv. 12 and 15 indicate that vv. 1-17 constitute the prophet's announcements of speeches by YHWH, whereas the 3rd-person references to YHWH throughout indicate that vv. 18-26 constitute a speech by the prophet himself. Thus both vv. 1-17 and 18-26 are speeches by the prophet, insofar as the prophet transmits YHWH's speeches in vv. 1-17. Nevertheless, this does not indicate the basic structure of vv. 1-26. Instead, the structure of vv. 1-26 is based on a modified form of the prophetic announcement of judgment in which the prophet announces the consequences of the people's actions in terms of both punishment and delayed deliverance. Consequently, the structure of vv. 1-26 comprises two basic parts: vv. 1-11, which focus on the people's wrongdoing in sending an embassy to Egypt, and vv. 12-26, which describe the consequences of this action as punishment (vv. 12-17) and YHWH's delayed deliverance (vv. 18-26).

Verses 1-11 constitute an oracular report concerning YHWH's dissatisfaction with the people's embassy to Egypt. The oracle formula in v. 1 and the 1st-person common singular address perspective (cf. vv. 1, 7), together with the imperative address in v. 8, indicate that the prophet is here transmitting a speech by YHWH. Although the three basic subunits of vv. 1-11 (vv. 1-5, 6-7, 8-11) lack syntactical links, internal references between the subunits indicate their relationship within the larger context of vv. 1-11.

The first subunit of vv. 1-11 is the oracular report of YHWH's woe oracle in vv. 1-5. The passage contains two basic components distinguished by syntax and content, including the oracular report of the woe statement proper in v. 1 and the specification of this statement in vv. 2-5. Although vv. 2-5 lack a conjunctive particle that would tie them to v. 1, the introductory participle *hahōlĕkîm,* "those who walk," clearly refers back to the "rebellious sons" of v. 1. Within vv. 2-5, v. 2 specifies the actions of the people, who are traveling to Egypt to seek sanctuary. Vv. 3-4, linked to v. 2 by the conjunctive *wĕhāyâ,* "and it [the refuge of Pharaoh] shall be," specifies the consequences of such an action for the people (shame). This is basically stated in v. 3. V. 4, linked to v. 3 by a causative *kî,* "because," states that the cause of such shame lies in the Egyptians' association with Zoan, the site of the exodus from Egypt (cf. Ps 78:12), and with On, the site of the temple of Re (Atum), Egypt's second largest shrine (see Dorsey, "On"). V. 5 lacks a syntactical connection to vv. 2 and 3-4 but provides a summation that reiterates the basic theme of vv. 2-5 that those who go to Egypt bring only shame, not aid.

The second major subunit of vv. 1-11 is the pronouncement *(maśśā')* concerning the beasts of the Negev in vv. 6-7. This passage is distinguished by its superscription in v. 6 and by the commands that introduce the following subunit in v. 8. It is linked to vv. 1-5, however, by the repetition of the phrase *'al-'am lō' yô'îlû,* "to a people that cannot profit them," which also appears in v. 5. As Weis indicates (pp. 248-49), vv. 6-7 "collapse the reasoning process of vv. 2-5 that lead from the statement of purpose in v. 2 to . . . v. 5a." Consequently, vv. 6-7 presuppose vv. 1-5 in that they make the point of vv. 1-5 specific. In this instance, the pronouncement in vv. 6-7 portrays the caravan that approaches an Egypt that will provide no aid. Following the superscription in v. 6a, the structure of the pronouncement proper in vv. 6b-7 falls into two basic parts. V. 6b describes the caravan, including the wild beasts of the land through which it travels (v. 6bα) and the actions of the caravaneers who carry goods for Egypt on the backs of pack animals (v. 6bβ). V. 7 contains an evaluation of the caravan as worthless. This is basically stated in v. 7a (i.e., Egypt is no help). In v. 7b YHWH states that consequently Egypt will be called "Rahab who sits," i.e., Rahab (Egypt) will do nothing.

The third major subunit of vv. 1-11 appears in vv. 8-11, which constitute YHWH's instructions to write. Although these verses lack a conjunctive particle to join them to vv. 6-7, the antecedents of the objects of the imperatives in v. 8 can refer back only to v. 7. Three commands appear in v. 8, "now go [*bô'*], write it [*kātĕbāh*] upon a tablet before them and upon a scroll inscribe it [*ḥuqqāh*]." The latter two imperatives each includes a 3rd-person feminine singular direct object. The antecedent for these objects can only be the statement YHWH made about Egypt in v. 7: "therefore, I will call this [*lāzō't*], 'Rahab who sits.' " "This" in v. 7, expressed as a 3rd-person feminine singular demonstrative pronoun, apparently refers to Egypt or to YHWH's statement about Egypt. Consequently, this statement about Egypt is what the prophet is commanded to write. Vv. 8-11 comprise two basic components: the command to write for a later day in v. 8, and the basis for the command in vv. 9-11. The basis for the command is that the people are rebellious. This is basically stated in v. 9, introduced by a causative *kî,* and elaborated on in vv. 10-11, which quote the people's order to cease prophesying the truth. The order includes both negative and positive statements. It is expressed negatively in v. 10a with prohibitions directed against the seers (v. 10aα) and against the visionaries (v. 10aβ). It is expressed positively in vv. 10b-11 with a series of imperative commands. These include a command to speak smooth things and delusions (v. 10b), a command to turn aside from the (true) path (v. 11a), and a command to remove the Holy One of Israel (v. 11b).

Isaiah 30:12-26 begins with *lākēn,* "therefore," which indicates that the following material presupposes what precedes. Whereas vv. 1-11 focus on YHWH's dissatisfaction with the people for their embassy to Egypt, vv. 12-26 focus on the outcome of YHWH's dissatisfaction, i.e., that the people will suffer punishment and that YHWH will delay their deliverance. The whole is cast as a prophetic announcement in which the prophet clearly quotes statements by YHWH (cf. vv. 12, 15) prior to delivering his own comments. The messenger formulas in vv. 12 and 15, together with the prophet's own speech beginning in v. 18, define the three major subunits of this passage, including vv. 12-14, 15-17, and 18-26. The three subunits are bound together not only thematically but also by their conjunctive links, including the introductory causative *kî* in v. 15 and the conjunctive *wĕlākēn*, "and therefore," in v. 18. Note also that the messenger formula in v. 15, *kî kōh-'āmar 'ădōnāy yhwh qĕdôš yiśrā'ēl*, "for thus says the Lord YHWH, the Holy One of Israel," recaps the messenger formula of v. 12, *lākēn kōh-'āmar qĕdôš yiśrā'ēl*, "therefore thus says the Holy One of Israel." Likewise, the introductory *wĕlākēn* of v. 18 calls to mind the introductory *lākēn* of v. 12.

The first major subunit of vv. 12-26 is the messenger speech. The passage is introduced by the messenger formula in v. 12aα. The speech by YHWH, cast as an announcement of judgment directed against the people (note the 2nd-person masculine singular address forms), follows in vv. 12aβ-14. The announcement begins with the basis for the punishment, introduced by the typical *ya'an*, "because," in v. 12aβ-b, which accuses the people of rejecting YHWH's word in order to trust what is worthless. The consequences, introduced by the typical *lākēn*, are expressed by two similes in vv. 13-14. The first compares their iniquity/punishment to a bulging wall that finally shatters under the strain (v. 13). The second, linked to v. 13 by a conjunctive *wāw*, compares the shattering of the wall to a potter's vessel so thoroughly smashed that it is impossible to find a shard that can hold even minute amounts of water (v. 14).

Verses 15-17 constitute the second major subunit of vv. 12-26 and present the basis for the consequences against the people by pointing to their rejection of repentance and humility. Again, the passage is constituted as a YHWH messenger speech based on the form of a prophetic announcement of punishment. The messenger formula appears in v. 15aα$_1$ and the speech by YHWH appears in vv. 15aα$_2$-17. It begins with an accusation in v. 15aα$_2$-16bα concerning the people's rejection of YHWH's conditions for deliverance. The conditions are stated in v. 15aα$_2$ as repentance, humility, quietness, and trust. Vv. 15b-16bα state the people's response. This section begins in v. 15b with a statement that the people rejected these conditions, followed by a quotation of their statement that they would flee by horse (note conjunctive *wattō'mĕrû*, "and you said," at the beginning of v. 16). The consequence, introduced by introductory *'al-kēn*, "therefore," is then stated in vv. 16bβ-17, which describes the people's pursuit by horses in three parts: their pursuers will be swift (v. 16bβ), many will flee before few (v. 17a), and "you" (the people) will be isolated like a flagstaff or ensign on top of a mountain (v. 17b).

The third major subunit of vv. 12-26 is the prophetic instruction concerning YHWH's future or delayed deliverance of the people in vv. 18-26. The 3rd-person masculine singular references to YHWH throughout and 2nd-person masculine singular and 2nd-person masculine plural address forms indicate that this is a speech by the prophet to the people. The contents indicate that it is based on an announcement of future salvation. The passage begins with a basic statement of the prophet's message (i.e., that YHWH will delay salvation for the people), although he is careful to state the need for patience because salvation will indeed come. The balance of the passage in vv. 19-26, introduced by a causative *kî*, elaborates on this theme by spelling out the sequence of events, ranging from suffering to ultimate deliverance, that the people will experience.

391

In this regard, vv. 19-26 provide a basis for the prophet's statement, "happy [*RSV* 'blessed'] are all of those who wait for him," in v. 18.

The syntactical structure of vv. 19-26 indicates that this passage has two basic parts. V. 19a constitutes a prohibition of weeping, including the basis for the prohibition, which is that the people will dwell in Zion, in v. 19aα, and the prohibition proper in v. 19bβ. The structure of vv. 19b-26 is based on the appearance of the imperfect verb *yāḥnĕkā,* "he will show favor to you," in v. 19b followed by the converted perfect verbs *wĕnātan,* "and he will give," in vv. 20 and 23 and *wĕhāyâ,* "and it shall come to pass," in vv. 25 and 26.

The result is a five-part structure that outlines the passage from suffering to salvation. It begins with a basic statement that YHWH will show favor in v. 19b. Vv. 20-22 then provide an account of the suffering inflicted on the people so that they will cast out their idols. This includes a statement that YHWH will cause affliction (v. 20a), a statement that the teachers will not be hidden (v. 20b), and a statement that the people will then hear the word (vv. 21-22). This last statement includes an introduction to the word in v. 21a followed by a quotation of the word, which constitutes a command to adhere to YHWH and to cast out idols, in vv. 21b-22. Vv. 23-24 constitute an account of YHWH's giving of rain and produce, which focuses on agriculture and produce in v. 23a and on cattle in vv. 23b-24. V. 25 contains a statement that there will be water on all the hills on the day of the slaughter of enemies, and v. 26 states that there will be light on the day that YHWH heals the wounds of the people.

Finally, the second major subunit of 30:1-33 is the theophanic announcement that YHWH will strike down Assyria in vv. 27-33. This unit is distinguished by its generic character and is syntactically independent of the preceding material. The prophet appears to be the speaker, since the passage refers to YHWH in the 3rd person throughout. The 2nd-person masculine plural address form in v. 29 indicates that the people are the addressees. The structure of the passage breaks down into two basic parts, vv. 27-28 and 29-33, based on thematic factors and the absence of a conjunction in v. 29. Vv. 27-28 constitute a typical description of YHWH's approach. It includes three basic statements that describe YHWH: YHWH is coming from afar (v. 27a), YHWH's lips are full of anger (v. 27b), and YHWH's overwhelming wind will reach up to the neck (v. 28).

Verses 29-33 then describe YHWH's victory over Assyria in the context of the celebration accompanying that victory. V. 29 describes the victory on the mountain of YHWH. Vv. 30-31 describe the manifestation of YHWH's power over Assyria. This description includes a basic statement of the manifestation of YHWH's power in v. 30. The reason for that manifestation, the defeat of Assyria, appears in v. 31, introduced by a causative *kî.* Vv. 32-33 return to a description of the celebration by those who smite Assyria. V. 32 describes the celebration, and v. 33, introduced by causative *kî,* states that the reason for the victory celebration is that vengeance was decreed in the past. This last point is particularly important in the present context, because it makes clear the association of the theophany with the preceding prophetic instruction. Because vv. 1-26 indicate a future deliverance for the people after some delay, the celebration of that victory, when it finally does come, calls to mind and validates the past word of YHWH.

Genre

As already noted, the overarching genre of this passage is prophetic INSTRUC-
TION. Although the genre has no fixed form, it may be identified by its interest
in examining a given situation in order to draw conclusions from it, and by the
presence of various wisdom elements that contribute to its instructional function.
INSTRUCTIONS are designed to fill a number of functions, such as providing
guidance to individuals or groups, giving rules of conduct, or answering questions. In the present instance, the primary aim is to demonstrate that YHWH
will delay the deliverance of the people from the Assyrian empire. The basis for
this delay is YHWH's dissatisfaction with the people for sending an embassy
to Egypt in order to strike an anti-Assyrian alliance, thereby rejecting YHWH's
guarantees for the security of Jerusalem/Zion.

The passage employs a number of wisdom elements. Chief among them
is the interest in the people's rejection of YHWH's Torah in vv. 8-17. Jensen's
examination of this passage (pp. 112-20) has demonstrated the wisdom background of the terminology and concepts employed here. He notes that *tôrâ* in
v. 9 lacks any reference to law or to priestly *tôrâ,* but that it is closely associated
with typical wisdom language in the present context, including the relation to
the rebellious and lying "sons" *(bānîm)* in v. 9 (cf. v. 1) who are unwilling to
hear (cf. v. 15), the people's refusal to hear "that which is right" *(nĕkōḥôt)* from
the seers and visionaries in v. 10, the use of the terms "way" *(derek)* and "road"
('ōraḥ) in v. 11 with reference to the people's choices of action, and other typical
wisdom terminology such as *bĕʿiqqēš wĕnālôz* (MT: *bĕʿōšeq wĕnālôz),* "what
is crooked and devious," in v. 12 and *bĕšûbâ wānaḥat,* "by waiting and by
calm," in v. 15. Altogether, this language points to the people's refusal to hear
YHWH's word and thereby establishes the cause for YHWH's decision to delay
deliverance. Furthermore, Whedbee (p. 132) points to the wisdom background
of vv. 1-5, which refer to the people's attempt to carry out "counsel" *(ʿēṣâ,* v. 1)
or to seek "advice" *(pî,* v. 2) that does not come from YHWH in their efforts
to seek protection from Egypt. The passage further points out that Egypt is "a
people that brings no profit" *(ʿam lōʾ yôʿîlû,* v. 5).

The prophetic INSTRUCTION can be quite fluid in its formulation. The
present example is no exception, especially since it employs a number of other
generic elements that influence the overarching structure of the passage and
facilitate its aims. One must keep in mind that the key element in defining the
generic character of ch. 30 is the prophet's INSTRUCTION, which points to the
delay in YHWH's salvation of the people in vv. 18-26. Nevertheless, the formulation of this passage appears to be based on the pattern of the PROPHETIC
JUDGMENT SPEECH and the PROPHECY OF SALVATION in that it first points to
the current situation of the people's actions in vv. 1-11 prior to announcing the
consequences or outcome of those actions in vv. 12-26 in terms of both judgment
(vv. 12-17) and salvation (vv. 18-26).

In addition, a number of subordinate generic elements contribute to this
formulation. For example, vv. 1-11 employ a WOE ORACLE in vv. 1-5 that
describes the current actions of the people and thereby aids in providing the
basis for YHWH's dissatisfaction. It is characterized by the typical introductory

hôy, "woe!" which is directed against the "rebellious sons" who are sending an embassy to Egypt. The appearance of the ORACULAR FORMULA *nĕ'um-yhwh,* "utterance of YHWH," identifies vv. 1-5 as the prophet's report of an oracular statement by YHWH, and thereby validates YHWH's dissatisfaction. The PROPHETIC PRONOUNCEMENT *(maśśā')* in vv. 6-7 reinforces vv. 1-5 by expressing YHWH's frustration with the people further. The PROPHETIC PRONOUNCEMENT is designed to point to YHWH's actions in human affairs (Weis). Here the PRONOUNCEMENT provides the basis for YHWH's dissatisfaction and decision to delay deliverance. Finally, the INSTRUCTION to write in vv. 8-11 contributes to establishing the basis for YHWH's dissatisfaction with the people, in that it provides a written record or witness of the basis for that dissatisfaction. As such, it provides a means to validate YHWH's actions in relation to the people, including initial punishment against them followed by deliverance from Assyria at a later time. An imperative COMMAND to write appears in v. 8. In quoting the people concerning their rejection of YHWH's Torah, vv. 10-11 employ an ORDER directed to the prophets expressing the will of the people, both negatively and positively, to stop the prophets from expressing YHWH's will.

Verses 12-26 likewise employ a variety of generic elements to express the outcome of the situation outlined in vv. 1-11. MESSENGER SPEECHES, characterized by the typical "thus says PN" formulation, appear in vv. 12-14 and vv. 15-17. Each expresses the prophet's transmission of a speech by YHWH, and each is formulated as a PROPHETIC JUDGMENT SPEECH to announce the consequences of the people's actions. The first states the people's rejection of YHWH's word (v. 12aβ-b) as the basis for their punishment (vv. 13-14), formulated as a pair of similes that liken the people's punishment to a shattered wall and a shattered pottery jug. The second states the people's rejection of YHWH's conditions (v. 15aα₂-16bα) as the basis for punishment (vv. 16bβ-17). Finally, the prophetic INSTRUCTION in vv. 18-26 is formulated as a PROPHETIC ANNOUNCEMENT OF SALVATION that states the ultimate outcome of this situation: YHWH will deliver the people at a future time.

The theophanic ANNOUNCEMENT that YHWH will strike down Assyria in vv. 27-33 validates the preceding scenario of punishment followed by delayed salvation. The THEOPANY REPORT typically describes in poetic form a theophany of YHWH as a means for offering praise. It generally includes two characteristic sections: a description of YHWH's approach, which appears here in vv. 27-28, and a description of the results of YHWH's coming, expressed here as a celebration of YHWH's defeat of Assyria in vv. 29-33. By describing YHWH's ultimate defeat of Assyria, the theophany confirms that the ultimate purpose of ch. 30 is to explain that YHWH's deliverance of the people will be delayed.

Setting

Although some have attempted to argue that portions of ch. 30 are postexilic, the references to cosmic change in relation to the deliverance of Jerusalem in vv. 19-26 hardly constitute grounds for such a late dating (cf. Kaiser, *Isaiah 13-39,* 298-310; Vermeylen, *Du prophète,* 411-20; Wildberger, *Jesaja,* 1193-94).

Such themes are not exclusively eschatological. Indeed, the interrelationship between the natural and human world was always presupposed in ancient Israelite and Judean thought (e.g., Jer 4:1-31, esp. vv. 23-26; Hosea 4; Zephaniah 1–3), and the welfare of Jerusalem was always a major concern in Judean traditions (e.g., Psalm 2). Instead, various features of Isaiah 30 point to the 7th-century Josianic redaction as the matrix that produced the present form of this text. This setting accounts only for vv. 19-33, however, in that vv. 1-18 appear to derive from the 8th-century prophet Isaiah. In this case, the Josianic redaction appears to have expanded an original 8th-century Isaianic text in order to reinterpret it and to apply it to the circumstances of Josiah's reign in the latter part of the 7th century.

Perhaps the most basic indication of the composite nature of this text is the abrupt shift in the overall thrust of the passage from condemnation and punishment in vv. 1-17 to salvation and deliverance in vv. 18-33. On the one hand, vv. 1-17 focus on the sending of a diplomatic mission to Egypt as an act of rebellion against YHWH and a rejection of YHWH's teaching and word. On the other hand, vv. 18-33 focus on YHWH's deliverance of the people from their oppressor and the restoration of the rains, agriculture, and cattle. There appears to be little in the way of explicit links or internal references between the two sections; rather, their relationship seems to be established primarily by literary juxtaposition. Indeed, there is some tension between the two sections. The promise of rain and fertility in vv. 20-24 does not address the problem posed in vv. 1-17, where the people seek a solution to a political problem. Furthermore, the reference to YHWH's deliverance from oppression in vv. 19-20 appears to respond to the oppression outlined in vv. 12-17, in which the people suffer the consequences of having failed to rely on YHWH. In this case, vv. 18-26 appear to address the disastrous outcome of the people's embassy to Egypt, but do not address the fundamental cause of their problems that prompted them to send for Egyptian aid in the first place. A subtle link does appear, however, in the instruction to record YHWH's pronouncement *(maśśā')* for a later day in v. 8, and in the reference to the funeral pyre that was arranged for Assyria (and for Molech) in v. 33. In this manner, the passage indicates that the announcements of salvation in the latter part of the chapter represent the ultimate outcome of the situation outlined in the first part of the chapter. Nevertheless, there is no explicit indication that either of these statements was composed in relation to the other.

The second major indication of the composite nature of this passage centers around the explicit reference to YHWH's defeat of Assyria in v. 31. This is particularly important because nowhere in the earlier parts of the chapter is there any indication that Assyria is the enemy that will punish the people. Although Assyria is the only viable candidate, the failure to mention Assyria in vv. 1-17 indicates that the identity of the oppressor is relatively unimportant; instead, the mere fact that the people will be pursued by attackers is foremost on the author's mind. Because of the explicit interest in the downfall of Assyria in v. 31, Barth (pp. 92-103) argues that the theophany in vv. 27-33 is a product of the Josianic redaction of Isaiah. In addition to the overall concern with the fall of Assyria in the time of King Josiah, Barth points to the fact that the celebration of that fall takes place at a night festival according to v. 29 ("You shall have a song as in the night when a holy feast is kept"). The only festival celebrated at night in biblical times was Passover (Exod 12:42; Deut 16:6-7; cf. Exod 34:25; Lev 23:5). The significance of such a Passover celebration becomes apparent when one recognizes that the observance of Passover was the primary celebration that marked the program of national and religious restoration sponsored by King Josiah in 622 when it was evident that the Assyrian empire was about to collapse (2 Kings 22-23, esp. 23:21-23). In such a context, the theophany in Isa 30:27-33 would express the Josianic perspective that the collapse of the Assyrian empire was an act of YHWH, who punished Assyria in accordance with the prophecies uttered by Isaiah a century before.

By contrast, Wildberger (*Jesaja,* 1210-15) argues that vv. 27-33 can be considered Isaianic. Much of the language is certainly that of Isaiah: "his breath is like an overflowing stream [*kĕnaḥal šôṭēp*] that reaches up to the neck [*'ad-ṣawwā'r*]" (v. 28; cf. 8:8; 10:22); "in furious anger and a flame of devouring fire [*wĕlahab 'ēš 'ôkēlâ*]" (v. 30; cf. 10:17; 29:6); "when he smites [Assyria] with his rod [*'aššûr baššēbeṭ yakkeh*] and every stroke of the staff [*maṭṭēh*] of punishment" (vv. 31-32; cf. 10:5, 15, 24-26; 28:27).

But Wildberger is forced to excise vv. 29 and 32, the very verses that testify to the Passover celebration, in order to reach this conclusion. Because the grounds for such excision are only thematic, it seems best to conclude that they should be retained, and that vv. 27-33 are the product of the Josianic redaction of Isaiah. This conclusion is further buttressed by the reference to the funeral pyre *(topteh)* prepared for Assyria (and Molech) in v. 33. A major feature of Josiah's reform was the destruction of Topheth (Heb. *tōpet*), the altar to Molech in the Hinnom Valley (2 Kgs 23:10). Josiah's destruction of this altar provides a fitting end to the child sacrifices and to the domination of the Assyrian empire.

Verses 18-26 (or vv. 19-26) are frequently considered to be postexilic because of their concern for the deliverance of Jerusalem and their portrayal of eschatological cosmic transformation (e.g., Vermeylen, *Du prophète,* 418-20; Wildberger, *Jesaja,* 1094). But the transformation of nature in vv. 25-26 is hardly eschatological; it merely highlights the divine healing announced in these verses. Likewise, the concern with the restoration of Jerusalem corresponds easily with the concerns of the Josianic redaction. The key consideration here is that much of the language and imagery does not appear to be Isaianic, but corresponds to that of the Deuteronomic writings that may well have been propagated during the reign of Josiah. Perhaps the most striking example is the promise of rain (*māṭār;* cf. Deut 11:11, 14, 17; 28:12, 24; 32:2), agricultural produce (*tĕbû'at hā'ădāmâ;* cf. Deut 14:22, 28; 16:15; 22:9; 26:12; 33:14), and cattle (*miqneh;* Deut 3:19) in v. 23. Other examples include the concern with idolatry in v. 22 (cf. Exod 32:4, 8, 17; Deut 9:12, 16; 27:15; cf. Judg 17:3, 4; 18:17, 18), and the concern in v. 21 with not deviating to the right or to the left from YHWH's correct path (Deut 2:27; 5:32; 17:11, 20; 28:14; cf. Josh 1:7; 23:6; 1 Sam 6:12; 2 Kgs 22:2). Altogether, these concerns correspond to those of the Josianic period, when a book believed to be an early form of Deuteronomy was reportedly found in the temple and subsequently served as the basis for the reform. Finally,

vv. 18-26 exhibit a shift in number in the 2nd-person address forms employed throughout the passage. Plural 2nd-person address forms appear in vv. 18, 20a, 21b, and 22; singular 2nd-person address forms appear in vv. 19, 20b, 21a, 22a (but see *BHS* on v. 22a; this form is probably due to the influence of the preceding verse). Such a shift in the number of the 2nd-person address forms is one of the primary characteristics of the Deuteronomic sermon forms.

One should note, however, that v. 18 is frequently excluded from vv. 19-26 due to its poetic form and the *wĕlākēn*, "and therefore," that ties it to v. 17 (Procksch, *Jesaja I–XXXIX,* 394-95; Kaiser, *Isaiah 13–39,* 397-98). The presence of a composite text at this point would be supported by the appearance of the awkward repetition of causative *kî* in both v. 18b and v. 19. If v. 18 is Isaianic, it would round out the judgmental material in vv. 1-17 with a promise of eventual salvation. V. 18 would thereby provide motivation for the prophet's audience to adopt the prophet's position by considering alternatives to sending an embassy to Egypt. The basis for the assertion that YHWH will act, i.e., that YHWH is a God of justice, and the statement "Happy [*RSV* 'blessed'] are all those who wait for him" would likewise reinforce the prophet's argumentative position. In this instance, v. 18 would then provide the basis for redactional expansion of this text in the Josianic period, in that vv. 19-26 and 27-33 would then elaborate on the implications of Isaiah's concluding statement in v. 18.

Finally, vv. 1-17 (18) may be considered the work of Isaiah ben Amoz. Most scholars do not contest this point, although the passage is frequently considered to be a redactional assemblage of short oracles because of their formal features. As the discussion of the structure of this passage indicates, however, vv. 1-5 are linked to vv. 6-7 by similar language and concerns, and vv. 8-11 contain instructions to record the pronouncement in vv. 6-7. Although Vermeylen (*Du prophète,* 411-16) has argued that vv. 9-11 are Deuteronomic, most of the characteristic language and themes in these verses appear also in Isaiah 1 and elsewhere. Vv. 12-14 and 15-17 lack specific reference to any other situation and would therefore be meaningless outside their present context. The only meaningful piece of historical information by which to date this text is the reference to an embassy sent to Egypt. Two occasions have been identified for such an embassy: the Philistine revolt of 713-711 and Hezekiah's preparations for revolt against Assyria in 705-701. The former may be excluded, however, because the Philistines appear to have been the ringleaders at that time; they might have had the opportunity to send an embassy to Judah, but Judah would have had little cause to entreat Egypt, especially since Judah appears to have avoided the conflict. It is more likely that this embassy was sent by Hezekiah in 705-701 as part of his efforts to ensure the success of his revolt. In such a situation, Hezekiah would have been the suitor and therefore would have needed to win the Egyptians to his side by sending lavish gifts (cf. vv. 6-7). Isaiah's argument is that the Egyptians are far away and therefore have little motivation to act effectively (vv. 4-5). In such a situation, the failure of the revolt is assured (vv. 12-14, 15-17). The better course of action is patience (vv. 15, 18).

Intention

The intention of this passage must be considered in relation to its various literary and historical settings. In the context of the 5th-century final form of the book of Isaiah, ch. 30 forms part of the oracles in chs. 28–33 that take up the punishment of Jerusalem and its subsequent restoration. Its primary function here is to explain the initial suffering that Jerusalem must endure in relation to the delayed salvation that the city is expected to experience during the early years of the Second Temple period. Such expectations must be seen in relation to the activities of Nehemiah and Ezra, who attempted to secure Jerusalem's existence as a holy city centered around the rebuilt temple in Jerusalem. Ch. 30 would play a similar role in the 6th-century edition of the book of Isaiah, except that the restoration of Jerusalem would entail the building of the Second Temple as well as the resettlement and agricultural prosperity of the city. In this context, the agricultural prosperity of the purified city would correspond to the expectations of the prophet Haggai, who argued that the rebuilding of the temple would lead to the material prosperity of Jerusalem at the center of the nations and the recognition of YHWH's world sovereignty.

The Josianic edition of ch. 30 must be considered in relation to the circumstances of the latter part of the 7th century, when it was evident that the Assyrian empire was about to fall and when King Josiah of Judah pursued his program for national restoration and religious reform. In this regard, ch. 30 emphasizes two major themes: the impending fall of the Assyrian empire and the futility of an alliance with Egypt. The significance of the former would seem to be self-evident; the fall of the Assyrian empire was taking place during the course of the reign of Josiah. The latter must be considered just as closely, however, in that the fall of Assyria left a power vacuum in the Syro-Palestinian corridor that Egypt threatened to fill. The rise of Egyptian power in the latter part of the 7th century obviously threatened Josiah's program for national restoration, for Judah was now faced with the prospect of exchanging an Assyrian suzerain for an Egyptian overlord. The extent to which the Egyptians were able to assert their power over Judah is debated, but it is clear that Josiah lost his life in 609 when Pharaoh Necho put him to death at Megiddo while on his way to support the Assyrians in their final stand against the Babylonian-Median coalition at Haran. The announcement of YHWH's intention to strike down Assyria and the warnings against involvement with the Egyptians would obviously have served Josiah's interests in reestablishing the former Davidic empire.

Two other features of ch. 30 are important for understanding the hermeneutics of the Josianic redaction. The first relates to v. 8, which contains an instruction to write this prophecy for a later time, and to v. 33, which refers to the fact that the destruction of Assyria had been arranged in the past. Insofar as these verses stem from Isaiah ben Amoz and the Josianic redaction respectively, they indicate the redaction's perspective that Isaiah ben Amoz addressed the situation of the 7th century even though he spoke nearly 100 years earlier. Such a perspective is bolstered by the fact that Assyria did not fall, as Isaiah stated that it would (30:18; cf. 10:5-34), in the late 8th century, but in the late 7th century.

In such an instance, the demise of Assyria during the reign of Josiah would serve as final confirmation of the validity of Isaiah's word and of Josiah as the object of Isaiah's promises concerning Davidic and Judean restoration (cf. 8:16–9:6 [*RSV* 7]). By this means, the delay in YHWH's promised salvation mentioned in 30:18-33 would account for the time between the reigns of Hezekiah and Josiah when Assyria continued to dominate Judah.

The second important feature concerns the references to the Egyptian cities Zoan and Heliopolis in v. 4, which provide the basis for relating this text to Josiah's concern with the celebration of Passover and the exodus tradition (2 Kgs 23:21-23; cf. Isa 11:11-16; note the use of the "ensign" [*nēs*] in both Isa 30:17 and 11:10, 12). Because Zoan was the site of YHWH's miracles during the exodus (Ps 78:12; cf. Exod 1:11; note that Zoan is identical with the store city Rameses), its appearance in v. 4 provides the basis to associate vv. 1-17 with both the general theme of Passover and deliverance of Judah in vv. 27-33 and that of deliverance from oppression combined with agricultural renewal in vv. 18-26. Here one should note that Passover commemorates both the deliverance of Israel from Egyptian bondage and the beginning of the harvest season in ancient Israelite agriculture.

With regard to the 8th-century edition of this text in vv. 1-18, the primary intention is to argue against Hezekiah's plans to ally with Egypt in preparation for a revolt against Assyria. Although many scholars have argued that these verses represent an assemblage of disparate, formally distinct, and previously independent texts, the elements that constitute vv. 1-18 lack sufficient reference to a specific setting apart from that defined in vv. 1-5. Without vv. 1-5, vv. 6-7, 8-11, 12-14, 15-17, and 18 (see above on v. 18) are meaningless. When considered together, however, they present a coherent rhetorical strategy designed to undermine confidence in the success of the embassy to Egypt and to advocate a policy of patience and delay while waiting for YHWH to resolve the situation.

Verses 1-5 set the basic theme of the passage by portraying the embassy to Egypt as a rebellion against YHWH that will result only in failure. The woe oracle addressed to the "rebellious children" *(bānîm sôrĕrîm)* highlights the rejection of YHWH by expressing the concluding of a treaty with Egypt with the phrase *wĕlinsōk massēkâ,* "and who make a league," in that the phrase means both "to weave a web," as in concluding a contract of alliance, and "to cast a molten image" or "to pour out a libation" to the Egyptian gods (see BDB, 651). In this regard, it is noteworthy that Isaiah mentions the city of Heliopolis (On), the primary temple of northern Egypt dedicated to the sun deity Re. It was the second most important temple in Egypt after the temple dedicated to Amun in Thebes, far to the south (see Dorsey, "On"). Because the request for Egyptian aid rejects the advice and shelter offered by YHWH, and presumably relies on the Egyptian gods, the association with Egypt will lead only to shame rather than to the expected aid and profit.

The pronouncement in vv. 6-7 backs up this initial claim. The passage describes the difficult journey through the Negev by the caravan and its pack animals laden with gifts to entreat the Egyptians. A pun involving the term *maśśā',* "pronouncement," establishes this function. The term means literally "burden" and relates to a play on words involving the verbal form *yiś'û,* "they bear/carry," in reference to the pack animals. The verb here governs several phrases ("they carry their riches on the backs of asses, and their treasures on the humps of camels, to a people that cannot profit them"). The last phrase is somewhat mistranslated in the *RSV.* The MT reads *'al-'am lō' yô'îlû,* literally "on a people that does not profit." In relation to the governing verb *yiś'û,* it should be translated, "they carry/rely on a people that does not profit." After stating that Egypt's help is worthless and empty, YHWH states that Egypt will be called "Rahab who sits still" *(rahab hēm šābet).* Although the precise meaning of the phrase is debated (cf. Wildberger, *Jesaja,* 1160-61), Rahab here functions as a mythological symbol for Egypt (cf. Ps 87:4) that was defeated by YHWH at creation (Isa 51:9; Ps 89:10). The phrase refers to Egypt's intentions to do nothing for Judah.

The instructions to write in vv. 8-11 apparently refer back to the statement concerning "Rahab who sits still" in vv. 6-7. The command to write in v. 8 employs 3rd-person feminine singular pronominal suffixes in reference to the object of writing (*kātĕbāh,* "write it"; *ḥuqqāh,* "inscribe it"). As noted above, the only possible feminine singular antecedent for these suffixes is the demonstrative *lāzō't,* "for this," in v. 7, which refers to the name for Egypt, "therefore I have called her [*lāzō't*]." The instructions seem to call for the recording of at least the pronouncement in vv. 6-7 for a later time. The recording of another prophetic pronouncement is mentioned in Hab 2:2. Likewise, Isa 8:1 and 16 refer to Isaiah's recording of the name Maher-shalal-hash-baz, and Jeremiah refers to the recording of Judah's sin (Jer 17:1) and restoration (Jer 30:2). In all cases, the recording of these prophetic words is intended to preserve them for future realization and validation. The recording of the pronouncement in vv. 6-7 serves as a means to witness to Judah's rejection of YHWH, and it further serves as a basis for announcing examples of the people's rebellious behavior in vv. 9-11.

Verses 12-14 and 15-17 describe the consequences of the people's behavior as a means to illustrate the prophet's point that the embassy to Egypt is futile. Vv. 12-14 liken the people to a bulging wall that is about to collapse and to a pottery jug that has been shattered so violently that no shards are large enough to carry even small amounts of water to put out the flames that Judah will presumably endure. Vv. 15-17 state that the people will receive precisely what they wish to avoid by entreating Egypt. If they flee on swift horses, they will be pursued by swift horses, and only a few pursuers will force many to flee. This portrayal of the people ends by rehearsing the remnant motif: only a few will be left "like a flagstaff on the top of a mountain, like a signal on a hill."

Finally, v. 18 gives the audience cause to adopt Isaiah's position that they should pursue a policy of patient waiting for deliverance. V. 18 states that YHWH will delay *(yĕḥakkeh)* showing favor to the people. This statement is further reinforced by the concluding statement, "happy are those who wait for him." According to Isaiah, Judah should not rush into an alliance with Egypt; the result would be only disaster. By pursuing a policy of caution that requires the people to wait for divine action, Isaiah apparently hopes to avoid a direct confrontation with the Assyrians, which the Egyptians may be unable or unwilling to join. By stating that the people should wait for YHWH to act, he apparently intends that other causes will draw the Assyrians away from Judah.

Bibliography

B. Couroyer, "Le nēs biblique: Signal ou enseigne?" *RB* 91 (1984) 5-29; D. A. Dorsey, "On," *Harper's Bible Dictionary* (ed. P. Achtemeier; San Francisco: Harper & Row, 1985) 730-31; J. C. Exum, "Of Broken Pots, Fluttering Birds, and Visions in the Night: Extended Simile and Poetic Technique in Isaiah," *CBQ* 43 (1981) 331-52; L. Laberge, "Is 30,19-26: A Deuteronomic Text?" *Église et Théologie* 2 (1971) 35-54; P. Reymond, "Un tesson pour 'ramasser' de l'eau à mare (Esaïe xxx,14)," *VT* 7 (1957) 203-7; L. Sabottka, "Is 30,27-33: Ein Übersetzungsvorschlag," *BZ* n.s. 12 (1968) 241-45; K.-D. Schunck, "Jes 30,6-8 und die Deutung der Rahab im Alten Testament," *ZAW* 78 (1966) 48-56; Weis (→ "Introduction to the Prophetic Literature"), 146-47, 248-49, 482.

PARENESIS CONCERNING RELIANCE ON EGYPTIAN AID AGAINST ASSYRIA, 31:1-9

Structure

I. Admonition against reliance on Egyptian aid:
   expanded woe oracle form   1-5
   A. Admonition proper: woe oracle against
      those who rely on Egypt   1-3
      1. Woe statement concerning trust in Egypt   1a
      2. Concerning trust in military power
         rather than in YHWH   1b
      3. Concerning wisdom and reliability of YHWH   2
      4. Concerning Egypt's nondivine status   3a
      5. Projected outcome: YHWH will punish
         both helper and helped   3b
   B. Basis for admonition: allegory illustrating
      YHWH's intention to punish Jerusalem himself   4-5
      1. Modified messenger speech formula $4a\alpha_1$
      2. Prophet's summation of YHWH's speech:
         allegory of lion with prey $4a\alpha_2$-5
         a. Allegory proper $4a\alpha_2$-α
            1) Portrayal of lion protecting prey $4a\alpha_2$
            2) Lion is not frightened away $4a\beta$
         b. Explanation of allegory   4b-5
            1) Concerning YHWH's action against Zion   4b
            2) Expanded explanation: YHWH's
               action compared to hovering birds   5
II. Exhortation to return to/rely on YHWH   6-9
   A. Exhortation statement proper   6
   B. Basis for exhortation: report of YHWH's
      oracle concerning abandonment of idols
      at fall of Assyria   7-9

Isaiah 31 is demarcated by its introductory *hôy* formulation in v. 1 and by its overall concern to convince its audience to abandon attempts to ally with Egypt during a time of threat by the Assyrians. Instead, ch. 31 proposes that the people trust in YHWH. Although concern with Egypt is not explicit in vv. 6-9, the reference to the fall of Assyria to a nonhuman sword in v. 8 provides a counterpoint to the statement that Egypt is human and not divine in v. 3. The introductory *hēn*, "behold," formulation of 32:1 marks the introduction to a new unit concerned with the righteous king.

The structure of ch. 31 is determined by its parenetic form. Parenesis is designed to persuade its audience to undertake a particular course of action; in this case it is designed to convince the audience to trust in YHWH during the time of Assyrian threat and not to trust in an alliance with Egypt. Parenesis frequently combines elements of admonition against the undesirable course of action and exhortation to the desired course of action. In ch. 31, the admonition against reliance on Egyptian aid to oppose the Assyrians appears in vv. 1-5. The exhortation to turn to YHWH appears in vv. 6-9, which are distinguished by their pronounced imperative masculine plural and 2nd-person masculine plural address forms directed to the *běnê yiśrā'ēl*, "children of Israel." The two sections likewise display a similar internal structure in that both the admonition proper (vv. 1-3) and the exhortation proper (v. 6) are followed by explanatory sections introduced by *kî*, "because."

The admonition against an Egyptian alliance in vv. 1-5 begins with the admonition proper in vv. 1-3 in the form of a woe oracle. The oracle begins with the woe statement proper in v. 1a, formulated according to the standard pattern of the genre with an introductory *hôy*, ("woe!") followed by the participle *hayyōrĕdîm*, which identifies the subject of the woe as "those who go down to Egypt for help." Although woe oracles can be addressed to those who are condemned (see D. R. Hillers, "*Hôy* and *Hôy*-Oracles: A Neglected Syntactic Aspect," in *The Word of the Lord Shall Go Forth* [*Fest.* D. N. Freedman; ed. C. L. Meyers and M. O'Connor; Philadelphia: American Schools of Oriental Research, 1983; Winona Lake: Eisenbrauns, 1983] 185-88), the 3rd-person formulation of this passage and its parenetic character suggest that the passage does not address those who are actually going to Egypt. Rather, it attempts to persuade the audience not to go to Egypt or not to join those who advocate an Egyptian alliance. Consequently, "those who go down to Egypt" are presented as a countertype that the audience is advised to avoid.

The initial woe statement in v. 1a is followed by a series of statements joined by *wāws* in vv. 1b-3. Scholars have noted that this is not a *wāw*-consecutive chain (Wildberger, *Jesaja*, 1227-28); instead, the following statements are distinguished

by their contents and by their individual syntactic structures. V. 1b begins with a
wāw-consecutive imperfect, *wayyibṭĕḥû*, "and they trusted," followed by the
perfect forms *wĕlō' šā'û*, "and they did not rely," and *lō' dārāšû*, "and they did
not consult," in order to portray the trust placed in military power rather than in
YHWH. V. 2 begins with an emphatic noun clause, "and yet he is wise," followed
by the *wāw*-consecutive *wayyābē'*, "and he brought," the perfect *lō' hēsîr*, "he did
not call back," and the converted perfect *wĕqām*, "and he will arise," to describe
YHWH's wisdom in bringing about the evil as required by his word and in
opposing that evil. V. 3a is constituted as a nonverbal statement that the Egyptians
are not divine and therefore that they cannot compare to YHWH. V. 3b employs a
chiastic syntactical structure of imperfect *yaṭṭeh*, "he will stretch out," converted
perfect *wĕkāšal*, "and he will stumble," converted perfect *wĕnāpal*, "and he will
fall," and imperfect *yiklāyûn*, "they will perish," to portray the projected outcome
that YHWH will strike down both the helper (Egypt) and the helped (Judah). The
sequence of statements in vv. 1-3 thereby presents a logical progression in an
argument that questions the wisdom of turning to an Egyptian alliance rather than
relying on YHWH.

The basis for the admonition appears in vv. 4-5, which are introduced by
an explanatory *kî*. The modified messenger speech formula in v. 4aα₁ demonstrates that vv. 4-5 are cast in the form of the prophet's report of a speech by
YHWH, but the 3rd-person references to YHWH in vv. 4aα₂-5 indicate that the
prophet does not quote the speech; he only reports its content. The content and
formulation demonstrate that it is an allegory designed to compare the action of
a lion protecting its prey to YHWH's actions in relation to Mt. Zion. The allegory
proper in v. 4aα₂-α is introduced by *ka'ăšer*, "just as," which establishes the
basis for the comparison. It portrays a lion protecting its prey while threatened
by shepherds in v. 4aα₂. V. 4aβ reports that the lion is not frightened away by
the shepherds. The explanation of the allegory appears in vv. 4b-5 as indicated
by the appearance of *kēn*, "thus" or "so," in vv. 4b and 5a. V. 4b explains that
YHWH's action against Zion may be compared to that of the lion. V. 5 then
compares YHWH's protection of Zion to that of hovering birds. Although this
allegory has been the cause of some confusion among scholars (see Barré), it
appears to portray YHWH's protection as that of a lion over prey or birds
hovering over their find; that is, the lion or birds protect their prey in order to
consume it themselves (see further under Intention).

The exhortation in vv. 6-9 is introduced by its masculine plural imperative formulation that calls on the children of Israel to return to YHWH. As
noted above, the exhortation proper appears in v. 6. The basis for the exhortation in vv. 7-9, introduced by an explanatory *kî*, appears in the form of the
prophet's report of an oracle from YHWH concerning the projected abandonment of idols at the fall of Assyria. The oracle proper appears in vv. 7-9a,
which are constituted by a *wāw*-consecutive verbal chain followed by a summary statement. V. 7 contains the imperfect form *yim'āsûn*, "they will reject,"
which serves as the basis for the chain, in order to announce the projected
abandonment of idols. V. 8a employs the converted perfect *wĕnāpal*, "and it
shall fall," to portray the projected fall of Assyria to a nonhuman sword. V. 8b
uses the converted perfect *wĕnās*, "and he shall flee," to portray Assyria's

flight. Finally, v. 9a breaks the pattern of *wāw*-consecutive formulation by returning to the imperfect form *ya'ăbôr,* "it shall pass." As such, it sums up the preceding material with a description of Assyria's abandonment of its positions and standards. V. 9b contains an expanded oracular formula identifying vv. 7-9a as an oracle by YHWH.

Genre

The overarching genre of ch. 31 is PARENESIS. PARENESIS employs no fixed literary form; rather, it is characterized by its persuasive intent with reference to a specific goal. In the present case, it intends to persuade the audience to avoid alliance with Egypt as the means to confront the Assyrian threat. Instead, it argues that reliance on YHWH is the necessary course of action since YHWH is the cause of the threat in the first place. Consequently, ch. 31 employs both ADMONITION against reliance on Egypt in vv. 1-5 and EXHORTATION to rely on YHWH in vv. 6-9. By focusing on both the negative aspects of alliance with Egypt and the positive aspects of reliance on YHWH, the passage presents a case for convincing the audience to follow the desired course of action.

The ADMONITION is characterized by its attempt to dissuade the audience from pursuing an alliance with Egypt as the means to counter the Assyrians. It employs several generic forms to achieve its goal. The most important is the WOE ORACLE form in vv. 1-3. The WOE ORACLE is characterized by its introductory *hôy* ("woe!"), followed by a participle formation describing the actions that serve as its object or occasion. This may be followed by statements that elaborate on that action. In the present instance, the woe is directed against those who go down (*hayyôrĕdîm*) to Egypt for aid. Although the woe form is frequently used to announce punishment, the parenetic context indicates that this is not the case here. Rather, the purpose of the present WOE ORACLE is persuasive in that it is designed to convince the audience not to ally with Egypt. The interest in achieving this goal is especially evident in vv. 1b-3. V. 1b indicates that those who rely on Egypt are impressed by military might, but they do not consult YHWH. V. 2 points to YHWH's wisdom and to the fact that YHWH caused the evil in the first place by fulfilling his divine word. Likewise, YHWH will stand against that evil. V. 3a points to the fact that the Egyptians are mortal, not divine like YHWH. Consequently, v. 3b points to the fact that YHWH will strike the helper and the helped. Because YHWH brought about the evil, presumably as a punishment, nothing will stand in the way of YHWH's purpose.

The basis for the ADMONITION is formulated as a PROPHETIC MESSENGER SPEECH. It employs a modified MESSENGER FORMULA in v. 4aα$_1$, but the following speech is a speech by the prophet, not by YHWH, which apparently summarizes the contents of YHWH's purported speech. The "speech" appears in the form of an ALLEGORY, a typical wisdom genre. In the present instance, the ALLEGORY employs the imagery of a lion protecting its prey when threatened by shepherds in order to explain YHWH's actions in relation to Zion. Just as a lion protects its prey when threatened, so YHWH will protect Zion from Egyptian intervention. But just as the lion protects his prey in order to eat it himself, so YHWH will protect Zion in order to punish it himself by bringing the Assyrians. The imagery of hovering birds reinforces this message, since birds likewise act to guard the carrion left over from the lion that they intend to consume.

The EXHORTATION in vv. 6-9 is designed to persuade the audience to rely on YHWH. It is constituted by a masculine plural imperative form, *šûbû* ("return!" in v. 6), which conveys the basic intent of the passage, and by the basis for the EXHORTATION (vv. 7-9), which provides reasons for the people to rely on YHWH, i.e., YHWH will eventually strike Assyria down. Vv. 7-9 are cast in the form of an oracle by YHWH, as indicated by the ORACULAR FORMULA *nĕ'um-yhwh*, "oracle of YHWH," in v. 9b.

Setting and Intention

Scholarly discussion of the setting and intention of ch. 31 has been greatly complicated by difficulties in establishing the meaning of the allegory concerning the lion and its prey in vv. 4-5 (for an overview of the discussion, see Kilian, *Jesaja 1–39*, 73-81). With the exception of v. 2, which is frequently regarded as an interpolation (Donner, 135-36; Childs, 33-35), scholars generally accept vv. 1-3 as authentic to the prophet Isaiah. By contrast, vv. 4-9 present problems in that vv. 5-9 are generally assigned to a later redaction during the Josianic (e.g., Barth, *Jesaja-Worte*, 77-92) or exilic/postexilic (cf. Vermeylen, *Du prophète*, 421-24) periods.

The problem centers around the fact that the image of the lion defending its prey is essentially judgmental, since the lion clearly represents a threat to the prey, whereas vv. 5-9 present a scenario of salvation. The issue is further complicated by the ambiguity of the statement that YHWH "will come to fight on [*lišbō' 'al*] Mt. Zion and on its hill" in v. 4. The verb *ṣb'* means "to assemble," "to muster," and is used in reference to an assembly for sacred worship (Num 4:23; 8:24; Exod 38:8; 1 Sam 2:22) or an assembly for war (Num 31:7; Isa 29:7, 8; Zech 14:12). When used in reference to an assembly for war, the preposition *'al*, "against," generally follows *ṣb'*. This suggests that the present passage must be understood to refer to a hostile threat against Mt. Zion. Nevertheless, the imagery of the hovering birds, with the associated terms for protection and the general tone of protection and reconciliation in vv. 6-9, suggests to many scholars that v. 4 must somehow refer to the protection of Zion (cf. Childs, 57-59). The frequent use of vocabulary that appears elsewhere in Isaiah, such as the references to "his idols of silver and his idols of gold" (*'ĕlîlê kaspô we'ĕlîlê zĕhābô*) in v. 7 (cf. 2:20), supports scholars who argue that vv. 6-9 are later additions to this text that are designed to change its judgmental character to one of salvation (Vermeylen, *Du prophète*, 423).

A second problem pertains to the appearance of v. 2, which disrupts the sequence of conjunctive verbs in vv. 1-3 with the statement "and yet he is wise" (*wĕgam hû' ḥākām*) in order to tout YHWH's wisdom in the midst of a threat. Because of these disruptions and because the references to the wicked employ vocabulary that appears most frequently in the psalms, Childs has argued that v. 2 is an interpolation into this text (pp. 33-35).

Yet these problems, and the fragmented reading of ch. 31 that results, stem from the failure of scholars to recognize the parenetic character of this passage. In general, the problem of the literary setting of these verses has been framed as a rigid choice between interpreting this material in terms of judgment or in terms of salvation. The analysis of the structure above notes that the elements of judgment and salvation in this text work together to produce an argument that is designed to persuade the audience that an alliance with Egypt will not help Jerusalem's situation. Rather than alleviating the threat against the city, alliance with Egypt would result in the defeat of both Egypt, the "helper," and Jerusalem, the "helped" (v. 3). In this instance, the exhortation in vv. 6-9 presents the alternative scenario: reliance on YHWH alone will bring about the downfall of the Assyrian invader. Such an interpretation has implications for the problems posed both by v. 2 and by v. 4.

With regard to v. 2, scholars have noted that the reference to YHWH's wisdom clearly disrupts the portrayal of the sin and punishment of those who would ally with Egypt. Yet this position assumes that the text is condemning this party for an action that has already taken place. Such a view ignores the perspective of the imperfect and converted perfect verbs in vv. 1a (*yišchsāʿēnû*, "they shall rely"), 2b (*wĕqām*, "and he shall rise"), and 3b (*yaṭṭeh*, "he shall extend," *wĕkāšal*, "and he shall stumble," *wĕnāpal*, "and he shall fall," *yiklāyûn*, "they shall perish"), which project reliance on Egypt and the subsequent downfall of both Egypt and Jerusalem as a future event. The *wāw*-consecutive imperfect and perfect verbs in vv. 1b (*wayyibṭĕḥû*, "and they trusted," *wĕlōʾ šāʿû ʿal*, "and they did not rely on," *lōʾ dārāšû*, "they did not consult") and 2a (*wayyābēʾ*, "and he brought," *lōʾ hēsîr*, "he did not rescind") refer to actions in the past that have led to the present situation of choice between Egypt and YHWH. As such, they provide the basis for deciding whether to ally with Egypt or trust in YHWH. As Whedbee points out (*Isaiah and Wisdom*, 132-35), YHWH's wisdom becomes the key issue here: YHWH brought the evil in the first place in accordance with his word and therefore provides the greatest opportunity for overcoming it. As v. 3 states, Egypt is not God, and one may hardly expect that Egypt's capabilities can resolve the threat posed by the invader. Egypt will be of no use whatsoever.

The analysis of the structure and genre of ch. 31 presented above also influences the interpretation of vv. 4-9. Many scholars view v. 4 as the beginning of a new unit (e.g., Wildberger, *Jesaja*, 1238), but the *kî* at the beginning of v. 4 and the syntactically independent imperative *šûbû* ("return!") at the beginning of v. 6 demonstrate that vv. 1-5 and vv. 6-9 constitute the two basic subunits of this chapter. One must consider vv. 4-5 in relation to vv. 1-3 since they provide the basis for the admonition. On the one hand, as noted above, the image of the lion and its prey in v. 4 is generally interpreted as a threat, especially since the phrase *lišbōʾ ʿal* means "to fight against." On the other hand, the hovering birds in v. 5 are generally regarded as a protective image: "Like birds hovering, so YHWH Sabaoth will protect Jerusalem; he will protect it and deliver it, he will spare and rescue it."

But this understanding fails to appreciate the role that the hovering birds play in relation to the protection described in the passage. The birds in fact build on the imagery of the lion and its prey in v. 4 in that the birds are those that always gather when a lion has taken prey. Lions rarely eat the entire kill at one time but return repeatedly until they are done. The dead prey invariably attracts the attention of scavenger birds who hope to feed on the lion's kill. Like the lion, they also protect the carcass. But this protection does not entail the salvation of the victim; rather, they hover over the scene to protect against another scavenger who might take the kill from them once the lion is finished. It is noteworthy that *wĕhiṣṣîl*, which means both "to snatch away" and "to deliver" (BDB, 664), indicates a wordplay that shifts the reader's perspective from one of rescue to one of threat. Likewise, *wĕhimlîṭ*, "and he escapes," indicates the threat posed by hovering birds who swoop down and then escape before they can be caught. Overall, the image presented here is one of threat. When applied to Jerusalem, it illustrates YHWH's intention to punish the city himself, without interference from the Egyptians or anyone else.

As noted above in the structural analysis, a clear shift takes place with v. 6. At this point, the passage turns from attempting to convince the audience to avoid an alliance with Egypt and turns toward its primary goal, which is to convince the audience to rely on YHWH. The unambiguous imperative in v. 6 makes this clear: "Turn to him from whom you have deeply revolted, O people of Israel!" The explanatory *kî* in v. 7 then introduces the basis for this exhortation in vv. 7-9, i.e., YHWH will bring down the Assyrian oppressor. Likewise, the reference to the fall of Assyria to a nonhuman sword highlights the contrast with the mortal Egyptians in v. 3a: YHWH has the power to relieve Jerusalem; Egypt does not. It is noteworthy that ch. 31 makes little sense without vv. 6-9. If the passage was designed to condemn alliance with Egypt, it can hardly succeed in that it fails to present an alternative strategy until vv. 6-9. Egyptian alliance is condemned, but the images of destruction in vv. 1-5 hardly provide a full basis for abandoning the position. As vv. 4-5 make clear, Jerusalem is doomed whether Egypt attempts to help or not. Vv. 6-9 provide the basis for positive action.

The parenetic character of this passage and the focus on the issue of alliance with Egypt at a time of threatened Assyrian invasion indicate that this passage must be set in relation to Hezekiah's revolt against Assyria in 705-701. Although Egypt was clearly behind Syro-Palestinian opposition to Assyria throughout the latter part of the 8th century, Hezekiah's revolt of 705-701 appears to be the most likely setting for this passage because this was the only time that Jerusalem was clearly threatened (cf. vv. 4-5). The intention of the passage is to persuade against alliance with Egypt and for reliance on YHWH alone. In effect, it argues against mounting the revolt at all, insofar as it counsels against military means to oppose the Assyrians (v. 1). The passage concedes that the Assyrians will come; in fact, they are brought by YHWH (v. 2). But it maintains that the Egyptians will be of no help because YHWH intends to punish the city before delivering it. The argumentative character of the passage, with its elements of admonition and exhortation, the use of allegory in vv. 4-5, and the reference to YHWH's wisdom in v. 2, indicate that the passage has a social setting in wisdom forms of argumentation and persuasion. This setting suggests that Isaiah had a role in the debate over Hezekiah's decision whether to ally with Egypt against the Assyrian empire. The best policy, Isaiah argued, would be to avoid a useless and costly confrontation in favor of waiting patiently for YHWH to complete the punishment that required the presence of the Assyrians in the first place. Once the punishment was completed, YHWH would act to destroy the Assyrian oppressors.

Although ch. 31 appears to have been composed in relation to the debates over Hezekiah's plans to revolt against Assyria in 705-701, the chapter also clearly functions in relation to later editions of the book. The admonition against alliance with Egypt and the announcement of the downfall of the Assyrian empire to a nonhuman sword obviously served the interests of the 7th-century Josianic redaction. The downfall of the Assyrian empire at this time would have been explained in relation to Isaiah's previous statement that this would take place. The corresponding rise of the Egyptian empire in the late 7th century, and the threat that this posed to the newly emerging Josianic kingdom, would likewise have been understood in relation to Isaiah's anti-Egyptian statements. In both cases, the downfall of Assyria and the rise of Egyptian power with its capacity to threaten Judah would have been taken as fulfillments of Isaiah's prophecy. Later editions of the book of Isaiah in the 6th and 5th centuries would have seen the passage largely in typological terms, insofar as the fall of Assyria would have symbolized the fall of the major empires that threatened Judah's existence: Babylon in the 6th century and the Persian-Median empire in the 5th century. Certainly, the appearance of an oracle against Assyria in 14:24-27, appended to the oracle against Babylon in 13:1–14:23, testifies to such typological interpretation. The interrelationship between chs. 1–39, which focus on Assyria as the major enemy of Judah, and chs. 40–55, which presuppose Babylon as the major enemy, likewise indicates such an understanding of the role of Assyria in ch. 31.

Bibliography

M. L. Barré, "Of Lions and Birds: A Note on Isaiah 31.4-5," in *Among the Prophets: Language, Image and Structure in the Prophetic Writings* (ed. P. R. Davies and D. J. A. Clines; JSOTSup 144; Sheffield: JSOT Press, 1993) 55-59; Childs, *Assyrian Crisis* (→ "Introduction to the Book of Isaiah"), 33-35, 57-59; Donner, *Israel unter den Völkern* (→ 1:4-9), 135-39; G. Eidevall, "Lions and Birds as Literature: Some Notes on Isaiah 31 and Hosea 11," *SJOT* 7 (1993) 78-87; M. A. Sweeney, "Parenetic Intent in Isaiah 31," in *Proceedings of the Eleventh World Congress of Jewish Studies, Division A: The Bible and Its World* (ed. D. Assaf; Jerusalem: World Union of Jewish Studies, 1994) 99-106.

PROPHETIC INSTRUCTION SPEECH CONCERNING THE ANNOUNCEMENT OF A ROYAL SAVIOR, 32:1-20

Structure

Isaiah 32 is demarcated initially by the particle *hēn*, "behold!" which introduces the unit with an exclamatory statement concerning the righteous rule of the new king. Although vv. 9-14 turn to a concern with mourning over the failure of the vintage, the unit continues with a description of the fertility, justice, and peace that will characterize the reign of the new king. The introductory *hôy*, "woe!" in 33:1 indicates the beginning of the next unit.

Many scholars employ a combination of thematic and formal criteria to define the three major subunits for this passage as vv. 1-8, 9-14, and 15-20 (e.g., Vermeylen, *Du prophète*, 424-48; Wildberger, *Jesaja*, 1251, 1264, 1274-75), but this division overlooks the syntactical features of the passage. The shift from 3rd-person descriptive language in vv. 1-8 to 2nd-person feminine plural address forms in vv. 9-14 certainly indicates that a major structural division occurs between vv. 8 and 9. Despite the thematic and formal shift at v. 15 from lamentation in vv. 9-14 to announcement of salvation in vv. 15-19, however, the introductory *'ad*, "until," in v. 15 indicates that these verses are connected to vv. 9-14 insofar as they define the duration of the time for lamentation and indicate its joyful aftermath. By contrast, the beatitude in v. 20 is syntactically independent from the preceding verses and is formulated with 2nd-person masculine plural address language. These considerations indicate that the three major subunits of ch. 32 are vv. 1-8, 9-19, and 20.

The disputational language and thematic focus on the just reign of the new king following previous desolation of the land and city indicate that the whole is formulated as a prophetic instruction speech concerning the announcement of a royal savior (see the discussion of Genre below). Within this context, vv. 1-8 constitute a disputational announcement of a royal savior, vv. 9-19 constitute a prophetic announcement of salvation from disaster, and v. 20 constitutes a beatitude that confirms the happiness of the righteous.

The disputational announcement of a royal savior in vv. 1-8 introduces the entire unit by announcing the righteous reign of a new king against the background of a dispute against a group of authorities, here characterized as "fools" and "misers" (see v. 5), who hold a pessimistic view of the future. As such, vv. 1-8 prepare the way for the following announcement in vv. 9-19 that salvation will follow a period of trouble. The structure of vv. 1-8 is determined by a combination of thematic, formal, and syntactical features. The announcement of a royal savior appears in vv. 1-2; two initial imperfect verbs in v. 1, *yimlāk*, "he [the king] shall rule," and *yāśōrû*, "they [officers] shall govern," are followed in v. 2 by a *wāw*-consecutive verb, *wĕhāyâ*, "and he [each] shall be." V. 1 therefore constitutes an announcement of the just rule of the new king and rulers, whereas v. 2 employs the image of wind and rain that provides relief from drought and heat to describe the characteristics of that rule.

Verses 3-8 then shift to disputational language to challenge the outlook of those with a pessimistic view of the future. Those who "see" and "hear" (v. 3), i.e., those in positions of authority, are apparently pessimistic in their outlook for the future. They are later characterized as "fools" and "misers" who advocate apostasy and error, and bring hunger, thirst, and oppression of the poor (vv. 5-7). Those previously characterized as rash and inarticulate gain understanding and clear speech (v. 4); their beneficent counsel establishes them as the true "nobles" or "benefactors" (v. 8).

The structure of these verses is determined by both theme and syntax. Vv. 3-4 employ imperfect verbal forms that basically state that those considered rash and inarticulate will overcome those authorities who see and hear. The eyes and ears of the authorities will be unable to function (v. 3), whereas the rash will gain understanding and the inarticulate will gain clear speech (v. 4). Vv. 5-8 follow up with an elaboration of this theme that maintains that the fools will no longer dominate. Although vv. 5-8 are not joined syntactically to vv. 3-4, the contrast between the "fool" *(nābāl)* and "miser" *(kîlay)* who is not really a "noble" *(nādîb)* on the one hand and the one whose beneficent counsel establishes a true "noble" *(nādîb)* on the other indicates that these verses form an appositional elaboration on vv. 3-4. V. 5 employs imperfect verbal statements to state the principle that the "nobles" will be recognized for what they truly are: "fools" and "misers." Vv. 6-8, introduced by an explanatory *kî,* "because," explain this principle in detail with a series of verbal statements connected by conjunctive *wāws.* V. 6 concerns the "fool" *(nābāl)* whose utterances lead to "wickedness" *(ḥōnep)* and "apostasy" *(tôʿâ),* as well as to "hunger" *(rāʿēb)* and "thirst" *(ṣāmēʾ).* V. 7 focuses on the "miser" *(kēlay)* whose evil counsel perverts "justice" *(mišpāṭ;* cf. v. 1) to the oppressed and poor. Finally, v. 8 concerns the true "noble" *(nādîb)* whose nobility is recognized by "beneficial" counsels and actions *(nědîbôt).*

Verses 9-19 constitute the prophetic announcement concerning the characteristics of the savior's reign as the emergence of salvation from disaster. Thematic, formal, and syntactical criteria indicate that two major subunits make up this section: vv. 9-14 constitute a call to mourn or lament directed to the "women who are at ease" *(nāšîm šaʾănannôt)* and the "complacent daughters" *(bānôt bōṭěḥôt;* cf. *BHS)* mentioned in v. 9; vv. 15-19 indicate that the lamentation will continue until a coming time of salvation. Insofar as vv. 15-19 present the coming salvation as the ultimate aftermath of the lamentation, they focus the concern of vv. 9-19 on the time of salvation and thereby return to the theme of the righteous reign of the new monarch in vv. 1-8 (see the discussion of Intention below).

The structure of the call to mourn or lament in vv. 9-14 is determined by the imperative verb forms in vv. 9 and 11, which introduce subunits in vv. 9-10 and 11-14. Vv. 9-10 comprise a call to instruction that functions as an introduction to a call to a public complaint service in vv. 11-14. The call to instruction proper in v. 9 employs three feminine plural imperatives *(qōměnâ,* "rise up"; *šěmaʿnâ,* "hear"; *haʾzēnnâ,* "give ear"), which call for the attention of the "women who are at ease/complacent daughters." Although v. 10 is syntactically independent of v. 9, the address to "you complacent women" *(bōṭěḥôt)* recapitulates the address to the "complacent *[bōṭěḥôt]* daughters" of v. 9. It therefore provides the basis for the call to instruction by pointing to the coming failure of the vintage.

The failure of the vintage also provides the cause for the call to a public complaint service in vv. 11-14. Again, vv. 11-14 are constituted initially by imperative verbs in vv. 11-12a *(ḥirdû;* "tremble" [masculine plural imperatives may be employed with feminine addressees, but see *BHS];* *rěgānâ,* "shudder"; *pěšōṭâ wěʿōrâ,* "strip and make yourselves bare"; *waḥăgôrâ,* "and gird sackcloth"), which constitute four commands to lament. The addressees of these commands are "you women who are at ease" *(šaʾănannôt)* and "you complacent ones" *(bōṭěḥôt),* recalling v. 9. The objects of lamentation are defined successively as the land in vv. 12b-13a and as the city in vv. 13b-14. In each case, the objects of lamentation are indicated by the particle *'al,* "for" (*RSV;* lit. "over"), but the introductory asseverative *kî,* "yea," in v. 13b indicates a minor structural shift that introduces a concern for the city and its buildings.

As noted above, vv. 15-19 are linked to vv. 9-14 by the particle *'ad,* "until," which defines the duration of the mourning. The structure of this passage is determined syntactically. The initial temporal statement in v. 15a states that the lamentation will last "until the wind [*RSV* 'Spirit') is poured upon us from on high." This is followed by a series of *wāw*-consecutive statements in vv. 15b-19 that describe the future circumstances of salvation. The structure of this segment is determined by the introductory formula *wĕhāyâ,* "and it shall come to pass," in vv. 15b and 17. Vv. 15b-16 describe the future transformation of nature with justice and righteousness, and vv. 17-18 describe the coming peace and security for the people.

Verse 19 is textually difficult (see *BHS*) and somewhat anomalous in the present context in that it projects the downfall of the Davidic dynasty (*yā'ar,* "forest"; cf. 22:8; 1 Kgs 7:2; 10:17, 21) and "the city" of Jerusalem *(hā'îr)* in relation to the coming peace. The appearance of both these terms in earlier verses of this passage presents difficulties for understanding v. 19. "City" appears in v. 14 in reference to the desolate conditions of the land; why refer to the downfall of the city in the context of coming salvation? "Forest" appears in v. 15 as part of the portrayal of the coming fertility of the land; why refer to the downfall of the forest in such a context? (Contra Barth, 212-13, who attempts to understand v. 19 as a reference to the fall of Assyria but fails to account for the role that the forest plays in the coming salvation; cf. Wildberger, *Jesaja,* 1275-76.) G. R. Driver ("Isaiah I–XXXIX," 52-53) attempted to employ Arabic cognates to read the verse as a description of the future idyllic conditions of the forest and city ("and the forest will be cool where it runs down [to the plain], and the city will laze in the [hot] lowlands"). But the difficulties engendered by this reconstruction and other attempts at emendation indicate that it is best to regard v. 19 as a gloss to vv. 17-18. V. 19 thereby recapitulates the theme of vv. 13b-14 in relation to the conditions of the early Persian period when Jerusalem lay in ruins and the Davidic dynasty ceased to rule (for a full discussion of the problems posed by this verse, see D. Barthélemy et al., *Critique Textuelle de l'Ancien Testament* [OBO 50/2; Fribourg: Éditions Universitaires; Göttingen: Vandenhoeck & Ruprecht, 1986] 223-24, who argue that the verse should not be emended or transposed; cf. Clements, *Isaiah 1–39,* 264; Duhm, *Jesaia,* 239; Kaiser, *Isaiah 13–39,* 332-36; Procksch, *Jesaja I–XXXIX,* 415-16; Wildberger, *Jesaja,* 1274-76). In relation to its present context, v. 19 suggests the need to humble the Davidic dynasty and the city of Jerusalem as the precondition for the coming salvation (cf. Nielsen, *There Is Hope,* 180).

Finally, the beatitude in v. 20 constitutes the third and final major subunit of ch. 32. It is syntactically independent of the preceding material, and the suffix pronoun of *'ašrêkem,* "happy are you," indicates that it is addressed to a masculine plural audience distinct from the feminine addressees of vv. 9-14. Although the meaning of the references to "those who sow beside all waters, who let the feet of the ox and the ass range free," is difficult to establish with any precision, the present context suggests that it refers to those who opposed the pessimistic outlook of the authorities mentioned in vv. 1-8. As such, it affirms the position of those who realized that salvation would emerge from the prior distress.

Genre

The overarching genre of ch. 32 is that of prophetic INSTRUCTION concerning the ANNOUNCEMENT OF A ROYAL SAVIOR (cf. Wildberger, *Jesaja,* 438-46). The ANNOUNCEMENT OF A ROYAL SAVIOR is a variation of the (→) prophecy of salvation. It is typically set in the royal courts of the ancient Near East, including Egypt and Mesopotamia, where it frequently functions as part of a prophecy to authorize the actions of a king (e.g., "Prophecy of Neferti," *ANET,* 444-46). Common elements include the announcement of a new king or a description of his coming, mention of his names, and the characteristics of his rule. Although mention of the king's names is lacking in ch. 32, elements of the genre appear in vv. 1-2 and 15-18. Vv. 15-18 likewise reiterate characteristics of the new king's rule mentioned in vv. 1-2, including "justice," "righteousness," and the "wind" or "spirit" that will bring this about, although the king is not mentioned in these verses (contra Stansell, "Isaiah 32"). In addition, the lamentation material in vv. 9-14 provides an appropriate contrast to the peaceful reign of the new king who is presented as overcoming past adversity.

Isaiah 32 is also characterized by its instructional character, which plays a role in relation to the ANNOUNCEMENT OF A ROYAL SAVIOR. Although the prophetic INSTRUCTION follows no fixed form, this identification is evident in part from the contents of the passage, which emphasize the coming just and peaceful reign of a new king following a time of trial, and from various features of the speech that are characteristic of wisdom instruction speeches. Foremost among them are the references to natural events, including the comparison of the king to the wind and rain in vv. 1-2, the failure of the vintage and its consequences for the welfare of the land and city in vv. 10 and 12-14, and the transformation of nature in vv. 15-19. The natural elements often play a role in the ANNOUNCEMENT OF A ROYAL SAVIOR in that they are frequently employed to describe both the desolate state of the land prior to the reign of the new king and its abundance once the new king takes the throne (see "Prophecy of Neferti," *ANET,* 444-46, esp. 445). They also play a role in relation to the instructional aspects of this text insofar as ancient Israelite wisdom frequently relied on observations of nature to provide the basis for understanding the world (cf. Job 12:7-25; Prov 24:30-34; 25:2-3; 26:1-3; 30:1-5, 24-28, 29-31). In each case, the natural elements interact with human elements so that the examples from nature provide a basis for formulating the various theses of the passage. Thus the righteousness and justice of the king sustain the human realm just as wind and rain sustain the natural world (cf. Prov 21:1). The failure of the vintage undermines life in the land and city, insofar as human society depends on the natural world's ability to provide food. Likewise, the transformation of nature to a luxurious state of fertility presages justice and peace for the people.

In addition to the interaction between the natural and human worlds, various wisdom forms, including the DISPUTATION (vv. 3-8), the CALL TO INSTRUCTION (vv. 9-10), and the BEATITUDE (v. 20), also indicate the instructional nature of this passage. These and the other generic elements that are included in the prophetic INSTRUCTION of ch. 32 will be discussed below.

The disputational ANNOUNCEMENT OF A ROYAL SAVIOR in vv. 1-8 represents a combination of two generic elements: the ANNOUNCEMENT OF A ROYAL SAVIOR and the DISPUTATION. In the present instance, the announcement of the new king and the description of his rule appear in vv. 1-2. The DISPUTATION appears in vv. 3-8, which advocate the position of those who see a positive outcome from the situation of disaster over against those who hold a pessimistic viewpoint. Although this does not appear to be a full example of the DISPUTATION form, in that it does not argue for a clearly articulated position, it does presuppose the conflicting views of the two parties and maintains that those previously considered rash and inarticulate are the ones who in fact possess true knowledge. The passage employs a typical wisdom contrast between the "fool" (nābāl) who lacks understanding (cf. Prov 17:7, 21; 30:22) and the "prince" or "benefactor" (nādîb) who provides the model for righteous action and wise counsel (cf. Prov 8:16; 17:7, 24-26; 19:6; 25:7).

The prophetic announcement concerning the characteristics of the new king's reign in terms of the emergence of salvation from disaster is defined by the announcement language of vv. 15-19 and by the thematic juxtaposition of disaster in vv. 9-14 and salvation in vv. 15-19. A number of generic subelements appear within this section.

The CALL TO MOURN in vv. 9-14 is introduced by the CALL TO ATTENTION in vv. 9-10. The form generally introduces a public address in a variety of contexts (especially wisdom instruction; see Prov 7:24) to attract the attention of the audience. It typically includes an invitation to listen, mention of the addressees, and an indication of the content of what is to be heard. In the present example, the invitation to listen is constituted by the feminine plural imperative verbs (qōmnâ, "rise up"; šĕma'nâ, "hear"; ha'zēnnâ, "give ear"), which solicit the attention of the audience, here defined by the vocative expressions nāšîm ša'ănannôt, "women who are at ease," and bānôt bōṭĕḥôt, "complacent daughters." The content of what is to be heard is expressed simply as qôlî, "my voice," and 'imrātî, "my speech," and by the reference to the coming failure of the vintage in v. 10. The CALL TO ATTENTION precedes the CALL TO A PUBLIC COMPLAINT SERVICE (vv. 11-14), which presents the primary content and is the basis for the generic identification of vv. 9-14 as a whole. This genre is employed in times of emergency to convene a liturgical complaint ceremony or fast (cf. 1 Kgs 21:9). It typically includes a sequence of imperatives to call the people together, mention of the people being called, and the reason for the complaint service. All three elements are present in vv. 11-14. The imperatives appear in v. 11 (ḥirdû; "tremble"; rĕgāzâ, "shudder"; pĕšōṭâ wĕ'ōrâ, "strip and make yourselves bare"; waḥăgôrâ, "and gird sackcloth") where they are directed to the "women who are at ease" and the "complacent women" mentioned in v. 9. The reason for the complaint ceremony, in vv. 12b-14, is that the welfare of the land and the city are threatened by the failure of the vintage mentioned in v. 10. In the present context, the CALL TO A PUBLIC COMPLAINT SERVICE conveys the experience of disaster that precedes the salvation announced in vv. 15-19.

Verses 15-19 announce that the lamentation will last until the coming of a future deliverance. A DESCRIPTION OF SALVATION appears in vv. 15b-19 and conveys the benefits of this future time. The DESCRIPTION OF SALVATION is normally a constituent element of the ANNOUNCEMENT OF SALVATION, but in the present context it relates to the ANNOUNCEMENT OF A ROYAL SAVIOR in vv. 1-2. Although the king is not mentioned in vv. 15b-19, the appearance of natural images to convey the upcoming salvation and the characterization of that time as one of "justice" *(mišpāṭ),* "righteousness" *(ṣĕdāqâ),* and "peace" *(šālôm)* call to mind the vocabulary and images employed to describe the righteous reign of the new king in vv. 1-2. In this sense, the coming age of salvation is identified with the coming reign of the new king.

Finally, the BEATITUDE in v. 20 represents a common form employed in wisdom literature to extol the fortunate lot of those whose behavior, knowledge, and outlook conform with that of the wise (Prov 3:13; 8:32, 34; 20:7; 28:14; 29:18; Job 5:17). It is typically introduced by the term *'ašrê,* "happy are," or "fortunate are," followed by the subject and a relative clause that describe the reason for their fortunate state. In the present instance, those who are happy sow seed on the waters and allow their animals to range free, apparently expressing the optimism and sense of security advocated in vv. 3-8.

Setting

Together with ch. 33, ch. 32 forms the conclusion to chs. 1–33 in the final form of the book of Isaiah. In addition, it concludes the Isaianic materials concerning the city of Jerusalem in chs. 28–33. As such, ch. 32 provides the hermeneutical perspective for understanding Isaiah's prophecies concerning the disasters that overtook Israel and Judah during the late 8th century. That perspective was that Judah would suffer a time of trial and tribulation, but the people would eventually be delivered from such distress by the reign of a new king who would usher in a period of justice, righteousness, and peace. In the context of the final 5th-century form of the book, this would anticipate the establishment of YHWH's rule over the entire world and the nations' recognition of Jerusalem as the center for YHWH's rule. In the 6th-century edition of the book, the theme of YHWH's rule would still be fundamental, but it would presuppose the demonstration of YHWH's power in the downfall of Babylon and the expectation of a new Davidic monarch. In either setting, ch. 32 would provide the basis for understanding the prior suffering of Judah in relation to YHWH's plan to establish Judah as the center of a righteous and peaceful world.

Isaiah 32 would play a similar role in relation to the 7th-century Josianic edition of the book of Isaiah, in that it would likewise provide the basis for understanding Isaiah's words in relation to the disasters that had overtaken Judah in the Assyrian period. In this case, Josiah would be the natural fulfillment of

YHWH's plans to restore Judah once the punishment at the hands of the Assyrian empire had been completed. A number of factors suggest that the present form of ch. 32 was composed precisely for this purpose. Although vv. 9-14 appear to stem from the 8th-century prophet, the chapter as a whole appears to be a redactional composition that was designed to conclude the Josianic edition of Isaiah's prophecies.

Barth (pp. 211-15) presents a number of arguments for assigning the bulk of ch. 32 to the Josianic or Assyrian redaction of the book of Isaiah. Most of them are are based on associations with other texts that he had already assigned to the Assyrian redaction (e.g., Isa 8:23b–9:6 [*RSV* 7]). His most forceful argument, however, is the contrast between the future salvation based on the monarchy and the past disasters that had overtaken the city of Jerusalem (pp. 214-15). He notes that the emphasis on an actual monarchical state requires that the terminus ad quem of this text be 587.

One might legitimately ask if such a text could also be set in the early Persian period when some Judean circles anticipated the restoration of the Davidic monarch (cf. Hag 2:20-23), but the failure to indicate any disruption of the monarchy in Isaiah 32 suggests that this text must be preexilic. On the basis of the 8th-century dating of Isa 8:16–9:6 (*RSV* 7) offered above, one might also ask if this text might refer to the future reign of Hezekiah in contrast to that of Ahaz. Despite Isaiah's initial support for Ahaz, Isa 8:16–9:6 (*RSV* 7) demonstrates that he anticipated that Ahaz's successor would provide a better model of righteous Davidic rule. One should note, however, that prior to Hezekiah's reign Isaiah never made any statement that would suggest that the security of the city of Jerusalem would be compromised. Although Isaiah was willing to concede that the land of Judah would be threatened, YHWH's guarantee of security for the city of Jerusalem and the Davidic dynasty formed the very basis of Isaiah's message (cf. 7:1-25; 8:1-15; 10:5-34). In fact, it was only when the Assyrian monarch threatened Jerusalem itself that Isaiah condemned the Assyrian empire, which he had previously portrayed as YHWH's tool to punish the errant people (cf. 10:5-34; 14:24-27). Isaiah's condemnations of the city of Jerusalem begin only during the reign of Hezekiah when the king attempts to form foreign alliances to oppose the Assyrians (28:7-22; 29:1-4; 30:1-14; 31:1-9) and when Isaiah begins to discuss the consequences of that action (1:2-9; 3:1–4:1; 22:1-25). Even then, the purpose of Isaiah's condemnations of Jerusalem is to motivate the people to return to YHWH so that YHWH's promised protection of the city will resume (28:23-29; 29:5-24; 30:15-33; 31:1-9). Because Isaiah never condemns the king directly, it is unlikely that Isaiah wrote this oracle to refer to Hezekiah; rather, it seems likely that the object of this passage is Josiah.

In addition to the focus on an actual monarchical state, two other features of this text support the identification of the monarch as Josiah. The first is the relation of this text to 11:1-16, which I identified above as a Josianic composition. Several important features of ch. 32 relate to those of ch. 11. The most important is the use of *rûaḥ*, "wind" or "spirit," in 32:2 and 15 and in 11:2 and 4. In both texts, "wind" or "spirit" serves as an agent associated with the king's righteous rule. In 32:2 and 15 it is employed as a natural element that brings about the conditions of fertility, as well as those of justice, righteousness, and peace in the land. In 11:2 and 4 it forms the basis for the king's wisdom that in turns brings about righteous rule. Although *rûaḥ* is located in the king in 11:2 and 4, v. 2 explicitly states that it stems from YHWH just as 32:15 states that *rûaḥ* is poured out on the people "from on high" (*mārôm*, i.e., "heaven"). Furthermore, both ch. 32 and ch. 11 emphasize the themes of wisdom, natural fertility/abundance in relation to the king's righteous reign, and peace in the land of Israel. Consequently, ch. 32 appears to stem from the same Josianic redaction as ch. 11. Although Stansell ("Isaiah 32," esp. 9-10) attempts to argue that vv. 15-18 (19-20) stem from a different redaction than that of vv. 1-5 (6-8), his arguments are not compelling. Based on the presence of the disputational material in vv. 1-5, he mistakenly assumes that vv. 1-5 focus on the transformation of an internal relationship whereas vv. 15-18 focus on the people as a whole. As demonstrated above, the issue in vv. 1-8 is competing interpretations of the future, which will be resolved in the coming time of peace (i.e., Josiah's reign) when the optimists are proved correct.

The second feature is the composite character of this text. Scholars have long noted that vv. 1-8 and 15-20 form a redactional framework around vv. 9-14 (see Stansell, "Isaiah 32," for a summary of positions). Vv. 9-14 clearly articulate a theme of judgment and disaster that betrays no awareness of the message of salvation found in vv. 1-8 and 15-20. Furthermore, the formulation of v. 15a, *'ad-yē'āreh 'ālênû rûaḥ mimmārôm*, "until the Spirit [lit. "wind"] is poured out upon us from on high," is clearly composed as a means to link vv. 9-14 to the following text. Whereas vv. 1-8 and 15-20 appear to be redactional, vv. 9-14 appear to be Isaianic. Indeed, the use of the imagery of the vintage and thorns and briars to describe the coming fate of the land and city is typical of the prophet (cf. 5:1-25). In fact, scholars generally term these verses "the last words of Isaiah" (Fohrer, *Jesaja,* 2:127). Wildberger's arguments (*Jesaja,* 1265-67; cf. Kaiser, *Isaiah 13–39,* 327-29) that vv. 9-14 must be understood as a retrospective view of the destruction of Jerusalem should be rejected. Although the passage clearly refers to Jerusalem as indicated by the mention of "the joyful city" *(qiryâ 'allîzâ)* in v. 13 and the "Ophel" (*'ōpel; RSV* "hill") in v. 14, his view that the text represents a *vaticinium ex eventu* ("prophecy after the fact") does not account for the use of the failed vintage to project the downfall of the city. Such a tactic would hardly be necessary after 587, when Judean thought focused on the downfall of Jerusalem as the product of the people's wrongdoing. In this case, the image of the ruined Jerusalem must be considered as a rhetorical device employed by the prophet to persuade the people that such an event was possible. The association of a failed vintage and the potential fall of Jerusalem provides little basis for dating vv. 9-14, but it appears likely that these verses formed part of Isaiah's polemic against Hezekiah's planned revolt against Assyria. According to 37:30-32, agricultural failure is associated with the Assyrian siege of Jerusalem.

Although the precise social setting of the Isaianic version of vv. 9-14 is not completely clear, the Josianic version of the final form of ch. 32 appears to be set in the court of King Josiah. The announcement of a royal savior is typically set in the royal court, where it functions as a means to confirm the legitimacy of the king's reign. Insofar as it presents the king as the means to overcome past adversity, it looks forward to a peaceful and prosperous reign for the new monarch. In relation to the prophecies of Isaiah, ch. 32 presents King Josiah as the fulfillment of the prophet's words. The new king is presented as the fulfillment of YHWH's plans to bring disaster upon the country followed by salvation.

Intention

The intention of ch. 32 is determined by a number of interrelated factors. Foremost among them is its generic character as an announcement of a royal savior, but the structure of the passage, its lamentation and disputation elements, its setting in the court of King Josiah, and its placement in its present literary context also play important supporting roles.

The generic character of ch. 32 as announcement of a royal savior plays the major role in defining the overall intention of this passage. As noted above, this genre plays the dominant role in defining the overall structure and contents of the chapter insofar as it appears in vv. 1-8 and 15-20. The new monarch is portrayed as the divinely inspired catalyst for a new age of justice, righteousness, peace, and natural abundance. The interaction of the natural elements, including wind and rain, as well as the wilderness, steppe *(karmel),* and forest, play an especially important role in relation to the genre, for they demonstrate cosmic or natural assent to the reign of the new king. Consequently, the entire natural world affirms the righteous rule of the new monarch. Likewise, the "wind/spirit on high" (v. 15) affirms divine support.

The lamentation elements in vv. 9-14 also play an important role in relation to the announcement of a royal savior. These verses appear to have been composed originally by the prophet to warn of future consequences for the people. Those consequences are expressed in terms of the failure of the vintage, but clearly the welfare of the land, city, and people are foremost in the prophet's mind. The danger is expressed initially in terms of agricultural failure, but the references to the "exultant city," "palace," and "hill/acropolis/Ophel" (*'ōpel)* indicate that the prophet envisions a threat against the city of Jerusalem. Although the specific occasion for this passage is difficult to reconstruct, the emphasis on security and complacency, combined with the focus on the image of a deserted city of Jerusalem, suggests that the prophet has in mind an invasion against the city as the main threat. The emphasis on the battlements of the city, including the "hill/acropolis" and "watchtower" (v. 14), suggests that a military attack is foremost on the prophet's mind. He is certainly known for expressing the threat of military invasion in terms of agricultural failure (cf. 5:1-30; cf. 10:5-34). In relation to the announcement of a royal savior, however, vv. 9-14 present a pointed contrast with the peaceful reign of the new monarch. Whereas the land, city, and people suffered deprivation in the past, the reign of the new monarch will put an end to such suffering. Vv. 9-14 thereby highlight the salvation offered by the new king and bolster the persuasive appeal of the passage.

The wisdom elements of the passage, including the disputational material in vv. 3-8 and the beatitude in v. 20, also contribute significantly to its persuasive appeal. In relation to the historical and social setting in the royal court of King Josiah, they aid in garnering support for the new monarch by characterizing those with a pessimistic outlook on his reign as "fools" and "misers," whereas those who are optimistic are characterized as the true "princes" or "benefactors" (*nādîb*). That the opponents appear to be persons in authority is also significant in that it may point to the fact that Josiah was installed as monarch by the "people of the land" in opposition to a rebellious group of officials under Josiah's father Amon who used their access to the royal house to murder the prior monarch (cf. 2 Kgs 21:19-26; 2 Chr 23:21-25). In such a volatile situation, the disputational material of ch. 32 would confirm not only the new monarch but also the actions of those who opposed the rebellious "servants" of the king. The concluding beatitude in v. 20, with its emphasis on those who sow seed and tend animals, confirms the position of those characterized as the optimists in vv. 3-8. Such a characterization lends support to the view that the new king's supporters are the "people of the land."

The literary setting of ch. 32 also plays an important role in defining its intention. As the concluding section (together with ch. 33) of the Josianic redaction of Isaiah's prophecies, ch. 32 presents the reign of the new king Josiah as the culmination of Isaiah's prophecies and YHWH's plans for Israel, Judah, and Jerusalem. The presentation of Josiah's ideal reign is presented as the means for understanding both the oracles of judgment and the oracles of salvation found in the Josianic edition of the book of Isaiah. Josiah represents the ideal monarch and the possibility of a glorious future for Zion and the people of Israel/Judah announced in various salvation oracles throughout the book (e.g., 8:16–9:6 [*RSV* 7]; 11:1-16). Likewise, the oracles of judgment against Israel, Judah, and even Jerusalem indicate YHWH's plans to punish the people as a means to purify them and the land in preparation for the righteous reign of the new monarch, who will represent YHWH's power to rule the nations and to restore Zion and the land of Judah/Israel as the center for divine recognition.

That material from Isaiah is employed in this chapter is particularly important in that it reveals some of the hermeneutical perspective of the Josianic redaction. Not only were Isaiah's prophecies considered to be true, but he was understood to have been speaking about the coming reign of the righteous king Josiah throughout his career in relation to the disasters that befell the land at the hands of the Assyrians. In the eyes of the Josianic redactors, Isaiah's prophecies and the experience of Assyrian invasions were the necessary preparation for the righteous reign of King Josiah, who would bring the period of tribulation to an end.

Finally, the literary setting of ch. 32 in relation to the 6th- and 5th-century editions of the book of Isaiah must also be considered. From the perspective of the 6th-century edition of the book, it was obvious that King Josiah's rule had failed to bring about the projected peace. But with the impending fall of Babylon, the opportunity for the reestablishment of Judah/Zion would have provided the context for understanding ch. 32. Its literary placement at the conclusion of the prophecies of Isaiah and prior to the materials from Deutero-Isaiah indicates that this chapter played an important role in defining the expectations expressed in chs. 40–55 (60–62), especially the expectation that the reign of King Cyrus of Persia would usher in an era of peace including the reestablishment of Zion/Judah and the recognition of YHWH among the nations. Such an era would then have been understood as the goal of YHWH's plans for punishing and restoring Israel and Jerusalem. Likewise, ch. 32 would play a similar role in the 5th-century edition of the book in that it would aid in providing the transition between the first part of the book and the second. Again, the projected righteous and peaceful reign of the new king would define the expected outcome of Isaiah's prophecies in both portions of the book. But the delay in realizing that ideal situation is evident in chs. 56–66. Although the people in 5th-century Judah might have wanted a new Davidic monarch, it appears more likely that the references to a monarch who would usher in an era of peace in this period might well be references to YHWH (cf. chs. 60–62; 66). In such a situation, YHWH's righteous and peaceful rule of Israel and the world would provide the basis for understanding ch. 32 in the context of the final form of the book.

Bibliography

Barth, *Jesaja-Worte* (→ "Introduction to the Book of Isaiah"), 211-15; J. W. Olley, "Notes on Isaiah xxxii 1, xlv 19, 23 and lxiii 1," *VT* 33 (1983) 446-53; J. J. M. Roberts, "The Divine King and the Human Community in Isaiah's Vision of the Future," in *The Quest for the Kingdom of God: Studies in Honor of George E. Mendenhall* (ed. H. B. Huffmon, F. A. Spina, and A. R. W. Green; Winona Lake: Eisenbrauns, 1983) 127-36; R. J. Sklba, " 'Until the Spirit from on High Is Poured out on Us' (Isa 32:15): Reflections on the Role of the Spirit in the Exile," *CBQ* 46 (1984) 1-17; G. Stansell, "Isaiah 32: Creative Redaction in the Isaian Tradition," in *SBL 1983 Seminar Papers* (ed. K. H. Richards; Chico: Scholars Press, 1983) 1-12; idem, *Micah and Isaiah* (→ 1:10-17), 62-63; Wegner, *Examination of Kingship* (→ "Introduction to the Book of Isaiah"), 275-301.

PROPHETIC ANNOUNCEMENT
OF A ROYAL SAVIOR, 33:1-24

Structure

I. Address to oppressor: woe oracle	1
A. Woe statement	1a
B. Announcement of punishment	1b
II. Address to YHWH: petition for relief from oppressor	2-4
A. Petitions to YHWH for relief	2
1. First petition: show favor	2a
a. Petition proper	2aα
b. Basis for petition: we have waited	2aβ
2. Second petition: strength and salvation	2b
a. Strength/arm	2bα

Isaiah 33 is demarcated initially by the introductory *hôy* ("woe!") in v. 1 directed against an unnamed oppressor. The body of the chapter presupposes the overthrow of this oppressor prior to the institution of YHWH's kingship. A new unit begins in 34:1 with an imperative address directed to the nations concerning the downfall of Edom.

Although ch. 33 begins with a concern for the overthrow of the unnamed oppressor in v. 1, it focuses ultimately on the institution of YHWH's kingship as its primary concern. Insofar as the passage is constructed to project the future overthrow of the oppressor and YHWH as the future king who will bring an end to oppression, it must be regarded as a prophetic announcement of a royal savior. The structure of this text is determined by the interaction of a variety of elements, especially its shifting forms of address, its changes in genre and theme, and its syntactical features. Five preparatory subunits build toward the climactic vv. 17-24, which describe YHWH's kingship over a secure Jerusalem and the cessation of oppression.

The first major subunit is v. 1, which is a woe oracle directed against the unnamed oppressor. It is clearly defined by the introductory *hôy* and by the 2nd-person masculine singular address forms, which can refer only to the oppressor. The verse includes the basic woe statement in v. 1a and an announcement of punishment in v. 1b stating that the oppressor will be punished in accordance with the devastation it brought upon others (*kahătimkā*, lit. "according to your finishing [off]/devastation"; *kannĕlōtĕkā*, lit. "according to your bringing to an end/extermination").

The second major subunit is vv. 2-4, which constitute an address to YHWH in the form of petitions for relief from oppression. The passage is defined by its 2nd-person masculine singular address forms in vv. 2 and 3. Although v. 4 contains a 2nd-person masculine plural address form (*šĕlalkem*, "your [pl.] spoil"), the lack of an apparent referent for this form and the lack of a comparative particle before *'ōsep hehāsîl*, "[as] the caterpillar gathers," like that in the parallel v. 4b (*kĕmaššaq gēbîm*, "as locusts leap") suggest that the verse should read *šālal kĕmô 'ōsep* (so *RSV;* cf. *BHS;* Duhm, *Jesaia,* 240; Wildberger, *Jesaja,* 1283; contra Barthélemy et al., *Critique textuelle de l'Ancien Testament* [OBO 50/2; Fribourg: Éditions Universitaires; Göttingen: Vandenhoeck & Ruprecht, 1986] 228-29).

Within the context of vv. 2-4, v. 2 is distinct because of its imperative syntactical structure and its use of 1st-person common plural forms ("we," "us") to identify the perspective of the speaker. Apparently, the speaker/prophet employs the 1st-person common plural to identify with the audience. The reference to YHWH in v. 2aα and the 2nd-person masculine singular address forms confirm that YHWH is the addressee. The imperative verbs constitute the basic structure of the verse as two petitions to YHWH for relief. V. 2a contains the first petition to "be gracious to us" *(ḥonnēnû)*, including the petition proper in v. 2aα and the basis for the petition, "we have waited for you," in v. 2aβ. V. 2b contains the second petition to "be their arm" *(hĕyēh zĕrōʿām;* v. 2bα) or "our salvation" *(yĕšûʿātēnû;* v. 2bβ). In v. 2bα "their arm" apparently refers to the "peoples" or "nations" who constitute Judah's enemies in v. 3; the "arm" refers to the "strength" necessary to repel them. Consequently, punishment of the enemies corresponds to "our salvation" in v. 2bβ. Vv. 3-4 then elaborate on the results of YHWH's intervention. As indicated by the conjunctive *wāw* in v. 4 *(wĕʾussap,* "and it [spoil] is gathered") and the contents of vv. 3-4, these verses form a subunit that elaborates on the results of YHWH's intervention by describing the defeat of the enemies. V. 3 states that the "peoples" or "nations" will be scattered, and v. 4 states that their spoil will be taken.

The third major subunit is vv. 5-6, which constitute an address to the audience concerning the exaltation of YHWH. These verses are syntactically independent from the preceding material, but they are connected together by the *wāw*-consecutive *wĕhāyâ,* "and he shall be," at the beginning of v. 6. Although v. 5 is formulated as an objective statement concerning the exaltation of YHWH, the 2nd-person masculine singular address form in v. 6 ("and he will be the stability of *your* times") indicates that vv. 5-6 are constituted as the prophet's address to the audience. Within the context of the chapter as a whole, vv. 5-6 begin to articulate YHWH's projected response to the petition in vv. 2-4. Vv. 5-6 include two parts: the basic statement concerning YHWH's exaltation in v. 5 and an enumeration of the benefits that will result from YHWH's exaltation in v. 6.

The fourth major subunit is vv. 7-13, which constitute the prophet's summation of circumstances leading to the royal savior. The passage is syntactically independent from the preceding material in that it is introduced by the exclamatory particle *hēn,* "behold!" It is defined by its descriptive 3rd-person language, which lacks any specific address forms, and by its generic pattern based in the prophetic announcement of punishment. Within the larger structure of ch. 33, vv. 7-13 constitute a descriptive announcement concerning the reasons for YHWH's intervention.

Verses 7-9 convey the basis for punishment as the prophet's description of the oppression caused by the unnamed oppressor. Although vv. 7-9 contain nine syntactically independent statements, thematic associations indicate that three basic parts appear here, each describing different aspects of the oppression. V. 7 focuses on the oppressors' warriors, who show no quarter to their victims by ordering them out (of their homes; lit. "their warriors cry, 'Out!' " contra *RSV*) and rebuffing their emissaries of peace (see the discussion of Intention below). V. 8 focuses on the disruption of human life, including the cessation of commerce, the breaking of the normal bounds of social order (lit., "[the] covenant is broken"; see further under Intention below), and the disregard for cities (MT; contra *RSV*) and human beings. Finally, v. 9 focuses on the disruption of nature, including the mourning of the land and the withering of Lebanon.

The last part of the fourth subunit is vv. 10-13, which constitute the prophet's announcement of YHWH's judgment speech, as indicated by the speech formula *yō'mar yhwh,* "says YHWH," in v. 10a and by the 1st-person singular formulation of the speech throughout vv. 10-13 that can refer only to YHWH. The speech is formulated with 2nd-person masculine plural address forms in vv. 11 and 13, which are apparently directed to the oppressor. V. 10 constitutes the first major element of the judgment speech in that the 1st-person common singular formulation with introductory *'attâ,* "now," of its three basic statements presents a general announcement that YHWH will rise up against the oppressor. Vv. 11-12 contain the prophetic announcement of punishment proper, employing the metaphors of childbirth, chaff, and fire. V. 11 employs 2nd-person masculine plural address forms directed to the oppressors which state that they shall bear chaff and that fire shall consume them. V. 12 is connected to v. 11 by the *wāw*-consecutive verb *wĕhāyû,* "and they shall be," which introduces a statement of the consequences. V. 13 employs both 2nd-person masculine plural and 1st-person common singular to address the oppressors and to identify YHWH as the speaker. The verse is formulated as a call to attention, which normally introduces the following material. But since v. 13 is formulated as YHWH's speech and vv. 14ff. are not, v. 13 can serve only as the conclusion to YHWH's speech in vv. 10-13. In this context, it serves as a concluding admonition that calls attention to YHWH's past deeds and power (cf. Wildberger, *Jesaja,* 1296).

The fifth major subunit of ch. 33 is vv. 14-16, which constitute the prophet's announcement concerning the approach of the royal savior. Like vv. 7-13, the overall structure of vv. 14-16 is formulated with descriptive announcement language that contains no specific address forms, but the generic pattern of the torah or entrance liturgy and the 1st-person common singular formulation of the entrance questions in v. 14b distinguish them from what precedes. One should note that in contrast to other examples of the entrance liturgy in Psalms 15 and 24, the qualities articulated in the response are not general ethical qualities but those of a righteous monarch (see further on Intention). Insofar as v. 16 identifies the heavens as the home of the monarch, vv. 14-16 prepare for the announcement of YHWH as the royal savior in vv. 17-24. The first component of this subunit is v. 14a, which introduces the passage by stating that "sinners" and "the godless" will be afraid in Zion. This is followed by the questions in v. 14b concerning the qualifications of one who wishes to enter the temple. The responses appear in vv. 15-16. V. 15 is formulated with the participles that are typical of the entrance liturgy form. They describe the attributes of a righteous monarch or ruler, including righteousness (v. 15a), the avoidance of corruption or bribes (v. 15bα), and the toleration of neither evil nor bloodshed (v. 15bβ). V. 16 employs finite verbs, which are not typical of the form, to describe the monarch's divine attributes, i.e., his dwelling place is above (v. 16a; cf. v. 5) and his sustenance (bread and water) is secure (v. 16b).

The sixth subunit of ch. 33, in vv. 17-24, constitutes the goal of the entire passage in the form of an announcement of the vision of the royal savior in vv.

17-24. This subunit is defined by its generic pattern based in the announcement of a royal savior, its 2nd-person masculine singular singular address forms directed to the audience throughout the passage, and its 1st-person common singular formulation employed by the speaker/prophet to identify with the audience addressed here. The identification of YHWH as king in v. 22 and the announcements concerning the relief from oppression in vv. 18-19 and 23-24 mark vv. 17-24 as the climax of the entire chapter. The structure of this subunit is determined by its shifting address patterns, its thematic foci, and its syntactical features.

Verse 17 sets the stage for the announcement by employing the image of what "your eyes" will see to describe to the audience a vision of "the king in his beauty" and "a land that stretches afar." Vv. 18-19 then shift to what "your mind" (lit. "heart") will perceive concerning the cessation of oppression. V. 18a introduces the issue with a basic statement that the mind/heart will meditate on the terror. Vv. 18b-19 then follow up with rhetorical questions concerning the disappearance of the oppressor who counted towers and weighed the tribute. The questions proper appear in v. 18b, and an appositional expansion in v. 19, introduced by the direct object particle 'et, focuses on the disappearance of the insolent and incomprehensible foreign oppressor. Vv. 20-22 then shift back to what "your eyes" will see, namely, a vision of a secure Jerusalem with YHWH as king. The announcement of the vision appears in v. 20 and is formulated with an imperative command (ḥăzēh, "look upon") to see the secure Zion in v. 20a followed by an elaboration in v. 20b that employs the metaphor of an immovable tent to describe the secure Jerusalem that "your eyes" will see. The basis for this vision appears in vv. 21-22, introduced by an emphatic causative kî, "for indeed." V. 21 employs the metaphor of ships that are unable to pass through YHWH's waters to describe the security that YHWH will provide the city. V. 22, introduced by a causative kî, "because," states that YHWH's rule provides the basis for such security.

Verses 23-24 are a special case due to a translational problem. In their present form, they employ a 2nd-person feminine singular address form to shift to a focus on Zion's relief from pain and suffering. V. 23a is particularly problematic in that scholars have confused its enigmatic vocabulary with nautical references that would refer to the ships mentioned in v. 23 (cf. RSV). Yet these scholars have failed to recognize the wordplay involving the noun ḥebel, which can mean "cord, rope," or "pain." In v. 20b it refers to tent ropes as part of the metaphor describing the security of Jerusalem. Because of this meaning, and because kēn-tornām and nēs in v. 23 can refer to the "base of a mast" and a "sail," respectively (cf. Ezek 27:5, 7), scholars have concluded that ḥăbālāyik in v. 23 must refer to the ropes that would be used to secure the mast and unfurl the sail of a ship. The antecedent for the 2nd-person feminine singular pronominal suffix in ḥăbālāyik, "your ropes," is taken to be the reference to the feminine 'ŏnî-šayiṭ, "galley with oars," in v. 21b, but this overlooks the masculine ṣî 'addîr, "stately ship," that immediately follows. It also overlooks the use of tōren, "staff," and nēs, "ensign," in 30:17, which refers to the ensign raised in times of distress to call for aid or to serve as a rallying point (cf. Exod 17:15; Isa 5:26; 11:10, 12; 13:2; 18:3; 31:9; 62:10; Jer 4:6, 21; 50:2; 51:12; Ps 60:6

[*RSV* 4]; cf. Num 26:10). If the 2nd-person feminine singular pronoun suffix is taken as an address to Zion/Jerusalem, however, the passage may be translated as a reference to Zion's relief from pain and oppression: "your pains are relieved [lit. "dispersed, loosened"], they shall not seize the base of the staff, an ensign shall not be unfurled." Consequently, v. 23a contains a basic statement concerning Zion's relief from pain. The introductory *'āz,* "then," indicates that vv. 23b-24, linked by a conjunctive *wāw* in v. 24, follow up with specifications of this statement. V. 23b states that the people will take much spoil (from the oppressor), v. 24a states that the inhabitant (of Zion) will be relieved from illness, and v. 24b states that "the people who dwell in it [i.e., Zion] will be forgiven their iniquity" (contra *RSV*).

Genre

Scholars have generally followed Gunkel in regarding ch. 33 as a (→) prophetic liturgy because of its diverse generic elements, but R. Murray has successfully argued that the chapter coheres around an unspecified royal ritual. Indeed, ch. 33 appears to be a somewhat mixed text in that its generic character is influenced by both the COMMUNAL COMPLAINT SONG (cf. Mowinckel) and the ANNOUNCE-MENT OF A ROYAL SAVIOR. The COMMUNAL COMPLAINT SONG is typically based on a PETITION to YHWH for relief from some threat; such a PETITION appears in vv. 2-4 and presupposes the WOE ORACLE against the oppressor in v. 1. Likewise, one could construe the material in vv. 5-24 as an affirmation of confidence that YHWH will respond to the PETITION, but these features appear to be subsumed into the general pattern of the ANNOUNCEMENT OF A ROYAL SAVIOR, which appears most clearly in vv. 17-24. The genre typically includes an announcement of the new king (v. 17), his name (v. 22), and a description of his reign (vv. 18-21, 23-24), all of which appear in vv. 17-24. One should note, however, that the ANNOUNCEMENT OF A ROYAL SAVIOR frequently describes the desperate circumstances that called for the appearance of a royal savior in the first place, including the breakdown of both the social and natural order (cf. "Prophecy of Neferti"; *ANET,* 444-46, esp. 445; cf. Isa 33:7-9). This would clarify the function of vv. 1, 2-4, and 7-9 in relation to the genre, in that these verses would establish the need for a royal savior. Likewise, other elements of the chapter, including vv. 5-6, 10-13, and 14-16, describe YHWH's characteristics, actions, and approach that would further inform the ANNOUNCEMENT OF A ROYAL SAVIOR. The climactic position of vv. 17-24, which describe YHWH's rule as the climax toward which the rest of the passage builds, confirms the constitutive role of the ANNOUNCEMENT OF A ROYAL SAVIOR in formulating this passage. One should also note that the chapter is formulated as a PROPHETIC ANNOUNCEMENT insofar as it employs the prophet's direct address language and a future orientation to convey its announcement of YHWH as a royal savior.

A variety of other generic elements also contribute to the overall genre of this passage, and modify the ANNOUNCEMENT OF A ROYAL SAVIOR. After all, this is not a typical example of the genre in that it proposes YHWH as the new king whose reign will inaugurate a reign of peace. Furthermore, Beuken demonstrates that ch. 33 serves as a sort of "mirror text," reflecting the themes, motifs, and vocabulary of both chs. 1–32 and 34–66. It thereby serves as a means to link the two major portions of the book of Isaiah and to draw out their major themes. This would explain the mixture of COMMUNAL COMPLAINT SONG and the ANNOUNCEMENT OF A ROYAL SAVIOR in ch. 33, insofar as the interaction of punishment and salvation serves as a major theme of the book together with that of the emerging role of YHWH as ruler of the world.

As noted above, the influence of the COMMUNAL COMPLAINT SONG is evident in the appearance of the WOE ORACLE in v. 1 and the PETITIONS in vv. 2-4. The WOE ORACLE is typically employed in prophetic literature to criticize or to announce punishment for some sort of action or attitude deemed incorrect by the prophet. It is formulated with two basic parts: the particle *hôy* ("woe!") followed by a participial formulation that describes the criticized actions or the offending party (cf. v. 1a), and a continuation that elaborates on the basic woe statement in some way. In the present instance, v. 1b states that the oppressor will be punished in accordance with its destruction of others. The PETITION is generally the basic element of any COMMUNAL COMPLAINT SONG. It is typically, but not exclusively, formulated in the imperative, and requests YHWH's intervention to relieve the petitioning party from some misfortune. It may also contain a basis for the PETITION that will establish the grounds for YHWH's intervention. In the present instance, v. 2a contains the basic PETITION to YHWH formulated in the imperative, *yhwh honnēnû,* "O YHWH, be gracious to us," followed by the basis for the PETITION, "we have waited for you" (contra *RSV*), which expresses the petitioners' dependence on and relation with YHWH. With its second imperative form, "be their [contra *RSV*] arm every morning, our salvation in the time of trouble," v. 2b constitutes a second PETITION that reinforces the basic PETITION of v. 2a. Vv. 3-4 simply elaborate on the results of YHWH's intervention.

The PROPHETIC ANNOUNCEMENT OF PUNISHMENT in vv. 7-13 builds on the COMMUNAL COMPLAINT elements in vv. 1, 2-4 by announcing YHWH's response to the PETITION for relief from oppression. More importantly, however, it follows an address to the audience concerning YHWH's exaltation in vv. 5-6 and thereby contributes to the ANNOUNCEMENT OF A ROYAL SAVIOR by demonstrating YHWH's intent to bring about just rule. The passage is formulated with its typical elements: vv. 7-9 rehearse the crimes of the oppressor and thereby provide the grounds for the punishment; vv. 10-13 are formulated as the prophet's announcement of a speech by YHWH (note the SPEECH FORMULA in v. 10, *yō'mar yhwh,* "says YHWH") expressing YHWH's intention to take punitive action against the oppressor. As noted in the discussion of the structure, vv. 11-12 employ the metaphors of childbirth, chaff, and fire to convey the pain, worthlessness, and destruction that will overtake the oppressor for its actions. A concluding CALL TO ATTENTION appears in v. 13. Although this genre is employed in both prophetic and wisdom contexts to call attention to material that will follow, it appears at the conclusion of the speech in its present context. In this context, the CALL TO ATTENTION serves as a means to reinforce the message of judgment delivered in vv. 10-12. Despite its placement at the end of YHWH's speech, its introductory function is still apparent to the reader, in that it serves as a rhetorical device that calls attention to the following subunits as well and thereby aids in maintaining the flow of the passage as a whole.

Verses 14-16 constitute a modified form of the ENTRANCE LITURGY. The genre is typically constituted by questions that ask after the righteousness or cultic purity of the addressee who wishes to enter the temple precincts. This is followed by a response, generally formulated with participles, which attests to the required attributes. Other examples of the genre appear in Psalms 15 and 24:3-5 (cf. Mic 6:5-8). Scholars generally maintain that the ENTRANCE LITURGY was employed to establish the cultic purity of those who wished to enter the temple. Upon arriving at the gate of the temple, pilgrims would establish their admissibility by stating their qualifications to a temple functionary within, who would enumerate the conditions of entry. Such a purpose is unlikely, however, in that it would be impossible to determine whether a pilgrim was actually righteous without extensive investigation, which would create havoc for a such a public event. Instead, it is more likely that the ENTRANCE LITURGY served as a means to assert the righteousness or cultic purity of liturgical participants, not to challenge it or to establish it. In the present instance, the qualities enumerated — righteousness, avoidance of bribes, prohibition of murder, etc. — are those that pertain to a righteous monarch; they are not the general ethical principles that appear in Psalms 15 and 24. This function indicates that the genre has been modified for its role in the present context; that is, it is designed to assert the righteousness of the monarch who approaches to assume rule. In this case, the references to the monarch's dwelling in the heavens (*mĕrômîm;* cf. v. 5) indicate that YHWH is the royal savior.

The basic ANNOUNCEMENT OF A ROYAL SAVIOR appears in vv. 17-24. As noted above, the constituent elements of the genre appear here, including the approach of the monarch (v. 17), his names (v. 22), and a description of his rule (vv. 18-21, 23-24). The genre was typically employed in the royal courts of the ancient Near East to confirm the rule of a new monarch with a portrayal of the blessings and order that his rule would bring. Because YHWH is the monarch, however, a modification is introduced in that the announcement is portrayed as a vision. This is evident from the COMMAND to "look on Zion" in v. 20a, which is formulated with the imperative verb *ḥăzēh.* The root *ḥzh* generally refers to prophetic visions. This perspective is reinforced by the references to what "your eyes" will see (vv. 12, 20b) and what "your heart/mind" will perceive (v. 18). One should note that the RHETORICAL QUESTIONS in v. 18b serve as a means to emphasize the disappearance of the oppressor at the onset of YHWH's reign.

Setting

The historical setting of ch. 33 has proved to be particularly problematic. Scholarly opinion runs the entire gamut of possibilities including the time of Isaiah (Roberts), the time of King Josiah (Mowinckel, 235, n. 1), the period of the Babylonian exile (Clements, *Isaiah 1–39,* 265), the Persian period (Wildberger, *Jesaja,* 1288), and the Hellenistic period (Kaiser, *Isaiah 13–39,*

342). The problem is rooted in the liturgical character of the passage and the absence of any definitive historical references. The passage clearly presupposes a situation of threat by a foreign oppressor, but that situation pertains to all the settings suggested above.

Despite the difficulties involved, it seems best to maintain that ch. 33 stems from the Persian period; specifically, it is the product of the 5th-century redaction that produced the final form of the book of Isaiah. A variety of considerations support this view, including its portrayals of the oppressor and of YHWH as king, its liturgical setting, and its literary character as a "mirror text" (*Spiegeltext,* so Beuken) within the book of Isaiah.

In arguing for Isaianic authorship of ch. 33, Roberts (pp. 15-16) points to the literary coherence of the chapter, its vague portrayal of the oppressor, and its use of the Zion tradition. He notes correctly that the passage should not be broken down into its smallest units and that the vague portrayal of the oppressor does not preclude Isaianic authorship. He further notes that the use of the Zion tradition is completely consistent with Isaiah's theology. But Roberts's argument fails on this last point in that YHWH is presented as the future king. Although Isaiah is certainly capable of conceiving YHWH in royal terms as the true power behind the Davidic throne (cf. ch. 6; 9:1-6 [*RSV* 2-7]), he consistently anticipates a real Davidic monarch on the throne in Jerusalem (8:23–9:6 [*RSV* 7]; cf. 7:10-17). But ch. 33 presents YHWH as the monarch; there is no suggestion of a real Davidic monarch in this passage. This lack would eliminate the passage from consideration as an Isaianic composition and as the product of the Josianic redaction, which likewise anticipates a real Davidic monarch on the throne (cf. 11:1-16; 32:1-20, contra Roberts). Indeed, such a perspective corresponds much more closely to the late-6th-century redaction of Isaiah that portrays YHWH as an arbitrator and judge among the nations (2:2-4), but that anticipates a real monarch, such as Cyrus (44:28; 45:1) or even Zerubbabel (cf. Hag 2:20-23).

Only in the context of the 5th-century edition of the book of Isaiah, when there is little hope for the establishment of a Davidic monarch, does one see the portrayal of YHWH as king (cf. chs. 65–66, esp. 66:1-2). During this period, Judah was forced to recognize the reality of Persian rule. Although it is unlikely that Jews abandoned hope for the possibility of independent Davidic kingship, the center of Jewish life began to shift from a focus on the interrelated institutions of the Davidic monarchy and the temple to one on the temple (reinforced by the Torah) alone.

At this point, the liturgical character of ch. 33, including the communal complaint song elements in vv. 1, 2-4, and the royal entrance liturgy in vv. 14-16, come into play along with the modified form of the announcement of a royal savior. Insofar as Ezra saw his return to Jerusalem to reestablish the "remnant" or "holy seed" of Judah as the fulfillment of prophecy in the book of Isaiah (Ezra 9:2, 8; cf. Isa 6:13; see K. Koch, "Ezra and the Origins of Judaism," *JSS* 19 [1974] 173-97), a royal liturgy such as Isaiah 33 that declares YHWH to be king would serve Ezra's interests. Although it draws on traditional elements of Zion theology that proclaim YHWH as king (Psalms 93; 95–100; note that Psalm 101 indicates that this tradition anticipated a real king who would declare his fitness according to qualities that mirror those of Isa 33:14-16), it would have presented no threat to the ruling Persian monarchy. Even though the image of the oppressor in ch. 33 may well preserve some memory of the Assyrians (Childs, 112-17, esp. 114-15; cf. R. Murray, 207), it would have applied to the Persians in a 5th-century context. Unlike the Babylonians, who completely destroyed Judah, the Persians acted as suzerains, disrupting normal life (vv. 7-9) and taking tribute (vv. 18-19); but the anonymous portrayal of the oppressor in ch. 33 would have presented no real threat to them. One should note that although the book of Isaiah is quite capable of identifying Judah's oppressors, it only does so for the Assyrians (10:5-34; 14:24-27), the Babylonians (13:1–14:23), and other nations in the oracles against the nations (chs. 13–23). The only major Near Eastern nation missing from the oracles against the nations in chs. 13–23 is Persia. King Cyrus of Persia was apparently regarded as YHWH's instrument for Judah's salvation in the 6th-century edition of Isaiah (cf. 44:28; 45:1), but the indications of upheaval in the world in chs. 65–66, Haggai, and Zechariah 1–8 suggest that Persia, too, would be targeted for overthrow by YHWH in the 5th century.

Although one cannot be certain, the emphasis on water imagery in v. 21 and the theme of YHWH's kingship suggest a possible association with the liturgy of the festival of Sukkot, or Booths. Sukkot marks the beginning of the rainy season in Israel and, according to some (e.g., Mowinckel), celebrates YHWH's kingship in Zion. One should note that Ezra first read the Torah to the people in Jerusalem at the festival of Sukkot (Nehemiah 8–10). It is possible that Isaiah 33, or even the entire book of Isaiah, played a role in relation to the observance of this festival.

The decisive arguments for the 5th-century setting of Isaiah 33, however, relate to its literary character and setting. In its present position, ch. 33 concludes the first half of the book of Isaiah (chs. 1–33), which contains the announcements of the prophet's oracles concerning the Assyrian period. Insofar as ch. 33 stands at the conclusion of chs. 1–33, and before chs. 34–66, which proclaim the prophet's message for the Babylonian and Persian periods, it is in an opportune position to summarize the first part of the book and to anticipate the second part, thereby serving as part of a literary bridge between the book's major components. Beuken's study of ch. 33 as "mirror text" points to this role, since it establishes that ch. 33 contains extensive allusions to the vocabulary and themes of the book. Beuken argues that composing such a "mirror text" is a common literary technique designed to link major components of a piece of literature and to summarize their ideas and concepts.

Beuken's study overlooks some important connections, however, that would strengthen his case. These include many references to ch. 1. Isa 33:24 mentions the despoiling of the oppressor, the relief from sickness, and the pardon from sin in contrast to the conditions outlined in 1:4, 5, and 7. The qualities of the righteous king mentioned in the entrance liturgy in vv. 14-16 correspond with the concerns raised in 1:16-17 and 21-26. Insofar as ch. 1 serves as a summary of the book of Isaiah by rehearsing its major themes of punishment and the anticipated restoration of Jerusalem (Fohrer, "Jesaja 1" [→ 1:1-31]), ch. 33 serves as its counterpart in that it, too, reviews these major concerns, but from the perspective of the expected downfall of the oppressor, rather than from the perspective of the coming punishment of Jerusalem as articulated in ch. 1.

But ch. 33 establishes links with other important organizing texts in Isaiah as well. Its use of *ḥebel*, "pains" or "labor pains," in v. 23a corresponds to the use of this term in 13:8; 26:17; and 66:7, where it describes the world's transformation and upheaval (cf. the verbal forms of *ḥbl*, "to destroy" or "to labor in childbirth," in 10:27; 13:5; 32:7; 54:16). The term *bĕrît*, "covenant," in v. 8 likewise plays a prominent role in describing the breakdown or establishment of world order in 24:5; 54:10; and 55:3, each of which concludes or introduces a major block of material. In addition to the lexical links with the major structural blocks of the book, the portrayal of YHWH as the king who overthrows oppression and inaugurates a new age takes up a central concern expressed at the beginning of the book (2:2-22) and at the end (66:1-24).

Clearly, ch. 33 plays a major role in establishing the structure of the entire book and in summarizing and conveying its ideas concerning YHWH's purposes in bringing about disaster and restoration for Jerusalem and the world. Such a role indicates that ch. 33 was composed as part of the 5th-century redaction that established the final form of the book as a whole.

Intention

The intention of ch. 33 is determined by its generic characteristics and liturgical setting on the one hand, and by its literary setting and characteristics on the other.

Although there is no evidence that ch. 33 functioned independently of its present literary setting as a liturgical text set in the temple, it is clear that liturgical forms, such as the communal complaint song and the announcement of a royal savior, play an important role in determining its overall intent. As demonstrated in the discussion of genre above, both genres influenced the present form of this text. The purpose of the communal complaint song is to appeal to YHWH for assistance in overcoming an enemy threat. The purpose of the announcement of a royal savior is to legitimize the rule of the king, especially with regard to his ability to overcome adversity and to establish a righteous and peaceful reign. Both of these purposes come together in the present text to present YHWH as the monarch who will overcome the threat posed by the unnamed oppressor and establish a peaceful and secure Jerusalem as the site for YHWH's rule.

The structure of the passage demonstrates a progression of thought that is directed toward the establishment of YHWH's peaceful rule. The future perspective indicates that the passage presupposes a current situation of crisis that will be resolved when YHWH's rule is established. It begins in v. 1 with a warning against the oppressor who will be overthrown in accordance with its own destructive crimes. Vv. 2-4 convey the petition of the people for YHWH's aid against the oppressor and describe its projected defeat. Vv. 5-6 describe YHWH's exaltation as the means to introduce YHWH's intervention and assumption of kingship. Vv. 7-13 employ the prophetic announcement of judgment to depict the oppressor's crimes and YHWH's response; because the oppressor has disrupted the human and natural order, YHWH will rise against the oppressor to destroy it. Vv. 14-16 employ a modified form of the entrance liturgy to describe YHWH's approach to the temple. Just as the king declared his righteous intention in the context of a royal temple ritual (cf. Psalm 101, which Kraus calls a "a king's vow of loyalty"; see H.-J. Kraus, *Psalms 60–150* [tr. H. C. Oswald; CC; Minneapolis: Augsburg, 1989] 277), so YHWH's righteousness is asserted by employing a genre that derives from a liturgical context. The vision of the overthrow of the oppressor and YHWH's establishment of peaceful rule in Jerusalem appears in vv. 17-24.

One should note that such a composition expresses the hopes of a community that wishes to overcome a difficult situation. In the context of the 5th century, that situation would be the overthrow of Persian rule and the establishment of YHWH's just reign in its place. Although some scholars might maintain that a purge of the wicked in Jerusalem is envisioned here, such a position relies on a mistranslation of v. 14 as "The sinners in Zion are afraid" *(RSV)*. But the syntactical construction of the sentence, *pāḥădû běṣîyôn ḥaṭṭā'îm*, "the sinners are afraid in Zion," does not support such an interpretation and instead points to an external threat to the city consistent with the image of the foreign oppressor. In this case, the anonymity of the oppressor and the identity of YHWH as the ruling monarch are important. As Zerubbabel and his supporters learned (see Haggai; cf. Zechariah 1–8), Persia was not willing to tolerate a challenge to its rule by the establishment of a Davidic monarch in Judah. Although some in Judah might look forward to an independent Judah, the identification of Persia as the oppressor or explicit calls for a real Davidic king might provoke the Persians to take punitive action. Consequently, the present form of Isaiah 33 expresses the repressed hopes of the Judean population.

Another aspect of the intention of this passage is evident in relation to its literary function within the book of Isaiah. As noted in the discussion of setting above, ch. 33 plays a key role as a "mirror text" in relation to the book as a whole. By alluding to vocabulary from various parts of the book, including its key structural texts, and by taking up its major themes, ch. 33 acts as a bridge that links the major segments of the book of Isaiah, chs. 1–33 and 34–66, together. By virtue of this function and its place at the conclusion of chs. 1–33, ch. 33 complements ch. 1, a text that summarizes the major concerns of the first half of the book. Whereas ch. 1 summarizes the themes of judgment against Jerusalem and Judah and the eventual restoration of Zion from the perspective of the coming punishment, ch. 33 looks forward to the end of that punishment and the resulting restoration of Zion as the site for YHWH's peaceful rule. The interaction of communal complaint song and the announcement of a royal savior clearly reflect this concern. Likewise, the formulation of the modified call to attention in v. 13, "Hear, you who are far off, what I have done; and you who are near, acknowledge my might," anticipates similar phraseology in the second half of the book (34:1; 40:21, 28; 41:1; 43:19; 44:18; 45:6; 46:12; 48:6, 8; 49:1, 26; 51:1, 7, 21; 55:2).

Isaiah 33 clearly plays a key role in establishing the structure and message of the book as a whole. In this regard, the anonymity of the oppressor and the identity of YHWH as the king who will bring peace by overthrowing the oppressor are crucial to the overall intention of this chapter. By presenting the oppressor as an anonymous figure, ch. 33 makes it possible to typologize the oppressors, such as Assyria and Babylon, who are named throughout the book. This typologizing enables the reader to apply oracles explicitly addressed to these figures in specific historical situations to different situations in times other than those of the original setting of the text. Here it is noteworthy that the Hebrew terms employed for the oppressor in 33:1, *šôdēd*, "destroyer," and *bôgēd*, "treacherous one," are drawn from 21:2, which employs them in reference to the Median/Persian attack against the Assyrians at Der in Babylonia in 720. Consequently, 33:1 employs a term that calls to mind a context that gathers together all three major conquerors of Judah in the book of Isaiah. The use of this term facilitates both the typologization of the oppressor in ch. 33 and the application of oracles that identify the oppressor explicitly to other situations.

Such a perspective is evident, for example, in 13:1–14:27, where an oracle concerning YHWH's projected destruction of Assyria (14:24-27) follows immediately upon an oracle against Babylon (13:1–14:23). This association indicates that the author intended to draw an analogy between Babylon and Assyria: just as Assyria was condemned and ultimately judged for its crimes, so the oracles in the book of Isaiah that condemn Assyria will condemn Babylon on the same principle. This analogy would explain why so little material condemning Babylon appears in the book when chs. 40ff. presuppose Babylon's punishment. It also explains why the punishment of Assyria in chs. 36–39 provides the background for the oracles concerning Babylon in chs. 40–48. Likewise, the identification of YHWH as king precludes the need to identify a real Davidic king as the fulfillment of the royal oracles in the first part of the book (9:1-6 [*RSV* 2-8]; 11:1-16; 32:1-20). In an age when the Davidic dynasty no longer ruled, YHWH's purposes could be accomplished with a Persian monarch such as Cyrus (44:28; 45:1) or with no monarch at all (cf. 55:3; 66:1-2). Such a hermeneutical perspective ensured a great deal of flexibility in applying the oracles of the book of Isaiah to later situations that had nothing to do with the Assyrian or Babylonian periods. Likewise, oracles announcing the rule of a Davidic monarch could be applied to other rulers or authority figures, such as the Hasmoneans, Jesus, or the Zealots of the Roman period.

Bibliography

W. A. M. Beuken, "Jesaja 33 als Spiegeltext im Jesajabuch," *ETL* 67 (1991) 5-35; Childs, *Assyrian Crisis* (→ "Introduction to the Book of Isaiah"), 112-17; L. Delekat, *Asylie und Schutzorakel am Zionheiligtum: Eine Untersuchung zu den privaten Feindpsalmen* (Leiden: Brill, 1967) 166-76; K. Galling, "Der Beichtspiegel: Eine gattungsgeschichtliche Studie," *ZAW* 47 (1929) 125-30; H. Gunkel, "Jesaia 33, eine prophetische Liturgie," *ZAW* 42 (1924) 177-208; S. Mowinckel, *Psalmenstudien II* (1921; repr. Amsterdam: P. Schippers, 1966) 235-38; R. Murray, "Prophecy and the Cult" (→ "Introduction to the Prophetic Literature"); Roberts, "Divine King" (→ 32:1-20); S. Schwantes, "A Historical Approach to the 'R'LM of Is 33:7," *AUSS* 3 (1965) 158-66; B. Stade, "Jes. 32. 33," *ZAW* 4 (1884) 256-71; S. Ö. Steingrimsson, *Tor der Gerechtigkeit: Eine literaturwissenschaftliche Untersuchung der sogenannten Einzugsliturgien im AT: Ps 15; 24,3-5 und Jes 33,14-16* (ATSAT 22; St. Ottilien: EOS, 1984); R. D. Weis, "Angels, Altars and Angles of Vision: The Case of *'r'lm* in Isaiah 33:7," in *Tradition of the Text* (*Fest.* D. Barthélemy; ed. G. J. Norton and S. Pisano; OBO 109; Freiburg: Universitätsverlag; Göttingen: Vandenhoeck & Ruprecht, 1991) 285-92; J. Ziegler, "Das Heuschreckengleichnis Is. 33,4," *Bib* 14 (1933) 460-64.

PROPHETIC INSTRUCTION CONCERNING YHWH'S POWER TO RETURN THE REDEEMED EXILES TO ZION, 34:1–35:10

Structure

I. Prophetic instruction concerning YHWH's power
over the nations: example of Edom 34:1-17
    A. First address to nations concerning destruction
of Edom: prophecy against a foreign nation 1-15
    B. Second address to nations concerning confirmation
of YHWH's power 16-17
II. Prophetic oracle of salvation concerning the return
of the redeemed to Zion 35:1-10
    A. Announcement of rejoicing/blossoming
in nature/Arabah 1-2
    B. Instruction to the weak concerning the
coming of YHWH and its results 3-10

Isaiah 34–35 is demarcated initially by the call to attention directed to the nations in 34:1-2, which employs masculine imperative verbs (*qirbû*, "draw near"; *haqšîbû*, "give ear") to instruct the world to hear about YHWH's anger against all the nations. Although ch. 35 lacks an explicit syntactical or generic connection to ch. 34, the two chapters function together in that the prophetic instruction concerning YHWH's power over the nations in ch. 34 serves as the necessary premise for the prophetic oracle of salvation concerning the return of the redeemed to Zion in ch. 35. The narrative material in ch. 36 marks the beginning of a new unit.

The basic structure of chs. 34–35 is determined by the presence of two generically distinct units: the prophetic instruction concerning YHWH's power over the nations in ch. 34, and the prophetic oracle of salvation concerning the return of the redeemed to Zion in ch. 35. A full discussion of the respective structures of each of these units appears under the treatment of each chapter below. The prophetic instruction in ch. 34 employs the example of Edom's destruction to demonstrate YHWH's power over the nations. The first address to the nations in 34:1-15, identified by the imperative address forms in v. 1, describes the destruction of Edom in lurid detail and identifies it as a manifestation of YHWH's vengeance on the "Day of YHWH" (cf. v. 8). The second address to the nations, identified by the imperative address forms in v. 16, confirms the destruction as a manifestation of YHWH's power by instructing the audience to read in "the book of YHWH," presumably the prophecies of Isaiah, in order to see that YHWH's commands have been fulfilled. The prophetic oracle of salvation in ch. 35 then announces the return of the redeemed to Zion. Isa 35:1-2 provide a cosmic perspective to the return by announcing the rejoicing or blossoming of the natural world. Vv. 3-10, which are demarcated by the masculine imperative verbs in vv. 3-4, then provide instruction to the weak concerning the coming of YHWH and its results; that is, they will return to Zion while all nature witnesses and rejoices.

Genre

The overarching genre of chs. 34–35 is prophetic INSTRUCTION. This is evident from the primary role played by the imperative verbs in the structure of these chapters (esp. in 34:1, 16; 35:3-4), which identify 34:1-17 and 35:3-10 as examples of the INSTRUCTION genre. It is also evident in the overall concern of these chapters to identify YHWH as the cause of the destruction of Edom, and thereby to project that YHWH's power will then be applied to return the redeemed exiles to Zion. To this end, the passage also employs the PROPHECY CONCERNING A FOREIGN NATION in 34:1-15 and the PROPHETIC ORACLE OF SALVATION in 35:1-10. A detailed discussion of the generic characteristics of each of these chapters appears below.

Setting

Isaiah 34–35 plays an important role in the final form of the book of Isaiah in that this unit introduces the second part of the book in chs. 34–66. The introductory role of this unit is evident from a number of formal features that associate chs. 34–35 with the two halves of the book (cf. Torrey, *Second Isaiah,* 92-104, 279-301; Gosse, "Isaïe 34-35"; for a full discussion, see the "Introduction to the Book of Isaiah" in this volume and the individual discussions of chs. 34 and 35 below).

Such features include the following: the parallel calls to attention in ch. 1 and ch. 34 (see Evans, "On the Unity"); the concern with the redemption of Zion in chs. 2–4; 28–33 and in chs. 35; 40; 49–54; the contrasting portrayals of Ahaz and Hezekiah at parallel times of crises in 6:1–9:6 (*RSV* 7) and chs. 36–39 (cf. Ackroyd, "Isaiah 36–39"); the association between the prophecy against Edom in 34:1-15 and the pronouncements concerning foreign nations in chs. 13–23, especially that against Babylon in ch. 13 (see Dicou); the association between the prophecy against Edom in 34:1-15 and the prophecy against Edom in 63:1-6 (cf. Dicou); the concern with the blind, deaf, and lame in 35:5-6 and in 6:9-10; 42:16-19; 43:8; and 44:18 (see Clements, "Unity"; idem, "Beyond Tradition History"); and the return of the redeemed to Zion by means of a second exodus through the wilderness in 35:8-10 and in 11:11-16; 27:12-13; 56:8; 62:10-12; 66:20 (cf. Vermeylen, *Du prophète,* 446; Steck, *Bereitete Heimkehr,* 67-68; Sweeney, *Isaiah 1–4,* 17-20). Altogether, chs. 34–35 presuppose the projected punishment of Jerusalem, Israel, and the nations together with the projected restoration of Zion announced in chs. 1–33. In introducing chs. 34–66, chs. 34–35 announce that the time for the realization of these prophecies has arrived. To this end, 34:16-17 commands the reader to "read from the book of YHWH," in order to confirm that the prior commands of YHWH have been realized.

As noted in the discussion of the setting of ch. 35, this chapter presupposes chs. 40–55, which indicates that it was composed during the late 6th century, probably as an introduction to the second part of the 6th-century edition of chs. 2–62*. Ch. 34 presupposes the 5th-century displacement of the Edomites by the

Nabateans, which indicates that the final composition of chs. 34–35 must be placed in association with the composition of the final form of the book of Isaiah. For full discussions of the composition of chs. 34 and 35, see the individual treatments of these chapters below.

Intention

The intention of chs. 34–35 must be considered in relation to their literary setting as the introduction to the second half of the book in chs. 34–66. In addition, one must consider the structure of chs. 34–35, their generic character as a prophetic instruction, and their historical setting in the 5th century.

This unit maintains that the prior prophecies of chs. 1–33 are about to be realized. Whereas chs. 1–33 project the punishment of Jerusalem, Israel, and the nations during the Assyrian period together with the restoration of Zion at a later time, chs. 34–66 maintain that punishment of Jerusalem, Israel, and the nations has already taken place by the Babylonian and early Persian periods, and that the restoration of Zion is imminent. The destruction of Edom during the 5th century is particularly important in this scenario, in that this serves as the basis to demonstrate that YHWH's plans will in fact take place, thereby confirming the validity of the prophetic words that precede. In this regard, the instruction to read in "the book of YHWH" in 34:16 is crucial to understanding the intent of these chapters in that such confirmation of the realization of YHWH's plans is made when one consults the previous words of the prophet and correlates them with current events. In this case, the 5th-century destruction of Edom confirms YHWH's words of punishment against the nations and demonstrates that YHWH's promises for the restoration of Zion at the center of the nations (cf. 2:2-4) will in fact take place.

Isaiah 34–35 sees the realization of YHWH's promises not only in the historical realm, in which Edom will be destroyed and Zion will be redeemed, but also in the cosmic or natural realm, in which all of creation will celebrate at the restoration of Zion (cf. 40:1-11). This portrayal indicates the ancient Judean view that the temple stands at the center of the creation, that the creation of the world takes place at Zion, and that the people of Israel thereby stand at the center of the nations of the world (cf. J. D. Levenson, "The Temple and the World," *JR* 64 [1984] 275-98; idem, *Sinai and Zion: An Entry into the Jewish Bible* [Minneapolis, Chicago, and New York: Winston, 1985]). In this regard, the punishment of Jerusalem, Israel, and the nations, and the restoration of Zion at the center of the nations, stands in the book of Isaiah as a cosmic event that demonstrates YHWH's sovereignty over the entire universe (cf. chs. 1; 2–4; 65–66).

Bibliography

→ bibliography at "Introduction to the Book of Isaiah." W. Caspari, "Jesaja 34 und 35," *ZAW* 49 (1931) 67-86; B. Dicou, "Literary Function and Literary History of Isaiah 34," *BN* 58 (1991) 30-45; H. Donner, " 'Forscht in der Schrift JHWHs und lest!' Ein Beitrag zum Verständnis der israelitischen Prophetie," *ZTK* 87 (1990) 285-98; Elliger, *Deutero-jesaja* (→ "Introduction to the Book of Isaiah"), 272-78; H. Graetz, "Isaiah XXXIV. and XXXV.," *JQR* 4 (1891) 1-8.

PROPHETIC INSTRUCTION CONCERNING YHWH'S POWER OVER THE NATIONS: EXAMPLE OF EDOM, 34:1-17

Structure

I. First address to nations concerning destruction of Edom: prophecy against foreign nations	1-15
A. Call to attention directed to nations and to world	1
B. First basis for call: anger of YHWH against nations	2-4
1. Basic statement	2
a. Concerning YHWH's anger against nations	2a
b. Appositional explication: YHWH has consigned them to slaughter	2b
2. Elaboration concerning their demise	3-4
a. Concerning dead bodies	3a
b. Concerning dissolving of mountains and host of heaven	3b-4aα
c. Concerning withering of heavens and host	4aβ-b
1) Simile concerning rolling up of nations like scroll of heaven	4aβ-bα
2) Simile concerning demise of their host like withering leaf	4bβ-γ
C. Second basis for call: YHWH's sword drenched with blood of Edom	5-6a
1. YHWH's statement that sword is directed against Edom	5b
2. Prophet's elaboration that sword is full of blood and fat of sheep, he-goats, and rams	6a
D. Third basis for call: YHWH's sacrifice in Bozrah/Edom	6b-7
1. Basic statement	6b
2. Concerning additional animals	7a
3. Concerning land soaked with blood	7b
E. Fourth and climactic basis for call: YHWH's day of vengeance against Edom and recompense for cause of Zion	8-15
1. Basic statement	8
2. Elaboration concerning ruin of land	9-15
a. Land turned to pitch and brimstone	9-10
1) Concerning ruin of streams and ground	9a
2) Consignment of land to pitch and brimstone	9b-10

Isaiah 34 is demarcated initially in v. 1 by the masculine plural imperatives that introduce a call to attention addressed to the nations. The masculine imperative verb in v. 16 indicates that vv. 16-17 resume this address to the nations and refer back to the preceding material against Edom. Isa 35:1 clearly introduces a new unit as indicated by the absence of a syntactical connection with the preceding verbs, the thematic shift to the rejoicing of the wilderness and desert, and the use of imperfect verbs. Although 34:1-15 contains material concerning YHWH's judgment against the nations in general (vv. 1-4) and against Edom in particular (vv. 5-15), the resumption of the address to the nations, together with the command to read in order to confirm YHWH's punishment against Edom in vv. 16-17, indicates that vv. 1-17 are to be read as a unit. In this case, vv. 16-17 draw out the purpose of the call to attention in v. 1 by indicating that the nations are to learn about YHWH's power to punish from the example of Edom. The speaker is the prophet throughout.

  The basic structure of ch. 34 is determined by the masculine plural imperative verbs in vv. 1 and 16, which define the chapter's two addresses to the nations. Considered in relation to their respective contents, the two addresses constitute an instructional speech concerning YHWH's power based on the fulfillment of an oracle of judgment against Edom. Vv. 1-15 constitute the first address to the nations concerning YHWH's judgment against Edom as an example that confirms YHWH's capacity to bring about judgment against the nations. Vv. 16-17 constitute the second address to the nations, which confirms YHWH's power by directing them to read YHWH's book where they will see that all of the statements concerning Edom are coming to pass.

Muilenburg has demonstrated that the appearance of the particle *kî* in vv. 2, 5, 6b, and 8 plays an important role in determining the structure of ch. 34. In fact, they determine the structure of the first address to the nations in vv. 1-15 in that they introduce a series of subunits that explain the basis for the initial call to attention directed to the nations in v. 1. Each of these subunits contributes an element to a logical progression of images that finds its climax in the depiction of YHWH's vengeance against Edom as "recompense for the cause of Zion" in vv. 8-15. Such a culmination indicates that vv. 1-15 are based in the prophecy concerning a foreign nation (see further under Genre), and that the punishment of Edom stands as an example for the nations to witness.

The first basis for the call to the nations appears in vv. 2-4, which focus on the anger of YHWH against the nations. The structure of this subunit is determined by an initial basic statement in v. 2 of YHWH's anger and consignment of the nations to slaughter, followed in vv. 3-4 by an elaboration that describes their demise. The basic statement includes the statement concerning YHWH's anger in v. 2a and an appositional explication in v. 2b that states that YHWH has consigned the nations to slaughter. The elaboration in vv. 3-4 is joined to v. 2 by an initial conjunctive *wāw*, but its structure is determined by a *wāw*-consecutive chain that builds on the paired imperfect verbs in v. 3a, *yušlākû*, "they shall be cast out," and *ya'ăleh*, "it shall rise." The elaboration focuses on their dead bodies (v. 3a), the dissolution of the mountains and the host of heaven (vv. 3b-4aα), the rolling up of the nations "like the scroll of heaven" and the withering of their host like a withering leaf (v. 4aβ-b).

The second basis for the call to the nations appears in vv. 5-6a, which focus on the image of YHWH's sword drenched in blood. V. 5 employs 1st-person common singular suffix pronouns, *ḥarbî*, "sword," and *ḥermî*, "my curse/ban," which indicate that YHWH is the speaker. Consequently, v. 5 constitutes a statement by YHWH that the divine sword is directed against Edom for judgment. V. 6 resumes the prophet's speech with an elaboration that states that YHWH's sword is full of the blood and fat of sheep *(kārîm)* and he-goats *('attûdîm)* and the innards of rams *('êlîm)*. The significance of the references to the sheep, goats, and rams may be that these terms are often employed in relation to the leaders of a people in the Hebrew Bible *(kār;* cf. 16:1; *'āttûd,* 14:9; Ezek 34:17; *'ayil,* Exod 15:15; 2 Kgs 24:15; Ezek 17:13; 31:11, 14; 34:17). Consequently, v. 6 contains a double entendre that refers both to animals for slaughter and to the leaders of Edom.

The third basis for the call to the nations appears in vv. 6b-7, which focus on YHWH's sacrifice in Bozrah or Edom. V. 6b basically states that YHWH will have a sacrifice in Bozrah, the capital of Edom, and a slaughter in Edom. Two explanatory statements, each introduced by a converted perfect verb, appear in v. 7a and 7b. V. 7a states that wild oxen and young steers will fall with the mighty bulls, i.e., the people will perish with their leaders. V. 7b states that the land will be drenched with blood.

The fourth basis for the call to the nations appears in vv. 8-15, which focus on YHWH's day of vengeance against Edom and year of recompense for the cause of Zion. Because this section is the climax of the series, it is the longest and describes the desolation of the land of Edom in detail. Following the basic statement of YHWH's day of vengeance and year of recompense in v. 8, vv. 9-15 elaborate on this concept by describing the destruction of Edom in terms reminiscent of the destruction of Sodom and Gomorrah. The structure of vv. 9-15 is constituted by a series of paired converted perfect verbs that convey a progression of images that trace the fall of Edom. Vv. 9-10 focus on the image of a land turned to pitch and brimstone. V. 9a states that Edom's streams and soil shall be turned to pitch and brimstone. Vv. 9b-10 develop this image by focusing on the land that has become burning pitch in v. 9b, whereas v. 10a and v. 10b employ appositional statements that describe the unquenchable smoke and its eternal desolation respectively. Vv. 11-12 focus on the resulting break-down of order. V. 11a states that various unclean animals (viz., the hawk, the porcupine, the owl, and the raven) shall possess the land. Vv. 11b-12 describe a situation of chaos in which no social order exists (cf. *BHS* and *RSV* notes on v. 12). V. 13 describes the desolate strongholds and fortresses that are overrun by weeds (v. 13a) and animals such as the jackals and ostriches (v. 13b).

Verses 14-15 break the pattern of paired converted perfect verbs by em-ploying a converted perfect and an imperfect in v. 14a followed by three em-phatic statements introduced by references to "there" that describe how the desert beasts will meet or inhabit the coastlands. This is basically stated in v. 14a with a reference to satyrs; v. 14b (*'ak-šām*, "indeed there") refers to the "night hag" (*lîlît*), v. 15a (*šāmmâ*, "there") describes the owl, and v. 15b (*'ak-šām*, "indeed there") describes the kite with her mate. The image of such creatures inhabiting the areas of Edom formerly inhabited by people completes the picture of destruction.

The second address to the nations concerning the confirmation of YHWH's power appears in vv. 16-17. The structure of this section begins with the basic instruction to read from the "book of YHWH" in v. 16aα constituted by the imperative verbs *diršû*, "seek," and *qěrā'û*, "read." The results are then de-scribed in vv. 16aβ-17 as a confirmation of YHWH's power. V. 16aβ-b states that not one of these animals is missing, i.e., everything described in the book is happening. This is basically stated in v. 16aβ and the cause, that YHWH has commanded it and gathered them, is stated in v. 16b. V. 17, connected to v. 16aβ-b by a conjunctive *wāw*, elaborates with statements that YHWH has determined this (v. 17a) and that they shall possess the land of Edom forever (v. 17b).

Genre

The overarching genre of ch. 34 is the prophetic INSTRUCTION. The prophetic character of this chapter is evident in its reliance on the PROPHECY CONCERNING A FOREIGN NATION (see below). Although the INSTRUCTION genre has no fixed form of expression, it is identified by its overall intent to provide guidance or instruction to an individual or group. In the present case, this intention is evident in its attempt to demonstrate YHWH's power over the nations and capacity to bring about judgment on them. It employs the case of the destruction of Edom as a specific example from which the nations should draw their general conclusions. The imperative mode of address (cf. vv. 1 and 16) appears frequently in instructional contexts. Here vv. 16-17 further establish the instructional character of the chapter by directing the addressees (i.e., the nations and other readers) to examine the "book of YHWH" to confirm the validity of the preceding material concerning Edom.

Isaiah 34 employs several additional generic elements that contribute to its overall character as a prophetic INSTRUCTION speech. The most important is the PROPHECY CONCERNING A FOREIGN NATION, in this case Edom, which governs the form of vv. 1-15. The PROPHECY CONCERNING A FOREIGN NATION derives from the (→) prophetic announcement, but it has no fixed structure and employs a great variety of different generic elements. Its basic content is the destruction of a foreign nation by some enemy, which is generally portrayed as currently taking place or expected in the near future. Its basic intent is to demonstrate that the destruction is an act of YHWH. In the present instance, this serves the overall instructional character of ch. 34, which intends to make this point to the nations.

Several other generic elements in ch. 34 also contribute to its overall instructional character. The CALL TO ATTENTION in v. 1 commonly opens a public address that calls the audience's attention to the speech that follows. It appears frequently in a wisdom or instructional context to introduce the words of a teacher (e.g., Prov 7:24). In the present case, it calls the nations' attention to the following material concerning the demise of Edom. The use of similes to compare a human situation to natural phenomena is also a typical device of wisdom instruction in that ancient thinkers founded their perception of the world on the principle that order found in the natural world also applied to the human world. V. 4 contains two examples of such similes, which liken YHWH's destruction of the nations to the rolling up of a scroll and the withering of their host to the withering of leaves from the garden or fig tree. Although Hillers attempts to argue that the portrayal of a destroyed Edom overrun with animals and weeds reflects a background in ancient Near Eastern treaty curses, no explicit treaty is evident here, since "the book of YHWH" in v. 16 appears to refer to a more general or foundational document for YHWH's relationship to the world. Rather, the imagery of animals overrunning Edom stems from more general ancient Near Eastern conceptions of the relationship between nature and the human world from which wisdom, ancient treaties, and the present text draw.

Setting

Torrey's study of Deutero-Isaiah (*Second Isaiah,* esp. 92-104, 279-301) not only challenged Duhm's hypothesis that a postexilic prophet designated as Trito-Isaiah authored chs. 56–66; it also initiated an extensive debate concerning the authorship of chs. 34–35 within the book of Isaiah. This debate led ultimately to a complete reevaluation of the book as a whole and the function of these chapters within it. Based on his extensive examination of the vocabulary and

441

ideas of chs. 34–35 in relation to that of chs. 40–66, Torrey concluded that chs. 34–35 were written by the Second Isaiah, a postexilic prophet in Jerusalem who wrote chs. 34–35 and 40–66 in approximately 400 B.C.E. Graetz had argued in an earlier study that although ch. 35 was written by Second Isaiah, ch. 34 was written by someone in a much later period.

The primary response to Torrey appeared with the publication of Elliger's study of Deutero-Isaiah in relation to Trito-Isaiah, as well as with works by other scholars that attempted to defend Duhm's hypothesis that chs. 56–66 constituted Trito-Isaiah. Elliger's reexamination of the vocabulary and ideas of chs. 34–35 in relation to chs. 40–66 (*Deuterojesaja,* 272-78) demonstrated that these chapters were composed by neither Deutero- nor Trito-Isaiah. Although chs. 34–35 employ a great deal of vocabulary characteristic of chs. 40–66, they also employ a significant number of distinctive terms that are not found in either Deutero- or Trito-Isaiah. Consequently, Elliger concluded that although the language and style of ch. 34 in particular are influenced by Deutero-Isaiah, chs. 34–35 were written by another prophet in the time of Trito-Isaiah.

Although Pope challenged Elliger's conclusions by arguing that chs. 34–35 are a unity written by Deutero-Isaiah, Steck has successfully demonstrated that ch. 34 stems from a different redactional layer than that of ch. 35 (*Bereitete Heimkehr,* 52). Unlike ch. 35, ch. 34 shows no direct literary reference to Deutero-Isaiah. Ch. 35 does not refer back to ch. 34; in fact, the eternal desolation depicted in ch. 34 contradicts the intentions of ch. 35 with its focus on the renewal of creation. Likewise, the blooming desert of ch. 35 leads to the return of Israel to Zion, whereas ch. 34 depicts worldwide judgment expressed specifically in relation to Edom. According to Steck, an earlier form of ch. 34 (vv. 1 and 5-15) joined ch. 33 as a conclusion to Proto-Isaiah, but vv. 2-4 and 16-17 were added as part of the final redaction of the book that placed ch. 35 as a literary bridge between the two major parts of the book.

Although chs. 34–35 are generally regarded as part of the conclusion to Proto-Isaiah (see Elliger, *Deuterojesaja,* 278; Procksch, *Jesaja I–XXXIX,* 427), a growing number of scholars follow Torrey in identifying these chapters as the introduction to the second half of the book of Isaiah (see Brownlee, *Meaning,* 257-59; Evans, "On the Unity"; Gosse, "Isaïe 34–35"; cf. Kiesow, *Exodustexte,* 156-57). Although Torrey's lexical and thematic grounds do not provide an adequate basis for this hypothesis, ch. 34 displays a number of literary links with chs. 1; 13; 63:1-6; and other texts (cf. Dicou) that demonstrate that, together with ch. 35, the chapter fills this role.

A number of lexical and thematic links indicate that the portrayal of YHWH's judgment against Edom and the nations in ch. 34 is designed to provide a complement and counterpoint to the portrayal of judgment against Israel and Zion in ch. 1 (cf. Evans, 134-35, who attempts to demonstrate the parallel between chs. 34–35 and chs. 1–5). Links listed by Evans include parallel calls to attention in 34:1 and 1:2; the focus on YHWH's "vengeance" in 34:8 and 1:24; unquenchable burning of Edom in 34:10 and of YHWH's enemies in 1:31; the "mouth" of YHWH that speaks in 34:16 and 1:20; YHWH's "sword" of punishment in 34:5, 6 and 1:20; and the sacrificial "blood" and "fat" of cattle in 34:6-7 and 1:11-15. To these one may add the motif of Sodom and Gomorrah in 34:9-10 and 1:7-9 and

10, and the parallel references to wilting leaves in 34:4 and 1:30. Just as ch. 34 employs these terms and motifs to announce YHWH's judgment against Edom and the nations as a preface to the redemption of Zion in ch. 35, so ch. 1 employs similar vocabulary and themes to portray YHWH's judgment of Israel and Jerusalem prior to the redemption of Zion outlined in chs. 2–4.

Likewise, the portrayal of judgment against Edom in ch. 34 complements the portrayal of judgment against Babylon in ch. 13. Vermeylen (*Du prophète,* 440-41) notes a number of links between these two texts. Chief among them is the identical plan of battle in both texts, including: the preparation for combat in 34:1 and 13:2-4; the carnage of the nations in 34:2-3 and 13:5-9, 14-16; cosmic upheaval in 34:4-5a and 13:10-13; the taking of the city and the massacre of its inhabitants in 34:5b-8 and 13:17-19; the steppe turning to desert in 34:9-10 and 13:20; and the appearance of wild animals in 34:11-15 and 13:21-22. Vermeylen also notes the divine sword in 34:5-6 and 13:5, the expression "from generation to generation" in 34:10 and 13:20, and the correspondence between the animals listed in 34:11-15 and 13:21-22 (cf. Gosse, "Isaïe 34–35," 400). To this one may add the motif of the "Day of YHWH" in 34:8 and 13:6. Just as YHWH's judgment against Edom symbolizes the judgment of all the nations in 34:1-4, so YHWH's judgment against Babylon symbolizes the judgment of all the earth in 13:3-5.

A similar parallel exists between the portrayal of YHWH's vengeance against Edom in ch. 34 and 63:1-6, which symbolizes YHWH's vengeance against the nations (v. 3). Again, Vermeylen (*Du prophète,* 441-42; cf. Dicou) points to the parallels. Both employ nearly identical language to describe YHWH's day of vengeance and year of recompense or redemption in 34:8 and 63:4; both refer explicitly to Bozrah, the capital of Edom, in 34:6 and 63:1; and both focus explicitly on the imagery of bloody sacrifice in 34:6-7 and 63:1-6. In the larger context of the second part of the book, YHWH's assault against Edom in 63:1-6 previews divine plans to bring about judgment against the entire world (cf. 59:16-21; 66:15-24).

Additional links appear in other texts that are important for establishing the overall structure of the book of Isaiah, including the following: the theme of YHWH's day of vengeance in 34:8 and 61:2; the wild animals and thorns that overrun structures and land in 34:11-15 and 32:13-14; and YHWH's defeat of the hosts of heaven together with the overturning of nature as a symbol for the defeat of the nations in 34:1-4 and 24:21-23.

All these links demonstrate that ch. 34 (and 35) plays an important role in the structure of the book of Isaiah, and is crucial in introducing the second half of the book. Not only does it reprise the motifs and themes of chs. 1–33, i.e., the projected judgment of the world as the counterpart to YHWH's judgment of Israel and Zion; it also conceives of such judgment as the preparation for YHWH's revelation to the world at Zion. Together with ch. 35, it introduces these themes as the key motifs of chs. 34–66.

Isaiah 34 was apparently composed for this setting. Steck's arguments for denying the common authorship of chs. 34 and 35 have already been noted above. His arguments for identifying an earlier anti-Edom oracle in vv. 5-15 must be rejected, however, in that they are based on his inability to understand why the nations would be called to be both witnesses and victims of YHWH's judgment, so that he could only understand the references to the judgment against the nations in vv. 2-4 and the instruction to search the scriptures in vv. 16-17 as redactional additions to a text that originally concluded Proto-Isaiah (see Steck, *Bereitete Heimkehr,* 52-54; cf. Dicou). But the discussion of the structure of ch. 34 demonstrates that the nations are called to witness the destruction of Edom, not as witnesses to a legal proceeding as many assume, but as witnesses to YHWH's power over all the nations. Consequently, YHWH's punishment of Edom serves as an example of what will come to the nations as well. Contrary to common opinion, the object of this passage is not the judgment of Edom but YHWH's capacity to judge the world at large. This means that one need not regard ch. 34 as a composite passage (see also Lust, who mistakenly argues that vv. 8-15 are directed against Zion). Unlike ch. 35, which presupposes only chs. 40–55 and perhaps 2–32, ch. 34 presupposes materials that constitute the final redaction of the book of Isaiah in chs. 1 and 56–66, and it builds on earlier materials such as ch. 13 (cf. Elliger, *Deuterojesaja,* 275, who argues that 63:1-6 serves as the *Vorlage* to ch. 34). Consequently, ch. 34 was written during the latter part of the 5th century as part of the final redaction of the book of Isaiah.

The portrayal of the demise of Edom corresponds well to a historical setting in the 5th century. Under the influence of ch. 34's links to chs. 40–55/56–66 and various traditions condemning the Edomites for their part, either as participants or as spoilers, in the destruction of Jerusalem by the Babylonians (cf. Jer 49:7-22; Ezek 25:12-17; Obad 1-21; Ps 137:7; Lam 4:21-22), a number of scholars argue that ch. 34 should be placed in the late 6th century (e.g., Fohrer, *Jesaja,* 2:144). This view is mistaken, however, in that the overall thrust of this passage is not to condemn Edom but to portray its demise as an example of YHWH's power to the nations. This purpose finds an ideal background in the situation of Edom during the 5th century. Although the details are still hazy, scholars have concluded that the kingdom of Edom gradually deteriorated during the course of the 5th century as the desert-dwelling Nabateans began to move into the Edomite homeland and displace its inhabitants. By the 4th century, the Nabatean kingdom had replaced that of the Edomites, although many Edomites may have been incorporated into the Nabatean realm (see J. R. Bartlett, "The Rise and Fall of the Kingdom of Edom," *PEQ* 104 [1972] 26-37; idem, "From Edomites to Nabataeans: A Study in Continuity," *PEQ* 111 [1979] 53-66; idem, *Edom and the Edomites* [JSOTSup 77; Sheffield: JSOT Press, 1989]; E. A. Knauf, *Ismael: Untersuchungen zur Geschichte Palestinas und Nordarabiens im 1.Jahrtausend v. Chr.* [Wiesbaden: Harrassowitz, 1985]; D. F. Graf, "The Origin of the Nabataeans," *ARAM* 2 [1990] 45-75). The portrayal of the desert, the wild animals, and the thorns overtaking Edom in ch. 34 provides a natural metaphor for Edom's demise in the 5th century.

Intention

In regard to the intention of ch. 34, one must consider a number of the chapter's important features discussed above: its literary form as an instruction speech constituted largely by the prophecy concerning a foreign nation, its historical setting in relation to the demise of Edom during the course of the 5th century, and its literary setting within the framework of the final form of the book of Isaiah. In conjunction with these features, one must consider several constitutive motifs: the analogy to the destruction of Sodom and Gomorrah, the portrayal of animal sacrifice, and the use of the "Day of YHWH" tradition.

As noted above, the form of ch. 34 is determined by its use of the instruction genre together with that of the prophecy concerning a foreign nation. The nations are called to observe the demise of Edom. Consistent with the prophecy concerning a foreign nation, the reasons for Edom's downfall are not given. In the present context, it is not important, because Edom's fate is to serve as an example of YHWH's power and capacity to judge all nations. It therefore serves notice to the nations concerning YHWH's plans for them as well.

The motifs mentioned above contribute to this overall intention. The "Day of YHWH" is a traditional motif from ancient Israelite thought that apparently derives from the holy war tradition (see G. von Rad, "The Origin of the Concept of the Day of YHWH," *JSS* 4 [1959] 97-108; for a full summary of discussion of the "Day of YHWH" motif, see A. J. Everson, "Day of the Lord," *IDBSup*, 209-10). Although the tradition is frequently turned against Israel in prophetic literature (e.g., Amos 5:18-20), it is generally directed against Israel's enemies for crimes committed against Israel and YHWH (see Joel 3:1-5 [*RSV* 2:28-32]; Obad 15-17; Zeph 1:14-18). In Isa 34:8 the motif expresses YHWH's intention to take vengeance against Edom for its crimes against Zion. As the context indicates, the "Day of YHWH" against Edom functions in relation to YHWH's judgment against the nations at large. In this regard, it is noteworthy that elsewhere in the book of Isaiah, the "Day of YHWH" motif functions as a means to express YHWH's judgment against the entire earth (2:6-21), against Babylon as the head of the nations (13:1-22), and against Edom as a symbol of YHWH's victory over the nations (63:1-6). Thus the motif functions not only to express YHWH's judgment against Edom and the nations in the immediate context of ch. 34, but also to link the chapter to the rest of the book in which it functions as a major expression of YHWH's plans for the world at large.

A second constitutive motif in ch. 34 is the analogy that is drawn between the destruction of Edom and the destruction of Sodom and Gomorrah (cf. Genesis 18–19). The motif appears in vv. 9-12, which describe the overturning of the land of Edom and the dissolution of social or governmental order. It is expressed by several key terms and images, including the verb *wĕnehepĕkû*, "and they shall be shall be turned [into]," in v. 9 (cf. Gen 19:21, 25, 29), the reference to *goprît*, "pitch," in v. 9 (cf. Gen 19:24), the reference to the "smoke" in v. 10 (cf. Gen 19:27-28), and the general reference to the reversal of creation expressed by the use of the phrase *tōhû wĕ . . . bōhû*, "waste and . . . void," in v. 11 (cf. the comment by Lot's daughters in Gen 19:31-32 which suggests that they thought all creation had been destroyed). The proximity of Edom to the southern tip of the Dead Sea, where Sodom and Gomorrah are traditionally located, apparently motivated the application of this motif to the portrayal of Edom's downfall (cf. Jer 49:17-22). Insofar as it expresses YHWH's capacity to destroy the earth (cf. v. 11), it builds on the motif of the "Day of YHWH," which immediately precedes. In this regard, the Sodom and Gomorrah motif not only expresses YHWH's capacity to punish the nations at large, but also ties ch. 34 into the structure of the book as a whole. The motif of the destruction of Sodom and Gomorrah appears elsewhere in Isaiah as a metaphor for YHWH's judgment against Zion (1:9, 10; cf. 3:9) and against Babylon and the nations (13:19). Likewise, YHWH's role as creator of the earth is expressed elsewhere in Isaiah with reference to YHWH's capacity either to overcome or to bring about chaos (*tōhû wĕ . . . bōhû,* v. 11; cf. 24:10; 29:21; 40:17, 23; 41:29; 44:9; 45:18, 19; 49:4; 59:4). Consequently, the Sodom and Gomorrah motif expresses YHWH's plans for the world in Isaiah.

Finally, one must consider the motif of animal sacrifice, in relation not only to the literary form of ch. 34 but also to its historical setting. The motif appears in vv. 2 and 5-7, with lurid descriptions of the blood of the sacrificial animals that will drench YHWH's sword and the land. This image is no doubt motivated in part by the wordplay on the Hebrew word for "red," *'ādôm,* which is very similar to that for "Edom," *'ĕdôm.* It also contributes to the general image of carnage in Edom as the action of YHWH in the context of ch. 34.

Just as important, however, are the social dimensions of the portrayal. As noted above, many of the terms for the sacrificial animals in v. 6 are frequently employed in Biblical Hebrew with reference to leaders of a people. The "clean" animals of the sacrifice portrayed in vv. 5-7 must be contrasted with the "unclean" animals from the desert in vv. 11-15 that will inhabit Edom once the slaughter is completed (note that the animals listed here are classified as "clean" or "unclean" in Deuteronomy 14). That the "unclean" animals from the wilderness or desert (cf. v. 14) replace the "clean" may well serve as a metaphor for the displacement of Edom by the Nabateans who entered Edom from the desert. Consequently, the image of Edom's demise in ch. 34 relates well to the social conditions in Edom during the course of the 5th century. In relation to this historical setting, ch. 34 asserts that the Nabatean displacement of Edom is an act of YHWH, and that the fall of Edom presages YHWH's actions against the nations at large. In this regard, the instruction to examine "the book of YHWH" in v. 16 apparently indicates that the statements in the book of Isaiah are coming true; with regard to Edom, not one of the animals mentioned in ch. 34 is lacking in Edom during the 5th century.

Bibliography

→ bibliography at "Introduction to the Book of Isaiah" and at 34:1–35:10. W. A. M. Beuken, "Isaiah 34: Lament in Isaianic Context," *OTE* 5 (1992) 78-102; J. A. Emerton, "A Note on the Alleged Septuagintal Evidence for the Restoration of the Hebrew Text of Isaiah 34:11-12," *ErIs* 16 (1982) 34*-36*; Hillers, *Treaty-Curses* (→ "Introduction to the Prophetic Literature"), 44-53; J. Lust, "Isaiah 34 and the *ḥerem,*" in *The Book of Isaiah/Le Livre d'Isaïe* (ed. J. Vermeylen; BETL 81; Leuven: Leuven University Press and Peeters, 1989) 275-86; J. Morgenstern, "The Loss of Words at the Ends of Lines in Manuscripts of Hebrew Poetry," *HUCA* 25 (1954) 41-83; J. Muilenburg, "The Literary Character of Isaiah 34," *JBL* 59 (1940) 339-65; M. Pope, "Isaiah 34 in Relation to Isaiah

35, 40-66," *JBL* 71 (1952) 235-43; V. Tanghe, "Der Schriftgelehrte in Jes 34,16-17," *ETL* 67 (1991) 338-45.

PROPHETIC ORACLE OF SALVATION CONCERNING THE RETURN OF THE REDEEMED TO ZION, 35:1-10

Structure

1) Emergence of holy highway   8aα
2) Unclean/fools will not travel it   8aβ-b
3) Predators will not travel it   9a
4) Redeemed shall return to Zion in joy   9b-10

Isaiah 35 is demarcated initially by its abrupt shift to the theme of rejoicing and blossoming in the wilderness in v. 1, as well as by the lack of any syntactical or formal connection to the preceding material. The motif of rejoicing (and blossoming) permeates the entire passage and appears again explicitly in v. 10 in relation to the return of the redeemed to Zion. It thereby forms a thematic inclusion with v. 1. Isa 36:1 begins the narrative report concerning Sennacherib's siege of Jerusalem.

The structure of ch. 35 is determined by a combination of generic, thematic, and syntactical factors. Although the passage is a prophetic oracle of salvation, its structure is based in instruction to convey a priestly oracle of salvation concerning YHWH's coming in vv. 3-4 and concerning the results of YHWH's coming in vv. 5-10. The whole is introduced by an announcement concerning the rejoicing and blossoming of the wilderness and desert, specifically the Arabah, a dry, desolate portion of the Jordan rift that extends from the southern end of the Dead Sea to the Gulf of Aqaba.

The announcement of the rejoicing and blossoming of nature and the Arabah appears in vv. 1-2. This subunit is characterized by its use of 3rd-person finite verbs to describe the rejoicing and blossoming of nature, specifically the Arabah. The structure of the passage is determined by a series of four syntactically independent statements that are linked together by interlocking thematic motifs and key words. The first is v. 1, which employs three 3rd-person imperfect verbs linked by conjunctive *wāw*s to describe the rejoicing and blossoming of the nature and the Arabah. V. 1a employs the 3rd-person masculine singular imperfect verb *yĕśuśûm,* "they shall be glad," to describe the rejoicing of the wilderness and desert. V. 1b then shifts to two 3rd-person feminine singular imperfect verbs, *wĕtāgēl,* "it shall rejoice," and *wĕtiprah,* "and it shall blossom," to describe the transformation of the Arabah. The second statement in v. 2aα then shifts exclusively to the blossoming and rejoicing of the Arabah. It is set off from v. 1 by the expression *kahăbaṣṣālet,* "like the lily," and by the absolute imperfect verbal construction *pārōah tiprah,* "it shall surely blossom"; but it is also linked to v. 1 by its inverted repetition of the verbs *tiprah,* "it shall blossom," and *wĕtāgēl,* "and it shall rejoice." The third statement in v. 2aβ states that the Arabah shall attain the "glory" and "majesty" of the Lebanon, the Carmel, and the Sharon, each of which refers to a distinctive area of the northern part of Israel known for its fecundity. The reference to the Sharon plain links this statement to the preceding statement in that the "lily" *(hăbaṣṣālet)* is commonly associated with the Sharon plain (cf. Cant 2:1). Finally, the fourth statement in v. 2b sums up the whole by stating that "they" (i.e., the wilderness, desert, and Arabah; cf. v. 1) will see the "glory" and "majesty" of YHWH, thereby repeating the key terms of v. 2aβ.

The second major subunit in vv. 3-10 is an instruction to the weak concerning the coming of YHWH and its results. The instruction itself appears in

vv. 3-4 as indicated by the masculine plural imperative verbs *ḥazzĕqû/'ammēṣû*, "strengthen/make firm," in v. 3 and *'imrû*, "say," in v. 4. V. 3 thereby constitutes an instruction to strengthen the weak, including the weak hands in v. 3a and the feeble knees in v. 3b. V. 4 constitutes an instruction to speak to the fainthearted. It includes an instruction command formula in v. 4aα and the instruction proper in v. 4aβ-b. The instruction proper is formulated as a priestly oracle of salvation with three basic components: the assurance formula, "be strong, fear not!" in v. 4aβ; the statement that YHWH comes *(yābô')* for vengeance in v. 4bα; and the statement that YHWH comes *(yābô')* to "save you" in v. 4bβ.

Verses 5-10 then focus on the results of YHWH's coming as indicated by the introductory occurrences of *'āz*, "then," in vv. 5 and 6. Overall, these verses state that the ultimate result of YHWH's coming is the restoration of the redeemed to Zion. This result is expressed initially in vv. 5-6a by reference to the restoration of the crippled in two statements introduced by *'āz*, "then." V. 5 refers to the restoration of the blind and deaf, and v. 6a refers to the restoration of the lame and mute.

Verses 6b-10, introduced by a causative *kî*, "for," then state the basis for this restoration in terms of the restoration of the cosmos. This is expressed initially by the outpouring of water in the wilderness or Arabah in v. 6b. This statement alone clearly does not explain the event; consequently two elaborations, each introduced by an introductory *wĕhāyâ*, "and it shall become/be," explain the significance of this image. The first elaboration in v. 7 focuses on the image of water in the wilderness or Arabah; v. 7a states that dry places will become wet, and v. 7b portrays the growth of swampland or an oasis with its snakes, reeds, and rushes. The second elaboration in vv. 8-10 then shifts to the restoration of the redeemed to Zion with four distinct images. V. 8aα focuses on the emergence of a holy highway; v. 8aβ-b states that the unclean and fools will not travel it; v. 9a states that predators will not travel it; finally, vv. 9b-10 borrow material from 51:10-11 to portray the return of the redeemed to Zion with joy and singing.

Genre

The overarching genre of ch. 35 is the prophetic ORACLE OF SALVATION. This is an adaptation of the priestly ORACLE OF SALVATION, which is generally identified by the presence of the ASSURANCE FORMULA, *'al-tîrā'û*, "fear not." The priestly ORACLE OF SALVATION was customarily delivered within the institutional framework of the Jerusalem temple worship to express divine grace. It may well have had a function in relation to holy war as well (cf. Deut 20:1-9, esp. v. 3). Although the ASSURANCE FORMULA appears in v. 4, the instructional context of this occurrence and the formulation of the entire passage as a PROPHETIC ANNOUNCEMENT indicate that Isaiah 35 is an adaptation of the standard priestly form. In this present case, it aids in expressing a future time of salvation when the redeemed will return to Jerusalem.

The prophetic ORACLE OF SALVATION in ch. 35 appears to have employed elements of INSTRUCTION and THEOPHANY REPORT as well. The instructional elements are evident in the COMMANDS in vv. 3-4 to strengthen the weak by informing them of the appearance of YHWH and its overall significance in relation to the transformation of nature and the return of the redeemed to Zion. One should note that the reference to opening eyes and ears also appears in wisdom instruction (Job 14:3; 27:19; Prov 20:13; cf. K. D. F. Römheld, *Wege der Weisheit: Die Lehren Amenemopes und Proverbien 22,17–24,22* [BZAW 184; Berlin and New York: de Gruyter, 1989] esp. 18-27; idem, *Die Weisheitslehre im alten Orient* [Biblische Notizen 4; Munich: Görg, 1989]). Theophanic elements are also evident in the references to the coming of YHWH and the results for both nature and humankind. The motif appears explicitly in the INSTRUCTION to the fainthearted in v. 4 and the results portrayed in vv. 5-10. Likewise, the transformation of the wilderness and desert in vv. 1-2 appears to draw on theophanic themes. Ch. 35 differs from the standard (→) theophany report forms, however, in that it does not describe the fear of creation or the defeat of enemies. Consequently, it is clear that the theophanic elements have been adapted into the overall form of the prophetic ORACLE OF SALVATION.

Setting

Isaiah 35 plays a definitive role within the structure of the final 5th-century form of the book of Isaiah. Together with ch. 34, it constitutes the introduction to the second half of the book, chs. 34–66. Unlike ch. 34, which focuses on the overthrow of Edom as a symbol of YHWH's power over against the nations, ch. 35 focuses on YHWH's capacities as redeemer and creator by emphasizing the renewal of creation and the return of the redeemed to Zion in a new exodus along a highway through the Arabah.

A number of scholars note that ch. 35 serves as a sort of "digest" of the prophecies of Deutero-Isaiah in chs. 40–55 in that it highlights the major themes of the writings of the exilic prophet (see Clements, "Unity," 121; cf. Graetz, "Isaiah XXXIV"); others argue that ch. 35 is part of the writings of Deutero-Isaiah (Torrey, *Second Isaiah*, 92-104, 295-301; Scott; Smart, 292-94). A number of considerations indicate that ch. 35 was not written by either Deutero-Isaiah or Trito-Isaiah. These include its distinctive vocabulary (e.g., *maslûl*, "highway," in v. 8, but *měsillâ*, "highway," in 40:3; 49:10; 62:10; see Elliger, *Deuterojesaja*, 272-78; Wildberger, *Jesaja*, 1358-59); its distinctive concepts, such as the redemption of all diaspora Jews rather than only those of Babylonia (Clements, *Isaiah 1–39*, 275) or the splendor of Lebanon, which is otherwise lacking in chs. 40–66; and its modified citation of 51:10-11 in 35:9b-10. The similarities in theme and vocabulary, and the citation of 51:10-11, indicate that ch. 35 presupposes Deutero-Isaiah, but the chapter was not written by the same hand.

Likewise, ch. 35 was not written by the same hand as ch. 34. As noted in the discussion of ch. 34, Steck (*Bereitete Heimkehr,* 52) points to fundamental contradictions in outlook that demonstrate the work of two different authors in these chapters. Thus the eternal destruction of the land of Edom in 34:10 contradicts the blooming of the Arabah in 35:1-10, and the world judgment and images of violence announced in ch. 34 contrast sharply against the restoration of the redeemed to Zion in ch. 35.

Steck also notes the redactional function of ch. 35 in that it summarizes many of the major themes pertaining to the highway employed for the redemption of Jewish exiles in 11:11-16 and 27:12-13 (cf. 19:23-24), as well as similar imagery in 40:1-11 and 62:10-12 (cf. 48:20-22; 49:8-13; 51:9-11; 52:11-12). Furthermore, he notes that 62:10-12, which announces the redemption of the exiles and their return to Zion, is the goal of the redactional layer in which ch. 35 functions (pp. 67-68; for an overview of his understanding of the composition of the book of Isaiah and the role of 62:10-12, see his "Trito-Jesaja im Jesajabuch," in *The Book of Isaiah/Le livre d'Isaïe* [ed. J. Vermeylen; BETL 81; Leuven: Leuven University Press and Peeters, 1989] 361-406; repr. in *Studien zu Tritojesaja* [BZAW 203; Berlin and New York: de Gruyter, 1991] 3-45). Yet Steck's observations can be expanded by noting that the imagery employed in ch. 35 is that of the exodus, which serves as one of the primary means to unite both portions of the book of Isaiah (cf. Kiesow, *Exodustexte*, 142-57; see Sweeney, *Isaiah 1–4*, 17-21, for a full discussion). As in the prophecies of Deutero-Isaiah, the goal of the Exodus in Israelite tradition was the land of Israel and YHWH's temple in Zion (Exod 15:13-18; Ps 78:54-55). When viewed from the perspective of the exodus tradition, it becomes clear that the return of the redeemed to Zion in ch. 35 and 62:10-12, among others, fulfills the invitation issued to Jacob in 2:5 to come to Zion and walk in the "light" of YHWH (cf. 60:1-3). Furthermore, the theme of Israel's blindness and deafness in 35:5-6 not only serves as another major link between the two parts of the book (cf. 6:9-10; 29:18; 32:3; 42:16, 18-9; 43:8; 44:18; see Clements, "Beyond Tradition History," 101-4; idem, "Unity," 125; Sweeney, *Isaiah 1–4*, 20-21; Aitken), but also indicates that the redeemed will finally see what YHWH has done.

Steck (*Bereitete Heimkehr,* 76-79) argues that ch. 35 is part of the final redaction of Isaiah during the Diodoche wars of the 4th century, based on his views of the composition of chs. 40–66 and the relation of ch. 35 to this material. But the links between ch. 35 on the one hand and chs. 40–55 and 60–62 on the other indicate that ch. 35 was composed specifically in relation to this material. Furthermore, the links with Proto-Isaiah demonstrate that ch. 35 functions as a redactional text that binds these chapters to Proto-Isaiah. Scholarly consensus maintains that chs. 40–55 date to the mid- to late 6th century (see J. A. Soggin, *Introduction to the Old Testament* [3rd ed.; tr. J. Bowden; Louisville: Westminster/John Knox, 1989] 365-78). Likewise, various studies demonstrate that chs. 60–62 date to the latter part of the 6th century (see Soggin, *Introduction,* 393-97; on the composition of chs. 60–62 within the context of chs. 56–66, see S. Sekine, *Die Tritojesajanische Sammlung [Jes 56–66] Redaktionsgeschichtlich Untersucht* [BZAW 175; Berlin and New York: de Gruyter, 1989] esp. 68-104). Inasmuch as ch. 35 presupposes these texts, it must have been composed at some time in the late 6th century, as part of the 6th-century redaction of the book of Isaiah. Whereas ch. 34 presupposes the upheaval of the Persian empire during the 5th century (cf. chs. 1; 56–59; 63–66), ch. 35 presupposes the coming peace and restoration for Zion offered by the newly established Persian rule. In such a context, its emphasis on the Arabah as the site of the new exodus not only draws on traditional elements of the exodus tradition, which places the returning Israelites in the Negev, Edom, and Moab; it also points to the potential return of exiles from Egypt in the years when the Persian empire prepared for its conquest of Egypt in 525.

Finally, the social or institutional setting of ch. 35 may well be the temple in Jerusalem, insofar as the exodus tradition and the renewal of creation presuppose the temple as the goal of the exodus and the locus of creation. Certainly, these motifs frequently play a role in liturgical contexts. But there is no clear evidence that ch. 35 ever functioned independently from its literary context in the book of Isaiah. Rather, the placement of ch. 35 within the book of Isaiah may indicate that the book was read within the context of a temple liturgy that celebrated the return to Zion. The festival of Sukkot emphasizes this theme in that its use of the motif of temporary dwellings in the wilderness calls to mind Israel's wandering in the wilderness for a forty-year period. Sukkot also marks the beginning of the rainy season in Israel and thereby provides a context for understanding the motif of the watering of the Arabah that appears in ch. 35. Tradition indicates that the altar of the Second Temple was dedicated in conjunction with the festival of Sukkot and that construction of the temple commenced at this time (see Ezra 3:1-7). Some of the visions connected with temple reconstruction in Zechariah 1–8 appear to presuppose a setting in the festival of Sukkot (e.g., the dedication of the altar and the ordination of the priest, Zech 2:1-4; 3:1-10; cf. Exod 29:1-46; the reading of the scroll, Zech 5:1-4; cf. Deut 31:9-13). Insofar as Zech 8:20-23 refers explicitly to material from Isaiah (Isa 2:2-4; 7:14), it seems likely that the 6th-century edition may well have been read as part of the liturgy for the dedication of the altar in 520. In such a setting, ch. 35 would have emphasized the theme of the return through the wilderness to Zion and thereby would have provided a context for understanding the prophecies of the book of Isaiah.

Intention

The intention of ch. 35 is determined by a combination of factors, including its structure and genre; its major motifs of the exodus, creation, and the blind, deaf, and lame; its social setting in the context of Sukkot worship and the dedication of the Second Temple; and its literary context in the book of Isaiah.

Most fundamentally, the structure and genre of ch. 35 indicate that its purpose is to announce salvation to Israel and the return of the exiles to Zion. As noted in the discussion of genre above, the priestly oracle of salvation has been adapted to its present context through the use of prophetic announcement and instruction forms so that the passage can fulfill this role. Normally, the oracle functions in a liturgical context to express an assurance of divine grace, but it can also be employed in a war situation to assure the army that YHWH will grant victory. In the present context, it serves as a means to instruct and to announce to the community that the hardships of foreign invasion and exile are over, and that the process of restoration is beginning.

Isaiah 35 employs several major motifs to convey this message, including the exodus tradition, the associated creation tradition, and the opening of the eyes and ears of the blind and deaf. The first two relate to the institutional setting of ch. 35 in the context of Sukkot worship. All three relate to the literary setting of ch. 35 as a redactional text that binds together and draws out the major salvation themes of the book.

The exodus motif appears most clearly in vv. 8-10, which describe the highway that the redeemed will travel on their journey through the Arabah to return to Zion. As such, this motif echoes the forty years of wilderness wandering after the exodus and the journey to the promised land by way of the King's Highway through the Arabah, Edom, and Moab (Num 20:17; 21:22; Deut 2:8). Insofar as the land of Israel and the temple in Jerusalem are the final goal of the exodus journey (Exod 15:13-18), the return of the exiles to Jerusalem in Isaiah 35 not only corresponds to the exodus tradition but also contributes to the overall concern to announce salvation. The fruitfulness of the desert or Arabah is often associated with the exodus tradition, especially in relation to the provision of water, manna, and quails (Exod 15:22–16:36; Numbers 11; 20; Psalm 105; cf. Isa 40:1-11, etc.), but the correlation of the exodus wandering and the fruitfulness of the desert is closest in the festival of Sukkot or Booths. Sukkot has a dual character in that it celebrates the end of the harvest season and commemorates the forty years of wandering in the wilderness. The "booths," or temporary dwellings in which the people live during the course of the festival, symbolize both the huts in which Israelite farmers lived while gathering the grape and olive harvests and the tents in which the people lived while wandering through the wilderness in the exodus tradition. More importantly, Sukkot marks the beginning of the rainy season, which is especially important to ensure the fertility of the land and future harvests.

In this respect, the blooming of the desert plays a particularly important role. The Arabah or desert is the last place that one would expect to obtain a good harvest or even water. But for a brief period during the rainy season, the desert of the land of Israel blooms in full splendor. As such, the desert symbolizes the potential fertility of the land like that of the ever fertile northern areas, such as the Lebanon range, the Carmel mountains, and the Sharon plain. The association with the desert/Arabah and the life-giving qualities of the rains corresponds nicely with the exodus wilderness wandering, in that the journey through the desert to Zion ensures the people's life and well-being in their own land of "milk and honey." When considered in relation to the setting of the Sukkot liturgy, Isaiah 35 brings out the motifs of the festival; its relation to the dedication of the altar of the Second Temple and the reconstruction of the temple itself (cf. Ezra 3:1-9) points to the role of the temple as both the goal of the exodus wandering and the locus of creation that ensures the fertility of the land and the life of its people.

This function is also important in relation to the literary setting of Isaiah 35 as a redactional text that binds together the two halves of the book. As noted in the discussion of setting above, ch. 35 functions as a literary "bridge" in that it takes up the motif of the return of the exiles to Zion mentioned in 11:11-16; 19:23-24; 27:12-13; 40:1-11; 48:20-22; 51:9-11; 52:11-12; 62:10-12. Likewise, the motif of the opening of the eyes and ears of the deaf and blind (vv. 5-6) takes up a concern that appears in 29:18; 32:3; 42:16; 42:18-19; 43:8; 44:18. In relation to the 6th-century edition of chs. 2–62*, ch. 35 serves as the introduction to the second half of the book (chs. 35–62*); together with ch. 34, it serves as the introduction to the second half (chs. 34–66) of the final 5th-century form of the entire book of Isaiah (chs. 1–66; cf. Gosse, "Isaïe 34–35"). In both cases, ch. 35 draws out the themes of salvation and the recognition of YHWH's power to save by the people as the means to introduce the message of salvation that appears in the writings of Deutero-Isaiah and Trito-Isaiah. Insofar as the 6th-century edition serves as part of the Sukkot liturgy of the dedication of the Second Temple altar, and insofar as the 5th-century edition serves in a similar capacity at Ezra's return to Jerusalem (Nehemiah 8–10), Isaiah 35 draws out the Sukkot themes that relate the book of Isaiah to the festival observance. Ch. 35 points to the potential for salvation and well-being represented by the reconstruction of the Jerusalem temple in the 6th century and by the institution of Mosaic Torah under Ezra in the 5th century. In doing so, it presents these events as respective fulfillments of the prophecies of Isaiah ben Amoz.

Bibliography

→ bibliography at 34:1–35:10 and at 34:1-17. Aitken, "Hearing and Seeing" (→ 28:1-29); J. A. Emerton, "A Note on Isaiah xxxv 9-10," *VT* 27 (1977) 488-89; A. T. Olmstead, "II Isaiah and Isaiah, Chapter 35," *AJSL* 53 (1936-37) 251-53; R. B. Y. Scott, "The Relation of Isaiah, Chapter 35, to Deutero-Isaiah," *AJSL* 52 (1935-36) 178-91; Smart, *History and Theology* (→ "Introduction to the Book of Isaiah"), 292-94.

ROYAL NARRATIVE CONCERNING HEZEKIAH, 36:1–39:8

Structure

I. Confrontation story concerning defeat of Sennacherib's threat against Jerusalem	36:1–37:38
II. Royal novella concerning Hezekiah's recovery from illness	38:1-22
III. Prophetic story concerning Isaiah's announcement of punishment against Hezekiah on occasion of Merodach-baladan's embassy: dialogue report	39:1-8

Isaiah 36–39 is an easily identifiable narrative block within the larger structure of the book of Isaiah. It is distinguished by its narrative form and by its concern with events pertaining to the reign of King Hezekiah, whereas the preceding and following material is poetic and lacks specific reference to historical persons or events. Another version of this narrative appears in 2 Kgs 18:13–20:19. As the following discussion and that of the individual units below will demonstrate, chs. 36–39 are a revised version of the earlier narrative in 2 Kings.

A combination of thematic concerns and formal indicators demonstrates that the structure of Isaiah 36–39 falls into three major units: chs. 36–37; ch. 38; and ch. 39. Each is introduced by a temporal formula that establishes its respective setting in time. These formulas tie the subunits together as three separate episodes that relate to the same basic event: Sennacherib's invasion of Judah in 701. Thus chs. 36–37 begin with the formula *wayěhî bě'arba' 'eśrēh šānâ lammelek ḥizkîyāhû,* "and it came to pass in the fourteenth year of King Hezekiah," and narrates the account of YHWH's defeat of Sennacherib's threat against Jerusalem following Hezekiah's plea for assistance. Ch. 38 begins with the formula *bayyāmîm hāhēm ḥālâ ḥizkîyāhû lāmût,* "in those days, Hezekiah was mortally ill," and narrates the account of how Hezekiah was cured by YHWH after praying for deliverance. Ch. 39 begins with the formula *bā'ēt hahî'* [see *BHS*] *šālaḥ měrōdak bal'ădān ben-bal'ădān melek-bābel sěpārîm ûminḥâ 'el-ḥizkîyāhû wayyišma' kî ḥālâ wayyeḥĕzāq,* "at that time Merodach-baladan, the son of Baladan, king of Babylon, sent letters and a present to Hezekiah when he heard that he was sick and that he had recovered." Ch. 39 then narrates the account of Isaiah's condemnation of Hezekiah on the occasion of the Babylonian delegation's visit. Discussions of the respective structures for each of these subunits appear below.

Not only do the initial temporal formulas relate each narrative to the same setting in time; the sequence of the narratives indicates that they present time retrospectively in that the events narrated in chs. 38 and 39 would have to precede those of chs. 36–37. Thus the account of Sennacherib's siege in chs. 36–37 begins the narrative sequence, but Hezekiah's illness as narrated in ch. 38 must precede the siege chronologically since it refers to YHWH's deliverance of Jerusalem as a future event (38:6). Likewise, the account of Merodach-baladan's embassy in ch. 39 presupposes Hezekiah's illness, but it must precede the account of the 701 siege of Jerusalem chronologically since Merodach-baladan's embassy could not have visited after 703 when Merodach-baladan was finally driven from his throne by Sennacherib (see J. A. Brinkman, "Merodach-Baladan II," in *Studies Presented to A. Leo Oppenheim, June 7, 1964* [eds. R. D. Biggs and J. A. Brinkman; Chicago: Oriental Institute, 1964] 6-53). Consequently, the present form of the narrative initially presents Sennacherib's siege of Jerusalem, but retrospectively presents Hezekiah's illness and Merodach-baladan's embassy as events that occurred prior to the siege. From the narrator's perspective, Hezekiah's illness and Isaiah's condemnation of Hezekiah constitute the background for the siege and inform its interpretation (see below on Intention).

Genre

The overarching genre of chs. 36–39 may be identified as ROYAL NARRATIVE insofar as the narrative block presents Hezekiah as an ideal figure of piety and success. The genre is somewhat modified, however, in that Hezekiah must rely on YHWH for deliverance in chs. 36–37 and ch. 38. Furthermore, Hezekiah's success is qualified by Isaiah's condemnation in ch. 39. Both of these circumstances serve the overall interests of the genre in that Hezekiah's reliance on

YHWH demonstrates his ideal piety. The condemnation by Isaiah does not affect Hezekiah personally, but it serves as a means to exemplify his piety again when he humbly accepts the judgment in 39:8. It further enables the narrator to employ the presentation of Hezekiah to address concerns of the second part of the book beginning in ch. 40. Hezekiah thereby serves as a model of piety for the future after the exile is realized.

The identification of chs. 36–39 as a ROYAL NARRATIVE differs from the generic identification of 2 Kings 18–20 as a (→) regnal resumé (Long, *2 Kings*, 192). Modifications to the text of 2 Kings 18–20 have changed its generic character. These modifications include both the removal of the narrative framework pertaining to the reign of Hezekiah in 2 Kgs 18:1-12 and 20:20-21 and the removal or alteration of various elements in 2 Kgs 18:13–20:19, resulting in an idealized portrayal of Hezekiah in the Isaiah version of the narrative. These modifications will be discussed specifically together with the individual treatments of the units of Isaiah 36–39. Subordinate genres will likewise be discussed below.

Setting

The setting of Isaiah 36–39 must be defined in relation to the parallel narrative in 2 Kgs 18:13–20:19. As the following discussions of the settings of the respective subunits of Isaiah 36–39 will demonstrate, Isaiah 36–39 is a modified version of 2 Kgs 18:13–20:19. The narrative in 2 Kgs 18:13–20:19 relates to the final edition of the DtrH produced in the mid-6th century. The Kings version of the narrative gives special attention to the deportation of King Jehoiachin, whose ultimate release from prison during the reign of Evil-merodach concludes the DtrH in 2 Kgs 25:27-30 (cf. 2 Kgs 24:10-17, esp. v. 13, which presents Jehoiachin's deportation as the fulfillment of YHWH's word). Prior to its incorporation into the DtrH, the Hezekiah narrative appears to have been composed in two stages: the account of Sennacherib's siege dates to the reign of King Josiah in that it presents the deliverance of Jerusalem from the Assyrians as an act of YHWH, and the accounts of Hezekiah's illness and Merodach-baladan's embassy date to the period 598-587 in that they presuppose the deportation of Jehoiachin but not the destruction of Jerusalem (see esp. R. E. Clements, "The Isaiah Narrative of 2 Kings 20:12-19 and the Date of the Deuteronomic History," in *Isac (sic) Leo Seeligmann Volume* [ed. A. Rofé and Y. Zakovitch; Jerusalem: E. Rubinstein, 1983] 209-20; Hardmeier, *Prophetie*, passim).

Despite the evident prehistory of the Hezekiah narratives, the incorporation of Isaiah 36–39 as a narrative block into the larger framework of the book of Isaiah must be attributed to the late-6th-century redaction of the book. Although an earlier form of the narrative concerning Sennacherib's siege of Jerusalem appears to have formed part of the Josianic edition of the book of Isaiah (see the treatment of chs. 36–37 below), chs. 36–39 as a whole form a literary bridge or transition between the Assyrian and Babylonian segments of the 6th-century edition (see Ackroyd, "Isaiah 36–39"; cf. idem, "Historians and Prophets," 121-51, 278-82; idem, "The Biblical Interpretation," 181-92, 287-88;

Conrad, *Reading Isaiah,* 34-51; Melugin, *Formation,* 82-84; Seitz, "Divine Council"; Sweeney, *Isaiah 1–4,* 32-34).

Several observations support this conclusion. First, the present form of 2 Kgs 18:13–20:19, from which Isaiah 36–39 derive, dates to the mid-6th century. Second, Isaiah 36–39 raises the issue of Babylonian exile by emphasizing the deportation of Hezekiah's descendants and wealth to Babylon in 39:6-7. Third, the idealization of Hezekiah in Isaiah 36–39 presents him as a transitional figure in relation to the 6th-century edition of the book. He serves as a model of piety in deliberate contrast to the portrayal of Ahaz in ch. 7 (see the discussion of Intention below) and thereby serves the ideology of Deutero-Isaiah who rejects the notion of royal self-reliance in favor of reliance on YHWH. Hezekiah's question as to when he might ascend to the house of YHWH in 38:22 responds to the invitation to acknowledge YHWH's sovereignty on Mt. Zion issued to the nations and to Israel in 2:2-4, 5, which date to the 6th-century edition of the book. Hezekiah thereby also serves as the model of piety presupposed throughout chs. 40–55, in which the Davidic monarchy no longer exists (44:28; 45:1) but the people of Israel are invited to join in the Davidic covenant (55:3).

The narrative does not appear to have been modified in the 5th-century edition of the book, in which it plays a similar transitional role.

Intention

The intention of chs. 36–39 must be defined in relation to both the 6th- and 5th-century editions of the book. With regard to the 6th-century edition, Ackroyd points to the significance of the theme of Babylonian exile in ch. 39 ("Interpretation," 152-71, 282-85). The narrative thereby presupposes that the Babylonian exile will be part of the ultimate outcome of the prophecies of Isaiah. But several aspects of this narrative, including the present arrangement of its constituent subunits, the idealization of Hezekiah, and its place in the larger structure of the book, point to the fact that deliverance and restoration, not exile, stand as the ultimate outcome of the prophet's words. The key is for the reader to accept the invitation to acknowledge YHWH that is presented in the 6th-century edition of the book of Isaiah.

As noted in the discussion of structure above, the present arrangement of chs. 36–39 initially presents the siege of Jerusalem followed by accounts of Hezekiah's recovery from illness and Isaiah's condemnation of Hezekiah for hosting Merodach-baladan's embassy. The order of presentation is significant in that it reflects the narrator's interest in chronological retrospection, i.e., the narrative concerning Hezekiah's illness and Merodach-baladan's recovery should precede that of Sennacherib's siege chronologically. In this regard, the narrator presents Hezekiah's recovery and condemnation as the background to YHWH's deliverance of Jerusalem from Sennacherib's siege. Two points become clear: Jerusalem (and Hezekiah) are saved due to Hezekiah's exemplary piety in time of crisis; and Hezekiah's (and the Davidic dynasty's) deliverance is temporary in that he is granted only fifteen more years of life, whereas

Jerusalem's deliverance is never qualified. The narrative thereby points to the fact that Jerusalem will be saved on account of Hezekiah's exemplary piety, but the Davidic dynasty will pass.

The idealization of Hezekiah is accomplished in part by the modification of the narrative in 2 Kgs 18:13–20:19 when it was taken over into the 6th-century edition of the book of Isaiah, but it is also accomplished by a deliberate contrast with the portrayal of Ahaz in Isaiah 7. When faced with similar circumstances of a potentially disastrous invasion of the land of Judah, the two kings react differently. Whereas Ahaz rejects YHWH's promises of security delivered by Isaiah and turns to the Assyrians for help, Hezekiah seeks out YHWH's promise of security through the prophet Isaiah. Whereas Ahaz's actions lead to the conquest of the northern kingdom of Israel and its eventual destruction by Assyria, Hezekiah's actions lead to the destruction of the Assyrian army and the deliverance of the city of Jerusalem.

Ackroyd demonstrates a number of points of comparison between Isa 6:1–9:6 (*RSV* 7) and chs. 36–39 that highlight the deliberate contrast between Ahaz and Hezekiah ("Isaiah 36–39," esp. 116-19). Both texts open with historical notes (6:1; 7:1; and 36:1) of which the latter two relate to the DtrH (cf. 2 Kgs 16:5 and 18:13). Both events are located at the same spot, by the water conduit near the highway of the Fullers' Field (Isa 7:3 and 36:2). Both narratives depend heavily on the use of prophetic signs (*'ôt;* in 7:11, 14 and 37:30; 38:7, 22), which Ahaz rejects and Hezekiah accepts. Both narratives employ the clause "the zeal of YHWH Sabaoth will accomplish this" at climactic points in the narrative (9:6 [*RSV* 7] and 37:30). The reference to the "steps of Ahaz" *(ma'ălôt 'āḥāz)* in 38:8 provides an obvious link to the Ahaz narrative. Other features of the two narratives illustrate the contrast between the two monarchs. For example, 7:2 and 4 make clear that the threat to Jerusalem in Ahaz's time is inconsequential, whereas ch. 36 presents the Assyrian threat as quite real. Likewise, both monarchs receive a message of comfort from Isaiah, but whereas Ahaz shows groundless fear, Hezekiah does not. The result is a presentation of Hezekiah's exemplary faith and piety in contrast to Ahaz's groundless fears and faithlessness in a similar situation of crisis.

The presentation of Hezekiah's exemplary piety indicates that chs. 36–39 present him as the fulfillment of Isaiah's words in the first part of the book. In relation to the Ahaz narrative, Hezekiah obviously is intended to serve as the ideal monarch presented in 9:1-6 (*RSV* 2-7), who serves as "the wonderful counsellor," "prince of peace," etc. As such, Hezekiah might also fulfill the royal ideal expressed in 11:1-16 and 32:1-20, although his failure to return the exiles of Judah and to establish a peaceful habitation may suggest that the authors of the book have something else in mind. It is noteworthy that Hezekiah's request for a sign that he will go up to the house of YHWH in 38:22 reflects the invitation to the nations in 2:2-4 and to Jacob (Israel) in 2:5 to go up to the house of YHWH on Zion in order to acknowledge YHWH's sovereignty. As noted in the discussion of these texts, they stem from the 6th-century edition of the book of Isaiah. Likewise, the discussion of the setting of ch. 38 notes that the form of Hezekiah's question in 38:22 has been modified from that in 2 Kgs 20:8 in order to reflect the text of Isa 2:2-4, 5. This modification indicates the redactors' intention to associate Hezekiah's request with the invitation to Jacob in Isa 2:5; i.e., Hezekiah becomes the ideal Jew who will accept YHWH's invitation to worship and accept YHWH as monarch. In this regard, the coming loss of the Davidic monarchy is inconsequential insofar as YHWH is the true monarch (cf. ch. 6) who authorized the monarchy in the first place. This portrayal would suggest that the 6th-century redaction of Isaiah saw YHWH, not a Davidic king, as the monarch who would restore the exiles (11:1-16) and establish peaceful habitations for the people with just rule (32:1-20).

Hezekiah's portrayal in chs. 36–39 also serves as the literary setting for the writings of Deutero-Isaiah in chs. 40–55 (Melugin, *Isaiah*, 82-84; Seitz, "Divine Council"). Chs. 40–55 are not presented as the writings of another prophet, but as the continuation of the writings of Isaiah in light of the events portrayed in chs. 36–39. It is therefore noteworthy that chs. 40–55 do not presuppose the continued existence of the Davidic monarchy, but envision YHWH's designated "messiah" or monarch as Cyrus of Persia (44:24-28; 45:1-8). As YHWH's surrogate, Cyrus will build the temple (44:28) and rule the nations (45:1), but YHWH will exercise true royal authority. In these circumstances, the invitation to Israel to join in the covenant of David in 55:3 is particularly striking. As in 2:5, Israel is invited to join in YHWH's plans, and it remains only for Israel to accept the invitation. In this regard, the portrayal of Hezekiah in chs. 36–39 presents the ideal Jew who stands ready to accept YHWH's invitation offered at the beginning (2:5) and the end (55:3) of the 6th-century edition of the book.

Much of the same might be said of the role of chs. 36–39 in relation to the 5th-century edition, in which these chapters serve in a similar transitional role between the two parts of the book. As noted by Seitz (*Zion's Final Destiny,* 176-82), Hezekiah's sickness in ch. 38 relates to the theme of Jerusalem's sickness in ch. 1. Like Jerusalem in ch. 1, Hezekiah in ch. 38 stands in need of healing, and Hezekiah's turn to YHWH presents a model for the stricken city to follow in order to achieve the redemption announced in 1:27-28. As noted in the discussion of ch. 1 above, the final edition of this chapter stems from the 5th-century redaction of the book of Isaiah. The portrayal of a sick city in need of healing conforms to the portrayal of YHWH's plans to create a new heaven and earth in chs. 65–66, in which the evil of the world will be cleansed in order to make way for YHWH's righteous rule. Again, the portrayal of Hezekiah in chs. 36–39 presents him as one who awaits that ideal period. The presentation of YHWH as the true monarch in 66:1 precludes the reestablishment of the Davidic monarchy.

Bibliography

→ bibliography at "Introduction to the Prophetic Literature" and at "Introduction to the Book of Isaiah." P. R. Ackroyd, "The Biblical Interpretation of the Reigns of Ahaz and Hezekiah," in *Studies in the Religious Tradition of the Old Testament* (London: SCM, 1987) 181-92, 287-88; idem, "Historians and Prophets," in *Studies,* 121-51, 278-82; L. Camp, *Hiskija und Hiskijabild: Analyse und Interpretation von 2 Kön 18–20* (Altenberg: Telos, 1990); C. Hardmeier, "Die Propheten Micha und Jesaja im Spiegel von Jeremia XXVI und 2 Regum XVIII–XX: Zur Prophetie-Rezeption in der nachjoshianischen Zeit," *Congress Volume, Leuven 1989* (ed. J. A. Emerton; VTSup 43; Leiden: Brill, 1991) 172-89; M. Hutter, *Hiskija König von Juda: Ein Beitrag zur judäischen Geschichte in assyrischer Zeit* (Grazer Theologische Studien; Graz: Universität Graz, 1982); A. Jepsen, *Die Quellen des Königsbuches* (2nd ed.; Halle: Niemeyer, 1956) 77; O. Kaiser, "Die Verkündigung des Propheten Jesaja im Jahre 701," *ZAW* 81 (1969) 304-15; S. L. McKenzie, *The Trouble with Kings: The Composition of the Book of Kings in the Deuteronomistic History* (VTSup 42; Leiden: Brill, 1991) 101-9; J. Meinhold, *Die Jesajaerzählungen: Jesaja 36-39: Eine historisch-kritische Untersuchung* (Göttingen: Vandenhoeck & Ruprecht, 1898); A. T. Olmstead, "The Earliest Book of Kings," *AJSL* 31 (1915) 169-214; H. M. Orlinsky, "The Kings-Isaiah Recensions of the Hezekiah Story," *JQR* 30 (1939-40) 33-49; I. W. Provan, *Hezekiah and the Books of Kings: A Contribution to the Debate about the Composition of the Deuteronomistic History* (BZAW 172; Berlin and New York: de Gruyter, 1988); E. Ruprecht, "Die ursprüngliche Komposition der Hiskia-Jesaja-Erzählungen und ihre Umstrukturierung durch den Verfasser des deuteronomistischen Geschichtswerkes," *ZTK* 87 (1990) 33-66; B. Stade, "Anmerkungen zu 2 Kö. 15-21," *ZAW* 6 (1886) 156-89.

CONFRONTATION STORY CONCERNING THE DEFEAT OF SENNACHERIB'S THREAT AGAINST JERUSALEM, 36:1-37:38

Structure

I. Report of Sennacherib's invasion of Judah	36:1
II. Report concerning Sennacherib's first message to Hezekiah/Jerusalem	36:2-22
A. Sennacherib sends Rabshakeh	2a
B. Rabshakeh stands by upper pool	2b
C. Judean officers come out	3
D. Rabshakeh's first speech: commission of messengers to Hezekiah	4-10
1. Speech formula	4aα
2. Speech proper: commission of messengers to Hezekiah	4aβ-10
a. Commission formula	4aβ
b. Message: messenger speech	4b-10
1) Messenger formula	4bα
2) Message proper: disputation speech	4bβ-10
a) Disputation of general premise: rhetorical question concerning confidence in revolt	4bβ-5a
(1) Rhetorical question proper	4bβ
(2) Counterpoint: words are no basis for war	5a
b) Disputation of subpremise: rhetorical question concerning unreliable supporters	5b-7

460

Isaiah 36–37 is demarcated initially by its narrative form with an introductory *wayĕhî*, "and it came to pass," which distinguishes the unit from the preceding poetic passage in ch. 35. The unit is governed throughout by a *wāw*-consecutive verbal formulation that establishes its prose narrative character. The temporal formula *bayyāmîm hāhēm*, "in those days," marks the beginning of the next unit in 38:1.

Scholars generally assume that the structure of this narrative is based on the two parallel accounts of Sennacherib's threats against the city of Jerusalem that appear within the passage (e.g., Long, *2 Kings*, 198-202). This view must be rejected in that it is not based on purely literary grounds, but on the source analysis of this material initiated by Stade ("Anmerkungen"; cf. Childs, *Assyrian Crisis*, 69-103). Source critics maintain that there are two separate accounts of Sennacherib's threat against Jerusalem in Isa 36:1–37:9a, 37-38 (= source B[1]) and 37:9b-36 (= source B[2]), and that these have been combined within the present literary context. Although it is likely that the two sources are present in the narrative (see Setting below), there are no clear formal features that suggest that the basic structure is determined by the two parallel encounters. Rather, the narrative demonstrates a relatively consistent *wāw*-consecutive form that focuses on the actions of the various characters that appear within.

The present form of the narrative presupposes a conflict between two major characters, YHWH and Sennacherib, who are mentioned only incidentally (cf. Fewell). The eventual death of Sennacherib as a result of his blasphemy against YHWH and the involvement of the prophet Isaiah as YHWH's major representative indicate that this narrative is based on the prophetic confrontation story (see the discussion of Genre below). The main action of the narrative is conveyed by subsidiary figures, including the Rabshakeh, Hezekiah, the Judean officers, the prophet Isaiah, the Assyrian messengers, and the angel of YHWH. Overall, the actions or interactions of these figures advance the plot step by step to its inevitable conclusion, which is the defeat and death of one of the major contestants, Sennacherib. Consequently, the structure of this narrative is based on a sequence of scenes in which the subsidiary characters interact with each other on behalf of or in conjunction with YHWH and Sennacherib.

The narrative reports seven major episodes that constitute the structure of this passage. It begins with a report of Sennacherib's invasion of Judah in 36:1 that sets the scene for what follows. Subsequent subunits convey the major stages of the confrontation between Sennacherib and YHWH. Isa 36:2-22 reports the conveyance of Sennacherib's first message to Hezekiah and Judah which demands their surrender. Isa 37:1-7 reports Hezekiah's reaction to this message by sending a delegation to request YHWH's intercession through the prophet Isaiah. Isa 37:8-13 reports Sennacherib's second message to Hezekiah and Judah in which he claims to be more powerful than YHWH, thus setting the challenge to which YHWH will respond. Isa 37:14-20 reports Hezekiah's prayer to YHWH for deliverance. Isa 37:21-35 reports YHWH's response to Hezekiah through Isaiah, which states that Sennacherib will be defeated and that Judah will be restored. Finally, 37:36-38 reports Sennacherib's defeat and assassination, which provides the climactic resolution to the conflict between the major characters.

Following the report of Sennacherib's invasion in 36:1, the report concerning Sennacherib's first message to Hezekiah/Judah in 36:2-22 conveys the first major stage of the conflict between Sennacherib and YHWH. The subunit focuses on the confrontation between Sennacherib's representative, the Rabshakeh, and Hezekiah's representatives, the Judean officers Eliakim ben Hilkiah, Shebna, and Joah ben Asaph. The structure and sequencing of this subunit are determined by the reports of the actions of each character. Isa 36:2a reports that Sennacherib sends the Rabshakeh to Hezekiah in Jerusalem. Isa 36:2b reports that the Rabshakeh stands by the upper pool by the Fuller's Field in order to confront the defenders of Jerusalem. Isa 36:3 reports the arrival of Hezekiah's officers. These three episodes thereby set the scene for the following speech by the Rabshakeh.

The report of the Rabshakeh's first speech in 36:4-10 conveys Sennacherib's basic demand for Hezekiah's and Jerusalem's surrender. It begins with a standard speech formula in v. 4aα followed by the speech proper in vv. 4aβ-10, which is formulated as a commission of the Judean officers to carry Sennacherib's message to Hezekiah. The commission formula appears in v. 4aβ and the message to be conveyed appears in vv. 4b-10 in the form of a messenger speech. The messenger formula appears in v. 4bα, and the message proper appears in vv. 4bβ-10 in the form of a diplomatic disputation (cf. Childs, *Assyrian Crisis,* 81, 85). The disputation begins by challenging the main premise of Hezekiah's revolt, Hezekiah's confidence that the revolt will succeed, in vv. 4bβ-5a. The disputation employs a rhetorical question in v. 4bβ that questions the basis for Hezekiah's confidence. This is followed by the counterpoint in v. 5a: the words (or promises) of supposed allies are no basis for a revolt. The disputation moves to a challenge of the first subpremise of the revolt, the reliability of Hezekiah's supporters, in vv. 5b-7. This portion of the disputation begins with a rhetorical question in v. 5b that asks whom Hezekiah has trusted. The counterpoints appear in vv. 6-7, which state that Egypt is an unreliable ally (v. 6) and that YHWH will not support Hezekiah (v. 7). The formulation of v. 7 includes a statement of Hezekiah's presupposition that YHWH will support him in v. 7a and a refutation of that presupposition in v. 7b based on Hezekiah's destruction of YHWH's altars. The disputation of the second subpremise, that Hezekiah has the strength to challenge Sennacherib, appears in vv. 8-9. It begins with a proposal in v. 8 that Hezekiah challenge Sennacherib, backed by an offer of two thousand horses if Hezekiah can find the men to place on them. This is followed by a rhetorical question in v. 9 that asserts that even under such conditions, Hezekiah could not defeat the least of Sennacherib's commanders. The final disputation of a subpremise appears in v. 10, formulated simply as a rhetorical question that asserts that YHWH supports the Assyrian king and ordered him to destroy Judah.

Isaiah 36:11 reports the response of the Judean officers to this speech. Rather than reply to its arguments, they request that the Rabshakeh speak in Aramaic so that the people on the wall will not understand the gravity of the threat posed against them. The speech formula appears in v. $11a\alpha_1$, followed by the speech proper in v. $11a\alpha_2$-b. The speech is parenetic in formulation, including a positive proposal to speak Aramaic (v. $11a\alpha_2$-β) and a negative proposal against speaking Judean (v. 11b). The Rabshakeh's counterresponse that he will continue to speak in Judean follows immediately in 36:12. The speech formula appears in v. $12a\alpha_1$. The speech proper appears in v. $12a\alpha_2$-b, which is formulated as a rhetorical question that asserts that the people on the wall are the ones who need to hear his words. These sections thereby prepare for the following second speech by the Rabshakeh.

The report of the Rabshakeh's second address in 36:13-20 indicates that it is directed to defenders of Jerusalem in an attempt to convince them to surrender. It begins with a description of the circumstances of the address in v. 13a that states that the Rabshakeh speaks Judean in a loud voice. The report of his speech appears in vv. 13b-20. It begins with a speech formula in v. $13b\alpha$, followed by the speech proper in vv. $13b\beta$-20, which is formulated as a parenetic attempt to persuade the Judeans to surrender. The speech proper begins with a call to attention in v. $13b\beta$.

The first of two messenger speeches appears in vv. 14-16a, including the messenger formula in v. $14a\alpha$ and the messenger speech proper in vv. $14a\beta$-16a, which is formulated as an attempt to dissuade the Judeans from trusting in Hezekiah. The grounds for discussion are laid out in vv. $14a\beta$-15. They include a warning not to be deceived by Hezekiah in v. $14a\beta$-b, constituted by a basic statement (v. $14a\beta$) and its reason, i.e., that Hezekiah cannot save them (v. 14b). The second ground appears in v. 15, which warns against relying on Hezekiah's trust in YHWH. The summation of the argument in v. 16a states simply, "Do not listen to Hezekiah."

The second messenger speech in vv. 16b-20 attempts to provide positive grounds for surrender by stating that the Assyrian king will provide lenient treatment to all who surrender. It begins with a messenger formula in v. $16b\alpha_1$, followed by the messenger speech proper in vv. $16b\alpha_2$-20. This attempt to persuade the people begins with a proposal for surrender in vv. $16b\alpha_2$-17. It includes the proposal proper (v. $16b\alpha_2$-α) and a statement of the time limits or conditions: the people will remain on their own land until they are taken to another equally pleasant land. Vv. 18-20 then provide the people with counterarguments against Hezekiah. V. 18 states that Hezekiah might try to convince them that YHWH will save them. Counterarguments appear in the form of two rhetorical questions in vv. 19-20. V. 19 asks where are the gods of other cities who were unable to stop Sennacherib. V. 20 asks who among the gods could save their lands in order to assert that YHWH cannot save Judah.

The subunit concludes with two additional scenes. V. 21 reports that the Judean officers responded to the Rabshakeh's speech with silence. This is basically stated in v. 21a. V. 21b reports that Hezekiah's command was the reason for the silence. The subunit concludes with v. 22, which narrates the report by the Judean officers to Hezekiah.

The third major episode of the narrative appears in 37:1-7, which shifts the focus to Hezekiah and his reaction to Sennacherib's challenge, i.e., he sends a delegation of officers to the prophet Isaiah in order to request assistance from YHWH. The structure of this subunit is defined by the actions of its major characters. It begins with a report that Hezekiah puts on mourning garb in v. 1, followed by a statement in v. 2 that he sends a delegation including Eliakim, Shebna, and the elders of the priests to the prophet Isaiah.

The delegation's speech to Isaiah appears in vv. 3-4, formulated as a report of a messenger speech. The speech formula appears in v. 3aα$_1$, followed by the messenger speech proper in vv. 3aα$_2$-4. The messenger formula appears in v. 3aα$_2$, followed by the speech proper in vv. 3aβ-4 that is formulated as an appeal to the prophet for YHWH's intercession. An assessment of the situation appears in v. 3aβ-b that states that it is a day of calamity. This is basically stated in v. 3aβ, and the reason follows in v. 3b in the form of a proverbial statement that there is no strength among the people to bear children. The appeal for a prayer by Isaiah for YHWH's intercession appears in v. 4. It states the condition, that perhaps YHWH has heard Sennacherib's reviling words, in v. 4a and the appeal proper in v. 4b.

The action then shifts to the movement of the delegation in v. 5 as they approach Isaiah to hear his answer. The report of Isaiah's response then follows in vv. 6-7. The speech formula appears in v. 6aα, and the speech proper follows in vv. 6aβ-7 in the form of a commissioning speech in which Isaiah commissions the delegation as messengers to Hezekiah. The commission formula appears in v. 6aβ, followed by the messenger speech to be transmitted to Hezekiah in vv. 6b-7. The messenger formula appears in v. 6bα$_1$, and the speech proper follows in vv. 6bα$_2$-7 in the form of a prophetic oracle of salvation. The oracle begins with the reassurance formula, *'al-tîrā'* . . . , "fear not . . . ," in v. 6bα$_2$-b, followed by the announcement of punishment and death for Sennacherib in v. 7.

The fourth major episode appears in 37:8-13, which reports Sennacherib's second message to Hezekiah and Jerusalem. Again, the sequence of action by the major characters determines the structure of the subunit. Isa 37:8 reports that the Rabshakeh returns to the Assyrian king at Libnah. V. 9a reports that the Assyrian king hears about the approach of Tirhakah, king of Ethiopia. Finally, vv. 9b-13 report that the Assyrian king sent messengers to Hezekiah. The report that the Assyrian king sent messengers appears in v. 9b, followed by the commissioning speech in vv. 10-13. The commission formula appears in v. 10aα, followed by the speech proper in the form of a disputation speech against trust in YHWH in vv. 10aβ-13. The basic premise to be disputed, YHWH's promise to deliver the city previously stated in 37:6b-7, is stated in v. 10aβ-b. The argumentation against this premise follows in vv. 11-13, organized in the form of three rhetorical questions. V. 11 asks how the people will be saved when the Assyrian king has been able to destroy other lands. The rhetorical question in v. 12 asserts that the other gods were unable to save their lands. Finally, the rhetorical question in v. 13 asserts that the kings of these lands were lost as a consequence of their (and their gods') inability to defend against the Assyrian kings.

The fifth major episode of this unit in 37:14-20 focuses on Hezekiah's prayer to YHWH as his response to the message from the Assyrian king. The sequence of action determines the structure. V. 14a reports that Hezekiah receives and reads the scroll containing the Assyrian king's message. V. 14b reports that he enters the temple and spreads out the scroll. Vv. 15-20 then report his prayer to YHWH. The prayer formula appears in v. 15, followed by the prayer proper, formulated as a standard complaint (cf. Wildberger, *Jesaja*, 1425), in vv. 16-20. The invocation in v. 16 includes the invocation proper in v. 16aα, a 2nd-person masculine singular address stating that YHWH alone is God to all the nations in v. 16aβ, and another 2nd-person masculine singular address asserting that YHWH made heaven and earth in v. 16b. V. 17 is a petition, formulated with masculine imperatives directed to YHWH, to hear and to see the reviling words of Sennacherib that occasioned the complaint. Vv. 18-19 state the motivation for the complaint with an imprecation of the Assyrian kings. V. 18 states that they have destroyed lands, and v. 19 states that they have destroyed gods. The complaint concludes with Hezekiah's petition to YHWH for deliverance, introduced by *wĕ'attâ*, "and now," in v. 20.

The sixth major subunit in 37:21-35 reports Isaiah's response to Hezekiah that conveys YHWH's oracle of judgment against Sennacherib. The response report formula appears in v. 21a, followed by the response proper in vv. 21b-35, formulated as two messenger speeches that together constitute a modified judgment speech against Sennacherib.

The first messenger speech appears in vv. 21b-32, which state the grounds for Sennacherib's judgment in vv. 21b-29 and the basis for Jerusalem's deliverance in vv. 30-32. The messenger formula appears in v. 21b, followed by the message proper in vv. 22-32. The introductory statements in vv. 22a and 30aα respectively identify the two components of the speech in vv. 22-29 and 30-32. V. 22a identifies the following material as YHWH's word concerning Sennacherib. The word proper in vv. 22b-29 is formulated as a taunt against the Assyrian king. The structure of the taunt is determined by the shifting sequence of topics and rhetorical questions. V. 22b states Jerusalem's derision of Sennacherib by describing the city as a woman scorning and shaking her head against the tyrant.

Verses 23-25 focus on Sennacherib's reviling of YHWH. V. 23 begins with a rhetorical question that accuses Sennacherib of reviling YHWH. Vv. 24-25 specify the charge by quoting Sennacherib's offending statements. V. 24aα contains the quotation formula, and vv. 24aβ-25 contain the quotations. They include Sennacherib's 1st-person statements that he has reached to the farthest limits of the heavens to cut down trees (v. 24aβ-b) and that he has dug, drunk, and dried up the waters of the Nile (v. 25).

Verses 26-28 then shift to YHWH's power. Like vv. 23-25, these verses begin with rhetorical questions in v. 26aα that demonstrate YHWH's power. The specification of this assertion follows in vv. 26aβ-28 with a series of four statements concerning YHWH's power. V. 26aβ asserts that YHWH is the creator; vv. 26b-27a state that YHWH controls the means for destruction; v. 27b illustrates the destructive power with the metaphor of grass before the wind; and v. 28 states that YHWH knows all about Sennacherib's activities.

Finally, v. 29 shifts to YHWH's word of judgment against Sennacherib. The basis for judgment, Sennacherib's raging pride, is stated in v. 29a with a typical introductory *ya'an*, "because of." The consequence follows in v. 29b: YHWH will place a hook in Sennacherib's nose in order to return him back from whence he came.

A prophetic announcement of a sign to Hezekiah follows in 37:30-32, which is linked as the second part of the preceding messenger speech by the conjunctive *wāw* at the beginning of v. 30. V. 30aα constitutes the introductory statement or declaration of a sign which identifies the following as a sign to Hezekiah. The sign proper appears in vv. 30aβ-32. Vv. 30aβ-31 constitute an instruction to eat the wild growth of the fields and to plant new produce. This includes the instruction proper to eat and plant in v. 30aβ, and the projected result that a remnant from the house of Judah will emerge from Jerusalem/Zion in v. 31. V. 31 is linked to v. 30aβ by the converted perfect verb *wĕyāsĕpâ*, "and there shall again be." V. 32, introduced by a causative *kî*, "because," states the basis for this sign, that a remnant will emerge from Jerusalem and survivors from Mt. Zion. This is basically stated in v. 32a and confirmed by the appositional statement in v. 32b that "the zeal of YHWH Sabaoth shall accomplish this."

The second messenger speech in vv. 33-35, which are joined to vv. 21b-32 by *lākēn*, "therefore," describe the consequences of the preceding material for Sennacherib in the form of an announcement of judgment. The messenger formula, modified by the addition of the initial *lākēn*, appears in v. 33aα. The message proper, formulated as an announcement of judgment against Sennacherib, appears in vv. 33aβ-35. V. 33aβ-b states a series of prohibitions concerning Sennacherib's threats against Jerusalem. The oracle formula *nĕ'ûm-yhwh*, "oracle of YHWH," in v. 34 indicates that vv. 34-35 constitute an oracle by YHWH stating that YHWH will turn Sennacherib aside (v. 34), and that YHWH will defend Jerusalem (v. 35). The two statements apparently presuppose the word against Sennacherib in vv. 21b-29 and the sign to Hezekiah and Jerusalem in vv. 30-32.

Finally, the seventh subunit in 37:36-38 reports the aftermath of the encounter between Sennacherib and YHWH, including Sennacherib's defeat and assassination. The structure of this subunit is determined by the narrative sequence of action. V. 36 reports that the "angel of YHWH" killed 185,000 troops in the Assyrian camp, thereby causing the defeat of Sennacherib's army. V. 37 reports Sennacherib's subsequent return to Nineveh. V. 38 reports Sennacherib's assassination by two of his sons while worshiping in the temple of his god Nisroch. This last point indicates Sennacherib's total defeat in his confrontation with YHWH. His own statements concerning YHWH's inability to defend Jerusalem are turned against him in that his own god Nisroch is unable to defend him from an attack by his own sons in the deity's temple.

Genre

Isaiah 36–37 is generally treated as a (→) historical narrative, a (→) prophetic narrative, or a (→) legend (cf. Long, *2 Kings,* 202), but such treatments fail to account adequately for the conflict between YHWH and Sennacherib in this passage. Historical considerations and legendary elements certainly play important roles in the interpretation of this narrative, but the conflict between YHWH (represented by the prophet Isaiah) and Sennacherib is the fundamental concern of this narrative. Sennacherib's threat against the city of Jerusalem appears at first to be the primary issue of the narrative, but this is easily resolved as a result of Isaiah's first oracle to Hezekiah's delegation in 37:6-7, in which the prophet states that YHWH will defeat Sennacherib. Rather, the primary issue is Sennacherib's blasphemy against YHWH in 37:10-13, in which Sennacherib challenges YHWH's word and maintains that he, not YHWH, holds the ultimate power to decide the fate of Jerusalem in his hands. YHWH's word against Sennacherib, transmitted through Isaiah in 37:22-29, makes clear that this is the fundamental issue. Here Sennacherib is portrayed as defying YHWH by claiming that he has the power to reach to the heights of heaven and to dig and dry up the waters of the earth (37:23-25). YHWH's response in 37:26-28 indicates that this claim strikes to the very heart of YHWH's role in that the Assyrian monarch effectively claims to be the creator of the universe. The issue now becomes not simply the deliverance of Jerusalem but a demonstration of the true power in the universe.

With these considerations in mind, it becomes evident that the genre of this narrative is based on the prophetic CONFRONTATION STORY. A subgenre of the prophetic (→) narrative, the prophetic CONFRONTATION STORY focuses on a confrontation between a prophet and his or her opponents in an attempt to legitimize the prophetic word by pointing to the demise of the opponents, who would deny its validity. Examples include Amos's confrontation with the Israelite high priest Amaziah at Bethel (Amos 7:10-17) and Jeremiah's confrontation with the prophet Hananiah (Jeremiah 27–28). In both cases, the death of the prophet's opponent verifies the validity of the prophet's message. In the present instance, however, it is not Isaiah but YHWH who is directly involved in the conflict. Nevertheless, a key characteristic of this narrative is that surrogates act on behalf of the major actants: the Rabshakeh and the messengers act on behalf of Sennacherib, the Judean officers act on behalf of Hezekiah, and Isaiah acts on behalf of YHWH. At the very basis of the narrative lies the validity of YHWH's word versus that of Sennacherib, just as the validity of YHWH's word lies at the basis of the prophetic CONFRONTATION NARRATIVES concerning Amos and Jeremiah. Like Amos and Jeremiah, Isaiah delivers that word. When Sennacherib challenges YHWH's word, he dies. Here one should note that the deliverance of Jerusalem is not the climactic act of the narrative; rather, the climactic act is the death of Sennacherib.

Although the prophetic CONFRONTATION STORY provides the basic generic identity of this narrative, a large number of subordinate genres also play important roles. The most basic generic form in chs. 36–37 is the REPORT, which is a 3rd-person narrative about a single event in the past. The REPORT interacts with the prophetic CONFRONTATION STORY to provide the basic structure and formulation of the narrative as an account of Sennacherib's attempt to obtain Jerusalem's surrender as the backdrop for the confrontation between YHWH and Sennacherib. The prophetic CONFRONTATION STORY has no specific form other than a description of a confrontation between the two major antagonists. Consequently, the INVASION REPORT, a specialized form of the larger REPORT genre, plays an important role in the formulation of the narrative (for a discussion of the INVASION REPORT, see Long, 2 Kings, 206). It appears in the framework of the narrative in both 36:1 and 37:36-38 in order to provide the setting for the confrontation between YHWH and Sennacherib that constitutes the main concern of the narrative. In typical fashion, 36:1 sets forth the major concerns of the INVASION REPORT: Sennacherib's invasion of Judah and its results, i.e., his capture of all the cities of Judah. Isa 37:36-38 returns to the concern by stating that Sennacherib's defeat, withdrawal, and death constitute the ultimate outcome of the confrontation.

The report of the Rabshakeh's first speech in 36:4-10 employs a number of generic elements. At its most basic level, it is formulated as a REPORT of a COMMISSION in that it reports the Rabshakeh's attempt to commission the Judean delegation to act as messengers to convey Sennacherib's message to Hezekiah. The commissioning of a messenger is not an independent genre but only part of a narrative concerning the sending of messengers. Nevertheless, it is easily identified by its INSTRUCTIONS to convey a message, in this case the COMMAND in v. 4a, *'imrû-nā' 'el-ḥizqîyāhû*, "say now to Hezekiah," followed by the stereotypical MESSENGER FORMULA in v. 4b, *kōh-'āmar* PN, "thus says PN." In the present instance, the commissioning of messengers relates to the diplomatic exchange in which each of the major parties to the discussion, Sennacherib and Hezekiah, is represented by delegates who must deliver, receive, and convey the messages. The message itself takes the form of a DIPLOMATIC DISPUTATION. In keeping with the general DISPUTATION genre, it is designed to challenge the premises or beliefs of the opposing party or audience and to convince that party instead that the speaker's position is correct. The RHETORICAL QUESTION plays an important role in this DISPUTATION, for it is designed not to evoke an answer but to assert a point by posing an unanswerable question or one that can be answered only in the desired manner. In the present instance, the DISPUTATION employs RHETORICAL QUESTIONS to attack Hezekiah's beliefs that his revolt will succeed and to assert the counterthesis that it will fail.

The first element of the DISPUTATION in vv. 4bβ-5a attacks the general premise of Hezekiah's confidence in the revolt by asserting that words, or in this case promises of allies, are no basis for war. The general basis for this argument is that Hezekiah can expect no assistance from his allies now that the

Assyrian army is on the scene. The subsequent elements of the DISPUTATION then attack the more specific points of the general premise. Vv. 5b-7 question the reliability of Hezekiah's supporters by pointing out that neither Egypt nor YHWH will come to his aid. Egypt is an unreliable ally at best, and Hezekiah has offended YHWH by tearing down YHWH's altars as part of his religious reform. Vv. 8-9 then challenge Hezekiah's ability to defend himself by pointing out that even with the gift of two thousand horses, Hezekiah could not find the men to use them; and even if he could, he still could not challenge the least of Sennacherib's commanders. Finally, v. 10 asserts that YHWH must support the Assyrian king, who could not have destroyed the land of Judah without YHWH's permission. Such argumentation is typical of Assyrian diplomatic exchanges (cf. Long, *2 Kings,* 217-20; Childs, *Assyrian Crisis,* 80-82; Cohen; H. W. F. Saggs, "The Nimrud Letters, 1952 — Part I," *Iraq* 17 [1955] 21-56; Wildberger, "Rede").

The diplomatic setting of the exchange in this narrative accounts for the presence of a PARENESIS in the REPORT of the Judean officers' response to the Rabshakeh in 36:11. Rather than respond directly to his challenge, they attempt to persuade him to speak Aramaic instead of Judean in order that the people on the walls will not understand. PARENESIS is an attempt to persuade with reference to a goal. It employs both positive forms, in this instance the proposal to speak Aramaic in v. 11aα_2-β, and negative forms, in this instance the request not to speak Judean in v. 11b. The setting of diplomatic exchange and disputation also accounts for the use of the RHETORICAL QUESTION in the REPORT of the Rabshakeh's response to this request in 36:12. Here he employs a RHETORICAL QUESTION to assert that the people on the walls are the ones who most need to hear his words. By this means, he provides the basis for rejecting the officers' proposal and thereby undermines Hezekiah's negotiating position by making Sennacherib's terms, and Hezekiah's desperate position, known to all.

The REPORT of the Rabshakeh's second speech in 36:13-20 likewise employs PARENESIS in an attempt to persuade the Judeans to surrender. It uses a typical CALL TO ATTENTION formula in v. 13bβ, *šimĕ'û 'et-dibrê hammelek haggādôl melek 'aššûr,* "hear the words of the great king, the king of Assyria." The formula typically opens a public address and functions as a means to attract the attention of the listeners to the following speech. In the present case, it employs the title (i.e., "the great king") typically used by the Assyrian monarchs in their diplomatic correspondence and public pronouncements (cf. Cohen, 38-39). Vv. 14-16a then focus on the negative elements of the PARENESIS in an attempt to dissuade the Judeans from trusting in Hezekiah. The speech is cast in a typical MESSENGER SPEECH form as indicated by the MESSENGER FORMULA in v. 14aα. Its argumentation is summed up by the PROHIBITION in v. 16a, "do not listen to Hezekiah." The positive elements of the PARENESIS appear in the form of a second MESSENGER SPEECH in vv. 16b-20. Following the MESSENGER FORMULA in v. 16bα$_1$, the speech attempts to persuade the Judeans to surrender by offering a pleasant life in a foreign land. The proposal is backed by further counterarguments against Hezekiah that apparently relate to disputation language as well as to the PARENESIS. In case Hezekiah attempts to convince the people that YHWH will save them, the Rabshakeh employs RHETORICAL QUES-

TIONS in vv. 19-20 to assert that YHWH cannot save the people of Jerusalem because other gods were unable to save their peoples from the might of the Assyrian king.

The REPORT concerning Hezekiah's reaction to the Rabshakeh's message in 37:1-7 likewise employs the MESSENGER SPEECH form to convey the message sent by Hezekiah to Isaiah. Rather than portraying the commissioning of the messengers, however, the text reports the delegation's encounter with the prophet in vv. 3-7. The delegation's speech to Isaiah, introduced by the MESSENGER FORMULA in v. 3aα₂, is formulated as an APPEAL for a prayer by the prophet to YHWH. APPEALS generally assume no obligation on the part of the party addressed. Consequently, the present instance lays out grounds for such an APPEAL in v. 3aβ-b by pointing to the calamity facing Jerusalem. The APPEAL for Isaiah's prayer follows in v. 4. The REPORT of Isaiah's response employs typical commissioning language, as indicated by the COMMISSIONING FORMULA in v. 6aβ and the MESSENGER FORMULA in v. 6bα₁. The prophet's response is formulated as an ORACLE OF SALVATION (cf. J. Begrich, "Das priesterliche Heilsorakel," *ZAW* 52 [1934] 81-92). Such oracles were generally delivered in a liturgical setting to express the assurance of divine favor, perhaps in response to a COMPLAINT. The oracle begins with the typical REASSURANCE FORMULA, *'al-tîrā'*, "fear not" (cf. Conrad, *Fear Not Warrior*, esp. 52-62), followed by an announcement that YHWH will turn Sennacherib away from Jerusalem and see to his death.

The REPORT concerning Sennacherib's second message in 37:8-13 employs generic forms like those of the first message. Vv. 10-13 are cast as a COMMISSION as indicated by the COMMISSIONING FORMULA in v. 10aα. The message itself in vv. 10aβ-13 is formulated as another DISPUTATION SPEECH. The basic premise to be disputed, that the Judeans should not trust YHWH's promise to deliver the city, is stated in v. 10aβ-b. The argumentation in vv. 11-13 again employs RHETORICAL QUESTIONS to assert the opposite view. V. 11 maintains that the people cannot be saved because the Assyrian king has destroyed other lands; v. 12 asserts that other gods were not able to save their lands; and v. 13 sums up by asking what happened to the other kings.

The REPORT of Hezekiah's prayer in 37:14-20 formulates Hezekiah's prayer as a COMPLAINT SONG OF AN INDIVIDUAL in vv. 16-20. COMPLAINT SONGS were employed in liturgical settings on behalf of an individual in distress in order to petition YHWH for relief. Although the prayer does not contain all the elements typically found in the genre, which indicates that it was composed specifically for its present literary context, the essential elements are present. The invocation appears in v. 16 in an expanded form that alludes to YHWH's roles as God of all the nations and creator of heaven and earth. Hezekiah petitions YHWH to see and hear the COMPLAINT in v. 17. Such a PETITION stems from the protestation of innocence, typical of the form as well as the imprecation of enemies. Vv. 18-19 contain the full imprecation of the Assyrian kings by referring to their destructive acts against other lands and gods. As such, vv. 18-19 provide motivation to YHWH to intercede. V. 20 contains the core of the COMPLAINT in the form of a PETITION to YHWH to deliver Hezekiah and his people from the Assyrians. The use of the 1st-person common plural pronoun ("deliver us") suggests that this COMPLAINT is conceived in communal terms.

The REPORT of Isaiah's response to Hezekiah in 37:21-35 is formulated with two MESSENGER SPEECHES, in vv. 21b-32 and vv. 33-35, which together constitute a modified PROPHETIC JUDGMENT SPEECH against Sennacherib. The first MESSENGER SPEECH, identified by its MESSENGER FORMULA in v. 21b, employs the PROPHETIC JUDGMENT SPEECH pattern in vv. 22-29 to specify the grounds for Sennacherib's judgment, and the PROPHETIC ANNOUNCEMENT OF A SIGN in vv. 30-32 to announce deliverance for Jerusalem. Together these subunits constitute an indictment of Sennacherib that projects his downfall by pointing to YHWH's capacity to save the city of Jerusalem. In fact, the crime of which Sennacherib is charged is his challenge of YHWH's power.

The word concerning Sennacherib, identified by its introduction in v. 22a, is formulated as a TAUNT against the monarch that depicts Jerusalem's derision of the tyrant. Vv. 23-25 focus on the accusation made against Sennacherib by employing RHETORICAL QUESTIONS to assert that the Assyrian monarch has reviled YHWH by claiming that he, not YHWH, is the ultimate power in the universe with the capacity to decide the fate of others. Vv. 26-28 then employ RHETORICAL QUESTIONS to assert YHWH's power in the universe with the capacity to create, to destroy, and to know all of Sennacherib's whereabouts. The discourse concludes with a word of judgment against Sennacherib in v. 29 that follows the general pattern of a PROPHECY OF PUNISHMENT AGAINST AN INDIVIDUAL. V. 29a states that the grounds for judgment are Sennacherib's raging pride or arrogance in asserting his power over that of YHWH; v. 29b states the consequence that YHWH will put a hook in Sennacherib's nose and return him from whence he came.

The PROPHETIC ANNOUNCEMENT OF A SIGN in vv. 30-32 functions as a means to verify both the preceding indictment of Sennacherib and the announcement of his punishment. It speaks to the issue of relative power raised in vv. 22-29 by pointing to YHWH's capacity to create in the natural world. Following the typical declaration of a sign in v. 30aα, the sign proper includes an INSTRUCTION to Hezekiah to eat the natural agricultural growth of the land for the next two years prior to planting a new crop in the third year. Such an INSTRUCTION highlights YHWH's capacity to provide for the people by natural means; and the agricultural metaphor highlights the social situation of the people of Judah who, like the crops, will be renewed when they again take root after the Assyrian threat has passed. This INSTRUCTION constitutes the typical description of the sign. In typical form, v. 32 addresses the significance of the sign by stating that "a remnant shall go forth from Jerusalem and survivors from Mt. Zion" and that "the zeal of YHWH Sabaoth shall accomplish this."

The second MESSENGER SPEECH in 37:33-35 constitutes a PROPHETIC ANNOUNCEMENT OF PUNISHMENT against Sennacherib and thereby completes the ORACLE OF JUDGMENT pattern initiated in vv. 21b-32. The MESSENGER FORMULA in v. 33aα is introduced by *lākēn,* "therefore," which is typical of the PROPHETIC ANNOUNCEMENT OF PUNISHMENT. The announcement itself employs PROHIBITIONS in v. 33aβ-b against Sennacherib's actions that threaten Jerusalem and an oracular form in vv. 34-35, identified by the ORACULAR FORMULA *nĕ'um-yhwh,* "oracle of YHWH," at the end of v. 34, to announce that YHWH will turn aside Sennacherib in order to defend the city of Jerusalem.

The oracle thereby takes up the concerns of both the word against Sennacherib in vv. 21b-29 and the sign for Hezekiah in vv. 30-32.

Finally, the REPORT of Sennacherib's defeat and death in 37:36-38 returns to the forms of the prophetic CONFRONTATION STORY and INVASION REPORT that introduce this narrative. It describes in sequence the defeat of Sennacherib's army by YHWH's angel, the return of Sennacherib to Nineveh, and Sennacherib's assassination in the temple of Nisroch by his own sons. The REPORT thereby confirms the announcements of 37:6-7, 29, and 33-35 that YHWH will return Sennacherib to his own land and that he will be killed. In relation to the INVASION REPORT, these verses describe the ultimate outcome of Sennacherib's invasion of Judah. In relation to the prophetic CONFRONTATION STORY, they describe the ultimate outcome of his confrontation with YHWH.

Setting

The narrative concerning the defeat of Sennacherib's siege of Jerusalem in chs. 36–37 presents tremendous opportunities and difficulties with respect to both its sociohistorical setting and its literary setting. It clearly relates to a well-known historical event from Isaiah's lifetime that is also reported in Sennacherib's Annals (*ANET*, 287-88), but its 3rd-person narrative form demonstrates that it is not the product of the prophet Isaiah. Rather, it stems from a writer who wished to portray Isaiah's role in relation to Sennacherib's siege of Jerusalem in 701. Although it would seem to offer insight into events pertaining to the siege of Jerusalem, various literary issues cloud its interpretation. Sennacherib's Annals present some striking parallels to the Isaiah narrative, but offer a very different view of the outcome of the siege.

A narrative that is nearly identical to Isaiah 36–37 appears in 2 Kgs 18:13–19:36, but this account differs from Isaiah 36–37 in that it includes a brief notice of Hezekiah's surrender to Sennacherib and his payment of tribute (2 Kgs 18:14-16). Other textual differences will be discussed below. Obviously, these differences raise questions about the historical character of the narrative. As part of the larger textual unit of Isaiah 36–39, the narrative plays an important transitional role in the overall structure of the book of Isaiah, but the appearance of the parallel narrative in 2 Kings raises questions as to whether it was composed for its setting in Isaiah, in Kings, or perhaps in another context. Furthermore, the text includes some important parallels to the texts concerning Isaiah's encounter with Ahaz during the Syro-Ephraimite War in Isaiah 7:1–9:6 (*RSV* 7), but the evidence suggests that 7:1–9:6 (*RSV* 7) was arranged in relation to chs. 36–37 and not vice versa.

Since the work of Stade ("Anmerkungen," esp. 170-86), it has become customary to treat the narrative concerning Sennacherib's siege of Jerusalem as a composite text. Based on the unparalleled appearance of a narrative concerning Hezekiah's submission to Sennacherib in 2 Kgs 18:14-16, the accounts of two Assyrian embassies to Hezekiah during the siege, and the report of the aftermath of the confrontation, Stade identified several separate literary sources pertaining to the narrative that have been modified somewhat in subsequent discussion.

Source A is a historically reliable account of Hezekiah's submission to Sennacherib in 18:13-16; source B_1 includes 18:17–19:9bα, 36-37; source B_2 includes 19:9b-20, 32aβ-b, 34-35 (cf. Gonçalves, 373-76, 445-48; for a discussion of the early debate, see Honor; for more recent discussion, see Seitz, *Zion's Final Destiny*, 47-118). Childs divides the sources so that B_1 includes 18:17-9a, 36-37 and B_2 includes 19:9b-35 (*Assyrian Crisis*, 73-76).

Although this source division represents the current scholarly consensus, various studies of the literary character of the narrative point to its compositional unity (e.g., Smelik; Fewell). Essentially, the argument turns on the fact that the repeated confrontation between Sennacherib's representatives and those of Hezekiah highlights the underlying confrontation between YHWH and Sennacherib. The second confrontation emphasizes the Assyrian monarch's hubris and blasphemy against YHWH by maintaining that he (the Assyrian monarch) must be considered the absolute power of the universe. The structural analysis offered above indicates that although the two confrontations play important roles in the narrative presentation, the structure of the narrative is ultimately based not on a presentation of two parallel confrontations but on a narrative sequence pertaining to the shifting focus on the actions of the characters portrayed in the narrative. The second confrontation simply heightens the dramatic tension of the encounter and provides a basis for YHWH's response through the prophet Isaiah that Sennacherib will be defeated and led back to his own land. It thereby demonstrates that YHWH actually controls the situation in Isa 37:22-29. Such tension likewise heightens the promises of a rejuvenated Jerusalem in 37:30-35. One should therefore reject the traditional source divisions of this narrative.

At first glance, the account of Sennacherib's siege of Jerusalem in chs. 36–37 and the parallel account in 2 Kgs 18:13–19:36 provide a potentially informative historical source for the diplomatic negotiations that took place between Sennacherib and Hezekiah during the Assyrian siege of Jerusalem in 701. Not only do Sennacherib's Annals include his account of the invasion of Judah and siege of Jerusalem with striking parallels to the biblical versions; a number of studies of the Rabshakeh's speeches demonstrate that they also reflect the language and practice of Assyrian diplomatic negotiation at this time. Such features include the use of intermediaries in negotiation, the title of the Assyrian king ("the great king, the king of Assyria," Isa 36:4), the portrayal of Egypt as "a broken reed" (36:6), and various elements of the disputational argumentation (see Cohen; cf. Childs, *Assyrian Crisis*, 80-85; Machinist; Long, *2 Kings*, 209-21).

Although these features might suggest that Isaiah 36–37 represents a transcript of the negotiations between Sennacherib and Hezekiah, various problems in this text raise questions about its historical character and demonstrate that it is not a fully accurate account of the events of 701.

First, the statement in 37:36 that the "angel of YHWH" smote the Assyrian army employs a legendary motif analogous to that of the exodus traditions to portray the defeat of the Assyrians and the death of 185,000 troops, an impossibly high number (cf. Exod 12:23). Although Herodotus (2.141) notes that the Assyrian army was overrun by rodents at this time, which suggests the possibility of plague, his account is somewhat garbled in that it incorporates a number of motifs relevant to Greek folklore, and it appears to reflect the legendary biblical account or perhaps an account of Esarhaddon's campaign against Egypt (cf. W. Baumgartner, "Herodots babylonische und assyrische Nachrichten," in *Zum alten Testament und seiner Umwelt* [ed. W. Baumgartner; Leiden: Brill, 1959] 282-331, esp. 305-9; Cogan and Tadmor, 250-51).

A second complicating factor appears in Jer 26:16-19, which states that Micah was the prophet who convinced Hezekiah to repent. This assertion naturally raises questions about the veracity of an account that attributes Hezekiah's decision to Isaiah's influence. Although various scholars have raised this issue (e.g., Ackroyd, "Isaiah I–XII," 85-86), one should note that Jer 26:16-19 quotes Mic 3:12, which predicts the destruction of Jerusalem, in order to defend the prophet Jeremiah for making similar statements. The purpose was to demonstrate that such a negative statement could have a positive outcome, in this case, Hezekiah's repentance. Isaiah never states that the city of Jerusalem will be destroyed, and therefore he could not have been cited as an example in this instance. But Micah's statement presents a perfect analogy to Jeremiah's Temple Sermon, for which he was tried for sedition. By combining Micah's statement with the tradition of Hezekiah's repentance, which is known only from the Isaiah narratives, Jeremiah's defenders were merely trying to cite a precedent in which announcements of Jerusalem's destruction could be taken as an exhortation to repentance (cf. Seitz, *Zion's Final Destiny*, 105-6). This example does not prove that Micah was originally the subject of such a narrative.

Second, two major anachronisms appear in the biblical account. The assassination of Sennacherib by his sons mentioned in Isa 37:38 did not take place until 681 (see now Parpola). Likewise, 37:9 states that Sennacherib heard a report of the approach of the Ethiopian pharaoh Tirhakah. Tirhakah's title may be anachronistic in that he did not ascend to the Egyptian throne until 690-689, but he would have been old enough to command an Egyptian relief force in 701 (see K. A. Kitchen, *The Third Intermediate Period in Egypt (1100-650 BC)* [Warminster: Aris and Phillips, 1973] 154-72, 387-93). Both the inclusion of the report concerning the assassination of Sennacherib and the reference to Tirhakah as the king of Ethiopia (Cush) indicate that the present narrative telescopes historical events ranging over several decades into a single account of Sennacherib's invasion of 701.

Third, the portrayal of an overwhelming Assyrian defeat in Isaiah 36–37/2 Kings 18–19 conflicts with Sennacherib's account of the siege (*ANET*, 287-88). Although some elements correspond, such as Sennacherib's claim to have taken 46 fortified Judean cities (cf. Isa 36:1; 2 Kgs 18:13) and the amount of tribute exacted from Hezekiah (30 talents of gold and 800 talents of silver; cf. 2 Kgs 18:14-16, which lists 300 talents of silver and 30 talents of gold), Sennacherib claims to have achieved a victory over Hezekiah. In addition to the silver and gold mentioned above, he lists as booty 200,150 captives, valuables such as precious stones, furnishings, etc., and even some of Hezekiah's daughters, concubines, and musicians. Sennacherib gives no hint of the defeat mentioned in Isaiah 36–37.

On the basis of these problems, some scholars have posited two Assyrian invasions, so that Sennacherib's Annals and 2 Kgs 18:14-16 portray an Assyrian victory in 701, whereas Isaiah 36–37/2 Kgs 18:13, 17–19:36 portray an Assyrian defeat some time after 689 (e.g., J. Bright, *History of Israel* [3rd ed.; Philadelphia: Westminster, 1981] 298-309 and the literature cited there; cf. Shea), but most scholars reject this position now. Assyrian records speak only of one invasion of Judah, and Sennacherib never claims to have taken the city of Jerusalem or to have removed Hezekiah from the throne. Furthermore, 2 Kgs 18:14-16 presents an account of Hezekiah's submission and payment of tribute to Sennacherib. It appears that Sennacherib was unable to force Hezekiah's surrender and concluded an agreement with him that allowed Hezekiah to maintain his throne while submitting to the Assyrian monarch as his overlord. In such a situation, both monarchs could claim victory: Sennacherib for forcing Hezekiah's submission and payment of tribute, and Hezekiah for saving the city of Jerusalem and his own throne (for discussion of the historical issues and sources, see B. Oded, "Judah and the Exile," in *Israelite and Judaean History* [ed. J. H. Hayes and J. M. Miller; OTL; Philadelphia: Westminster, 1977] 446-51; cf. Cogan and Tadmor, 246-51). In comparison to the straightforward account of Hezekiah's submission in 2 Kgs 18:14-16, the historically telescoped and legendary account in Isaiah 36–37/2 Kgs 18:13, 17–19:36 appears to be the product of late theological reflection and literary embellishment.

Indeed, the literary character of Isaiah 36–37 plays a major role in its interpretation, but the fact that it appears in two distinct literary contexts (Isaiah 36–39; 2 Kgs 18:13–20:19) complicates the matter. Although the narratives are nearly identical, divergences between them indicate that each has been tailored to fit its respective literary context. The issue is further complicated by the identification of several sources that make up the final form of the narrative. Obviously, each of these issues must be examined in order to specify the literary setting of this text and its composition.

As noted in the overview of Isaiah 36–39, these chapters play an important transitional role within the final form of the entire book of Isaiah. Although the narrative begins with consideration of the Assyrian period, insofar as it portrays events pertaining to Sennacherib's invasion of Judah in 701, the reference to the carrying off of Judean wealth and Hezekiah's offspring to Babylon (39:6-7) shifts the reader's attention to the period of Babylonian exile that is presupposed throughout the balance of the book (chs. 40ff.). Furthermore, Ackroyd ("Isaiah 36–39") notes the textual correspondences between 6:1–9:6 (*RSV* 7) and chs. 36–39 that signal a deliberate contrast between the actions of the faithful Hezekiah and those of the faithless Ahaz when faced with a similar situation of foreign invasion (cf. Sweeney, *Isaiah 1–4*, 12-13). Both confrontations take place at the same location, "by the conduit of the upper pool on the highway to the Fullers' Field" (7:3; 36:2). Both kings are offered an oracle of salvation introduced by the reassurance formula "fear not" (*'al-tîrā'*; 37:6; 7:4; cf. Conrad, *Reading Isaiah*, 34-51) and including signs of YHWH's faithfulness in time of crisis, which Ahaz rejects (7:11, 14) and Hezekiah accepts (37:30; 38:7, 22). Both narratives employ the phrase "the zeal of YHWH Sabaoth will accomplish this" (9:6 [*RSV* 7]; 37:32). Finally, 38:8 refers to the "dial of Ahaz" in the context of Hezekiah's acceptance of YHWH's promise of a cure from his sickness, which emphasizes the contrast of the two kings. Other correspondences with the book of Isaiah include the following references to cities that the Assyrian king has conquered and his arrogance in threatening Jerusalem (36:19; 37:13; cf. 10:5-15, esp. vv. 9-11; Clements, *Isaiah and Deliverance*, 36-39); the reference to Shebna, identified as the "scribe" in 36:3 and 37:2, and as the officer "over the household" in 22:15; the references to the "remnant of the house of Judah" (37:31), which reflects similar concerns with the remnant throughout First Isaiah; and the statement "Have you not heard that I determined it long ago? I planned from days of old what now I bring to pass" (37:26; cf. 40:21, 28; 48:8).

Although these considerations might suggest that chs. 36–39 were composed for their transitional role in the book of Isaiah, a closer examination of the evidence indicates that this is not the case. First, Clements demonstrates that the reference to the carrying off of Judean wealth and Hezekiah's sons in 39:6-7 must be understood in reference to the first Babylonian deportation of 597, when King Jehoiachin and other leading Judeans were carried off as hostages to Babylonia. Ch. 39 contains no reference to the destruction of Jerusalem and the temple in 587 and therefore cannot be understood in relation to the later period of Babylonian exile that chs. 40–55 presuppose (Clements, "The Isaiah Narrative of 2 Kings 20:12-19 and the Date of the Deuteronomic History," in *Isac (sic) Leo Seeligmann Volume* [eds. A. Rofé and Y. Zakovitch; Jerusalem: E. Rubinstein, 1983] 209-20). Second, the correspondence between 6:1–9:6 (*RSV* 7) and chs. 36–39 does not indicate that chs. 36–39 were composed in relation to 6:1–9:6 (*RSV* 7); rather, the editorial arrangement of 6:1–9:6 (*RSV* 7), which mixes 1st- and 3rd-person narrative forms with poetry and which combines materials stemming from the prophet Isaiah with those from later writers, indicates that 6:1–9:6 (*RSV* 7) was assembled in relation to chs. 36–39.

Other references that might presuppose statements in Isaiah do not correspond exactly, thereby indicating that although the author of chs. 36–39 may have been familiar with the Isaiah tradition, this text was not composed for a place in the book of Isaiah. The references to the Assyrian king's hubris and the cities that he claims to have taken do not correspond. Isa 36:19 lists Hamath, Arpad, Sepharvaim, and Samaria, and 37:13 lists Hamath, Arpad, Sepharvaim, Henna, and Ivva. Isa 10:9-11 lists Carchemish, Calno, Arpad, Hamath, Damascus, and Samaria. The lack of correspondence indicates that the author of chs. 36–37 may have had 10:5-15 in mind when composing the narrative concerning Sennacherib's siege, but there is no evidence of direct dependence that would indicate that chs. 36–37 were composed for a setting in the book of Isaiah. The same applies to the reference to Shebna as the scribe in 36:3 and 37:2. He is identified as the officer who is "over the house" in 22:15 (see the commentary on these verses above). If chs. 36–37 were composed in relation to earlier material in Isaiah, one would expect greater precision in the identification of Shebna's office.

The reference to the "remnant of the house of Judah that remains" (*pĕlêṭat bêt-yĕhûdâ hanniš'maarâ*) in 37:31 is unique. Elsewhere the book of Isaiah refers to the "remnant" (*pĕlêṭâ*) of "Israel" (4:2), "the house of Jacob" (10:20), "Moab" (15:9); the "rest" (*šĕ'ār*) of "Israel" (10:20), "Jacob" (10:21) and "his people" (11:11, 16; 28:5), and "that which is left" (*hanniš'ār*) of "the remnant of Israel in Zion" (4:3). None of these statements, however, refers to a remnant of Judah; rather, they refer to the remnant of Israel, Jacob, or even Moab.

Finally, the formula in 37:26 corresponds only generally to its counterparts in Second Isaiah. If this narrative was composed with the intention of placing it in the book of Isaiah, one might expect greater correspondence in its references to other Isaianic texts.

The parallel version of Isaiah 36–39 in 2 Kgs 18:13–20:21 also plays an important role within the present form of Kings. The prose narrative formulation corresponds to that of the rest of Kings, and the concern with the exile of Hezekiah's sons to Babylon relates to the conclusion of Kings, which portrays Evil-merodach's release of King Jehoiachin from prison (2 Kgs 25:27-30). In this instance, the narrative in 2 Kgs 18:13–20:21, with its references to Hezekiah's stripping of the temple and the deportation of his descendants to Babylon, forms a sort of prelude to the narratives concerning the destruction of the temple and the Babylonian exile in 2 Kings 25. The Rabshakeh's reference to Hezekiah's reform measures (2 Kgs 18:22-25/Isa 36:7-10) not only serves as a basis for his argument that YHWH sent the Assyrian army to punish Hezekiah, but also refers to the notice given concerning Hezekiah's reform measures in 2 Kgs 18:4. Such notice is entirely lacking in the book of Isaiah. Furthermore, the language employed in this notice reflects the use of typical Deuteronomistic literature in the narrative (cf. Ben Zvi). Such considerations have led the majority of scholars since Gesenius to conclude that the original setting of this narrative is in the books of Kings.

Nevertheless, there is little basis for this conclusion (cf. Seitz, *Zion's Final Destiny*, 48-61). Again, the notice of the carrying off of wealth and Hezekiah's sons to Babylon presupposes not the events of 587 but those of 597. Likewise, the narrative is combined with a conflicting account of Hezekiah's submission to Sennacherib in 2 Kgs 18:14-16. In the present context, the inclusion of this notice highlights Sennacherib's arrogance by indicating that he demanded further concessions even after Hezekiah had surrendered.

One must conclude, however, that the combination of these narratives represents redactional juxtaposition. 2 Kgs 18:14-16 consistently employs the shortened form of Hezekiah's name, *ḥizqîyâ*, and the title *melek yěhûdâ*, "king of Judah" (e.g., 18:14), in contrast to 2 Kgs 18:17–20:21/Isa 36:2–39:8, which employs the long form, *ḥizqîyāhû*, and the title *hammelek*, "the king" (e.g., 2 Kgs 19:1/Isa 37:1). The formulation of the notice of Hezekiah's submission to Sennacherib in 2 Kgs 18:14-16 corresponds to that of 18:1-12, which relates the DtrH's account of Hezekiah's reign. Apparently, the narrative concerning the defeat of Sennacherib's siege of Jerusalem, Hezekiah's sickness, and the Babylonian delegation to Hezekiah was worked into the larger framework of DtrH's narrative concerning Hezekiah's reign. Exceptions to the pattern occur in 2 Kgs 18:9 and 20:20-21, both of which employ the form *ḥizqîyāhû*. Both instances, however, may be attributed to the influence of 2 Kgs 18:13, 17–20:19/Isa 36:1–39:8. Furthermore, Seitz (*Zion's Final Destiny*, 57) notes the similarity between the formulation of the narrative concerning Ahaz's submission to Tiglath-pileser in 2 Kgs 16:5, 7-9 and that concerning Hezekiah's submission to Sennacherib in 2 Kgs 18:14-16, which emphasizes continuity between the two monarchs rather than the contrast that is found in the Isaiah tradition. Such continuity diminishes Hezekiah to some extent and aids in preparing for the narrative concerning Josiah, who is described in superlative language (e.g., 2 Kgs 23:25, "before him there was no king like him . . . nor did any like him arise after him"). In the overall scheme of the DtrH, no king, Hezekiah included, rivaled Josiah. This picture contrasts with the portrayal of Hezekiah as the ideal monarch, especially over against Ahaz, in the book of Isaiah.

In fact, the discrepancies between the Isaiah and Kings versions of this narrative suggest that Isaiah 36–39 was drawn from 2 Kgs 18:13–20:19 and modified to idealize Hezekiah prior to its placement in the book of Isaiah (see Sweeney, *Isaiah 1–4,* 12-16). The modifications tend to remove any sense of wrongdoing or lack of faith on Hezekiah's part, and they accentuate the role of YHWH rather than Hezekiah as the main actor of the narrative and opponent of Sennacherib. The narrative concerning Hezekiah's submission to Sennacherib in 2 Kgs 18:14-16 obviously does not appear, but this may be attributed to DtrH. Isaiah 36–37 mentions only the Rabshakeh, whereas 2 Kings 18–19 includes three Assyrian delegates, the Tartan, the Rab-saris, and the Rabshakeh, who correspond to Hezekiah's three representatives, Eliakim ben Hilkiah who is over the house, Shebna the scribe, and Joah ben Asaph the recorder (2 Kgs 18:18/Isa 36:3). In the context of Kings, the appearance of three representatives of Sennacherib balances those of Hezekiah and indicates that Hezekiah and Sennacherib are the major actors of the narrative. But in the context of Isaiah, the inclusion of only the Rabshakeh as the messenger of Sennacherib balances the role of Isaiah as the messenger of YHWH, thereby identifying YHWH and Sennacherib as the major actors of the narrative and relegating Hezekiah to a subsidiary role. Within the context of Kings, which focuses on the monarchs, it is easy to understand why Hezekiah would be given a prominent role. But in the context of the book of Isaiah, it is difficult to understand why Hezekiah would be given any role at all, unless he was taken over from the Kings narrative. He is never mentioned elsewhere in the book except in the superscription in Isa 1:1. By contrast, YHWH is the major actor of the book of Isaiah. It therefore follows that the Kings narrative was modified for a place in Isaiah rather than vice versa.

Other discrepancies support this pattern of a modification as well. Isa 36:17-18 modifies 2 Kgs 18:32 in order to water down a statement that charges Hezekiah with misleading the people ("do not listen to Hezekiah because [*RSV* 'when'] he will mislead you"/"unless Hezekiah misleads you, saying YHWH will deliver us"). Isa 37:36 eliminates the statement "and it came to pass that night" in 2 Kgs 19:35 when describing the blow struck by the "angel of YHWH" against the Assyrian camp, thereby eliminating any suggestion that YHWH delayed in carrying out the promised deliverance. Isa 38:4-5 eliminates any suggestion that YHWH delayed in responding to Isaiah in 2 Kgs 20:4-5 by eliminating the reference to Isaiah's leaving the inner court. Likewise, Isa 38:5-6 eliminates the reference in 2 Kgs 20:5-6 to YHWH's healing of Hezekiah after he goes to the temple on the third day. The removal of 2 Kgs 20:6b-8 and 9b-11a from Isa 38:6-7 eliminates doubts about Hezekiah's faithfulness by placing his questions concerning the fulfillment of YHWH's sign at the end of the narrative (Isa 38:21-22). The addition of the Psalm of Hezekiah in Isa 38:9-20, completely

482

lacking in the Kings narrative, enhances the portrayal of Hezekiah as a loyal servant of YHWH. Finally, Hezekiah's question in Isa 39:8, "for there will be peace and truth in my days?" (contra *RSV*, which does not construe this as a question), eliminates the conditional formulation of the corresponding question in 2 Kgs 20:19, "shall there not be peace and truth in my days?" and any indication that Hezekiah doubts the prophet's word.

In sum, these modifications of the Kings narrative in the Isaiah version present an idealized portrayal of Hezekiah while enhancing the role of YHWH as the major actor in all portions of the narrative. Such modifications tailor the narrative to fit the overall concerns of the book of Isaiah.

Nevertheless, the above considerations indicate that the narrative seems to have been composed neither for the book of Kings nor for the book of Isaiah; rather, it appears to have been composed independently for some other context. This situation raises the question of the setting of such a narrative and the possibility that it appeared in some earlier form. Clements's observations that Isaiah 39 relates to the Babylonian deportation of King Jehoiachin in 597 have already been noted, and a strong case has been made that the narrative cycle, which includes the account of YHWH's deliverance of Jerusalem, Hezekiah's illness, and the embassy of Merodach-baladan, addresses the situation of Judah after Jehoiachin's deportation but prior to the destruction of Jerusalem *(Prophetie)*. Although there is no firm evidence that any of the narratives circulated independently from the others, there is evidence of redactional activity within the cycle. Ackroyd ("Interpretation," 153-54) points to the redactional nature of the temporal headings that introduce each narrative (36:1, "and it came to pass in the fourteenth year of King Hezekiah"; 38:1, "in those days"; 39:1, "at that time"), which indicates the possibility of their separate origins.

It is noteworthy, therefore, that the concerns of ch. 39 differ greatly from those of the preceding narratives, in that they imply some wrongdoing or misjudgment on the part of Hezekiah, who is condemned by the prophet Isaiah for inviting the Babylonian delegation to Jerusalem. Both the narrative concerning Sennacherib's siege and that of Hezekiah's sickness focus on Hezekiah's faithfulness in YHWH's promises of salvation, and both emphasize YHWH's promises to protect the city of Jerusalem and the Davidic dynasty (37:35; 38:5-6). Both narratives point to Hezekiah's triumphs over adversity, and neither contains any hint of potential danger to the dynasty or the city such as that which appears in ch. 39. Ch. 39 appears to temper the portrayal of Hezekiah by pointing to potential problems that resulted from his handling of the Assyrian crisis; in this instance, his negotiations with Merodach-baladan set the stage for later Babylonian threats to Jerusalem and the Davidic dynasty. When viewed in relation to ch. 39, chs. 36–37 and 38 appear to provide some hope that continued faithfulness in YHWH's promises of protection will overcome the threat posed by Babylon. Nevertheless, the differing concerns of these narratives point to the conclusion that the narratives concerning Sennacherib's siege of Jerusalem and Hezekiah's illness existed in some form prior to the inclusion of the narrative concerning Merodach-baladan's embassy to Hezekiah.

It is essential to note that these narratives emphasize Hezekiah's faithfulness in relation to YHWH's promises of protection to the city of Jerusalem and the Davidic dynasty. They also point to the downfall of Assyria, the assassination of Sennacherib, and the reign of Esarhaddon. It is also essential to note that such concerns advise a course of action in situations of threat. Such a concern presupposes a situation in which potential threats exist for the city and the dynasty. The Babylonian exile might provide the occasion for such a concern, but the destruction of the city of Jerusalem would undermine the credibility of divine promises for its protection. Otherwise, two settings suggest themselves: Jerusalem's submission to Babylon and the deportation of Jehoiachin in 597, and Manasseh's submission to Assyria during the period of Assyrian hegemony over Jerusalem.

The above discussion has already demonstrated that the narratives concerning Sennacherib's invasion and Hezekiah's illness do not appear to have been composed in relation to the narrative concerning the Babylonian embassy; rather, the opposite is the case. Although these narratives relate to the concern with the events of 597, they appear to presuppose an earlier situation when read in relation to the narrative concerning the Babylonian embassy. Seitz (*Zion's Final Destiny*, 96-116) argues that the composition of chs. 36–37 must be set in the reign of Manasseh. He maintains that the work was produced early in his reign in order to provide the young monarch with the model of an idealized Hezekiah as a basis for his own reign. Although Seitz dismisses Manasseh's failure to live up to this model as irrelevant, his actions are precisely to the point in understanding the function of such a narrative in relation to Manasseh's reign. Manasseh was judged to be the worst king of Judah by the DtrH; his actions prompted YHWH's decision to destroy Jerusalem (see 2 Kgs 21:1-18). 2 Chr 33:10-13 reports that Manasseh was forced to submit to Assyria when he was dragged in fetters before the Assyrian king. This report may well indicate the reason why Manasseh suppressed opposition to his reign, which was marked by a policy of submission to Assyria. Obviously, such a policy contradicts the course of action outlined in Isaiah 36–37 (38), and poses a threat to Jerusalem and to the dynasty. In such circumstances, the parties who propagated the narrative of Sennacherib's siege of Jerusalem would be the very groups that were suppressed under Manasseh.

Although the causes of Amon's assassination and the motives of those who killed his assassins are unclear, the resulting reign of King Josiah (640-609) sees a monarch whom the DtrH portrays as fulfilling the model of the ideal Hezekiah; in fact, the portrayal of Hezekiah's reign in 2 Kings 18–20 becomes the model for the portrayal of Josiah's reign in 2 Kings 22–23 (see R. D. Nelson, "Josiah in the Book of Joshua," *JBL* 100 [1981] 531-40; cf. idem, *The Double Redaction of the Deuteronomistic History* [JSOTSup 18; Sheffield: JSOT Press, 1981]; I. W. Provan, *Hezekiah and the Books of Kings* [BZAW 172; Berlin and New York: de Gruyter, 1988] esp. 153-55). It therefore seems reasonable to conclude that the narrative concerning Sennacherib's siege of Jerusalem was written against the background of the threats to Jerusalem and the Davidic dynasty realized during the reign of Manasseh, in order to provide a role model for the young king Josiah that would emphasize faithfulness in YHWH's promises to deliver the city and the dynasty. The impending downfall of Assyria and the opportunity to restore Jerusalem's and the Davidic dynasty's position at the

center of a renewed Davidic empire provide added incentive for the promulga-
tion of such a tradition to the young Josiah (on the royal educational function
of such traditions, see A. Lemaire, "Vers l'histoire de la Rédaction des Livres
des Rois," *ZAW* 98 [1986] 221-36).

Although the above discussion indicates that Isaiah 36–37 (38) does not
appear to have been composed for a place in the book of Isaiah, it is likely that
it was appended to the Josianic edition of the book. The discussion of 7:1–9:6
(*RSV* 7) above demonstrates that this pericope was assembled in relation to chs.
36–38, and that it formed part of the Josianic edition of chs. 5–12. In this regard,
the contrast between Ahaz and Hezekiah would provide either a further instructional basis for Josiah or a means to legitimize his policy for restoring the
Davidic empire, which policy was based on YHWH's promises transmitted
through Isaiah for the security and the central roles of Jerusalem and the Davidic
dynasty. The downfall of the Assyrian empire during the course of his reign
would further confirm such an understanding of the prophecies of Isaiah.

Intention

Although chs. 36–37 present an account of Sennacherib's siege of Jerusalem,
the above discussion demonstrates that it is no mere transcript or report of a
historical event. Rather, chs. 36–37 present a highly theologized account of
the siege in order to present a message concerning YHWH's promise of
protection and the appropriate response to that promise. One must take account of the narrative function of these chapters in relation to various historical and literary settings from the time of their composition in the mid-7th
century. Despite the shifting contexts of this text, several of its features remain
constant, including YHWH's promises to secure the city of Jerusalem and the
Davidic dynasty, Hezekiah's faithful acceptance of YHWH's promises, the
downfall of the Assyrian empire, and the emergence of a renewed remnant
from Jerusalem.

When read in relation to the final 5th-century edition of the book of Isaiah,
chs. 36–37 function as part of a larger textual block in chs. 36–39. As noted
above, chs. 36–39 play an important transitional role within the book of Isaiah
by shifting the focus of attention from the Assyrian period to the aftermath of
the Babylonian exile. In this regard, the presentation of Sennacherib and Assyria
as the major enemies of Judah, and the presentation of Hezekiah as the major
protagonist, after YHWH, must be taken as typological. Persia had replaced
Babylon as the foremost temporal power of the time, exercising hegemony over
Jerusalem and preventing the restoration of the Davidic monarchy. In such a
situation, ch. 39 provided the primary means to understand the current status of
Jerusalem and the dynasty in that past reliance on temporal powers had reduced
Judah to its current state of dependency. Chs. 36–37 in particular counseled sole
reliance on YHWH, which was the trademark of Ezra's and Nehemiah's reforms,
as the means to overcome the current situation. Faithful reliance on YHWH,
like that of Hezekiah, would bring about the downfall of the Persian empire and
the restoration of the Davidic house. The reference to a restored remnant in

Jerusalem corresponds to similar concerns expressed in Ezra and Nehemiah for a restored remnant of the people (Ezra 9:8, 13, 14, 15; Neh 1:2). As such, Isaiah 36–39 provides the backdrop or foundation for the promises that are expressed in chs. 40–66 for the restoration of Zion and the sovereignty of YHWH over the nations. The death of Sennacherib in this narrative is an element of the prophetic confrontation story in which it serves as a means to legitimize the prophetic message. In the context of the book of Isaiah, the prophetic confrontation story in chs. 36–37 legitimizes the program of the entire book.

Isaiah 36–37 plays a similar role in relation to the 6th-century edition of the book of Isaiah, except there Babylon, not Persia, was the major enemy of Judah. Again, the narrative concerning Sennacherib's downfall functions as part of the larger narrative in chs. 36–39 that speaks directly to the circumstances of the Babylonian exile. The references to the carrying off of Judah's wealth and royal descendants to Babylon naturally addressed the situation of the Davidic monarchs. Whether Jehoiachin was still alive at the time of the composition of the 6th-century edition of Isaiah is debatable, but his own sons would certainly have been looking for the opportunity to reclaim the throne and to reestablish Jerusalem in the wake of Cyrus's defeat of the Babylonians. In this regard, the message of faithful reliance on YHWH and the restoration of "the remnant of the house of Judah . . . for the sake of my servant David" (37:31, 35) would have been particularly significant following the surrender of Babylon. Again, the transitional function of the narrative comes into play in that the major characters of the narrative must be considered typologically. As a précis to the promises of Second Isaiah in chs. 40–55, the narrative concerning Sennacherib's defeat would provide a backdrop for the promised restoration of Jerusalem, the rebuilding of the temple, and YHWH's rule through Cyrus (cf. 44:24-28; 45:1-8).

Isaiah 36–37 appears to function as part of the Josianic edition of the book of Isaiah, albeit in an earlier form than now appears either in Isaiah or 2 Kings. This function obviously complicates the issue, particularly when one considers that the narrative was not composed for this role. Isaiah 36–37 (38) would have concluded the Josianic edition of Isaiah and thereby would have provided the means to read the preceding prophecies of Isaiah. At this juncture, Isaiah 36–37 points to the fulfillment of YHWH's promises in the time of Josiah, and it legitimizes these promises by pointing to the demise of Sennacherib when he attempted to confront YHWH. Although Isaiah's prophecies were delivered in the time of the Assyrian crisis, they address the circumstances of Josiah's restoration. By presenting Hezekiah in contrast to Ahaz, the narrative focuses on Hezekiah as a model for righteous action and thereby provides the model for Josiah's reign in the aftermath of the fall of the Assyrian empire. In this regard, it is noteworthy that the prophecy concerning the rejuvenation of the remnant of the house of Judah in 37:30-32 employs the imagery of a "root" (*šōrēš*) reestablishing itself in order to produce fruit. The same imagery is employed in 11:1-16, which describes the renewed vigor of the house of David, the return of the exiles of Israel and Judah, and the restoration of the Davidic empire.

Finally, one must consider Isaiah 36–37 in and of itself. It appears to have been composed as an independent narrative that presupposes the problems inherent in Manasseh's reign of Judah, especially since Assyria's hegemony in this period posed a threat to the city of Jerusalem and the Davidic dynasty. Chs. 36–37 advise that trust in YHWH will see the city and the dynasty through the crisis so that they can take root again. As noted above, this text may well have functioned as an educational tool that defined the perspective of the young king Josiah.

Bibliography

→ bibliography at "Introduction to the Book of Isaiah" and at 36:1–39:8. P. R. Ackroyd, "The Death of Hezekiah: A Pointer to the Future?" in *Studies in the Religious Traditions of the Old Testament* (London: SCM, 1987) 172-80, 285-87; idem, "An Interpretation of the Babylonian Exile: A Study of II Kings 20 and Isaiah 38–39," *SJT* 27 (1974) 329-52 (repr. in *Studies,* 152-71, 282-85); A. Alt, "Die territorialgeschichtliche Bedeutung von Sanheribs Eingriff in Palästina," in *Kleine Schriften zur Geschichte des Volkes Israel* (Munich: Beck, 1953) 2:242-49; R. D. Barnett, "The Siege of Lachish," *IEJ* 8 (1958) 161-64; E. Ben Zvi, "Who Wrote the Speech of Rabshakeh and When?" *JBL* 109 (1990) 79-90; J. A. Brinkman, "Sennacherib's Babylonian Problem: An Interpretation," *JCS* 25 (1973) 89-95; K. Budde, "The Poem in 2 Kings xix 21-28 (Isaiah xxxvii 22-29)," *JTS* 35 (1934) 307-13; C. F. Burney, "'The Jews' Language': 2 Kings xviii 26 = Isa. xxxvi 11," *JTS* 13 (1912) 417-23; M. Burrows, "The Conduit of the Upper Pool," *ZAW* 70 (1958) 221-27; Clements, *Isaiah and Deliverance* (→ 22:1-25); idem, "The Prophecies of Isaiah to Hezekiah Concerning Sennacherib: 2 Kings 19.21-34//Isa. 37.22-35," in *Prophetie und geschichtliche Wirklichkeit im alten Israel* (*Fest.* S. Herrmann; ed. R. Liwak and S. Wagner; Stuttgart: Kohlhammer, 1991) 65-78; M. Cogan and H. Tadmor, *II Kings* (AB 11; Garden City, NY: Doubleday, 1988); C. Cohen, "Neo-Assyrian Elements in the First Speech of the Biblical Rab-Šāqē," *IOS* 9 (1979) 32-48; D. Conrad, "Einige (archäologische) Miszellen zur Kultgeschichte Judas in der Königszeit," in *Textgemäss: Aufsätze und Beiträge zur Hermeneutik des Alten Testaments* (*Fest.* E. Würthwein; ed. A. H. J. Gunneweg and O. Kaiser; Göttingen: Vandenhoeck & Ruprecht, 1979) 28-32; P. E. Dion, "Sennacherib's Expedition to Palestine," *Église et Théologie* 20 (1989) 5-25; D. N. Fewell, "Sennacherib's Defeat: Words at War in 2 Kings 18.13–19.37," *JSOT* 34 (1986) 79-90; K. Fullerton, "Isaiah's Attitude in the Sennacherib Campaign," *AJSL* 42 (1925) 1-25; Gonçalves, *L'expédition de Sennachérib* (→ 1:4-9); G. Götzel, "Hizkia und Sanherib," *BZ* 6 (1908) 133-54; H. Haag, "La campagne de Sennachérib contre Jérusalem en 701," *RB* 58 (1951) 348-59; J.-G. Heintz, "Lettres royales à la divinité en Mésopotamie et en Israël antiques: esquisse d'un genre littéraire," *RHR* 181 (1972) 111-13; L. L. Honor, *Sennacherib's Invasion of Palestine: A Critical Source Study* (New York: Columbia University Press, 1926); A. K. Jenkins, "Hezekiah's Fourteenth Year: A New Interpretation of 2 Kings xviii 13–xix 37," *VT* 26 (1976) 284-98; O. Kaiser, "Die Verkündigung des Propheten Jesaja im Jahre 701," *ZAW* 81 (1969) 304-15; C. Van Leeuwen, "Sanchérib devant Jérusalem," *OTS* 14 (1965) 245-72; J. Le Moyne, "Les deux ambassades de Sennachérib à Jérusalem: Recherches sur l'évolution d'une tradition," in *Mélanges Bibliques* (*Fest.* A. Robert; Paris: Bloud et Gay, 1956) 149-53; P. Machinist, "Assyria and Its Image in First Isaiah," *JAOS* 103 (1983) 719-37; N. Na'aman, "Sennacherib's Campaign to Judah and the Date of the *lmlk* Stamps," *VT* 29 (1979) 61-86; S. Parpola, "The Murder of Sennacherib," in *Death in Mesopotamia: Papers read at the xxvie rencontre assyriologique internationale* (ed. B. Alster; Copenhagen: Akademsk, 1980) 171-82; A. Rofé, *The Prophetical Stories* (Jerusalem: Magnes, 1988) 88-95; H. H. Rowley, "Hezekiah's Reform and Rebellion," in *Men of God: Studies in Old Testament History and Prophecy* (London: Nelson, 1963) 98-132; W. H. Shea, "Sennacherib's Second Palestinian Campaign," *JBL* 104 (1985) 401-18; K. A. D. Smelik, "Distortion of Old Testament Prophecy: The Purpose of Isaiah xxxvi and xxxvii," *OTS* 24 (1986) 70-93; idem, "King Hezekiah Advocates True Prophecy: Remarks on Isaiah xxxvi and xxxvii//II Kings xviii and xix," *OTS* 28 (1992) 93-128; W. von Soden, "Sanherib vor Jerusalem 701 v. Chr.," in *Bibel und Alter Orient* (ed. H.-P. Müller; BZAW 162; Berlin and New York: de Gruyter, 1985) 149-57; S. Stohlmann, "The Judaean Exile after 701 B.C.E.," in *Scripture in Context II: More Essays on the Comparative Method* (ed. W. W. Hallo et al.; Winona Lake: Eisenbrauns, 1983) 147-75; A. Strus, "Interprétations des noms propres dan les oracles contre les nations," *Congress Volume, Salamanca 1983* (ed. J. A. Emerton; VTSup 36; Leiden: Brill, 1985) 272-85; R. de Vaux, "Jérusalem et les Prophètes," *RB* 73 (1966) 481-509; E. Vogt, *Der Aufstand Hiskias und die Belagerung Jerusalems 701 v. Chr.* (AnBib 106; Rome: Biblical Institute Press, 1986); H. Wildberger, "Die Rede des Rabsake vor Jerusalem," *TZ* 35 (1979) 35-47.

ROYAL NOVELLA CONCERNING HEZEKIAH'S RECOVERY FROM ILLNESS, 38:1-22

Structure

I. Narrative introduction concerning the circumstances of Hezekiah's recovery	1-8
A. Concerning Hezekiah's sickness	1
1. Hezekiah's mortal illness	1a
2. Isaiah's message to Hezekiah	1b
a. Isaiah comes to Hezekiah	$1b\alpha_1$
b. Isaiah speaks to Hezekiah	$1b\alpha_2$-β
1) Speech formula	$1b\alpha_{2a}$
2) Speech proper: messenger speech	$1b\alpha_{2b-\beta}$
a) Messenger formula	$1b\alpha_{2b}$
b) Message: command to inform house that Hezekiah will die	$1b\alpha_{2c}$-β
B. Concerning Hezekiah's reaction: petition to YHWH	2-3
1. Turns face to wall	2a
2. Prays to YHWH	2b
3. Hezekiah's speech: petition to YHWH	3a
a. Speech formula	$3a\alpha_1$
b. Speech proper: petition to YHWH	$3a\alpha_{2-\beta}$
4. Hezekiah's weeping	3b
C. Concerning YHWH's word to Hezekiah through Isaiah: prophetic announcement of salvation/healing	4-8
1. Prophetic word formula	4

	a) Question proper	15a
	b) Speaker's destitute position	15b
	3) Second petition: grant life	16
	a) Speaker's dependence on years	16a-bα
	b) Petition proper	16bβ
c.	Account of Hezekiah's salvation	17-20a
	1) Bitterness turned to peace	17a
	2) Address to YHWH concerning saving act	17b-19
	a) Statement of YHWH's deliverance	17b
	(1) Statement proper	17bα
	(2) Manifestation: cast away sins	17bβ
	b) Reason: dead do not praise YHWH but living do	18-19
	(1) Dead do not praise YHWH	18
	(a) Sheol/death does not praise	18a
	(b) Dead do not wait for YHWH's truth	18b
	(2) Living do praise YHWH	19
	(a) Living praise YHWH	19a
	(b) Living father instructs sons in YHWH's truth	19b
	3) Concluding affirmation of YHWH's deliverance	20a
d.	Communal declaration of praise with music	20b
B. Narrative aftermath: Hezekiah's healing		21-22
1.	Isaiah's prescription of a remedy	21
2.	Hezekiah's request for a sign that he will ascend to house of YHWH	22

Isaiah 38 is demarcated initially by the temporal formula *bayyāmîm hāhēm,* "in those days," in 38:1. The dominant narrative form of the unit and its concern with Hezekiah's illness and recovery extend through 38:22. The temporal formula *bā'ēt hahî'* (see *BHS*), "at that time," in 39:1 marks the beginning of a new unit.

The structure of ch. 38 is determined by factors of both form and content. The dominant form of the chapter is prose narrative governed by *wāw*-consecutive imperfect verbs, but this form is seemingly disrupted by "the letter [*miktāb*] of Hezekiah," a poetic composition with its own superscription in vv. 9-20. Although vv. 9-20 clearly differ in form from vv. 1-8 and 21-22, and lack a syntactical connective to join them to the preceding verses, the conjunctive *wāw*-consecutive formulation of vv. 21-22 provides the syntactical links that work vv. 9-20 into the overall narrative form. Indeed, Hezekiah's thanksgiving song of the individual in vv. 9-20 constitutes the focal point of the unit. When read in context, it provides Hezekiah's response to the healing promised to him by YHWH in vv. 1-8; the following statements in vv. 21-22 are anticlimactic in that they report speeches and actions that follow from Hezekiah's song. The structure of the unit therefore falls into two basic parts. Vv. 1-8 constitute a narrative introduction concerning the circumstances of Hezekiah's recovery, and vv. 9-22 constitute a narrative report of Hezekiah's thanksgiving song and its aftermath. The unit may therefore be characterized as a prophetic legend concerning Hezekiah's recovery from illness (see the discussion of Genre below).

The structure of vv. 1-8 is determined by the *waw*-consecutive imperfect narrative form and the sequence of action concerning the circumstances of Hezekiah's recovery from illness culminating in YHWH's word of salvation to Hezekiah reported in vv. 4-8.

Verse 1 describes the circumstances of Hezekiah's illness, including the report of his illness in v. 1a and the report of Isaiah's message to Hezekiah in v. 1b that he should prepare for death. V. 1b contains two components based on the *waw*-consecutive verbal forms: v. 1bα_1 states that Isaiah came to Hezekiah (*wayyābô'*, "and he came"), and v. 1bα_2-β states that Isaiah spoke to Hezekiah (*wayyō'mer*, "and he said"). The report of Isaiah's speech includes the speech formula in v. 1bα_{2a} and the speech proper in v. 1bα_{2b}-β. The speech is formulated as a messenger speech, including the messenger formula in v. 1bα_{2b} and the message, a command to Hezekiah to inform his household that he will die, in v. 1bα_{2c}-β.

Verses 2-3 report Hezekiah's reaction to the news that he will die, viz., he petitions YHWH to remember his faithful service, presumably to plea for his life. Again, the basic structure of the subunit is determined by the sequence of action as indicated by the *wāw*-consecutive imperfect verbs. Hezekiah turns his face to the wall in v. 2a (*wayyassēb*, "and he turned"), and he prays to YHWH in v. 2b (*wayyitpallēl*, "and he prayed"). V. 3a reports Hezekiah's speech (*wayyō'mer*, "and he said"), here formulated as a petition to YHWH. The speech formula appears in v. 3aα_1, and the speech proper appears in v. 3aα_2-β. V. 3b concludes the subunit with a report that Hezekiah wept (*wayyēbk*, "and he wept").

Verses 4-8 report the conveyance of YHWH's word of salvation and healing to Hezekiah through Isaiah, and thereby serve as the culmination of vv. 1-8. In keeping with the overall form of the narrative, this subunit is introduced by the *wāw*-consecutive imperfect verb *wayyĕhî*, "and it was." The structure of the subunit is determined by the distinction between the prophetic word formula in v. 4 and the word proper in vv. 5-8, here formulated as a commission to Isaiah to deliver YHWH's word to Hezekiah. The commissioning formula appears in v. 5aα_1, and the content of the commission appears in v. 5aα_2-8, here formulated as a messenger speech. The messenger formula appears in v. 5aα_2, and the message appears in v. 5aβ-8, here formulated as an oracle of salvation or healing with a sign. V. 5aβ-γ constitutes YHWH's acknowledgment of Hezekiah's complaint or petition, including 1st-person statements addressed to Hezekiah that YHWH has heard his prayer (v. 5aβ) and that YHWH has seen his tears (v. 5aγ). The oracle of salvation or healing with the prophetic sign follows in vv. 5b-8. The oracle of salvation or healing, formulated in a 1st-person address to Hezekiah, appears in vv. 5b-6 and consists of two parts. V. 5b states that YHWH will add fifteen years to Hezekiah's life, and v. 6 states that YHWH will deliver this city, i.e., Jerusalem. Vv. 7-8 contain the prophetic announcement of a sign. The 3rd-person announcement addressed to Hezekiah in v. 7 indicates that it constitutes the prophet's introductory statement or identification of the sign, and the 1st-person announcement in v. 8 contains the sign proper, which states that the shadow of the dial of Ahaz will return ten steps.

The second major section of ch. 38 is the narrative report of Hezekiah's letter to YHWH and its aftermath in vv. 9-22. Its structure is determined in terms of both form and content. The poetic composition with superscription in vv. 9-20 constitutes the report of the letter of Hezekiah as the first major subunit, and the narrative in vv. 21-22 constitutes the second, which relates statements and events that follow from the preceding letter.

The fundamental structure of the report of Hezekiah's letter in vv. 9-20 is determined by the distinction between the superscription in v. 9, which identifies the following material as the letter *(miktāb)* of Hezekiah when he recovered from his illness, and vv. 10-20, which constitute the letter proper. The letter itself contains elements of both the individual complaint and the thanksgiving song, but it must be regarded as a thanksgiving song in that this element constitutes the overall aim of the composition. The song is formulated primarily as a 1st-person address to YHWH, although at times it refers to YHWH in the 3rd person (vv. 11a, 14b, 15a, 16a, 20a). The structure of the song includes four basic parts determined on thematic grounds.

Verses 10-13 contain an account of the singer's (Hezekiah's) distress addressed to YHWH, including four elements that are grouped in pairs according to their parallel formulations. V. 10 contains a statement of the singer's passing life. It is formulated with an introductory *'ănî 'āmartî,* "I have indeed said," and includes references to the passing days of the singer in v. 10a and his passing years in v. 10b. A parallel statement, as indicated by the introductory *'āmartî,* "I said," appears in v. 11. This verse focuses on the passing existence of the singer by referring to his inability to see YHWH in the land of the living in v. 11a and his inability to see human beings from the grave in v. 11b. V. 12 contains the singer's first address to YHWH as indicated by the formula *mîyôm 'ad-layĕlâ tašlîmēnî,* "from day to night you finish me." The address begins with a simile comparing the situation of the singer to that of a shepherd's tent that has been uncovered and removed in v. 12a. A second simile, which compares the situation of the singer to that of a weaver's cloth that has been rolled up and trimmed, appears in v. 12bα. Finally, the formulaic address to YHWH appears in v. 12bβ. A second address to YHWH, parallel to the first as indicated by the appearance of the formula *mîyôm 'ad-layĕlâ tašlîmēnî,* appears in v. 13. It begins with a statement that the singer is still (v. 13aα). A simile that compares the situation of the singer to that of a lion's victim appears in v. 13aβ. Again, the formulaic address "from day until night you finish me" appears in v. 13b.

The singer's petition to YHWH for relief in vv. 14-16 is the second major part of vv. 9-22. Its structure is determined by the imperative verbs, which constitute the first and second petitions, respectively, in vv. 14 and 16, and which bracket the rhetorical question that reinforces the singer's appeal in v. 15. The first petition to grant security in v. 14 begins with a simile that compares the singer to a chirping bird in v. 14a and thereby conveys the singer's need to speak. This is followed by a statement that the singer's eyes look to heaven for help in v. 14bα. Finally, the petition and its cause appear in v. 14bβ, which states that "my Lord has oppressed me" (contra *RSV*) and employs the imperative verb *'ārĕbēnî,* "pledge security to me," to express the singer's appeal. The rhetorical question in v. 15 reinforces that appeal by pointing to the singer's destitute position. The question proper in v. 15a indicates that the singer can say no more to YHWH other than what YHWH has already said and done. V. 15b then points to the speaker's flying years and bitterness of soul. The second petition to grant life appears in v. 16. It begins with a statement of the speaker's dependence on his years for life in v. 16a-bα, followed by the petition proper in v. 16bβ, formulated with the verbs *wĕtaḥălîmēnî wĕhaḥăyēnî,* "you shall make me strong, and grant life."

The account of the singer's salvation appears in vv. 17-20a. V. 17a, introduced by *hinnēh,* "behold," states that the singer's bitterness has turned to peace. This is followed by an address to YHWH, formulated in 2nd-person masculine singular address form and joined to v. 17a by the conjunctive *wĕ'attâ,* "and you," in vv. 17b-19. V. 17b constitutes a statement of YHWH's deliverance of the singer, including both the statement proper in v. 17bα and a verification of the deliverance, introduced by *kî,* "for," which states that YHWH has cast away the singer's sins. The reason for the deliverance appears in vv. 18-19, introduced by a causative *kî,* "because." V. 18 states that the dead do not praise YHWH, including statements that Sheol and death do not praise YHWH (v. 18a) and that the dead do not wait for YHWH's truth (v. 18b). V. 19 states that the living do praise YHWH (v. 19a) and that a (living) father instructs his sons in YHWH's truth (v. 19b). Finally, there is a concluding affirmation of YHWH's deliverance in v. 20a, formulated in objective language like v. 17a. The song concludes with a communal declaration of praise with music formulated in 1st-person common plural forms.

Verses 21-22 convey the narrative aftermath of Hezekiah's song in that they report the actions and statements that follow from Hezekiah's song of thanksgiving. V. 21 reports Isaiah's prescription of a remedy for the monarch, and v. 22 reports Hezekiah's request for a sign that he will ascend to the house of YHWH. These verses thereby point to the healing of Hezekiah and to his gratitude to YHWH.

Genre

The overarching genre of ch. 38 is royal NOVELLA, which focuses on the commendable qualities of the king in an effort to justify his rule (cf. Clements, *Isaiah 1–39,* 289). Although Hezekiah appears to be the focal point of this narrative, one should note that this is a modified form of the narrative concerning Hezekiah's illness and recovery from 2 Kgs 20:1-11 in which the prophet Isaiah plays an instrumental role. The earlier form of this narrative in 2 Kgs 20:1-11 appears to be a (→) prophetic legend (Rofé, *Prophetic Stories,* 137-39; Long, *2 Kings,* 235-41), but changes in the Isaiah version of this narrative have shifted its generic character. The inclusion of Hezekiah's Psalm in vv. 9-20 and other modifications downplay the role of the prophet in order to emphasize Hezekiah's piety as the motivating factor in YHWH's decision to cure the king (see below on Setting). Although the prophet still plays an important role in the present form of the narrative, the edificatory function of the narrative is heightened by the increased attention to the piety of the monarch. It thereby employs the example of Hezekiah to point to individual piety as a characteristic that the deity will reward. The legendary character of this narrative is evident from both its form and its content, which focuses on a miraculous event that is aimed at the edification of the audience. The narrative presents Hezekiah as near death due to an unspecified illness, but his overwhelming piety becomes the basis for his miraculous cure by YHWH.

Various subordinate genres appear in vv. 1-8, which contribute to the association of the royal NOVELLA form with the PROPHETIC LEGEND in 2 Kgs 20:1-11. The REPORT of the MESSENGER SPEECH in v. 1b, identified by the MESSENGER FORMULA in v. 1bα$_{2b}$, plays a major role in conveying the gravity of Hezekiah's illness. Although v. 1a has already informed the reader that Hezekiah's illness is terminal, YHWH's imperative COMMAND to Hezekiah to inform the royal household of the king's impending death emphasizes the divine role in the matter and indicates that Hezekiah's fate is sealed. The REPORT of Hezekiah's PETITION to YHWH in v. 3a, identified by its supplicatory language, 'ānnâ yhwh zĕkor-nā', "please YHWH, remember," emphasizes Hezekiah's faithful and good service as king, and thereby provides a basis for YHWH to reconsider the king's death.

The REPORT of the conveyance of YHWH's word to Hezekiah through Isaiah in vv. 4-8 employs a number of generic elements to convey the reversal of YHWH's decision. The PROPHETIC WORD FORMULA, wayĕhî dĕbar-yhwh 'el-yĕša'yāhû lē'mōr, "and the word of YHWH was unto Isaiah saying," identifies YHWH as the source of the following statements and thereby lends them divine authority. In keeping with this purpose, vv. 5-8 are formulated as a COMMISSION, indicated by the COMMISSIONING FORMULA in v. 5aα$_1$, which again identifies YHWH as the source of the following word. The COMMISSION itself is formulated as a MESSENGER SPEECH, as indicated by the MESSENGER FORMULA in v. 5aα$_2$, and again lends divine authority to the statement. YHWH's word is formulated as a PROPHETIC ORACLE OF SALVATION combined with a PROPHETIC ANNOUNCEMENT OF A SIGN. This is evident in vv. 5b-6, which announce YHWH's intention both to heal Hezekiah and to deliver this city (Jerusalem). The PROPHETIC ANNOUNCEMENT OF A SIGN in vv. 7-8 is identified by a typical example of the introductory formula, wĕzeh-lĕkā hā'ôt mē'ēt yhwh 'ăšer ya'ăśeh yhwh 'et-haddābār hazzeh 'ăšer dibbēr, "and this is the sign for you from YHWH that YHWH will accomplish this thing that he has said" (cf. 1 Kgs 13:3; Jer 44:29-30). The sign itself follows in v. 8, introduced by hinnî mēšîb, "behold, I am returning."

Past interpreters have classified 38:9-20 as a (→) petition, a (→) song of illness, and a (→) thanksgiving song (for summaries of opinions see Begrich, 2-3; Watts, 124-25), and more recently as a "confession" of trust (de Boer, 185), (→) hymn of praise (Seybold, Gebet, 147-53), or a (→) psalm of thanksgiving (see Nyberg; Wildberger, Jesaja, 1455). Begrich (pp. 6-16) notes correctly that the psalm is a combination of both COMPLAINT and THANKSGIVING elements. Although the psalm does not conform to the ideal form of any genre, Wildberger is correct to conclude that it is fundamentally a THANKSGIVING SONG in that the elements of COMPLAINT and PRAISE lend themselves to the overall intention to express gratitude to YHWH for deliverance from calamity. The statements *ʾănî ʾāmartî*, "I indeed have said," and *ʾāmartî*, "I have said," at the beginning of vv. 10 and 11, respectively, indicate a summary of past afflictions that are typical of THANKSGIVING SONGS OF THE INDIVIDUAL (Begrich, 54). V. 17 likewise presupposes that YHWH has brought about deliverance. V. 17a is especially important in that it states that peace has replaced the singer's bitterness (*hinnēh lĕšālôm mar-lî mār*, "behold, bitterness that is bitter to me has become peace"). This is reinforced by the statement in v. 17b that YHWH has favored the singer and cast away the singer's sins. This verse thereby states the premise of the entire psalm, that YHWH has relieved the singer from affliction. V. 19, "the living, the living, he shall thank you, like me today," then expresses the singer's gratitude.

Several subordinate generic elements contribute to the THANKSGIVING SONG of Hezekiah. First is the SUPERSCRIPTION in v. 9, which identifies the song as a "letter" of Hezekiah. Although the term *miktāb*, "letter," is disputed, it likely refers simply to a composition by the monarch. In any case, the genre of ROYAL LETTERS or compositions to deities is known in ancient Mesopotamia, where the letters generally appear inscribed on statues or stelae. In many cases, they are appeals to the deity for deliverance from calamity or sickness, or they thank the deity addressed for such deliverance (see Hallo for a full discussion).

Second are the COMPLAINT elements that appear in vv. 10-13 in order to provide an account of the singer's distress. The COMPLAINT elements follow no fixed form, but they do employ metaphorical language in the form of similes to convey the singer's desperate situation. The singer is compared to a shepherd's tent that has been removed (v. 12a), a rolled-up weaver's cloth that has been trimmed (v. 12b), and the victim of a lion (v. 13a). Another simile in v. 14, which compares the singer to a chirping bird who can no longer remain still (cf. v. 13), provides the basis for the PETITIONS that follow in vv. 14-16.

Third are the PETITIONS that appear in vv. 14-16. Two specific examples appear in this text formulated as masculine singular imperatives directed to YHWH. The first is the imperative verb *ʾārĕbēnî*, "pledge security to me," in v. 14b. The Piel form of *ʿrb* is a technical legal term that refers to taking something in pledge as a guarantee of security for debts (Prov 11:15; 20:16; 27:13), mortgages (Neh 5:3), or personal safety (Gen 43:9; 44:32). In the present context, it is noteworthy that the preceding statement in v. 14b, "my Lord has oppressed me," employs the verb *ʿšq*, which is a technical legal term for extortion (Lev 5:23; Deut 24:14; Amos 4:1; Jer 7:6, etc.). This indicates that the PETITION functions as a righteous demand for relief from a wrong committed against the singer. The RHETORICAL QUESTION in v. 15 reinforces the singer's PETITION by pointing to the fact that nothing more can be said; the case is clear. Finally, the second PETITION in v. 16bβ gets to the heart of the matter by employing a 2nd-person masculine singular imperfect combined with a masculine singular imperative, *wĕtaḥălîmēnî wĕhaḥăyēnî*, "you shall make me strong and give me life." The essential demand of the singer is thereby made clear. Although PETITIONS generally appear as an element of the COMPLAINT, they function as a means to describe the calamity from which the singer is delivered in the present instance.

Fourth is the AFFIRMATION OF CONFIDENCE in v. 20a that appears at the conclusion of the account of the singer's salvation in vv. 17-20a. The AFFIRMATION typically appears in the COMPLAINT. Here it reinforces the deliverance for which the singer gives thanks.

Setting

Any consideration of the setting of ch. 38 must account for the fact that this narrative appears in two distinct forms (2 Kgs 20:1-11 and here). Although scholars tend to treat these texts as if they constituted one narrative, the appearance of the Psalm of Hezekiah in Isa 38:9-20 and the extensive differences between the two versions indicate that each must be treated separately. Clearly, one version grew out of the other. Although the differences between the two versions mandate a separate setting for each, the setting of each version must be considered in relation to the other.

In keeping with Gesenius's conclusion concerning the priority of 2 Kgs 18:13–19:37 over Isaiah 36–37, most scholars maintain that Isaiah 38 is a reworked version of 2 Kgs 20:1-11 (e.g., Clements, *Isaiah 1–39*, 288; Kaiser, *Isaiah 13–39*, 400; Sweeney, *Isaiah 1–4*, 14-15). The narrative form of the chapter plays a major role in this decision, insofar as Isaiah 38 is largely prose narrative like the books of Kings, whereas the book of Isaiah is largely composed of poetic oracles. But the key argument turns on the differences between the Kings and Isaiah versions of the narrative, insofar as the Isaiah version shows a tendency to idealize Hezekiah and to emphasize YHWH's immediate response to Hezekiah's exemplary piety. The several differences between the two versions of the narrative illustrate this tendency.

2 Kings 20:4-5 states, "and Isaiah had not gone out from the middle court when the word of YHWH was unto him saying, 'Return and you shall say to Hezekiah, prince of my people. . . .'" Isa 38:4-5 states simply, "and the word of YHWH was unto Isaiah saying, 'go and you shall say to Hezekiah. . . .'" The longer version in Kings suggests some delay in YHWH's response to Hezekiah's prayer. It portrays the prophet leaving the inner court, and it introduces YHWH's word with the command "return," suggesting that Isaiah had already left the king's presence. This portrayal points to an interest on the part of the Isaiah writer to emphasize that YHWH's response to Hezekiah's prayer in Isa 38:2-3 was immediate (cf. 2 Kgs 20:2-3).

When reporting YHWH's word to Hezekiah, 2 Kgs 20:5-6 states, "Behold, I am healing you, on the third day you shall go up to the house of YHWH, and I shall add upon your days fifteen years." Isa 38:5 reads simply, "Behold, I am adding upon your days fifteen years." Again, the Kings version suggests some delay in YHWH's response to Hezekiah in that he will be healed only after three days, whereas there is no delay in the Isaiah version. Furthermore, the absence of any reference to Hezekiah's ascending to the temple eliminates any suggestion that his piety is motivated by his personal welfare.

2 Kings 20:6-9 contains a number of statements that differ extensively from their counterparts in Isaiah 38 and appear in completely different positions.

2 Kgs 20:6 states that YHWH will heal Hezekiah "for my sake and the sake of my servant David." This motivation does not appear at all in the Isaiah version of the narrative, for it would contradict the focus on Hezekiah's piety as the motivating factor for YHWH's healing. Likewise, the references to Isaiah's application of the remedy and Hezekiah's request for a sign that he shall be healed and ascend to the house of YHWH in 2 Kgs 20:7-8 appear only at the end of the Isaiah narrative (Isa 38:21-22). Again, the Kings version of the narrative associates Hezekiah's healing with his desire to go to the temple, and suggests that the healing provides the basis for his piety. The application of the remedy in Isa 38:21 appears only after Hezekiah has expressed his piety in the Psalm of Hezekiah in Isa 38:9-20, and thus eliminates this potential motivation. His question concerning the sign that he will go to the temple in Isa 38:22 contains no association of this act with his healing. Furthermore, 2 Kgs 20:9 begins with a reference to the fact that Isaiah states the sign to Hezekiah. In Isa 38:6-7 such reference does not appear, thereby emphasizing that the sign comes from YHWH. The priority of the 2 Kings account is evident in the fact that Isa 38:7 formulates the promised sign with 3rd-person references to YHWH, despite the fact that it is presented as a speech by YHWH. But 2 Kgs 20:9 formulates the promised sign as a speech by Isaiah, and thereby gives greater emphasis to the prophet's role in the interchange.

2 Kings 20:9b-11a contains an exchange between Isaiah and Hezekiah in which the king states that he will choose a more difficult sign than that offered by Isaiah: whereas Isaiah states that the shadow on the dial of Ahaz will advance ten steps, Hezekiah demands that it move backward ten steps. Such a demand suggests skepticism on the part of Hezekiah and raises questions about his faithfulness. This exchange is completely lacking in the Isaiah version of the narrative, thereby preserving Hezekiah's piety. The statement that Isaiah called to YHWH in 2 Kgs 20:11a prior to the narrative report of the return of the shadow is likewise absent from the Isaiah version. Isa 38:8 presents the return of the shadow by ten steps as part of the statement by YHWH of the sign to Hezekiah. Again, Isaiah's role in the encounter is diminished.

The Psalm of Hezekiah appears in Isa 38:9-20, but it is entirely absent from the Kings version of the narrative. As noted above, it is a song of thanksgiving that accentuates the singer's (Hezekiah's) confidence in YHWH's promise to heal. Here it is noteworthy that the psalm appears prior to the application of the remedy in Isa 38:21. Hezekiah has received only the promise that he will be healed, and he responds with piety before the cure is effected.

In all cases, the differences between the Isaiah and the Kings versions of this narrative point to an effort in the Isaiah version to idealize Hezekiah's piety, to emphasize YHWH's immediate response to the faithful monarch, and to diminish the role of the prophet in the interchange between Hezekiah and the deity. Although little noticed, the 3rd-person reference to YHWH in Isa 38:7, in a context in which YHWH is the speaker, plays an important role in that the Kings version portrays Isaiah as the speaker of this statement (2 Kgs 20:9). These considerations demonstrate that the Kings version of the narrative has been modified by a later redactor.

Seitz has recently challenged this view; he maintains the priority of the

Isaiah account on several grounds (*Zion's Final Destiny*, 149-91, esp. 162-82). He states that the differences between the Kings and Isaiah versions of the narrative are meaningless because both narratives depict Hezekiah in ideal terms (p. 160). He is correct to note that the Kings and Isaiah versions of the narrative have different concerns (p. 161). But by formulating the issue in black-and-white terms, he underestimates the significance of the differences between them for determining the priority of composition. According to Seitz, the idealization of Hezekiah in Isaiah 38 does not entail the nonidealization of Hezekiah in 2 Kgs 20:1-11. Instead, he offers the following arguments.

First, the narrative concerning Hezekiah's illness cannot be considered, with the account of Merodach-baladan's embassy to Hezekiah, as a supplement to the account of Sennacherib's siege. Unlike the account of the Babylonian embassy, it does not raise the issue of exile; rather, its fundamental concern is like that of the Sennacherib narrative in that it associates Hezekiah's recovery with YHWH's decision to defend the city of Jerusalem (2 Kgs 20:6; Isa 38:6). The composition and setting of the account of Hezekiah's illness must therefore be considered in relation to the account of Sennacherib's siege. According to Seitz, this would be in association with an early-7th-century version of the book of Isaiah.

Second, the narrative in 2 Kgs 20:5 and 8 conflates the mention of two distinct signs in Isa 38:1-22: that concerning Hezekiah's recovery in Isa 38:7-8 and that concerning his visit to the temple in 38:22. Scholars have noted that Hezekiah's request for a second sign in 38:22 is somewhat anomalous since he has already received a sign that he will be healed. According to Seitz, such conflation can be understood only if one posits that the Isaiah version is earlier and that the account in 2 Kgs 20:1-11 resolves a difficult reading. Likewise, the appearance of the Psalm of Hezekiah in Isa 38:9-20 is not intrusive; rather, it occupies a logical position in the flow of the narrative in that it expresses Hezekiah's piety following the promise of healing. The inclusion of vv. 21-22 immediately following the psalm does not indicate a redactional attempt to preserve elements of an original tradition in 2 Kgs 20:1-11; rather, it testifies to the gradual growth of the tradition in Isaiah 38.

Still other elements of the narrative point to an original setting in the book of Isaiah, according to Seitz. The references to Hezekiah's illness recall the portrayal of a sick Jerusalem in Isa 1:5b-6, and Hezekiah's recovery contrasts with the notice of Sennacherib's death in 37:36-38. The placement of the Psalm of Hezekiah at the end of the Proto-Isaiah material in its present context testifies to the practice of placing poetic material at the end of large tradition blocks (e.g., Genesis 49; Deuteronomy 32–33; 2 Sam 22:1–23:7).

Nevertheless, Seitz's contention for the priority of the Isaiah narrative over that of Kings must be rejected. Obviously, the relationship between the narrative of Hezekiah's illness and those concerning Sennacherib's invasion and the embassy of Merodach-baladan has little bearing on the issue since both Kings and Isaiah contain all three episodes. Likewise, the association between Hezekiah's sickness and the sickness of Jerusalem portrayed in Isaiah demonstrates only a motific association. Such a vague connection cannot stand as evidence that the narrative was composed originally for its present position in the book of Isaiah; it only suggests that the author of the narrative may have been aware of the Isaianic motif. Likewise, the position of the Psalm of Hezekiah does not argue for the compositional priority of the Isaiah narrative; such placement may also result from redactional work that adapted an original narrative in 2 Kgs 20:1-11 to the literary context of the book of Isaiah.

The key to Seitz's position is obviously his argument that 2 Kgs 20:1-11 has conflated the two originally separate signs pertaining to Hezekiah's recovery and his visit to the temple in Isa 38:7-8 and 38:22, respectively. Hezekiah's question in 38:22 makes little sense if one relates his request for a sign only to his healing; the combination of the signs in 2 Kgs 20:5-6 would obviously resolve a difficult Isaianic text. Although the two signs appear to be unrelated, one should note that the issues of healing a boil *(šĕḥîn)* and ascending to the temple are closely related in ancient Israelite thought. The presence of a boil indicates the possibility of leprosy, which would render a person unclean and therefore unfit to participate in temple worship and sacrifice. Lev 13:18-23 defines the procedures for examining a boil to determine the cleanliness of the afflicted person, and Leviticus 14 defines the sacrificial procedure by which one so afflicted resumes the right to appear for worship at the temple. The issues of Hezekiah's healing and his visit to the temple are hardly separate; in fact, they are closely associated in relation to Israelite religious practice. The narrative in 2 Kgs 20:1-11 presupposes such a relationship; Hezekiah's healing enables him to resume worship at the temple.

The issue does not turn on the reason why the narrator in 2 Kings 20 would combine the two issues, for they are naturally two aspects of the same issue. Instead, the issue turns on the reason why the narrator of Isa 38:1-22 would separate them. The solution appears when one considers the unusual placement of Hezekiah's question concerning a sign that he shall ascend to the temple in Isa 38:22. In its present position, Hezekiah's question in 38:22 functions as a rhetorical question for which no answer is forthcoming. As such, it highlights Hezekiah's piety, as many have argued.

But Hezekiah's question also highlights the issue of ascent to the house of YHWH, or participation in temple worship, in and of itself. In this respect, it is noteworthy that this issue also dominates Isaiah 2–4, especially the portrayal of the nations' ascent to Mt. Zion in 2:2-4 and the invitation to Jacob to ascend to the house of YHWH in 2:5. In fact, the statement attributed to the nations in 2:3, *lĕkû wĕnaʿăleh ʾel-har-yhwh ʾel-bêt ʾĕlōhê yaʿăqōb,* "Come, and let us go up to the mountain of YHWH, to the house of the God of Jacob," employs vocabulary quite similar to that of Hezekiah's question, "What is the sign that I shall go up [*ʾeʿĕleh*] to the house of YHWH [*bêt yhwh*]?" Such lexical correspondences are also evident in the account of the sign given to Hezekiah in connection with the deliverance of Jerusalem in 37:30-32: "a remnant shall go out from Jerusalem and a band of survivors [*pĕlêṭâ*] from Mt. Zion." This statement corresponds to 2:3b: "Torah [*RSV* 'the law'] shall go out from Zion, and the word of YHWH from Jerusalem." Here it is noteworthy that 4:2-6, the concluding pericope of chs. 2–4, refers to the remnant left in Jerusalem as *pĕlêṭat yiśrāʾēl* (cf. *pĕlêṭâ* in 37:32). Such lexical correspondence, as well as the evidence that the signs of 2 Kgs 20:1-11 were separated in Isa 38:1-22, suggests that a redactor of the book of Isaiah deliberately modified the narrative of 2 Kgs 20:1-11 (or 2 Kgs 18:13–20:19) in order to place it into the book of Isaiah and thereby to associate it with Isaiah 2–4. Isaiah 2–4 defines the role of Zion as the location of the temple of YHWH and invites Jacob, defined in chs. 2–4 as the remnant of Israel, to join in worship of YHWH at Zion.

As argued above, chs. 2–4 are the product of the late-6th-century redaction of the book of Isaiah that constitutes chs. 2–55. This edition of the book of Isaiah was produced in relation to the construction of the Second Temple as a means to garner support among the Jewish population by convincing the people that the reconstruction of the temple signaled YHWH's sovereignty over the entire world (cf. Haggai). As such, it invited Jews both to return to Jerusalem and to acknowledge YHWH's power by worshiping at the new temple. This concern appears at the beginning (2:2-4, 5) and at the end of the book (ch. 55), where the people are invited to partake of water, wine, and bread, and thereby to renew the covenant of David. When considered in relation to this 6th-century edition of the book of Isaiah, ch. 38 presents Hezekiah as the ideal model of pious action called for in the book. He has been healed from his sickness, as the 6th-century Jews were healed from the affliction of the Babylonian exile, and he now stands ready to ascend to the house of YHWH. Consequently, the modified version of the narrative concerning Hezekiah's illness and recovery must be attributed to the late-6th-century redaction of the book of Isaiah.

Chapter 38 not only presents Hezekiah as the model of pious action in this context but also forms part of the larger complex of narratives in chs. 36–39 that joins the Proto-Isaianic traditions in chs. 2–33 to those of Deutero-Isaiah in chs. 34–55. It performs a similar function in the 5th-century edition of the book as a whole. The final redaction of the book of Isaiah highlighted this role by placing ch. 1, with its portrayal of Jerusalem as a sick city in need of redemption, at the beginning of the book.

Having defined the setting of ch. 38 in the context of the book of Isaiah, I still must define the settings of the earlier text traditions on which the Isaianic form of this narrative is based. They include the narrative in 2 Kgs 20:1-11 and the Psalm of Hezekiah in Isa 38:9-20.

2 Kings 20:1-11 is an integral part of the Hezekiah narratives in 2 Kings 18–20, and it therefore forms a major component of the DtrH. The relation of this narrative to that of Sennacherib's invasion of Judah (2 Kgs 18:13–19:37) is clear by its introductory temporal formula, "in those days," and by the association of Hezekiah's recovery with YHWH's decision to deliver the city of Jerusalem (20:5-6). The narrative also provides the premise for the embassy of Merodach-baladan to Hezekiah in 20:12-19 by virtue of the introductory temporal formula in 20:12, "at that time," and by the statement that Hezekiah's sickness served as the occasion of the embassy.

Many scholars consider these narratives to be a unified compositional block, even though the narratives concerning Hezekiah's illness and Merodach-baladan's delegation may well be based on earlier traditions (e.g., Ackroyd, "Interpretation"; Smelik, "Distortion"). Seitz argues (*Zion's Final Destiny,* 149-91), however, that the composition of the narrative concerning Hezekiah's healing must be associated with that of Sennacherib's siege of Jerusalem, which he places in the early 7th century. He maintains that the narrative therefore predates that concerning Merodach-baladan's embassy in that there is no redactional association between the two other than a superficial association with Hezekiah's illness, and none at all between the narrative of the embassy and that of the siege of Jerusalem. The narrative concerning Hezekiah's illness does not take up the issue of exile that appears in the Merodach-baladan narrative; rather, Hezekiah's sickness must be seen in relation to Sennacherib's threat to Jerusalem. Just as the city is saved by Hezekiah's exemplary piety, so Hezekiah himself is saved for the same reason. The narrative is text-generated, not event-generated, in that it is composed to present the pious and delivered Hezekiah in deliberate contrast to the arrogant Sennacherib, who is assassinated by his own sons in the temple of his own god. Insofar as the question of the historicity of Hezekiah's illness is irrelevant, the literary portrayal of his illness takes on overwhelming importance. Like the narrative concerning Sennacherib's threat to the city, the narrative concerning Hezekiah's sickness presents the reader with a model of pious action that motivates YHWH's deliverance. The narrative concerning Merodach-baladan's embassy offers a corrective to this positive portrayal in the light of the Babylonian threat to Jerusalem and the Davidic dynasty in 597-587.

Although Seitz makes a number of cogent observations and arguments, he overlooks one fundamental point in the interpretation of this narrative: Hezekiah is healed from his sickness, but his deliverance is limited in that he is allowed only fifteen more years. In the context of the book of Kings, Hezekiah stands as the model of a Davidic monarch of exemplary piety; nevertheless, in the DtrH presentation the Davidic line will suffer punishment for its wrong-doings (cf. 2 Sam 7:14-15).

Two observations must be made with regard to this important point. First, the narrative concerning Hezekiah's illness tempers that of the deliverance of the city from Sennacherib. Indeed, Jerusalem and Hezekiah are saved, but Hezekiah will eventually succumb. As noted above, the account of Sennacherib's siege of the city appears to have been written to instruct the young Josiah, and it functioned subsequently as a means to support his reform. The narrative concerning Hezekiah's illness, however, tempers the expectations of deliverance. In this regard, Clements's observation (*Isaiah and Deliverance*, 67) that the narrative concerning Merodach-baladan's embassy reflects the Babylonian deportation of King Jehoiachin in 598, but predates the full exile of 587, is to the point. Hezekiah is saved, but the dynasty must nevertheless suffer. Whereas the intent of the Sennacherib narrative is entirely positive, that of the healing of Hezekiah is not. Rather, it corresponds to the intent of the Merodach-baladan narrative, which portrays the coming deportation of the Davidic monarch to Babylon.

Second, the DtrH concludes with a notice of Jehoiachin's release from prison (2 Kgs 25:27-30). This notice provides an element of hope at the end of the narrative following the description of the Babylonian exile. When read in the context of the DtrH, the account of Hezekiah's illness and recovery presages the situation of Jehoiachin. YHWH has assured the dynasty of eternal rule, but it will suffer punishment when necessary (2 Samuel 7). Hezekiah then becomes a model of suffering and hope for the hapless Jehoiachin. The dynasty's and Jerusalem's chances for the future may well depend on Jehoiachin's ability to show faith in YHWH during a time of crisis in the same way that his ancestor Hezekiah did.

These observations suggest that the narrative concerning Hezekiah's illness was composed in the aftermath of Jehoiachin's deportation to Babylon. In its immediate literary context, it continues the theme of deliverance put forward in the narrative concerning Sennacherib's invasion of Judah, but it also corresponds to the impending threat contained in the narrative concerning Merodach-baladan's embassy to Hezekiah. It would appear that the depiction of Hezekiah's cure was intended as a means to represent the DtrH's contention that YHWH had made an eternal promise to the house of David. Despite the exile suffered by Jehoiachin and the people of Judah in 598 and again in 587, Jehoiachin and his descendants should have faith in YHWH's ability to save. Although the narrative may well have been composed in the aftermath of Jehoiachin's deportation and before the destruction of Jerusalem, as Clements maintains, it clearly plays an important role in the final form of the DtrH, which dates to the mid-6th century. It was from this source that the late-6th-century redaction of Isaiah reformulated the narrative.

Finally, scholars have posited an independent origin for the Psalm of Hezekiah in 38:9-20. Although it is impossible to prove with any certainty, the separate superscription for the psalm and its distinctive form suggest that this is the case. In the absence of proved examples of Hezekiah's writings, it is likewise impossible to prove or to disprove Hezekiah's authorship or sponsorship of the psalm. Nevertheless, Hallo's study of the royal letter inscriptions suggests that the psalm may well have existed as a royal letter inscription of Hezekiah. It is not impossible that a stele containing this psalm was erected by Hezekiah in Jerusalem following the withdrawal of Assyrian forces from the vicinity in 701. As Hallo notes, it is not unusual for monarchs to express their political calamities in terms of personal illness. Likewise, the Siloam Inscription indicates Hezekiah's capacity for monumental inscriptions. The appearance of such a stele could well have played a role in motivating the composition of the accounts of YHWH's deliverance of Jerusalem from Sennacherib and Hezekiah from illness.

Intention

One must consider the intention of ch. 38 in relation to its structure, generic character, and setting; in relation to its immediate literary context in chs. 36–39; and in relation to the 5th- and 6th-century editions of the book of Isaiah as a whole.

The above discussion indicates clearly that a major concern of ch. 38 is to accentuate the exemplary piety of King Hezekiah when faced with mortal illness. This concern is evident in the first instance from its generic character as a royal novella, which emphasizes the exemplary qualities of a monarch. More importantly, however, this concern is evident from the special position given to the Psalm of Hezekiah within the structure of the chapter. As noted above, the placement of the psalm is somewhat disruptive in that it interrupts the narrative form of the chapter. Yet this serves the larger narrative purpose of drawing attention to the psalm and to the piety that it represents. When considered in relation to the sequence of events as presented in the chapter, this concern takes on special significance. When considered in relation to the parallel narrative in 2 Kgs 20:1-11, the divergences in the Isaiah 38 narrative point to an interest in emphasizing that Hezekiah's Psalm is motivated not by his impending cure but by his unquestioned faith in YHWH. Hezekiah's Psalm appears after the promised healing by YHWH and before the cure is effected. Likewise, the Isaiah version of the narrative takes special care to present YHWH's actions as an immediate response to Hezekiah's pious actions and statements, and it diminishes the role of the prophet in the interchange, thereby pointing to a more direct relationship between deity and monarch as a result of Hezekiah's faithfulness. In this regard, Hezekiah's final question concerning the sign that he shall go up to the temple points to his desire to respond to YHWH's actions.

When viewed in relation to the narrative block in chs. 36–39, ch. 38 clearly plays a transitional role. Scholars have noted the close association between the narrative concerning YHWH's deliverance of Jerusalem in chs. 36–37 and YHWH's cure of Hezekiah in ch. 38. The temporal formula "in those days" at the beginning of the chapter associates Hezekiah's illness with the siege of Jerusalem, and the motif of the deliverance of the city appears together with that of YHWH's promise to cure Hezekiah in 38:6. Furthermore, the two narratives demonstrate a similar narrative structure (cf. Laato, 277-79). In both cases, Hezekiah is faced with a crisis and he appeals piously to YHWH for assistance. The prophet Isaiah plays the role of intermediary and delivers a word of salvation to the monarch that includes a prophetic announcement of a sign (37:30-32; 38:7-8). The result is the same: Jerusalem is delivered in chs. 36–37 and Hezekiah is cured in ch. 38. In addition, Seitz (*Zion's Final Destiny,* 172-76) notes that Hezekiah's piety is intended to contrast with the arrogance of Sennacherib, and whereas Sennacherib dies by the hands of his sons in the temple of his own god, Hezekiah is delivered to stand in the temple of his God.

But one must also consider ch. 38 in relation to the narrative concerning Merodach-baladan's embassy to Hezekiah in ch. 39, which concludes with Isaiah's statement that Hezekiah's sons will be carried off to exile in Babylonia (see Ackroyd, "Interpretation"). Obviously, this statement presents a threat and thereby contrasts with the message of deliverance presented in chs. 36–37. Although Hezekiah is delivered from illness in a manner that parallels Jerusalem's deliverance in chs. 36–37, one must note that his deliverance is temporary in that he is granted only fifteen more years. Hezekiah's piety wins him a reprieve from death, but it is only a reprieve, and he must eventually succumb to his fate.

In this regard, one must consider Hezekiah's role as a member of the Davidic house. As Clements notes (*Isaiah and Deliverance,* 67), the projected deportation of Hezekiah's sons in ch. 39 points to the crisis suffered by the Davidic dynasty in 598 when Jehoiachin was deported to Babylon. Two facets of this observation must be noted. First, Hezekiah is presented as a model of exemplary piety that will enable the dynasty (Jehoiachin and his successors) to recognize that YHWH will guarantee its security. Hezekiah then becomes an exemplar of faith in YHWH's promise of security for the dynasty when faced with overwhelming crisis. Second, the dynasty never regained full control of the throne in Jerusalem. Jehoiachin was succeeded by his uncle Zedekiah, who was nothing more than a Babylonian puppet. After the failed revolt of 587, not even a Babylonian puppet occupied the throne. Although Hezekiah was cured, his cure was only temporary. When considered in relation to the Josianic narratives concerning the deliverance of Jerusalem in chs. 36–37 and Merodach-baladan's embassy in ch. 39, ch. 38 points to the fact that, following Josiah's much-heralded attempt to restore the Davidic empire, the dynasty never recovered from that program's ultimate failure. Although Josiah's program offered new hope for the recovery of the Davidic dynasty and the land of Judah following a century of Assyrian hegemony, that recovery was only temporary.

Isaiah 36–39 plays an important transitional role in the larger structure of the book of Isaiah in that it provides part of the literary bridge between the material pertaining to the Assyrian period in chs. 1–33 and that pertaining to the Babylonian and Persian periods in chs. 34–66. As noted in the discussion of the overview of chs. 36–39, the image of Hezekiah presents a distinct contrast with that of Ahaz in 7:1–9:6 (*RSV* 7). When faced with similar situations of outside invasion, Hezekiah's exemplary piety and faith in YHWH carried him and Jerusalem through the crisis, whereas Ahaz's refusal to trust in the Davidic promise led to disaster. In contrast to Ahaz, who refused to ask for a sign in 7:10-17, Hezekiah pointedly asks for a sign in 38:22, which highlights his desire to praise YHWH in the temple and expresses his trust in YHWH's promises.

When considered in relation to the 5th-century form of the book of Isaiah, this narrative, with its portrayal of Hezekiah's exemplary piety in the face of illness, takes on special significance in that it presents Hezekiah as a model for the Jewish community of Jerusalem during the period of Ezra's reforms. During the latter part of the 5th century, Ezra and the Jewish community of Jerusalem faced an uphill struggle to reconstitute Jewish life in Jerusalem around the temple. Jerusalem still suffered from the effects of the Babylonian destruction, and, in the absence of the Davidic monarch, only the temple served as a means to focus Jewish identity and national life. The narrative of Hezekiah's illness takes up the motif of a sick Jerusalem in ch. 1 (cf. Seitz, *Zion's Final Destiny,* 176-82), which served as the introduction to the 5th-century edition of the book. It likewise expressed the hope for a new future, or a new heaven and earth based around the temple in Jerusalem with YHWH as monarch, as depicted in chs. 65–66, that would be realized only after tremendous suffering and upheaval. Hezekiah thereby presents a model of faithfulness to the Jewish community, assuring that trust in YHWH, expressed through temple worship, would see the community through its period of crisis.

Although the historical circumstances differ, the narrative plays a similar role in relation to the 6th-century edition of the book in chs. 2–55. Hezekiah's question concerning the sign that he will go up to the temple of YHWH relates to the projected ascent of the nations to YHWH's temple in Jerusalem as depicted in 2:2-4, and the invitation to Jacob to join the nations in 2:5. A similar theme is expressed in the invitation to the people to taste the waters in ch. 55 and thereby to reconstitute the Davidic covenant. When considered in relation to the return to Jerusalem and the rebuilding of the temple in the late 6th century, the narrative concerning Hezekiah's illness again presents the Jewish community with a model of piety and trust that YHWH's promises will be realized. The possible reestablishment of the Davidic dynasty under Zerubbabel (cf. Hag 2:20-23) would only reinforce this message of trust.

Bibliography

→ bibliography at 36:1–37:28. J. Begrich, *Der Psalm des Hiskia: Ein Beitrag zum Verständnis von Jesaja 38, 10-20* (FRLANT 42; Göttingen: Vandenhoeck & Ruprecht, 1926); W. H. Bellinger, *Psalmody and Prophecy* (JSOTSup 27; Sheffield: JSOT Press, 1984) 79-81; P. A. H. de Boer, "Notes on the Text and Meaning of Isaiah XXXVIII 9-20," *OTS* 9 (1951) 170-86; M. J. Gruenthaner, "Two Sun Miracles of the Old Testament," *CBQ* 10 (1948) 271-90; W. H. Hallo, "The Royal Correspondence of Larsa: I. A Sumerian Prototype for the Prayer of Hezekiah," in *Kramer Anniversary Volume: Cuneiform Studies in Honor of Samuel Noah Kramer* (ed. B. L. Eicher; AOAT 25; Kevelaer: Butzon & Bercker; Neukirchen-Vluyn: Neukirchener, 1976) 209-24; C. Jeremias, "Zu Jes. XXXVIII 21f," *VT* 21 (1971) 104-11; R. Kasher, "2 Kings 20:1-11 — Isaiah 38:1-22," *Shnaton* 7-8 (1983-84) 75-89 (in Hebrew); Laato, *Who Is Immanuel?* (→ 7:1–8:15), 277-79; H. S. Nyberg, "Hiskias Danklied Jes. 38,9-20," *ASTI* 9 (1974) 85-97; Seitz, *Zion's Final Destiny* (→ "Introduction to the Book of Isaiah"), 149-91; K. Seybold, *Das Gebet des Kranken im Alten Testament* (BWANT 99; Stuttgart: Kohlhammer, 1973) 147-53; H. Tadmor, "Sennacherib's Campaign to Judah: Historical and Historiographical Considerations," *Zion* 50 (1985) 65-80 (in Hebrew); R. Tournay, "Relectures bibliques concernant la vie future et l'angélologie," *RB* 69 (1962) 481-505, esp. 482-89; J. W. Watts, *Psalm and Story: Inset Hymns in Hebrew Narrative* (JSOTSup 139; Sheffield: JSOT Press, 1992) 118-31.

PROPHETIC STORY CONCERNING ISAIAH'S ANNOUNCEMENT OF PUNISHMENT AGAINST HEZEKIAH ON THE OCCASION OF MERODACH-BALADAN'S EMBASSY: DIALOGUE REPORT, 39:1-8

Structure

I. Report concerning circumstances of dialogue: Merodach-baladan's embassy to Hezekiah	1-2
A. Merodach-baladan's embassy to Hezekiah	1
1. Report that Merodach-baladan sent embassy	1a
2. Report of reason: Hezekiah's illness and recovery	1b
B. Hezekiah's reception of embassy	2
1. Receives favorably	2aα
2. Shows them wealth	2aβ-b
a. Basic statement	2aβ

Isaiah 39 is demarcated initially by the temporal formula *bā'ēt hahî'* (see *BHS*), "at that time," which introduces the unit. The narrative form and concern with events related to Merodach-baladan's embassy to Hezekiah continues through 39:8. Isa 40:1 begins a poetic oracle that instructs the prophet to announce comfort to the people.

Isaiah 39 is formulated as a prose narrative that employs *wāw*-consecutive imperfect verbs to convey the main elements of the action. The structure is determined in part by the shifts in the subjects of these verbs. Vv. 3-8 focus on a dialogue between Isaiah and Hezekiah, and vv. 1-2 provide the circumstances in which the dialogue takes place. Because the dialogue represents the major action of the narrative, the unit contains two major components: the report concerning the circumstances of the dialogue in vv. 1-2, and the report of the dialogue itself in vv. 3-8.

The report of the circumstances of the dialogue contains two major subunits as indicated by the change in subjects. V. 1 contains a report of Merodach-baladan's embassy to Hezekiah, which includes the report proper that he sent the embassy in v. 1a and the report in v. 1b that Hezekiah's illness and recovery was the reason for the embassy. V. 2 reports Hezekiah's reception of the embassy. V. 2aα states that he received them favorably, and v. 2aβ-b states that he showed them all his wealth. V. 2aβ contains the basic statement, and v. 2b contains an appositional explication stating that nothing was excluded.

The structure of the report of the dialogue between Isaiah and Hezekiah (vv. 3-8) is determined by the shifts in subject between Isaiah and Hezekiah. Each subunit of the dialogue report contains a question or statement by Isaiah followed by a response or statement by Hezekiah. The first exchange appears in v. 3. The report of Isaiah's question in v. 3a-bα includes a report of Isaiah's coming to Hezekiah in v. 3a and the report of his question to Hezekiah concerning the origin of the men of the embassy in v. 3bα. The report of Hezekiah's answer (that they are from Babylon) follows in v. 3bβ. The second exchange appears in v. 4. V. 4a contains the report of Isaiah's second question concerning what the men saw, and v. 4b contains Hezekiah's response that they saw everything in his house and in the storehouses. Finally, the third exchange appears in vv. 5-8. The report of Isaiah's announcement of punishment against Hezekiah appears in vv. 5-7, including the speech report formula in v. 5a and the speech proper in vv. 5b-7. The speech is formulated as an announcement of punishment that includes a call to attention in v. 5b and the announcement of punishment proper in vv. 6-7. V. 6 contains the statement of YHWH's intervention, which announces that everything in Hezekiah's house and storehouses will be carried off to Babylon, and v. 7 announces that Hezekiah's sons will serve as eunuchs in the palace of the Babylonian king as a result. The report of Hezekiah's twofold response, each part of which is introduced by a speech formula, then follows in v. 8. In the first report in v. 8a, Hezekiah states that YHWH's word is good. In the second report in v. 8b, Hezekiah states that the reason why YHWH's word is good is that there will be peace and truth in his days.

Genre

The overarching genre of this narrative is PROPHETIC STORY. This is a special form of the genre HISTORICAL STORY that employs a prophet as the central figure in order to convey motifs central to the narrator's concerns. In ch. 39, Isaiah delivers the ANNOUNCEMENT OF PUNISHMENT to Hezekiah in order to introduce concern with exile to Babylonia. This announcement helps to prepare the reader for the oracles beginning in ch. 40 that presuppose the Babylonian exile. One should note that the HISTORICAL STORY and the PROPHETIC STORY have no particular interest in entertaining, edifying, or instructing in the manner of a (→) legend. They may employ a rudimentary plot, such as the present sequence of events leading to Isaiah's condemnation of Hezekiah, but their main purpose is simply to report events (cf. Rofé, *Prophetical Stories*, 95-97, who considers ch. 39 to be an example of prophetic historiography).

Subordinate genres appear in vv. 5-7, which contain Isaiah's ANNOUNCEMENT OF PUNISHMENT against Hezekiah. The announcement is introduced by the CALL TO ATTENTION FORMULA in v. 5b, "hear the word of YHWH Sabaoth." The formula contains its typical elements: the invitation to listen introduces the formula; the addressee Hezekiah is evident from the context; and the word of YHWH Sabaoth is identified as what is to be heard. The ANNOUNCEMENT OF

PUNISHMENT proper appears in vv. 6-7. The ANNOUNCEMENT OF PUNISHMENT is typically the climactic element of a PROPHETIC JUDGMENT SPEECH, but it may stand alone as in the present instance. It usually contains a statement of YHWH's intervention, frequently introduced by *hinnēh,* "behold!" and a statement of the results of that intervention. In the present instance, v. 6 constitutes the former and v. 7 the latter.

Setting

Most commentaries tend to focus on the historical background to Merodach-baladan's embassy to Hezekiah in an attempt to establish the setting of this narrative. Merodach-baladan (i.e., Marduk-apla-iddina) was a Chaldean prince of the tribe of Bit-Yakin who ruled Babylon intermittently during the years 722-710 and 704-703 (see J. A. Brinkman, "Merodach-Baladan II," in *Studies Presented to A. Leo Oppenheim, June 7, 1964* [eds. R. D. Biggs and J. A. Brinkman; Chicago: Oriental Institute, 1964] 6-53). Together with Hezekiah, Merodach-baladan planned a confrontation with the Assyrian empire that resulted in a combined Babylonian/Judean revolt against Sennacherib in 705-701 and the siege of Jerusalem in 701. Consequently, a meeting between Merodach-baladan's envoys and Hezekiah would have taken place at some time prior to the revolt. It is difficult to pinpoint with any accuracy the time for such a meeting, or to verify its relation to Hezekiah's illness and recovery as the narrative states (Isa 39:1b). Scholars may posit a specific setting for the visit to Jerusalem by the Babylonian embassy, and undoubtedly it took place. But the absence of clear evidence for such a meeting and the narrative's primary focus on the exile of Hezekiah's sons to Babylon indicate that such a concern is secondary.

The setting of ch. 39 is determined to a large extent by its concern with exile to Babylon. On the one hand, Ackroyd ("Interpretation"; see also idem, "Isaiah 36–39") argues that this concern must relate to the overall concern with the Babylonian exile in the second half of the book of Isaiah insofar as chs. 36–39 serve as a transitional text between the two parts of the book. On the other hand, Clements ("Isaiah Narrative"; *Isaiah and Deliverance,* 63-71; cf. Hardmeier, *Prophetie*) points to the fact that ch. 39 says nothing about the destruction of the temple and Jerusalem by the Babylonians in 587, but focuses on the fate of the Davidic dynasty in that the sons or descendants of Hezekiah and the royal treasury will be taken to Babylon. He concludes consequently that the narrative is concerned with the deportation of King Jehoiachin to Babylon in 598/597, and that this narrative must have been written after Jehoiachin's deportation and before the events of 587.

The discussion of the setting of ch. 39 must also take account of the role that this narrative plays as a part of the block of Hezekiah narratives that appear in 2 Kings 18–20 and Isaiah 36–39. Although some scholars treat these narratives as a single block (e.g., Ackroyd, "Interpretation"), Seitz (*Zion's Final Destiny,* 150) points out that there is no compositional or redactional relationship between chs. 36–37 and ch. 39, since the former is concerned with the deliverance of the city of Jerusalem whereas the latter is concerned with the deportation of the monarchy. Ch. 38 supplies such a connection insofar as Merodach-baladan's embassy to Hezekiah takes place after he has recovered from his illness (39:1b), but the connection appears to be artificial. Seitz argues that ch. 38 was composed together with chs. 36–37, and that ch. 39 was added to this block at a later time, but the discussion of ch. 38 above indicates that the narrative concerning Hezekiah's recovery was composed in order to link the narrative concerning Merodach-baladan's embassy with that concerning the deliverance of Jerusalem from Sennacherib's siege (see above on ch. 38). Because the narrative concerning the Babylonian embassy was composed between 598 and 587, its incorporation into the Hezekiah narratives of 2 Kings 18–20/Isaiah 36–39 would have to have taken place at a later time.

The narrative appears to have been incorporated into the Kings version of the cycle in the mid-6th century as part of the composition of the final edition of the DtrH. The Isaiah version of the narrative appears to have been produced in relation to the late-6th-century edition of the book of Isaiah. Several lines of evidence support these contentions.

First, Jehoiachin appears to be a primary concern of the DtrH's portrayal of the Babylonian exile. The DtrH concludes with a notice of Jehoiachin's release from prison by Evil-merodach in 2 Kgs 25:27-30, which signals DtrH's interest in the possible restoration of the monarchy. Insofar as Evil-merodach (i.e., Amel-Merodach, son of Nebuchadrezzar; see Cogan and Tadmor, *II Kings,* 328) ruled from 562 to 560, this would place the composition of the final form of the DtrH at approximately the middle of the 6th century. Furthermore, DtrH signals its interest in the present narrative and its connection to Jehoiachin by noting that Jehoiachin's deportation to Babylon fulfilled Isaiah's prophecy (2 Kgs 24:10-17, esp. v. 13; cf. Begg, "2 Kings 20:12-19"; "The Reading").

Second, the Isaiah version of the narrative is not concerned with Jehoiachin, since this monarch is never mentioned in the book of Isaiah. Rather, the book of Isaiah is concerned with the issue of the Babylonian exile of 587 and its impact on the Davidic dynasty in general. This focus is evident in that the second half of the book presupposes the exile of the Jewish community, but lacks any concern with a specific Davidic monarch. Rather, the book focuses on Cyrus as the "anointed" of YHWH and the temple builder (44:24-28; 45:1-7), on the application of the Davidic covenant to the people as a whole (55:3; cf. 62:3), and on YHWH as the true monarch (66:1). Such images suggest a different and later concern than that of Kings, and indicate that ch. 39 focuses on the Babylonian exile of 587, not on the earlier deportation of Jehoiachin. As noted in the discussion of ch. 38 above, this concern with a new concept of the monarchy and the corresponding focus on the temple point to the late 6th century as the period in which the Hezekiah narratives were incorporated into a late-6th-century edition of Isaiah comprising chs. 2–55. In the context of such an edition, the concern with the Babylonian exile enables the Hezekiah narratives to form a major literary transition between the two parts of the book.

Third, a number of differences between the Kings and Isaiah versions of the Hezekiah narratives point to the fact that the Isaiah version of the narratives derived from that in Kings (see also the discussion of Setting for ch. 38 above). In the case of Isaiah, only one major difference comes into play, but it supports the overall thesis of the priority of the Kings narrative. In Isa 39:8b Hezekiah's response to Isaiah's announcement of judgment states: *kî yihyeh šālôm we'ĕmet bĕyomāy*, "because there will be peace and truth in my days." The response in 2 Kgs 20:19b reads: *hălô' 'im-šālôm we'ĕmet yihyeh bĕyomāy*, "shall there not be peace and truth in my days?" Scholars have speculated as to whether Hezekiah's response represents self-interested cynicism, *après moi la déluge* (Ackroyd, "Interpretation," 158), but such discussion misses the point. In both cases, Hezekiah recognizes that there will be disaster, but that it will come later. When one considers that the Babylonian embassy is intended in part to prepare for the confrontation with Babylon depicted in Isaiah 36–37, the king's response indicates his confidence that YHWH will enable Judah to succeed. Hezekiah's statement demonstrates his faith.

The difference in formulation between the two versions, however, is telling in regard to their compositional priority. On the one hand, the statement in 2 Kgs 20:19b is formulated as a question with the interrogative particle *hălô' 'im*, suggesting some doubt on the part of Hezekiah. On the other hand, the statement in Isa 39:8b is formulated as an unquestioned assertion with a causative *kî*, "because," which states without qualification that there will be peace. As noted in the discussions of chs. 36–37 and ch. 38 above, this statement corresponds with an overall interest in idealizing the character of Hezekiah in the Isaiah version of the narratives, thereby enabling the redactor of the 6th-century edition of Isaiah to present Hezekiah as the model of piety to the Judean audience.

Intention

The interpretation of the intention of ch. 39 centers on its concern with exile to Babylon, its transitional role within the book of Isaiah as part of the larger block of Hezekiah narratives in chs. 36–39, and its concern to present Hezekiah as a model of piety.

In the context of the book of Kings and the DtrH, the narrative concerning Merodach-baladan's embassy to Hezekiah in 2 Kgs 20:12-19 presages coming disaster. Isaiah's condemnation of Hezekiah and prediction that his sons will be deported to Babylon have obvious ramifications for Jehoiachin, the Davidic dynasty as a whole, and the theological presentation of Judah's destruction as a judgment by YHWH. Although Manasseh receives primary blame for YHWH's decision to destroy Jerusalem and the temple (2 Kgs 21:10-15), Hezekiah's actions in meeting with the Babylonians also plays a role in that it provides the pretext for the deportation of Jehoiachin to Babylon in 24:13. As such, the narrative concludes a sequence in 18:13–20:19 in which Hezekiah's character is called into question despite his overall high evaluation; he does surrender to Sennacherib and strip the temple without a fight (18:14-16), and he receives a foreign delegation despite YHWH's guarantees for Jerusalem's and the dynasty's security (2 Samuel 7). Such acts help to explain why Jerusalem and Judah were destroyed despite the efforts of exemplary monarchs. Even Hezekiah had his flaws.

The book of Isaiah presents a somewhat different picture. As noted in the discussions of chs. 36–37, 38, and 39 above, the text of these narratives was modified in the redaction of the late-6th-century edition of the book of Isaiah in order to eliminate any question concerning Hezekiah's exemplary piety. The reason for such a presentation becomes clear when one considers his role in the book as a model of piety for the Jewish community of the late 6th century. The late-6th-century edition of Isaiah presents a scenario for the restoration of Judah and Jerusalem in which the temple is to be rebuilt, but the Davidic dynasty is not to be restored. The temple serves as the focal point for the demonstration of YHWH's world sovereignty (2:2-4), and Jews are invited to join the nations in recognizing YHWH's sovereignty (2:5; ch. 55). Yet no Davidic monarch is envisioned, in keeping with the realities of Persian rule at this time. Instead, Cyrus serves as YHWH's anointed or monarch (44:28; 45:1), and the Davidic covenant is applied to the entire people rather than to a king of the Davidic line (55:3). The guarantee to the people is therefore based on the old Davidic covenant, but the guarantee of security is applied to them, not the monarch. In such circumstances, Hezekiah is presented as a model of faith. Despite the fact that his sons will be deported to Babylon, he continues to show faith in YHWH just as he did through the crises of the Assyrian siege and his own illness. As such, he serves as a model for showing faith in YHWH's promises of security despite the overwhelming tragedy of the loss of the land, Jerusalem, the temple, and the monarchy. According to the late-6th-century edition of Isaiah, Jews will return to the land, Jerusalem and the temple will be rebuilt, and the Davidic promise still holds. One needs only to show faith (and patience!) to see the full realization of the divine plan.

When read in relation to the 5th-century edition of the final form of the book of Isaiah, such conceptions still govern the intention of this narrative. Jerusalem had been resettled and the temple had been rebuilt, but in the time of Ezra and Nehemiah the full promises of restoration had not been realized. Hezekiah still serves as a model of faithfulness for the realization of the divine promises. YHWH's saving acts will eventually be manifested with the full restoration of Israel.

Bibliography

→ bibliography at "Introduction to the Book of Isaiah" and at 36:1–37:28. C. T. Begg, "2 Kings 20:12-19 as an Element of the Deuteronomistic History," *CBQ* 48 (1986) 27-38; idem, "The Reading at 2 Kings xx 13," *VT* 36 (1986) 339-41; R. E. Clements, "The Isaiah Narrative of 2 Kings 20:12-19 and the Date of the Deuteronomic History," in *Isac (sic) Leo Seeligmann Volume* (ed. A. Rofé and Y. Zakovitch; Jerusalem: E. Rubinstein, 1983) 209-20.

GLOSSARY

GENRES

ACCOUNT (Erzählung, Bericht). A term nearly synonymous with (→) report. Generally longer and more complex than a simple report, an account may consist of several briefer reports, statements, descriptions, and so on, organized according to a common theme. Accounts aim at some degree of explanation rather than simple narration of events. Like reports, accounts employ a 3rd-person narrative style. Examples include Judg 1:16, 17; 1 Kgs 6:1–7:51; Isa 7:1–8:15.

ACCUSATION (Anklage). One of the (→) trial genres. The accusation functions as part of the trial speech in which the accuser acts as prosecutor and the accused acts as defendant. The accusation normally specifies the offense for which the accused is being brought to trial. The accusation often serves as an element of the (→) prophetic judgment speech, the (→) prophetic announcement of punishment against an individual, or the (→) prophetic announcement of punishment against the people. In this capacity, the accusation functions as a means for the prophet to convey the reasons for YHWH's punishment of the accused.

Related genres: (→) Trial Genres.

ACROSTIC POEM (Akrosticher Psalm). A poem whose structure is guided by alphabetic considerations. Each unit (one line, Psalms 111; 112; two lines, Psalm 34; eight lines, Psalm 119) begins with a consecutive letter of the Hebrew alphabet. Cf. Prov 31:10-31; Psalms 9; 10; 25; 34; 37; 111; 112; 145; and perhaps Nah 1:2-10. The term does not designate a genre per se, but an aesthetic literary technique that has nothing to do with the genre or intention of the poem. The setting of acrostic compositions can be either communal worship or the wisdom tradition.

ADDRESS (Anrede). A speech directed to a particular audience. The audience is specified either in the speech itself, normally as a vocative, or in the literary context in which the speech is placed.

ADMONITION (Ermahnung gegen . . .). A speech designed to dissuade an individual or a group from a particular kind of behavior. It is closely related to (→) instruction, and, together with (→) exhortation, it constitutes (→) parenesis. It is not easily distinguished from statements that prohibit particular actions. Admonition appears in both prophetic discourse (e.g., Isa 1:16-17; Jer 25:3-7; Amos 5:4-5, 6-7) and didactic literature (e.g., Prov 6:20-21; 7:1-15). The genre is probably not the creation of either the prophets or the wisdom teachers, but more likely reflects modes of discourse that stem from a family or tribal setting.

Related genres: (→) Exhortation; (→) Instruction; (→) Parenesis; (→) Prohibition.

AFFIRMATION OF CONFIDENCE (Vertrauensäusserung). A characteristic element of the (→) complaint songs that expresses trust in YHWH's ability and willingness to intervene on behalf of the singer. Insofar as the (→) complaint songs are employed in times of distress to call upon YHWH for deliverance or relief, the affirmation of confidence both confirms the singer's faith in YHWH and aids in providing motivation for YHWH to act.

Eberhard S. Gerstenberger, *Psalms, Part I, with an Introduction to Cultic Poetry* (FOTL XIV; Grand Rapids: William B. Eerdmans, 1988) 244.

ALLEGORY (Allegorie). Not strictly a genre, but rather a speech form closely related to figurative or metaphorical language. The details of an allegory are chosen and shaped against the background of the interpretation or application so that each detail of the allegory recurs in the interpretation. The shortest form of the allegory is the metaphor, with just one motif calling for interpretation (Isa 3:14; Ezek 18:2); a longer form is the allegorical story, in which each detail has its bearing on the interpretation (Isa 5:1-7; Ezekiel 16; 34). An allegorical form of speech calls for allegorical interpretation. Allegory occurs in a variety of contexts, such as a dream report (cf. Gen 37:7; 41:17-24; Dan 7:2-14), a (→) vision report (cf. Dan 8:1-14 and the visions of Zechariah), a psalm (cf. Ps 80:9-20 [*RSV* 8-19]), a prophetic discourse (Isa 5:1-7; Ezekiel 16; 34), and a self-contained narrative (Judg 9:8-15).

ANNOUNCEMENT OF JUDGMENT (Gerichtsankündigung, Gerichtsansage). Ordinarily, the element in the (→) prophetic judgment speech in which punishment is announced. Also occurs as an independent genre. Its essence is the statement that a disaster (death, war, captivity, etc.) is imminent as YHWH's punishment for crimes or sins.

Most frequently, the announcement of judgment is framed and styled as a speech of YHWH through a prophet; thus it is usually introduced by means of the (→) messenger formula and concluded with the (→) oracular formula. The most common style is a 1st-person speech of YHWH that states what YHWH is about to do. Passive or impersonal formulations are known as well (cf. Amos 4:2-3).

In older terminology, the genre was known as the "threat."

Related genre: (→) Prophetic Judgment Speech.

E. Balla, *Die Droh und Scheltwörte des Amos* (Leipzig: A. Edelmann, 1926); C. Westermann, *Basic Forms of Prophetic Speech* (tr. H. C. White; Philadelphia: Westminster, 1967; repr. Cambridge: Lutterworth; Louisville: Westminster/John Knox, 1991).

ANNOUNCEMENT OF REPRIEVE (Ankündigung von Strafaufschub, Strafmilderung, Begnadigung). A type of (→) prophetic announcement that states that God intends to mitigate a promised punishment. Typically, it includes: (1) an allusion to some act of penitence taken by the person in question; (2) the reasons for God's intended actions; (3) the reprieve or mitigated punishment (see 1 Kgs 21:29; 2 Kgs 22:18-20; 2 Chr 12:7-8). The announcement of reprieve occurs commonly as part of a longer narrative now arranged into a stereotyped sequence called (→) schema of reprieve. The social setting for the announcement of reprieve is unclear, beyond the general one of prophetic activity. Its history may begin only with written narrative traditions that seek to interpret royal and national affairs as religious, divine/human drama.

Related genres: (→) Prophetic Announcement; (→) Prophetical Story.

ANNOUNCEMENT OF A ROYAL SAVIOR (Ankündigung eines Königes der Heilszeit). A special form of the (→) prophetic announcement of salvation. As part of the new period of salvation, the role of a just and righteous king is announced and described. Constituent elements of this genre may include: (1) a description of chaos in the land; (2) an announcement of the new king and a description of his coming; (3) mention of his names; and (4) description or characteristics of his rule. In Judean examples (cf. Isa 11:1-10; Jer 23:5-6; 33:15-16; Mic 5:1-4), the language is similar to that used in the royal cult in Jerusalem (cf. Ps 72:2, 4, 13).

The genre has its roots in Egypt and Mesopotamia, where similar oracles were pronounced at royal courts. It was frequently employed retroactively to legitimize the rule of a new monarch or usurper.

Related genre: (→) Prophetic Announcement of Salvation.

H. Wildberger, *Jesaja 1–12* (BKAT X/1; Neukirchen-Vluyn: Neukirchener, 1972) 438-42.

ANNUNCIATION OF BIRTH (Geburtsankündigung). A speech, commonly delivered by YHWH or a representative of YHWH, announcing the imminent birth of a child. The speech is typically introduced with *hinnēh*, "behold," and comprises two parts: (1) prediction of conception and birth of a child hinting at miraculous circumstances; and (2) designation of a special name and destiny for the child. The annunciation of birth appears frequently as part of the annunciation scene in which a divine emissary, usually an angel, announces the birth against the background of the woman's infertility or other difficulties (Gen 16:11-14; 18:1-15; Judg 13:3-5; 2 Kgs 4:11-17; cf. 1 Sam 1:9-20; 1 Kgs 13:2; 1 Chr 22:9-10; Isa 7:14-17). The child generally becomes one of the key figures or leaders in the subsequent narrative.

APPEAL (Anrufung, Berufung). An urgent request for action, assistance, intervention, or the like. Unlike (→) command, (→) prohibition, (→) petition, and (→) parenesis, an appeal may assume no special relationship of obligation between the person making the appeal and the party to whom it is made.

AUDITION REPORT (Auditionsbericht). In terms of structure, setting, and intention, simply one kind of (→) vision report. The audition report is distinguished only by the exclusive use of auditory means, rather than visual, to convey the vision.

Related genre: (→) Vision Report.

AUTOBIOGRAPHY (Selbstbiographie). The narration of a person's life or major life events, written by him- or herself in 1st-person form. No full autobiography occurs in the Hebrew Bible, but accounts of specific events do occur in autobiographical form (e.g., Isaiah 6; 8:1–9:6 [*RSV* 7]; Neh 1:1–7:5; 11:1–13:31).

BEATITUDE (Seligpreisung, Gratulation). A short formulaic speech that extols the fortunate or blessed state of an individual or whole people. Typically, the utterance begins with *'ašrê,* "fortunate" or "blessed," followed by the subject and any special qualifiers, often in the form of relative clauses (so 1 Kgs 10:8, "Happy ['*ašrê*] are your wives! Happy [*'ašrê*] are these your servants who continually stand before you . . ."; see Ps 2:12; Prov 8:34; 16:20). These basic elements can be expanded with the addition of elaborate clauses (e.g., Ps 1:1-2; Prov 3:13-14), or worked into more lengthy collections of sayings (e.g., Matt 5:3-11 in the NT). Beatitude is related to (→) blessing and praise, but remains distinct. It does not invoke God's blessing or utter God's praises, but describes one who is fortunate by reason of upright behavior or blessings already derived from God. Egyptian parallels are known. Most examples in the Hebrew Bible suggest that it was a form of wisdom teaching, didactic example, or precept. Occurrences in Isa 30:18; 32:20; and 56:2 demonstrate that it could be adapted into a prophetic context as well.

J. Dupont, " 'Beatitudes' égyptiennes," *Bib* 47 (1966) 185-222; W. Janzen, "'*ašrê* in the Old Testament," *HTR* 58 (1965) 215-26; E. Lipinski, "Macarismes et psaumes de congratulation," *RB* 75 (1968) 321-67.

BLESSING (Segen, Segnung). A pronouncement cast in either the imperative or indicative mode, designed to call down divine power through the spoken word. Blessing can be introduced or concluded with a formula employing the participle *bārûk,* "blessed," followed by the person who is to be blessed. Good examples appear in Gen 24:60 and Num 24:5-9. Blessing apparently derived from a tribal ethos (so Gen 24:60; 27:27-29), but was also at home in organized cultic affairs (e.g., 1 Kgs 8:14). Blessing should be distinguished from (→) beatitude (e.g., Ps 2:12; 1 Kgs 10:8), which acclaims blessings already received and becomes a type of didactic saying — as indeed some formulas with *bārûk* have become (e.g., Jer 17:7). Blessing is also different from praise (e.g., Ps 72:18; Exod 18:10), which, though beginning with a *bārûk* formula, always has God as its object, and so offers praise to God rather than invoking divine blessing on humanity.

CALL FOR A COMMUNAL COMPLAINT (Aufruf zur Volksklage). A call to the community to assemble for a complaint service. It may be triggered by any crisis of wide and devastating impact on the community (e.g., drought, Jer 14:1ff.; locust plague, Joel 1:5ff.; military threat, 2 Chronicles 20). The fundamental intention is to convene the community for an appropriate cultic response to the crisis at hand. This response normally leads to a petition for YHWH to intervene in order to remove the source of danger.

The genre is highly stylized and usually has three constituent elements: (1) the call itself in the form of a sequence of imperatives; (2) the direct address to the specific groups involved; and (3) the reason or motivation for the complaint service (cf. Joel 1:5-14). The genre is often found in the prophetic literature (cf. Isa 14:31; 23:1-14; 32:11-14; Jer 6:26; 25:34; 49:3; Zeph 1:11; Zech 11:2).

Related genres: (→) Call to Mourn; (→) Communal Complaint.
H. W. Wolff, "Der Aufruf zur Volksklage," *ZAW* 76 (1964) 48-56.

CALL NARRATIVE (Prophetischen Berufungsbericht). → VOCATION ACCOUNT.

COMMAND (Gebot). A direct commission, based on authority such as custom, law, or decree. It is usually expressed by an imperative or by forms with an imperative function, and it may be accompanied by a motive clause (cf. Isa 1:16-17; Prov 4:1-2).

Command is the opposite of (→) prohibition and a subgenre of order, which combines command and prohibition.

COMMISSION (Beauftragung, Sendung). An authoritative charge given by a superior to a subordinate. Commission may include a variety of elements such as direct command or specific instructions, depending on the particular role envisioned by the one who gives order, e.g., military envoy (2 Sam 11:18-21, 25), messenger (Gen 32:3-5; 1 Kgs 14:7-11), a royal official (2 Kgs 19:2-7). Commission often appears in narratives about prophets (e.g., Exod 3:7-10; 1 Kgs 12:22-24; 19:15-16; 21:17-19; Amos 7:15-17) and in the prophetic (→) vocation accounts (e.g., Isa 6:9-10; Jer 1:4-10; Ezek 3:1-11). Thus commission became an important way to represent the prophet as YHWH's messenger and to organize collections of prophetic words. In this context, reports

516

of a prophet's mission display several typical elements: (1) the (→) prophetic word formula, "the word of YHWH came to . . ."; (2) the (→) commissioning formula, "go, speak"; (3) the (→) messenger formula, "Thus says YHWH"; and (4) the message itself, usually some kind of (→) oracle addressed to individuals or the nation (see Isa 7:3-9; Jer 2:1-3; 7:1-7; 26:1-6; 1 Kgs 12:22-24; 19:15-18; 21:17-19; cf. 2 Kgs 9:1-3).

COMMUNAL COMPLAINT SONG (Volksklagelied, Klagelied des Volkes). A (→) song sung by the Israelite/Judean community in which YHWH is petitioned to avert the forthcoming disaster. The plea or petition for help is the decisive element that all other features support.

The cultic ceremonies in which the genre was used were not regularly scheduled, but occurred when the community as a whole was threatened by death, drought, famine, plague, or the like. The ceremonies included the seeking of (→) oracles (to determine the reason for the danger and the means to avert it), processions, sacrifices, and ablutions (cf. Jer 14:2-22; Joel; Psalms 44; 60; 79; 80; 83).

The (→) lamentation (cf. Lamentations; Psalms 44; 60; 79; 89) is a closely related genre, but different primarily in that it was sung after a calamity had occurred.

H. Gunkel and J. Begrich, *Einleitung in die Psalmen* (Göttingen: Vandenhoeck & Ruprecht, 1933) 117-39; S. Mowinckel, *The Psalms in Israel's Worship* (tr. D. R. Ap-Thomas; 2 vols.; Nashville: Abingdon, 1962) 1:193-246.

COMMUNAL THANKSGIVING SONG (Danklied des Volkes). A (→) song sung at a special service following a recent intervention by YHWH on behalf of the people. The song celebrates the event and praises YHWH for saving activity. The main elements are: (1) a call to sing (or to give thanks or to praise); (2) an account of the past trouble and salvation; (3) praise for YHWH (or YHWH's works); (4) announcement of sacrifice; (5) blessings; and (6) a vow or pledge. Often the song is antiphonal. Examples include Psalms 66 and 118. Special types of the communal thanksgiving song are the victory song (cf. Psalm 68; Exod 15:1-21; Judges 5) and the harvest hymn (cf. Psalms 65; 67).

The ceremonies that called for communal thanksgiving songs were not part of the regular ritual calendar, but were held to celebrate a victory, a deliverance from calamity, a bountiful harvest, or the like. The psalm was sung by a priest, a leader, a choir, or the people as a whole.

The genre is closely related to the (→) hymn of praise, differing primarily in terms of its special setting and its frequent inclusion of an account of past trouble and salvation. It is related to the (→) communal complaint song in that the community, when threatened with disaster, often vowed to give thanks if YHWH heard their complaint and delivered them.

F. Crüsemann, *Studien zur Formgeschichte von Hymnus und Danklied in Israel* (WMANT 32; Neukirchen-Vluyn: Neukirchener, 1969); C. Westermann, *Praise and Lament in the Psalms* (tr. K. R. Crim and R. N. Soulen; 2nd ed.; Atlanta: John Knox, 1981).

COMPLAINT (Klage). A statement that describes personal or communal distress, often addressed to God with a plea for deliverance (Job 3; Hab 1:2-4; etc.). The description of the distress is characterized by vivid language (cf. the so-called confessions of Jeremiah, e.g., Jer 12:1ff.), and by the use of the question "why?"

CONFRONTATION STORY (Konfrontierungsgeschichte). A subgenre of the (→) prophetic story that focuses on a confrontation between the prophet and his or her opponents. Constituent elements include: (1) the deliverance of the message by the prophet; (2) the confrontation by the opposition, who denies the validity of the message or the authority of the prophet; and (3) the punishment of the opponent that vindicates the prophet. Examples appear in Amos 7:10-17; Jeremiah 6; 19:1-2; 26; 27–28; 36 (cf. 1 Kgs 22:1-40; Isaiah 36–37). The purpose of the narratives is to legitimize the authority of the prophet and the validity of the prophet's message.

DESCRIPTION OF PUNISHMENT (Strafbeschreibung). A subgenre of (→) prophetic announcement, which in turn is an element of the (→) prophetic announcement of punishment. The punishment is normally announced as YHWH's intervention, which is then followed by results. The description of the results occurs occasionally as an independent genre. It essentially portrays the disaster that will come as the result of YHWH's punishment for crimes or sins (see 1 Kgs 21:23-24; 2 Kgs 9:36; Ezek 9:1-11).

DESCRIPTION OF SALVATION (Heilsbeschreibung). A subgenre of the (→) prophetic announcement of salvation. The salvation is not announced in a sentence with YHWH speaking in the 1st person; rather, it constitutes only the second part of the announcement of salvation or, when included together with the results, the third part (cf. Jer 31:23-25).

DIALOGUE (Dialog, Zweigespräch). An exchange of speech between two parties, each in response to the other. Dialogue may be verbal or written, and it may occur in various social settings and literary contexts, such as wisdom disputation (e.g., Job), prophetic speech (e.g., Hab 1:2–2:20), and narrative literature (e.g., Genesis 24; cf. Isaiah 36–37). There is no specific literary genre of dialogue in the Hebrew Bible; rather, dialogue serves as a literary device that aids in defining the structure of a text or the social reality reflected in a text.

DIPLOMATIC DISPUTATION (Diplomatische Disputationswort). A specific type of (→) disputation set in the context of diplomatic exchange (see 2 Kgs 18:13–19:37; Isaiah 36–37).
     Related genres: (→) Dialogue; (→) Disputation.
     B. S. Childs, *Isaiah and the Assyrian Crisis* (SBT 2/3; London: SCM, 1967) 76-93.

DIRGE (Leichenlied, Leichenklage, Leichenklagelied). A funeral song that bewails the loss of the deceased, describes his or her merits, and calls for further mourning. The dirge typically appears in the 3/2 *qînâ* meter. Its characteristic formulation includes the exclamation *'êk* (or *'êkâ*), "how," "alas," a contrast between former glory and present tragedy, and imperatives that call for mourning.

The dirge was ordinarily performed by hired women or gifted individuals after a death, and it was usually sung in the presence of the corpse as part of the funeral preparations. Examples appear in 2 Sam 1:19-27; 3:33-34. Prophets frequently adapted the dirge, often mockingly, to announce the fate of a king or personified nation (e.g., Isa 14:4-23; Ezek 19:1-14; 27:1-36; Amos 5:1-3).

E. Gerstenberger, *Psalms, Part 1; with an Introduction to Cultic Poetry* (FOTL XIV; Grand Rapids: Eerdmans, 1988) 10-11; H. Jahnow, *Das hebräische Leichenlied* (BZAW 36; Giessen: Töpelmann, 1923).

DISPUTATION (Disputationswort, Streitgespräch). A general term used to designate a dispute between two or more parties. The genre is rooted in the wisdom tradition, where it is employed as a device to examine contrasting points of view (e.g., Job), and it functions in a legal setting as a means to resolve conflicting legal claims (cf. Gen 31:36-43). Most examples appear in prophetic literature and present only the prophet's speech, which attempts to persuade the audience to abandon its position or belief and adopt that of the prophet (Isa 8:16–9:6 [*RSV* 7]; 40:12-17, 18-20, [+25-26], 21-24, 27-31; 44:24-28; 45:9-13, 18-25; 46:5-11; 48:1-11, 12-15; 49:14-25; 50:1-3; Jer 2:23-28; 3:1-5; 31:29-30; 33:23-26; Ezek 11:2-12; 11:14-17; 12:21-28; 18:1-20; 20:32-44; 33:10-20; 33:23-29; 37:11b-13; Mic 2:6-11; Hag 1:2-11; Mal 1:2-5; 1:6–2:9; 2:10-16; 2:17–3:5; 3:6-12; 3:13-21 [*RSV* 3:13–4:3]; cf. Nahum). The genre is based in a two-part structure that includes a statement of the opponent's viewpoint and argumentation in which the speaker attempts to refute that viewpoint and argue for another. Constitutive elements of prophetic examples of the genre include: (1) the thesis to be disputed; (2) the counterthesis for which the speaker argues; and (3) the dispute or argumentation proper.

Related genres: (→) Trial Genres; (→) Dialogue.

J. Begrich, *Studien zu Deuterojesaja* (TBü 20; Munich: Kaiser, 1963) 48-53; A. Graffy, *A Prophet Confronts His People* (AnBib 104; Rome: Biblical Institute Press, 1984); D. F. Murray, "The Rhetoric of Disputation: Re-examination of a Prophetic Genre," *JSOT* 38 (1987) 95-121; E. Pfeiffer, "Die Disputationsworte im Buche Maleachi," *EvT* 19 (1959) 546-68; M. A. Sweeney, "Concerning the Structure and Generic Character of the Book of Nahum," *ZAW* 104 (1992) 364-77.

DOXOLOGY (Doxologie). A pithy, highly lyrical acclamation of divine glory and righteousness (e.g., 2 Sam 7:29; 1 Chr 17:27) that often functions in relation to (→) hymns of praise (e.g., Psalm 135) and (→) communal thanksgiving songs (e.g., Psalms 118; 136). The doxology appears to be rooted in cultic poetry, but it can serve as a device that aids in defining the structure and liturgical character of prophetic books (e.g., Amos 1:2; 4:13; 5:8-9; 8:8; 9:5-6; cf. Isa 42:10-13; 44:23; 45:8; 48:20-21; 49:13; 51:3; 52:9-10; 54:1-3).

Related genres: (→) Hymn; (→) Communal Thanksgiving Song.

J. L. Crenshaw, *Hymnic Affirmation of Divine Justice: The Doxologies of Amos and Related Texts in the Old Testament* (SBLDS 24; Missoula: Scholars Press, 1975); K. Koch, "Die Rolle der hymnischen Abschnitte in der Komposition des Amos-Buches," *ZAW* 86 (1974) 504-37; F. Matheus, *Singt dem Herrn ein neues Lied* (SBS 141; Stuttgart: Katholisches Bibelwerk, 1990); C. Westermann, *Sprache und Structur der Prophetie Deuterojesajas* (2nd ed.; CTM 11; Stuttgart: Calwer, 1981).

ENTRANCE LITURGY (Tempeleinlassliturgie). A liturgy of inquiry and response used to announce the admissibility of worshipers to the temple precincts. The genre presupposes the need for pilgrims to establish their cultic purity prior to entering the temple grounds. It therefore presents the procedure in the form of a question (e.g., Ps 24:3, "Who shall ascend the hill of YHWH? And who shall stand in his holy place?"), followed by an answer that enumerates the qualities required for admission to the temple. Examples include Psalms 15; 24; and Isa 33:14-16.

K. Koch, "Tempeleinlassliturgien und Dekaloge," in *Studien zur Theologie der alttestamentlichen Überlieferungen* (*Fest.* G. von Rad; ed. R. Rendtorff and K. Koch; Neukirchen-Vluyn: Neukirchener, 1961) 45-60.

EXHORTATION (Ermahnung zu . . . , Mahnrede). An (→) address form employed to persuade an audience to adapt a particular course of action. It is the opposite of (→) admonition, which attempts to persuade an audience against a particular course of action. Together, exhortation and admonition constitute (→) parenesis. The form appears to derive from wisdom or cultic instruction (see Prov 1:8-19; Psalms 1; 50; 95), although it may appear in any situation of public or private address in which the speaker attempts to persuade the audience to follow a course of action (e.g., Deuteronomy 6–11; Josh 1:2-9; 1 Kgs 2:2-9; 1 Chr 28:8, 20-21; 2 Chr 15:7).

Exhortation appears in prophetic literature (e.g., Isaiah 1; 31; 55; Zeph 2:1-3), although its status as an independent prophetic genre is contested. The debate is bound up with the issue of whether the prophets called for repentance from their audiences, in which case exhortation serves as a viable prophetic form, or whether they simply announced judgment against them.

Related genres: (→) Admonition; (→) Parenesis.

A. Vanlier Hunter, *Seek the Lord! A Study of the Meaning and Function of the Exhortations in Amos, Hosea, Isaiah, Micah, and Zephaniah* (Baltimore: St. Mary's Seminary and University, 1982); K. A. Tångberg, *Die prophetische Mahnrede* (FRLANT 143; Göttingen: Vandenhoeck & Ruprecht, 1987); T. M. Raitt, "The Prophetic Summons to Repentance," *ZAW* 83 (1971) 30-49; G. Warmuth, *Das Mahnwort* (BBET 1; Frankfurt: Lang, 1976); H. W. Wolff, "Das Thema 'Umkehr' in der alttestamentlichen Prophetie," *ZTK* 48 (1951) 129-48.

HISTORICAL NARRATIVE (Historische Erzählung). → HISTORICAL STORY.

HISTORICAL REVIEW (Geschichtliche Revue). The rehearsing of salient facts in the past experience of Israel or of the individual being addressed. The genre normally appears in narrative form. DtrH employs it as a testimonial farewell speech for Joshua (Josh 24:2-13) and Samuel (1 Sam 12:7-12), and as a rationale for the dynastic promise to David (2 Sam 7:6-9; cf. 1 Chr 17:5-8). It also appears in the Chronicler's History (2 Chr 15:2-7; 20:7-9) and in Nehemiah's prayer (Neh 9:7-31). It frequently aids in persuading people to follow a specific course of action or to adapt a specific viewpoint. It can therefore appear in prophetic literature as a means to justify an (→) announcement of judgment (e.g., Isa 9:7-20 [*RSV* 8-21]).

HISTORICAL STORY (Historische Erzählung). A specific type of (→) narrative that presents a purportedly historical episode. It is unimportant whether the episode actually occurred as reported. Most examples of the historical story in the prophetic literature appear as (→) prophetic story (e.g., Isaiah 7; 20; 36–39; Amos 7:10-17).

> Related genres: (→) Narrative; (→) Prophetic Story.
>
> B. O. Long, *1 Kings; with an Introduction to Historical Literature* (FOTL IX; Grand Rapids: Eerdmans, 1984) 2-8.

HYMN OF PRAISE (Hymn, Loblied). A joyful song of choir or community extolling the greatness, kindness, and righteousness of YHWH and YHWH's dwelling place. Hymns function in various capacities: they praise creation and creator (Psalms 8; 19; 104); they praise YHWH's glorious deeds in history (Psalms 68; 105); they admire YHWH's abode in Mt. Zion (Psalms 46; 48; 76); and they jubilate at YHWH's just reign (Psalms 24; 47; 93; 96). They sometimes appear in the prophetic literature, where they aid in defining the liturgical character and literary structure of the prophetical books (e.g., Isaiah 12; 42:10-13; 44:23; 45:8; 48:20-21; 49:13; 51:3; 52:9-10; 54:1-3; Amos 1:2; 4:13; 5:8-9; 8:8; 9:5-6).

> Related genre: (→) Doxology.
>
> F. Crüsemann, *Studien zur Formgeschichte von Hymnus und Danklied in Israel* (WMANT 32; Neukirchen-Vluyn: Neukirchener, 1969); E. Gerstenberger, *Psalms, Part 1; with an Introduction to Cultic Poetry* (FOTL XIV; Grand Rapids: Eerdmans, 1988) 16-19; C. Westermann, *Praise and Lament in the Psalms* (tr. K. R. Crim and R. N. Soulen; 2nd ed.; Atlanta: John Knox, 1981).

INCLUSION (Inclusio). A rhetorical device in which a compositional unit begins and ends with the same or similar theme, refrain, vocabulary, or other mode of expression.

INDICTMENT SPEECH (Anklageerhebung). One of the (→) trial genres. The indictment speech is a component of the trial speech. It is a statement formally handed down by a judicial authority charging a person with committing an act punishable under the provisions of the law. It is presented either on approval of an accusation or in its own right.

Because of the particular structure of Israel's and Judah's judicial system, the judicial authorities who issue an indictment may function as both accuser and judge, such as a king or a tribal judge (cf. 1 Sam 15:17-19; 22:13; 1 Kgs 2:42-43; 18:17; 22:18; 2 Kgs 20:2, 36). Other officials may also bring an indictment against someone before a judicial authority (cf. Jer 36:20; 2 Sam 19:22).

A modified form of the indictment speech can also be employed in prophetic literature as the accusation or the reason for punishment in the (→) prophetic judgment speech (Isa 8:6; Jer 11:9-10; Mic 3:9-11), the (→) prophetic announcement of punishment against an individual (Amos 7:16; Jer 23:1), and the (→) prophetic announcement of punishment against the people (Isa 30:12; Hos 2:7-8).

Related genres: (→) Prophetic Announcement of Punishment against an Individual; (→) Prophetic Announcement of Punishment against the People; (→) Prophetic Judgment Speech; (→) Trial Genres.

H. J. Boecker, *Redeformen des Rechtslebens im Alten Testament* (2nd ed.; WMANT 14; Neukirchen-Vluyn: Neukirchener, 1970); J. Harvey, *Le plaidoyer prophétique contre Israël après la rupture de l'alliance* (Montreal: Bellarmin, 1967); C. Westermann, *Basic Forms of Prophetic Speech* (tr. H. C. White; Philadelphia: Westminster, 1967; repr. Cambridge: Lutterworth; Louisville: Westminster/John Knox, 1991).

INSTRUCTION (Instruktion, Unterweisung). A writing or discourse, chiefly in imperative mode, that offers guidance to an individual or group by setting forth particular values or prescribing rules of conduct. Instruction typically tends to deal with universals: broad values, traditional rules for conduct, or aphoristic knowledge drawn from wide experience. The settings and occasions of use for instruction must have been quite diverse. In Israel and Judah, instructions were probably created by persons of some official or aristocratic standing, such as lawgiver, priest, prophet, scribe, wisdom teacher, or even king. In Egypt, the best examples derive from scribes who formulated didactic works to summarize accepted knowledge or, in some cases, produced instruction in the guise of an after-the-fact testament from a king to his successor, with propagandistic overtones (*ANET,* 414-19; more generally, see M. Lichtheim, *Ancient Egyptian Literature* [3 vols.; Berkeley: University of California, 1973-81] 1:58-80). Similarly, the clearest examples from the Hebrew Bible are in the didactic literature (e.g., Prov 1–9; 22:17–24:22). Prophetic examples tend to be employed for persuasive purposes, and they become somewhat more specific by focusing on the wisdom of continued adherence to YHWH, who promises to defend Zion and the Davidic house, and on the opportunities for national restoration presented to Judah by YHWH's bringing about catastrophe (e.g., Isa 8:16–9:6 [*RSV* 7]; 28:1–33:24).

Related genres: (→) Admonition; (→) Exhortation; (→) Parenesis.

INVASION REPORT (Invasionsbericht). A brief report concerning an invasion followed by the actions taken to deal with it or, more simply, the results of the invasion. Typically, the report opens with an invasion formula, X (name of a king or an army) "came against" *('ālâ bĕ/'al)* Y (reference to the place, often a city). This formula is sometimes extended with verbs such as "besiege" *(ṣûr)* or "fight against" *(nilḥām)*. The report may be developed with a brief statement concerning the immediate result (e.g., "he took it" *[lākad/tāpas]* or, more often, a longer summary of, e.g., defeat, exile, or successful suing for relief.

Examples appear in 1 Kgs 14:25-28; 2 Kgs 12:18-19; 16:6-9; 17:5-6; 24:10-17; Isa 36:1 (cf. Isa 7:1; Jer 39:1-10). Some examples of invasion reports, or at least certain of their literary formulas, appear in the Bible as integral parts of longer accounts of military events (e.g., 1 Kgs 16:17; 20:1; 2 Kgs 6:24). Unlike a battle report, a report of invasion avoids description of battle, although occasionally it will mention the gathering of forces (e.g., 2 Kgs 6:24). The precise chronistic reckonings in 1 Kgs 14:25-28; 2 Kgs 18:13-16; and 24:10-17 suggest that invasion reports probably originated in the activities of royal scribes who maintained records of the king's actions that they could then draw on to write royal inscriptions, chronicles, annals, and history.

LAMENTATION (Volksklage, Untergangsklage, Klagelied, Klage). A song in which the community bewails its fate following a national catastrophe. Typical elements include a description of the former bliss and happiness, and an account of the present desolation. Exhortations to mourn and (→) petitions to save the remnant are also frequently employed. The formulaic expressions *'êk* and *'êkâ* ("how," "alas"), as used in the (→) dirge, are common.

The setting of the genre was a public service following a disaster such as a plague or the destruction of a city or tribe. The people were called to mourn, repent, and possibly to move God to save the remnant. The ritual usually included fasting (cf. 1 Sam 7:6; Joel 1:14; Judg 20:26). The lamentation itself could be sung by the people as a whole, a choir, or a soloist. Examples include Lamentations 1; 2; 4; and 5. Psalms 44; 60; and 79 reflect similar situations.

The lamentations should be distinguished on the one hand from the (→) dirge, which mourns the death of an individual, and on the other hand from the (→) communal complaint song, which is used before the calamity. Consequently, in the complaint song the plea predominates; in the lamentation it is subdued (if it occurs at all).

E. Gerstenberger, *Psalms, Part 1; with an Introduction to Cultic Poetry* (FOTL XIV; Grand Rapids: Eerdmans, 1988) 10-11.

LEGEND (Legende, Heiligenerzählung, Wundererzählung). A narrative concerned primarily with the wondrous, miraculous, and exemplary. Legend is aimed at edification rather than merely entertainment, instruction, or even imaginative exploration of the storyteller's art. Thus legends often encourage awe for a holy place (e.g., Judg 6:19-24), ritual practice (2 Macc 1:19-22), and holy men and women (e.g., Gen 22:1-19; 1 Kgs 12:33–

13:34; 14:1-18; 17:1–19:21; 2 Kgs 1:2-16; 2:1-25), who may be models of devotion or virtue. Legend differs from history and (→) historical story in its refusal to be bound by a (→) story, thereby giving less attention to developed points of narrative interest, such as description, artistic structure, and plot. Legends took varied forms, and were told in royal courts, at religious shrines, in family and tribal settings, and on pilgrimages to holy sites.

LITURGY (Liturgie). A comprehensive category that denotes widely varying complexes of cultic acts and words set in a stylized sequence and normally intended for use in worship. The constitutive elements may themselves be originally independent genres (e.g., hymn, prayer, complaint, oracle, thanksgiving song, blessing, doxology) that are now interwoven into different patterns depending on setting and intention. Examples include: liturgies of complaint (see Psalms 12; 60; Joel 1–2; Jeremiah 14), liturgies of praise (see Psalms 66; 95), liturgies of thanksgiving (see Psalm 118), processional liturgies (see Psalms 24; 132), entrance liturgies (see Psalms 15; 24), and prophetic liturgies (see Isaiah 33; Habakkuk; Nahum).

E. Gerstenberger, *Psalms, Part 1; with an Introduction to Cultic Poetry* (FOTL XIV; Grand Rapids: Eerdmans, 1988) 2-22; H. Gunkel and J. Begrich, *Einleitung in die Psalmen* (Göttingen: Vandenhoeck & Ruprecht, 1933, repr. 1966); J. Jeremias, *Kultprophetie und Gerichtsverkündigung* (WMANT 35; Neukirchen-Vluyn: Neukirchener, 1970); A. Johnson, *The Cultic Prophet and Israel's Psalmody* (Cardiff: University of Wales, 1979); S. Mowinckel, *Psalmenstudien III* (repr. Amsterdam: P. Schippers, 1966); R. Murray, "Prophet and Cult," in *Israel's Prophetic Tradition* (*Fest.* P. R. Ackroyd; ed. R. Coggins et al.; Cambridge: University Press, 1982) 200-216.

MESSENGER SPEECH (Botenspruch, Botenrede). The message delivered by a messenger. It is styled as a literal repetition of the words that were given to the messenger at the time that the messenger was commissioned by the sender (cf. Gen 32:1-5). The messenger speech begins with the (→) messenger formula, and the message itself takes the form of a direct speech by the sender. Use of the form presupposes that the person who delivers the message speaks on behalf of the sender.

S. Meier, *The Messenger in the Ancient Semitic World* (HSM 45; Atlanta: Scholars Press, 1988); idem, *Speaking of Speaking: Marking Direct Discourse in the Hebrew Bible* (VTSup 46; Leiden: Brill, 1992) 273-98; R. Rendtorff, "Botenformel und Botenspruch," *ZAW* 74 (1962) 165-77; C. Westermann, *Basic Forms of Prophetic Speech* (tr. H. C. White; Philadelphia: Westminster, 1967; repr. Cambridge: Lutterworth; Louisville: Westminster/John Knox, 1991) 98-115.

MOTIVE CLAUSE (Begründungssatz). A statement often employed with another genre, such as a (→) prohibition, (→) instruction, or (→) exhortation that is designed to reinforce the persuasive thrust of the statement. It is generally introduced by *kî*, "for, because," or *pen*, "lest, unless," and it provides the authoritative basis for the statement, the reason for adapting its viewpoint, or the reason for acting in accordance with its recommendation or instructions.

B. Gemser, "The Importance of the Motive Clause in Old Testament Law," *Congress Volume, Copenhagen 1953* (VTSup 1; Leiden: Brill, 1953) 50-66; R. Soncino, *Motive Clauses in Hebrew Law* (SBLDS 45; Chico: Scholars Press, 1980).

NARRATIVE (Erzählung). A broad generic designation for an (→) account of action communicated directly. It includes various subgenres, such as (→) etiology, (→) fable, (→) history, (→) legend, (→) myth, (→) novella, (→) report, (→) saga, (→) story, and (→) tale. Narrative is concerned with action or movement, and it includes the interplay of emotions and ideas. It is informative, in that it is not primarily concerned with moving the audience to action, creating an attitude in it, or developing an idea for it. Narrative may be historical, insofar as it communicates activity that is plausible within the normal realm of human experience; or it may be nonhistorical, insofar as the action communicated transcends, precedes, or follows normal human experience.

G. W. Coats, *Genesis; with an Introduction to Narrative Literature* (FOTL I; Grand Rapids: Eerdmans, 1983) 2-10.

NOVELLA (Novelle). A long prose (→) narrative produced by a literary artisan for a particular purpose or purposes. Its fundamental purpose is entertainment, but the author may use the novella to address theological questions, such as YHWH's adherence to the covenant with Abraham (Genesis 11–22), or moral questions, such as the propriety of the king's behavior and its effect on the royal house of David (2 Samuel 11–1 Kings 2). The structure of the novella depends upon the author's ability to develop suspense and to resolve it in particular directions. Subplots and interweaving motifs may provide depth to the major plot line. Even within the major plot line, multiple structures can facilitate a wider range of goals than would normally be the case in traditional narrative. Characterization can develop subtle tones. Thus the entire piece gives the reader a total impression of an event as a complex and subtle process. Figures in the process are subordinated to the crucial character of the process itself.

The setting of the novella lies in the literary activity of the author, who may draw on traditional (→) narratives with settings in various institutions. However, the qualifying characteristic of the novella is the unique shape given to the subject matter by the author. In that sense, the novella is not simply a stage in the history of typical traditional material, but an original creation (e.g., Genesis 37–47).

Related genre: (→) Narrative.

G. W. Coats, *Genesis; with an Introduction to Narrative Literature* (FOTL I; Grand Rapids: Eerdmans, 1983) 8.

OATH (Eid, Schwur). A formal pronouncement, cast as either cohortative or indicative, which binds the oath taker to a particular course of action, attitude, or stance by invoking sanctions by the deity. Typically, an oath is introduced by the (→) oath formula, "As YHWH lives" (*ḥāy yhwh;* e.g., Ezek 18:3; cf. Isa 8:19). Then follows what the person who takes the oath will or will not do. Most frequently, an oath is a form of self-curse.

ORACLE (Orakel). A broad generic category that designates communication from a deity, often through an intermediary such as a priest, seer, or prophet. It has no specific form, although it may include the (→) oracular formula *nĕ'ûm-yhwh,* "utterance of YHWH." An oracle may be delivered in response to an oracular inquiry (Num 22:7-12; Josh 7:6-15; 2 Sam 5:23-24; Ezek 14:1-3), but it may also come unsolicited. Prophetic speeches presented as YHWH's own words may be classified as unsolicited oracles. The oracle appears to have originated in a setting of formal inquiry of the deity through a priest or prophet, which may include the divinatory use of lots (Urim) or incubation rituals. 1 Sam 28:6 mentions dreams, Urim, and prophets as possible sources for seeking an oracle.

J. Begrich, "Das priesterliche Heilsorakel," in *Gesammelte Studien zum alten Testament* (TBü 21; Munich: Kaiser, 1964) 217-31 (repr. from *ZAW* 52 [1934] 81-92); K. Koch, *The Growth of the Biblical Tradition* (tr. S. M. Cupitt; New York: Scribner's, 1969) 171-82.

ORACLE OF SALVATION (Priesterliches Heilsorakel). An oracle form, postulated by J. Begrich, from which the (→) prophetic announcement of salvation is believed to have developed. Prophetic forms of the genre occur in Isa 41:8-13, 14-16; 43:1-7; and 44:1-5 (cf. 7:4-9; 37:5-7). The form is typically introduced by the formula "Do not fear," followed by a formal statement by a priest or other cultic official that assures divine favor. Because no independent examples of the priestly form occur in the Hebrew Bible, Kilian has challenged the existence of the form in a setting of individual complaint. But the regularized use of the assurance formula in prophetic contexts and frequent references to divine response in the Psalms (cf. Psalms 12; 35; 91; 121) suggest the likelihood of such an oracle. In this regard, it is noteworthy that the oracle in Isa 37:5-7 apparently comes in response to an inquiry made to the prophet Isaiah, who elsewhere responds to Hezekiah's prayer in the temple (Isa 37:14-35).

Related genre: (→) Prophetic Announcement of Salvation.

J. Begrich, "Das priesterliche Heilsorakel," in *Gesammelte Studien zum alten Testament* (TBü 21; Munich: Kaiser, 1964) 217-31 (repr. from *ZAW* 52 [1934] 81-92); E. Gerstenberger, *Psalms, Part 1; with an Introduction to Cultic Poetry* (FOTL XIV; Grand Rapids: Eerdmans, 1988) 253; R. Kilian, "Ps 22 und das priesterliche Heilsorakel," *BZ* 12 (1968) 172-85.

ORDER (Befehl). A forthright expression of will (e.g., *miswâ*), which may be positive (→ Command) or negative (→ Prohibition). Like all expressions of will, an order can have various settings, including legal narratives, wisdom teaching, and prophetic discourse.

PARENESIS (Paräneses). An address to an individual or a group that seeks to persuade with reference to a goal. It may be composed of several genre elements and characteristic stylistic features, in a flexible arrangement (cf. Deuteronomy 6–11; Prov 1:8-19; Isaiah 1; 31). It generally combines (→) admonition, which aims to dissuade an audience from a particular course of action or belief, with (→) exhortation, which attempts to persuade an audience to adopt a particular course of action or set of beliefs. (→) Commands, (→) prohibitions, (→) instructions, etc., may also be mixed into a parenetic address. (→) Motive clauses are frequently included.

PETITION (Petition, Bittrede, Bittschrift). A request or plea from one person to another asking for some definite response. The petition may occur in contexts that express ordinary, day-to-day situations. In such cases the structure of the petition includes both the basis for the petition and the petition proper, expressed directly or indirectly (e.g., Gen 18:3-4; 23:4; 1 Kgs 2:15-17; 5:17-20). The petition also occurs as the central element of all (→) complaints, in which the supplicant asks for divine help. It is usually formulated in the imperative, but the jussive, imperfect, and cohortative are also employed to express the supplicant's "wish."

    E. Gerstenberger, *Psalms, Part 1; with an Introduction to Cultic Poetry* (FOTL XIV; Grand Rapids: Eerdmans, 1988) 254; B. O. Long, *2 Kings* (FOTL X; Grand Rapids: Eerdmans, 1991) 307.

PRAYER (Gebet). Any communication by a human being toward a deity. It is ordinarily a direct address to God in the 2nd-person singular. In the Hebrew Bible, prayer encompasses a great variety of modes of expression, motivations, and intentions, and reflects many distinct settings. Consequently, it includes many different specific genres. While all prayer tends to be ritualistic to some degree, one may distinguish broadly between free, personal prayer and cultic prayer. The latter is predominant in the Hebrew Bible; furthermore, the free, personal prayers usually employ modes of expression and motifs known in the cult. Hezekiah's prayer to YHWH in Isa 37:14-20, e.g., is a standard (→) complaint form set in the temple, which presents a (→) petition to YHWH for deliverance from the Assyrian invasion.

PRESENCE VISION REPORT (Visionsschilderung). See (→) Vision Report.

PRIESTLY TORAH (Priesterliche Tora). An authoritative instructional form, postulated by J. Begrich, from which prophetic (→) instruction (prophetic torah) is believed to have developed. The priestly form seems to have focused on instruction concerning cultic purity, i.e., proper separations between clean and unclean and between holy and profane. Priestly torah was given by priests in response to a question about such matters. Hag 2:11-13 demonstrates both this teaching aspect of the priestly office and prophetic utilization of the form. The instruction could take various shapes, and these were often employed by prophets: a command or prohibition (Isa 1:11; Ezek 45:8b-9; Amos 5:5a), a statement of YHWH's desire (Amos 5:21-22), the determination of a judgment (Isa 1:13), or a description of consequences (Amos 4:5).

Related genre: (→) Instruction.

J. Begrich, "Die priesterliche Tora," in *Werden und Wesen des Alten Testaments* (BZAW 66; ed. P. Volz et al.; Berlin: Töpelmann, 1936) 63-88; C. Westermann, *Basic Forms of Prophetic Speech* (tr. H. C. White; Philadelphia: Westminster, 1967; repr. Cambridge: Lutterworth; Louisville: Westminster/John Knox, 1991) 203-4.

PROHIBITION (Verbot). A direct forbidding of an action or a thing, based on an authority such as custom, law, or decree. It is usually expressed by the phrase "you shall not," which employs *lō'* or *'al* with the jussive (vetitive or prohibitive form). It carries its force within itself, but is frequently accompanied by a (→) motive clause (e.g., Prov 22:22–23:18). A prohibition can appear alone (e.g., Exod 22:17; Isa 1:13) or in a series (e.g., Exod 20:2-17).

A prohibition is a negative (→) command. Both prohibition and command are subgenres of order (cf. 2 Sam 13:28).

The prohibition occurs frequently in the wisdom teaching (→ instruction, admonition), as well as in legal narratives. It may also be employed by prophets, generally in conjunction with instructional or persuasive forms. The authoritative character of the prohibition, the absence of specific legal penalties for its violation, and its frequent association with instructional forms indicate that the basic function of the prohibition is to instruct or to persuade. The setting presupposes an authoritative source, such as the family, clan, or tribe, the priesthood, the monarchy, the wisdom teachers, or the prophets.

Related genres: (→) Admonition; (→) Command; (→) Instruction.

J. Bright, "The Apodictic Prohibition: Some Observations," *JBL* 92 (1973) 185-204; E. Gerstenberger, *Wesen und Herkunft des "apodiktischen Rechts"* (WMANT 20; Neukirchen-Vluyn: Neukirchener, 1965); W. Richter, *Recht und Ethos* (Studien zum Alten und Neuen Testament 15; Munich: Kösel, 1966).

PROPHECY (Prophetie). See (→) Prophetic Announcement.

PROPHECY CONCERNING A FOREIGN NATION (Fremdvolkerorakel, Fremdvölkerspruch). A prophetic speech form that announces punishment or disaster against a foreign nation. It presents the destruction as an act of YHWH that is presently taking place or that will take place in the immediate future. Although the form is generally styled as an address to the foreign nation or its king, the actual addressee is Israel or Judah. Prophecies concerning foreign nations usually appear in series (Isaiah 13–23; Jeremiah 46–51; Ezekiel 25–32; Amos 1–2; Zeph 2:4-15), but they may also appear individually (Isa 10:5-34; 34; Obadiah; Nahum). There is no specific structure, and they may employ a variety of forms, including the (→) taunt (Isa 14:4-23), the (→) prophetic pronouncement (Isaiah 13–23), the (→)

dirge (Ezek 27:1-36; 32:1-16), the (→) lamentation (Isa 15:1-9), and the (→) summons to war (Isa 13:2-5).

The setting lies initially in execration rituals to curse enemies (1 Kings 22; Numbers 22–24) and later in liturgical announcements of YHWH's sovereignty (Psalms 2; 46; 48; 76). The form flourished in the Assyrian, Babylonian, and Persian periods, when Israel and Judah experienced invasion by outside armies composed of units from nations throughout the ancient Near East. The various series of prophecies concerning foreign nations presuppose YHWH's world sovereignty on the pattern of imperial rulers of the time and YHWH's capacity to visit destruction on Israel's and Judah's enemies.

Related genres: (→) Prophetic Announcement; (→) Prophetic Pronouncement.

D. L. Christensen, *Transformations of the War Oracle in Old Testament Prophecy* (HDR 3; Missoula: Scholars Press, 1975); J. H. Hayes, "The Oracles against the Nations in the Old Testament" (Diss., Princeton Theological Seminary, 1964); D. L. Petersen, "The Oracles against the Nations: A Form-Critical Analysis," in *SBL 1975 Seminar Papers* (vol. 1; ed. G. McRae; Missoula: Scholars Press, 1975) 39-61; C. Westermann, *Basic Forms of Prophetic Speech* (tr. H. C. White; Philadelphia: Westminster, 1967; repr. Cambridge: Lutterworth; Louisville: Westminster/John Knox, 1991) 204-5.

PROPHECY OF PUNISHMENT AGAINST AN INDIVIDUAL (Gerichtsankündigung über den Einzelnen). See (→) Prophetic Announcement of Punishment against an Individual.

PROPHECY OF PUNISHMENT AGAINST THE PEOPLE (Gerichtsankündigung über das Volk). See (→) Prophetic Announcement of Punishment against the People.

PROPHECY OF SALVATION (Prophetische Heilsankündigung). See (→) Prophetic Announcement of Salvation.

PROPHETIC ANNOUNCEMENT (Prophetische Ankündigung). A broad collecting generic term for an unsolicited (in contrast to a solicited prophetic oracle) announcement of a prophet concerning future events or future actions of YHWH.

Prophetic announcement includes a variety of subgenres: (→) prophetic announcement of punishment; (→) prophetic announcement of punishment against an individual; (→) prophetic announcement of punishment against the people; (→) prophetic announcement of salvation; (→) prophetic announcement of a sign; (→) announcement of a royal savior; (→) prophecy concerning a foreign nation; (→) prophetic proof saying.

PROPHETIC ANNOUNCEMENT OF PUNISHMENT (Prophetische Gerichtsankündigung). The essential element of the (→) prophetic judgment speech, the

(→) prophetic announcement of punishment against an individual, and the (→) prophetic announcement of punishment against the people. When employed as part of these genres, the prophetic announcement of punishment follows an (→) accusation or other indication of the grounds for the punishment (Isa 22:17-24; Ezek 16:3-34, 36-43). It may also appear by itself as an independent genre (Isa 37:29; Ezek 5:14-15, 16-17). It is typically introduced by the (→) messenger formula, and it typically comprises intervention and results. The former heralds YHWH's coming acts in the 1st person, often introduced by *hinnēh,* "behold," and the latter presents the consequences of those acts in the 2nd or 3rd person.

Related genres: (→) Prophetic Announcement of Punishment against an Individual; (→) Prophetic Announcement of Punishment against the Nation; (→) Prophetic Judgment Speech.

C. Westermann, *Basic Forms of Prophetic Speech* (tr. H. C. White; Philadelphia: Westminster, 1967; repr. Cambridge: Lutterworth; Louisville: Westminster/John Knox, 1991) 149-61.

PROPHETIC ANNOUNCEMENT OF PUNISHMENT AGAINST AN INDIVIDUAL   (Gerichtsankündigung an den Einzelnen). A subgenre of the (→) prophetic announcement that announces disaster against an individual (cf. 1 Sam 2:27-36; Isa 22:16-24; Amos 7:14-17; Jer 20:1-6) or a group of individuals (cf. 1 Kgs 14:7-11; Jer 23:2, 9-12, 13-15) as punishment for a specified offense. It is distinguished from the (→) prophetic judgment speech in that it employs a more direct form of the (→) accusation against the individual. The basic two-part structure appears to be based on the sequence of an Israelite or Judean judicial proceeding: (1) the accusation in which the individual is confronted with the offense; and (2) the (→) prophetic announcement of punishment proper, which specifies YHWH's punishing actions as the consequence of the offense. The latter is typically introduced by *lākēn,* "therefore," and the (→) messenger formula. The genre serves as the basis for the (→) prophetic announcement of punishment against the people.

Related genres: (→) Prophetic Announcement; (→) Prophetic Announcement of Punishment against the People.

K. Koch, *The Growth of the Biblical Tradition* (tr. S. M. Cupitt; New York: Scribner's, 1969) 210-13; C. Westermann, *Basic Forms of Prophetic Speech* (tr. H. C. White; Philadelphia: Westminster, 1967; repr. Cambridge: Lutterworth; Louisville: Westminster/John Knox, 1991) 129-68; H. W. Wolff, "Die Begründungen der prophetischen Heils- und Unheilssprüche," in *Gesammelte Studien zum Alten Testament* (TBü 22; Munich: Kaiser, 1964) 9-35 (repr. from *ZAW* 52 [1934] 1-22).

PROPHETIC ANNOUNCEMENT OF PUNISHMENT AGAINST THE PEOPLE (Gerichtsankündigung über das Volk). A subgenre of the (→) prophetic announcement punishment against the entire nation (Amos 2:1-3, 4-5; 4:1-3; Hos 2:7-9; Isa 30:12-14; Mic 3:1-4) for a specified offense. It appears to be a later development from the (→) prophetic announcement of punishment against an individual. The structure is much more varied, but the basic components are the same and continue to reflect the sequence of Israelite and Judean court procedure: (1) a statement of the reasons for the punishment, generally in the form of an (→) accusation that accuses the nation of some offense deserving punishment; and (2) a (→) prophetic announcement of punishment proper, which specifies the consequences of the offense. Again, the latter is typically introduced by *lākēn*, "therefore," and the (→) messenger formula. The two components may be inverted to produce the (→) prophetic explanation of punishment (e.g., Isa 3:1-11; Jer 2:26-28; Amos 9:8-10).

Related genres: (→) Prophetic Announcement; (→) Prophetic Announcement of Punishment against an Individual; (→) Prophetic Explanation of Punishment.

K. Koch, *The Growth of the Biblical Tradition* (tr. S. M. Cupitt; New York: Scribner's, 1969) 210-13; C. Westermann, *Basic Forms of Prophetic Speech* (tr. H. C. White; Philadelphia: Westminster, 1967; repr. Cambridge: Lutterworth; Louisville: Westminster/John Knox, 1991) 169-89; H. W. Wolff, "Die Begründungen der prophetischen Heils- und Unheilssprüche," in *Gesammelte Studien zum Alten Testament* (TBü 22; Munich: Kaiser, 1964) 9-35 (repr. from *ZAW* 52 [1934] 1-22).

PROPHETIC ANNOUNCEMENT OF SALVATION (Prophetische Heilsankündigung). A subgenre of the (→) prophetic announcement of salvation or blessing to individuals, groups, or the nation (Isa 7:7-9; 29:22-24; Jer 28:2-4; 31:2-6; 34:4; Amos 9:11-12, 13-15; Mic 5:10-20). Westermann maintains that the genre is properly termed the "proclamation of salvation," and argues that the basic pattern includes a proclamation of deliverance followed by a blessing. The form has a long history, and it is employed to express the promise of the land (Exod 3:6-8), the promise of a king (Gen 49:10-12), the promise of a son (1 Sam 1:17-20, 21-28), and the promise of rescue from enemies (1 Sam 7:3-15). A crucial development in the genre takes place in the exilic period when Deutero-Isaiah derives the (→) oracle of salvation (Isa 41:8-13, 14-16; 43:1-7; 44:1-5) from an earlier priestly form. The new form included three elements: (1) the (→) reassurance formula, "fear not"; (2) the "basis of reassurance in the perfect tense or nominal form"; and (3) the "future-oriented basis, which is identical with the "proclamation of salvation" (Westermann, *Prophetic Oracles*, 42-43). This development sets the pattern for the independent examples of the form that announce deliverance from exile throughout the exilic and postexilic periods. The original setting is uncertain, although the association with the oracle of salvation suggests cultic oracular inquiry.

Related genres: (→) Prophetic Announcement; (→) Oracle of Salvation.

K. Koch, *The Growth of the Biblical Tradition* (tr. S. Cupitt; New York: Scribner's, 1969) 206-15; C. Westermann, *Prophetic Oracles of Salvation in the Old Testament* (tr. K. R. Crim; Louisville: Westminster/John Knox, 1991); H. W. Wolff, "Die Begründungen der prophetischen Heils- und Unheilssprüche," in *Gesammelte Studien zum Alten Testament* (TBü 22; Munich: Kaiser, 1964) 9-35 (repr. from *ZAW* 52 [1934] 1-22).

PROPHETIC ANNOUNCEMENT OF A SIGN (Prophetisches Zeichenankündigung). A subgenre of the (→) prophetic announcement that announces a future event as a means to confirm a prophetic word. Examples appear in 1 Kgs 13:3; Isa 7:14-17; 37:30-32 (= 2 Kgs 19:29-31); 38:7-8 (= 2 Kgs 20:9-10); Jer 44:29-30. Normally, the prophetic announcement of a sign comprises three major elements: (1) a declaration of an event as a "sign" from YHWH, e.g., "this is the sign to you from YHWH" (Isa 38:7a); (2) a subordinate clause that gives the significance of the sign, e.g., "that YHWH will do this thing that [YHWH] has promised" (38:7b); and (3) the description of the event that is to be taken as the sign. Sometimes the second element is missing, as the context supplies the significance (e.g., 37:30-32). The settings of such announcements would vary according to the circumstances in which prophets were active or accounts about them were written. The original setting for such announcements may have been related to oracular inquiry.

Related genre: (→) Prophetic Announcement.

PROPHETIC BOOK (Prophetisches Buch). The literary presentation of the sayings of a particular prophet. There is some question concerning the number of prophetic books in the Hebrew Bible because of uncertainty as to whether the "Book of the Twelve Prophets" constitutes a single prophetic book or twelve individual books. Each book begins either with a (→) superscription that identifies the following material as the "words," "vision," "pronouncement," of the prophet or with some variation that associates the following material with the prophet. The (→) superscription may also identify the historical circumstances of the prophet. Narratives may also be provided that aid in establishing the context of the prophet's activity and in expressing the prophet's message (e.g., Isa 6:1–9:6 [*RSV* 7]; 36–39; Jeremiah 26–29; 32–44; Ezekiel 1–11; Hosea 1–3; Amos 7:10-17; Jonah; Haggai; Zechariah 1–8). The examples of Isaiah and Zechariah demonstrate clearly that it is not necessary that all the material in the book is written by or about the prophet, even though the prophetic books present their contents as such.

The form of the prophetic book varies considerably because of the large number of generic elements that may be included. Prophetic books are collections only in the broadest sense of the term, insofar as they constitute a collection of the prophet's sayings. Research into the specific forms of entire prophetic books is just beginning, but it suggests that they are deliberately organized in accordance with the intentions of the editors who composed them. Thus Isaiah focuses on the fate or destiny of Zion; Jeremiah is portrayed as a prophet like Moses; and Ezekiel focuses on the purification of Jerusalem as the necessary prelude for restoration of the temple. Many scholars presuppose that prophetic books are organized according to a typical three-part pattern: (1) judgment against Israel; (2) judgment against the nations; and (3) eschatological blessings for Israel and the world (cf. Ezekiel; Jeremiah [LXX]). Other organizing principles may be implemented, such as the chronological arrangement (Ezekiel; Haggai; cf. Zechariah 1–8), a narrative sequence (Jonah), or generic patterns such as the (→) exhortation (Isaiah; Zephaniah), the (→) disputation (Nahum), or the (→) prophetic pronouncement (Habakkuk).

The liturgical character or contents of many of the prophetic books (e.g., Isaiah 12; 33; Joel; Habakkuk 3; Nahum) suggests that the setting for their composition and use was in the temple. During the Second Temple period, prophets appear to have served as functionaries in the temple rituals, and prophetic books appear to have been read as part of the liturgy.

R. E. Clements, "Patterns in the Prophetic Canon," in *Canon and Authority* (ed. G. W. Coats and B. O. Long; Philadelphia: Fortress, 1977) 42-55; idem, "The Prophet and His Editors," in *The Bible in Three Dimensions* (ed. D. J. A. Clines et al.; JSOTSup 87; Sheffield: JSOT Press, 1990) 203-20; R. M. Hals, *Ezekiel* (FOTL XIX; Grand Rapids: Eerdmans, 1989) 352-53.

PROPHETIC EXPLANATION OF PUNISHMENT (Prophetische Erklärung für Bestrafung). A modification of the (→) prophetic announcement of punishment in which the prophet explains that a current situation of disaster is a punishment imposed by YHWH and provides the reason for that punishment. Essentially, the form reverses the two constituent elements of the prophetic announcement of punishment by presenting the announcement of punishment first, followed by the reasons for the punishment. Examples appear in Isa 3:1-11; Jer 2:26-28; Ezek 22:23-31; 23:5-10; and Amos 9:8-10. The genre is both analytical and instructional in that it presupposes a current or past situation of disaster, identifies it as an act of YHWH, and then determines the causes that prompted YHWH to bring about the punishment in the first place. The setting is unclear, although it appears to relate to oracular or prophetic inquiry.

Related genres: (→) Prophetic Announcement; (→) Prophetic Announcement of Punishment against an Individual; (→) Prophetic Announcement of Punishment against the People.

PROPHETIC JUDGMENT SPEECH (Prophetische Urteilsrede, Prophetische Urteilswort). A subgenre of the (→) prophetic announcement in which the prophet speaks on behalf of YHWH to announce judgment against an individual, group, or nation. Examples appear in Isa 8:5-8; Jer 11:9-12; and Mic 3:9-12. The main elements of the genre are: (1) a statement of the reasons for judgment; (2) a logical transition, such as *lākēn,* "therefore," with the (→) messenger formula; and (3) the (→) prophetic announcement of punishment. Other elements, such as the (→) call to attention or the (→) oracular formula, may also appear. In the prophetic judgment speech, the prophet presents the reasons for judgment in his or her own words, followed by the prophet's report of the announcement of punishment by YHWH. This indirect means of stating the punishment and its grounds is the chief distinction between this genre and the (→) prophetic announcement of punishment, which generally employs direct address language to accuse and announce punishment.

Related genres: (→) Prophetic Announcement; (→) Prophetic Announcement of Punishment against an Individual; (→) Prophetic Announcement of Punishment against the People.

G. M. Tucker, *Form Criticism of the Old Testament* (Philadelphia: Fortress, 1971); C. Westermann, *Basic Forms of Prophetic Speech* (tr. H. C. White; Philadelphia: Westminster; repr. Cambridge: Lutterworth; Louisville: Westminster/John Knox, 1991) 129-209.

PROPHETIC LEGEND (Prophetenlegende). A subgenre of (→) narrative that focuses on the prophet as the main character and exemplar of virtue, goodness, piety, and divine favor. It is employed for a variety of purposes, chiefly to edify or inculcate religious devotion. A variety of subtypes have been identified: (1) the simple legenda (2 Kgs 2:19-22, 23-24; 4:1-7, 38-41, 42-44; 6:1-7; 13:20-21), which focuses on miracles to demonstrate the prophet's power; (2) elaborations on the legenda (2 Kgs 1:2-17a; 4:8-37), which display a more fully developed plot; (3) the vita (1 Kgs 19:19–2 Kgs 13:19), which presents a life of the prophet; (4) the political legenda (2 Kgs 6:8-23; 6:24–7:20), in which the prophet overcomes an enemy in the realm of politics who attempts to belittle the holy man; (5) prophetic historiography (1 Kings 9–10; 2 Kgs 18:13–19:37; cf. Isaiah 36–37), which focuses on the prophet as the central figure of a historical narrative; (6) prophetic biography (Jeremiah 26–36; 37–43), which attempts to present a historical account of the prophet's activities; (7) the ethical legenda (Num 20:1-13; 2 Kgs 4:1-7, 18-37; 5; 20:1-11; cf. Isaiah 38), which emphasizes the power of prayer; (8) the exemplum (1 Kings 22), which employs a historically recognized prophet as a means to teach moral lessons or proper conduct; (9) the (→) parable (Jonah; 1 Kings 13), which instructs by means of an imaginary incident; (10) the epic (1 Kgs 16:29–19:18), which focuses on an idea that governs the prophet's life; and (11) the martyrology (Jer 38:28b; 39:3, 11-14; 40:1-6), which presents a believer who risks his or her life by testifying to nonbelievers.

The setting for the prophetic legend appears to have been in the support groups that sometimes formed around a prophet and created the legends to venerate the master. A secondary setting appears to be in the historiographical tradition of Judah that produced historical works such as the DtrH.

Related genres: (→) Legend; (→) Narrative; (→) Prophetical Story.
A. Rofé, *The Prophetical Stories* (Jerusalem: Magnes, 1988).

PROPHETIC LITURGY (Prophetische Liturgie). See (→) Liturgy.

PROPHETIC PRONOUNCEMENT *(maśśā').* A prophetic discourse in which the prophet attempts to explain how YHWH's actions are manifested in the realm of human affairs. The genre is identified primarily by content and the specification of the text as a *maśśā'*, "pronouncement," in a (→) superscription (see Isa 13:1; 14:28; 15:1; 30:6; Nah 1:1; Hab 1:1; Zech 9:1; 12:1; Mal 1:1). The prophetic pronouncement is spoken in response to a particular situation in human events; it is analytical in character in that it examines past and present events in an attempt to draw conclusions about YHWH's activity and intentions. The pronouncement appears to be based on a revelatory experience or vision, which may indicate that the setting is to be found in relation to oracular inquiry or incubation rituals (see Jer 23:16-40; cf. Num 24:3, 21, 23).

Related genre: (→) Prophecy Concerning a Foreign Nation.

R. D. Weis, "A Definition of the Genre *Maśśā'* in the Hebrew Bible" (Diss., Claremont Graduate School, 1986).

PROPHETIC PROOF SAYING (Prophetisches Erweiswort). A subgenre of the (→) prophetic announcement in which the prophet, speaking on behalf of YHWH, announces punishment against an individual, group, or nation, and argues that this punishment will convince the recipient to recognize YHWH's sovereign identity. This genre appears in 1 Kgs 20:13, 28; very frequently in Ezekiel (e.g., Ezek 25:2-3, 6-7, 8-11, 15-17; 26:2-6); and in Isa 41:17-20; 49:22-26.

The main elements are: (1) the (→) prophetic announcement of punishment and (2) the recognition formula. These two combine to constitute a two-part prophetic proof saying (e.g., Ezek 12:19-20). When, as is often the case, a statement of the reason for punishment and a logical transition are prefixed to the prophetic announcement of punishment, the result is a three-part prophetic proof saying (e.g., Ezek 25:6-7, 8b-11).

Related genre: (→) Prophetic Announcement.

R. M. Hals, *Ezekiel* (FOTL XIX; Grand Rapids: Eerdmans, 1989) 353-54; W. Zimmerli, "The Word of Divine Self-manifestation (Proof-Saying): A Prophetic Genre," in *I Am YHWH* (tr. D. W. Stott; Atlanta: John Knox, 1982) 99-110; idem, *Ezekiel 1* (tr. R. E. Clements; Hermeneia; Philadelphia: Fortress, 1979) 38-39.

PROPHETIC SPEECH (Prophetische Rede). Any speech given by a prophet. The term is thus a broad functional one, defined sociologically. Because it has no other specific defining characteristics, it is too comprehensive to serve as a specific genre designation. Prophetic speech may be formulated as any specific speech form: (→) messenger speech, (→) oracle, (→) prophetic announcement, etc.

K. Koch, *The Growth of the Biblical Tradition* (tr. S. Cupitt; New York: Scribner's, 1969) 183-220; G. M. Tucker, "Prophetic Speech," *Int* 32 (1978) 31-45; C. Westermann, *Basic Forms of Prophetic Speech* (tr. H. C. White; Philadelphia: Westminster, 1967; repr. Cambridge: Lutterworth; Louisville: Westminster/John Knox, 1991); idem, *Prophetic Oracles of Salvation in the Old Testament* (tr. K. Crim; Louisville: Westminster/John Knox, 1991).

PROPHETIC STORY (Prophetenerzählung). A type of (→) historical story in which a prophetic figure plays a central role and carries the interpretative motifs that express the narrator's interests (e.g., Isaiah 39). According to Long, the prophetic story is similar in many respects to the (→) prophetic legend, except that it intends simply to report a historically plausible event rather than to edify, entertain, or instruct. It may therefore be identified with the prophetic historiography or prophetic biography that Rofé identifies as a subcategory of prophetic legend.

Related genres: (→) Prophetic Legend; (→) Historical Story.

B. O. Long, *2 Kings* (FOTL X; Grand Rapids: Eerdmans, 1991) 301; A. Rofé, *The Prophetical Stories* (Jerusalem: Magnes, 1988).

PROPHETIC TORAH (Prophetische Tora). See (→) Priestly Torah.

QUESTION-AND-ANSWER SCHEMA (Frage und Antwort Schema). A literary device that projects a question and its answer as a means of describing a future situation. One type assumes a disaster and assigns reasons and responsibility for it, thus elaborating on implicit admonitions to avoid the behavior which will lead to such an end. Typical are Jer 22:8-9; 1 Kgs 9:8-9; and Deut 29:21-24. All of these are from the Deuteronomistic writers who placed national destruction in the context of broken covenant and realized covenantal curses. Parallels are in the commemorative royal inscriptions of Ashurbanipal (e.g., *ANET,* 300). A second type appears as a divine speech addressed to a prophet, envisions a situation in which someone will ask a question, and suggests the answer that will be given. Examples are Jer 23:33; 5:19; 13:12-14; Ezek 21:12; and 37:19. Literary function varies according to biblical context. Models for this device derive apparently from situations in which a person sought oracles through a prophet.

B. O. Long, "Two Question and Answer Schemata in the Prophets," *JBL* 90 (1971) 129-39.

REPORT (Bericht). A brief, self-contained prose narrative, usually in 3rd-person style, about a single event or situation in the past. In contrast to story or (→) legend, a report has no developed plot or imaginative characterization. Insofar as there is action, report differs from statement or description. Varying in length from a very short notice to a longer, even composite account, reports can carry diverse content. Some types of report, defined by structure and content, take on special importance in the Hebrew Bible, such as (→) theophany report, (→) vision report, or (→) report of a symbolic action. The setting for report would vary according to content and purpose.

REPORT OF AN EXPRESSIVE ACTION (Bericht Einer Ausdruckshandlung). A report of a gesture or simple bodily action used to express or accompany an emotion or message. In contrast to the relatively complex (→) report of a symbolic action, this genre portrays a relatively simple gesture or action, such as clapping the hands or stamping the foot (cf. Ezek 6:11) to embody or enhance the power of a prophetic message.

Related genre: (→) Report of a Symbolic Action.

R. M. Hals, *Ezekiel* (FOTL XIX; Grand Rapids: Eerdmans, 1989) 354.

REPORT OF A SYMBOLIC ACTION (Symbolische Handlung). The report of an incident in which a prophet accompanies a pronouncement with an action understood as a symbolic sign. The action functions as a dramatic means to symbolize YHWH's intentions or actions toward the people and to confirm the prophetic statement. Examples appear in Hosea 1–3; Isa 7:3; 8:1-4; 20:1-6; Jer 13:1-11; Ezek 4:1–5:17, etc. (cf. 1 Kgs 22:11). The genre typically includes three basic elements: (1) an instruction to perform a symbolic act; (2) the report that the act was performed; and (3) a statement that interprets the significance of the act. Although Fohrer relates the form to sympathetic magic that compels action in the prescribed manner, Stacey's analysis of its dramatic and cultic elements indicates that these actions function merely to introduce and express divine action, thereby reinforcing the prophet's message.

Related genres: (→) Report; (→) Prophetic Legend.

G. Fohrer, "Die Gattung der Berichte über symbolische Handlungen der Propheten," in *Studien zur alttestamentlichen Prophetie (1949-1965)* (BZAW 99; Berlin: Töpelmann, 1967) 92-112 (repr. from *ZAW* 64 [1952] 101-20; idem, "Prophetie und Magie," in ibid., 265-93; idem, *Die symbolischen Handlungen der Propheten* (2nd ed.; ATANT 54; Zurich: Zwingli, 1968); W. D. Stacey, *Prophetic Drama in the Old Testament* (London: Epworth, 1990).

RHETORICAL QUESTION (Rhetorische Frage). A question asked for its rhetorical or telling effect that does not require a reply. It occurs frequently in argument and persuasion, and as a subgenre in numerous genres of the Hebrew Bible. It appears often in Isaiah's speeches (e.g., Isa 1:5a; 1:12b; 3:15a; 5:4; 8:19b; 10:8-9). The supposition is that the answer is clear, usually the only one possible, and a deeper impression is made on the hearer by the question form than by the statement.

D. Sweeney, "What's a Rhetorical Question?" *Lingua Aegyptia* 1 (1991) 315-31.

ROYAL LETTER (Königsbrief). A type of royal inscription known in ancient Mesopotamia. It is generally addressed to deities as a means to appeal for deliverance from calamity or sickness, or to thank the deity for deliverance. Hezekiah's "letter" in Isa 38:9-20 appears to be a Judean example of a royal letter formulated as a (→) thanksgiving song of the individual, in this case for deliverance from sickness.

W. W. Hallo, "The Royal Correspondence of Larsa: I. A Sumerian Prototype for the Prayer of Hezekiah," in *Kramer Anniversary Volume* (ed. B. L. Eicher; AOAT 25; Kevelaer: Butzon & Bercker; Neukirchen-Vluyn: Neukirchener, 1976) 209-24.

ROYAL NARRATIVE (Königsnovelle). A genre of ancient Egyptian literature that presents the king as an ideal figure of strength, piety, and success. The literary forms vary, but the intent is clearly propagandistic. Examples appear in M. Lichtheim, *Ancient Egyptian Literature* (3 vols.; Berkeley: University of California, 1973-81) 1:115-18, 2:57-72; and J. H. Breasted, ed., *Ancient Records of Egypt* (5 vols.; Chicago: University of Chicago, 1906-1907) 2:131-66; 3:251-81. The portrayal of David's Rise in 1-

2 Samuel may well represent an Israelite example of this genre. Other examples appear in 1 Kings 3–11 and Isaiah 38 (cf. Isaiah 36–37).

S. Herrmann, "Die Königsnovelle in Ägypten und in Israel," in *Gesammelte Studien zur Geschichte und Theologie des Alten Testaments* (TBü 75; Munich: Kaiser, 1986) 120-44 (repr. from *Wissenschaftliche Zeitschrift der Univ. Leipzig,* 3 Jg. Ges. u. sprachwiss. Reihe Heft 1 [1953-54] 51-62).

ROYAL PSALM (Königspsalm, Königslied). Not an indigenous genre, but any psalm type (e.g., complaint, thanksgiving, hymn) that is adapted to fit royal etiquette and court ritual. Examples from the Psalter appear in Psalm 18 (→ communal thanksgiving song); Psalm 21 (an intercession oracle for the king); Psalm 45 (a royal wedding song); Psalm 72 (a prayer for the king). Isa 9:1-6 (*RSV* 2-7) and 38:9-20 represent two examples of a royal psalm of thanksgiving, the former for the birth of a new king and the latter for deliverance from sickness.

E. S. Gerstenberger, *Psalms, Part 1; with an Introduction to Cultic Poetry* (FOTL XIV; Grand Rapids: Eerdmans, 1988) 19.

ROYAL PSALM OF THANKSGIVING (Königsdanklied). A psalm that combines elements of the (→) royal psalm and the (→) thanksgiving song of the individual in order to celebrate the enthronement of a new king (e.g., Isa 9:1-6 [RSV 2-7]).

SCHEMA OF REPRIEVE (Schematische Darstellung von Strafaufschub, Strafmilderung, or Begnadigung). A pattern of literary motifs characteristic of the final shape of heavily redacted portions of the Hebrew Bible. Typically, it includes: (1) description of penitence that follows on an event of divine punishment, or the promise of such; and (2) a (→) prophetic announcement of salvation that mitigates the punishment, or a report of such an event. The language is stereotyped. Penitents "rend" their garments, dress in sackcloth, and fast. The prophecy, which typically includes an allusion to penitence, gives the justification for reprieve, and then announces that the punishment has been set aside or mitigated in some way. Examples are: 1 Kgs 21:27-29; 2 Kgs 22:19-20; 2 Sam 12:13-14; and 2 Chr 12:7-8. Although schema of reprieve may be a kind of "stock scene" at home with Israelite storytellers, it appears more likely that this literary scheme had its origin in the redacting and shaping hands that organized large blocks of biblical tradition.

SELF-DISCLOSURE ORACLE (Prophetisches Erweiswort). See (→) Prophetic Proof Saying.

SIMILE (Similie). A speech form closely related to figurative or metaphorical language in which two essentially unlike things are compared. The purpose of the genre is to instruct the reader or listener by means of the comparison. The form employs the preposition *kĕmô,* "like," or the prefixed form *kĕ,* "like," to establish the comparison.

SONG (Lied). A poetic composition intended for public performance by an individual singer or a group. The performance of songs could be accompanied by musical instruments. The Hebrew Bible includes various noncultic songs, such as working songs (Num 21:17-18; Judg 9:27), love songs or wedding songs (Canticles; Psalm 45), drinking songs (Amos 6:4-6; cf. Isa 5:11-13), battle songs (Exod 15:20-21; Num 10:35-36; 1 Sam 18:6-7), funeral songs (→ dirge), and mocking songs (Isa 14:4b-23; 23:15-16; Num 21:27-30).

SONG OF PRAISE (Loblied). See (→) Hymn of Praise.

SPEECH (Rede). A general term employed for any oral communication. Speeches may appear in a wide variety of forms depending on the circumstances of the speaker, the addressee, the situation addressed, and the setting of the speech.

SUMMARY-APPRAISAL (Zusammentassende Abschlussformel). A statement attached to the end of a literary unit that offers both a summary and an appraisal of the preceding material. The formula consists of a demonstrative pronoun (e.g., *zeh, zō't,* "this"), and usually has a bicolon structure. It is reflective and didactic in character, and it often contains technical wisdom terminology. Its setting appears to be in wisdom instruction (see Prov 1:19; Job 8:13; 18:21; 20:29; Qoh 4:8; Ps 49:14), but it is also employed by prophets (cf. Isa 14:26; 17:14; 28:29; Jer 13:25).

    B. S. Childs, *Isaiah and the Assyrian Crisis* (SBT 2/3; London: SCM, 1967) 128-36; J. W. Whedbee, *Isaiah and Wisdom* (Nashville: Abingdon, 1971) 75-79.

SUMMONS TO WAR (Aufforderung zum Kampf). A speech form employed in the context of holy war to call warriors to battle. The basic form includes: (1) the summons proper; and (2) the motivation, which usually refers to imminent intervention by YHWH (cf. Judg 3:28; 4:6-7, 14; 7:9).

    The prophets frequently employ the genre in the context of an (→) announcement of judgment. Prophetic versions generally include a mobilization call, expressed with masculine plural imperative verbs, which refer to attack (Jer 46:9; 49:14, 28, 31; 50:29; 51:27; Joel 4:9), preparation of weapons (Jer 46:4; 50:14; 51:11; Joel 4:10 [*RSV* 3:10]), or the destruction of the enemy (Jer 5:10; 6:5; 50:16, 21, 26; Mic 4:13). An announcement of judgment then follows in which the speaker can be YHWH (Jer 49:15; Joel 4:12 [*RSV* 3:12]; Mic 4:13) or the prophet (Isa 13:4; Jer 46:10; Joel 4:14 [*RSV* 3:14]).

    R. Bach, *Die Aufforderung zur Flucht und zum Kampf im alttestamentlichen Prophetenspruch* (WMANT 9; Neukirchen: Neukirchener, 1962) 51-91.

SUPERSCRIPTION (Überschrift). A statement prefixed to a literary work, such as a book, collection, song, oracle, etc. The term refers to the place of this statement in the structure of a work, namely, preceding its body (as opposed to a subscription, which follows the conclusion of the body).

The superscription may consist of a variety of elements, such as author, addressee, title, date, location, or genre. While the composition of most of these elements can vary, superscriptions in the Hebrew Bible ordinarily identify the character of the work, either in the concise definition form of a title ("This Is the Book of the Generations of Adam," Gen 5:1; 2:4a; "A Psalm of David," Ps 101:1; "The Proverbs of Solomon, Son of David, King of Israel," Prov 1:1), or in a more elaborate form (e.g., Jer 1:1-3). Superscriptions normally appear at the beginning of the prophetic books in various forms, which generally include a brief indication of author, date, and subject (e.g., Isa 1:1; Amos 1:1; Mic 1:1; Zech 1:1). They also may appear before textual blocks within the book (e.g., Isa 2:1 [chs. 2–4]; 13:1 [chs. 13–23]; Jer 46:1 [chs. 46–51]) or before individual compositions within the book (e.g., Isa 14:28; 15:1; 38:9; Jer 7:1; 11:1; Hab 3:1; Hag 2:1; Zech 1:7; 9:1; 12:1).

Although superscriptions may function as titles (cf. 2 Chr 32:32; Isa 1:1), they differ from titles generically in that a title refers to the distinguishing name of a work, whether it is a superscription or not. Superscriptions apparently find their setting in the scribal activity of the tradents of biblical literature, who studied, interpreted, composed, and transmitted the works to which superscriptions were added.

G. M. Tucker, "Prophetic Superscriptions and the Growth of the Canon," in *Canon and Authority* (ed. G. W. Coats and B. O. Long; Philadelphia: Fortress, 1977) 56-70.

TAUNT (Verspottung, Verhöhnung). An utterance or composition designed to denigrate its object. The taunt may appear in a war setting, in which opponents battle with words prior to the actual combat (e.g., 1 Sam 17:43, 44; 1 Kgs 20:11), in the context of negotiations in which one party wishes to intimidate the other (e.g., 1 Kgs 12:10b), or in prophetic speech in which the prophet attempts to belittle the addressee (Isa 23:15-16; Jer 22:14-15). The taunt may also take the form of a mocking or taunting song (e.g., Isa 14:4-23).

THANKSGIVING SONG OF THE INDIVIDUAL (Danklied des Einzelnen). A psalm sung by or on behalf of an individual recently delivered from personal distress, which expresses gratitude to YHWH for intervention and deliverance. The elements are the same as those of the (→) communal thanksgiving song: (1) a call to sing (or to give thanks or praise); (2) an account of the past trouble and salvation; (3) praise for YHWH (or YHWH's works); (4) announcement of sacrifice; (5) blessings; and (6) a vow or pledge. The (→) thanksgiving formula, "I thank thee . . . ," commonly appears as part of the song.

The setting appears to have been in the context of the temple, in which the individual presented thanks and sacrifices to YHWH for deliverance. Examples appear in Psalms 30; 32; 92; and Jonah 2. The (→) royal psalm is a special type reserved for the king (e.g., Isa 9:1-6 [*RSV* 2-7]; 38:9-20).

Related genres: (→) Communal Thanksgiving Song; (→) Hymn of Praise.

W. Beyerlin, "Die tôdâ der Heilsvergegenwärtigung in den Klageliedern des Einzelnen," *ZAW* 79 (1967) 208-44; F. Crüsemann, *Studien zur Formgeschichte von Hymnus und Danklied in Israel* (WMANT 32; Neukirchen: Neukirchener, 1969); E. Gerstenberger, *Psalms, Part 1; with an Introduction to Cultic Poetry* (FOTL XIV; Grand Rapids: Eerdmans, 1988) 14-16; C. Westermann, *Praise and Lament in the Psalms* (tr. K. R. Crim and R. N. Soulen; 2nd ed.; Atlanta: John Knox, 1981).

THEOPHANY REPORT (Gotteserscheinung). A genre that depicts the manifestation of YHWH, generally in poetic form. It contains two characteristic elements: (1) a description of YHWH's approach; and (2) a description of the accompanying natural upheaval, such as wind, fire, storm, etc., together with reactions of fear and awe. Examples appear in Deut 33:2; Judg 5:4-5; Amos 1:2; Mic 1:3-4; Ps 68:8-9; cf. 1 Kgs 19:9-14. Either element may be expanded with additional motifs (cf. Isa 19:1; 26:21; 30:27-33; Nah 1:2-6; Hab 3:3-12; Pss 97:2-5; 114:3-7). The original setting may have been in celebrations of military victory intended to praise YHWH for granting success. Elements of the theophany report appear in various literary contexts, such as (→) hymns (Ps 97:2-5), narrative literature (1 Kgs 19:9-14), and prophetic texts (Isa 19:1-4; 26:21; Ezek 1:4-28).

J. Jeremias, *Theophanie: Die Geschichte einer alttestamentlichen Gattung* (WMANT 10; Neukirchen-Vluyn: Neukirchener, 1965).

TRIAL GENRES (Gerichtsreden). A collecting term for generic elements related to legal procedure and the context of the law court. The setting may be the jurisdiction of the civil courts held at the gates of a city (cf. Ruth 4:1-12), the sacral jurisdiction of the sanctuaries (Joshua 7; Jeremiah 26), or the royal court (2 Sam 12:1-6; 1 Kgs 3:16-28). Legal genres and formulas appear in many situations of daily life; they are especially prevalent in the prophets, where they appear to have had some influence on the (→) prophetic announcements of punishment, the (→) prophetic judgment speech, and prophetic forms of (→) instruction.

One characteristic prophetic form of the trial genres is the so-called trial speech, often identified as the "*rîb*-pattern" or the "(covenant) lawsuit" form. Examples appear in Isaiah 1; Jeremiah 2; Hosea 4; Micah 6; and various other texts, especially in Deutero-Isaiah. The term *rîb* means "controversy" and can refer to a legal case brought by one party against another; in the case of the prophets, it typically refers to YHWH's case against Israel for violation of the terms of the covenant between YHWH and Israel (cf. Isa 3:13; Jer 2:9; Hos 4:1; Mic 6:1-2). Characteristic elements might include a (→) call to attention (Isa 1:2; Hos 4:1; Jer 2:4; Mic 6:1-2); an appeal for a legal proceeding (Isa 1:18-20); an (→) accusation (Isa 1:2-20; 3:12-15; Hos 4:4-8; Jer 2:5-34); (→) rhetorical questions (Isa 1:5, 12; 3:15; Jer 2:5, 14, 31-32); and, finally, an (→) announcement of judgment (Jer 2:35-37; Hos 4:4-10) or some form of (→) instruction in proper behavior (Isa 1:10-17; Mic 6:6-8).

H. J. Boecker, *Redeformen des Rechtslebens im Alten Testament* (2nd ed.; WMANT 14; Neukirchen-Vluyn: Neukirchener, 1970); J. Harvey, *Le plaidoyer prophétique contre Israël après la rupture de l'alliance* (Montreal: Bellarmin, 1967); K. Nielsen, *Yahweh as Prosecutor and Judge* (JSOTSup 9; Sheffield: JSOT Press, 1978).

VISION REPORT (Visionsbericht, Visionsschilderung). The description by a prophet of what he or she sees (vision) or hears (audition) in an inner prophetic perception. Visual elements are frequently introduced by *hinnēh,* "behold," and auditory elements are frequently introduced by an indication of a speech by YHWH. Horst identifies three basic types: (1) the "presence vision," which recounts the prophet's experience of the presence of YHWH (Isaiah 6; Jer 1:4-10; Ezek 1:4-28); (2) the "word assonance vision," in which the vision is based on a wordplay or an object that symbolizes a word of YHWH (Jer 1:11-12, 13-15; Amos 8:1-3); and (3) the "event vision," in which the vision is conveyed through the depiction of a future event (Isa 13:4-5; 21:1-9; Nah 3:1-3). Long's analysis likewise results in three types: (1) the "oracle vision," which employs a question-and-answer dialogue to present the meaning of a simple image (Amos 7:7-8; Jer 1:11-14); (2) the "dramatic word vision," which depicts a heavenly scene to convey a word of YHWH (Amos 7:1-6; Isaiah 6; Ezek 9:1-10); and (3) the "revelatory-mysteries-vision," in which a divine guide conveys the secrets of YHWH's activity and future events (Zech 2:3-4; 4:1-6a; cf. Daniel 8; 10–12).

The original setting of prophetic vision reports may have been in the context of divination or oracular inquiry. In their literary contexts, they authenticate and convey the prophetic message.

F. Horst, "Die Visionsschilderungen der alttestamentlichen Propheten," *EvT* 20 (1960) 193-205; B. O. Long, "Reports of Visions Among the Prophets," *JBL* 95 (1976) 353-65; M. Sister, "Die Typen der prophetischen Visionen in der Bibel," *MGWJ* 78 (1934) 399-430.

VOCATION ACCOUNT (Prophetischer Berufungsbericht). A genre in which a prophet or the prophetic tradition refers to the initiatory commission of the prophet. The vocation account may be presented in an autobiographical (e.g., Isaiah 6; Jeremiah 1; Ezekiel 1) or an objective narrative form (e.g., Exodus 3; Judges 6; 1 Kings 22). There are two basic types: the first focuses on the visionary element in which the prophet sees the heavenly court of YHWH (1 Kings 22; Isaiah 6; Ezekiel 1); the second subordinates all elements to the word of YHWH (Exodus 3; Jeremiah 1; Ezek 2:1–3:15). Habel identifies a number of relatively consistent elements, including: (1) a divine confrontation; (2) an introductory word; (3) a (→) commission; (4) an objection by the prophet; (5) a reassurance; and (6) a sign. In general, the vocation account authenticates the prophet as a spokesperson for YHWH, and aids in expressing the prophet's overall message.

N. Habel, "The Form and Significance of the Call Narratives," *ZAW* 77 (1965) 297-323; W. Richter, *Die sogenannten vorprophetischen Berufungsberichte* (FRLANT 101; Göttingen: Vandenhoeck & Ruprecht, 1970); H. Wildberger, *Jesaja 1–12* (BKAT X/1; Neukirchen-Vluyn: Neukirchener, 1972) 234-39; W. Zimmerli, *Ezekiel 1* (tr. R. E. Clements; Hermeneia; Philadelphia: Fortress, 1979) 97-100.

Vow (Gelübde). A solemn promise to God usually including a protasis, often introduced by *'im,* "if," or *'im-lō,* if not," and an apodosis. During affliction it was customary to make a promise to YHWH (cf. Gen 28:20-22; Judg 11:30-31; 2 Sam 15:7-8). Consequently, (→) complaint songs and (→) thanksgiving psalms reflect this usage and give it a liturgical form, in which the vow may become an element of prayer (Pss 22:26 [RSV 25]; 56:13 [RSV 12]; 61:6, 9 [RSV 5, 8]; 116:14, 18).

WISDOM SAYING (Weisheitsspruch). A short didactic saying, based on experience or tradition, that inculcates some value or lesson. It occurs most commonly in Proverbs (e.g., Proverbs 10), where it is expressed in various kinds of parallelism. In contrast to the proverb, however, the wisdom saying is directly didactic; it teaches, and does not leave an issue as an open question. It can appear in the prophetic literature as well (e.g., Isa 3:10-11; cf. 2:22).

WOE ORACLE (Wehruf). A type of (→) prophetic announcement used to criticize particular actions or attitudes of the people, and to announce punishment against them. Woe oracles may appear as individual units (Amos 5:18-20; Isa 1:4; 3:11; 10:5; Nah 3:1; Hab 3:1) or in a series (Isa 5:8-24; 28–33; Hab 2:6-20). The form is identified by the "woe statement," which includes the introductory exclamation, *hôy,* "woe!" followed by a participle or noun that characterizes the action or people in question negatively, and additional material that elaborates on the initial woe statement with a variety of forms. The origins of the genre are disputed; proposals include wisdom circles (Gerstenberger, Wolff, Whedbee), the curse (Westermann), and the funeral ritual (Clifford, Janzen, Hardmeier, Wanke, Williams). Apart from its origin, it functions basically as a rhetorical device in prophetic literature to catch the attention of the audience (see, e.g., Zech 2:10 [*RSV* 6]).

R. J. Clifford, "The Use of *HÔY* in the Prophets," *CBQ* 28 (1966) 458-64; E. Gerstenberger, "The Woe-Oracles of the Prophets," *JBL* 81 (1962) 249-63; C. Hardmeier, *Texttheorie und biblische Exegese* (BEvT 79; Munich: Kaiser, 1978); W. Janzen, *Mourning Cry and Woe Oracle* (BZAW 125; Berlin and New York: de Gruyter, 1972); G. Wanke, "*'ôy* und *hôy,*" *ZAW* 78 (1966) 215-18; C. Westermann, *Basic Forms of Prophetic Speech* (tr. H. C. White; Philadelphia: Westminster, 1967; repr. Cambridge: Lutterworth; Louisville: Westminster/John Knox, 1991) 190-98; J. W. Whedbee, *Isaiah and Wisdom* (Nashville: Abingdon, 1971) 80-110; J. G. Williams, "The Alas-Oracles of the Eighth Century Prophets," *HUCA* 38 (1967) 75-91; H. W. Wolff, *Amos the Prophet: The Man and His Background* (tr. F. R. McCurley; Philadelphia: Fortress, 1973) 17-34.

ZION HYMN (Zionshymnus). A derivative form of the (→) hymn of praise that focuses on Zion as the abode of YHWH and the principal locale of Israelite and Judean worship (e.g., Psalms 46; 48; 76; 84; 87; 122; 132; 137; cf. Isa 2:2-4). Because of the interrelationship between monarchy and temple, Zion hymns are generally considered as part of the (→) royal psalms.

> E. Gerstenberger, *Psalms, Part 1; with an Introduction to Cultic Poetry* (FOTL XIV; Grand Rapids: Eerdmans, 1988) 19, 258.

FORMULAS

bayyôm hahû' FORMULA (*bajjom hahu'* Formel). A characteristic prophetic formula employed at the beginning of (→) Prophetic Announcements concerning some future event. The formula generally appears as b*ayyôm hahû'*, "in that day," *wĕhayâ bayyôm hahû'*, "and it shall come to pass in that day," or some variation.

CALL TO A PUBLIC COMPLAINT SERVICE (Aufruf zur Volksklage). A public announcement that calls the population to a public complaint ceremony in cases of a national emergency (drought, Jer 14:1ff.; enemy from the outside, 2 Chronicles 20). In this ceremony, YHWH is invoked to intervene in order to "proclaim" or to "sanctify a fast" (*qārā'* or *qiddaš ṣôm;* cf. 1 Kgs 21:9, 12; Joel 1:14; 2:15).

CALL TO ATTENTION FORMULA (Aufmerksamkeitsruf, Aufforderung zum Hören, Lehreröffnungsformel). A formula that opens a public presentation or address, and intends to attract the attention of the hearers to the speech that follows. The constituent elements are: (1) an invitation to listen; (2) mention of the addressee(s); and (3) an indication of what is to be heard.

> This call would commonly be employed by a singer (cf. Judg 5:3), a wisdom teacher (cf. Prov 7:24), or an official envoy (cf. 2 Kgs 18:28-29). It appears frequently in the prophetic literature in various forms, often expanded by relative clauses (see Amos 3:1; Hos 4:1; Mic 6:1; Isa 1:10; Ezek 6:3).

> K. Koch, *The Growth of the Biblical Tradition* (tr. S. Cupitt; New York: Scribner's, 1969) 205; B. O. Long, *2 Kings* (FOTL X; Grand Rapids: Eerdmans, 1991) 319; I. Lande, *Formelhafte Wendungen der Umganssprache im Alten Testament* (Leiden: Brill, 1949) 13-14; H. W. Wolff, *Hosea* (tr. G. Stansell; Hermeneia; Philadelphia: Fortress, 1974) 65-66; S. J. De Vries, *1 and 2 Chronicles* (FOTL XI; Grand Rapids: Eerdmans, 1989) 437.

CALL TO FLEE FORMULA (Aufforderung zur Flucht). A formula employed to alert the people to take refuge from danger in times of war (e.g., 1 Sam 15:6). Its setting is holy war, and it is frequently imitated by Jeremiah in his announcements concerning foreign nations (e.g., Jer 48:6-8, 18; 49:30;

50:8-10; 51:6, 45; cf. Zech 2:10-13). Constituent elements include: (1) an indication of the addressee and masculine plural imperatives urging flight from an imminent disaster; and (2) reference to the disaster, introduced by *kî*, "for," "because."

Related genre: (→) Summons to War.

R. Bach, *Die Aufforderungen zur Flucht und zum Kampf im alttestamentlichen Prophetenspruch* (WMANT 9; Neukirchen: Neukirchener, 1962).

CALL TO MOURN FORMULA (Aufforderung zum Trauern). See (→) Call for a Communal Complaint.

CALL TO WORSHIP FORMULA (Ruf zur Anbetung, Aufruf zum Lob). A formula that summons the people to sing, play, give thanks, shout, or clap hands in honor of YHWH. The basic form is:

Sing to YHWH:
Yea, he is great!

Examples appear in Exod 15:21b; Deut 32:43; Isa 12:4-6; Jer 20:13; Pss 9:12-13 (*RSV* 11-14); 106:1; 107:1; 117:1-2; 118:1-4; and 136:1. These imperative summons were probably voiced by an officiant while the second line containing the praise proper would have been sung or shouted by the community. It likely served as the introductory or closing part of hymn singing.

COMMISSIONING FORMULA (Aussendungsformel). The essential part of an authoritative charge to a messenger or emissary to deliver a message on behalf of the sender. The standard wording is "Go and say to PN" plus the identification of the addressee. The (→) messenger formula and message then normally follow. Examples appear in Gen 32:5; 1 Kgs 14:7a; 2 Kgs 18:19; 19:6; Isa 7:3-4; 36:4; 37:6; 38:4; Ezek 3:1b, 4b, and 11a.

EXCLAMATION OF DISTRESS (Schreckensruf). A stereotypical exclamation that expresses the speaker's distress, fear, or horror. Components include the outcry (*'ôy*, "woe"), followed by *lĕ* ("to") with a suffix indicating the person involved, and a phrase usually beginning with *kî* ("for") that mentions the cause of the exclamation. Examples appear in Num 21:29; 1 Sam 4:7; Isa 3:9, 11; 6:4; Jer 4:13 and 31. The exclamation of distress is sometimes formulated as a question (e.g., Num 24:23; 1 Sam 4:8; Jer 13:27).

G. Wanke, *"'ôy und hôy,"* ZAW 78 (1966) 215-18.

IMPRECATION FORMULA (Böseformel). The formula *'im-lō'*, "if not," or "surely," which expresses the emphatic affirmative to imply retribution in cases where a vow or oath is not fulfilled (Gen 24:37-38; Ps 131:2; cf. Ps 132:1-5). The imprecation formula sometimes appears in the context of prophetic speech, where it is spoken by YHWH to emphasize the surety of divine action (Isa 5:9; 14:24-25; 22:14; Jer 15:11; 49:20-21).

MESSENGER FORMULA (Botenformel). The formula *kōh 'āmar PN,* "Thus says PN," which normally introduces a (→) messenger speech. It seems to have originated in the ancient and widespread practice of the oral transmission of a message by means of a third party. The formula normally occurs twice in the following sequence: (1) it is spoken by the sender who commissions and instructs the messenger (cf. Gen 32:5; 45:9); (2) it is reiterated by the messenger at the delivery of the message (cf. 2 Kgs 18:29/Isa 36:14; Num 22:15-16).

In some prophetic books, the specific messenger formula "Thus says YHWH" *(kōh 'āmar yhwh)* occurs frequently (especially in Jeremiah and Ezekiel, but not in Hosea, Joel, Habakkuk, or Zechariah). This usage implies that a prophet delivering a message is understood in analogy with the practice of commissioning, instructing, and sending a messenger.

The shorter formula, *'āmar yhwh,* "says YHWH," which is derived from the messenger formula, is used like the (→) oracular formula in the beginning, at the end, or in the middle of a word of God.

Related genre: (→) Messenger Speech.

S. Meier, *The Messenger in the Ancient Semitic World* (HSM 45; Atlanta: Scholars Press, 1988); idem, *Speaking of Speaking: Marking Direct Discourse in the Hebrew Bible* (VTSup 46; Leiden: Brill, 1992) 273-98; C. Westermann, *Basic Forms of Prophetic Speech* (tr. H. C. White; Philadelphia: Westminster, 1967; repr. Cambridge: Lutterworth; Louisville: Westminster/John Knox, 1991) 98-115.

OATH FORMULA (Schwurformel). The formula *ḥāy yhwh,* "as YHWH lives," which usually introduces an (→) oath.

ORACULAR FORMULA (Gottesspruchformel). The formula *ně'ûm-yhwh,* "utterance of YHWH," which labels a prophetic speech (or a part of it) as a word of God. Its place may be at the beginning, the middle, or the end of a prophetic speech. The setting of the formula appears to be the (→) vision report of the seer (cf. 2 Sam 23:1; Num 24:3).

Related genre: (→) Oracle.

F. Baumgartel, "Die Formel *ně'um JHWH,*" *ZAW* 73 (1961) 277-90; S. Meier, *Speaking of Speaking: Marking Direct Discourse in the Hebrew Bible* (VTSup 46; Leiden: Brill, 1992) 298-314; R. Rendtorff, "Zum Gebrauch der Formel *ně'ûm jhwh* im Jeremiabuch," *ZAW* 66 (1954) 27-37.

PROPHETIC UTTERANCE FORMULA (Prophetische Offenbarungsformel). See (→) Oracular Formula.

PROPHETIC WORD FORMULA (Wortereignisformel, Offenbarungsformel). A combination of the phrase *děbar yhwh,* "the word of YHWH," with the verb *hāyâ,* "to be, happen," plus the preposition *'el,* "to," followed by the name of the prophet or a pronoun suffix that refers to the prophet. It may be employed in narratives that relate the reception of a prophetic word (e.g., 1 Sam 15:10; 1 Kgs 6:11) or as the introduction to a prophetic word in prophetic literature (e.g., Jer 7:1; 11:1). It may serve as a redactional device (e.g., Jer 33:19, 23;

35:12; 42:7), or it may be formulated as a 1st-person report of a prophet (e.g., Jer 1:4, 11; 2:1; Ezek 6:1; 7:1). It may also appear in the (→) superscription to a (→) prophetic book (Hos 1:1; Joel 1:1; Mic 1:1; Zeph 1:1).

S. M. Meier, *Speaking of Speaking: Marking Direct Discourse in the Hebrew Bible* (VTSup 46; Leiden: Brill, 1992) 314-19.

REASSURANCE FORMULA (Beruhigungsformel, Bestätigungsformel). The formula *'al-tîrā'*, "fear not," sometimes with name and object, followed by *kî*, "because," which introduces the reason. The reason is often expressed with the assistance formula, "I am with you." The intention is to encourage a person (or persons) in fear to regain composure.

No original setting can be defined; the formula appears in very different situations. The examples in Isaiah (7:4-9; 10:24-27; and 37:6-7) are delivered as part of (→) prophetic announcements of salvation that promise relief from a foreign oppressor. The speaker can be a prophet, speaking for him- or herself or for YHWH (cf. 2 Kgs 6:16; Isa 7:4-9; 10:24-27; 35:4; 40:9; 41:10); YHWH (cf. Gen 15:1; 26:24; Deut 3:2; Josh 8:1); or people from all ways of life (cf. Gen 35:17; 42:23; Num 14:9; 1 Sam 22:23; 23:17; Job 5:21-22).

Related genres: (→) Oracle of Salvation; (→) Prophecy of Salvation.

E. W. Conrad, *Fear Not Warrior: A Study of 'al tîrā' Pericopes in the Hebrew Scriptures* (BJS 75; Chico: Scholars Press, 1985); P. E. Dion, "The 'Fear Not' Formula and Holy War," *CBQ* 32 (1970) 565-70.

SPEECH FORMULA (Redeformel). A broad general term to indicate a formal marker of a (→) speech. Speech formulas may employ any verb or noun that indicates speech, especially the verbs *'mr,* "to say," *dbr,* "to speak," and *'nh,* "to answer," or nouns such as *dābār,* "word," and *n'm,* "utterance." Specific generic types are included, such as the (→) messenger formula, the (→) oracular formula, and the (→) prophetic word formula.

S. M. Meier, *Speaking of Speaking: Marking Direct Discourse in the Hebrew Bible* (VTSup 46; Leiden: Brill, 1992).

THANKSGIVING/OFFERTORY FORMULA (Dank-/Opferdarbringungsformel). The expression "I will give you thanks" (*'ôdĕkā;* cf. Pss 43:4; 108:4 [*RSV* 3]; 118:21; Isa 12:1; cf. Isa 38:19). The formula marks the dedication of the sacrificial animal to YHWH when it is sacrificed, and it designates the act of giving thanks in worship in the context of a thanksgiving song (cf. Pss 30:13 [*RSV* 12]; 35:18; 52:11 [*RSV* 9]; 54:8 [*RSV* 6]; 86:12; 111:1; 138:1).

F. Crüsemann, *Studien zur Formgeschichte von Hymnus und Danklied in Israel* (WMANT 32; Neukirchen-Vluyn: Neukirchener, 1969) 267-79.